Portrait of
America

PORTRAIT OF AMERICA

FIFTH EDITION

VOLUME I

*From the European Discovery
to the End of Reconstruction*

STEPHEN B. OATES

UNIVERSITY OF MASSACHUSETTS, AMHERST

HOUGHTON MIFFLIN COMPANY
BOSTON   DALLAS   GENEVA, ILLINOIS
PALO ALTO   PRINCETON, NEW JERSEY

Again, for Greg and Stephanie with my love

Cover research by ROSE CORBETT GORDON.
Picture research by PEMBROKE HERBERT/
PICTURE RESEARCH CONSULTANTS.

Cover: Boston Harbor *by J.W.A. Scott (1854). Courtesy of*
The Bostonian Society/Old State House.

PRINTED IN THE U.S.A.
LIBRARY OF CONGRESS CATALOG CARD NUMBER: 90-83000
ISBN: 0-395-55427-6
BCDEFGHIJ-B-987654321

Contents

XIII   THE DEATH OF SLAVERY

XIV   A CRUEL WAR, A TROUBLED PEACE

PREFACE TO THE FIFTH EDITION

Like its predecessors, the Fifth Edition of this anthology stresses the human side of history, suggesting how the interaction of people and events shaped the course of the American past. As I compiled selections for *Portrait of America,* my primary criteria were that they be well written and suffused with human interest and insight. I chose essays, narratives, and biographical portraits that humanize American history, portraying it as the story of real people who actually lived, who struggled, enjoyed triumphs, suffered failures and anxieties, just like people in our own time. I hope that the anthology is an example of humanistic history at its best, the kind that combines scrupulous and engaging scholarship with a compelling narrative style. My feeling is that, since college survey audiences are not professional ones, they might enjoy reading history if it presents the past in exciting and readable form.

The Fifth Edition of Volume I has been considerably revised. Although it retains the best and most popular selections of the previous edition, I have rewritten the introductions to several of them. The Fifth Edition also features nine new selections, some of which — John C. Miller's account of the Salem witchcraft scare, Brian McGinty's treatment of the 1787 constitutional convention, and James MacGregor Burns's essay on Reconstruction as a failed revolution — replace and improve upon earlier selections on similar subjects. Other new selections focus on topics not previously covered — the Indian view of the European discovery of America, the great European migration to the New World, the lives and contributions of Abigail Adams and John Marshall, social

customs and patterns of the early Republic, and the railroads and the "go-ahead" age. I hope that *Portrait of America* is now more balanced than ever, for it offers samplings of virtually every kind of history — men's and women's, black and white, social and cultural, political and military, urban and economic, national and local — so that students can appreciate the rich diversity of the American experience.

The anthology is intended for use largely in college survey courses. It could be utilized as a supplement to a textbook or to a list of paperback readings. Or it could serve as the basic text. The book is organized into fourteen parts according to periods or themes; each part contains two or three related selections. This organization allows readers to make comparisons and contrasts between different events or viewpoints. Introductions set the selections in proper context and tie them all together so that they can be read more or less as connected episodes.

Study questions following the selections are designed to raise thought-provoking issues and to help students make comparisons and contrasts between the selections. The questions also help students review the readings and suggest points for class discussion.

In putting the Fifth Edition together, I drew on the expertise of congenial and enthusiastic colleagues across the country. I owe special thanks to Professor Charles J. Errico of Northern Virginia Community College, who provided generous critiques of both volumes, reported the response of his students to previous editions, and offered cogent critical suggestions. My gratitude, too, to

Dr. Karen Smith, who wrote study questions for the new selections, composed captions for the illustrations, and offered constructive criticism. I am indebted to Professor Betty L. Mitchell of Southeastern Massachusetts University for contributing the original study questions and giving excellent advice about selections on women's history. Professor Joyce Berkman of the University of Massachusetts, Amherst, also counseled me on women's history. I am indebted to the following professors for reviewing one or both volumes:

Fred W. Anderson
University of Colorado at Boulder

James Cook
Floyd Junior College

Howard C. Ellis
Lorain County Community College

Graham Hawks
Western Michigan University

F. Jack Hurley
Memphis State University

Ronald Isetti
St. Mary's College

Allen Kohrman
Massasoit Community College

Thomas Lewis
Mount Senario College

Larry MacLeitch
Mendocino College

Lessing Nohl
American River College

Herbert Rissler
Indiana State University

I want to thank my assistants, Lisa May, Liang He, and Dan Costello, who brought me countless articles and books, photocopied materials, gave advice, and performed many other indispensable tasks. Finally, I am grateful to the many students who have offered praise and suggestions for *Portrait of America,* for they are invaluable arbiters of how effectively it teaches them about our past.

S.B.O.

I

THE
EUROPEAN
DISCOVERY

I

Columbus, the Indians, and Human Progress

HOWARD ZINN

Contrary to legend, the European discovery of America took place quite by accident. The story of that discovery begins in the fifteenth century, when the European world was slowly spinning its way out of the Middle Ages, slowly becoming aware of the treasures — and mysteries — of distant Asia. There were many who dreamed of the fabled Orient, but none with more enterprise than a Genoese sailor named Christopher Columbus, who was certain that he could reach the Orient by sailing westward across largely uncharted waters. The nation that financed his project, Columbus contended, would enjoy the shortest route to the riches of Japan and India — silks, gems, tapestries, and highly prized spices.

Since the Crusades, Europeans had bought these luxuries from Italian merchants, who got them from Arab traders in the Holy Land. But in the thirteenth and fourteenth centuries, travelers like Marco Polo reported that Asia was the source of the succulent goods the Italians brought out of the Near East. After the rise of Europe's nation states, Portugal sought an ocean route to Asia's fortunes; in the fifteenth century, her hardy navigators, pioneers of nautical astronomy, sailed around the African Cape and opened a sea route to India. Meanwhile, Columbus dreamed of a western route across the Atlantic — which was not infeasible, since intelligent Europeans in the fifteenth century knew the world was round. Finally, he persuaded the king and queen of Spain to commission him Admiral of the Ocean Sea and to provide money, men, and ships for his voyage. He would sail under the flag of Spain and would receive a share of the profits secured from whatever lands he reached in Asia.

Most of us have certain preconceptions about Columbus and his fabled voyage: every Columbus Day we commemorate the myth of the bold, visionary hero who

2

defied contemporary superstition and plunged across a storm-tossed Atlantic against all odds, discovered America, and made the United States possible. In reality, of course, Columbus did not "discover" America; the Native Americans, or Indians, had done that some thirty thousand years before. And other Europeans had probably seen the New World before Columbus embarked on his voyage. What is more, Columbus never believed that he had found a new continent, instead insisting that he had seen islands of the Orient — proof of all his theories, goal of all his dreams. In sum, he realized none of his dreams save that of navigating the Atlantic. He died in 1506, unaware that his explorations had given Spain a claim to a vast New World and opened it for the profit and glory of the Old.

To be sure, Columbus had courage, imagination, and persistence, and he was a superior navigator. But his significance was considerably different from what most Americans realize. Named after Saint Christopher, the legendary pagan turned saint who became the "Christ-bearer," Columbus conceived it his destiny to carry Christianity across the ocean to the "pagan" countries of the Orient. In executing his divine mission, the great explorer was the flagbearer of European values and aspirations, which he unwittingly transported to the shores of the New World. In fact, Columbus's "Christian expeditionary force" established the first outpost of European civilization there, inaugurating three centuries of exploration and conquest that changed the course of modern history. Indeed, the European discovery of America had a profound impact on the Old World: not only did the opening of this enormous new frontier stimulate the European imagination, as reflected in both artistic and scientific expression; it also brought about a clash of imperial energies as Spain, Portugal, France, and eventually England all vied with one another in staking out claims to the New World.

But there was another side to the European discovery of America, a dark side. From the viewpoint of the first Americans, to whom Columbus gave the name Indios, the European invasion of their world was a catastrophe. Columbus himself set the example for subsequent Europeans, initiating a policy of enslavement and killing that was to result in the near extermination of the first Americans. Even Columbus's otherwise sympathetic biographer, Samuel Eliot Morison, admitted that the "cruel policy" begun by Columbus and pursued by his successors amounted to "genocide." To make matters worse, the Indians were not immune to the communicable viruses the Europeans carried to the New World. Epidemics of measles, typhoid, smallpox, dysentery, tuberculosis, and alcoholism were to sweep through the original Americans, killing them by the countless thousands. Modern demographers estimate that in 1492 some 12 million Indians inhabited the New World north of Mexico; in the ensuing centuries of white conquest, the number of Indians fell by about 90 percent.

Most of you have probably read about Columbus and "the discovery of America" from the standpoint of the European leaders and conquerors, for much of traditional *history has been written that way. Modern historians, however, are turning more and more to the underside of history, to the Indians and the slaves, the workers and the immigrants, the women and the children, in order to gain a deeper understanding of the past. In the following selection, historian and political scientist Howard Zinn attempts such an approach. He tells the story of the "discovery of America" from the perspective of the victims — the gentle Arawaks who greeted Columbus, the Powhatans and the Pequots who stood in the way of the English settlers of Virginia and Massachusetts. In the process, Zinn reminds us of what was destroyed in the name of progress for Western civilization.*

ARAWAK MEN AND WOMEN, naked, tawny, and full of wonder, emerged from their villages onto the island's beaches and swam out to get a closer look at the strange big boat. When Columbus and his sailors came ashore, carrying swords, speaking oddly, the Arawaks ran to greet them, brought them food, water, gifts. He later wrote of this in his log:

They . . . brought us parrots and balls of cotton and spears and many other things, which they exchanged for the glass beads and hawks' bells. They willingly traded everything they owned. . . . They were well-built, with good bodies and handsome features. . . . They do not bear arms, and do not know them, for I showed them a sword, they took it by the edge and cut themselves out of ignorance. They have no iron. Their spears are made of cane. . . . They would make fine servants. . . . With fifty men we could subjugate them all and make them do whatever we want.

These Arawaks of the Bahama Islands were much like Indians on the mainland, who were remarkable (European observers were to say again and again) for their hospitality, their belief in sharing. These traits did not stand out in the Europe of the Renaissance, dominated as it was by the religion of popes, the government of kings, the frenzy for money that marked Western civilization and its first messenger to the Americas, Christopher Columbus.

Columbus wrote:

As soon as I arrived in the Indies, on the first Island which I found, I took some of the natives by force in order that they might learn and might give me information of whatever there is in these parts.

The information that Columbus wanted most was: Where is the gold? He had persuaded the king and queen of Spain to finance an expedition to the lands, the wealth, he expected would be on the other side of the Atlantic — the Indies and Asia, gold and spices. For, like other informed people of his time, he knew the world was round and he could sail west in order to get to the Far East.

Spain was recently unified, one of the new modern nation-states, like France, England, and Portugal. Its population, mostly poor peasants, worked for the nobility, who were 2 percent of the population and owned 95 percent of the land. Spain had tied itself to the Catholic Church, expelled all the Jews, driven out the Moors. Like other states of the modern world, Spain sought gold, which was becoming the new mark of wealth, more useful than land because it could buy anything.

Pages 1–22 from *A People's History of the United States.* Copyright © 1980 by Howard Zinn. Reprinted by permission of Harper & Row, Publishers, Inc.

There was gold in Asia, it was thought, and certainly silks and spices, for Marco Polo and others had brought back marvelous things from their overland expeditions centuries before. Now that the Turks had conquered Constantinople and the eastern Mediterranean, and controlled the land routes to Asia, a sea route was needed. Portuguese sailors were working their way around the southern tip of Africa. Spain decided to gamble on a long sail across an unknown ocean.

In return for bringing back gold and spices, they promised Columbus 10 percent of the profits, governorship over new-found lands, and the fame that would go with a new title: Admiral of the Ocean Sea. He was a merchant's clerk from the Italian city of Genoa, part-time weaver (the son of a skilled weaver), and expert sailor. He set out with three sailing ships, the largest of which was the *Santa Maria,* perhaps 100 feet long, and thirty-nine crew members.

Columbus would never have made it to Asia, which was thousands of miles farther away than he had calculated, imagining a smaller world. He would have been doomed by that great expanse of sea. But he was lucky. One-fourth of the way there he came upon an unknown, uncharted land that lay between Europe and Asia — the Americas. It was early October 1492, and thirty-three days since he and his crew had left the Canary Islands, off the Atlantic coast of Africa. Now they saw branches and sticks floating in the water. They saw flocks of birds. These were signs of land. Then, on October 12, a sailor called Rodrigo saw the early morning moon shining on white sands, and cried out. It was an island in the Bahamas, the Caribbean sea. The first man to sight land was supposed to get a yearly pension of 10,000 maravedis for life, but Rodrigo never got it. Columbus claimed he had seen a light the evening before. He got the reward.

So, approaching land, they were met by the Arawak Indians, who swam out to greet them. The Arawaks lived in village communes, had a developed

Far from idealizing Christopher Columbus as a bold adventurer, Ghirlandaio's portrait suggests instead the determined ascetic, an appropriate image for the voyager whose self-appointed mission was to carry Christianity to the heathen peoples of the New World. (Scala Art Resource, New York)

agriculture of corn, yams, cassava. They could spin and weave, but they had no horses or work animals. They had no iron, but they wore tiny gold ornaments in their ears.

This was to have enormous consequences: it led Columbus to take some of them aboard ship as prisoners because he insisted that they guide him to the source of the gold. He then sailed to what is now Cuba, then to Hispaniola (the island which today consists of Haiti and the Dominican Republic). There, bits of visible gold in the rivers, and a gold mask presented to Columbus by a local Indian chief, led to wild visions of gold fields.

On Hispaniola, out of timbers from the *Santa Ma-*

ria, which had run aground, Columbus build a fort, the first European military base in the Western Hemisphere. He called it Navidad (Christmas) and left thirty-nine crewmembers there, with instructions to find and store the gold. He took more Indian prisoners and put them aboard his two remaining ships. At one part of the island he got into a fight with Indians who refused to trade as many bows and arrows as he and his men wanted. Two were run through with swords and bled to death. Then the *Nina* and the *Pinta* set sail for the Azores and Spain. When the weather turned cold, the Indian prisoners began to die.

Columbus's report to the Court in Madrid was extravagant. He insisted he had reached Asia (it was Cuba) and an island off the coast of China (Hispaniola). His descriptions were part fact, part fiction:

Hispaniola is a miracle. Mountains and hills, plains and pastures, are both fertile and beautiful . . . the harbors are unbelievably good and there are many wide rivers of which the majority contain gold. . . . There are many spices, and great mines of gold and other metals. . . .

The Indians, Columbus reported, "are so naïve and so free with their possessions that no one who has not witnessed them would believe it. When you ask for something they have, they never say no. To the contrary, they offer to share with anyone. . . ." He concluded his report by asking for a little help from their Majesties, and in return he would bring them from his next voyage "as much gold as they need . . . and as many slaves as they ask." He was full of religious talk: "Thus the eternal God, our Lord, gives victory to those who follow His way over apparent impossibilities."

Because of Columbus's exaggerated report and promises, his second expedition was given seventeen ships and more than twelve hundred men. The aim was clear: slaves and gold. They went from island to island in the Caribbean, taking Indians as captives. But as word spread of the Europeans' intent they found more and more empty villages. On Haiti, they found that the sailors left behind at Fort Navidad had been killed in a battle with the Indians, after they had roamed the island in gangs looking for gold, taking women and children as slaves for sex and labor.

Now, from his base on Haiti, Columbus sent expedition after expedition into the interior. They found no gold fields, but had to fill up the ships returning to Spain with some kind of dividend. In the year 1495, they went on a great slave raid, rounded up fifteen hundred Arawak men, women, and children, put them in pens guarded by Spaniards and dogs, then picked the five hundred best specimens to load onto ships. Of those five hundred, two hundred died en route. The rest arrived alive in Spain and were put up for sale by the archdeacon of the town, who reported that, although the slaves were "naked as the day they were born," they showed "no more embarrassment than animals." Columbus later wrote: "Let us in the name of the Holy Trinity go on sending all the slaves that can be sold."

But too many of the slaves died in captivity. And so Columbus, desperate to pay back dividends to those who had invested, had to make good his promise to fill the ships with gold. In the province of Cicao on Haiti, where he and his men imagined huge gold fields to exist, they ordered all persons fourteen years or older to collect a certain quantity of gold every three months. When they brought it, they were given copper tokens to hang around their necks. Indians found without a copper token had their hands cut off and bled to death.

The Indians had been given an impossible task. The only gold around was bits of dust garnered from the streams. So they fled, were hunted down with dogs, and were killed.

Trying to put together an army of resistance, the Arawaks faced Spaniards who had armor, muskets, swords, horses. When the Spaniards took prisoners they hanged them or burned them to death. Among the Arawaks, mass suicides began, with cassava poison. Infants were killed to save them from the Spaniards. In two years, through murder, mutilation, or suicide, half of the 250,000 Indians on Haiti were dead.

When it became clear that there was no gold left, the Indians were taken as slave labor on huge estates, known later as *encomiendas*. They were worked at a ferocious pace, and died by the thousands. By the year 1515, there were perhaps fifty thousand Indians left. By 1550, there were five hundred. A report of the year 1650 shows none of the original Arawaks or their descendants left on the island.

The chief source — and, on many matters the only source — of information about what happened on the islands after Columbus came is Bartolomé de las Casas, who, as a young priest, participated in the conquest of Cuba. For a time he owned a plantation on which Indian slaves worked, but he gave that up and became a vehement critic of Spanish cruelty. Las Casas transcribed Columbus's journal and, in his fifties, began a multi-volume *History of the Indies.* In it, he describes the Indians. They are agile, he says, and can swim long distances, especially the women. They are not completely peaceful, because they do battle from time to time with other tribes, but their casualties seem small, and they fight when they are individually moved to do so because of some grievance, not on the orders of captains or kings.

Women in Indian society were treated so well as to startle the Spaniards. Las Casas describes sex relations:

Marriage laws are non-existent: men and women alike choose their mates and leave them as they please, without offense, jealousy or anger. They multiply in great abundance; pregnant women work to the last minute and give birth almost painlessly; up the next day, they bathe in the river and are as clean and healthy as before giving birth. If they tire of their men, they give themselves abortions with herbs that force stillbirths, covering their

shameful parts with leaves or cotton cloth; although on the whole, Indian men and women look upon total nakedness with as much casualness as we look upon a man's head or at his hands.

The Indians, Las Casas says, have no religion, at least no temples. They live in

large communal bell-shaped buildings, housing up to 600 people at one time . . . made of very strong wood and roofed with palm leaves. . . . They prize bird feathers of various colors, beads made of fishbones, and green and white stones with which they adorn their ears and lips, but they put no value on gold or other precious things. They lack all manner of commerce, neither buying nor selling, and rely exclusively on their natural environment for maintenance. They are extremely generous with their possessions and by the same token covet the possessions of their friends and expect the same degree of liberality. . . .

In Book Two of his *History of the Indies*, Las Casas (who at first urged replacing Indians by black slaves, thinking they were stronger and would survive, but later relented when he saw the effects on blacks) tells about the treatment of the Indians by the Spaniards. It is a unique account and deserves to be quoted at length:

Endless testimonies . . . prove the mild and pacific temperament of the natives. . . . But our work was to exasperate, ravage, kill, mangle and destroy; small wonder, then, if they tried to kill one of us now and then. . . . The admiral, it is true, was blind as those who came after him, and he was so anxious to please the King that he committed irreparable crimes against the Indians. . . .

Las Casas tells how the Spaniards "grew more conceited every day" and after a while refused to walk any distance. They "rode the backs of Indians if they were in a hurry" or were carried on ham-

Illustrated works like Père Bartolomé de Las Casas' Very Brief Account of the Destruction of the Indies *helped spread the story of Spanish atrocities against the Indians in the New World. The Spaniards, Las Casas reported, "thought nothing of knifing Indians by tens and twenties and of cutting slices off them to test the sharpness of their blades." (William L. Clements Library, University of Michigan)*

mocks by Indians running in relays. "In this case they also had Indians carry large leaves to shade them from the sun and others to fan them with goose wings."

Total control led to total cruelty. The Spaniards "thought nothing of knifing Indians by tens and twenties and of cutting slices off them to test the sharpness of their blades." Las Casas tells how "two of these so-called Christians met two Indian boys one day, each carrying a parrot; they took the parrots and for fun beheaded the boys."

The Indians' attempts to defend themselves failed. And when they ran off into the hills they were found and killed. So, Las Casas reports, "they suffered and died in the mines and other labors in desperate silence, knowing not a soul in the world to whom they could turn for help." He describes their work in the mines:

. . . mountains are stripped from top to bottom and bottom to top a thousand times; they dig, split rocks, move stones, and carry dirt on their backs to wash it in the rivers, while those who wash gold stay in the water all the time with their backs bent so constantly it breaks them; and when water invades the mines, the most arduous task of all is to dry the mines by scooping up pansful of water and throwing it up outside. . . .

After each six or eight months' work in the mines, which was the time required of each crew to dig enough gold for melting, up to a third of the men died.

While the men were sent many miles away to the mines, the wives remained to work the soil, forced into the excruciating job of digging and making thousands of hills for cassava plants.

Thus husbands and wives were together only once every eight or ten months and when they met they were so exhausted and depressed on both sides . . . they ceased to procreate. As for the newly born, they died early because their mothers, overworked and famished, had no milk to nurse them, and for this reason, while I was in Cuba, 7000 children died in three months. Some mothers even drowned their babies from sheer desperation. . . . In this way, husbands died in the mines, wives died at work and children died from lack of milk . . . and in a short time this land which was so great, so powerful and fertile . . . was depopulated. . . . My eyes have seen these acts so foreign to human nature, and now I tremble as I write. . . .

When he arrived on Hispaniola in 1508, Las Casas says, "there were 60,000 people living on this island, including the Indians; so that from 1494 to 1508, over three million people had perished from war, slavery, and the mines. Who in future generations will believe this? I myself writing it as a knowledgeable eyewitness can hardly believe it. . . ."

Thus began the history, five hundred years ago, of the European invasion of the Indian settlements in the Americas. That beginning . . . — is conquest, slavery, death. When we read the history books given to children in the United States, it all starts with heroic adventure — there is no bloodshed — and Columbus Day is a celebration. . . .

What Columbus did to the Arawaks of the Bahamas, Cortés did to the Aztecs of Mexico and Pizarro to the Incas of Peru. [Though not so brutal as the Spaniards, the English settlers of North America nevertheless followed the Spanish pattern of violence when dealing with the native population. That pattern was set early against the Powhatans in Virginia.] . . . In 1585, before there was any permanent English settlement in Virginia, Richard Grenville landed there with seven ships. The Indians he met were hospitable, but when one of them stole a small silver cup, Grenville sacked and burned the whole Indian village.

Jamestown itself was set up inside the territory of an Indian confederacy, led by the chief, Powhatan. Powhatan watched the English settle on his people's land, but did not attack, maintaining a posture of coolness. When the English were going through their "starving time" in the winter of 1610, some of them ran off to join the Indians, where they would at least be fed. When the summer came, the governor of the colony sent a messenger to ask Powhatan to return the runaways, whereupon Powhatan, according to the English account, replied with "noe other than prowde and disdaynefull Answers." Some soldiers were therefore sent out "to take Revendge." They fell upon an Indian settlement, killed fifteen or sixteen Indians, burned the houses, cut down the corn growing around the village, took the queen of the tribe and her children into boats, then ended up throwing the children overboard "and shoteinge owtt their Braynes in the water." The queen was later taken off and stabbed to death.

Twelve years later, the Indians, alarmed as the English settlements kept growing in numbers, apparently decided to try to wipe them out for good. They went on a rampage and massacred 347 men, women, and children. From then on it was total war.

Not able to enslave the Indians, and not able to live with them, the English decided to exterminate them. Edmund Morgan writes, in his history of early Virginia, *American Slavery, American Freedom:*

Since the Indians were better woodsmen than the English and virtually impossible to track down, the method was to feign peaceful intentions, let them settle down and plant their corn wherever they chose, and then, just before harvest, fall upon them, killing as many as possible and burning the corn. . . . Within two or three years of the massacre the English had avenged the deaths of that day many times over. . . .

When the Pilgrims came to New England they too were coming not to vacant land but to territory inhabited by tribes of Indians. The governor of the Massachusetts Bay Colony, John Winthrop, created the excuse to take Indian land by declaring the area legally a "vacuum." The Indians, he said, had not "subdued" the land, and therefore had only a "natural" right to it, but not a "civil right." A "natural right" did not have legal standing.

The Puritans also appealed to the Bible, Psalms 2:8: "Ask of me, and I shall give thee, the heathen for thine inheritance, and the uttermost parts of the earth for thy possessions." And to justify their use of force to take the land, they cited Romans 13:2: "Whosoever therefore resisteth the power, resisteth the ordinance of God: and they that resist shall receive to themselves damnation."

The Puritans lived in uneasy truce with the Pequot Indians, who occupied what is now southern Connecticut and Rhode Island. But they wanted them out of the way; they wanted their land. And they seemed to want also to establish their rule firmly over Connecticut settlers in that area. The murder of a white trader, Indian-kidnaper, and troublemaker became an excuse to make war on the Pequots in 1636.

A punitive expedition left Boston to attack the Narragansett Indians on Block Island, who were lumped with the Pequots. As Governor Winthrop wrote:

They had commission to put to death the men of Block Island, but to spare the women and children, and to bring them away, and to take possession of the island; and from thence to go to the Pequods to demand the murderers of Captain Stone and other English, and one thousand fathom of wampom for damages, etc. and some of their children as hostages, which if they should refuse, they were to obtain it by force.

The English landed and killed some Indians, but the rest hid in the thick forests of the island and the English went from one deserted village to the next, destroying crops. Then they sailed back to the mainland and raided Pequot villages along the coast, destroying crops again. One of the officers of that expedition, in his account, gives some insight into the Pequots they encountered: "The Indians spying of us came running in multitudes along the water side, crying, What cheer, Englishmen, what cheer, what do you come for? They not thinking we intended war, went on cheerfully. . . ."

So, the war with the Pequots began. Massacres took place on both sides. The English developed a tactic of warfare used earlier by Cortés and later, in the twentieth century, even more systematically: deliberate attacks on noncombatants for the purpose of terrorizing the enemy. . . .

So the English set fire to the wigwams of the village. By their own account: "The Captain also said, We must Burn Them; and immediately stepping into the Wigwam . . . brought out a Fire Brand, and putting it into the Matts with which they were covered, set the Wigwams on Fire." William Bradford, in his *History of the Plymouth Plantation* written at the time, describes John Mason's raid on the Pequot village:

Those that scaped the fire were slaine with the sword; some hewed to peeces, other rune throw with their rapiers, so as they were quickly dispatchte, and very few escaped. It was conceived they thus destroyed about 400 at this time. It was a fearful sight to see them thus frying the fyer, and the streams of blood quenching the same, and horrible was the stincke and sente there of, but the victory seemed a sweete sacrifice, and they gave the prayers thereof to God, who had wrought so wonderfully for them, thus to inclose their enemies in their hands, and give them so speedy a victory over so proud and insulting an enimie. . . .

Forty years after the Pequot War, Puritans and Indians fought again. This time it was the Wampanoags, occupying the south shore of Massachusetts Bay, who were in the way and also beginning to trade some of their land to people outside the Massachusetts Bay Colony. Their chief, Massasoit, was dead. His son Wamsutta had been killed by Englishmen, and Wamsutta's brother Metacom (later to be called King Philip by the English) became chief. The English found their excuse, a murder which they attributed to Metacom, and they began a war of conquest against the Wampanoags, a war to take their land. They were clearly the aggressors, but claimed they attacked for preventive purposes. As Roger Williams, more friendly to the Indians than most, put it: "All men of conscience or prudence ply to windward, to maintain their wars to be defensive."

. . . The elite of the Puritans wanted the war; the ordinary white Englishman did not want it and often refused to fight. The Indians certainly did not want war, but they matched atrocity with atrocity. When it was over, in 1676, the English had won, but their resources were drained; they had lost six hundred men. Three thousand Indians were dead, including Metacom himself. Yet the Indian raids did not stop.

For a while, the English tried softer tactics. But ultimately, it was back to annihilation. The Indian population of 10 million that was in North America when Columbus came would ultimately be reduced to less than a million. Huge numbers of Indians would die from diseases introduced by the whites. A Dutch traveler in New Netherland wrote in 1656 that "the Indians . . . affirm, that before the arrival of the Christians, and before the smallpox broke out amongst them, they were ten times as numerous as they now are, and that their population had been melted down by this disease, whereof nine-tenths of them have died." When the English first settled Martha's Vineyard in 1642, the Wampanoags there numbered perhaps three thousand. There were no wars on that island, but by 1764, only 313 Indians were left there. Similarly, Block Island Indians numbered perhaps 1,200 to 1,500 in 1662, and by 1774 were reduced to fifty-one.

Behind the English invasion of North America, behind their massacre of Indians, their deception, their brutality, was that special powerful drive born in civilizations based on private property. It was a morally ambiguous drive; the need for space, for land, was a real human need. But in conditions of scarcity, in a barbarous epoch of history ruled by competition, this human need was transformed into the murder of whole peoples. . . .

What did people in Spain get out of all that death and brutality visited on the Indians of the Americas? For a brief period in history, there was the glory of a Spanish Empire in the Western Hemisphere. As Hans Koning sums it up in his book *Columbus: His Enterprise*:

For all the gold and silver stolen and shipped to Spain did not make the Spanish people richer. It gave their kings an edge in the balance of power for a time, a chance to hire more mercenary soldiers for their wars. They ended up losing those wars anyway, and all that was left was a deadly inflation, a starving population, the rich richer, the poor poorer, and a ruined peasant class.

Beyond all that, how certain are we that what was destroyed was inferior? Who were these people who came out on the beach and swam to bring presents to Columbus and his crew, who watched Cortés and Pizarro ride through their countryside, who peered out of the forests at the first white settlers of Virginia and Massachusetts?

Columbus called them Indians, because he miscalculated the size of the earth. In this [account] we too call them Indians, with some reluctance, because it happens too often that people are saddled with names given them by their conquerors.

And yet, there is some reason to call them Indians, because they did come, perhaps 25,000 years ago, from Asia, across the land bridge of the Bering Straits (later to disappear under water) to Alaska. Then they moved southward, seeking warmth and land, in a trek lasting thousands of years that took them into North America, then Central and South America. In Nicaragua, Brazil, and Ecuador their petrified footprints can still be seen, along with the print of bison, who disappeared about five thousand years ago, so they must have reached South America at least that far back.

Widely dispersed over the great land mass of the Americas, they numbered 15 or 20 million people by the time Columbus came, perhaps 5 million in North America. Responding to the different environments of soil and climate, they developed hundreds of different tribal cultures, perhaps two thousand different languages. They perfected the art of agriculture, and figured out how to grow maize (corn), which cannot grow by itself and must be planted, cultivated, fertilized, harvested, husked, shelled. They ingeniously developed a variety of other vegetables and fruits, as well as peanuts and chocolate and tobacco and rubber.

On their own, the Indians were engaged in the great agricultural revolution that other peoples in Asia, Europe, Africa were going through about the same time.

While many of the tribes remained nomadic hunters and food gatherers in wandering, egalitarian communes, others began to live in more settled communities where there was more food, larger populations, more divisions of labor among men and women, more surplus to feed chiefs and priests, more leisure time for artistic and social work, for building houses. About a thousand years before Christ, while comparable constructions were going on in Egypt and Mesopotamia, the Zuñi and Hopi Indians of what is now New Mexico had begun to build villages consisting of large terraced buildings, nestled in among cliffs and mountains for protection from enemies, with hundreds of rooms in each village. Before the arrival of the European explorers, they were using irrigation canals, dams, were doing ceramics, weaving baskets, making cloth out of cotton.

By the time of Christ and Julius Caesar, there had developed in the Ohio River Valley a culture of so-called Moundbuilders, Indians who constructed thousands of enormous sculptures out of earth, sometimes in the shapes of huge humans, birds, or serpents, sometimes as burial sites, sometimes as fortifications. One of them was 3½ miles long, enclosing 100 acres. These Moundbuilders seem to have been part of a complex trading system of ornaments and weapons from as far off as the Great Lakes, the Far West, and the Gulf of Mexico.

About A.D. 500, as this Moundbuilder culture of the Ohio Valley was beginning to decline, another culture was developing westward, in the valley of the Mississippi, centered on what is now St. Louis. It had an advanced agriculture, included thousands of villages, and also built huge earthen mounds as burial and ceremonial places near a vast Indian metropolis that may have had thirty thousand people. The largest mound was 100 feet high, with a rectangular base larger than that of the Great Pyramid of Egypt. In the city, known as Cahokia, were toolmakers, hide dressers, potters, jewelrymakers, weavers, saltmakers, copper engravers, and magnificent ceramists. One funeral blanket was made of twelve thousand shell beads.

From the Adirondacks to the Great Lakes, in what is now Pennsylvania and upper New York, lived the most powerful of the northeastern tribes, the League of the Iroquois, which included the Mohawks (People of the Flint), Oneidas (People of the Stone), Onondagas (People of the Mountain), Cayugas (People at the Landing), and Senecas (Great Hill People), thousands of people bound together by a common Iroquois language.

In the vision of the Mohawk chief Hiawatha, the legendary Dekaniwidah spoke to the Iroquois: "We bind ourselves together by taking hold of each other's hands so firmly and forming a circle so strong that if a tree should fall upon it, it could not shake nor break it, so that our people and grandchildren shall remain in the circle in security, peace and happiness."

In the villages of the Iroquois, land was owned in common and worked in common. Hunting was done together, and the catch was divided among the members of the village. Houses were considered common property and were shared by several families. The concept of private ownership of land and homes was foreign to the Iroquois. A French Jesuit priest who encountered them in the 1650s wrote: "No poorhouses are needed among them, because they are neither mendicants nor paupers. . . . Their kindness, humanity and courtesy not only makes them liberal with what they have, but causes them to possess hardly anything except in common."

Women were important and respected in Iroquois society. Families were matrilineal. That is, the family line went down through the female members, whose husbands joined the family, while sons who married then joined their wives' families. Each extended family lived in a "long house." When a woman wanted a divorce, she set her husband's things outside the door.

Families were grouped in clans, and a dozen or more clans might make up a village. The senior women in the village named the men who represented the clans at village and tribal councils. They also named the forty-nine chiefs who were the ruling council for the Five Nation confederacy of the Iroquois. The women attended clan meetings, stood behind the circle of men who spoke and voted, and removed the men from office if they strayed too far from the wishes of the women.

The women tended the crops and took general charge of village affairs while the men were always hunting or fishing. And since they supplied the moccasins and food for warring expeditions, they had some control over military matters. As Gary B. Nash notes in his fascinating study of early America, *Red, White, and Black*: "Thus power was shared between the sexes and the European idea of male dominancy and female subordination in all things was conspicuously absent in Iroquois society."

Children in Iroquois society, while taught the cultural heritage of their people and solidarity with the tribe, were also taught to be independent, not to submit to overbearing authority. They were taught equality in status and the sharing of possessions. The Iroquois did not use harsh punishment on children; they did not insist on early weaning or early toilet training, but gradually allowed the child to learn self-care.

All of this was in sharp contrast to European values as brought over by the first colonists, a society of rich and poor, controlled by priests, by governors, by male heads of families. For example, the pastor of the Pilgrim colony, John Robinson, thus advised his parishioners how to deal with their children: "And surely there is in all children . . . a stubbornness, and stoutness of mind arising from natural pride, which must, in the first place, be broken and beaten down; that so the foundation of their education being laid in humility and tractableness, other virtues may, in their time, be built thereon.''

Gary Nash describes Iroquois culture:

No laws and ordinances, sheriffs and constables, judges and juries, or courts or jails — the apparatus of authority in European societies — were to be found in the northeast woodlands prior to European arrival. Yet boundaries of acceptable behavior were firmly set. Though priding themselves on the autonomous individual, the Iroquois maintained a strict sense of right and wrong. . . . He who stole another's food or acted invalourously in war was "shamed" by his people and ostracized from their company until he had atoned for his actions and demonstrated to their satisfaction that he had morally purified himself.

Not only the Iroquois but other Indian tribes behaved the same way. In 1635, Maryland Indians responded to the governor's demand that if any of them killed an Englishman, the guilty one should be delivered up for punishment according to English law. The Indians said:

It is the manner amongst us Indians, that if any such accident happen, wee doe redeeme the life of a man that is so slaine, with 100 armes length of Beades and since that you are heere strangers, and come into our Countrey, you should rather conform yourselves to the Customes of our Countrey, than impose yours upon us. . . .

So, Columbus and his successors were not coming into an empty wilderness, but into a world which in some places was as densely populated as Europe itself, where the culture was complex, where human relations were more egalitarian than in Europe, and where the relations among men, women, children, and nature were more beautifully worked out than perhaps any place in the world.

They were people without a written language,

but with their own laws, their poetry, their history kept in memory and passed on, in an oral vocabulary more complex than Europe's, accompanied by song, dance, and ceremonial drama. They paid careful attention to the development of personality, intensity of will, independence and flexibility, passion and potency, to their partnership with one another and with nature.

John Collier, an American scholar who lived among Indians in the 1920s and 1930s in the American Southwest, said of their spirit: "Could we make it our own, there would be an eternally inexhaustible earth and a forever lasting peace.''

Perhaps there is some romantic mythology in that. But the evidence from European travelers in the sixteenth, seventeeth, and eighteenth centuries, put together recently by an American specialist on Indian life, William Brandon, is overwhelmingly supportive of much of that "myth." Even allowing for the imperfection of myths, it is enough to make us question, for that time and ours, the excuse of progress in the annihilation of races, and the telling of history from the standpoint of the conquerors and leaders of Western civilization.

QUESTIONS TO CONSIDER

1 Howard Zinn describes the lives and customs of both Arawaks and fifteenth-century Spanish explorers. Do you see a fundamental irony in the behavior of the ''Christian'' expeditionary forces in the New World? How do they compare to the "savages"? What internal and external pressures led Columbus and his men to enslave the peoples of the Americas? How might these Europeans have vindicated their actions.

2 Consider Governor Winthrop's claim that New England lands existed in a vacuum. Under what theory did the Puritans justify their seizure of Indian lands? Where did they claim to find the authority for exercising sovereignty over local tribes?

3   Describe the achievements of scattered Indian tribes and nations up to the time of the European discovery. How did these achievements parallel progress in other parts of the world?

4   Zinn seems to believe that many American Indian tribes were culturally superior to the European people who conquered them. Describe the social and political traits that Zinn finds so appealing. Would our country be better off if the first settlers from Europe had absorbed rather than obliterated earlier cultures?

5   How does Zinn's treatment of the European discovery expand our understanding of this historical epoch? Why is it important for us to look at history from points of view other than those of conquerors? Does the ideal of progress justify conquest? What is progress, anyway?

2

From These Beginnings

PAGE SMITH

For a time, it seemed that Spain would become the dominant imperial power in the New World. While Portugal received Brazil, thanks to an edict from the pope in 1493, Spain claimed the rest of South and Central America and sent out explorers to look for gold and silver there. By the 1550s powerful Spain had a sprawling colonial empire that comprised most of South America, Central America, Mexico, the Caribbean islands, Florida, and the American Southwest from Texas to California.

Meanwhile French explorers searched eastern Canada for the Northwest Passage, a legendary waterway that was supposed to connect the Atlantic and Pacific oceans and that, under France's control, would give France access to the luxuries of Asia. Unable to find such a passage, France was content to establish a fur-trading empire in Canada, with her explorers, traders, and missionaries advancing west to the Great Lakes and then southward down the Mississippi to New Orleans.

England, however, was slow to join the race for colonies, although John Cabot's voyage to North America in 1497 had given England a claim to the New World. Finally, under Queen Elizabeth, the English challenged Spain's rule of the oceans and her domination of the New World. Adventurous "sea dogs" under John Hawkins raided Spanish commerce on both the Atlantic and the Pacific; and in 1588, in a dramatic sea battle, the English navy defeated the Spanish Armada, a victory that gave England virtually undisputed control of the seas. Thanks to the persuasive arguments of Sir Walter Raleigh, Sir Humphrey Gilbert, and Richard Hakluyt, all champions of colonization, England at last began to build a New World empire. After an abortive attempt to found a colony on Roanoke Island, North Carolina, Queen Elizabeth and her successor James I authorized private corporations called joint stock companies to establish the Jamestown, Plymouth, and Massachusetts Bay colonies. As the number of colonies increased in the seventeenth century, a great migration began to English North America. That migration is the subject of the following selection by historian Page Smith, who writes from the standpoint of the European immigrants, thus giving you a different perspective from that in the opening selection. With a vivid pen and an eye for telling detail, Smith discusses the remarkable hodgepodge of humanity that streamed into the English colonies from more than a dozen European countries. Among them, of course, were hardy farmers, aspiring merchants, indentured servants, and visionary religious groups in search of better secular and spiritual lives. But the unfortunate and the disreputable came as well, ranging from English boys who were stolen and sold into bondage, to convicted felons and "rogues and vagabonds" shipped out to the colonies by the British government. As Smith explains, "rogues and vagabonds" included a variety of outlawed folk — beggars, prostitutes, drunkards, dancers, fiddlers, fencers, actors, jugglers, dice players, minstrels, fortunetellers, charlatans, tinkers, peddlers, and loiterers, all of whom played some part in the drama of colonization. From farmers to felons, this diverse assortment of individuals went on to seize the eastern coast of North America and to forge a new nation in the wilderness.

THE AMERICAN COLONISTS came from a variety of backgrounds. . . . What united them was the wilderness to which they came, a vast land . . . [that] was, literally, incomprehensible; it reached beyond the mind's imagining, threatening and promising, larger than all of Europe: coastal shelf and then mountains and endless plains and more mountains and, finally, the Pacific. No one could measure its extent. The English settlers for their part clung to its eastern margins, to the seacoast strip that faced the ocean highway to the Old World. Even here there were terrains, climates, and topographies as

Extracts from *A People's History of the American Revolution*, Vol. II: *A New Age Begins*, pages 28–47, copyright McGraw-Hill Publishing Company. Used by permission of the publisher.

dramatically different as one could imagine — from the rocky, frigid shores of New Hampshire to the sunny beaches of South Carolina.

There was a kind of mad presumption about the whole venture: a few thousand, and then a few hundred thousand, and finally a few million souls scattered along almost two thousand miles of coastline. And in truth it could be said that those who made this strange odyssey to the new World were as diverse as the land they inhabited. Those from England itself represented every class and condition of men. And then there were the Swedes, who settled on the Delaware long before William Penn and his followers arrived, and the stolid and intractable Dutch, reputed to have bought Manhattan from the [Indians] for a few strings of beads — the most famous real estate deal in history. And the French

Huguenots, Protestants fleeing from persecution in a Catholic country; the Catholics of Maryland, fleeing persecution in a Protestant country; the Quakers, fleeing the harassments of the Anglican establishment, the Church of England; and Germans from innumerable principalities, fleeing military draft and the various exactions of petty princes.

Within the British Isles themselves — Ireland, Scotland, England and Wales — there was striking diversity among the New World emigrants. The Separatists — the Pilgrims under William Bradford — wanted, in essence, to be separate; the Puritans wanted to found a Bible Commonwealth and redeem a fallen world. When Cromwell and the Puritans dominated England and beheaded Charles I, certain Royalists found refuge in Virginia and New York. When the restoration of the monarchy brought Charles II to the English throne and re-established the Stuart line, the regicides — those involved in the execution of Charles I — found refuge in Puritan New England. When the Scottish Covenanters, or Presbyterians, so akin in spirit to the Puritans of New England, rose against the high-handed and tyrannical actions of the re-established monarchy, they were crushingly defeated . . . and cruelly repressed. Many, in consequence, came to America. And they continued to come for a hundred years. . . .

And then there were the Irish. They were a special case. They fled famine and rent-wracking landlords. . . . A Catholic people, they fled their Protestant masters. But above all they fled poverty, the poverty of a ruthlessly exploited peasantry. Generation after generation, the Irish came to the American colonies, primarily to Maryland and Pennsylvania, where they gravitated to the frontier areas. In addition to the Catholic Irish, Scotch-Irish Presbyterians came in substantial numbers to the colonies throughout the eighteenth century. The Scotch-Irish were those Covenanters, or militant Presbyterians, who had been forced by the bitter divisions in Scotland itself to seek the protection of the En-

glish armies in Northern Ireland (hence Scotch-Irish). For many of them, Ireland was little more than a way station to the colonies, where they showed a marked preference for Pennsylvania and settled, typically, on the frontier. . . .

So the immigrants came in an ever-growing tide — the hungry, the oppressed, the contentious, the ambitious, those out of power and out of favor, the losers, whether in the realm of politics or of economics. And America could accommodate them all: Irish peasant and his land-poor master, Scottish Highlander and Lowlander, persecuted Protestant and persecuted Catholic, fortune-seeker and God-seeker, they found their places, their kinfolk, the familiar accents of their home shires or counties or countries.

But the essence of them all, of all that human congress, the bone and marrow, the unifying principle, the prevailing and pervasive spirit was English. Like the others who came, the English came . . . for a number of reasons. Most of them shared some particular expectation, whether for spiritual or material betterment or, happily, both. Many of those who came later shared, of course, the hopes of the original settlers. Many more came because conditions were desperately hard in England and Ireland for poor people, even for those who had not yet sunk into the pit of abandoned hopelessness that was the lot of the most wretched.

It has been estimated that London in the eighteenth century had 6,000 adult and 9,300 child beggars. In the entire country of some 10,000,000 persons, there were estimated to be 50,000 beggars, 20,000 vagrants, 10,000 idlers, 100,000 prostitutes, 10,000 rogues and vagabonds, 80,000 criminals, 1,041,000 persons on parish relief. Indeed, over half the population was below what we would call today "the poverty line," and many, of course, were profoundly below it — below it to the point of starvation. An estimate of the different classes — and class lines were almost impassable — in 1688 suggests that nobility, gentry, merchants, professionals, free-

German Immigrants in Georgia. "The immigrants came in an ever-growing tide," Page Smith writes, "the hungry, the oppressed, the contentious, the ambitious, those out of power *and out of favor, the losers, whether in the realm of politics or of economics." (New York Public Library, Rare Book Room, Astor, Lenox and Tilden Foundations)*

holders (those who held land on their own), craftsmen, and public officials constituted 47 per cent of the population; while common sailors and soldiers (recruited, for the most part, from the lowest levels of British society and enduring desperately hard conditions of service), laborers, servants, paupers, and all those other remarkable subdivisions that we have listed above such as rogues and vagrants made up 53 per cent of the population. The colonies, for their part, had a virtually inexhaustible demand for labor.

Anyone willing to work could be put to worthwhile labor, and might (and often did) in a few years establish himself as an independent farmer or artisan.

Yet it was one thing to be an undernourished London apprentice who hated his master and another to find a way to get to America. Some indication of the situation of the working class in the larger cities may be discerned from the condition of pauper children in London in the early eighteenth century. Orphaned, or more frequently illegitimate and abandoned at birth, they were sent to workhouses and to parish nurses. A Parliamentary study found that of all such infants born or received in London's workhouses in a three-year period, only seven in every hundred were alive at the end of that time. As part of the "surcharge of necessitous people," orphaned and impoverished children who were public charges were sporadically dispatched to the colonies as indentured servants. People worked, typically, from six in the morning until eight at night for a pittance that barely supported life. They had no holidays except at Christmas, Easter, and on hanging days, when everyone might be entertained and edified by watching wretches hanged for crimes that, in many instances, would be classed as misdemeanors today.

Despite the cruelty of punishments, London had a large criminal class and was infested with prostitutes. The working class drowned its miseries in bad gin and beer. There were some 7,000 ginshops in the suburbs of London and, by 1750, 16,000 in the city itself (only 1,050 of which were licensed); most of them were in the poorest sections of the city, whose horrors are vividly recorded in Hogarth's etchings of Gin Lane. The hard liquor consumed in one year (1733) in London alone amounted to 11,200,000 gallons, or some 56 gallons per adult male.

Next to public hangings, the principal entertainments available to the poor — and enjoyed by the rich as well — were cockfighting, bullbaiting, and badger baiting. In such circumstances there was ample incentive to emigrate almost anywhere. . . . But to the penniless, the question was: How? The growing need for labor in the colonies supplied the answer, and a system of indenture, based on the long-established apprenticeship, was devised. Agents paid for the ship's passage of improvident men and women who were willing to contract themselves in America to work off the cost of their transportation. By this means, tens of thousands of English

and Irish workers of both sexes found their way across the ocean.

The system was easily and often abused. A class of men "of the lowest order," called spirits and crimps, arose, who spirited away unwilling lads and sold them into bondage. . . . One spirit boasted that he had been spiriting persons for twelve years at a rate of five hundred persons a year. He would give twenty-five shillings to anyone who would bring him a likely prospect, and he could sell such a one to a merchant at once for forty shillings. Often spiriting was a profitable sideline for a brewer, hostler, carpenter, or tavern keeper. The tavern keeper was in an especially advantageous position, since a drunken patron was an easy victim. So dreaded were these dismal agents that mothers frightened their children into obedience by warning them that a spirit would carry them off if they were bad. It was no idle threat. In 1653 Robert Broome secured a warrant for the arrest of a ship's captain charged with carrying off his son, aged eleven, who had been spirited aboard. A few years later, a commission going aboard the *Conquer* found that eleven out of nineteen servants had been "taken by the spirits." Their average age was nineteen. Not all spirits were depraved men, however, and even the worst of them often performed a useful service in arranging transportation for a servant who wished to emigrate to the colonies against the wishes of parents or a master. . . .

For a time it proved easier to get women servants than men servants. . . . Mathew Cradock, captain of the *Abraham*, sailing for Virginia, made elaborate preparations for carrying a shipload of servants, men and women alike, to Virginia on a four-year indenture. On his ship's arrival in various English ports, . . . he rounded up forty-one men and twenty women, the latter "from 17 to 35 yeares and very lustye and strong Boddied. . . ."

Clothing, "peppar and Gingar," and three-and-a-half pounds of tobacco for the men were all purchased before the ship set sail, and a midwife was hired to make sure none of the women were pregnant. Soon after the ship sailed it was driven into the harbor of Cowes, and it was a month before it got favorable winds. By that time, three of the women were pregnant and were sent home; some who were put ashore to do the washing ran away and had to be tracked down at a cost of ten shillings; and another was found "not fette to be entertained havinge the frentche dizeas [gonorrhea]" and was sent packing.

If a female indentured servant became pregnant during her service, her misdeed represented a loss to her master, so that an indentured servant guilty of bastardy was required to pay the usual charges levied against unwed mothers as well as to indemnify her master for the loss of her services during the later stages of her pregnancy and her lying-in. Not infrequently, the master was the culprit. In Maryland, Jacob Lumbrozo, a Portuguese Jew, alias Dr. John, was charged with having made persistent overtures to his maid, Elisabeth Weales, and when rebuffed, "hee tooke her in his armes and threw her upon the bed she went to Cry out hee plucked out his handerchif of his pocket and stope her mouth and force her whether shee will or noe when hee know that she was with Child he gave her fickes to distroy it and for anything shee know hee would distroy her too. . . ." By the time the case came to court, Lumbrozo had married Elisabeth Weales, who became a prominent if contentious figure in the affairs of the county. In Virginia, a statute was passed to prevent a master who had impregnated his servant girl from claiming extra service from her beyond her indenture: "Late experiments shew that some dissolute masters have gotten their maides with child, and yet claime the benefitt of their service." However, the maid got off no better. After the end of her indenture she was to be sold by the church wardens for the use of the parish for two years. . . .

The terms of indenture required the master to provide food and clothing for his servants and, often in the case of German or Swiss servants, to take the responsibility for seeing that they learned English during the term of their indenture. At the end of their terms they were to be provided with a stated sum of money and a suit of presentable clothes so that they could make a proper start in life. South Carolina required that a female servant at the expiration of her service be given a waistcoat and petticoat, a new shift of white linen, shoes and stockings, a blue apron and two white linen caps. In some colonies, indentured servants received land at the end of their term of indenture. Thus in North Carolina during the proprietary period a servant's "freedom dues" were fifty acres of land and afterward three barrels of Indian corn and two new suits of a value of at least five pounds. . . ."

Whether wickedly abused or treasured and rewarded — and certainly they experienced both cruelty and kindness — indentured servants made up more than half the immigrants to the middle and southern colonies. During the twenty-five-year period between 1750 and 1775, some 25,000 servants and convicts entered Maryland, and a comparable number arrived in Virginia. Abbott Smith estimates that during the same period at least twice as many servants and redemptioners entered Pennsylvania, of whom perhaps a third were German and the rest, in large part, Irish. The Irish, in addition to being contentious, dirty, and strongly inclined to drink, were Catholics. To Protestants, this fact made the Irish the least desirable of all immigrant groups. The more substantial class of immigrants, especially the Germans and the Swiss, came as redemptioners. Redemptioners were carried to America by a ship captain with the understanding that after they reached the colonies, they would undertake to sell themselves to the highest bidder and then pay the captain the cost of their passage. Most of the redemptioners were craftsmen whose skills were much in demand in the colonies and who could thus sell themselves on favorable terms to a master. If they could not sell themselves, it was the shipmaster's right to undertake to sell them, often at highly disadvantageous terms. Since a master could buy much cheaper from a ship captain, collusion between prospective buyers and the captain was not uncommon.

The story of indentured servants is one of the most dramatic in colonial America. While many of those who came under indenture were the "scum and off-scourings of the earth" — convicts, paupers, runaway apprentices, prostitutes and the like — many, particularly among the non-English, were respectable and decent people who had fallen on hard times or simply wished to improve their fortunes. We also know that in the rude conditions of colonial life, many of the dissolute were redeemed.

In seventeenth- and eighteenth-century England, crime was endemic. The alarm of the more prosperous classes was expressed in cries for law and order. The penalty of death was prescribed for all felonies. In seventeenth-century England, almost three hundred crimes were classed as felonies; a conviction for anything, indeed, from housebreaking and the theft of goods worth more than a shilling must result in the sentence of death by hanging, since the judge had no discretionary power in felony cases. The benefit of clergy and royal pardon were the only mitigations. A convicted felon could "call for the book," ususally a Bible, and if he could read it, he was freed of the penalty of death, branded on the thumb, and released. The practice stemmed from medieval times, when generally speaking only those in holy orders were able to read, and they were subject to their own ecclesiastical courts. The benefit of clergy was undoubtedly a great incentive to the development of a literate criminal class, but in a time when a vast majority of the poor were illiterate, it had little else to recommend it. The simple fact was that if you were poor and illiterate you might be hanged for stealing a few shillings' worth of cloth, while a villainous cutpurse who could decipher a simple text would be branded and then would go free. . . .

The royal pardon was the only amelioration of a murderous system. Again in a typically English accommodation, judges who thought sentences too severe could send up a list of those convicted felons they considered worthy of mercy, and these would be pardoned by the king. For many years more than half of those sentenced to hang were pardoned, and increasingly it came to be the practice to issue such pardons on the condition that the culprit agreed to leave the country. From the middle of the seventeenth century until early in the eighteenth, thousands of convicts left England under this arrangement. Of these, a substantial majority found their way to the English colonies in the West Indies and in North America. In 1717, Parliament passed a law permitting the "transportation" out of the realm of certain classes of offenders "in clergy." From 1619 to 1640 all felons reprieved by royal pardon were transported to Virginia to help make up the toll of those settlers lost by disease, and between 1661 and 1700 more than 4,500 convicts were dispatched to the colonies. In the years form 1745 to 1775, 8,846 convicts, 9,035 servants, and 3,324 slaves landed at Annapolis, Maryland.

Convicts were certainly not ideal settlers. In one contingent, twenty-six had been convicted for stealing, one for violent robbery, and five for murder. . . . The character of such settlers is indicated by the career of Jenny Voss, who was eventually hanged at Tyburn after having been transported to the colonies, where "she could not forget her old Pranks, but used not only to steal herself, but incited all others that were her fellow Servants to Pillfer and Cheat," so that her master was glad to be rid of her, the more so since "she had wheadled in a Son of the Planters, who used to Lye with her and supply her with Moneys. . . ."

Virginia and Maryland, which had been the principal outlets for transported felons, had passed laws forbidding their importation by the end of the seventeenth century. . . . But despite such [laws], Parliament in 1717 passed a statute that overrode colonial efforts to stem the tide of undesirables. A total of thirty thousand convicted felons were shipped from England in the fifty-year period prior to the Revolution, of whom the greater number apparently went to Maryland and Virginia. Since convicts were bound into servitude for seven or fourteen years, which often proved to be a lifetime, the colonists usually bid actively for the most likely ones. The men sold for from eight to twenty pounds or, roughly, twenty-five to fifty dollars. Women brought slightly less, while the old and infirm were given away or, if no taker could be found, a subsidy was paid to anyone who would take them in.

It was not a humane or enlightened system, and the most that can be said for it is that the majority of the transported felons who were sold into white semislavery were slightly better off alive than dead. For those who escaped their masters, fled to other colonies, and established themselves as respectable citizens, it was a handsome bargain. Those willing to work and fortunate enough to have a kind master, had a far better life than the one they had left behind in England. It is safe to surmise that a substantially higher proportion of women than men were redeemed to a decent life — from which it would presumably follow that a substantial number of Americans who trace their line of decent back to colonial times have an ancestress or two who arrived here as a convicted felon, a sneak thief, or a prostitute.

Three or four times a year, the convicts to be transported were marched in irons though the streets of London from Newgate Prison to Blackfriars. This procession provided, like hangings, a popular form of entertainment for mobs who would hoot at the convicts and, when the convicts replied with obscene epithets, sometimes pelt them with mud and stones. The more prosperous convicts could buy special privileges. Thus in 1736, four felons rode to the point of embarkation in two hackney coaches, and another, "a Gentlemen of Fortune, and a Barrister at Law," convicted of stealing books

from the Trinity College library, had a private coach to carry him in style. These men paid their own passage and shared a private cabin.

Besides the large number of convicted felons, there were many other Englishmen who fell in the rather commodious category of "rogues and vagabonds." Although they came from a very different economic stratum, these were the hippies and dropouts of seventeenth- and eighteenth-century English society, the men and women so alienated from the dominant culture that they had devised their own. They lived on the margins of the law, devoted to preying in a thousand ingenious ways on the public. A statute of Parliament defined them as [beggars, drunkards, prostitutes, dancers, fiddlers, fencers, actors, jugglers, dice players, minstrels, fortunetellers, charlatans, tinkers, peddlers, and loiterers]. . . . Punishments were meant to be exemplary and painful. All beggars were to be stripped to the waist and whipped until they were bloody, then sent home or to the grim confines of a house of correction. Moreover, any rogue who appeared to be a hardened and dangerous character would be sent to such places beyond the seas as the Privy Council might designate.

By these provisions, incorrigible lawbreakers could be shipped out of the mother country even more readily than convicts throughout the colonial period. How "manie Drunkards, Tossepottes, whoremoisters, Dauncers, Fidlers and Minstrels, Diceplaiers, & Maskers" were dispatched to the colonies is not revealed by British court records. On the other hand, we know of enough charlatans, fortunetellers, minstrels, jugglers, tinkers, and actors in the colonies to assume that a good many of these roguish varieties made their way to America and provided lively if not always discreet entertainment for the less sophisticated colonists. What seems remarkable is that the colonies (like Virginia and Maryland) receiving the largest numbers of indentured servants and convicted felons were not utterly submerged and demoralized by these successive waves of human flotsam. Vicious and depraved as many of them must have been, the great majority made the adjustment to colonial life with reasonable success. Otherwise it is hard to see how these colonies could have survived, let alone prospered in their material and spiritual endeavors.

The transatlantic voyage from England to America was a terrible ordeal for most of those who made the crossing. Indentured servants signed up by crimps and spirits embarked on small, poorly equipped, and often dirty sailing vessels that took from one to as much as five months, depending on prevailing winds, to make the crossing. The *Sea-Flower*, with 106 passengers aboard, took sixteen weeks; forty-six of her passengers died of starvation, and of these, six were eaten by the desperate survivors. The long crossing meant bad food; the water stank and grew slimy, meat spoiled, and butter turned rancid. If the captain or owner was a profiteer, the food was often rotten to begin with. In small boats tossed by heavy seas, seasickness was commonplace. One passenger on such a crossing wrote a crude verse describing the effects of a storm on his fellow voyagers: Soon after the storm began, "there was the odest scene betwixt decks that I ever heard or seed. There was some sleeping, some spewing . . . some damning, some Blasting their legs and thighs, some their liver, lungs, lights and eyes. And for to make the scene the odder, some curs'd Father, Mother, Sister, and Brother."

A French Protestant named Durand sailed for Virginia after the revocation of the Edict of Nantes and the resumption of active persecution of the Huguenots. There were fifteen prostitutes on board ship, headed, hopefully, for a new life in the New World. During the passage, they spent their time singing and dancing and making love with the sailors and the indentured servants aboard. Durand, kept awake by their revels, wrote: "Certainly their insolence wrought a change in my nature, for my acquaintances would no doubt impute to me, as my greatest failing, an exaggerated love of the fair sex,

& to tell the truth I must admit that in my youth there was no injustice in this accusation. Not that I was ever low enough or coarse enough to feel an affection for prostitutes, but I am obliged to confess I did not abhor their debauchery as I should have. . . . But when I saw those wenches behave so shockingly with the sailors and others, in addition to the distress caused by their songs and dances, it awakened within me so intense a hatred of such persons that I shall never overcome it." Durand's wife died at sea, the food ran out, and the captain proved to be a knave and a bully. Their voyage took nineteen miserable weeks, long enough for weakness and hunger to quiet the gaiety of the prostitutes.

In the German principalities, the counterparts of the English "spirits" were the Newlanders, agents who tried to persuade guileless countryfolk to set sail for America. Gottlieb Mittelberger, a German immigrant from Enzweiningen who arrived in Philadelphia in 1750, gave a vivid account of his crossing of the Atlantic. He was bitter about the "sad and miserable condition of those traveling from Germany to the New World, and the irresponsible and merciless proceedings of the Dutch traders in human beings and their man-stealing emissaries — I mean the so-called Newlanders. For these at one and the same time steal German people under all sorts of fine pretexts, and deliver them into the hands of the great Dutch traffickers in human souls." The trip meant "for most who undertake it the loss of all they possess, of freedom and peace, and for some the loss of their very lives and, I can even go so far as to say, of the salvation of their souls." Mittelberger's journey took six months, the people "packed into the big boats as closely as herring. . . ." The water distributed to thirsty passengers was often "very black, thick with dirt and full of worms." Mittelberger's description of conditions on the ship refers to "smells, fumes, horrors, vomiting . . . boils, scurvy, cancer, mouthrot . . . caused by the age and the highly-salted state of the food, especially of the meat. . . . Add to all that shortage of food, hunger, thirst, frost, heat, dampness, fear, misery, vexation, and lamentation . . . so many lice . . . that they have to be scraped off the bodies. All this misery reaches its climax when in addition to everything else one must suffer through two or three days and nights of storm . . . all the people on board pray and cry pitifully together.'' Under such circumstances, what little civility there might have been collapsed completely. People grew so bitter ''that one person begins to curse the other, or himself and the day of his birth, and people sometimes come close to murdering one another. Misery and malice are readily associated, so that people begin to cheat and steal from one another.'' It is hardly surprising that America, when the immigrants reached it, seemed a land of deliverance; ''When at last after the long and difficult voyage the ships finally approach land,'' Mittelberger wrote, ''for the sight of which the people on board had longed so passionately, then everyone crawls from below to the deck, in order to look at the land. . . . And the people cry for joy, pray, and sing praises and thanks to God. The glimpse of land revives the passengers, especially those who are half-dead of illness. Their spirits, however weak they had become, leap up, triumph, and rejoice. . . .

As difficult as were the conditions under which indentured servants and redemptioners crossed the Atlantic, the circumstances of the prisoners were, as might be imagined, substantially worse. They were chained below decks in crowded, noisome ranks. One observer who went on board a convict ship to visit a prisoner wrote: ''All the states of horror I ever had an idea of are much short of what I saw this poor man in; chained to a board in a hole not above sixteen feet long, more than fifty with him; a collar and padlock about his neck, and chained to five of the most dreadful creatures I ever looked on.'' Living conditions were little better than those obtaining on slave ships, and before the voyage was over it was not uncommon to lose a quarter of the human cargo, most frequently to the ravages of

smallpox. (Only half as many women as men died on these hell ships, a fact attributed by merchants in the convict trade to their stronger constitutions.) Convicts so often arrived in the colonies more dead than alive that Parliamentary statutes finally set minimum allowances of bread, cheese, meat, oatmeal, and molasses per passenger — with two gills of gin issued on Saturdays.

The feelings of the colonists concerning the apparently endless stream of transported felons and vagabonds are indicated by a passage in the *Virginia Gazette* of May 24, 1751: ''When we see our Papers fill'd continually with Accounts of the most audacious Robberies, the most cruel Murders, and infinite other Villanies perpetrated by Convicts transported from Europe,'' the correspondent wrote, ''what melancholy, what terrible Reflections must it occasion! What will become of our Posterity? These are some of thy Favours, Britain! Thou are called our Mother country; but what good Mother ever sent Thieves and Villains to accompany her children; to corrupt some with their infectious Vices and murder the rest? . . . In what can Britain show a more Sovereign contempt for us than by emptying their Jails into our Settlements. . . .'' Whatever the colonists' feelings, the English were delighted with the practice of transporting their convicts to America. By such a procedure, the criminal was separated from evil companions and from the usually deplorable conditions that had induced him to take up a life of crime.

Not all convicts appreciated, by any means, the opportunity afforded them to start life over in the colonies. Not a few found their way back home (risking certain death, if caught) and declared that they would rather be hanged than return to America.

Servants and convicts who had served out their indentures often drifted to the frontier areas of the colonies, particularly to the southern frontier. Some took up cattle ranching in western Carolina, where the cattle were turned loose to graze, rounded up yearly into pens (hence Cowpens, South Carolina), and driven to the seacoast markets for meat and hides. Some, like the Hatfields and the McCoys, would in time feud with each other for decades; others lived lives of lawlessness and banditry, preying on staid planters in more settled areas and becoming, in some instances, the ancestors of the southern mountain folk, who for successive generations resisted the incursions of tax collectors.

A number, of course, gathered in the seaport towns of Baltimore, Philadelphia, New York, Charles Town, and Boston, where they drank excessively, did occasional labor, committed petty crimes, rioted, and formed the nucleus of revolutionary mobs. The truth was that with few exceptions, they belonged to that class of people whose feelings lie very close to the surface. Violent and passionate by nature, they were peculiarly susceptible to both religious conversion and revolutionary ardor. Restless and rootless, they were readily swept up by any emotional storm. Many of them were converted at the time of the Great Awakening [a series of Protestant revivals lasting from about 1725 to 1770] into pious Presbyterians, Methodists, and, somewhat later, Baptists. These denominations, with their emphasis on personal experience, were perfectly suited to the psychological needs of such individuals. Thus a substantial number of servants and ex-convicts accommodated themselves to the Protestant Ethic and became in time indistinguishable from their orthodox neighbors.

Less colorful, but equally important, were those settlers who came on their own initiative and at their own expense. By a process of natural selection, such individuals were usually aggressive, ambitious, and, as we would say today, highly motivated. Prominent among them were the Scotch-Irish. . . . [They were] independent yeoman farmers who were stout Presbyterians, often shared a common Scottish aversion to the British, and were now removed in turn to the congenial atmosphere of the colonies, particularly Pennsylvania. Hardy, enterprising Cal-

vinists, they made their way in large numbers westward, where land was plentiful and cheap. There, serving as "the guardians of the frontier," they were constantly embroiled with eastern land speculators or various Indian tribes over ownership of land.

There was a special affinity between native Lowland Scots and the inhabitants of the middle and eastern colonies. This led to a substantial immigration of Scotch-Irish in the middle years of the eighteenth century preceding the Revolutionary crisis. Never large in numbers, the Scots nonetheless, like the Jews and Huguenots, played a disproportionately important role in colonial affairs and were prominent in the patriot cause.

The Rhineland country in present-day Germany was in the eighteenth century divided into a number of principalities, including the Rheinpfalz or Rhenish Palatinate, Württemberg, Baden, and Brunswick. These petty states were constantly embroiled in European conflicts, and many German peasants, most of them pious Lutherans, fled from the exactions of their princes: from conscription, heavy taxes, and a condition of chronic insecurity. The majority came to Pennsylvania, with some in New York, Virginia, and the Carolinas. In Penn's colony, they established tight-knit, self-contained farming communities, where they clung to their language and their folk traditions. Travelers noted that they were stolid, hard-working, and usually more tidy than their English or Scotch-Irish neighbors. From *Deutsch*, they became Pennsylvania Dutch, developing their own patois and, by clinging stubbornly to their folk traditions, making their villages into small fortresses of cultural separatism. The most conspicuous and long-lived of the German immigrant groups that came to America were the Moravians, a pietist sect. . . . This group settled primarily in Salem, North Carolina, and Bethlehem, Pennsylvania, and to this day they preserve a rich tradition of church music, especially that of Johann Sebastian Bach. The Dunkers, who excelled in choral singing and book-making, and their close cousins the Mennonites also came largely to Pennsylvania. Today, forbidden by their religion to wear clothes with buttons, to drive cars, to use electricity, radios, or television, the Mennonite men with their chin hair, plain black clothes, and broad-brimmed black hats, and the women with their long skirts and bonnets, still farm the rich and carefully tended soil of central Pennsylvania and are frequently embroiled with the state over their determination not to send their children to public schools. . . .

As Protestant England had persecuted its Catholics, so Catholic France persecuted its Protestants (known as Huguenots). In consequence many Huguenots looked to the New World. Since they were denied entry into New France, a number were strung out from Boston to Charles Town, favoring the toleration and commercial opportunities offered by these port towns. Peter Faneuil, the rich merchant who built Faneuil Hall, Boston's "Cradle of Liberty," and who was both a good patriot and a public benefactor, was of Huguenot ancestry, as were Paul Revere and — in South Carolina — the Rhetts, the Gadsdens, the Ravenels, the Laurenses, the Deveaux and the L'Enfants.

A handful of Jews came to the American colonies in the seventeenth and eighteenth centuries, with Pennsylvania and Rhode Island as the preferred locations. The first American synagogue was built in Providence, Rhode Island. Aaronsburg, Pennsylvania, was founded by Jewish settlers, and in Philadelphia the wealthy Gratz family contributed generously to the patriot cause. A Jewish scholar taught Hebrew at Harvard in the middle of the eighteenth century.

[Ultimately] . . . this collection of astonishingly diverse individuals, from a dozen countries and twice as many religious sects and denominations, spread out over a vast territory and coalesced into a nation and eventually into a united people. . . .

QUESTIONS TO CONSIDER

1 Sixteenth-century immigrants to the American colonies came from England, Scotland, Ireland, France, Germany, Holland, and Sweden. What characteristics does Page Smith suggest they had in common?

2 How did conditions in seventeenth- and eighteenth-century England fuel emigration to the colonies? Describe the system of indenture. How did convicted felons, rogues, and vagabonds end up coming to America?

3 Describe the ordeal of the ocean crossing for indentured servants and for convicts. If they arrived safely, how did these immigrants make their way in American society? In what ways did the system of indenture discriminate against women?

4 By the mid-eighteenth century established colonists had begun to protest the dumping of England's human refuse on American shores. Why do you suppose the colonies were not simply overwhelmed by the flood of undesirables? Where did these and other colonial protests against English highhandedness eventually culminate?

5 Page Smith says that many of the felons, rogues, and vagabonds were converted to solid citizens in the religious revivals of the mid-eighteenth century. In what ways were these immigrants particularly susceptible to conversion?

II

SEEDTIME OF
A NATION

3

The First Century of the Modern World

CARL N. DEGLER

In all, Americans lived for 169 years under British rule. To place the colonial era in chronological perspective, this is the number of years that elapsed between Jefferson's election to the presidency in 1800 and the first moon landing in 1969. As Carl Degler observes, the first hundred years of colonial life had a significant effect on what Americans would think and do for generations afterward. Synthesizing from an array of modern writings and adding trenchant insights of his own, Degler explores the crucial themes of seventeenth-century America. He discusses the profound impact of the abundance and availability of land on the growth of indigenous American institutions. He also traces the development of representative government and the Protestant work ethic in America, an ethic that found secular expression in Benjamin Franklin's maxims in Poor Richard's Almanac: *"Early to Bed, and early to rise, makes a Man healthy, wealthy, and wise." "He that riseth late must trot all Day, and shall scarce overtake his Business at Night." "Sloth makes all Things difficult, but Industry all easy." "Laziness travels so slowly, that Poverty soon overtakes him." "Women and Wine, Game and Deceit, Make the Wealth Small and the Wants Great." (We look more closely at Franklin in selection 6.)*

Degler deals with two other topics that merit special attention. One concerns the question, "Were the Puritans 'Puritanical'?" Alas for them, the Puritans have received a bad rap in American popular literature. In Playboy Magazine *some years ago, Hugh Heffner summed up the popular misconception, referring to the Puritans as grim bigots who hated pleasure in any form and who turned America into a land of rigid sexual repression, censorship, and conformity. Like many others, Heffner confused the Puritans with the Victorians of the late nineteenth and early twentieth centuries, who did not discuss sensual matters in polite company and who advocated a strict moral code, even if they did not always practice it. The Victorians were so prudish that they referred to piano legs as* limbs, *because the word "legs" was too licentious for them. At any rate, Degler sets the Puritans' record straight, pointing out that they proscribed excesses of enjoyment, not enjoyment itself.*

Finally, Degler examines the origins of racial slavery in America, pointing out that this hateful system not only degraded our black forebears but created a moral problem for all Americans that has persisted to this day. It might be instructive to compare the white Europeans' violent treatment of the Indians, as described in the first selection, to the white Europeans' enslavement of blacks. Clearly Christian charity did not extend to dark-skinned people who were neither Christian nor European.

IN MORE WAYS THAN IS OFTEN RECOGNIZED, the one hundred years after the death of Elizabeth I in 1603 comprise the first century of the modern world. A number of developments peculiar to modern European thought cluster within these years: the true beginnings of modern science in the work of Galileo and Newton, Harvey and Boyle; the first expression of modern democratic ideas by the Levelers and in the Army Debates of the English Civil Wars; the decisive break in a millennium of religious dominance with the end of the wars of religion and the acceptance of the principle of religious tolerance; the achievement of lasting constitutional and representative government in England with the Glorious Revolution of 1688. It was also the time of the first permanent settlement of English colonists.

For America, its origin in this first century of New World, the future was still fluid. Europe's ways, both the new and the old, could be planted in America free of the choking weeds of outmoded

Pages 1–38 from *Out of Our Past: The Forces That Shaped Modern America* by Carl N. Degler. Copyright © 1959, 1970 by Carl N. Degler. Reprinted by permission of Harper & Row, Publishers, Inc.

habits. America would be a testing ground, but it would be difficult to predict what would happen. Some of the European ways would wither; some would strike root; still others would change and adapt to the new environment. For a good part of the century this plasticity was characteristic. But then, by the end of the century, the mold had hardened. In a number of ways what Americans would be for generations to come was settled in the course of those first hundred years.

☆

CAPITALISM CAME IN THE FIRST SHIPS

To men coming from the "tight little isle" the vast land of America, though untamed and dense with forest, was remarkably like the old, both in the flora that covered it and in the crops that it would yield. Although in a region like New England settlers would soon discover the soil to be thin and unfertile compared with that of the more southern colonies, it was not a desert, and from the beginning a well-organized group like the Massachusetts Bay people were able to wring a comfortable, if not opulent, living from the lean and rocky soil. The Chesapeake colonies had better soil and, as it turned out, a climate conducive to the production of a staple of world-wide appeal — the infamous weed, tobacco.

A land endowed with such promise could not fail to attract a continuous stream of men and women from the shops and farms of Europe. For centuries the problem in Europe had been that of securing enough land for the people, but in the New World the elements in the equation were reversed. "I hear . . . that servants would be more advantageous to you than any commodity," wrote a Londoner to a Virginian in 1648. For over three centuries, through wars and revolutions, through economic disaster and plague, the underlying, insistent theme of American history was the peopling of a continent.

Though the pervasive influence which Frederick Jackson Turner attributed to the frontier in the shaping of the American character can be overestimated, the possibility of exaggeration should not hide the undeniable fact that in early America, and through most of the nineteenth century, too, land was available to an extent that could appear only fabulous to land-starved Europeans. From the outset, as a result, the American who worked with his hands had an advantage over his European counterpart. For persistent as employers and rulers in America might be in holding to Old World conceptions of the proper subordination of labor, such ideas were always being undercut by the fact that labor was scarcer than land.

The imagination of men was stretched by the availability of land in America. Though land was not free for the taking, it was nearly so. In seventeenth-century New England there were very few landless people, and in the Chesapeake colonies it was not unusual for an indentured servant, upon the completion of his term, to receive a piece of land. Thus, thanks to the bounty of America, it was possible for an Englishman of the most constricted economic horizon to make successive jumps from servant to freeman, from freeman to freeholder, and, perhaps in a little more time, to wealthy speculator in lands farther west. Not all men were successful in America, to be sure, but, as the emigration literature reveals, enough were to encourage most men in the new land to strive hard for wealth and success.

In America the availability of land rendered precarious, if not untenable, those European institutions which were dependent upon scarcity of land. Efforts to establish feudal or manorial reproductions in the New World came to nothing. The Dutch, for example, tried to set up an ambitious system of patroons, or great landowners, whose broad acres along the Hudson were intended to be worked by tenants. In keeping with the manorial practices common in Europe, the patroon was to dispense justice and administer in his own right the government of his little kingdom. But contrary to the popular tradition that sees these patroonships carrying over into the period of English rule after 1664, only two of the Dutch grants outlasted New Netherland, and of them, only one was in existence ten years later. Under English rule only Rensselaer retained his original grant; all the others returned or forfeited them to the Dutch West Indies Company. It is significant that the other land-granting policy of the Dutch, that of individual small holdings, was much more successful.

At the beginning, Lord Baltimore's attempt to erect manors in Maryland and to create a feudal aristocracy enjoyed more success than that of the Dutch. Some sixty manors were established in the province during the seventeenth century, the lords of which constituted a kind of new Catholic aristocracy. On at least one of these manors, that of St. Clement, manorial courts-leet (for tenants) and baron (for freeholders) were actually held, private justice being dispensed by the lord. But here too the experiment of transplanting European social ways to the free and open lands of America was to prove futile. Slavery and the plantation were much more efficient ways for utilizing land than the outmoded manor; moreover, tenants were restive in the face of free lands to the west.

The failure in New York and Maryland to reconstitute the manors of Europe did not prevent the founders of the Carolinas from making one more attempt. In the Fundamental Constitutions of 1669 provisions were included for "leet-men" who would not be able "to go off from the land of their particular lord" without permission. Moreover, it was decreed that "all children of leet-men shall be leetmen, and so to all generations." Atop this lowest stratum of hereditary tenants was erected a quasi-feudal hierarchy of caciques and landgraves, capped by a palatine. It seems hardly necessary to add that this design, so carefully worked out in Europe, was implemented in America only to the extent of conferring titles upon the ersatz nobility; the leetmen, so far as the records show, never materialized. Indeed, the Fundamental Constitutions caused much friction between the settlers and the proprietors. Even though the hereditary nature of leetmen was discarded in 1698, the popular assembly never accepted the revised Constitutions. By the opening years of the eighteenth century, the baronies which had been taken up ceased to exist, having become simply estates or farms, none of which enjoyed the anticipated array of tenants.

Thus in those areas where an attempt was made to perpetuate the social system of Europe, it was frustrated almost from the beginning. Quite early in the colonial period, great disparities of wealth appeared in the agricultural South, as elsewhere, but this was stratification resting initially and finally upon wealth, not upon honorific or hereditary conceptions derived from Europe. As such, the upper class in America was one into which others might move when they had acquired the requisite wealth. And so long as wealth accumulation was open to all, the class structure would be correspondingly flexible.

In New England there was no experimentation with feudal or manorial trappings at all. The early history of that region is a deliberate repudiation of European social as well as religious practices. As early as 1623, for example, William Bradford wrote that communal property arrangements had failed in Plymouth and that as a consequence the governing officials divided the land on an individual basis. Individual ownership of land, so typical of American land tenure ever since, was thus symbolically begun. The larger colony of Massachusetts Bay, in its first codification of laws, the Body of Liberties of 1641, made explicit its departure from feudal and manorial incidents upon landholding. "All our lands and heritages shall be free from all fines and licenses upon Alienations, and from all hariots, wardships, Liveries, Primerseisins, yeare day and wast, Escheates and forfeitures. . . ."

The failure of America to inherit a feudal aristocracy carried implications for the future which transcended the mere matter of land tenure. The very character of the society was affected. As we have seen already, it meant that wealth, rather than family or tradition, would be the primary determinant of social stratification. Furthermore, the absence of a feudal past in America has meant that there are no classes which have a vested interest in the social forms of an earlier age. American society, as a consequence, has never split into perpetually warring camps of reactionaries and radicals in the way, for example, French society has been riven ever since the Great Revolution. Moreover, without a feudal past America offers only the thinnest of soils into which a conservatism of the European variety can sink its roots. Almost all Americans, regardless of class, have shared a common ideology of Lockean or Whig liberalism. The so-called conservatives of the American past have been only more cautious liberals. There has been in America no widely held tradition analogous to the conservatism of Edmund Burke. Burke's considerable doubts about the hopefulness of progress, the efficacy of reason, and the value of revolution have found few sympathetic ears in America. Only some ante-bellum Southerners like Thomas Dew and George Fitzhugh showed any signs of a Burkean conservative outlook. And those murmurings were killed off with the end of slavery. The conservativism of a Senator Barry Goldwater of the 1960's or of a Ronald Reagan of the 1980's is really only a species of nineteenth-century liberalism, as their emphasis upon laissez faire and individualism makes clear.

There are economic as well as political consequences which flow from the fact that America was born free of the medieval tradition of aristocracy. These are seen in purest form if we contrast the attitudes of French and American businessmen of today. (It is not so true of Englishmen because participation in trade never carried the taint it did in France.) Recruitment into management has often been hampered in France, John Sawyer has shown, because of the tradition of family enterprises. Businesses, as a result, were confined to a limited group of potential entrepreneurs and managers, "much like hereditary fiefs." Instead of being able to draw upon the population at large for the best men available, French business enterprises have often been handicapped by adherence to a feudal-like familism. Moreover, a feudally derived aristocratic disdain for trade and business still permeates French thought. As a consequence, the French businessman, unlike the American, is beset by a nagging feeling that success in business carries little prestige, and is perhaps a sign of unfashionable materialism. Hence he does not drive to expand his business or to make a lot of money; he is satisfied with a comfortable, gentlemanly living. As Sawyer concluded, "the French businessman has *himself* been unable to slough off the anti-capitalist sentiment in his social inheritance." Devoid of such an inheritance, America was also free of such inhibitory attitudes; from the beginning, to paraphrase a President of the United States, the main business of America has been business.

In place of medieval and aristocratic notions about the degrading nature of trade and business, seven-

teenth-century Englishmen brought to America two forms of that bourgeois spirit which Max Weber has called the Protestant ethic: Puritanism and Quakerism. It is possible to overemphasize the extent to which Puritanism departed from medieval conceptions of a just price, prohibitions on interest, and so forth, for such restrictions on unfettered capitalism also formed a part of Puritan economic practice in Massachusetts. But the general loosening of economic restraints which Puritanism unquestionably condoned, and its strong accent on work and wealth accumulation, bestowed religious sanction upon business enterprise. The backward-looking and forward-looking economic attitudes of Puritanism are both apparent in a Massachusetts statute of 1633. The first part of the law, in keeping with medieval practices, prescribed the proper wages for bricklayers, wheelwrights, and other skilled craftsmen, while the second part of the statute ordered "that noe person, hawse-holder or other, shall spend his time idely or unprofflably, under paine of such punishment as the Court shall thinke meet to inflicte. . . ." The close connection the Puritans saw between godliness and worldly success is implied in a story told by Governor Winthrop in his *History*. The story concerns one Mansfield who arrived in Massachusetts poor but "godly." With the help of a local rich man, "this Mansfield grew suddenly rich, and then lost his godliness, and his wealth soon after."

The calling or occupation of a Christian was an important conception in Puritan thought; it also serves as an illuminating instance of the tight linkage between religion and economics. To the Puritan, a Christian's work was a part of his offering to God. "As soon as ever a man begins to look toward God and the way of his Grace," the Reverend John Cotton taught, "he will not rest til he find out some warrantable calling and employment." No matter what the calling, "though it be but of a day laborer," yet he will make of it what he can, for "God would not have a man receive five talents and gain but two; He would have his best gifts improved to the best advantage.'' To work hard is to please God. As Cotton Mather, the grandson of Cotton, said at the end of the century, ''Would a man *Rise* by his Business? I say, then let him Rise to his Business. . . . Let your *Business* ingross the most of your time.''

Important, but often overlooked in the Puritan conception of the calling, was the idea of social obligation. For a calling to be ''warrantable,'' John Cotton emphasized, a Christian ''would see that his calling should tend to public good.'' Moreover, he continued, ''we live by faith in our vocations, in that faith, in serving God, serves man, and in serving man, serves God.'' Cotton Mather at the end of the century put it even more succinctly. One should have a calling ''so he may Glorify God by doing Good for *Others*, and getting of *Good* for himself.'' It was this cementing of social conscience to thoroughgoing individualism which saved Puritanism from degenerating into a mere defense of economic exploitation.

If the earliest New England divines, like John Cotton, had some doubts about the trader because — as the medieval schoolmen had contended — he bought cheap and sold dear, later Puritans easily accepted the new economic order. Cotton Mather, in good Calvinist fashion, argued that there ''is every sort of law, except the Popish, to justify a regulated *usury*. 'Tis justified by the law of necessity and utility; humane society, as now circumstanced, would sink, if all *usury* were impracticable.'' By the end of the century the bulging warehouses, the numerous ships in Boston Harbor, and the well-appointed mansions of the merchants bore ample testimony to the compatibility of Puritanism and wealth-getting.

Widely recognized as the dominance of Puritan economic ideals may be in New England, it is less often acknowledged that the thriving commercial center of Philadelphia owed much of its drive to a similar ethic among the Quakers. It was William Penn, not John Winthrop, who advised his children to ''cast up your income and live on half; if you can, one third; reserving the rest for casualties, charities portions.'' Simple living, as the bewigged Cotton Mather reminds us, was more a trait of Quakers in the seventeenth and eighteenth century than of Puritans. Indeed, so concerned were the Friends over the vices of ostentation and vanity that they would not permit portraits to be painted of themselves. The only concessions to the ego were black silhouettes. ''Be plain in clothes, furniture and food, but clean,'' William Penn told his children, ''and the coarser the better; the rest is folly and a snare.'' Furthermore, he counseled, diligence ''is the Way to Wealth: *the diligent Hand makes Rich. . . . Frugality* is a Virtue too, and not of little Use in Life, the better Way to be Rich, for it has less Toil and Temptation.''

As early as the seventeenth century, ''the legend of the Quaker as Businessman'' was widely accepted. This view, which was very close to the truth, pictured the Friends as shrewd, canny traders, ''singularly industrious, sparing no Labour or Pains to increase their Wealth,'' as one seventeenth-century observer put it. Much like the Puritans, the Quakers were eminently successful in the counting-house, preaching and practicing that doctrine of the calling which united religion and bourgeois economic virtues in happy and fruitful marriage.

As New Englanders fanned out into the upper Middle West in the late eighteenth and early nineteenth centuries, the seed of Puritanism, now stripped of its theological skin, was planted across America. Furthermore, if one recognizes that the doctrine of the calling was Calvinist before it was Puritan, then the numbers of people imbibing that economic precept with their religious milk swells to impressive proportions. At the time of the Revolution, Ralph Barton Perry has calculated, one out of every two white Americans was a Calvinist of some persuasion.

Though no longer clothed in theological vestments, the virtue of work and wealth has remained with Americans. As Max Weber pointed out, the advice of Franklin's Poor Richard is but the Puritan ethic shorn of its theology; in Franklin the Puritan has become the Yankee. No longer anxious about unearthly salvation, but keenly concerned about a good bargain, the American still carries the tell-tale brand of Puritanism.

☆

WERE THE PURITANS "PURITANICAL"?

To most Americans — and to most Europeans, for that matter — the core of the Puritan social heritage has been summed up in Macaulay's well-known witticism that the Puritans prohibited bearbaiting not because of torture to the bear, but because of the pleasure it afforded the spectators. And as late as 1925, H. L. Mencken defined Puritanism as "the haunting fear that someone, somewhere, may be happy." Before this chapter is out, much will be said about the somber and even grim nature of the Puritan view of life, but quips like those of Macaulay and Mencken distort rather than illumine the essential character of the Puritans. Simply because the word "Puritan" has become encrusted with a good many barnacles, it is worth while to try to scrape them off if we wish to gain an understanding of the Puritan heritage. Though this process is essentially a negative one, sometimes it is clarifying to set forth what an influence is *not* as well as what it is.

Fundamental to any appreciation of the Puritan mind on matters of pleasure must be the recognition that the typical, godly Puritan was a worker in the world. Puritanism, like Protestantism in general, resolutely and definitely rejected the ascetic and monastic ideals of medieval Catholicism. Pleasures of the body were not to be eschewed by the Puritan, for, as Calvin reasoned, God "intended to provide not only for our necessity, but likewise for our pleasure and delight." It is obvious, he wrote in his famous *Institutes,* that "the Lord have endowed flowers with such beauty . . . with such sweetness of smell" in order to impress our senses; therefore, to enjoy them is not contrary to God's intentions. "In a word," he concluded, "hath He not made many things worthy of our estimation independent of any necessary use?"

It was against excess of enjoyment that the Puritans cautioned and legislated. "The wine is from God," Increase Mather warned, "but the Drunkard is from the Devil." The Cambridge Platform of the Church of 1680 prohibited games of cards or dice because of the amount of time they consumed and the encouragement they offered to idleness, but the ministers of Boston in 1699 found no difficulty in condoning public lotteries. They were like a public tax, the ministers said, since they took only what the "government might have demanded, with a more *general imposition* . . . and it employes for the welfare of the publick, all that is raised by the *lottery.*" Though Cotton Mather at the end of the century condemned mixed dancing, he did not object to dancing as such; and his grandfather, John Cotton, at the beginning saw little to object to in dancing between the sexes so long as it did not become lascivious. It was this same John Cotton, incidentally, who successfully contended against Roger Williams' argument that women should wear veils in church.

In matters of dress, it is true that the Massachusetts colony endeavored to restrict the wearing of "some new and immodest fashion" that were coming in from England, but often these efforts were frustrated by the pillars of the church themselves. Winthrop reported in his *History,* for example, that though the General Court instructed the elders of the various churches to reduce the ostentation in

Henry Darnell III as a Child. Justus Engelhardt Kuhn's painting graphically illustrates the gap between white aristocrats and African slaves in colonial America. Young Darnell is dressed in jewelled platform shoes, a brocaded coat and lace scarf, and a luxurious cape that befit his status as a member of a developing landed aristocracy. The painter's choice of costume, accoutrements, and a backdrop of palatial dwellings catered to his aristocratic clientele, who liked to see themselves as transplanted European gentry, but who were rarely so wealthy as the painting suggests. By contrast to Henry Darnell, the African American wears a silver collar that symbolizes his servitude. His kneeling position and humble expression also indicate his inferior rank. (Maryland Historical Society)

dress by "urging it upon the consciences of their people," little change was effected, "for divers of the elders' wives, etc., were in some measure partners in this general disorder."

We also know now that Puritan dress — not that

made "historical" by Saint-Gaudens celebrated statue — was the opposite of severe, being rather in the English Renaissance style. Most restrictions on dress that were imposed were for purposes of class differentiation rather than for ascetic reasons. Thus long hair was acceptable on an upper-class Puritan like Cromwell or Winthrop, but on the head of a person of lower social status it was a sign of vanity. In 1651 the legislature of Massachusetts called attention to that "excess of Apparell" which has "crept in upon us, and especially amongst people of mean condition, to the dishonor of God, the scandall of our profession, the consumption of Estates, and altogether unsuitable to our poverty." The law declared "our utter detestation and dislike, that men and women of mean condition, should take upon them the garb of Gentlemen, by wearing Gold or Silver Lace, or Buttons, or Points at their knees, or to walk in great Boots; or Women of the same rank to wear Silk or Tiffany hoods, or Scarfes, which tho allowable to persons of greater Estates, or more liberal education, is intolerable in people of low condition." By implication, this law affords a clear description of what the well-dressed Puritan of good estate would wear.

If the Puritans are to be saved from the canard of severity of dress, it is also worth while to soften the charge that they were opposed to music and art. It is perfectly true that the Puritans insisted that organs be removed from the churches and that in England some church organs were smashed by zealots. But it was not music or organs as such which they opposed, only music in the meetinghouse. Well-known American and English Puritans, like Samuel Sewall, John Milton, and Cromwell, were sincere lovers of music. Moreover, it should be remembered that it was under Puritan rule that opera was introduced into England — and without protest, either. The first English dramatic production entirely in music — *The Siege of Rhodes* — was presented in 1656, four years before the Restoration. Just before the end of Puritan rule, John Evelyn noted in his diary that he went "to see a new opera, after the Italian way, in recitative music and scenes. . . ." Furthermore, as Percy Scholes points out, in all the voluminous contemporary literature attacking the Puritans for every conceivable narrow-mindedness, none asserts that they opposed music, so long as it was performed outside the church.

The weight of the evidence is much the same in the realm of art. Though King Charles' art collection was dispersed by the incoming Commonwealth, it is significant that Cromwell and other Puritans bought several of the items. We also know that the Protector's garden at Hampton Court was beautified by nude statues. Furthermore, it is now possible to say that the Puritan closing of the theaters was as much a matter of objection to their degenerate lewdness by the 1640's as an objection to the drama as such. As far as American Puritans are concerned, it is not possible to say very much about their interest in art since there was so little in the seventeenth century. At least it can be said that the Puritans, unlike the Quakers, had no objection to portrait painting.

Some modern writers have professed to find in Puritanism, particularly the New England brand, evidence of sexual repression and inhibition. Though it would certainly be false to suggest that the Puritans did not subscribe to the canon of simple chastity, it is equally erroneous to think that their sexual lives were crabbed or that sex was abhorrent to them. Marriage to the Puritan was something more than an alternative to "burning," as the Pauline doctrine of the Catholic church would have it. Marriage was enjoined upon the righteous Christian; celibacy was not a sign of merit. With unconcealed disapprobation, John Cotton told a recently married couple the story of a pair "who immediately upon marriage, without ever approaching the *Nuptial* Bed," agreed to live apart from the rest of the world, "and afterwards from one another, too. . . ." But, Cotton advised,

such behavior was "no other than an effort of blind zeal, for they are the dictates of a blind mind they follow therein and not of the Holy Spirit which saith, *It is not good that man should be alone.*" Cotton set himself against not only Catholic asceticism but also the view that women were the "unclean vessel," the tempters of men. Women, rather than being "a necessary Evil are a necessary Good," he wrote. "Without them there is no comfortable Living for Man. . . ."

Because, as another divine said, "the Use of the Marriage Bed" is "founded in man's Nature" the realistic Puritans required that married men unaccompanied by wives should leave the colony or bring their wives over forthwith. The Puritan settlements encouraged marriages satisfactory to the participants by permitting divorces for those whose spouses were impotent, too long absent, or cruel. Indeed, the divorce laws of New England were the easiest in Christendom at a time when the eloquence of a Milton was unable to loosen the bonds of matrimony in England.

Samuel Eliot Morison in his history of Harvard has collected a number of examples of the healthy interest of Puritan boys in the opposite sex. Commonplace books, for example, indicate that Herrick's poem beginning "Gather ye rosebuds while ye may" and amorous lines from Shakespeare, as well as more erotic and even scatological verse, were esteemed by young Puritan men. For a gentleman to present his affianced with a pair of garters, one letter of a Harvard graduate tells us, was considered neither immoral nor improper.

It is also difficult to reconcile the usual view of the stuffiness of Puritans with the literally hundreds of confessions to premarital sexual relations in the extant church records. It should be understood, moreover, that these confessions were made by the saints or saints-to-be, not by the unregenerate. That the common practice of the congregation was to accept such sinners into church membership without further punishment is in itself revealing. The civil law, it is true, punished such transgressions when detected among the regenerate or among the nonchurch members, but this was also true of contemporary non-Puritan Virginia. "It will be seen," writes historian Philip A. Bruce regarding Virginia, "from the various instances given relating to the profanation of Sunday, drunkenness, swearing, defamation, and sexual immorality, that, not only were the grand juries and vestries extremely vigilant in reporting these offences, but the courts were equally prompt in inflicting punishment; and that the penalty ranged from a heavy fine to a shameful exposure in the stocks . . . and from such an exposure to a very severe flogging at the county whipping post." In short, strict moral surveillance by the public authorities was a seventeenth-century rather than a Puritan attitude.

Relations between the sexes in Puritan society were often much more loving and tender than the mythmakers would have us believe. Since it was the Puritan view that marriage was eminently desirable in the sight of God and man, it is not difficult to find evidence of deep and abiding love between a husband and wife. John Cotton, it is true, sometimes used the Biblical phrase "comfortable yoke mate" in addressing his wife, but other Puritan husbands come closer to our romantic conventions. Certainly John Winthrop's letters to his beloved Margaret indicate the depth of attachment of which the good Puritan was capable. "My good wife . . . My sweet wife," he called her. Anticipating his return home, he writes, "So . . . we shall now enjoy each other again, as we desire. . . . It is now bed time; but I must lie alone; therefore I make less haste. Yet I must kiss my sweet wife; and so, with my blessing to our children . . . I commend thee to the grace and blessing of the lord, and rest. . . ."

Anne Bradstreet wrote a number of poems devoted to her love for her husband in which the sentiments and figures are distinctly romantic.

To my Dear and loving Husband
I prize thy love more than whole Mines of gold
Or all the riches that the East doth hold.
My love is such that Rivers cannot quench,
Nor aught but love from thee give recompense

In another poem her spouse is apostrophized as

My head, my heart, mine Eyes, my life, nay more
My joy, my Magazine of earthly store

and she asks:

If two be one, as surely thou and I,
How stayest thou there, whilst I at Ipswich lye?

Addressing John as "my most sweet Husband," Margaret Winthrop perhaps epitomized the Puritan marital ideal when she wrote, "I have many reasons to make me love thee, whereof I will name two: First, because thou lovest God and, secondly, because thou lovest me. If these two were wanting," she added, "all the rest would be eclipsed."

It would be a mistake, however, to try to make these serious, dedicated men and women into rakes of the Renaissance. They were sober if human folk, deeply concerned about their ultimate salvation and intent upon living up to God's commands as they understood them, despite their acknowledgment of complete depravity and unworthiness. "God sent you not into this world as a Play-House, but a Work-house," one minister told his congregation. To the Puritan this was a world drenched in evil, and, because it truly is, they were essentially realistic in their judgments. Because the Puritan expected nothing, Perry Miller has remarked, a disillusioned one was almost impossible to find. This is probably an exaggeration, for they were also human beings; when the Commonwealth fell, it was a Puritan, after all, who said, "God has spit in our faces." But Professor Miller's generalization has much truth in it. Only a man convinced of the inevitable and eternal character of evil could fight it so hard and so unceasingly.

The Puritan at his best, Ralph Barton Perry has said, was a "moral athlete." More than most men, the Puritan strove with himself and with his fellow man to attain a moral standard higher than was rightfully to be expected of so depraved a creature. Hence the diaries and autobiographies of Puritans are filled with the most tortuous probing of the soul and inward seeking. Convinced of the utter desirability of salvation on the one hand, and equally cognizant of the total depravity of man's nature on the other, the Puritan was caught in an impossible dilemma which permitted him no rest short of the grave. Yet with such a spring coiled within him, the Puritan drove himself and his society to tremendous heights of achievement both material and spiritual.

Such intense concern for the actualization of the will of God had a less pleasant side to it, also. If the belief that "I am my brother's keeper" is the breeding ground of heightened social conscience and expresses itself in the reform movements so indigenous to Boston and its environs, it also could and did lead to self-righteousness, intolerance, and narrow-mindedness, as exemplified in another product of Boston: Anthony Comstock. But this fruit of the loins of Puritanism is less typical of the earthy seventeenth-century New Englander than H. L. Mencken would have us think. The Sabbatarian, antiliquor, and antisex attitudes usually attributed to the Puritans are a nineteenth-century addition to the much more moderate and essentially wholesome view of life's evils held by the early settlers of New England.

To realize how different Puritans could be, one needs only to contrast Roger Williams and his unwearying opponent John Cotton. But despite the range of differences among Puritans, they all were linked by at least one characteristic. That was their belief in themselves, in their morality and in their mission to the world. For this reason, Puritanism was intellectual and social dynamite in the seventeenth century; its power disrupted churches, defied tyrants, overthrew governments, and beheaded kings.

The Reformation laid an awesome burden on the souls of those who broke with the Roman Church. Proclaiming the priesthood of all believers, Protestantism made each man's relationship to God his own terrifying responsibility. No one else could save him; therefore no one must presume to try. More concerned about his salvation than about any mundane matter, the Puritan was compelled, for the sake of his immortal soul, to be a fearless individualist.

It was the force of this conviction which produced the Great Migration of 1630–40 and made Massachusetts a flourishing colony in the span of a decade. It was also, ironically, the force which impelled Roger Williams to threaten the very legal and social foundations of the Puritan Commonwealth in Massachusetts because he thought the oligarchy wrong and himself right. And so it would always be. For try as the rulers of Massachusetts might to make men conform to their dogma, their own rebellious example always stood as a guide to those who felt the truth was being denied. Such idividualism, we would call it today, was flesh and bone of the religion which the Puritans passed on. Though the theocracy soon withered and died, its harsh voice softened down to the balmy breath of Unitarianism, the belief in self and the dogged resistance to suppression or untruth which Puritanism taught never died. Insofar as Americans today can be said to be individualistic, it is to the Puritan heritage that we must look for one of the principal sources.

In his ceaseless striving for signs of salvation and knowledge of God's intentions for man, the Puritan placed great reliance upon the human intellect, even though for him, as for all Christians, faith was the bedrock of his belief. "Faith doth not relinquish or cast out reason," wrote the American Puritan Samuel Willard, "for there is nothing in Religion contrary to it, tho' there are many things that do transcend and must captivate it." Richard Baxter, the

English Puritan, insisted that "the *most Religious*, are the *most* truly, and *nobly rational.*" Religion and reason were complementary to the Puritan, not antithetical as they were to many evangelical sects of the time.

Always the mere emotion of religion was to be controlled by reason. Because of this, the university-trained Puritan clergy prided themselves on the lucidity and rationality of their sermons. Almost rigorously their sermons followed the logical sequence of "doctrine," "reasons," and "uses." Conscientiously they shunned the meandering and rhetorical flourishes so beloved by Laudian preachers like John Donne, and in the process facilitated the taking of notes by their eager listeners. One of the unforgivable crimes of Mistress Anne Hutchinson was her assertion that one could "feel" one's salvation, that one was "filled with God" after conversion, that it was unnecessary, in order to be saved, to be learned in the Bible or in the Puritan writers. It was not that the Puritans were cold to the Word — far from it. A saint was required to testify to an intense religious experience — almost by definition emotional in character — before he could attain full membership in the Church. But it was always important to the Puritans that mere emotion — whether it be the anarchistic activities of the Anabaptists or the quaking of the Friends — should not be mistaken for righteousness or proper religious conduct. Here, as in so many things, the Puritans attempted to walk the middle path — in this instance, between the excessive legalism and formalism of the Catholics and Episcopalians and the flaming, intuitive evangelism of the Baptists and Quakers.

Convinced of reason's great worth, it was natural that the Puritans should also value education. "Ignorance is the mother (not of Devotion but) of Heresy," one Puritan divine declared. And a remarkably well-educated ministry testified to the Puritan belief that learning and scholarship were necessary for a proper understanding of the Word of God. More than a hundred graduates of Cambridge and Oxford Universities settled in New England before 1640, most of them ministers. At the same date not five men in all of Virginia could lay claim to such an educational background. Since Cambridge University, situated on the edge of Puritan East Anglia, supplied most of the graduates in America, it was natural that Newtown, the site of New England's own college, would soon be renamed in honor of the Alma Mater. "After God had carried us safe to New-England," said a well-known tract, some of its words now immortalized in metal in Harvard Yard, "one of the next things we longed and looked after, was to advance learning, and perpetuate it to posterity; dreading to leave an illiterate ministry to the churches, when the present ministers shall lie in the dust." "The College," founded in 1636, soon to be named Harvard, was destined to remain the only institution of higher learning in America during almost all the years of the seventeenth century. Though it attracted students from as far away as Virginia, it remained, as it began, the fountainhead of Puritan learning in the New World.

Doubt as one may Samuel Eliot Morison's claims for the secular origins of Harvard, his evidence of the typically Renaissance secular education which was available at the Puritan college in New England is both impressive and convincing. The Latin and Greek secular writers of antiquity dominated the curriculum, for this was a liberal arts training such as the leaders had received at Cambridge in England. To the Puritans the education of ministers could be nothing less than the best learning of the day. So important did education at Harvard seem to the New Haven colony in 1644 that the legislature ordered each town to appoint two men to be responsible for the collection of contributions from each family for "the mayntenaunce of scolars at Cambridge. . . ."

If there was to be a college, preparatory schools had to be provided for the training of those who were expected to enter the university. Furthermore, in a society dedicated to the reading of the Bible, elementary education was indispensable. "It being one chief project of that old deluder Satan to keep men from the knowledge of the Scriptures" began the first school laws of Massachusetts (1647) and Connecticut (1650). But the Puritans supported education for secular as well as religious reasons. The Massachusetts Code of 1648, for instance, required children to be taught to read inasmuch "as the good education of children is of singular behoof and benefit to any Common-wealth."

The early New England school laws provided that each town of fifty families or more was to hire a teacher for the instruction of its young; towns of one hundred families or more were also directed to provide grammar schools, "the master thereof being able to instruct youths so far as they may be fitted for the University." Though parents were not obliged to send their children to these schools, if they did not they were required to teach their children to read. From the evidence of court cases and the high level of literacy in seventeenth-century New England, it would appear that these first attempts at public-supported and public-controlled education were both enforced and fruitful.

No other colony in the seventeenth century imposed such a high educational standard upon its simple farming people as the Puritans did. It is true, of course, that Old England in this period could boast of grammar schools, some of which were free. But primary schools were almost nonexistent there, and toward the end of the seventeenth century the free schools in England became increasingly tuition schools. Moreover, it was not until well into the nineteenth century that the English government did anything to support schools. Primary and secondary education in England, in contrast with the New England example, was a private or church affair.

Unlike the Puritans, the Quakers exhibited little impulse toward popular education in the seventeenth and early eighteenth centuries. Because of their accent on the Inner Light and the doctrine of universal salvation, the religious motivation of the [Quakers] for learning was wanting. Furthermore, the Quakers did not look to education, as such, with the same reverence as the Puritans. William Penn, for example, advised his children that "reading many books is but a taking off the mind too much from meditation." No Puritan would have said that.

Virginia in the seventeenth century, it should be said, was also interested in education. Several times in the course of the century, plans were well advanced for establishing a university in the colony. Free schools also existed in Virginia during the seventeenth century, though the lack of village communities made them inaccessible for any great numbers of children. But, in contrast with New England, there were no publicly supported schools in Virginia; the funds for the field schools of Virginia, like those for free schools in contemporary England, came from private or ecclesiastical endowment. Nor was Virginia able to bring its several plans for a college into reality until William and Mary was founded at the very end of the century.

Though the line which runs from the early New England schools to the distinctly American system of free public schools today is not always progressively upward or uniformly clear, the connection is undeniable. The Puritan innovation of public support and control on a local level was the American prototype of a proper system of popular education.

American higher education in particular owes much to religion, for out of the various churches' concern for their faiths sprang a number of colleges, after the example of the Puritans' founding of Harvard. At the time of the Revolution, there were eight colleges besides Harvard in the English colonies, of which all but one were founded under the auspices of a church. William and Mary (1693) and King's College, later Columbia (1754), were the work of the Episcopalians; Yale (1701) and Dartmouth (1769) were set up by orthodox Congregationalists dissatisfied with Harvard; the College of

New Jersey, later Princeton (1747), was founded by the Presbyterians; Queens College, later Rutgers (1766), by the Dutch Reformed Church; the College of Rhode Island, later Brown (1764), by the Baptists. Only the Academy of Philadelphia, later the University of Pennsylvania (1749), was secular in origin.

The overwhelming importance of the churches in the expansion of American higher education during the colonial period set a pattern which continued well into the nineteenth century and to a limited extent is still followed. Well-known colleges like Oberlin, Wesleyan, Haverford, Wittenberg, Moravian, Muhlenberg, and Notre Dame were all founded by churches in the years before the Civil War. By providing a large number of colleges (recall that England did not enjoy a third university until the nineteenth century), the religious impulses and diversity of the American people very early encouraged that peculiarly American faith in the efficacy and desirability of education for all.

When dwelling on the seminal qualities of the seventeenth century, it is tempting to locate the source of the later American doctrine of separation of Church and State and religious freedom in the writings of Roger Williams and in the practices of provinces like New York, Maryland, and Pennsylvania. Actually, however, such a line of development is illusory. At the time of the Revolution all the colonies, including Rhode Island, imposed restrictions and disabilities upon some sects, thus practicing at best only a limited form of toleration, not freedom of religion — much less separation of Church and State. Moreover, Roger Williams' cogent and prophetic arguments in behalf of religious freedom were forgotten in the eighteenth century; they could not exert any influence on those who finally worked out the doctrine of religious freedom enshrined in the national Constitution. In any case, it would have been exceedingly difficult for Williams to have spoken to Jefferson and the other Virginians who fought for religious freedom. To Williams the Puritan, the great justification for freedom of religion was the preservation of the purity of the Church; to the deistic Virginians, the important goal was the removal of a religious threat to the purity and freedom of the State.

☆

RIGHTS OF ENGLISHMEN

For one who cherishes American political institutions, the manner in which representative government began in the seventeenth century might well make him shudder as well as wonder. The process was largely "accidental," arbitrary and hardly to be anticipated from the nature of things. This is especially true of Virginia, where the whole precedent of self-government in America was first worked out. When in 1619 the Virginia Company suggested that the colonists "might have a handle in the governinge of themselves," there was, as Charles Andrews has pointed out, "no sufficient reason, legal or other, why a popular assembly should be set up in Virginia." It was all that casual.

The precarious existence of this first representative assembly in America was emphasized in 1624, when the Crown, for various reasons, revoked the Company's charter, the King declaring that "the Government of the Colonies of Virginia shall immediately depend upon Our Selfe." Thus was terminated the legal authority for an assembly. Three times between 1625 and 1629 the planters held "conventions" for specific purposes, but these were neither regular nor legitimate assemblies. Beginning in 1630, however, and each year thereafter, without any encouragement from the Crown, the Virginians held an Assembly and presumed to legislate. Interestingly enough, in the light of the later Revolution, among their earliest laws was a prohibition upon the Governor and the Council — both of whom were appointed by the Crown — to "lay any taxes or impositions, upon the colony, theire land or commodities, otherwise then [sic] by the authoritie of the Grand Assembly.'' The legal authority for the Assembly, however, was still in doubt, for the King had not assented to its existence, and no one disputed his final and complete authority. Then in 1637 the royal instructions to the Governor contained a call for an Assembly, but the failure to provide for annual sessions indicated that the Crown was still undecided on the matter. Finally, the Governor's instructions in 1639 made it clear that the King had responded favorably to the colony's persistent requests for a continuing representative assembly.

The importance of this decision as a precedent can hardly be exaggerated. Virginia was the first English settlement to fall under the direct control of the Crown, and its forms of government could not fail to influence, if not determine, those of subsequent royal colonies — and, it should be remembered, in time all but four of the thirteen colonies would be royal.

The evolution of Massachusetts' government was somewhat different; the fact that the charter was brought with the settlers insured that events in America would be determining factors. The narrow limits of the charter, which was intended for the running of a corporation, not a community, came under attack in the first year, when over a hundred settlers applied for the rights of freemen. At that point the decision was made to open the coveted rank to ''such as are members of some of the churches within the lymitts of'' the colony. This broadening of the franchise signalized the transformation of the corporation into a true commonwealth, composed of citizens with rights and duties. In practice, confining citizenship to church members was not as restrictive as might at first be supposed, for this was, after all, a Puritan venture. There were towns like Roxbury in 1638–40, for example, which consisted of sixty-nine householders, of whom fifty-nine were church members and voters.

For the first four years Massachusetts was governed by the magistrates, who, in turn, were elected by the whole body of freemen; there being no representative assembly, the magistrates made the laws. It is more than coincidental, however, that at about the same time the Virginia Assembly was putting itself on record as opposing taxation by the executive, a similar remonstrance was afoot in Massachusetts. Early in 1632, Winthrop tells us, a group of ministers and elders of Watertown ''delivered their opinion, that it was not safe to pay moneys'' levied upon the people by the Governor and the assistants, ''for fear of bringing themselves and posterity into bondage.'' The coincidence, of course, is not accidental, for it simply underscores the common English origins of the two widely separated colonies. For centuries Englishmen had jealously guarded their right to levy their taxes locally; they continued to do so in the New World. Moreover, in the first part of the seventeenth century the issue of taxation and representative government was before the eyes of the whole nation as King and Parliament carried on their struggle for supremacy. It was to be expected that history and current events would both be reflected in the two English colonies in America.

As the number of settlers in Massachusetts increased, thereby rendering it more and more difficult for all freemen to meet together, it became necessary either to abandon the meeting of freemen, a step which men like Governor Winthrop apparently urged, or else to elect deputies or proxies who would act for the general body of freemen. At the insistence of the freemen, the latter method was accepted at the same time that it was agreed that taxes would be levied only by the legislature. Thus, in May, 1634, the first representative assembly met in Boston, with each town sending three deputies. It was understood that they ''shall have full power and voice of all and said freemen,'' except for the election of the magistrates.

The history of constitutional development in both Massachusetts and Virginia makes it quite apparent that the ordinary man's dogged insistence upon self-government in America was perhaps the most important single factor in the establishment of the representative government we esteem today. Even an opponent of popular government, John Winthrop, expressed grudging admiration for the people's ingenious if illogical pursuit of their own governance. Noting their appeal to the patent or charter in a recent dispute with the magistrates, Winthrop wryly commented that it "may be observed how strictly the people would seem to stick to their patent, where they think it makes for their advantage, but are content to decline it, where it will not warrant such liberties as they have taken up without warrant from thence."

If representative government can be said to have triumphed in the seventeenth century, it can also be said that the idea of democracy, defined as government by the consent of all the governed, was born in that century. The line to the present, however, is more tenuous, the traces fainter; not until the nineteenth century was democracy in full flower. But the beginnings of the democratic idea are already to be found in the Puritan's conception of the covenant. The idea of an agreement between the ruler and the ruled as the basis for government was very well understood in seventeenth-century Protestant America, not only because of the contemporary theological use of it, but because the extensive and close reading of the Bible among all classes made the idea common coin. The covenants with Adam, with Noah, and with Abraham were well-known Biblical agreements between God and men. Only by the agreement of all concerned, read the Cambridge Church Platform of 1648, could "we see . . . how members can have Church-power over one another mutually." It was natural that this religious or Biblical example should be extended to civil affairs, especially in a new land where the usual sanctions for government were wanting. Thomas Hooker of Connecticut fame, for example, applied the covenant idea directly to government when he wrote,

"there must of necessity be a mutual agreement . . . before, by any rule of God," men "have any right or power, or can exercise either, each toward the other."

Since the Church, according to Puritan thought, could be brought into existence only by the action of the whole membership, and the minister was called and ordained by the congregation, it was hardly to be expected that the state would long remain outside such popular participation. It was this germ of democracy which never ceased to ferment within the hard shell of Puritan government. In a very real sense, Puritanism, with its doctrines of individualism and the covenant, contained the seeds of its own destruction as an authoritarian government.

"Nothing is more striking to a European traveler in the United States than the absence of what we term the government, or the administration," wrote Alexis de Tocqueville after his tour of the United States in the 1830's. "Written laws exist in America, and one sees the daily execution of them; but although everything moves regularly, the mover can nowhere be discovered." The reason for this, Tocqueville concluded, was the great importance and strength of local government in America. Over a century later local self-rule still means much to Americans, as the appeals to its principles by modern conservatives and opponents of centralized government make evident.

It is not to be doubted that the strength of local government in America derives from the English heritage of the first settlers. Immigrants brought with them a long experience in local self-rule in the shires and towns of old England. But the distribution of the two primary forms of local government in the United States — the town of New England and the county of Virginia — is largely the result of geography and the motivations of the people who settled in the two sections of English America. When the Puritans landed in Massachusetts, they laid out their settlements in a form that best secured the object of their coming — that is, the practice of their religion. Instead of the spreading out over the land in individual farms — a procedure which would have hampered church attendance and hindered control over the religious and moral life of the people — the seventeenth-century settlements took the shape of compact villages, with the farming land stretching around the periphery. Though such a nucleated village was similar to those in England and on the Continent, the fact that settlers in Virginia evolved a much different scheme of settlement makes it clear that religious and social aims, not the European inheritance, were the controlling factors.

The Englishmen who settled in Virginia, once the dangers of Indian attacks and starvation had been surmounted, spread themselves out on individual farms, forsaking the village settlement so familiar to many of them in England. (It is true that in the western part of England, especially in Devon, whence some settlers came to Virginia, separate farmsteads were well known, but even there the nucleated village was common.) The settlers in Virginia quickly found that large plantations situated along the great rivers of the tidewater were best suited to the growing of tobacco. These widely separated plantations became so typical of the colony that by the end of the century Virginian historian Robert Beverley was regretting they had ever gotten started. "This Liberty of taking up Land and the Ambition each Man had of being Lord of a vast, tho' unimproved Territory, together with the Advantage of many Rivers, which afforded a commodious Road for shipping at every Man's Door, has made the Country fall into . . . an unhappy Settlement and course of Trade." As a result, he continued, "to this Day they have not any one place of Cohabitation among them, that may reasonably bear the Name of a Town."

The forms of local government adopted in both Virginia and New England reflected the configuration of the settlements. With population spread thin by the centrifugal forces of geography and economy, the county, with its sheriffs, justices of the peace, and county court, all inherited from England, became the Virginian, and by extension, the southern form of local government. In New England, geographical forces were largely neutral — there were no navigable rivers to encourage the spreading out of population — while religion acted as a powerful cohesive force. Though as early as 1650 a Connecticut law spoke of the "great abuse of buying and purchasing home lots and laying them together, by means, whereof great depopulations are like to follow," the village or town, clustering around the all-important meetinghouse, was the typical New England form of local government, with town meeting and selectmen.

Since the church was self-governing in New England, it was to be anticipated that the town meeting, which was in some seventeenth-century towns indistinguishable in membership from the church, should be also. Indeed, it might be said with justice that the town meeting, so peculiar to New England and so remarkable to Tocqueville, was the natural offspring of the religion and geography of New England. In practice the town meeting was one of the most democratic features of seventeenth-century life. All residents of the Massachusetts town, whether they were church members or not, could speak at meeting, though before 1647 only "saints" could vote. After that date and at the instance of the freemen, it was provided that all male residents over twenty-three could vote, be elected to town offices, and serve on juries, regardless of church membership. Recent investigations make it clear that all through the Puritan era most men in Massachusetts could participate in town government if they wished to. The New England town was truly a training ground for responsible and democratic government.

From what has been said up to now regarding the political institutions of the seventeenth-century colonists, it is apparent that they were formative for modern Americans. But the adaptation of English political ways to America, especially the representative assembly, exercised a further influence upon the course of American history. The very rhetoric and framework within which the revolutionary crisis of 1765–76 was carried out stemmed from the political forms which Americans had evolved in the wilderness. Indeed, without this particular development of representative assembly, local government, and political freedom, the Revolution, if it took place at all, would have had different goals and different slogans. For this reason, if for no other, this haphazard, often accidental, transfer of English political ways to America is suffused with a significance which origins otherwise rarely enjoy.

☆

BLACK PEOPLE IN A WHITE PEOPLE'S COUNTRY

As the germ of the revolution is to be detected in the political history of the seventeenth century, so the genesis of the Civil War is implicit in its social history. In late August, 1619, said John Rolfe, a Dutch ship dropped off "twenty Negars" at Jamestown. But, contrary to popular history, the American race problem did not begin then. It would be another half century before slavery, as it was to be known later, was clearly established in America. As late as 1671 the Governor of Virginia estimated that Negroes made up less than 5 per cent of the population.

For most of the seventeenth century, Virginia society consisted largely of small, independent, landowning farmers; slave plantations as they would be known in the eighteenth century were not only few in number but their owners were relatively insignificant politically and socially.

Not until the opening years of the eighteenth century were land holding yeomanry and indentured servants displaced to any appreciable degree by Negro slaves. Whereas in 1671, 5 per cent of the population was black, in 1715 the figure was up to 24

per cent, and by 1756 Negro slaves accounted for over 40 percent of the population. (By 1724, Negro slaves outnumbered whites more than two to one in South Carolina.) As slavery grew in importance, so did the great planter; by the end of the seventeenth century, the landed squire with his scores of slaves had superseded the sturdy yeoman in the political and social affairs of Virginia. The causes for this sharp shift in class power in the province do not concern us here. The reason for discussing it at all is in order to make clear that for most of the century neither the institution of slavery nor the Negro was an important part of the life of Virginians.

Yet it must be said that slavery and racial discrimination began in the seventeenth century. A century and a half ago, that most perspicacious student of America, Alexis de Tocqueville, pointed to slavery as the origin of the American prejudice toward the black man. Contrary to the situation in antiquity, he remarked, "among the moderns the abstract and transient fact of slavery is fatally united with the physical and permanent fact of color." Furthermore, he added, in the North "slavery recedes, but the prejudice to which it has given birth is immovable." More modern historians have also stressed this causal connection between the institution of slavery and the color prejudice of Americans. And it is patent to anyone conversant with the nature of American slavery, especially as it functioned in the nineteenth century, that the impress of bondage upon the future of black people in this country has been deep and enduring.

But if one examines the early history of slavery in the English colonies and the reaction of Englishmen toward black people, it becomes evident that the assumption that slavery is responsible for the low social status of Negroes is open to question. For one thing, the institution of slavery, as it was to be delineated in law by the end of the seventeenth century, apparently did not prevail when the first Negroes came to Jamestown. Or at least it did not appear in the statute books of Virginia until 1660.

Indeed, it is this late appearance of the status of slavery in law that has led some historians to argue that prior to the 1660's Negroes enjoyed a status equal to that of white indentured servants. To historians of that persuasion slavery was the force that dragged down the Negro to social inferiority and discrimination. Unfortunately for this view, the scholarship of Winthrop Jordan concludes that the exact status of Negroes during the first decades in America cannot be known for certain, given the available sources. One reason that the status cannot be surely known is that there is some cause to believe that Negroes were discriminated against long before the institution of slavery appeared in the law. In short, if one is seeking to uncover the roots of racial prejudice and discrimination against blacks in America, the soundest procedure would be to abandon the idea that slavery was the causal factor. In place of it, one ought to work on the assumption that discrimination preceded slavery and by so doing helped to reinforce it. Under this assumption American race prejudice originated in the discriminatory social atmosphere of the early seventeenth century, long before slavery was written into law. When slavery did appear in the statutes, it could not help but be shaped by the folk bias within which it grew. Thus legal slavery in the English colonies reinforced and helped to perpetuate the discrimination against the black man that had prevailed from the beginning of settlement.

Simply because the Negro differed from the Englishman in a number of ways, it was unlikely that men of the seventeenth century would accord the black man an equal status with Englishmen. Even Irishmen, who were white, Christian, and European, were held to be literally "beyond the Pale," and some were even referred to as "slaves." The African, after all, was a heathen at a time when "Christian" was a title of import. Moreover, he was black and culturally different. As one sixteenth-century English observer of Africans phrased it, "although the people were blacke and naked, yet they were civill." In Shakespeare's play, Brabantio's horror at his daughter's elopement with the black Othello reflects the seventeenth-century Englishman's consciousness of the Negro's differences. "Damned as thou art, thou hast enchanted her," exclaims the outraged father, ignoring the fact of Othello's Christianity. Only in a bewitched state, he argues, would his daughter shun "the wealthy curled darlings of our nation . . . to incur a general mock" and leave her family in order to seek "the sooty bosom of such a thing as thou." Desdemona herself admitted that she perceived the Moor's "visage in his mind" — an acknowledgment that his difference in countenance would have been a serious obstacle to a love less profound than hers. In *Titus Andronicus* Tamora is reviled by Bassianus for loving the Moor Aaron. "Believe me, queen, your swarth Cimerian doth make your honour of his body's hue, spotted, detested and abominable." Why, he asks her, are you wandering in the forest "with a barbarous Moor"?

But a feeling that Englishmen and Negroes were different did not depend upon vague impressions gained from chance or occasional contact with black men or Moors in England. The fact that Negroes arrived in English America as the cargo of the international slave trade unquestionably fostered a sense of superiority among Englishmen. If the noble and commanding Othello could be stigmatized as a "thing," how much more likely it was that degrading terms be applied to those wretches newly spilled out of the slave ships! It was to be anticipated that from the beginning a special inferior position would be assigned black people.

Such, indeed, was the fact even though the Virginia and Maryland records in the years between 1620 and 1660 rarely refer to "slaves" but speak mainly of "Negroes." The failure to use the term "slave" should not blind us to the real possibility that the status for which it stood was already in being. The legal definition of the inferior status which the English in America — both in New England and in the Chesapeake colonies — were building for Negroes was imprecise in those early years. But that an inferior status was in the process of being worked out seems undoubted. Moreover, the treatment accorded another dark-skinned heathen people, the Indians, offers further evidence that enslavement was early the lot reserved for blacks. Indian slavery was practiced in all the English settlements almost from the beginning; rarely were any distinctions made between Indians and Negroes when discriminatory legislation was enacted. But let us now turn to the beginnings of slavery in the English colonies.

The colonies of Virginia and New England had ample opportunity to learn of discriminatory practices against Negroes from island settlements of English like Bermuda and New Providence in the Caribbean. As early as the 1620's and 1630's these colonies provided a discriminatory or outright slave status for Negroes. In 1623, for example, the Assembly of Bermuda passed an act restraining "the insolencies of the Negroes," limiting the black man's freedom of movement and participation in trade, and denying him the right to bear arms. The Puritan venture of New Providence Island in the western Caribbean was notorious for its pirating of Negro slaves from the Spanish colonies in order to sell them or use them on its plantations. By the 1640's, according to the contemporary historian Richard Ligon, Barbados, another Caribbean English settlement, was using blacks as outright slaves.

There is evidence as early as the 1630's and 1640's that Virginia and Maryland were singling out Negroes for discriminatory treatment as compared with white indentured servants. One Hugh Davis in Virginia in 1630 was "soundly whipped before an assembly of Negroes and others for abusing himself to the dishonor of God and the shame of Christians, by defiling his body in lying with a Negro." An act passed in Maryland in 1639 enumerated the rights of "all Christian inhabitants (slaves excepted)." The slaves referred to could have been only Indians or Negroes since all white servants

were Christians. Negroes were specifically denied the right to bear arms in Virginia in 1640 and in Maryland in 1648, though no such prohibition was put upon white servants; indeed, in statutes that prohibited Negroes from being armed, masters were directed to arm the white servants.

Two cases for the punishment of runaway servants in Virginia throw some light on the status of Negroes by 1640. The first case concerned three runaways, of whom two were white men and the third a Negro. All three were given thirty lashes, and the white men had the terms owed their masters extended a year, at the completion of which they were to work for the colony for three more years. The other, "being a Negro named *John Punch* shall serve his said master or his assigns for the time of his natural Life here or elsewhere." It is obvious that the Negro's punishment was the most severe and that his penalty, in effect, was reduction to slavery, though it is also clear that up until his sentencing he must have had the status of a servant.

The second case, also of 1640, suggests that by that date some Negroes were already slaves. This one also involved six white men and a Negro who had plotted to run away. The punishments meted out varied, but Christopher Miller, "a dutchman (a prince agent in the business)," was given the harshest treatment of all: thirty stripes, burned with an "R" on the cheek, a shackle on his leg for a year "and longer if said master shall see cause," and seven years of service for the colony upon completion of his time due his master. The only other one of the plotters to receive the stripes, the shackle, and the burning of the "R" was the Negro Emanuel, but, significantly, he did not receive any sentence of work for the colony. Apparently he was already serving his master for a lifetime — i.e., he was a slave.

In early seventeenth-century inventories of estates there are two distinctions which appear in the reckoning of the value of servants and Negroes. Uniformly, the Negroes are more valuable, even as children, than any white servant. Secondly, the naming of a servant is usually followed by the number of years yet remaining to his service; for the Negroes no such notation appears. Thus, in an inventory in Virginia in 1643, a twenty-two-year-old white servant, with eight years still to serve, was valued at 1,000 pounds of tobacco, while a "Negro boy" was rated at 3,000 pounds; a white boy with seven years to serve was listed as worth 700 pounds. An eight-year-old Negro girl was calculated to be worth 2,000 pounds. On another inventory in 1655, two good men servants with four years to serve were rated at 1,300 pounds of tobacco, and a woman servant with only two years to go was valued at 800 pounds. But two Negro boys, who had no limit set to their terms, were evaluated at 4,100 pounds apiece, and a Negro girl was said to be worth 5,500 pounds.

Such wide differences in the valuation of Negro and white "servants" strongly suggest, as does the failure to indicate term of service for Negroes, that the latter were slaves. Beyond a question, there was some service which these blacks were rendering which enhanced their value — a service moreover, which was not or could not be exacted from the whites. Furthermore, a Maryland deed of 1649 suggests slave status not only of lifetime term but also of inheritance. Three Negroes "and all their issue both male and female" were deeded.

More positive evidence of true slavery is afforded by the court records of the 1640's and 1650's. In 1646, for example, a Negro woman and a Negro boy were sold to Stephen Charlton to be of use to him and "his heyers etc. for ever." A Negro girl was sold in 1652 to one H. Armsteadinger "and his heyers . . . forever with all her increase both male and female." One investigator, Susie Ames, describes the case of two Negroes brought into the eastern shore of Virginia in 1635. Over twenty years later, in 1656, the widow of the master was bequeathing the child of one of the original Negroes and the other Negro and her children. This was more than mere servitude — the term was longer than twenty years and apparently the status was inheritable.

It is true that, concurrently with these examples of onerous service or actual slavery exacted from Negroes, some black people did gain their freedom. But such instances do not deny the existence of discrimination or slave status; they simply testify to the unsteady evolution of a status for black people. Indeed, the tangential manner in which recognition of Negro slavery first appeared in the Virginia statutes strengthens the supposition that the practice long preceded the law. In 1660, in a statute dealing with punishments for runaway servants, only casual reference was made to "those Negroes who are incapable of making satisfaction by addition of time." Apparently, everyone at the time knew what was meant by the circumlocution.

But as legal questions of status arose from time to time, clarification of the Negroes' position had to be written into law. Thus in 1662 Virginia declared that the status of offspring would follow that of the mother in the event of a white man getting a Negro with child. When Maryland in 1664 prescribed service for Negroes *durante vita* and included hereditary status through the *father*, it also prohibited unions between the races. The preamble of the statute offers a clue as to the motives behind this separation of the races. Prohibition of intermarriage is necessary because "divers free born *English* women, forgetful of their free condition, and to the disgrace of our nation, do intermarry with Negro slaves," from which fact questions of status of issue have arisen. Therefore, the law was enacted in order to prevent harm to masters and "for deterring such free-born women from such shameful matches. . . ." Interestingly enough, the South Carolinian slave code of 1712 justified special legislation for Negroes on grounds of cultural difference. "The Negroes and other slaves brought unto the people of this province . . . are of barbarous, wild, savage natures, and such as renders them wholly unqualified to be governed by the laws, customs, and practices of this province. . . .''

Regardless of the reasoning behind the singling out of Negroes, as early as 1669 the law in Virginia implicitly viewed Negroes as property. An act of that year assured masters that they would not be held responsible for the accidental death of a slave as a result of punishment because it should be presumed that no man would ''destroy his owne estate.'' But it still would be a long while before the legal status of slave property would be finally settled. In 1705, for example, Virginia law declared slaves to be real estate, though with many exceptions. Similarly, in South Carolina slaves were first denominated real estate in 1690 and then chattels in 1740. By 1750, the law in the southern colonies had settled on chattels as the proper designation of slave property.

The important point is not the evolution of the legal status of the slave, but the fact that discriminatory legislation regarding the Negro long preceded any legal definition of slavery. Equally important, in view of the commonly held view that numbers of Negroes determined the inferior status imposed upon the black, is the evidence of discrimination long before numbers were large. In 1680 Virginia enacted a series of regulations which were very close to the later slave codes in restricting the movement of Negroes, prohibiting their bearing arms, and providing capital punishment for those who ran away or offered resistance to whites. Yet it would be another twenty years before the Negroes would make up even a fifth of the total population of Virginia. In short, long before slavery was an important part of the labor system of the South, blacks had been fitted into a special and inferior status.

Some historians have recently argued that, despite the evidence of a more lowly status for blacks than whites in the seventeenth-century Chesapeake re-

gion, it was slavery that was the true source of what later would be called racism, and the emphasis upon racial differences was part of the effort of the white ruling class to control unruly lower-class whites. There are two objections to this explanation for the emergence of racial discrimination in America, aside from the evidence we have already examined. The first is that only black people were reduced to the position of slaves. It is true, as these revisionist historians point out, that other ethnic groups, notably the Irish, were also looked down upon and exploited. But only blacks and some Indians — another colored population — were ever reduced to actual slavery, that is, to property. The second reason is that outside the Chesapeake region, in areas where slaves were not and never would be important in the economy, blacks were also enslaved and free blacks were also discriminated against. In short, the peculiar social conditions of Virginia — such as the unruliness of white servants — cannot explain the emergence of social discrimination against blacks in New England or the middle colonies.

So few Negroes were imported into New England during the seventeenth century that references to their status are scattered, but those pieces of evidence which are available suggest that from the earliest years an especially low status, if not slavery itself, was reserved for the Negro. One source of 1639, for example, tells of a Negro woman being held as a slave on Noddles Island in Boston Harbor. Her master sought to mate her with another Negro, but, the chronicler reported, she kicked her prospective lover out of bed, saying that such behavior was ''beyond her slavery.'' It is also well known that the first Massachusetts legal code, the Body of Liberties of 1641, permitted enslavement of those who are ''sold to us,'' which would apply to Negroes brought by the slave ships.

Nor was the use of Negroes as slaves unknown or undesirable to the Puritans. One correspondent of John Winthrop in 1645, for instance, talked of the desirability of war against the Indians, so that captives might be taken who could be exchanged "for Moores [Negroes], which will be more gayneful pilladge for us then [*sic*] wee conceive, for I doe not see how wee can thrive until wee get into a stock of slaves sufficient to doe all our business, for our children's children will hardly see this great Continent filled with people. . . ." Moreover, he went on, "servants" will not stay but "for verie great wages. And I suppose you know verie well how we shall maynteyne 20 Moores cheaper than one English servant." The following year the United Colonies (Massachusetts, Plymouth, New Haven, and Connecticut colonies) decreed, in order to save prison costs, that contumacious Indians would be delivered up to those they had injured or "be shipped out and exchanged for Negroes" as the case might justify. That enslavement of Negroes was well known in New England by the early 1650's is evident from the preamble of a Rhode Island statute of 1652. It was said that it "is a common course practised amongst Englishmen to buy Negers, to that end they may have them for service or slaves forever. . . ."

Though the number of Negroes in New England was exceedingly small, the colonies of that region followed the same path as the southern provinces in denying arms to the blacks in their midst. In 1652, Massachusetts had provided that Indians and Negroes should train in the militia the same as whites. But this ruling apparently caused friction, for in 1656 the earlier law was countermanded by the words "henceforth no Negroes or Indians, although servants of the English, shalbe armed or permitted to trayne." Connecticut in 1660 also excluded Indians and "Negar servants" from the militia and "Watch and Ward," although as late as 1680 it was officially reported to London that there were no more than thirty "slaves" in the colony.

Edward Randolph as commissioner of the Crown reported in 1676 that there were a few indentured servants in Massachusetts, "and not above two hundred slaves in the colony," by which he meant Negroes, for he said they "were brought from Guinea and Madagascar." Yet not until 1698 did the phrase "Negro slave" appear in the Massachusetts statutes. Practice was preceding law in New England just as it had in the South. In 1690, discrimination against the few Negroes in Connecticut reached the point where all Negroes were forbidden to be found outside the town bounds without "a ticket or a pass" from either master or the authorities, the restriction applying equally to free Negroes and slaves. Furthermore, it was provided that ferrymen would be fined if they permitted Negroes without passes to use their ferries. And though as early as 1680 official reports to London were distinguishing between slaves and servants, statute law barely defined the institution of slavery. In 1704, for example, the Governor gave it as his opinion that all children born of "Negro bond-women are themselves in like condition, i.e. born in servitude," but he admitted that no law had so provided. Legislation, he said, was "needless, because of the constant practice by which they are held as such. . . ." In 1703, Massachusetts provided that "molatto and Negro slaves" could be set free only if security was given that they would not be a charge on the community, and two years later a prohibition against sexual relations between Negroes and whites was enacted. In 1717, Negroes were barred from holding land in Connecticut.

Thus, like the southern colonists, the New Englanders enacted into law, in the absence of any prior English law of slavery, their recognition of blacks as different in race, religion, and culture. It should be especially noted that in many instances discriminations were made against all Negroes, whether slave or free — a fact which reinforces the argument that the discrimination preceded slavery and was not simply a consequence. Unquestionably, the coincidence of slavery with discrimination fastened still more firmly the stigma of inferiority upon the Negro, but slavery must be absolved of starting the cycle.

Once the sense of difference between the two peoples was embodied in law, the logic of the law widened the differences. All through the early eighteenth century, judges and legislatures in all the colonies elaborated the law along the discriminatory lines laid down from the beginning. In this, of course, especially in the South, they had the added incentive of perpetuating and securing a labor system which had become indispensable to the economy. As a consequence, the cleavage between the races was deepened and hardened.

In time the correspondence between the black man and slavery would be so perfect that it would be difficult to realize that the Negro was not always and everywhere in a degraded status. Thus began in the seventeenth century the Negro's life in America. With it commenced a moral problem for all Americans which still besets us at the close of the twentieth century. Though started casually, thoughtlessly, and without any preconceived goal, the web became so interwoven, so complex, so tightly meshed that John C. Calhoun could say, in 1850, slavery "has grown with our growth, and strengthened with our strength." . . .

QUESTIONS TO CONSIDER

1 Degler believes that during the first hundred years of settlement in the British colonies, Europeans were transformed into Americans. What Old World ways were discarded or altered in the New World? What ways, if any, survived intact?

2 Discuss the many ways the abundance and availability of land in America shaped American character, thought, and politics.

3 How did Puritanism and Quakerism embody the bourgeois spirit that Max Weber called the Protestant ethic? Was this ethic merely a religious justification for ruthless materialism, or was it something more? How was the Protestant ethic transformed into the American work ethic?

4 Discuss the reality of the widely held belief that Puritan society was grim, colorless, bigoted, and sexually repressed. How would Degler respond to H. L. Mencken's 1925 definition of Puritanism as "the haunting fear that someone, somewhere, may be happy"?

5 Discuss the evolution of the legal status of black slaves in America. How does Degler answer the question of which came first, slavery or racial discrimination? What are the implications of his answer for race relations in modern America?

4

Courtship, Marriage, and Children

JOHN C. MILLER

*Modern Americans, living in an age of divorce and family fragmentation, might be
surprised by how dominant a role the family played in Colonial America. The central
unit of social organization, the family served the colonists in several vital capacities:
it was the main source of recreation and association, the major instrument of education,
a self-sustaining economic unit, often the leading producer of food and manufactured
goods, and a powerful stabilizing influence in a turbulent frontier with a rapidly
expanding population. Because the family was rigidly patriarchal, the colonial man
was truly the master of his house, able to command the wages of his children and
owning virtually all of his wife's property. An average family numbered twenty or
thirty people and included not only parents and a brood of children but dependent
relatives, free and bonded servants, and slaves.*

*So essential was family life that colonists everywhere viewed "the selfish luxury
of solitary living" with suspicion. Some areas even discriminated against unmarried
people: in New Haven, for example, single men and women, proscribed from living
alone, were obliged to board with a household approved by the court or a magistrate.
Few men could afford to live alone anyway, for children constituted a cheap and
indispensable labor force. Moreover, in a society with a surplus of men and laws that
forbade bonded servants from marrying, wedlock was a symbol of status and respectability. As a southern colonist observed, "an Old Maid or an Old Bachelor are as
scarce among us and reckoned as ominous as a Blazing Star."*

*In the following narrative, biographer and historian John C. Miller describes the
highlights of colonial family life, from courtship and marriage to the role and status*

of women and children. The result is a striking portrait of those early colonists, whose experiences speak to us across the decades.

☆ **1** ☆

IN COLONIAL AMERICA, most parents considered marriage too serious a matter to be left to the young people directly concerned. Because of its financial and social consequences, the choice of a life partner was often made by parents for their offspring — a choice that the young men and women were expected to ratify dutifully. Law and custom required that a suitor make application to the parents for permission to court the young lady. If permission were not forthcoming, the young man proceeded at his peril, for the law was prepared to deal with the pertinacious swain who would not take no — from the girl's father rather than from the girl herself — for an answer. Of course, when a dowry was at issue, fathers could discourage unwanted suitors by letting it be known that they intended to withhold financial assistance if their daughters married without parental consent. . . .

To account the world well lost for love was a maxim seldom acted upon by upper-class Americans or those who aspired to enter the upper class. Rather, the principal objectives of marriage were wealth, social position and love — usually in that order. Laced as they were with dowries and jointures, marriages resembled business arrangements more that plighted troths.

The manner in which negotiations were carried on is shown in the following exchange of letters

Excerpts from *The First Frontier: Life in Colonial America* by John C. Miller, copyright © 1966 by John C. Miller. Used by permission of Dell Books, a division of Bantam, Doubleday, Dell Publishing Group, Inc.

between John Walker and Bernard Moore of Virginia:

May 27, 1764.

Dear Sir: — My son, Mr. John Walker, having informed me of his intention to paying his addresses to your daughter, Elizabeth, if he should be agreeable to yourself, lady, and daughter, it may not be amiss to inform you what I think myself able to afford for their support in case of an union. My affairs are in an uncertain state; but I will promise one thousand pounds, to be paid in the year 1765, and one thousand pounds to be paid in the year 1766; and the further sum of two thousand pounds I promise to give him, but the uncertainty of my present affairs prevents my fixing on a time of payment. The above sums are all to be in money or lands and other effects at the option of my said son, John Walker.

I am, Sir, your humble servant.
John Walker

To: Col. Bernard Moore, Esq. in King William.

May 28, 1764.

Dear Sir: Your son, Mr. John Walker, applied to me for leave to make his addresses to my daughter, Elizabeth. I gave him leave, and told him at the same time that my affairs were in such a state that it was not in my power to pay him all the money this year that I intended to give my daughter, provided he succeeded; but would give him five hundred pounds next spring, and five hundred pounds more as soon as I could raise or get the money; which sums, you may depend, I will most punctually pay to him. I am, sir, your obedient servant,

Bernard Moore

No family of colonial Virginia made more advantageous marriages than did "the marrying Carters." By dint of judiciously uniting their sons and daughters in matrimony with Burwells, Harrisons, Pages, Fitzhughs, and the other First Families of Virginia, the Carters acquired wealth, social position and political influence. Moreover, they did not shirk their duty in replenishing the earth. John Carter, the lusty founder of the clan, was married five times and had twelve children. About 50,000 of his descendants are alive today — a statistic that puts him in the same class with Pocahontas and the passengers on the *Mayflower*.

Samuel Sewall's courtship of Madam Winthrop illustrates the businesslike frame of mind with which a fortunehunter embarked upon matrimony. In 1722, when Sewall laid siege to Madam Winthrop, the well-provided-for widow of Governor Winthrop, he had lost by death two wives, ten of his fourteen children and ten of his grandchildren. Undaunted by these repeated strokes of adversity, Sewall was eager and fresh for marriage. But Madam Winthrop drove a hard bargain: as the price for her hand, she demanded that Sewall promise to keep a coach. From a purely monetary point of view, Sewall calculated that he would lose money by consenting to Madam Winthrop's terms. He therefore broke off negotiations and later married a less exacting widow. Madam Winthrop died in 1725. Samuel Sewall, the most assiduous funeral-goer in Boston, served as a pallbearer.

The long winters and the small and inadequately heated houses of New England and New York created a serious problem for unmarried men and women. Where could the rites of courtship be performed? The family fireside, around which the entire family usually congregated, was too public for the kind of intimacy the circumstances demanded, yet to remove any distance from its benign glow was apt to chill the ardor of even the most hot-blooded lover. A solution was found in the ancient and parentally approved custom of bundling. A young man and woman, fully clothed, lay down together in bed, crawled under the blankets and exchanged confidences and, insofar as possible, endearments. Bundling was governed by a rigorous code that even the most amorous were expected to observe: "Thus far and no farther" was a motto that might appropriately have been hung at the head of a bed reserved for bundling.

Lieutenant Francis Anbury, a British officer who served in America during the War of Independence, described bundling as he knew it from personal experience:

The night before we came to this town [Williamstown, Mass.] being quartered at a small log hut, I was convinced in how innocent a view the Americans look upon that indelicate custom they call *bundling*. Though they have remarkable good feather beds, and are extremely neat and clean, still I preferred my hard mattress, as being accustomed to it; this evening, however, owing to the badness of the roads, and the weakness of my mare, my servant had not arrived with my baggage at the time for retiring to rest. There being only two beds in the house, I inquired which I was to sleep in, when the old woman replied, "Mr. Ensign," here I should observe to you, that New England people are very inquisitive as to the rank you have in the army; "Mr. Ensign," says she, "our Jonathan and I will sleep in this, and our Jemima and you shall sleep in that." I was much astonished at such a proposal, and offered to sit up all night, when Jonathan immediately replied, "Oh la! Mr. Ensign, you won't be the first man our Jemima has bundled with, will it Jemima?" when little Jemima, who, by the bye, was a very pretty, black-eyed girl, of about sixteen or seventeen, archly replied, "No, father, not by many, but it will be with the first Britisher" (The name they give to Englishmen). In this dilemma, what could I do? The smiling invitation of pretty Jemima — the eye, the lip, the — Lord ha' mercy, where am I going to? But wherever I may be going now, I did not go to bundle with her — in the same room with her father and mother, my kind *host* and *hostess* too! I thought of that — I thought of more besides — to struggle with the passions of nature; to clasp Jemima in my arms — to — do what? you'll ask — why, to do — nothing! for amid all these temptations, the lovely Jemima had melted into kindness, she had been outcast from the world — treated with contempt, abused by violence, and left perhaps to perish! No, Jemima; I could have endured all this to have been blest with you, but it was too vast a sacrifice, when you were to be the victim! Suppose how great the test of virtue must, or how cold the American constitution, when this unaccountable custom is in hospitable repute, and perpetual practice.

Bundling began to go out of fashion about the time of the French and Indian War — perhaps because the British soldiers quartered in the colonies did not abide by the rules of the game. Clergymen began to take disapproving note of the practice in their sermons; what had once been regarded as a harmless and comfortable way of courting was stigmatized as a sin. Moreover, the construction of larger and better-heated houses in New England weakened the case for bundling. And so, after over a century of popularity, the custom was loaded with obloquy and banished from the land. Not until the advent of the automobile did young Americans recover one of the freedoms they had lost in the colonial period.

After bundling fell into disrepute, the Yankees and the Dutch each claimed that they had learned the practice from the other but the young people of both sections were more disposed to praise than to blame the originators. New Englanders also charged that the Dutch used bundling as a cover for sexual irregularities. Certainly the penalties meted out to transgressors against the code of bundling were more severe in New England than in New Netherland. Among the Puritans, couples who had children a suspiciously short time after marriage were often compelled to confess publicly in church that they had indulged in premarital relations. More easygoing in such matters, the Dutch permitted men and women to live together after they had published the marriage bans.

Death provided almost as much occasion for remarriage as divorce does today. It sometimes happened that a man or woman remarried so soon after the death of his or her partner that they were consoled upon the death of the late lamented and congratulated upon the choice of a successor at the same time. The first marriage celebrated in Plymouth was that between Edward Winslow, a widower of seven weeks standing, and Susanna White, who had lost her husband less than twelve weeks previously. The governor of New Hampshire married a widow ten days after she buried her husband. Before he was forty-seven years old, Samuel Washington, George's brother, had been married five times. Although colonial Americans did not quite attain the multiplicity of wives enjoyed by the patriarchs in Biblical times, they were not far behind their illustrious predecessors in that regard, even though their wives did come in sequence. . . .

Instead of getting on in the world by hard work, thrift and frugality, many young Americans preferred to make their fortune in an easier way — by marrying a rich widow. The high mortality rate ensured a plentiful supply of widows and, since they inherited at least one-third of their deceased husband's estate, many were accounted wealthy by the standards of the time. When a widow remarried, her property passed into the legal possession of her new husband. In consequence, an enterprising young man, provided he did not fear comparison with his predecessor, could set himself up for life by marrying a widow blessed with a sizeable jointure.

For the same reason that an unmarried woman was looked upon as a sad quirk of nature, so confirmed bachelors were thought to shirk their duty to God, the community and womankind. In some colonies, a special tax was levied upon bachelors in order to drive home the lesson that two could live more cheaply than one. Thus American men were presented with a hard choice, between accepting the certain penalties of the law or risking the uncertain penalties of the married state.

So brisk was the demand for widows that some Americans marveled that the maidens ever found husbands. And, indeed, the girls had reason to complain that the widows got the cream of the crop. For example, Thomas Jefferson married a wealthy widow who brought him property worth over 100,000 dollars, including 135 slaves; by this advantageous marriage, Jefferson doubled his estate. In Martha Custis, whom he married seven months after the death of Daniel Custis, Washington landed a rich prize. All of Martha's property was vested in her new husband and he was free to dispose of it as he pleased.

In the pursuit of rich widows, bachelors were given hot competition by widowers. For, by the same token that there were many widows, there were also many widowers; indeed, death, aided by excessive childbearing, tended to cut down in their prime more women than men. Particularly when they were left with the care of small children, widowers were inclined to assume that they had prior claims upon the favors, fortunes and services of widows.

Even so, few girls went unmarried, and most were wives and mothers before they were out of their teens. William Byrd observed that matrimony throve so well in Virginia that "an Old Maid or an Old Bachelor are as scarce among us and reckoned as ominous as a Blazing Star." When his eldest daughter at the age of twenty-three had not found a husband, he was inclined to write her off as an "antique Virgin." He worried lest she become "the most calamitous creature in nature" — an old maid. On the other hand, Byrd might well have rejoiced that his daughter was still alive: his sister,

Ursula, married at sixteen, had died in childbirth a year later.

☆ 2 ☆

In seventeenth-century New England, marriage was wholly a civil matter: couples were united in wedlock by a magistrate without the sanctifying presence of a clergyman. The Pilgrims, having learned this custom in Holland, brought it with them to Plymouth but it owed its wide acceptance in New England to the fact that the Puritans found no evidence either in the Bible or in the practices of the first Christians that clergymen were authorized to perform the marriage ceremony. The secular side of marriage — the property settlements and legal obligations it entailed — reinforced the view that marriage was a function of the state rather than of the church. Marriages might be made in Heaven, but they were not valid until the fees had been paid and the entry duly made in the town records. Not until 1692 were ministers in Massachusetts authorized to perform marriages. Even so, it remained essentially a secular act: when clergymen solemnized marriages they acted as agents of the state.

By modern standards, a New England marriage ceremony was a pretty bleak affair. There was no wedding dress, no throwing of rice, no bridesmaids, music, ring, prayers or benediction. The couple simply clasped hands before a magistrate and heard themselves pronounced man and wife — a fitting introduction to life in colonial New England: plain, simple and unadorned.

In the Southern colonies, marriage was usually solemnized according to the rites of the Church of England, although, in deference to the large number of dissenters in those colonies, civil marriage was permitted. Among the Quakers, marriage took place in the presence of the assembled meeting without benefit of clerical or secular authorities. The parties simply indicated their intention of entering the married state and this declaration sufficed to make them man and wife. Nevertheless, the Quakers, like other religious groups in colonial America, required the publication of bans to guard against the danger of a hasty and ill-considered match.

Because of their scarcity in early America, women were more highly valued than in the Old World, where they were relatively abundant. In 1619, for example, the Virginia House of Burgesses addressed itself to the weighty question: Which, in a new plantation, "be the most necessary, man or woman?" Ultimately the legislators decided that one could not get along without the other: therefore the immigration of women was encouraged by granting 50 acres of land to every married woman who came to the colony.

But scarcity alone did not produce romantic idealization of women. The fact was, women were valued, among other things, as helpmates; without them, no farm or plantation could be wholly successful. From a purely utilitarian point of view, therefore, a woman around the house was indispensable, and it was this aspect of marriage, rather than romantic love, which was emphasized in colonial America.

Childbearing and childrearing, domestic drudgery, farm duties — these were the lot of most women during the colonial period. For them, life was not enlivened by women's clubs and community activities. While servants were comparatively cheap, those who could not afford them had no recourse to labor-saving appliances. Of colonial women it has been eloquently said:

Generations of them cooked, carried water, washed and made clothes, bore children in lonely peril, and tried to bring [them] up safely through all sorts of physical exposure without medical or surgical help, lived themselves in terror of the wilderness, and under the burden of a sad and cruel creed, sank at last into nameless graves, without

any vision of the grateful days when millions of their descendants should rise up and call them blessed.

The kind and amount of labor performed by a married woman depended upon her station in life. Far more toil was exacted from a pioneer woman than from the wife of a wealthy planter or a middle-class townsman. Besides making the family clothing, soap and candles, and other duties that, in more affluent households, were left to indentured servants and slaves, the pioneer woman was expected to labor in the fields and to do work commonly assigned to draft animals. William Byrd met a frontier woman whom he described as

a very civil woman and shews nothing of ruggedness or Immodesty in her carriage, yett she will carry a gun in the woods and kill dear, turkeys, &c. shoot down wild cattle, catch and tye hoggs, knock down beeves with an ax and perform the most manfull Exercises as well as most men in those parts.

Even though the wife of a Southern planter was spared this menial labor, running a large household, even with the aid of a housekeeper and numerous slaves, was often a frustrating and nerve-wracking task. Moreover, since the planters always entertained guests at home, the main burden of providing Southern hospitality fell upon their wives.

At the same time, law and custom relegated women to an inferior status. In the eyes of the common law, a married woman had no existence apart from her husband; she was his chattel to do with very much as he pleased. She could not make a valid contract, bring suit or be sued in court, execute a deed, administer an estate or make a will. She could exercise no legal rights over her children. The most she could ask of them was reverence and respect. Women were expected to look upon their husbands with reverence, love and fear — the same emotions with which they approached their Maker. Insofar as the law and custom could make them so, husbands were as gods upon earth.

Except in New England, where a husband was not permitted to beat his wife, and, with fine impartiality, a wife was not permitted to beat her husband, the law specified how much corporal punishment a husband could inflict upon his wife. When he beat her — as, indeed, on occasion, the law recognized, he must — the stick must be no larger than a finger in diameter. When applying the rod, a husband was enjoined to bear in mind that, after all, she was his wife and that her services would again be required. It was therefore forbidden to kill or permanently incapacitate a woman, no matter how much provocation she gave her liege lord. During the colonial period, it was a fair question to ask a man if he had stopped beating his wife.

From the number of cases in colonial courts of wives seeking protection against their spouses, it is apparent that some husbands abused their privilege of administering wholesome and character building chastisement. In such instances, the courts compelled the husband to give bond for his future good behavior and occasionally imposed a fine to teach him better conjugal manners.

Even when buying her clothes, a woman was expected to defer to the judgment of her husband. William Byrd recorded in his diary how violently he and his wife quarreled when he learned that she had made unauthorized purchases of finery from England. George Washington avoided this kind of trouble by personally ordering his wife's and his stepdaughter's clothing. He also chose the furniture, carpets, wallpaper, and even the color of the curtains for Mount Vernon. He even directed where the furniture was to be placed. Although Martha brought him a great deal of money, she was left in no doubt as to who was running the establishment.

Even though the Puritans permitted women to become church members, they did not allow them to speak in church: if they had questions they were advised to put them to their husbands and be guided by their superior wisdom. The fate of Anne Hutchinson . . . in Massachusetts, who was banished from the colony and scalped by the Indians on Long Island, was often cited as a warning to women not to meddle with theology or other matters beyond their powers of comprehension.

John Winthrop put women in the place he supposed God intended them to occupy:

The women's own choice makes such a man her husband; yet being so chosen, he is her lord and she is to be subject to him, yet in a way of liberty, not of bondage, and a true wife accounts her subjection her honour and freedom, and would not think her condition safe and free but in her subjection to her husband's authority. Such is the liberty of the church under the authority of Christ, her king and husband; his yoke is so easy and sweet to her as a bride's ornaments; and if through forwardness or wantonness, etc. she shake it off at any time, she is at no rest in her spirit until she take it up again; and whether her lord smiles upon her and embraceth her in his arms, or whether he frowns, or rebukes, or smites her, she apprehends the sweetness of his love in all and is refreshed, supported, and instructed by every such dispensation of his authority over her.

It was very much a man's world but, even with law and custom on their side, some husbands were unable to exercise the authority that was their due. Masterful, domineering wives cut these would-be patriarchs down to size and they submitted to petticoat government with hardly more than a whimper of protest.

Occasionally, unhappy wives ran away from insupportable husbands. In that event, the husband usually advertised in the newspapers — the notice appeared alongside advertisements for the return of fugitive servants and slaves — announcing his intention of prosecuting anyone who knowingly gave the fugitive shelter. After all, the wife, however much she might dislike her husband's bed and board, was his legal property and he had a right to her services, of which he could be deprived only by the law.

Divorce was easier in New England than in those colonies where the Church of England was established. From 1664 until the American Revolution, not a single divorce was legalized in the colony of New York. In that province and in the Southern colonies, a marriage could be dissolved only by act of the royal governor and council. As a result, many couples dragged out a loveless existence. But the courts occasionally mitigated this intolerable state of affairs by ordering legal separations and, in cases of excessive cruelty, desertion and nonsupport, required the errant husband to provide separate maintenance.

In one respect, at least, women enjoyed equality with men in colonial America: they were usually punished with equal severity for crimes and misdemeanors. Women were pilloried, ducked, whipped publicly and, for a particularly heinous offense such as the murder of a husband, burned to death. Around 1720, a woman was put to death in Philadelphia for burglary. And, as always, women who sinned against the moral code received the brunt of the punishment.

For one capital crime, witchcraft, the penalty was meted out almost exclusively to women. Only one male suffered death for selling his soul to the Devil; the rest of the victims of the witchcraft mania were women. Indeed, by definition, a "witch" was a woman; a man guilty of dealings with Satan was called a "wizard." Among the many disagreeable results of growing old, women faced the very real hazard of being taken for a witch — for old women were considered particularly susceptible to the wiles of the Evil One.

The romantic aura with which Southerners surrounded their womenfolk and the chivalry that they traditionally exhibited toward all members of the weaker sex were not always in evidence during the colonial period. In 1676, when Nathaniel Bacon and

his men were under attack by Governor Berkeley's partisans in Jamestown, they made a protective shield of the wives of their enemies behind which they made good their escape. Colonel Parke, the father-in-law of William Byrd II, threatened to drag Mrs. Blair, the wife of the Commissary of the Church of England in Virginia, bodily out of her pew in full view of the congregation because she gossiped about his well-known adultery. Nevertheless, the conditions of life in the Southern colonies — the threat of violence always present in the wilderness, the hostility of the Indians and the presence of large numbers of unpredictable black slaves — caused men to take an extraordinarily protective attitude toward women. In the nineteenth century, the novels of Sir Walter Scott helped prepare the way for the cult of womanhood and the elaborate courtesy and refinement of sentiment displayed by Southern males that led some travelers to conclude that, in the Southland, knighthood was again in flower.

But in colonial America it was the absolute authority enjoyed by the husband rather than the veneration accorded women that impressed European travelers. In 1780, comparing American social gatherings with the salons of Paris, Barbé Marbois remarked that the equality of the sexes had been carried much further in France than in America:

Nothing is so rare as an unsatisfactory household; the women are sincerely and faithfully attached to their husbands; they have few pleasures outside their families, but enjoy all those which a domestic and retired life have to offer. They live in the midst of their children, feed them, and bring them up themselves. Strangers are received well here, but are rarely admitted into the intimacy of the family. Accustomed to an extreme deference for women, a European finds it hard to get used to seeing the husband the absolute master of his household. Some people believe that it is their autocratic rule which keeps the customs of this society so pure, and that the equality to which Europeans have admitted their wives has produced first laxity and then corruption.

As was to be expected in a country as desperately short of labor as was colonial America, women played an important part in activities outside the home. Women ran taverns and retail stores, operated ferries, managed plantations, and the practice of obstetrics was almost monopolized by midwives. The formidable figure of the schoolmarm began to loom over the formative years of colonial children, but custom, based on hoary prejudice, barred women's entry into such high matters as politics, church affairs, literature and the professions.

Until Aaron Burr undertook to make his daughter, Theodosia, the most erudite and accomplished woman of her generation, few Americans were prepared to agree with Mrs. John Adams when she said that "if we mean to have heroes, statesmen and philosophers, we should have learned women." Nevertheless, during the eighteenth century, the educational revolution began to catch up with women. More and more, girls were taught to write as well as to read. Increasing wealth and leisure redounded to the benefit of upper-class colonial girls, many of whom were sent to dancing schools and even to "female seminaries" where they were taught music, drawing, French and manners. The ideal of the well-brought-up young lady had undergone a drastic change since John Winthrop laid down the law as to how the "females" of Boston should conduct themselves.

Indeed, before the colonial period came to a close, some travelers were ready to pronounce American women superior to American men. Of course, American men did not always rate very high: Nicholas Creswell, for example, considered Yankees to be "the nastiest Devils in creation." Even English ladies sometimes drew invidious comparisons between American men and women. A "Lady of Quality" who came to North Carolina in 1774 observed that many of the ladies she encountered "would make a figure in any part of the world" whereas even men of the better sort seemed no better than peasants. "To be a good marksman is the highest ambition of youth," she said, "while to those enervated by age or infirmity drinking grog remained a last consolation." When she encountered a man of breeding and manners she remarked: "tho' I believed him an American, I could not help owning he had the look of a gentleman."

☆ 3 ☆

"The population explosion" that began in western Europe in the eighteenth century was most strikingly manifested in the British American colonies. Families of ten or twelve children were not unusual and the arrival of an additional member of the family was almost an annual event. Sir William Phips, governor of Massachusetts, was one of 26 children, all born of the same mother; William Rawson had 20 children by one wife; Robert "Councillor" Carter of Virginia had 17 children and Charles Carter of Shelby had 23 children by two marriages. Benjamin Franklin came from a family of 17, and John Marshall, later Chief Justice of the United States Supreme Court, was the first of 15 brothers and sisters. A South Carolina woman was credited with having brought 34 children into the world — an achievement that would certainly entitle her to be acclaimed as the All-American Mother. Yet records in this field of endeavor were made only to be broken: in 1742, a New England woman died leaving five children, 61 grandchildren, 182 great-grandchildren and 12 great-great-grandchildren.

In colonial America, large families were the rule not because there was no effective method of birth control, but because the abundance of land and the scarcity of labor made children a valuable asset. Not only did Americans feel they could afford to have numerous children: they felt that they could *not* afford not to have them. Then, too, the heavy toll taken in childhood by disease necessitated a large number of offspring to ensure the survival of the family. But the main reason was economic: on American farms, the labor of children and young adults was indispensable. Boys did field chores and learned trades while girls were occupied with the housework, milking cows and during the harvest they helped to bring in the crops. As early as 1630, Francis Higginson of Salem pointed out that "little children here by setting of corn may earn much more than their own maintenance."

It is also true that Americans married young and had children in rapid succession because they did not fear that they would be unable to provide for them. If there was not land in the immediate neighborhood, the empty region to the west offered a seemingly inexhaustible supply of virgin soil. Thomas Jefferson said that it would take at least two centuries for Americans to fill up the country and he, of course, envisaged the people living on their own farms, not piled on top of one another in great cities. Had Thomas Robert Malthus been an American, it is hardly possible that he would have conceived the idea that population threatened to outrun the food supply.

Americans seemed to have assumed that they had been specially commissioned to replenish the earth and that no time could be lost in accomplishing this mission. The Reverend Charles Woodmason found that, on the Carolina frontier, every cabin contained ten or twelve young children and that often the children and grandchildren of the same couple were of the same age; uncles and nephews, aunts and nieces all frolicked together in the mud. The Indians could have read their doom in the census figures.

At an early age, children learned — no doubt, to their dismay — that they had been brought into the world to labor and that there was no lack of employment in America. The adage that the Devil found employment for idle hands seemed to parents to be particularly applicable to children. To guard against this danger, sport and other recreations were kept at a minimum. The Reverend John Cotton of Boston recommended that children be permitted to spend the first seven years at "lawful recreation" but thereafter, he added portentously, work must begin in earnest and the choice of a "calling" ought not be postponed beyond the twelfth year. Thus religion sanctioned a practice made necessary by the hard conditions of life in a pioneering age.

Reverence for God and parents was instilled in colonial children from an early age. In their infancy, they were taught that their parents "do bear a singular image of God, as he is the Creator, Sustainer and Governor." Their first duty was obedience; as Poor Richard said, teach your child to obey and you can teach him anything. . . .

For Puritan parents, the sweetness and innocence of childhood were marred by the doctrines of infant damnation and original sin. It was impressed upon every Puritan parent that they must see to the conversion of their offspring before they were taken by death — for if they died without being redeemed by religion they were the lawful prize of the Devil. Orthodox Calvinism afforded little hope to bereaved parents that infants could enter Heaven. The best that the Reverend Michael Wigglesworth could promise them was that the easiest room in hell was reserved for infants. But no Puritan was willing to accept either for himself or for his children an apartment in hell as a consolation prize for the mansions of Paradise. . . .

Eradicating original sin in children required liberal use of the rod by Puritan parents. Every schoolmaster, likewise, included among the paraphernalia of his profession a switch made of birch twigs and, for obstinate cases, a walnut stick. It did no good for a child who had been whipped at school to complain to his parents; in that event, he was likely to get a

As this eighteenth-century portrait of the Cheney family suggests, large families, with children born about two years apart, were common in colonial America. The abundance of land and the scarcity of labor made multiple children a real economic asset. (National Gallery of Art, Gift of Edgar William and Bernice Chrysler Garbisch)

whipping at home for good measure. "Better whipped than damned," said [the Reverend] Cotton Mather; and many parents laid on the rod with right good will, persuaded that they were thereby literally beating the Devil out of the child.

But Cotton Mather did not leave parents with the stark option of sparing the rod and thereby allowing Satan to gain the upper hand; precept and example, he contended, were more effective than chastisement as a means of bringing children to glory. "When you lay them in your bosoms and dandle them on your knees," he advised his parishioners, "try by little and little to infuse good things, holy truths, into them." Anne Bradstreet, the New England poetess, treated her children with love and understanding and, perhaps partly for that reason, succeeded in bringing all seven of them to maturity. She remarked:

Diverse children have their different natures. Some are like flesh which nothing but salt will keep from putrefaction; some again like tender fruits that are best preserved with sugar: those parents are wise that can fit their nurture according to their nature.

To vanquish this brutishness, Puritan children at an early age — their elders were inclined to believe the earlier the better — were confronted with the terrors of Hell and their own loathsomeness in the sight of God. When his daughter Kathy reached the age of four, Cotton Mather took her upon his knee and told her what every girl ought to know about Hell. Nor did he conceal from her his opinion that unless she wholly changed her nature she was assuredly destined for that place of eternal torment. In his diary, Mather recorded:

I sett before her the sinful condition of her nature and charged her to pray in secret places every day. That God for the sake of Jesus Christ would give her a new heart.

Samuel Sewall's impressionable young daughter, Betty, treated to similar straight talk about Hell and damnation, reacted in a way that astonished her parents:

When I came in, past 7 at night, my wife met me in the Entry and told me Betty had surprised them. I was surprised with the Abruptness of the Relation. It seems Betty Sewall had given some signs of dejection and sorrow; but a little while after dinner she burst into an amazing cry which caus'd all the family to cry too. Her mother ask'd the Reason, she gave none; at last said she was afraid she should go to Hell, her Sins were not pardon'd. She was first wounded by my reading a sermon of Mr. Norton's; Text, Ye shall seek me and shall not find me. And those words in the Sermon, Ye shall seek me and die in your Sins, ran in her Mind and terrified her greatly. And staying at home, she read out of Mr. Cotton Mather — Why hath Satan filled thy Heart? which increas'd her Fear. Her Mother asked her whether she pray'd. She answered Yes, but fear'd her prayers were not heard, because her sins were not pardoned.

Puritan parents were haunted by the fear that the punishment for their transgressions — and in New England, thoughts could be fully as sinful as deeds — might fall upon their children. When Cotton Mather's child fell into the fire, he exclaimed in an agony of contrition: "Alas for my sin, the just God throws my child into the fire." In his sermons, he urged parents whose children had met with bodily harm or death to look into their own souls — and when they saw the depravity and sin therein they would understand why God had struck down their children. Thus the sins of one generation descended to the next generation, and mankind was caught in an eternal cycle of wrongdoing and punishment in which children were the ultimate victims.

Naturally, therefore, the conviction of sin lay heavily upon children as well as upon adults. A New England conscience was usually acquired in childhood and no one pretended that it was a pleasant experience. A child's eyes were described as being "red and sore from weeping on his sins" and a two-and-a-half-year-old girl "as she lay in her cradle would ask herself the Question: What is my Corrupt Nature? and would answer herself: It is empty of Grace, bent unto Sin, and only to Sin, and that Continually." Many children might well have echoed her lament:

> What pity such a pretty maid
> As I should go to hell. . . .

And yet despite all the evidence that children were inherently depraved, Puritans believed that even these "limbs of Satan" could be saved by education and intensive religious instruction. The Reverend Thomas Hooker urged parents to bring children "as near to Heaven as we can. It is in our power to restrain them, and reform them, and that we ought to do." But admittedly, the task was not easy: childhood was conceived of as a race between death and damnation on one side and conversion and salvation on the other.

Too often, epidemics gave the victory to death. Cotton Mather offered the children of New England good advice, but comparatively few of them lived long enough to act upon it:

You may die in your Childhood, but you should be ambitious, that if it should be so, you die an hundred years old; have as much Knowledge and Virtue, as many men of an hundred years old.

It would have been extraordinary indeed had all Puritan children submitted docilely to a code so antithetical to their normal instincts. The truth is, the behavior of the young never ceased to give anxiety to their elders; they would have been the first to admit that Puritanism had not solved the problem of how to make the manners and morals of the younger generation a carbon copy of that of their parents. The familiar lament in Puritan New England was that each generation of children was a little worse than its predecessor. The decline was uninterrupted: no one ever said that the children were better behaved, more moral and more religious than their parents. Instead, the "Lusty and Wanton Frolicks of the Young People" seemed to become progressively more lusty and wanton. Some Puritan elders arrived at the conclusion that only the Second Coming could stop this woeful deterioration.

For evidence to support this discouraging prognosis, Puritans could point to such instances as that of the young lady who pounded a constable with a Bible and the New Hampshire girl who, when accused of wearing a headdress that violated the law, told the magistrates that she "would pull off her head clothes, and come in her hair to them, like a parcel of pitifully beggarly curs as they were." Young men were guilty of similar acts of defiance: in 1700, Lord Bellamont reported that there were "a great many young men educated at the College of Cambridge, who differ much in their principles from their parents."

The Dutch in New Netherland took a more lenient attitude toward the vagaries of children. One of the reasons the Pilgrims left Holland in 1620 was that they feared that their children were in danger of being corrupted by the example set them by the relatively emancipated Dutch boys and girls. In New Netherland, the Dutch burghers carried on this tradition of their homeland: adolescent behavior was viewed with a philosophical resignation almost wholly lacking in Boston. The first master of the Latin School in New Amsterdam did not share this equanimity: he complained that he was unable to keep order in school because some parents forbade him to punish their children. As a result, he said, the students, "beat each other and tore the clothes from each other's back."

The brooding anxiety with which Puritan parents watched over the spiritual state of their children was not generally shared by the Southern planters. Heaven was always easier of attainment in the South than in New England; for that ascent, the Church of England afforded a more convenient and commodious launching-pad than did the Congregational churches. Baptism — granted in the Puritan colonies only to the children of church members — was freely bestowed in the Church of England, where it was held to be one of the sureties of grace.

In consequence, while Southern planters did not neglect the religious education of their children, they dwelt less upon the terrors of Hell and the innate depravity of man than did the seventeenth-century Puritans. It was not merely the more indulgent climate of the South that accounted for this comparatively relaxed frame of mind. Religion was the principal determinant: the Presbyterians of the Southern colonies shared the New England Puritans' views of original sin and they, too, looked askance upon "Pretexes for what is called innocent (tho' in Reality damnable) Recreations."

If the children of Puritan New England reflected, even though to a lesser degree, their parents' besetting concern with religion and morals, so the children of Southern planters tended to duplicate their parents' passion for sport, hunting and horse racing. While the Southern planting society produced few paragons of religious zeal, it did create boys and girls who loved an outdoor life and who excelled in the accomplishments deemed befitting young people of the upper class.

William Fitzhugh, an eighteenth-century Virginia planter, summed up the point of view of his place, time, and class when he said that children had "better be never born than ill-bred." The good breeding was supplied by parental example and by etiquette books, imported translations of French and Italian manuals. The books were designed to turn out the complete gentleman and the perfect lady: besides teaching correct manners — how to bow or curtsey — they sought to inculcate such virtues as courage, integrity, justice, piety and chivalry in young men, and the qualities of chastity, modesty, loyalty and submissiveness to the superior wisdom of husbands in young ladies.

QUESTIONS TO CONSIDER

1   Describe courtship and marriage customs in colonial America. How does geography affect these customs? What does the simple, rather bleak New England marriage ceremony indicate about Puritan attitudes toward matrimony?

2   What was the legal status of colonial women? Why does Miller think that seventeenth-century America "was very much a man's world"? How can we reconcile women's status in the colonies with what Degler described in selection 3 as the growth of the spirit of democracy?

3   Why did colonial Americans tend to have large families? How do the availability of land and the scarcity of labor that Carl Degler emphasized in selection 3 affect population statistics in the colonies?

4   Compare colonial and modern attitudes toward children and child-raising practices. Can you explain why some of these attitudes and practices have changed? For example, why is the trend in America today toward smaller families?

5   How can you explain the paradox of seventeenth-century America: the growth of democracy, egalitarianism, and the ideal of government by the consent of those governed existing with the growth of black slavery and an inferior status for women?

III

COLONIAL CRUCIBLE

5

The Malice of Hell:
Satan Comes to Salem Village

JOHN C. MILLER

As both Carl Degler and John C. Miller have noted, seventeenth-century America had its unseemly sides. Among the worst were the witch scares that rocked New England, particularly Puritan Massachusetts. The most appalling outbreak was that in Salem Village in 1692, where the frightened citizenry accused as many as fifty "witches" a day. The Salem scare sent a total of twenty people to the gallows for practicing what was then a capital crime, and it plunged Massachusetts into a reign of terror.

Just why the witch panic occurred has been hotly debated for generations. But the best evidence suggests a combination of factors. First of all, as John C. Miller explains in the following selection, the witch hysteria was symptomatic of the age, a time when people were plagued with superstitions and monstrous fears — fears of the unknown, of demons, and of the Devil — which spawned religious persecutions and witch hunts on both sides of the Atlantic. In the absence of scientific explanations for baffling events, Protestants and Roman Catholics alike ascribed them to Satan, who, they believed, could seduce human souls through the medium of witches.

Secondly, the Salem hysteria must be placed in the context of a society in the throes of severe change. By the 1680s, the Puritan movement had lost much of its fervor and sense of mission, Puritan youth had become disenchanted and alienated from the world of their parents, and scores of other people had become increasingly preoccupied with material pleasure and comfort. The colony even lost the political and religious autonomy it had established under its original charter. In 1691, the Crown converted

Massachusetts into a royal colony — henceforth the king would appoint both governor and judges — and ended the exclusive status of the Puritan churches. Now Massachusetts Puritans had to respect the right of all Protestants, including members of the Church of England, to worship according to their consciences. Even more unsettling was the growing fear, in Massachusetts and elsewhere, that Roman Catholics were plotting to wipe out the Protestant religion, which had grown out of the Reformation — the sixteenth-century movement to reform the Roman Catholic church. The "great fear" of a Catholic conspiracy, Miller maintains, helped create a climate of anxiety and suspicion that produced the specter of witchcraft.

The powerful Puritan ministers, Increase and Cotton Mather, also contributed to the atmosphere of fear. In the 1680s, the Mathers convinced themselves that many of their followers took witchcraft too lightly. To Cotton Mather, who saw signs of evil even in a toothache, the Devil had apparently invaded the Puritan colony. The minister was so aroused that in 1686 he had a vision in which God called him to combat Satan in Massachusetts, whereupon, after fasting and prayer, Mather produced an impassioned polemic exposing "the whole Plot of the Devil against New England in every branch of it." Through their books and sermons, both Mathers worsened the tensions that gripped the colony, including Salem Village. Just why the witchcraft panic began there is the subject of Miller's judicious and compelling account. He begins with a prologue that places the Salem hysteria in the context of witchcraft in Europe.

☆

[PROLOGUE:
THE HISTORICAL CONTEXT]

SALEM WITCHCRAFT was merely an episode . . . in the history of an ancient superstition, for evidences of belief in the malefic power of certain indi-

viduals has been found in the most primitive societies. But it was not until the late Middle Ages, when witchcraft was identified with heresy and therefore came within the purview of the Holy Inquisition, that a witchcraft mania really began. The Reformation intensified the zeal of the witch-hunters. While Roman Catholics and Protestants disagreed upon many points, they agreed in holding witches in abhorrence and in putting an end to their existence as summarily as possible. In the sixteenth and seventeenth centuries . . . over 100,000 people charged with having leagued themselves with the Devil were put to death.

Witchcraft was believed to originate in a bargain

between a man or a woman and the Devil by which he or she agreed to sell his or her soul to Satan. This transaction, of course, was a great victory for Satan: he had turned against God one of God's own creatures and ensured the damnation of a human being. It was supposed that the Devil insisted that his victims sign a book agreeing to renounce the Christian religion, pay homage to the Prince of Darkness, and join in celebrating the Black Mass. Not until it was all down in writing did Satan feel that the bargain was truly consummated. Everything was neat, orderly and legal, the Devil having served his apprenticeship in Heaven where making contractual obligations — or so the Puritans believed — was the approved procedure. After the signatories signed the "contract," they were permitted to have carnal intercourse with devils, join in the witches sabbat, revel with the Devil himself, and enjoy the power to subvert God's order on earth. Women who put their signatures to this horrid affidavit became witches; men who joined the Devil's legion were known as wizards.

Witchcraft was therefore treated as a legal crime — an offense against God — which merited the death penalty. Every country in Christendom enacted laws against witchcraft and hauled suspects into civil or ecclesiastical courts to stand trial. No less an ornament of the English bar than Sir Edward Coke, the Elizabethan champion of the rights of Parliament against the Crown, defined a witch as "a person who hath conference with the Devil, to consult with him or to do some act." The act need not be malefic or destructive: if it were proved to have been performed through "conference with the Devil," it became a capital offense.

Witches were held responsible for storms, droughts, the death of cattle, sexual impotence, epidemics — and all the veils, in short, that the Devil chose to inflict upon mankind. But, clearly, malice, spite, and unreasoning fear played an important part in determining who were the Devil's agents. Unpopular eccentrics and "far-out" people were al-

ways candidates for suspicion. Old women were particularly vulnerable: being accused of practicing witchcraft was one of the hazards of being old, ugly, and unwanted. . . .

As a rule, outbreaks of witch-hunting occurred especially in countries distinguished by clerical power, popular ignorance, the breakdown of government, and the use of torture. Germany, where all these conditions existed, was the site of the most sanguinary efforts to suppress witchcraft. At the height of the mania, no one was safe from the suspicion of being in league with the Devil. The estates of wealthy people made them particularly vulnerable, and a lenient judge was liable to incur the charge of being an accomplice of the accused. Even the expression of disbelief in witchcraft was apt to be construed as circumstantial evidence of guilt. . . .

In whipping the people into a frenzy of fear of witches, intellectuals played a vital role. The belief in witches and the determination to stamp them out was in part a by-product of the scholarship of the age: the more learned and religious the individual, the more zealous and remorseless was his attitude toward witches likely to be. In the great witch hunts of the sixteenth and seventeenth centuries, the prime instigators were men of learning who instilled their fear of the prevalence of witchcraft into the minds of the common people.

Vast ingenuity was expended by scholars upon the problem of determining how a witch could be detected. While such signs as moles or warts, an insensitive spot which did not bleed when pricked, a capacity to float in water, and an inability to recite the Lord's Prayer constituted only circumstantial evidence, they gave witch-hunters a clear lead in tracking down the Devil's agents.

On the European continent, torture was used to extract confessions from those accused of witchcraft. The rack, red-hot pincers, thumbscrews, scourges, leg-crushing machines — the familiar appurtenances of torture — together with a novel instrument, the witches' chair (a seat under which a

In England, thousands of women like those shown in this 1655 drawing were convicted of witchcraft and hanged. The hangman (A) is checking to make certain that the four women on the gallows are dead. Three more women await execution while others watch from the barred window of the prison in the background. Looking on are the belman (B) and two sergeants (C). On the right, the witchfinder (D) is getting paid for his work. (Drawing discovered by R. Gardiner, New York Public Library)

fire was kindled), were the ultimate resorts of judges and inquisitors confronted with people who obstinately protested their innocence. By express order of the Pope, issued in 1468, there were no limits upon the amount or degree of torture that could be applied. But the inquisitors were not content with a confession procured under torture: the accused had to be tortured until he or she confessed voluntarily.

In England, although those accused of witchcraft were not tortured, they were subjected to intensive interrogation, sometimes lasting for weeks or even months without benefit of habeas corpus. Those convicted in England were hung rather than burned at the stake — a distinction which, however finely drawn, was important to those who suffered the penalty. Moreover, King James I and other authorities on witchcraft enjoined judges and juries strictly to observe the rules of evidence. Even so, about 30,000 people were convicted of witchcraft in the British Isles.

During the centuries when witchcraft was in flower, the professional witch-hunter and informer flourished in Europe. Judges welcomed the services of these itinerants who ferreted witches out of their

73

deepest lairs. One of the most successful witch-hunters on record was Matthew Hopkins, who, during the 1640s, was personally responsible for the death of over 200 English witches. But Hopkins enjoyed an unfair advantage over his rival witch-hunters: he was said to have secured the Devil's own list of witches commissioned to operate in England.

As a result of the bloodletting of the period 1600–1660, when the mania reached its height, a reaction against witch-hunting set in. On the Continent, torture had been carried to such lengths that the confessions which had brought thousands of men and women to their deaths seemed worthless. During this period, thousands of people saw one or more of their relatives suffer death under one of the most terrible charges that could be made against a human being — selling his or her soul to the Devil and contracting to aid the Devil against God.

Being the most militant of English Protestants in the struggle against the Roman Catholic Counter Reformation, the Puritans were peculiarly prone to believe in witchcraft and the ubiquitous power of Satan. Literal believers in the Bible, they took the injunction "Thou shalt not suffer a witch to live" to mean that they were under a religious duty to exterminate witches. [Said John Calvin, whose theology of predestination was the basis of Puritan dogma:] "The Bible teaches that there are witches and that they must be slain. . . . God expressly commands that all witches and enchantresses shall be put to death; and this law of God is an universal law." In Geneva, Calvin suited the action to the word. Before he came to that city, little had been heard of witchcraft, but in the 60 years that followed, over 150 witches were burned. It is not therefore merely coincidental that the most destructive witch craze in English history occurred during the period of Puritan ascendancy.

By the last quarter of the seventeenth century, the maniacal phase of witchcraft was clearly on the wane. Fewer and fewer of the "Accursed tribe"

were sent to the stake or the gallows. As Montaigne said, "After all, it is rating one's conjectures at a very high price to roast a man alive on the strength of them." In the late seventeenth century, Holland abolished witchcraft trials altogether. In Geneva, the final witch burning occurred in 1652, and the last mass holocaust took place in Germany in 1679 when the Archbishop of Salzburg consigned 97 witches to the flames. In 1672, Louis XIV of France ordered that all prisoners recently condemned to death for witchcraft by the Parlement of Rouen should have their sentences commuted to banishment.

But the belief in witchcraft could not yet be dismissed as a mere peasant superstition. What had really changed was not the belief in witchcraft but confidence in the effectiveness of the methods used to detect it. While few doubted that many of those who perished at the stake were genuine witches who richly deserved their fate, it began to dawn upon the sober-minded, particularly after the mania had spent itself, that many had fallen victim to biased evidence, rumor, hearsay, envy, and malice.

☆

THE DEVIL IN MASSACHUSETTS

What is truly remarkable about Salem witchcraft is that it occurred so late in the history of an ancient superstition. Far from playing a leading part in the mania, the Puritans did not enter upon the stage until the final act. That, in part, is why they became so conspicuous: most of the other actors, having already played out their terrible parts, had left the scene.

In Puritan New England, the outbreak of witchcraft occurred in a social context characterized by instability, clerical power, tension, and fear. . . . The "great fear" abroad in the land was the fear of crypto–Roman Catholics in high places who were believed to be plotting the overthrow of the Protestant religion. It is significant that the witch hunt was preceded by a hunt for Roman Catholics. To a marked degree, Salem witchcraft was a continuation of the anti–Roman Catholic agitation. Puritans would have been hard-pressed to tell which of the two — Roman Catholics or witches — was more malefic. In any event, at the very time that the threat of Roman Catholicism was approaching its climax, the country was infested with swarms of witches.

In Salem Village — now Danvers, Massachusetts — the anxiety and apprehension felt by all the people of the colony were aggravated by dissension between the pastor and his congregation (just before the outbreak of witchcraft, two ministers had successively taken their parishioners to court to collect their salaries, and both had won judgments); by educational backwardness; by petty squabbles among the villagers over land, animals, and crops; and by the presence of Tibuta, a slave woman of mixed black and Indian ancestry whose mind was filled with the primitive lore of her people. Tibuta was a slave in the household of the Reverend Samuel Parris, who had come to Salem Village in 1689 and who, like his predecessors, had quarreled with his parishioners over his salary. The Reverend Mr. Parris's family consisted of his wife, his daughter, and his niece. Tibuta regaled these highly impressionable adolescents with tales of the occult: Salem witchcraft was the product of the conjunction of African superstition with the Christian superstition of Western Europe.

The Reverend Mr. Parris was a firm believer in witchcraft, and his young daughter and niece had probably learned at his knee all about black magic and the Invisible World. It certainly seemed very real to them; at the age of twelve they were experts on demonology. Growing up in the narrow world of a country parsonage in an intellectual atmosphere that came straight from the Middle Ages, with overtones of voodooism, and living in a backward, tension-ridden, credulous, quarrelsome community, these girls were in a strategic position to start a witch hunt. Not surprisingly, they were seized with fits and convulsions, pinched and choked by unseen hands, pricked with invisible pins and needles, and visited by specters who tried to entice them into selling their souls to the Devil.

In 1691, few people doubted that the long-heralded assault on New England by the Invisible World had begun. For His own inscrutable purposes, the Almightly had apparently permitted Satan to launch an attack upon the chosen people. The most dismal predictions of the jeremiads [Puritan sermons reproving the people for their sins] seemed mild in comparison with the horrible reality. Cotton Mather declared that ''prodigious Witch-Meetings'' were being held all over the country at which ''a fearful knot of proud, ignorant, envious and malicious creatures'' volunteered for the Devil's service. But Mather was not surprised by this untoward event: ''Where,'' he asked rhetorically, ''will the Devil show most Malice, but where he is hated, and hateth most?'' Mather rejoiced at the prospect of a decisive encounter with his old enemy who, he was persuaded, had sent the witches ''as a particular Defiance unto *my* poor *Endeavours* to bring the Souls of men unto Heaven.''

Confronted by these ''horrible Enchantments and Possessions,'' Cotton Mather first tried to drive out the Devil by fasting and prayer, a method he had used successfully in previous cases of witchcraft. But events moved too fast: before he could employ this antidote, the country was assailed by a monstrous regiment of witches. Satan's objective, Mather felt certain, was to root the Christian religion out of New England. ''I believe,'' he said, ''there never was a poor Plantation, more pursued by the *wrath* of the *Devil,* than our poor *New England.*'' But at least the enemy was identifiable. From reports he had heard, Mather pieced together a picture of the Devil: ''a short and a Black Man . . . no taller than an ordinary Walking-Staff,'' wearing ''a High-Crowned Hat, with strait Hair, and had one Cloven-Foot.''

In May 1692, at the advice of the clergy, Governor [William] Phips appointed a special court of oyer and terminer in which those accused of witchcraft could be tried. This court was composed of merchants, public officials, and doctors. Most of the members were college graduates. There was not a lawyer among them, but this circumstance was not accounted important: college graduates were deemed sufficiently learned in the law to qualify as judges, and in any event, the problem of ridding the country of witches was thought to transcend the skill and erudition of any mere lawyer. Only the most pious, God-fearing men could cope with this assault.

In the Salem witch trails, despite the strong sense of urgency and crisis, no precipitate action was taken. There was a three-month delay between the first accusations and the first trial. During this interval, the bodies of the accused were carefully examined for such telltale evidence of guilt as insensitive spots, supernumerary teats, warts, or moles. The physical checkup over, the accused were asked to recite the Lord's Prayer. If they stammered, stuttered, or missed a word, it was all up with them, for it was a well-known fact that the Devil could not get through the Lord's Prayer without stumbling. Inability to shed tears was likewise accounted an incriminating sign, since the Devil was incapable of feeling remorse for any of his misdeeds. Those who failed to clear themselves of suspicion were indicted and bound over for trial. Without legal counsel, they conducted their own defense — no easy task in view of the fact that the judges and jurors, who were all church members, were strongly inclined to regard them as guilty until proved innocent.

Among the accused was a backwoods preacher, the Reverend George Burroughs. Burroughs was alleged to be the "black man" who sounded the trumpet that summoned the witches to their rendezvous, and he was also accused of having successively murdered his two wives by incantation. The first witness against Burroughs was his own granddaughter! During his examination and trial, spectators cried out that he was biting them — and, wonderful to relate, marks made by his teeth were found on their arms even though he had not stirred from the dock. Evidence was presented that Burroughs had performed feats of running and weightlifting clearly beyond the powers of mortal man unless aided by the Devil.

For Cotton Mather, the clinching evidence against Burroughs was supplied by five witches from Andover who testified that he was their ringleader and that in that capacity he had presided over their infernal get-togethers. Thenceforth, Mather took a personal interest in seeing Burroughs brought to the gallows, unusual as it was for one clergyman to display such zeal for putting a halter around the neck of another wearer of the cloth.

Burroughs was duly convicted and sentenced to death. But as he was being prepared for the noose, he made a moving plea of innocence and recited the Lord's Prayer without making a single mistake, and the spectators were almost persuaded that Burroughs was not a wizard after all. At this point, Cotton Mather, mounted on a horse, proved that he was as effective an orator in the saddle as in the pulpit. He turned the crowd against Burroughs by pointing out that the condemned man was not really an ordained minister and that all the persons hitherto executed had died by a righteous sentence. Burroughs was strung up, and Cotton Mather rode home satisfied with having done a good day's work for the Lord.

A convicted witch could save herself by confessing; indeed, the object of the prosecution was not to kill witches but to extract confessions from them. Some of the accused took this easy way out, implicating others in their accounts of their dealings with the Devil. These confessions brought an ever-widening circle of people under suspicion. As in England, torture was not used to procure confessions, but wizard or witch could go to the gallows protesting his or her innocence or stubbornly refusing to speak.

Confession, while it usually saved a person's life, led to forfeiture of property. Giles Cory, who would have been found guilty in an ordinary court of law of nothing more serious than eccentricity, refused to answer his accusers when charged with entering into a compact with the Devil — in the hope thereby of preserving his estate for his heirs. By English law (not repealed until 1772), *peine forte et dure* — pressing by weights until a confession, or death, was forthcoming — was prescribed for those who stood mute. The weights were placed upon Cory, and after several days of torture, he died without opening his lips. At that incredible cost, he made it possible for his heirs to inherit his property.

Salem witchcraft was not merely the result of a welling up of ignorance, superstition, and fear from the depths of society. The clergy, the magistrates (including Governor Phips himself), and educated people in general shared the conviction of the most ignorant and deluded people that they were witnessing an outbreak of "horrible Enchantments and Possessions" instigated by Satan.

As long as the accusations were made against friendless old women and people of low degree, the clergy hallooed on the witch-hunters and sanctified the good work by quoting the injunction of the Book of Exodus: "Thou shalt not suffer a witch to live." In the trials, every kind of "evidence" — hearsay, gossip, old wives' tales — was admitted provided that it indicated the guilt of the accused. Some of this so-called evidence went back many years and obviously originated in personal spite. None of the defendants had counsel to raise objections to the admission of this kind of evidence or, indeed, to question the legality of the procedure or the jurisdiction of the court. As a result, there was no one to contest the legality of "spectral evidence."

In their confessions, or in giving evidence on the witness stand, many people alleged that they had been approached by people who passed as respectable members of society yet who now appeared in the guise of the Devil's agents urging their victims to sign the Devil's book and to commit other enormities. This was "spectral evidence," and if it were indiscriminately admitted to be valid, there was obviously no limit to the number of people who might be accused of witchcraft. The weighty question raised by spectral evidence was whether or not the Devil could assume the shape of an innocent person or whether or not every person who appeared to be afflicted actually served the Devil's purposes.

When their opinion was asked, the Mathers recommended that the judges observe "a very critical and exquisite caution" lest they be taken in by the Devil's legerdemain. Caution was especially important, they warned, in cases of "persons formerly of an unblemished reputation." "It was better for a guilty witch to live," said Increase Mather, "than for an innocent person to die." Cotton Mather admitted that the Devil might, by God's permission, appear in the shape of an innocent person, but he thought that this permission was rarely given.

In essence, Cotton Mather took the position that spectral evidence merely offered grounds for suspicion and, at most, a presumption of guilt but that corroborative evidence was required before a verdict could be rendered. The immediate danger, as he saw it, was that evil spirits would confuse the judges by appearing in the guise of innocent people thereby permitting bona fide witches to escape scot-free. Chief Justice Stoughton, much as he revered the Mathers, did not accept their views on the admissibility of spectral evidence. In his opinion, the fact that the Devil assumed the form of a respectable individual, even though he was a pillar of the community, must mean that that individual had sold his soul, for, he declared, the Devil could not impersonate an innocent man or woman. He therefore instructed the jury that "as the Devil had appeared in the form of many of the accused, according to the eye-witnesses there, the defendants must be guilty."

William Stoughton, Chief Justice of the Court of Oyer and Terminer and a generous contributor to Harvard. In one of the low points of the witch trials, this stubborn, overweening juror insisted that Rebecca Nurse be hanged. He objected bitterly when the trials of witches ended, asserting that "We were in a way to have cleared the land of them. Who it is that obstructs the cause of justice I know not; the Lord be merciful to this country!" While some jurors and witnesses later repented their parts in the Salem proceedings, Stoughton went to his grave convinced that he had been right. (Harvard University Portrait Collection, given by John Cooper to Harvard College in 1810)

This instruction resulted in the conviction of several of the accused.

Nor did the people follow the Mathers in drawing these fine distinctions regarding the admissibility of spectral evidence. To them, any person who took the form of a specter must be an agent of Satan. In consequence, Massachusetts was gripped by a reign of terror. Ties of friendship and of blood ceased to matter. It was a case of every man for himself and the Devil take the hindmost. Wives tes-

tified against their husbands; children charged their parents with practicing witchcraft; a wife and daughter gave evidence against their husband and father in order to save themselves; and a seven-year-old girl helped send her mother to the gallows. When two young men would not confess, they were tied together by the neck until they accused their own mother. The role of specters began to read like a *Who's Who* of New England. Captain John Alden, the eldest son of John and Priscilla Alden, was accused of being a wizard on the strength of spectral evidence, but the resourceful captain escaped from jail. Dudley Bradstreet, the son of a former governor, fled the colony before he could be brought to trial. The wife of the Reverend John Hale, secretary of the colony of Connecticut, was denounced as a witch, and one woman who was hung at Salem was a church member. Cotton Mather himself was not safe: in October 1693, a young woman swore that Mather's image threatened and molested her. "I cried unto the Lord," Mather wrote in his Diary, "for the Deliverance of my *Name*, from the Malice of Hell." Thus the work of casting out devils seemed likely to lead to the depopulation of Massachusetts. Who would be alive to hang the last witch?

Clearly, events were escaping from the control of the clergy and magistrates. Witch-hunting had reached the height of mass hysteria: the people clamored for more victims, and no one was safe from their zeal and fear.

To add to the danger, although Salem Village continued to be "the Chief Seat of these Diabolical Vexations," witches began to expand their operations until all Massachusetts reeled under "the horrible Assaults made by the Invisible World." The citizens of Gloucester, expecting to be attacked by an army of witches, took refuge in a stockade. In Andover, where an epidemic was blamed on witches, more than 50 people were accused of having had dealings with the Devil. One of the magistrates who dared to defy public opinion by refusing to institute proceedings against the suspects was himself accused of sorcery. But the mania was short-lived: one of the accused instituted action for defamation of character against his accusors. "This wonderfully quenched zeal," it was observed, "the accusers saw *his* spectre no more."

By September 22, 1692, the Salem judges had tried 27 suspects, one-third of them church members; all had denied being witches. All 27 had been sentenced to death, and of this number 19 had been hanged and 1 pressed to death. A man accused of bewitching a dog barely escaped with his life, but the dog, presumably possessed by devils, was killed. None of the 50 who confessed that they were witches had been executed; 100 persons accused of being witches were in jail awaiting trial; and an additional 200 had been accused but had not yet been imprisoned. Two judges had resigned from the court of oyer and terminer to protest the course the proceedings had taken. Among the suspects were Lady Phips, the wife of the Governor of the province, and the Reverend Samuel Willard of Boston, the president of Harvard College. Willard was under suspicion because he had questioned some of the evidence presented at the trials.

On September 22, 1692, at the advice of the clergy, now thoroughly alarmed by the use to which spectral evidence was being put, Governor Phips suspended the proceedings of the court of oyer and terminer. In December the accused were brought before the Superior Court for trial. Spectral evidence was sparingly admitted, with the result that of the 52 persons brought to trial, 49 were acquitted. Only three were found guilty and condemned, but Phips first reprieved them and then granted a general pardon to all under suspicion. In 1957, the Massachusetts Legislature adopted a resolution absolving all the Salem witches of wrongdoing.

Chief Justice Stoughton bitterly lamented the decision to call a halt to the trials: "We were in a way to have cleared the land of them," he said. "Who it is that obstructs the cause of justice I know not; the Lord be merciful to this country!"

It is ironical that Cotton Mather, who wished to be known above all as a man of God and a do-gooder, should be remembered chiefly for his part in the Salem witch trials and therefore held to be typical of all that was most narrow, bigoted, and repellent in Puritanism — the very epitome of the black-frocked, bluenosed zealot. He was by no means the most remorseless and bloodthirsty of the witch-hunters; indeed, his position on spectral evidence marks him as a moderate and a stickler for the observance of legal formalities. The people, and some of the clergy, demanded more witch trials and more executions, but Mather tried to calm the storm he had helped create. In his poem dealing with Salem witchcraft, Longfellow makes Mather say:

> Be careful. Carry the knife with such exactness,
> that on one side no innocent blood be shed
> by too excessive zeal, and, on the other,
> no shelter given to any work of darkness.

Yet Cotton Mather did not question the justice of the verdicts handed down at Salem, nor did he doubt that all who had been executed were guilty. Those who asked God to attest to their innocence were guilty, in his opinion, of "monstrous impudence." Lest it be supposed that innocent people had been condemned on the basis of inadequate evidence, Mather wrote a book entitled *Wonders of the Invisible World* (1692). Yet Mather was not as sure as he professed to be that justice had been done: in 1696, he recorded in his diary his fear that God was angry with him for "not appearing with Vigor enough to stop the proceeding of the Judges, when the Inextricable Storm from the Invisible World assaulted the Country."

The period of the Salem witchcraft marked the last occasion on which witches and wizards were executed in the colonies, but the belief in witchcraft did not end, nor did the indictment and trial of suspects stop. In Virginia in 1705, a woman was accused of practicing witchcraft. The court ordered that her body be examined for witch marks and that she be subjected to the trial by water. The incriminating marks were found, and she floated while bound — strong evidence of guilt. Nevertheless, she was not tried as a witch, nor, for that matter, was she given an opportunity to clear her reputation.

Nevertheless, even during the trials at Salem, doubts had been expressed by one of the judges and by some clergyman regarding the guilt of some of the condemned. Not, however, that they doubted the existence of the Devil and of witchcraft: their reservations extended only to the kinds of evidence held admissible by the court. Yet the feeling gained ground that New England lay under the heavy indictment of having shed innocent blood. For this reason, some of the jurors and witnesses publicly repented their part in the proceedings at Salem. In 1697, Judge Samuel Sewall stood before his congregation and acknowledged his "blame and shame . . . asking pardon of men, and especially desiring prayers that God, who has unlimited authority, would pardon that sin and all others his sins." On the other hand, Chief Justice Stoughton went to his death insisting that he had been in the right.

It was the educated [laymen] rather than the clergy who took the lead in discrediting witchcraft. In 1700, Robert Calef, a Boston merchant, published *More Wonders of the Invisible World,* an attack upon Cotton Mather and witchcraft. Calef believed that a great deal of innocent blood had been shed at Salem, and he held Cotton Mather primarily responsible for it. The girls who had started the frenzy he called "a parcel of possessed, distracted, or lying Wenches, accusing their Innocent Neighbours." Cotton Mather denounced Calef's book as "a firebrand thrown by a madman," and Increase Mather, as president of Harvard College, ordered the book publicly burned in the college yard.

The eighteenth century Enlightenment [with its emphasis on the power of reason] completed the rout of witchcraft. Science shifted the attention of educated men from the supernatural to the natural world, thereby resuming a process which, having begun with the Renaissance, had been interrupted by the Reformation. Satan suffered the second of the two great disasters that befell him in his long and checkered career: having been cast out of Heaven, his power to control human events now began to be questioned. In short, Satan lost the thing upon which his power over [human beings] had always depended — his credibility. Witchcraft, after a long and bloody history, was relegated to the ignominious status of a mere superstition, and the thousands of men and woman who had perished in the flames or on the scaffold were seen to have been the victims of a great delusion.

QUESTIONS TO CONSIDER

1   According to John Miller, what social and political conditions were most likely to produce witchcraft hysteria? Describe the European context of witch-hunts in the seventeenth century. What larger lessons does the witchcraft experience teach us about human nature, especially during times of stress?

2   Children were frequently the victims of alleged witchcraft and subsequently became the "witches'" chief accusers. What relationship, if any, is there between the Puritan child-rearing tactics described by Miller in selection 4 and children's direct participation in the witchcraft hysteria?

3   In what ways did Cotton Mather's fear of witches become a self-fulfilling prophecy? How did Cotton and Increase Mather worsen the witchcraft hysteria in Massachusetts? Why did Cotton Mather and others finally retreat from their extreme position on witches?

4   Miller relates the Salem witchcraft hysteria to the waning of Puritan culture in Massachusetts. What kind of religious and social conditions would allow ignorant villagers to accuse the governor's wife, the president of Harvard, and the sons of John Alden and former governor Bradstreet and even to be believed for a time?

5   How has the idea of witches and witchcraft changed since the seventeenth century? Has fear of the supernatural and the unexplained disappeared, or has the twentieth century found new substitutes for witches and witch-hunts?

6

Meet Dr. Franklin

RICHARD B. MORRIS

Benjamin Franklin, who called himself "the printer of Philadelphia," was one of the most remarkable human beings colonial America ever produced. He not only personified the frugality, hard work, restlessness, and occasional irreverence of colonial Americans, but he came to symbolize their growing sense of nationality as well. In his long lifetime, he tried his hand at virtually every trade and profession young America had to offer — among other things, he was a farmer, a printer, a scientist, an author, a philosopher, a statesman, a diplomat, and a connoisseur of women. In the last capacity, he composed an article on the cultivation of a mistress and became a legendary womanizer. According to one anecdote, he sired so many children that a colleague was moved to quip that it was not Washington but Benjamin Franklin who was "the real father of our country." Franklin would have appreciated the anecdote, for he had a consummate sense of humor. But above all, he had an unflagging love for liberty and the natural rights of man.

Still, Franklin was a complex and often contradictory person. As Richard B. Morris demonstrates in his lively and candid portrait, Franklin went through identity crises like anyone else, indulged in literary pranks, and had ambivalent attitudes about women. Though he abhorred violence, he was a devious individual who rebelled against convention and authority and in time became a leading American revolutionary. At the same time, Franklin regarded himself as truly a citizen of the world who hoped one day "that not only the Love of Liberty, but a thorough Knowledge of the Rights of Man, may pervade all the Nations of the Earth, so that a Philosopher may set his Foot anywhere on its Surface, and say, 'This is my Country.'"

DECEPTIVELY SIMPLE AND DISARMINGLY CAN-DID, but in reality a man of enormous complexity, [Benjamin] Franklin wore many masks, and from his own time to this day each beholder has chosen the mask that suited his fancy. To D. H. Lawrence, Franklin typified the hypocritical and bankrupt morality of the do-gooder American with his stress upon an old-fashioned Puritan ethic that glorified work, frugality, and temperance — in short, a "snuff-coloured little man!" of whom "the immortal soul part was a sort of cheap insurance policy." Lawrence resented being shoved into "a barbed-wired paddock" and made to "grow potatoes or Chicagoes." Revealing in this castigation much about himself and little insight into Franklin, Lawrence could not end his diatribe against the most cosmopolitan of all Americans without hurling a barbed shaft at "clever America" lying "on her muck-heaps of gold." F. Scott Fitzgerald quickly fired off a broadside of his own. In *The Great Gatsby,* that literary darling of the Jazz Age indicted *Poor Richard* as midwife to a generation of bootleggers.

If Lawrence and Fitzgerald were put off by Franklin's commonsense materialism which verged on crassness or if Max Weber saw Franklin as embodying all that was despicable in both the American character and the capitalist system, if they and other critics considered him as little more than a methodical shopkeeper, they signally failed to understand him. They failed to perceive how Franklin's materialism was transmuted into benevolent and humanitarian ends, how that shopkeeper's mind was enkindled by a ranging imagination that set no bounds to his intellectual interests and that continually fed an extraordinarily inventive and creative spark. They failed to explain how the popularizer of an American code of hard work, frugality, and moral re-

straint had no conscientious scruples about enjoying high living, a liberal sexual code for himself, and bawdy humor. They failed to explain how so prudent and methodical a man could have got caught up in a revolution in no small part of his own making.

Franklin would have been the first to concede that he had in his autobiography created a character gratifying to his own vanity. "Most people dislike vanity in others, whatever share they have of it themselves," he observed, "but I give it fair quarter where I meet it." Begun in 1771, when the author had completed a half-dozen careers and stood on the threshold of his most dramatic role, his autobiography constitutes the most dazzling success story of American history. The penniless waif who arrived in Philadelphia disheveled and friendless, walking up Market Street munching a great puffy roll, had by grit and ability propelled himself to the top. Not only did the young printer's apprentice manage the speedy acquisition of a fortune, but he went on to achieve distinction in many different fields, and greatness in a few of them. In an age when the mastery of more than one discipline was possible, Franklin surpassed all his contemporaries as a well-rounded citizen of the world. Endowed with a physique so strong that as a young man he could carry a large form of type in each hand, "when others carried but one in both hands," a superb athlete and a proficient swimmer, Franklin proved to be a talented printer, an enterprising newspaper editor and publisher, a tireless promoter of cultural institutes, America's first great scientist whose volume on electricity turned out to be the most influential book to come out of America in the eighteenth century, and second to none as a statesman. Eldest of the Founding Fathers by a whole generation, he was in some respects the most radical, the most devious, and the most complicated.

From the available evidence, mainly provided by the subject himself, Franklin underwent two separate identity crises, when, as modern-day psychoan-

From pp. 6–30 in *Seven Who Shaped Our Destiny* by Richard B. Morris. Copyright © 1973 by Richard B. Morris. Reprinted by permission of the author.

Joseph Duplessis painted Franklin from life in 1787 and later made this copy from it. Franklin was a complex, contradictory individual, now witty and self-confident, now deceitful and given to literary pranks. Even so, he succeeded in everything he tried, from publishing a Philadelphia newspaper and Poor Richard's Almanack *to charming the women of Paris. (New York Public Library)*

alysts suggest, the subject struggles for a new self and a new conception of his place in the world. In adolescence Franklin experienced a psychological crisis of the kind that Erik Erikson has so perceptively attributed to personages as disparate as Martin Luther and Mahatma Gandhi. Again, Franklin, the middle-aged man seeking a new image of himself, seems the prototype of Jung's classic case. As regards the first crisis, Franklin's autobiography reveals a sixteen-year-old rebelling against sibling rivalry and the authority of his household, using a variety of devices to maintain his individuality and sense of self-importance.

Born in Boston in 1706, the tenth son of Josiah and Abiah Folger Franklin, and the youngest son of the youngest son for five generations, Franklin could very easily have developed an inferiority complex as one of the youngest of thirteen children sitting around his father's table at one time. Everything about the home reduced Franklin's stature in his own eyes. When his father tried to make a tallow chandler and soap boiler out of him, he made it clear that his father's trade was not to his liking. His father then apprenticed the twelve-year-old lad to his brother James, who had started a Boston newspaper, the *New England Courant,* in 1721. For the next few years Benjamin was involved in one or another kind of rebellion.

Take the matter of food. Benjamin, an omnivorous reader, devoured a book recommending a vegetarian diet. Since his brother James boarded both himself and his apprentices at another establishment, Franklin's refusal to eat meat or fish proved an embarrassment to his elder brother and a nuisance to the housekeeper. Franklin, to save arguments which he abhorred, worked out a deal with his brother, who agreed to remit to him half the money he paid out for him for board if he would board himself. Concentrating on a frugal meatless diet, which he dispatched quickly, Franklin, eating by himself, had more time to continue his studies. While eating one of his hastily prepared meals he first feasted on Locke's treatise *On Human Understanding.*

A trivial episode, indeed, but this piece of self-flagellation forecast a lifelong pattern of pervasive traits. Benjamin Franklin did not like to hurt anyone, even nonhuman creatures. He avoided hostilities. Rather than insisting upon getting the menu he preferred, he withdrew from the table of battle and arranged to feed himself. This noncombative nature, masking a steely determination, explains much of Franklin's relation with others thereafter. Even his abandonment of the faddish vegetarian diet provides insights into the evolving Franklin with his pride in rational decision. On his voyage from Boston to Philadelphia, he tells us, his ship became becalmed off Block Island, where the crew spent their idle moments catching cod. When the fish were opened, he saw that smaller fish came out of the stomachs of the larger cod. "Then, thought I," he confessed in his autobiography, "If you eat one another, I don't see why we mayn't eat you." With that, he proceeded to enjoy a hearty codfish repast and to return at once to a normal flesh-eating diet. With a flash of self-revelation, he comments, "So convenient a thing it is to be a *reasonable creature,* since it enables one to find or make a reason for everything one has a mind to do."

Franklin's rebellion against authority and convention soon assumed a more meaningful dimension. When, in 1722, his brother James was jailed for a month for printing critical remarks in his newspaper about the authorities, the sixteen-year-old apprentice pounced on the chance to achieve something on his own. He published the paper for his brother, running his own name on the masthead to circumvent the government. Continually quarreling with his overbearing brother, Franklin determined to quit his job, leave his family and Boston, and establish himself by his own efforts unaided. The youthful rebel set forth on his well-publicized journey to Philadelphia, arriving in that bustling town in October, 1723, when he was little more than seventeen years of age.

To carve out a niche for himself in the printing trade, Franklin had to keep a checkrein on his rebellious disposition. For weeks he bore without ill temper the badgering of his master Keimer. When the blow-up came, Franklin, rather than stay and quarrel, packed up and lit out. Once more he was on his own. "Of all the things I hate altercation," he wrote years later to one of his fellow commissioners in Paris with whom he was continually at odds. He would write sharp retorts and then not mail the letters. An operator or negotiator *par excellence,* Franklin revealed in his youthful rebellion against family and employers the defensive techniques he so

skillfully utilized to avoid combat. Yet there was little about Franklin's behavior which we associate with neurotics. He was a happy extrovert, who enjoyed the company of women, and was gregarious and self-assured, a striking contrast to Isaac Newton, a tortured introvert who remained a bachelor all his life. Suffice to say that Franklin never suffered the kind of nervous breakdown that Newton experienced at the height of his powers, and as a result his effectiveness remained undiminished until a very advanced age.

If Franklin early showed an inclination to back away from a quarrel, to avoid a head-on collision, if his modesty and candor concealed a comprehension of his own importance and a persistent deviousness, such traits may go far to explain the curious satisfaction he took in perpetrating hoaxes on an unsuspecting and gullible public. The clandestine side of Franklin, a manifestation of his unwillingness to engage in direct confrontation, hugely benefited by his sense of humor and satirical talents. An inveterate literary prankster from his precocious teens until his death, Franklin perpetrated one literary hoax after another. In 1730, when he became the sole owner of a printing shop and proprietor of the *Pennsylvania Gazette,* which his quondam boss Keimer had launched a few years earlier, Franklin's paper reported a witch trial at Mount Holly, New Jersey, for which there is no authority in fact.

Franklin's greatest hoax was probably written in 1746 and perpetrated the following year, when the story ran in London's *General Advertiser.* Quickly it was reprinted throughout England, Scotland, and Ireland, and in turn picked up by the Boston and New York papers. This was his report of a speech of Polly Baker before a Massachusetts court, in defense of an alleged prosecution for the fifth time for having a bastard child. "Can it be crime (in the nature of things I mean) to add to the number of the King's subjects, in a new country that really wants people?" she pleaded. "I own it, I should think it as praiseworthy, rather than a punishable action.'' Denying that she had ever turned down a marriage proposal, and asserting that she was betrayed by the man who first made her such an offer, she compared her role with that of the great number of bachelors in the new country who had ''never sincerely and honourably courted a woman in their lives'' and insisted that, far from sinning, she had obeyed the ''great command of Nature, and of Nature's God, *Encrease and Multiply*.'' Her compassionate judges remitted her punishment, and, according to this account, one of them married her the very next day.

How so obviously concocted a morality tale as that one could have gained such wide credence seems incredible on its face. Yet the French sage, the Abbé Raynal, picked it up for his *Histoire Philosophique et Politique,* published in 1770. Some seven years later, while visiting Franklin at Passy, Raynal was to be disabused. ''When I was young and printed a newspaper,'' Franklin confessed, ''it sometimes happened, when I was short of material to fill my sheet, that I amused myself by making up stories, and that of Polly Baker is one of the number.''

When some years later Franklin's severe critic John Adams listed Polly Baker's speech as one of Franklin's many ''outrages to morality and decorum,'' he was censoring not only Franklin's liberal sexual code but the latter's ability to throw off bad habits in old age. Franklin's penchant for pseudonymous writing was one side of his devious nature and evidenced his desire to avoid direct confrontation. He continued in later life to write a prodigious number of letters under assumed names which appeared in the American, English, and French press, some still undetected. His sly ''Edict by the King of Prussia,'' appearing in an English newspaper in 1773, was a parody, in which Frederick the Great threatened reprisals against England for failing to emancipate the colonists from Germany that originally settled the island. As commissioner in Paris Franklin reputably wrote a vitriolic hoax, *The Sale of the Hessians,* in which a Count

de Schaumbergh expressed delight that 1605 of his Hessians had been killed in America, 150 more than Lord North had reported to him. This was a windfall, since he was entitled to a sum of money for every fatality suffered by the mercenaries he had sold to George III. In the midst of delicate negotiations with the British to end the war of the American Revolution the irrepressible Franklin fabricated a hoax about the scalping of Americans by Indians in the pay of the British, and then printed it in the guise of a *Supplement to the Boston Independent Chronicle.* Gruesome propaganda indeed, but Franklin justified his deception to the censorious Adams by remarking that he believed the number of persons actually scalped ''in this murdering war by the Indians to exceed what is mentioned in invoice.''

The image of himself Franklin chose to leave us in his unfinished autobiography was of a man on the make, who insincerely exploited popular morality to keep his printing presses running. Yet he himself, perhaps tongue in cheek, would have said that the morality of *Poor Richard* was foreshadowed by the plan of conduct Franklin had put down on paper on a return voyage in 1726 to Philadelphia from London, where he had spent almost two years in an effort to be able to buy equipment to set himself up as a printer. Later in life Franklin praised the plan as ''the more remarkable, as being formed when I was so young, and yet being pretty faithfully adhered to quite through to old Age.'' The plan stressed the practice of extreme frugality until he had paid his debts, as well as truthfulness, industry, and the avoidance of speaking ill of others.

Franklin, the sixteen-year-old apprentice, absorbed the literary styles of his brother James and other New England satirists running their pieces in the *Courant,* and he clearly used the *Spectator* as his literary model. He produced the Silence Dogood letters, thirteen in a row, until, he admitted, ''my small fund of sense for such performances was pretty well exhausted.'' Until then even his own brother was not aware of the identity of the author. Typical was No. 6, which criticized pride in apparel, singling out such outlandish fashions as hoop petticoats, "monstrous topsy-turvy *Mortar-Pieces*. . . neither fit for the Church, the Hall, or the Kitchen," and looming more "like Engines of War for bombarding the Town, than Ornaments of the Fair Sex."

If the Dogood letters satisfied Franklin's itch for authorship, *Poor Richard* brought him fame and fortune. Lacking originality, drawing upon a wide range of proverbs and aphorisms, notably found in

a half-dozen contemporary English anthologies, Franklin skillfully selected, edited, and simplified. For example, James Howell's *Lexicon Tetraglotton* (London, 1660), says: "The greatest talkers are the least doers." *Poor Richard* in 1733 made it: "Great talkers, little doers." Or Thomas Fuller's *Gnomolonia* (London, 1732): "The way to be safe is never to be secure"; this becomes in *Poor Richard*, 1748: "He that's secure is not safe." Every so often one of the aphorisms seems to reflect Franklin's own views. Thus, *Poor Richard* in 1747 counseled:

Poor Richard, *which brought Franklin fame and fortune, offered readers a broad range of aphorisms and proverbs. The ones shown here are fairly tame. Others reflected Franklin's* bawdy sense of humor and taste for pungent language. (Yale University Art Gallery)

"Strive to be the *greatest* Man in your Country, and you may be disappointed; Strive to be the *best,* and you may succeed: He may well win the race that runs by himself." Again, two years later, *Poor Richard* extols Martin Luther for being "remarkably *temperate* in meat and drink," perhaps a throwback to Franklin's own adolescent dietary obsessions, with an added comment, *"There was never any* industrious *man who was not a* temperate *man."* To the first American pragmatist what was moral was what worked and what worked was moral.

If there was any priggish streak in the literary Franklin it was abundantly redeemed by his bawdy sense of humor and his taste for earthy language. Thus, to *Poor Richard,* foretelling the weather by astrology was "as easy as pissing abed." "He that lives upon Hope dies farting." The bawdy note of reportage guaranteed a good circulation of Franklin's *Gazette.* Thus in 1731:

We are credibly inform'd, that the young Woman who not long since petitioned the Governor, and the Assembly to be divorced from her Husband, and at times, industriously solicited most of the Magistrates on that Account, has at last concluded to cohabit with him again. It is said the Report of the Physicians (who in Form examined his *Abilities,* and allowed him to be in every respect *sufficient*) gave her but small Satisfaction; Whether any Experiments *more satisfactory* have been try'd, we cannot say; but it seems she now declares it as her Opinion, That *George is as good as de best.*

Franklin's ambivalent views of women indubitably reflected his own personal relations with the other sex. In his younger days he took sex hungrily, secretly, and without love. One of his women — just which one nobody knows for sure — bore him a son in 1730 or 1731. It was rumored that the child's mother was a maidservant of Franklin's named Barbara, an accusation first printed in 1764 by a political foe of Franklin's, reputedly Hugh Williamson. Whether it was this sudden responsibility or just the boredom of sowing his wild oats, Franklin came to realize that "a single man resembles the odd half of a pair of scissors." Having unsuccessfully sought a match with a woman who would bring him money, Franklin turned his thoughts back to Deborah Read, the girl he had first courted in Philadelphia and then jilted. Rebounding from that humiliation, Deborah married a potter named Rogers who quickly deserted her. Then she did not even bother to have the marriage annulled, relying instead on the rumor that her husband had left behind him a wife in England. Franklin, so he tells us in his autobiography, conveniently overlooked "these difficulties," and "took her to wife, September 1st, 1730." The illegitimate child, William, whether born before or after Franklin's common-law marriage to Deborah, became part of the household, a convenient arrangement for Franklin while a constant reminder to Deborah of her spouse's less than romantic feeling about her. Soon there arose between Deborah and William a coldness bordering on hostility.

The married Franklin's literary allusions to women could be both amicable and patronizing; he could treat them as equals but show downright hostility at times. He portrayed the widow Silence Dogood as frugal, industrious, prosaic, and earthy, but somehow retaining her femininity. Such inferiority as women appeared to have must be attributed to their inferior education. While believing in the moral equality of the sexes, Franklin did not encourage women to enter unconventional fields of activity. He stuffed his *Almanack* with female stereotypes, perhaps charging off his own grievances to the sex in general. He frequently jabbed at "domineering women," with Richard Saunders the prototype of all henpecked husbands and Bridget, his "shrewish, clacking" wife. Scolding, gossipy women and talkative old maids are frequent targets of Franklin's jibes. A woman's role in life, he tells us, is to be a wife and have babies, but a man has a more versatile role and therefore commands a higher value.

Franklin's bagatelles "On Perfumes" and "On Marriages," frequently if furtively printed, kept under wraps for years by the Department of State, attained a clandestine fame, but few in the nineteenth century dared to print either. With the sexual revolution of the twentieth century and the penchant for scatological vocabulary, Franklin's letter on marriage and mistresses attained respectability and wide circulation. In essence, Franklin, in a letter dated June 25, 1745, commended marriage as the state in which a man was "most likely to find solid Happiness." However, those wishing to avoid matrimony without foregoing sex were advised to choose "*old Women to young ones.*" Among the virtues of older women he listed their more agreeable conversation, their continued amiability to counteract the "Diminution of Beauty," the absence of a "hazard of Children," their greater prudence and discretion in conducting extra-marital affairs, and the superiority of techniques of older women. "As in the dark all Cats are grey, the Pleasure of corporal Enjoyment with an old Woman is at least equal, and frequently superior, every Knack being by Practice capable of Improvement." Furthermore, who could doubt the advantages of making an old woman *"happy"* against debauching a virgin and contributing to her ruin. Finally, old women are *"so gratefull!!!"*

How much this advice reflected Franklin's own marriage of convenience remains for speculation. *Poor Richard* is constantly chiding cuckolds and scolding wives, and suggesting that marital infidelity is the course of things. "Let thy maidservant be faithful, strong, and homely." "She that paints her Face, thinks of her Tail." "Three things are men most liable to be cheated in, a Horse, a Wig, and a Wife." Or consider poor Lubin lying on his deathbed, both he and his wife despairing, he fearing death, she, "that he may live." Or the metaphor of women as books and men the readers. "Are

Women Books? says Hodge, then would mine were an *Almanack,* to change her every Year."

Enough examples, perhaps, have been chosen to show that Franklin's early view of women was based on a combination of gross and illicit sexual experiences and a less than satisfying marriage with a wife neither glamorous nor intellectually compatible.

Abruptly, at the age of forty-two, Franklin retired from active participation in his printing business. He explained the action quite simply; "I flattered myself that, by the sufficient tho' moderate fortune I had acquir'd, I had secured leisure during the rest of my life for philosophical studies and amusements." These words masked the middle-age identity crisis that he was now undergoing. Seeking to project himself on a larger stage, he did not completely cut his ties to a less glamorous past, including a wife who was a social liability, but conveniently eluded it. Now he could lay aside the tools of his trade and the garments of a petit bourgeois and enter the circles of gentility. Gone were the days he would sup on an anchovy, a slice of bread and butter, and a half-pint of ale shared with a companion. His long bouts with the gout in later life attest to his penchant for high living, for Madeira, champagne, Parmesan cheese, and other continental delicacies. Sage, philanthropist, statesman, he became, as one critic has remarked, "an intellectual transvestite," affecting a personality switch that was virtually completed before he left on his first mission (second trip) to England in 1757. Not that Franklin was a purely parochial figure at the time of his retirement from business. Already he had shown that passion for improvement which was to mark his entire career. Already he had achieved some local reputation in public office, notably in the Pennsylvania Assembly. Already he had displayed his inventive techniques, most notably his invention of the Pennsylvania fireplace, and had begun his inquiries into the natural sciences.

Now, on retirement from private affairs, he stood on the threshold of fame. In the subsequent decade he plunged into his scientific investigations and into provincial politics with equal zest. Dispatched to England in 1757 to present the case of the Pennsylvania Assembly against the proprietor, he spent five of the happiest years of his life residing at the Craven Street residence of Mrs. Margaret Stevenson. Mrs. Stevenson, and especially her daughter Mary, provided for him a pleasant and stimulating home away from home. Reluctantly he returned to Philadelphia at the end of his five-year stay, so enraptured of England that he even contemplated settling there, "provided we can persuade the good Woman to cross the Seas." Once more, in 1764, he was sent abroad, where he stayed to participate in all the agitation associated with the Grenville revenue measures. Snugly content in the Stevenson ménage, Franklin corresponded perfunctorily with his wife back in Philadelphia. Knowing that Deborah was unwilling to risk a sea voyage to join him in London, Franklin did not insist. And although he wrote his wife affectionate letters and sent her gifts, he never saw her again. She died of a stroke in December, 1774, without benefit of Franklin's presence.

It was in France after the American Revolution had broken out that Franklin achieved more completely that new identity which was the quest of his later years. There the mellow septuagenarian, diplomat, and peacemaker carried out a game with the ladies of the salon, playing a part, ironic, detached but romantic, enjoying an *amitié amoureuse* with his impressionable and neurotic neighbor, Mme. Brillon in Passy, flirting in Paris with the romantically minded Comtesse d'Houdetot, and then in the rustic retreat of Auteuil falling in love with the widow of Helvétius, whom he was prepared to marry had she been so inclined. In the unreal world of the salon Franklin relished the role of "papa." Still he avoided combat or confrontation even in his flirtation. Where he scented rejection, he turned witty, ironic, and verbally sexual.

He found time, while engaged in the weighty affairs of peacemaking during the summer of '82, to draw up a treaty of "eternal peace, friendship, and love" between himself and Madame Brillon. Like a good draftsman, Franklin was careful to preserve his freedom of action, in this case toward other females, while at the same time insisting on his right to behave without inhibitions toward his amiable neighbor. Some months before he had written her:

I often pass before your house. It appears desolate to me. Formerly I broke the Commandment by coveting it along with my neighbor's wife. Now I do not covet it any more, so I am less a sinner. But as to his wife I always find these Commandments inconvenient and I am sorry that they were ever made. If in your travels you happen to see the Holy Father, ask him to repeal them, as things given only to the Jews and too uncomfortable for good Christians.

Franklin met Mme. Brillon in 1777, and found her a beautiful woman in her early thirties, an accomplished musician, married to a rich and tolerant man, twenty-four years her senior. To Mme. Brillon Franklin was a father figure, while to Franklin she combined the qualities of daughter and mistress. Part tease, part prude, Mme. Brillon once remarked: "Do you know, my dear papa, that people have criticized the sweet habit I have taken of sitting on your lap, and your habit of soliciting from me what I always refuse?" In turn, Franklin reminded her of a game of chess he had played in her bathroom while she soaked in the tub.

If Franklin was perhaps most passionately fond of Brillon, other ladies of the salon set managed to catch his eye, among them the pockmarked, cross-eyed Comtesse d'Houdetot, who made up in sex appeal what she lacked in looks. Unlike Rousseau, who cherished for the Comtesse an unrequited passion, which he widely publicized in his posthumous *La Nouvelle Héloise*, Franklin's relations with her never seemed to border on close intimacy. Contrariwise, Franklin carried on a long flirtation with the widowed Mme. Helvétius. Abigail Adams, John's strait-laced wife, was shocked at the open intimacies between the pair. Franklin complained that since he had given Madame "so many of his days," she appeared "very ungrateful in not giving him one of her nights." Whether in desperation or because he really felt the need to rebuild some kind of family life, he proposed to her. When she turned him down, he wrote a bagatelle, recounting a conversation with Madame's husband in the Elysian Fields, as well as his own encounter with his deceased wife Deborah. He then dashed into print with the piece, an odd thing to do if he were deadly serious about the proposal. As Sainte-Beuve remarked of this episode, Franklin never allowed himself to be carried away by feeling, whether in his youth or in old age, whether in love or in religion. His romantic posture was almost ritualistic. He almost seemed relieved at the chance to convert an emotional rebuff into a literary exercise.

Franklin's casual attitude toward sexual morality was shared by his son and grandson. Himself illegitimate, William, who sought to efface the cloud over his origin by becoming an arrant social climber and most respectable Tory, also sired an illegitimate son, William Temple Franklin, whose mother remains as much a mystery as William's own. Temple, engaged at Franklin's behest by the American peace commissioners as secretary in Paris, had an affair with Blanchette Caillot, a married woman by whom he had a child and whom he abandoned on his return to America.

If Temple was a playboy, that charge could never fairly be leveled at his grandfather. The Old Doctor, an irrepressible activist and dogooder, embodied in his own career that blend of practicality and idealism which has characterized Americans ever since. Convinced from early youth of the values of self-improvement and self-education, Franklin on his return to Philadelphia from his first trip to England organized the Junto, a society half debating, half social, attesting both to the sponsor's belief in the potentialities of continued adult education and to his craving for intellectual companionship not provided in his own home. Then came the subscription library, still flourishing in Philadelphia. Franklin's plans for an academy, drawn up in 1743, reached fruition a decade later, and were a positive outgrowth of his conviction that an English rather than a classical education was more suitable to modern man and that most colleges stuffed the heads of students with irrelevant book knowledge. Then, too, the Pennsylvania Hospital project drew upon his seemingly inexhaustible fund of energy, hospitalization being defended by him as more economical than home care. So did his organization of a local fire company, and his program for a tax-supported permanent watch, and for lighting, paving, sweeping, draining, and deicing the streets of Philadelphia. Convinced of the virtues of thrift and industry, Franklin could be expected to take a dim view of poor relief, and questioned "whether the laws peculiar to England which compel the rich to maintain the poor have not given the latter a dependence that very much lessens the care of providing against the wants of old age." Truly, this revolutionary, if he returned to us today, might well be aghast at the largess of the modern welfare state with its indifference to the work ethos.

Franklin evolved what he called his "moral algebra" to explain his code of ethics, a system which clearly anticipated Jeremy Bentham. In a letter to Joseph Priestley written in 1772 he outlined his method of marshaling all the considerations pro and con for a contemplated decision, setting them down in parallel columns, and then pausing for a few days before entering "short hints" for or against the measure. Subtracting liability from assets, one would come up with a moral or political credit or debit. Franklin never narrowed down the springs of human conduct to pain and pleasure, as did Bentham, but assumed a more complex set of motives. Franklin's moral algebra stemmed in part from his bookkeeping mentality, in part from his desire to reduce life to an orderly system.

That the oldest of American Revolutionaries should be committed to controlled, orderly change takes on larger significance when one seeks explanations as to why the American Revolution did not pursue the violent, even chaotic, course of the French. Nowhere is this better illustrated than in Franklin's evolving view about the Negro and slavery, in neither of which subjects did he show any active interest until well after middle life (after due allowance for the fact that as printer he published a few antislavery tracts in his earlier years). By shrewd calculation he demonstrated that the labor of a slave in America was dearer than that of an iron or wool worker in England. Embodying these calculations in what turned out to be a seminal paper on American demography, written when he was forty-five, Franklin did not let himself get actively drawn into the Negro question for another twenty years, and then he agreed to serve as a trustee for an English fund to convert Negros. As a Deist he could hardly have been passionately aroused by the prospect of saving souls, but many have consented to serve because of the degree of respectable public exposure involved. Earlier, in 1764, he was prepared to concede that some Negroes had "a strong sense of justice and honour," but it was not until 1772, when he was sixty-six years old, that he became aroused about the slave trade, that "detestable commerce." By the next year he was on record sympathizing with the movement to abolish slavery, and in 1787 he became president of the Pennsylvania Abolition Society, the oldest society of its kind in the world. He soon proposed a program for the education of free blacks in trades and other employment to avoid "poverty, idleness, and many vicious habits."

Franklin's last public act before his death was the signing of a memorial to Congress from his own Abolition Society asking for justice for the blacks and an end in the "traffic in the persons of our fellowmen." When Southern congressmen de- nounced the measure he sent to the press one of the last writings to come from his pen, a fictional account of an observation by an official of Algiers in 1687 denying a petition of an extremist sect opposing the enslaving of Christians. Accordingly, the divan resolved, in Franklin's tongue-in-cheek reporting, "The doctrine that plundering and enslaving the Christians is unjust, is, at best, problematical; but that it is the interest of the state to continue the practice, is clear: therefore let the petition be rejected."

A man of the Enlightenment, Franklin had faith in the power and beneficence of science. In moments snatched from public affairs during the latter 1740's and early 1750's — moments when public alarms interrupted his research at the most creative instant — he plunged into scientific experimentation. While his lightning kite and rod quickly made him an international celebrity, Franklin was no mere dilettante gadgeteer. His conception of electricity as a flow with negative and positive forces opened the door to further theoretical development in the field of electromagnetism. His pamphlet on electricity, published originally in 1751, went through ten editions, including revisions, in four languages before the American Revolution. Honors from British scientists were heaped upon him, and when he arrived in England in 1757 and again in 1764, and in France in 1776, he came each time with an enlarged international reputation as a scientist whom Chatham compared in Parliament to "our Boyle" and "our Newton."

Pathbreaking as Franklin's work on electricity proved to be, his range of scientific interest extended far beyond theoretical physics. He pioneered in locating the Gulf Stream, in discovering that northeast storms come from the southwest, in making measurements of heat absorption with regard to color, and in investigating the conductivity of different substances with regard to heat. A variety of inventions attested to his utilitarian bent — the Franklin stove, the lightning rod, the flexible metal catheter, bifocal glasses, the glass harmonica, the smokeless chimney. Indefatigable in his expenditure of his spare time on useful ends, he made observations on the nature of communication between insects, contributed importantly to our knowledge of the causes of the common cold, advocated scientific ventilation, and even tried electric shock treatment to treat palsy on a number of occasions.

To the last Franklin stoutly defended scientific experimentation which promised no immediate practical consequences. Watching the first balloon ascension in Paris, he parried the question, "What good is it?" with a characteristic retort, "What good is a newborn baby?"

Committed as he was to discovering truth through scientific inquiry, Franklin could be expected to be impatient with formal theology. While not denigrating faith, he regretted that it had not been "more productive of Good Works than I have generally seen it." He suggested that, Chinese style, laymen leave praying to the men who were paid to pray for them. At the age of twenty-two he articulated a simple creed, positing a deistic Christian God, with infinite power which He would abstain from wielding in arbitrary fashion. His deistic views remained unchanged when, a month before his death, Ezra Stiles asked him his opinion of the divinity of Jesus. Confessing doubts, Franklin refused to dogmatize or to busy himself with the problem at so late a date, since, he remarked, "I expect soon an opportunity of knowing the truth with less trouble."

Unlike the philosophers who spread toleration but were intolerant of Roman Catholicism, Franklin tolerated and even encouraged any and all sects. He contributed to the support of various Protestant churches and the Jewish synagogue in Philadelphia, and, exploiting his friendship with the papal nuncio in Paris, he had his friend John Carroll made the first bishop of the Catholic Church in the new United States. He declared himself ready to welcome a Muslim preacher sent by the grand mufti in Constantinople, but that exotic spectacle was spared Protestant America of his day.

Although he fancied the garb of a Quaker, a subtle form of reverse ostentation that ill-accorded with his preachments about humility, Franklin was no pacifist. During King George's War he urged the need of preparedness upon his city and province, praising "that *Zeal* for the *Publick Good,* that *military prowess, and* that *undaunted Spirit,"* which in past ages had distinguished the British nation. Like most of the Founding Fathers he could boast a military experience regardless of its brevity, and in Franklin's case it lasted some six weeks. Following Braddock's disastrous defeat in December, 1755, Franklin as a civilian committeeman marched into the interior at the head of an armed force, directing an improvised relief program for the frontier refugees who had crowded into Bethlehem and seeing about the fortifying of the Lehigh gap. Back in Philadelphia he organized a defense force known as the "Associators," of which he was elected colonel. As in his other projects, he entered into these military arrangements with gusto, all to the annoyance of the proprietor, who regarded Franklin as a dangerous political rival and who regularly vetoed all tax bills which included military levies on the proprietary estate of the Penn family.

Once again, almost a decade later, he took command of a military force — this time to face down a frontier band known as the Paxton Boys who in 1764 set out on a lawless march to Philadelphia to confront the government with a demand for protection against the Indians. Franklin issued a blazing pamphlet denouncing the Paxton Boys for their attacks on peaceful Indians and organized and led a force to Germantown, where he confronted the remonstrants and issued a firm warning. The Paxton Boys veered off, and order was finally restored. "For about forty-eight hours," Franklin remarked, "I was a very great man, as I had been once some years before in a time of public danger."

Franklin's brief exposure as a military figure,

combined with his leadership of the antiproprietary party, and his general prominence and popularity had by now made him anathema to proprietors and conservatives alike. Standing out against the Establishment, Franklin was heartened by the enemies he had made. A thorough democrat, Franklin had little use for proprietary privileges or a titled aristocracy. In his Silence Dogood letters written as far back as 1723 he had pointed out that "Adam was never called *Master* Adam; we never read of Noah *Esquire,* Lot *Knight* and *Baronet,* nor the *Right Honourable* Abraham Viscount Mesopotamia, Baron of Carian; no, no, they were plain Men." Again, *Poor Richard* engaged in an amusing genealogical computation to prove that over the centuries it was impossible to preserve blood free of mixtures, and "that the Pretension of such Purity of Blood in ancient Families is a mere Joke." With perhaps pardonable inconsistency Franklin took the trouble to trace his own family back to stout English gentry, but his basic antiaristocratic convictions stood the test of time. When, in the post-Revolutionary years, the patrician-sounding Society of the Cincinnati was founded in America, Franklin in France scoffed at the Cincinnati as "hereditary knights" and egged on Mirabeau to publish an indictment of the Order which set off an international clamor against its hereditary character.

For courts and lawyers, defenders of property and the status quo, Franklin reserved some of his most vitriolic humor. His *Gazette* consistently held up to ridicule the snobbery of using law French in the courts, excessive legal fees and court costs, and the prolixity and perils of litigation. For the lawyers who "can, with Ease, Twist Words and Meanings as you please," *Poor Richard* shows no tolerance. Predictably, Franklin took the side of the debtor against the creditor, the paper-money man against the hard-currency man.

Franklin's support of paper money did not hurt him in the least. As a matter of fact, the Assembly gave him the printing contract in 1731 for the £40,000 in bills of credit that it authorized that year. This incident could be multiplied many times. Franklin ever had an eye for the main chance. Whether as a poor printer, a rising politician, or an established statesman-scientist, he was regarded by unfriendly critics as a man on the make of dubious integrity. One of the improvements Franklin introduced as deputy postmaster general of the colonies was to make the carrying of newspapers a source of revenue and to compel his riders to take all the papers that were offered. On its face a revenue producer and a safeguard against monopoly, the ruling could hardly damage Franklin, publisher or partner of seven or eight newspapers, a chain stretching from New York to Antigua, and even including a German-language paper in Pennsylvania.

Accumulating a tidy capital, Franklin invested in Philadelphia town lots, and then, as the speculative bug bit him, plunged into Nova Scotian and western land ventures. His secretive nature seemed ideally suited to such investments, in which he followed a rule he laid down in 1753: "Great designs should not be made publick till they are ripe for execution, lest obstacles are thrown in the way." The climax of Franklin's land speculations came in 1769 when he joined forces with Samuel Wharton to advance in England the interests of the Grand Ohio Company, which was more British than colonial in composition. This grand alliance of speculators and big-time politicians succeeded in winning from the Privy Council of July 1, 1772, a favorable recommendation supporting their fantastic dream of a colony called Vandalia, to be fitted together from the pieces of the present-day states of Pennsylvania, Maryland, West Virginia, and Kentucky. There Franklin's love of order would replace that frontier anarchy which he abhorred.

Standing on the brink of a stunning success, the Vandalia speculators were now put in jeopardy by Franklin's rash indiscretion in turning over to his radical friends in Massachusetts some embarrassing letters of Governor Thomas Hutchinson which had been given to him in confidence. Indignant at Franklin's disloyalty, the Crown officers refused to complete the papers confirming the grant to the Grand Ohio Company. With his usual deviousness, Franklin, in concert with the banker Thomas Walpole, publicly resigned from the company. In reality Walpole and Franklin had a private understanding by which the latter would retain his two shares out of the total of seventy-two shares of stock in the company. As late as April 11, 1775, Franklin, Walpole and others signed a power of attorney authorizing William Trent to act on their behalf with respect to the grant, hardly necessary if Franklin was indeed out of the picture. In the summer of 1778 Franklin had a change of heart and decided to get back his original letter of resignation. When Walpole complied, Franklin added thereto a memorandum asserting: "I am still to be considered as an Associate, and was called upon for my Payments as before. My right to two shares, or two Parts of 72, in that Purchase still continues . . . and I hope, that when the Trouble of America is over, my Posterity may reap the Benefits of them." Franklin's posterity, it should be pointed out, stood a much better chance were England to retain the Old Northwest and the Crown validate the Grand Ohio claim than were title thereto to pass to the new United States, whose claim to that region Franklin would be expected by Congress to press at the peacemaking. Such an impropriety on Franklin's part was compounded by his casual attitude about his carrying on a correspondence with a British subject in wartime while officially an American commissioner to France.

Franklin's critics denounced his penchant for nepotism, his padding the postmastership payroll with his relatives, the pressure he exercised on his fellow peace commissioners to have the unqualified Temple Franklin appointed as secretary to the Commission, and his willingness to have his grandnephew Jonathan Williams set up as a shipping agent at Nantes. Franklin's conduct of his office in France continued to supply grounds for ugly charges. What is significant is not that Franklin was guilty as charged but rather that the suspicion of conflict of interest would not die down despite his own disclaimer. At best, Franklin in France was untidy and careless in running his office. What can be said about a statesman whose entourage numbered a secretary who was a spy in British pay, a maître d'hôtel who was a thief, and a grandson who was a playboy! Only a genius could surmount these irregularities and achieve a stunning triumph. And Franklin had genius.

Because of Franklin's prominence in the Revolutionary movement it is often forgotten that in the generation prior to the final break with England he was America's most notable imperial statesman, and that the zigzag course he was to pursue owed more to events than to logic. As early as 1751 he had proposed an intercolonial union to be established by voluntary action on the part of the colonies. Three years later, at Albany, where he presented his grand design of continental union, he included therein a provision for having the plan imposed by parliamentary authority. A thorough realist, Franklin by now saw no hope of achieving union through voluntary action of the colonies, and, significantly, every delegate to the Albany Congress save five voted in favor of that provision. Twenty years later a number of these very same men, chief of them Franklin himself, were to deny Parliament's authority either to tax or to legislate for the colonies.

Franklin's Plan of Union conferred executive power, including the veto, upon a royally appointed president general, as well as the power to make war and peace and Indian treaties with the advice and consent of the grand council. That body was to be chosen triennially by the assemblies of the colonies in numbers proportionate to the taxes paid into the general treasury. Conferring the power of election upon the assemblies rather than the more aristocratic and prerogative-minded governor's councils constituted a notable democratic innovation, as was his proposal for a central treasury for the united colonies and a union treasury for each colony.

Each intensely jealous of its own prerogatives, the colonial assemblies proved cool to the plan while the Privy Council was frigid. As Franklin remarked years later, "the Crown disapproved it as having too much weight in the democratic part of the constitution, and every assembly as having allowed too much to the prerogative; so it was totally rejected." In short, the thinking of the men who met at Albany in 1754 was too bold for that day. In evolving his Plan of Union Franklin had shown himself to be an imperial-minded thinker who placed the unity and effective administration of the English-speaking world above the rights and rivalries of the separate parts. Had Franklin's Plan of Union been put in operation it would very likely have obviated the necessity for any Parliamentary enactment of taxes for the military defense and administration of the colonies.

If Britain did not come up with a plan of union of her own soon enough to save her own empire, the Americans did not forget that momentous failure of statesmanship. Franklin's plan constituted the basic core of that federal system that came into effect with the First Continental Congress and, as proposed in modified form by Franklin in 1775, provided a scheme of confederation pointing toward national sovereignty. While the Articles of Confederation drew upon notions embodied in the Albany Plan, such as investing the federal government with authority over the West, it rejected Franklin's proposal to make representation in Congress proportional to population, a notion which found recognition in the federal Constitution. Writing in 1789, Franklin was justified in his retrospective judgement about his Albany Plan of Union. His was a reasonable speculation that had his plan been adopted "the different parts of the empire might still have remained in peace and union."

Franklin's pride in the Empire survived his letdown in 1754. In April, 1761, he issued his famous Canada pamphlet, "The Interest of Great Britain," wherein he argued the case for a plan which would secure for Great Britain Canada and the trans-Appalachian West rather than the French West Indian islands, arguments upon which Lord Shelburne drew heavily in supporting the Preliminary Articles of Peace of 1762 that his sponsor Lord Bute had negotiated with France.

For Franklin, 1765 may be considered the critical year of his political career. Thereafter he abandoned his role as imperial statesman and moved steadily on a course toward revolution. Some would make Franklin out as a conspirator motivated by personal pique, and while one must concede that Franklin's reticence and deviousness endowed him with the ideal temperament for conspiracy and that his public humiliation at the hands of Crown officials provided him with all the motivation that most men would need, one must remember that, above all, Franklin was an empiricist. If one course would not work, he would try another. Thus, Franklin as agent for Pennsylvania's Assembly in London not only approved the Stamp Act in advance, but proposed many of the stamp collectors to the British government. To John Hughes, one of his unfortunate nominees who secured the unhappy job for his own province, Franklin counseled "coolness and steadiness," adding

. . . a firm Loyalty to the Crown and faithful Adherence to the Government of this Nation, which it is the Safety as well as Honour of the Colonies to be connected with, will always be the wisest Course for you and I to take, whatever may be the Madness of the Populace or their blind Leaders, who can only bring themselves and Country into Trouble and draw on greater Burthens by Acts of rebellious Tendency.

But Franklin was a fast learner. If the violence and virtual unanimity of the opposition in the colonies to the Stamp Act took him by surprise, Franklin quickly adjusted to the new realities. In an examination before the House of Commons in February, 1766, he made clear the depth of American opposition to the new tax, warned that the colonies would refuse to pay any future internal levy, and intimated that "in time" the colonists might move to the more radical position that Parliament had no right to levy external taxes upon them either. Henceforth Franklin was the colonists' leading advocate abroad of their rights to self-government, a position grounded not only on his own eminence but on his agency of the four colonies of Pennsylvania, New Jersey, Massachusetts, and Georgia. If he now counseled peaceful protest, it was because he felt that violent confrontations would give the British government a pretext for increasing the military forces and placing the colonies under even more serious repression. A permissive parent even by today's lax standards, Franklin drew an interesting analogy between governing a family and governing an empire. In one of his last nostalgic invocations of imperial greatness, Franklin wrote:

Those men make a mighty Noise about the importance of keeping up our Authority over the Colonies. They govern and regulate too much. Like some unthinking Parents, who are every Moment exerting their Authority, in obliging their Children to make Bows, and interrupting the Course of their innocent Amusements, attending constantly to their own Prerogative, but forgetting Tenderness due to their Offspring. The true Act of governing the Colonies lies in a Nut-Shell. It is only letting them alone.

A hostile contemporary, the Tory Peter Oliver, denounced Franklin as *the instar omnium* of Rebellion" and the man who "set this whole Kingdom in a flame." This is a grotesque distortion of Franklin's role. While he was now on record opposing the whole Grenville-Townshend North program as impractical and unrealistic, the fact is that his influence in government circles declined as his reputation in radical Whig intellectual circles and in the Ameri-

can colonies burgeoned. It must be remembered that, almost down to the outbreak of hostilities, he still clung to his post of absentee deputy postmaster general of the colonies, with all the perquisites thereto attached. All that dramatically changed in the years 1773–74, a final turning point in Franklin's political career.

Franklin had got his hands on a series of indiscreet letters written by Thomas Hutchinson and Andrew Oliver, the governor and lieutenant governor of Massachusetts Bay respectively, and addressed to Thomas Whately, a member of the Grenville and North ministries. The letters, which urged that the liberties of the province be restricted, were given to Franklin to show him that false advice from America went far toward explaining the obnoxious acts of the British government. Tongue in cheek, Franklin sent the letters on to Thomas Cushing, speaker of the Massachusetts House of Representatives, with an injunction that they were not to be copied or published but merely shown in the original to individuals in the province. But in June, 1773, the irrepressible Samuel Adams read the letters before a secret session of the House and later had the letters copied and printed.

The publication of the Hutchinson-Oliver letters, ostensibly against Franklin's wishes, caused an international scandal which for the moment did Franklin's reputation no good. Summoned before the Privy Council, he was excoriated by Solicitor General Alexander Wedderburn. The only way Franklin could have obtained the letters, Wedderburn charged, was by stealing them from the persons who stole them, and, according to one account, he added, "I hope, my lords, you will mark and brand the man" who "has forfeited all the respect of societies and of men." Henceforth, he concluded, "Men will watch him with a jealous eye; they will hide their papers from him, and lock up their escritoires. He will henceforth esteem it a libel to be called a man of letters; *homo trium literarum!*" Of course, everyone in the audience knew Latin and recognized the three-lettered word Wedderburn referred to as *fur,* or thief.

Discounting Wedderburn's animosity, the solicitor general may have accurately captured the mental frame of mind of Franklin at this time when he remarked that "Dr. Franklin's mind may have been so possessed with the idea of a Great American Republic, that he may easily slide into the language of the minister of a foreign independent state," who, "just before the breaking out of war . . . may bribe a villain to steal or betray any state papers." There was one punishment the Crown could inflict upon its stalwart antagonist, and that was to strip him of his office as deputy postmaster general. That was done at once. Imperturbable as was his wont, Franklin remained silent throughout the entire castigation, but inwardly he seethed at both the humiliation and the monetary loss which the job, along with his now collapsed Vandalia scheme, would cost him. He never forgot the scorching rebuke. He himself had once revealingly remarked that he "never forgave contempt." "Costs me nothing to be civil to inferiors; a good deal to be submissive to superiors." It is reported that on the occasion of the signing of the treaty of alliance with France he donned the suit of figured blue velvet that he had worn on that less triumphal occasion and, according to an unsubstantiated legend, wore it again at the signing of the preliminary Peace Treaty by which Great Britain recognized the independence of the United States.

Believing he could help best by aiding Pitt in his fruitless efforts at conciliation, Franklin stayed on in England for another year. On March 20, 1775, he sailed for America, convinced that England had lost her colonies forever. On May 6, 1775, the day following his return to Philadelphia, he was chosen a member of the Second Continental Congress. There he would rekindle old associations and meet for the first time some of the younger patriots who were to lead the nation along the path to independence.

An apocryphal story is told of Franklin's journey from Nantes to Paris, to which he was to be dispatched by Congress. At one of the inns in which in stayed, he was informed that the Tory-minded Gibbon, the first volume of whose *History* had been published in the spring of that year, was also stopping. Franklin sent his compliments, requesting the pleasure of spending the evening with the historian. In answer he received a card stating that notwithstanding Gibbon's regard for the character of Dr. Franklin as a man and a philosopher, he could not reconcile it with his duty to his king to have any conversation with a rebellious subject. In reply Franklin wrote a note declaring that "though Mr. Gibbon's principles had compelled him to withhold the pleasure of his conversation, Dr. Franklin had still such respect for the character of Mr. Gibbon, as a gentleman and a historian, that when, in the course of his writing a history of the *decline and fall* of empires, the *decline and fall* of the British Empire should come to be his subject, as he expects it soon would, Dr. Franklin would be happy to furnish him with ample materials which were in his possession."

QUESTIONS TO CONSIDER

1 Compare Benjamin Franklin in this selection to Columbus in selection 1. In what ways were they both representative men of their time, men who reflected and helped to shape the values of their culture?

2 Morris says that Franklin was an enormously complicated man who wore many masks, which disguised the real Franklin from his contemporaries as well as from future scholars and biographers. What were these masks, and how successful is Morris in uncovering the man behind them?

3 How does the available evidence support or detract from Morris's thesis that Franklin underwent two separate identity crises? What do you think are the strengths and weaknesses of trying to apply twentieth-century psychoanalytic theories to eighteenth-century lives?

4   Morris calls Franklin "the first American pragmatist," a person who defined morality by what worked and concluded that what worked must be moral. In what sense does Franklin embody the seventeenth-century Puritan ethic described by Degler in selection 3? In what important ways did Franklin alter the ethic?

5   In what ways, if any, would you consider Franklin a revolutionary? Do you agree with Morris that if Franklin "returned to us today" he would be "aghast at the largess of the modern welfare state with its indifference to the work ethos"?

IV

"WHEN IN THE COURSE OF HUMAN EVENTS . . ."

7

A New Kind of Revolution

CARL N. DEGLER

The first American revolution, identified by historian Clinton Rossiter, occurred long before Thomas Jefferson wrote the Declaration of Independence. The first revolution was a social or cultural one, as American colonists over the decades developed their own customs and institutions until they came to have a sense of common nationality.

All this took place during a period of "salutary neglect," when the British imperial government allowed the colonies to develop without rigid and consistent government control. After 1763, however, the imperial government abandoned salutary neglect and attempted to do what it had every legal right to do: rule the British Empire, including the thirteen colonies, forcefully and consistently. Unaccustomed to such interference from faraway London, colonial Americans protested bitterly. As it turned out, Britain's decision to end salutary neglect proved fateful for colonies and mother country alike.

Historian Carl Degler describes the awakening of American nationality before 1763 and goes on to explain, through an imaginative use of metaphor, how the final break with England was indeed a new kind of revolution.

☆

AMERICANS HAVE NEW RIGHTS

"IT IS . . . TO ENGLAND that we owe this elevated rank we possess," remarked Crèvecoeur, "these noble appellations of freemen, freeholders, citizens; yes it is to that wise people we owe our freedom. Had we been planted by some great monarchy, we should have been mean slaves of some distant monarch." It was for sound historical reasons that during the Revolutionary crisis the colonials stoutly asserted their claims to the "rights of Englishmen." Yet despite the English substance at the core of colonial political forms, the colonists departed in a number of ways from the example of the mother country. Frequently these deviations were merely novel twists given to English institutions; sometimes they were new institutions called into being by the new conditions in America. But whatever the nature of the changes, by the middle of the eighteenth century the forsaking of English practices was in evidence and the American constitutional system of the future was visible.

A common political vocabulary can certainly serve to bind together a colony and a mother country. But when the meaning behind the words is different, then the stage is set for misunderstanding, recrimination, and conflict. During the 1850's, the North and the South found themselves in this dangerous position; the colonists and the English in the years immediately preceding the American Revolution also fell into this predicament. Steeped as they were in the English political language, the colonials spoke in what they thought was the common intellectual idiom of the Empire, neglecting to observe that the American experience had given the words

Pages 63–78 from *Out of Our Past: The Forces That Shaped Modern America* by Carl N. Degler. Copyright © 1959, 1970 by Carl N. Degler. Reprinted by permission of Harper & Row, Publishers, Inc.

a content quite different from that accepted by the Englishmen with whom they debated. That Americans and Britons were saying different things when they employed the same words did not become apparent until after 1765, but the actual differences in political and constitutional practices of the two peoples were there long before the Stamp Act.

It is true, of course, as Crèvecoeur implied, that in many respects the political institutions of England were reproduced in close detail in the colonies. By the middle of the eighteenth century, for instance, all of the mainland colonies except four were headed by a Royal Governor, appointed by the King and therefore bearing a relation to the people of the colony similar to that of the King to the British people. Moreover, each of the thirteen colonies enjoyed a representative assembly, which was consciously modeled, in powers and practices, after the British Parliament. The resemblance to the English example was carried still further in the division of the colonial assemblies into upper and lower houses in emulation of the House of Commons and the House of Lords. In both England and the colonies, furthermore, the suffrage was exercised only by property holders; in all the colonies, as in England, it was an axiom, as an act of South Carolina put it in 1716, that "none but such persons who have an interest in this Province shall be capable to elect or be elected."

Though in the letter the English and colonial constitutions were similar, in the spirit they were moving in different directions. For example, English constitutional development from the earliest years of the seventeenth century had been sometimes drifting, sometimes driving, but always moving in pursuit of the absolute power of Parliament. The most unmistakable sign of this tendency was the assertion that the King was under the law, as exemplified in the Petition of Right in 1628, the judgment and execution of Charles I in 1649, and finally the *de facto* deposition of James II in 1689. Together with this resolute denial of the divine right of kings went the assertion that Parliament was unlimited in its power; that it could change even the Constitution by its ordinary acts of legislation, just as it had created the Constitution by its past acts. By the eighteenth century, as today, the British accepted the idea that the representatives of the people were omnipotent; that, as the aphorism has it, "Parliament can do anything except change a man into a woman and a woman into a man."

The colonials did not look upon the English Parliament with such fond eyes, nor — equally important for the future — did they concede that their own assemblies possessed such wide powers. There were good historical reasons for this. Though to the English the word "Constitution" meant nothing more nor less than the whole body of law and custom from the beginning of the kingdom, to the colonials it meant a written document, enumerating specific powers. This distinction in meaning is to be traced to the fact that the foundations of government in the various colonies were written charters granted by the Crown. These express authorizations to govern were tangible, definite things. Over the years the colonials had often repaired to the timeless phrases and sonorous periods in their charters to justify themselves in the struggle against rapacious Governors or tyrannical officials of the Crown. More than a century of government under *written* constitutions convinced the colonists of the necessity for and efficacy of protecting their liberties against government encroachment by explicitly defining all governmental powers in a document.

Even before the Stamp Act was passed, James Otis of Massachusetts articulated the striking difference between the colonial and British conceptions of Parliamentary power and the nature of constitutions. "To say the Parliament is absolute and arbitrary is a contradiction," he asserted. Parliament cannot alter the supreme law of the nation because "the Constitution is fixed; and . . . the supreme legislative . . . cannot overlap the Bounds of it without destroying its own foundation." Here, long before the Revolution, was a succinct expression of what was to become the cardinal principle of American constitutionalism, clearly setting it off from the English in both practice and theory.

It is worth emphasizing that it was English practice which was moving away from colonial. Earlier in the seventeenth century, in the minds of jurists like Sir Edward Coke, Otis's arguments would have carried much weight, but now the mutability of the Constitution was widely accepted in England. The colonials in the middle of the eighteenth century, as we shall have occasion to notice during the Revolutionary crisis, were following the old-fashioned and more conservative line.

There was another way in which English and colonial constitutional developments were drifting apart. The intimate relation between the executive and Parliament, so characteristic of English and continental democracies today, was already taking shape in the middle of the eighteenth century. The executive was the cabinet of ministers, who were drawn from the Parliament itself; as a result there was no separation of powers, the executive and legislative branches being merely different manifestations of the same body. This development, however, did not take place in America. The existence, for one thing, of a royally appointed Governor made such a development impossible; he could not be readily supplanted by a cabinet or ministerial council. Moreover, by having written constitutions or charters, the colonies were limited to the forms provided in earlier days. Under such circumstances it is not surprising that the colonial leaders entirely overlooked what was happening in England. From their distance they remained convinced that the King — like their own Royal Governors — was the real executive. Thus, because of the peculiarly American experience, the colonists were committed to a conception of government quite at variance with the English.

An important corollary to the English doctrine of parliamentary absolutism was the assumption that the colonies were subject to the legislative power of that body. For most of the seventeenth century the doctrine was no more than an assumption, and so the colonies did not feel it. This was partly because parliamentary supremacy was achieved late in the century — in 1689 — and partly because the British government, embroiled in successive wars with Holland and France, did not seek to test its authority with the colonies.

This practice of "salutary neglect," as [Edmund] Burke named it, provided a long period during which the colonies developed self-reliance and their own ideas of government. The representative assembly in each of the provinces was widely viewed as the focus of government, peculiarly American, and constitutionally competent for all internal legislative purposes. The sole political tie of any consequence between the colonies and England was through the Royal Governor, and in four of the thirteen provinces there was not even this connection. It was to be expected, therefore, that the colonies should grow to think of their little assemblies as bearing the same relation to the Crown as the Parliament of Great Britain. Such a conception of colonial equality with England, however, ran counter not only to the strong current of parliamentary absolutism we have already noticed; it also flew in the face of a growing movement to centralize the government of the Empire in London.

There is irony in the growing divergence between England and the colonies regarding the power of representative assemblies. No institution introduced into the New World was probably more English than the representative assembly; yet it was this very political form, transformed by the American experience, which, more than anything else, served to bring about a break between the colonies and the Mother of Parliaments.

With the franchise, as with the parliamentary power, the colonists took a typically English institution and remade it into a wedge which drove the two peoples apart. Though both England and the colonies based the franchise on property holding, in the mother country this practice produced a small electorate. In America, however, the same requirement resulted in a quite different effect. Since property was widely distributed, even the use of property qualifications identical with those in England resulted in the colonies in a large electorate, occasionally even approaching universal manhood suffrage. The studies of Robert Brown in the history of colonial Massachusetts, for example, have made it clear that in both provincial and town elections well over a majority of men — perhaps 80 per cent — could vote. When Thomas Hutchinson was defeated in Boston in 1749 he said of the 200 votes he received: "they were the principal inhabitants, but you know we are governed not by weight but by numbers." At another time Hutchinson remarked with obvious distaste: "The town of Boston is an absolute democracy. . . ." Even allowing for some exaggeration on the part of a defeated politician, these statements of a contemporary indicate that large numbers of men could vote in colonial Massachusetts.

Though some of the other colonies probably could not boast as wide a franchise as Massachusetts or other New England provinces, the franchise in the eighteenth century in all the colonies was considerably wider than is often supposed. Richard McCormick, for example, has shown that in New Jersey the property qualifications were quite easy for the great majority of the adult males to meet. Indeed, he has uncovered instances where the regulations at the polls were so lax that women, boys, and even Negroes voted. Milton Klein has shown that in New York as many as 55 per cent of the adult white males actually voted, suggesting that the eligible actually reached proportions close to 100 per cent. In Pennsylvania, Albert McKinley has estimated, at least one half of the males in a farming area outside Philadelphia could vote, though the figure would be lower in the city itself. Robert and Katherine Brown have found a wide participation in elections in Virginia, often taken as an aristocratically inclined province in the colonial period and after. In a general survey of the colonial suffrage, Chilton Williamson has found that in virtually all areas, where figures are available, the proportion of adult white males who could vote was at least 50 per cent. In some places, as we have seen, it reached 75 per cent. Furthermore, unlike Virginians and other colonists, South Carolina voters also enjoyed the democratic device of the secret ballot. In short, the forms of political democracy were already beginning to appear in the colonial period. . . .

Related to both the political and constitutional innovations of the colonials was their defense of freedom of the press against the arbitrary power of government. The trial of John Peter Zenger in New York in 1735 is justly considered a landmark in the history of freedom. Under the English and colonial law of that time, the sole responsibility of a jury in a trial for seditious libel was to determine whether the accused had in fact written the alleged libel. Whether the material was in fact libelous was left up to the judge to decide. Since, in Zenger's case, Judge De Lancey was a creature of the Governor against whom the alleged libel was directed, the results of the trial seemed a foregone conclusion. This high probability was further enhanced when Zenger and his attorneys announced that they conceded Zenger's responsibility for writing and printing the article in question.

The drama and long-range significance of the case, however, turns upon the action of Andrew Hamilton, who assumed the leadership of the defense. Contending that the truth of Zenger's charges was the crux of the case, Hamilton argued that a press, unfettered by official control, was indispensable in a society claiming to be free. Truth, he said, was a legitimate, nay, a necessary defense in a libel suit. Almost casually he conceded Zenger's authorship of the offending piece. But then he turned to the jury and, in a masterful presentation, urged upon the jurors a new course. Disregarding the law and appealing to their love of liberty, Hamil-

ton challenged the jurors to decide the larger question of whether the charges Zenger levied against the Governor were true or not. If they were, Hamilton advised, then the jury should acquit the printer. Despite its sure knowledge that it was affronting a powerful and partisan judge, the jury nobly matched Hamilton's boldness and found Zenger not guilty.

It is true that censorship of the press, particularly by the assemblies, and even trial for libel in which truth was not accepted as a defense, occurred after the Zenger case. But there were no more trials for seditious libel in New York for the rest of the colonial period. Moreover, the trial and its outcome produced repercussions in England. Radicals and Whigs, won over by the brilliant colonial innovation in behalf of a free press, began a campaign in support of American liberty which was to reach its full power at the time of the Revolution in the voices of Burke, [Charles] Fox, John Wilkes, Dr. [Richard] Price, and Colonel [Isaac] Barré.

The principle inherent in the Zenger decision was not quickly implemented in America, as Leonard Levy has pointed out. It was not until 1798, during the Jeffersonians' powerful attacks upon the theory of the Sedition Act that the modern view of freedom of the press was worked out. Heretofore, all sides to the question, including the Jeffersonians themselves, had accepted the idea that a government had a right to suppress statements critical of its officials. The new view, going beyond that set forth in Zenger, asserted that if a society was to be considered free it could not suppress criticism under the old rubrics of "seditious libel" or "a licentious press." In fact, the crime of seditious libel, *i.e.,* bringing government into disrepute by attacking its officials, was abandoned. The concept that truth was a defense in a libel suit — the central principle in the Zenger case — was established in New York law in the case of Henry Coswell in 1804 through the joint efforts of Alexander Hamilton and James Kent. The doctrine was reinforced by legislative act in 1805 and inserted, for good measure, in the state constitutions of 1821 and 1846. [But] it was not until 1791, however . . . that English juries were granted the right to determine whether the writing in question was libelous or not, and it was not until 1843 that truth was accepted as a defense in a libel suit under English law.

☆

"ALL OF US AMERICANS"

In the course of the Zenger trial Andrew Hamilton had chided the attorney general for his constant citing of English precedent. "What strange doctrine is it to press everything for law here which is so in England," the clever Philadelphian exclaimed. Hamilton knew full well that the law of England prevailed in the colonies, but he was playing upon the colonials' growing pride of country.

In the years after 1740 the colonials became increasingly conscious of themselves as Americans. To be sure, there were very few outright demands for independence. It would take a good number of years, during which a consciousness of kind was only dawning, before the idea of independence would be thought of, much less advocated. Nevertheless, for two decades or more before the Revolutionary crisis of the late 1760's, Americans were expressing the feeling that they were different from Europeans, that they had a destiny of their own.

Ironically enough, the most obvious manifestations of this budding sense of Americanism appear in the course of the wars with France in the 1740's and 1750's, when colonials fought side by side with the English. During most of the century-long struggle against France in the seventeenth and eighteenth centuries, Britain had not demanded that the American colonies contribute anything more than the defense of their home areas and perhaps an occasional foray into adjacent French-held Canada. But beginning with the so-called War of Jenkins' Ear in 1739, which was first waged against Spain and then (as King George's War) against France, Britain stepped up her expectations of colonial military support. In 1741 the home government succeeded in goading the colonials to assist in the mounting of an offensive against Cartagena, the great port of the Spanish Main.

In part because the enterprise was a colossal fiasco, but largely because American and European soldiers were thrown together under novel circumstances, the differences between Americans and Europeans were sharply illuminated for both sides. Admiral Vernon, the British commander of the expedition, for example, consistently referred to the colonials as "Americans." The colonials, in turn, referred to their supposed blood brothers, the English, as "Europeans." The words, of course, had been used before, but never so generally or consistently as at this time. The failure of the Cartagena expedition added its bit to the splitting apart of the two national groups. The Americans came away convinced that the English were callous and cruel in their treatment of colonials, and the English soldiery and officers were disgusted with what they stigmatized as the cowardice and ineffectiveness of the colonial soldier.

When the New Englanders under Sir William Pepperell succeeded in capturing the French fortress at Louisbourg [on the Atlantic coast of Nova Scotia] in 1745, the colonials' incipient pride of country burst forth. To some it seemed to prove, as one bit of doggerel put it, that in valor

> . . . the British Breed
> In Western Climes their Grandsires far exceed
> and that New England Schemes the Old
>   Surpass.
>   As much as Gold does tinkling Brass;
> And that a Pepp'rell's and a Warren's name,
> May vie with Marlb'rough and a Blake for
>   Fame.

With the fall of Quebec in 1759, there was loosed a flood of prophecies that the star of American destiny was in the ascendant. "A new world has arisen," exulted the *New American Magazine,* "and will exceed the old!" It is noteworthy, considering its nationalistic name, that the magazine was then in its first year of publication. One scholar, Richard Merritt, in examining the colonial press of the mid-eighteenth century, found a remarkable increase in the early 1760's in references to "America" and "Americans" at the same time that there was a falling off in references to the connection with England. He finds, in short, a rise in American self-awareness prior to the catalyst of the Stamp Act crisis in 1765.

Meanwhile a developing American nationality was evident — perhaps less spectacularly, but nonetheless profoundly — in other ways. Under the influences of distance and the new environment, the mother tongue of the colonists was undergoing change. New words from the Dutch and Indian languages, for example, were constantly being added to the speech of the English in America; words like "boss," "stoop," "cruller," "crib," "scow," and "spook" came from the Dutch. The Indian names were all over the land, and they made America exotic for Englishmen as they still do for Europeans.

Americans also made up words, some of which reflected the new environment. "Back country" and "backwoods" were designed to describe the novelty of the frontier. Bullfrog, canvasback, lightning bug, razorback, groundhog, potato bug, peanut, and eggplant are similar colonial name tags for new natural phenomena.

Familiar English words sometimes assumed new meanings in America. "Lumber" in eighteenth-century England meant unused furniture, but in the colonies it was applied to the raw wood — and so it has remained. "Pie" in England, to this day, means a meat pie, but in the colonies that was a "potpie"; "pie" was reserved for fruit pastry. Dry goods in England included all nonliquids, like corn or wheat;

the colonials, however, changed the meaning to textiles only. The same alteration took place with the word "rock," which in England denoted a large mass; in America as early as 1712 it was being applied to a stone of any size. "Pond" was an English word meaning an artificial pool, but in unkempt America it came to mean any small lake. Certain words obviously attached to the English environment were lost in America, where their referents did not exist: fen, heath, moor, wold, bracken, and downs. It is not to be wondered, therefore, that in 1756 lexicographer Samuel Johnson was talking of an American dialect.

The burgeoning sense of Americanism was reflected also in the colonials' image of themselves. When Eliza Pinckney of South Carolina was presented at King George's Court in 1750, she insisted upon being introduced as an "American." That same year an advertisement in a Boston paper advertised beer as "American" and urged that Bostonians should "no longer be beholden to Foreigners for a Credible [*sic*] Liquor, which may be as successfully manufactured in this country." It is not the self-interest which is important here, but the fact that the advertiser obviously felt he could gain by making an appeal to a sense of American pride among his potential customers. This feeling among Americans that they were different from Europeans was put forth explicitly by a Carolinian in 1762. Speaking about the question of sending young colonials to England for their education, he said it would be most surprising if a British education should suit Americans, "because the Genius of our People, their Way of Life, their circumstances in Point of Fortunes, and Customs, and Manners and Humours of the Country, difference us in so many important Respects from Europeans. . . ." Such an education could not be expected to fit Americans, he went on, any more "than an Almanac, calculated for the Latitude of London, would that of Williamsburg."

As relations between the colonies and the mother country worsened after 1765, expressions of Americanism became more explicit and sometimes belligerent. Colonial students at Edinburgh University before 1765 commonly designated themselves as from the various provinces, but at the time of the Stamp Act, Samuel Bard wrote, he and several others began to style themselves "Americans" and the precedent was followed by many in subsequent years. About the same time Ezra Stiles of New Haven drew up a plan for an "American Academy of Science," which was designed, he said, "for the Honor of American Literature, contemned by Europeans." He stipulated that only native-born Americans should be members. And at the Stamp Act Congress, Christopher Gadsden of South Carolina urged the gathered colonial leaders to take cognizance of their common nationality. "There ought to be no New England man, no New Yorker, known on the Continent," he advised, "but all of us Americans. . . ."

The magic of the moment and the atmosphere in the new country were so potent that John Morgan, newly arrived at Philadelphia from London in 1765, declared, only a year later, "I consider myself at once as a Briton and an American." Such an ambivalent attitude must have been common among colonials in the early stage of the crisis between the colonies and the mother country. But regardless of Morgan's own ambiguous feelings, his work in helping to establish the new medical school at Philadelphia was hailed by Benjamin Rush as an aid to the growing self-consciousness of the people of America. Pointedly calling Britain an alien land, Rush wrote Morgan that no longer would the colonial student have to tear "himself from every tender engagement" and brave the dangers of the sea "in pursuit of knowledge in a foreign country."

One of the most curious but very clear manifestations of a growing American awareness of differences between the peoples of the Old and New Worlds was the widespread belief that English society was morally inferior, even decadent, when compared with the social character of the colonies. As early as 1735 Lewis Morris, visiting England, wrote

in his diary that he and his party "wish'd ourselves in our own Country, far from the deceits of a court." London appeared to Ebenezer Hazard as at once a wonderful "little World" and a "Sink of Sin." In 1767, English social conditions appeared shocking to William S. Johnson, who found the extremes of wealth and misery "equally amazing on the one hand and disgusting on the other." Benjamin Rush wrote from Edinburgh in 1767 that "every native of Philadelphia should be sent abroad for a few years if it was only to teach him to prize his native country above all places in the world."

Standing out against the decadence of England in the minds of colonials and of some Englishmen was the example of America as the hope of the world. In 1771, John Penn, who was certainly no radical, wrote that he considered Great Britain "as an Old Man, who has received several strokes of the Palsy, and tottering upon the brink of the Grave, whereas America was growing daily toward perfection." In 1745 a writer in the *Gentleman's Magazine* drew the lesson from the American success at the siege of Louisbourg that the colonials were truly in the classical tradition so dear to the men of the eighteenth century. He saw the colonists in "the great image of the ancient Romans leaving the plow for the field of battles, and retiring after their conquests to the plow again." For many Englishmen, America seemed to be utopia in actuality. But it was the Americans who above all were convinced of the moral superiority of their society. Colonials returned from Europe overflowing with tales of the iniquities they had witnessed in London or commenting on the manifest corruption of British politics. As early as 1748, Josiah Quincy was saying he was fearful that the venality of English political life would ruin the country. The self-righteousness of Americans toward Britain in the 1750's and 1760's reminds one of nothing so much as an adolescent's indignant strictures against his parent's timeworn but now suddenly recognized foibles. The American people were coming of age.

Along with adolescent carping, assertions of moral superiority, and self-righteousness in the years before 1765, there were also a few strong hints that independence was coming. The war against the French in Canada prompted some Americans to anticipate separation from England. Peter Kalm, for example, traveling through the colonies in 1748, was told that after the French were expelled from the western borders of the colonies, independence would come in a matter of thirty to fifty years. Once the "Gallicks" are removed, John Adams thought in 1755, the colonies would be able to go it alone. "The only way to keep us from setting up for ourselves," he wrote, "is to disunite us."

In 1760 and after, when the British government was wrestling with the question of whether or not the French should be expelled completely from the North American continent, there was much speculation as to the effect such expulsion would have upon the restive colonies. Though the canny Franklin blandly assured Parliament that the removal of the French would bind the colonies still closer to Britain, less suspect parties, like Comptroller Weare, pointed out that never before in history had an industrious and favored people like the Americans hesitated to break away from their mother country when they had the power to do so. It is highly likely, he added, "that a thousand leagues distance from eye and strength of government" would suggest just that "*to a people accustomed to more than British liberty.*" Also of this opinion was a correspondent of the *Gentlemen's Magazine* in 1760. "If the people of our colonies find no check from Canada, they will extend themselves, almost without bounds into the inland parts. . . . What the consequences will be," he added ominously and prophetically, "to have a numerous, hardy, independent people possessed of a strong country, communicating little, or not at all with England, I leave to your own reflections."

There was more behind the thought of independence than the removal of the French threat. There was the coming to climax of the whole history of a geographically separate and different people in America. English traveler Andrew Burnaby noticed it in 1759 when he pointed out that the growing cities of the coast were already turning their citizens into "great republicans" and that the farm dwellers too had "fallen into the same errors in their ideas of independency. . . ."

In sum, by the early 1760's the colonists were ready in a vague cultural sense for the parting of the ways with Britain. What remained was for something to happen that would cause them to be sharply aware of those vague differences and to force them to develop consciously those "country" ideas they had been ruminating over for years. The occasion came after 1763, when Britain sought to find a new basis for its relations with the continental colonies. Then the differences between the two peoples were translated into political and ultimately into military terms. That is the story of the coming of the American Revolution.

☆

A NEW KIND OF REVOLUTION

Though the colonists had long been drifting away from their allegiance to the mother country, the chain of events which led to the Revolutionary crisis was set in motion by external factors. The shattering victory of the Anglo-American forces over the French in the Great War for the Empire (1754–63), as Lawrence Gipson has rechristened the French and Indian War, suddenly revealed how wide the gulf between colonists and mother country had become. The very fact that the feared French were once and for all expelled from the colonial backdoor meant that another cohesive, if negative, force was gone. At least one friend of Britain, looking back from the fateful days of 1776, thought that "had Canada remained in the hands of the French, the colonies would have remained dutiful subjects. Their fears for themselves in that case," he reasoned, "would have supplied the place of the pretended affection for this nation. . . ." What actual effect the removal of the French produced upon the thinking of the colonists is hard to weigh, but there can be little doubt that the Great War for the Empire opened a new era in the relations between the colonies and the mother country.

Great Britain emerged from the war as the supreme power in European affairs: her armies had swept the once-vaunted French authority from two continents; her navy now indisputably commanded the seven seas. A symbol of this new power was that Britain's ambassadors now outranked those of France and Spain in the protocol of Europe's courts. But the cost and continuing responsibilities of that victory were staggering for the little island kingdom. Before the war the annual expenditures for troops in America and the British West Indies amounted to £110,000; now three times that sum was needed to protect the western frontier, suppress Indian revolts and maintain order. Furthermore, the signing of the peace found Britain saddled with a debt of £130 million, the annual charges of which ran to another £4 million. Faced with such obligations, the British government was compelled to reassess its old ways of running an empire, particularly in regard to the raising of new revenues.

Before the war, the administration and cost of the Empire were primarily, if not completely, a British affair. Imperial defense on the high seas was in the hands of the Royal Navy, and though the colonies were called upon from time to time to assist in the war with France, the bulk of the fighting was sustained by British troops. In return, the colonies had acquiesced in the regulation of their trade through a series of so-called Navigation Acts, which were enacted and enforced by the British authority; no revenues, however, except those collected as import or export duties, were taken from the colonies by Britain.

Under the pressure of the new responsibilities, the British authorities began to cast about for a new theory and practice of imperial administration into which the colonies might be fitted as actively contributing members. Prior to the war the government had been willing to protect the West Indian sugar interests at the expense of the rest of the Empire. But now, in the interest of increased revenue, the old protective duty, which was much too high to bring any return, was cut in half, thus permitting French molasses to compete with British West Indian in the English and colonial markets. In 1766, this molasses duty, in a further effort to increase revenue, was cut to two-thirds of what it had been before the war. In short, the need for imperial revenues, not private interests, was now dictating legislation. The Stamp Act of 1765 and the Townshend duties of two years later were similar efforts to spread the financial burdens of the Empire among the beneficiaries of the British triumph over the French.

It seemed only simple justice to London officialdom that the colonies should share in the costs as well as the benefits to be derived from the defeat of the ancient enemy. At no time, it should be noticed, were the colonies asked to contribute more than a portion of the price of their own frontier defense. The stamp duty, for instance, was envisioned as returning no more than a third of the total military expenditures in America; the remainder would be borne by the home government. And because the colonists had difficulty scraping together the specie with which to pay such duties, the British government agreed to spend all the revenue obtained from the stamp tax in the colonies in order to avoid depleting the scanty colonial money supply. Nor were Americans heavily taxed; it was well known that their fiscal burden was unique in its lightness. In 1775 Lord North told the House of Commons that the per capita tax payments of Britons were fifty times those of the Americans. It was not injustice or the economic incidence of the taxes which prompted the colonial protest, it was rather the novelty of the British demands.

The new imperial policies of the British government caught the Americans off guard. Reveling in the victory over the French, the colonists confidently expected a return to the lax, uninterested administration of the prewar years and especially to their old freedom from any obligation to support the imperial defenses. Therefore, when the first of the new measures, the Sugar Act of 1764, became law, the Americans protested, but on a variety of grounds and without sufficient unity to command respect. By the time of the Stamp Act in the following year, however, the colonists were ready.

The essential colonial defense, from which the colonies never deviated, was a denial that the British Parliament had any right in law or custom to lay taxes upon the colonies for revenue purposes. Such taxes, the colonials insisted, could only be levied by the colonial legislatures. Actually, this expression of the colonial constitutional position was as novel as the imperial policy. Never before had there been an occasion for such an assertion simply because England had heretofore confined her colonial legislation to the regulation of trade. It is true that the Pennsylvania Charter of 1681 specifically reserved to the British Parliament the right to tax the colony; but since Parliament had never used this power, the colonists had a case when they said the new British taxes were historically unknown and therefore unconstitutional. The details of this controversy, in which merit is by no means the exclusive possession of either side, do not concern us here. The important fact is not whether the Americans or the British were right in their respective readings of imperial constitutional history, but that the colonials believed they were right and acted accordingly. Regardless of the constitutional niceties involved, it is patent that the English had waited too long to assert their

authority. Too many Americans had grown accustomed to their untrammeled political life to submit now to new English controls. In brief, the colonists suddenly realized that they were no longer wards of Britain, but a separate people, capable of forging their own destiny.

This conviction runs all through the polemics of the Revolutionary crisis. For underlying the constitutional verbiage which Englishmen and Americans exchanged were two quite different assumptions about the nature of the British Empire and the character of the American people. Whereas Englishmen saw America as a part of an Empire in which all elements were subordinate to Britain, the Americans, drawing upon their actual history, saw only a loose confederation of peoples in which there were Britons and Americans, neither one of whom could presume to dictate to the other. The colonials, in effect, now felt themselves Americans, not displaced, subordinate Englishmen. Jefferson suggested this to the King himself when he wrote in his *Summary View of the Rights of British America:* "You are surrounded by British counsellors. . . . You have no minister for American affairs, because you have none taken from us." Furthermore, even after 1776 many a Loyalist exiled in Britain found the English annoying and strange — evidence of the fact that residence in America had worked its influence even upon those loyal to the Crown. "It piques my pride, I must confess," wrote one expatriated Loyalist, "to hear us called 'our colonies, our plantations,' in such terms and with such airs, as if our property and persons were absolutely theirs, like the [villeins] in their cottages in the old feudal system."

The imperial view so confidently advanced by Grenville and others of the British administration came too late; the Americans were not interested in making a more efficient Empire to be manipulated from Whitehall. Because of this basic conflict in assumptions, American demands continued to leapfrog ahead of British concessions right up to the Carlisle Peace Mission in the midst of the Revolu-

On July 2, 1776, as this painting shows, a committee consisting of Thomas Jefferson, Benjamin Franklin, Robert Livingston, Roger Sherman, and John Adams submitted a draft of the Declaration of Independence to the Second Continental Congress. Jefferson (second from the right) is laying the document before John Hancock. Franklin stands to Jefferson's left, Livingston, Sherman, and Adams to his right. (Oil painting by John Trumbull, copyright Yale University Art Gallery)

tionary War. Even ministerial assurances in 1769 that there would be no further imperially imposed taxes failed to divert the colonial drive toward equality with Britain. The child was truly asserting himself, and, as so often happens, the parent was reluctant to strike him down.

Measured against the age of Hitler and Stalin, the British overlords of the eighteenth century appear remarkably benign in their dealings with the colonies in the years after 1763. For it is a fact that the colonies were in revolt against a potential tyrant, not an actual one. As the American Tory Samuel Seabury wrote in 1774, the colonists were convinced that the ministers of the Crown "have laid a regular plan to enslave America; that they are now deliberately putting it in execution. This point has never been proved," Seabury added, "though it has been asserted over, and over, and over again." As Bernard Bailyn has pointed out in a survey of some 400 tracts from the Revolutionary era, Americans were convinced that a conspiracy was afoot in Britain to deprive them of their liberties. Historians, however, can find no real basis for such fears. To the politically sensitive colonists, who had steeped themselves in the "country party" philosophy of the early-eighteenth-century pamphleteers, the intention behind the British legislation of the pre-Revolutionary years seemed all too clear. For in the country party philosophy, which, after the Revolution, would become the philosophy of republicanism, any government of power was a constant danger to individual liberty. And England with a court party of wealth, power, and corruption was perceived by Americans as a growing and obvious threat to liberty. On the other hand, the British could never bring themselves to enforce, with all the power at their command, what they believed was the true nature of the Empire, that is, the subordinate position of the colonies. More than once General Thomas Gage, commanding the British troops in America, reported that his forces were too scattered to preserve proper order and government in the colonies. "I am concerned to find in your Lordship's letters," he wrote from New York in 1768, "that irresolution still prevails in our Councils; it is time to come to some determination about the disposition of the troops in this Country."

Part of this irresolution was born of British confusion as to what should be the government's purpose, as the hasty repeals of the stamp and Townshend duties testify on the one hand, and the remarkably inept Tea Act reveals on the other. Part of it stemmed from the fact that within their own house, so to speak, were Americans: at times Lord Chatham himself, at all times Edmund Burke, Colonel Issac Barré, John Wilkes, and Dr. Price, who insisted that Americans possessed the rights of Englishmen. "The seditious spirit of the colonies," George Grenville wryly complained on the floor of Commons in 1776, "owes its birth to the factions in this House."

Divided as to aims and devoid of strong leadership, the British permitted the much more united colonists, who were blessed with superb and daring leadership, to seize and hold the initiative. Not until the very end — after the destruction of the tea at

Boston Harbor in 1773 — did the patience of the British ministry run dry. By then, however, the years of acrimony, suspicion, and growing awareness of the differences between the two peoples had done their work, and the harsh coercive measures taken against Massachusetts only provoked counterviolence from all the colonies. Lexington and Concord, Bunker Hill and Independence Hall, were then not far behind.

By implication, the interpretation of the coming of the Revolution given here greatly subordinates the role of economic factors. Since the economic restrictions imposed upon the colonies have traditionally played a large role in most discussions of the causes of the Revolution, they deserve some comment here. Those who advance an economic explanation for the Revolution argue that the series of economic measures enacted by Britain in the century before 1750 actually operated to confine, if not stifle, the colonial economy. Therefore, it is said, the colonies revolted against Britain in an effort to break through these artificial and externally imposed limits. On the surface and from the assumptions of twentieth-century economic life, the mercantilistic system appears severe and crippling and worthy of strong colonial opposition.

Yet empirical investigations of the effects of the system by modern historians do not find much merit in the argument. Lawrence Harper and others have conclusively shown that the limitations placed on colonial manufactures by British laws did not seriously harm American interests or restrict American economic aspirations. The Navigation Laws, it is true, placed a burden upon colonial trade, especially of staples like tobacco and rice, perhaps amounting to as much as $7 million a year, according to one calculation. Yet very few objections to the Navigation Laws appear in the voluminous literature thrown up by the crisis. In fact, so acceptable did the system seem to that jealous American, Benjamin Franklin, that in 1774 he suggested to Lord Chatham that all the basic Navigation Laws be re-enacted by the colonial legislatures as an earnest of colonial loyalty. Furthermore, in October of that year, the first Continental Congress publicly declared the colonies willing to "cheerfully consent to the operation of such acts of the British Parliament, as are bona fide, restrained to the regulation of our external commerce, for the purpose of securing the commercial advantages of the whole empire to the mother country, and the commercial benefits of its respective members. . . ." In short, the navigation system was acceptable. Certainly laws the repressive nature of which no one was disturbed about can hardly be accepted as the grounds for a revolution.

No better economic argument can be made for taxation as a cause for the Revolution. Despite the tradition of oppressive taxation which the myth of the Revolution has spawned, the actual tax burden of the colonies was much heavier in the seventeenth century than in the years immediately before the conflict. On a per capita basis, taxes were five times greater in 1698 than they were in 1773. The lightness of the British taxes in the pre-Revolutionary period is also shown by the fact that the duty on molasses in 1766 was only a penny a gallon, or less than the duty the federal government imposed in 1791. As Lord North pointed out in 1775, taxation of the Americans was neither excessive nor oppressive.

From the unconvincing character of the economic explanations for the coming of the Revolution, it would appear, therefore, that the underlying force impelling the break was the growing national self-consciousness of the Americans. "The Revolution was effected before the war commenced," John Adams remarked years afterward. "The Revolution was in the minds and hearts of the people. . . ." The origins of the "principles and feelings" which made the Revolution, Adams thought, "ought to be traced back . . . and sought in the history of the country from the first plantations in America." For a century and a half the Americans had been growing up and now they had finally come of age. Precisely because the Revolution was the breaking away of a young people from a parent, the substance of the Revolution was political. The argument concerned the question of parental authority, because that is the precise point at which tension appears as the child approaches maturity and seeks to assert his independence. Unfortunately for Britain, but like so many modern parents, the mother country had long before conveniently provided the best arguments in favor of freedom. And the colonists had learned the arguments well. For this reason, the rhetoric of the Revolutionary argument was in the language of British political and constitutional thought, though not, significantly, that of the ruling "court party."

As children enjoying a long history of freedom from interference from their parent, the Americans might well have continued in their loose relationship, even in maturity, for they were conservative as well as precocious. History, however, decreed otherwise. Britain's triumph in the Great War for the Empire put a new strain on the family relationship, and so intense was the pressure that Americans could not fail to see, as the argument increased in acrimony, that they were no longer members of the English family, but rather a new people, with their own separate destiny. Some Americans saw it earlier than others; a good many saw it by 1776. John Penn, while in England in 1773, was struck by the English ignorance "with respect to *our* part of the world (for I consider myself more American than English). . . ." To South Carolinian Henry Laurens, the Boston Port Act hit at "the liberty of all Americans," not just at that of the people of Massachusetts. Once they were convinced of their essential difference as a people and that British obduracy would not melt, Americans could not accept the old familiar arrangements. Anything less than their independence as a people was unacceptable; it would take Englishmen another generation to realize that the disagreement was as deep as that.

At no time during the ten-year crisis, however, were most Americans spoiling for a rupture with England merely for the sake of a break. Indeed, no one can run through the constitutional arguments of that day without being struck with the reluctance — almost misgivings — with which Americans reached the conclusion of independence. After attending the Continental Congress in 1774, Washington, for example, was "well satisfied that" independence was not "desired by any thinking man in all North America." And, as late as July 6, 1775 — over two months after the embattled farmers made their stand at the "rude bridge" — Congress denied any "designs of separation from Great Britain and establishing independent states."

This was no heedless, impetuous overthrow of an oppressor; rather it was a slowly germinating determination on the part of Americans to counter and thwart a change in their hitherto established and accepted ways of governing. Except for the long-deferred assertion of independence, the whole corpus of Revolutionary rhetoric — and nothing lends itself more to radicalism than words — was conservative, expressive of the wish to retain the old ways as they understood them. The demands made upon Britain were actually pleas for a return to the old relationship: repeal the Stamp Act, the Townshend Acts, the Mutiny Acts; restore trial by jury as abrogated by the expanded admiralty courts; remove the restrictions recently placed upon western migration. One needs only to run through that famous list of grievances in the Declaration of Independence to be forcefully reminded that what these revolutionaries wanted was nothing but the *status quo ante bellum.*

"We have taken up arms," the Continental Congress carefully explained in July, 1775, two months after Lexington, "in defense of the freedom that is our birth-right, and which we ever enjoyed till the late violation of it. . . ." These men had been satisfied with their existence, they were not disgruntled agitators or frustrated politicians; they were a strange new breed — contented revolutionaries.

QUESTIONS TO CONSIDER

1   During the Revolutionary crisis, colonials asserted their "rights" as Englishmen and claimed that Parliament had violated these rights. Parliament and the king just as adamantly denied any violation of rights. Explain the roots of this misunderstanding between American colonists and the mother country.

2   Compare the similarities and differences between English and colonial American political institutions and constitutional practices. How did the American experience shape the colonists' political institutions and give new meaning to commonly shared English political language?

3   Examine the reasons American colonists in the eighteenth century felt a sense of mission, a sense that America was "the hope of the world." Compare this feeling with the seventeenth-century Puritan notion of building "a city upon a hill." Do you see any traces of this kind of missionary zeal today in America?

4   Comment on the appropriateness of Degler's metaphor comparing American colonists in the 1750s and 1760s with rebellious adolescents who are "coming of age."

5   Why did the first American revolution — the social and cultural revolution — lead ultimately to the second (and final) political and military revolution? Consider the impact of both external and internal forces.

8

England's Calamitous War

R ICHARD M. K ETCHUM

Certainly the American Revolution was full of people on both sides who were distin-
guished for heroism and courage against adversity. But this is only half the story.
Throughout the Revolution, English and Americans alike were plagued with difficul-
ties. The Americans, for their part, were hardly united about fighting for indepen-
dence. Many people opposed the rebellion and remained loyal British subjects, and
many others were indifferent to the whole thing. Although the Americans may have
had the best general in George Washington, colonial volunteers often fought without
regard for rules, discipline, or orders, charging forward with all the organization of
stampeding cattle. And cattle would have been immeasurably easier to drill. Baron
von Steuben, the Prussian drillmaster, became so exasperated with the sloppiness and
indifference of colonial troops that he once screamed at them in French: "Viens,
Walker, mon ami, mon bon ami! Sacré! Goddam de gaucheries of dese baudats! Je
ne puis plus. I can curse dem no more!" Then, as if lack of discipline were not bad
enough, many volunteers set out for home after battles, thinking that the war was
over or claiming that crops had to be harvested. During the eight years of war, an
estimated 400,000 men fought in the colonial army; yet the turnover was so rapid
that at no single time did Washington have more than 18,000 troops in the field.
At the same time, he was beset with chronic shortages of money, guns, and supplies.
Still, despite the odds, the American rebels fought on with grim determination, because
the distant goal of freedom — a powerful and appealing ideal — was far preferable
to a return to the status quo.

The British had even more agonizing problems than the Americans had. As Rich-
ard M. Ketchum, a noted historian of the Revolution, points out in the graceful

account that follows, England's political and military leaders were arrogantly optimistic at the start of hostilities, certain that the upstart colonials could be smashed by a single, overwhelming blow. Shunning any effort at conciliation, the king and the ministry of Lord North committed themselves to a war in a savage wilderness 3,000 miles from home. For the British, it was a calamity. Plagued with insurmountable logistical problems, British troops (including German mercenaries) suffered from supply shortages, low morale, and inept leadership. Moreover, the "colonial war" became increasingly unpopular back home, with many of England's leading politicians — and some of her generals as well — advocating colonial independence. As the Americans fought doggedly on, the British simply lost the will to fight. Overconfident, blundering, and indecisive by turns, the British government, Ketchum suggests, helped ensure the ultimate American victory.

BRITAIN, ON THE EVE OF [THE AMERICAN REVOLUTION], was the greatest empire since Rome. Never before had she known such wealth and power; never had the future seemed so bright, the prospects so glowing. All, that is, except the spreading sore of discontent in the American colonies that, after festering for a decade and more, finally erupted in violence at Lexington and Concord on April 19, 1775. When news of the subsequent battle for Bunker Hill reached England that summer, George III and his ministers concluded that there was no alternative to using force to put down the insurrection. In the King's mind, at least, there was no longer any hope of reconciliation — nor did the idea appeal to him. He was determined to teach the rebellious colonials a lesson, and no doubts troubled him as to the righteousness of the course he had chosen. "I am not sorry that the line of conduct seems now

chalked out," he had said even before fighting began; later he told his prime minister, Lord North, "I know I am doing my Duty and I can never wish to retract." And then, making acceptance of the war a matter of personal loyalty, "I wish nothing but good," he said, "therefore anyone who does not agree with me is a traitor and a scoundrel." Filled with high moral purpose and confidence, he was certain that "when once these rebels have felt a smart blow, they will submit. . . ."

In British political and military circles there was a general agreement that the war would be quickly and easily won. "Shall we be told," asked one of the King's men in Commons, "that (the Americans) can resist the powerful efforts of this nation?" Major John Pitcairn, writing home from Boston in March, 1775, said, "I am satisfied that one active campaign, a smart action, and burning two or three of their towns, will set everything to rights." The man who would direct the British navy during seven years of war, the unprincipled, inefficient Earl of Sandwich, rose in the House of Lords to express his opinion of the provincial fighting man. "Suppose the Colonies do abound in men," the First Lord of the Admiralty asked,

From Richard M. Ketchum, "England's Vietnam," *American Heritage* (June/July 1971), Vol. 12, No. 4. © 1971 by American Heritage, a division of Forbes, Inc. Reprinted by permission from *American Heritage*.

"what does that signify? They are raw, undisciplined, cowardly men. I wish instead of forty or fifty thousand of these *brave* fellows they would produce in the field at least two hundred thousand; the more the better, the easier would be the conquest; if they did not run away, they would starve themselves into compliance with our measures. . . ." And General James Murray, who had succeeded the great [James] Wolfe in 1749 as commander in North America, called the native American "a very effeminate thing, very unfit for and very impatient of war." Between these estimates of the colonial militiaman and a belief that the might of Great Britain was invincible, there was a kind of arrogant optimism in official quarters when the conflict began. "As there is not common sense in protracting a war of this sort," wrote Lord George Germain, the secretary for the American colonies, in September, 1775, "I should be for exerting the utmost force of this Kingdom to finish the rebellion in one campaign."

Optimism bred more optimism, arrogance more arrogance. One armchair strategist in the House of Commons, William Innes, outlined for the other members an elaborate scheme he had devised for the conduct of the war. First, he would remove the British troops from Boston, since that place was poorly situated for defense. Then, while the people of the Massachusetts Bay Colony were treated like the madmen they were and shut up by the navy, the army would move to one of the southern colonies, fortify itself in an impregnable position, and let the provincials attack if they pleased. The British could sally forth from this and other defensive enclaves at will, and eventually "success against one-half of America will pave the way to the conquest of the whole. . . ." What was more, Innes went on, it was "more than probable you may find men to recruit your army in America." There was a good possibility, in other words, that the British regulars would be replaced after a while by Americans who were loyal to their king, so that the army fighting the rebels would be Americanized, so to speak, and

the Irish and English lads sent home. General James Robertson also believed that success lay in this scheme of Americanizing the combat force: "I never had an idea of subduing the Americans," he said, "I meant to assist the good Americans to subdue the bad."

This notion was important not only from the standpoint of the fighting, but in terms of administering the colonies once they were beaten; loyalists would take over the reins of government when the British pulled out, and loyalist militiamen would preserve order in the pacified colonies. No one knew, of course, how many "good" Americans there were; some thought they might make up half or more of the population. Shortly after arriving in the colonies in 1775, General William Howe, for one, was convinced that "the insurgents are very few, in comparison with the whole of the people."

Before taking the final steps into full-scale war, however, the King and his ministers had to be certain about one vitally important matter: they had to be able to count on the support of the English people. On several occasions in 1775 they were able to read the public pulse (that part of it, at least, that mattered) by observing certain important votes in Parliament. The King's address to both Houses on October 26, in which he announced plans to suppress the uprising in America, was followed by weeks of angry debate; but when the votes were counted, the North ministry's majority was overwhelming. Each vote indicated the full tide of anger that influenced the independent members, the country gentlemen who agreed that the colonials must be put in their place and taught a lesson. A bit out of touch with the news, highly principled, and content in the belief that the King and the ministry must be right, none of them seem to have asked what would be best for the empire; they simply went along with the vindictive measures that were being set in motion. Eloquent voices — those of Edmund Burke, Charles James Fox, the Earl of Chatham, John Wilkes, among others — were raised in

The conciliatory advice of wise Parliamentarians like Burke and Pitt could not prevail over the war party headed by George III and his political cronies. In this prophetic cartoon from a British magazine of 1774, the spark of American rebellion seems destined to become an unquenchable blaze. (Trustees of the British Museum)

opposition to the policies of the Crown, but as Burke said, ". . . it was almost in vain to contend, for the country gentlemen had abandoned their duty, and placed an implicit confidence in the Minister."

The words of sanity and moderation went unheeded because the men who spoke them were out of power and out of public favor; and each time the votes were tallied, the strong, silent, unquestioning majority prevailed. No one in any position in power in the government proposed, after the Battle of Bunker Hill, to halt the fighting in order to settle the differences; no one seriously contemplated conversations that might have led to peace. Instead the government — like so many governments before and since — took what appeared to be the easy way out and settled for war.

George III was determined to maintain his empire, intact and undiminished, and his greatest fear was that the loss of the American colonies would set off a reaction like a line of dominoes falling. Writing to Lord North in 1779, he called the contest with America "the most serious in which any country was ever engaged. It contains such a train of consequences that they must be examined to feel its real weight. . . . Independence is [the Americans'] object, which every man not willing to sacrifice every object to a momentary and inglorious peace must concurr with me in thinking this country can never submit to. Should America succeed in that, the West Indies must follow, not in independence, but for their own interest they must become dependent on America. Ireland would soon follow, and [England] reduced to itself, would be a poor island indeed."

Despite George's unalterable determination, strengthened by his domino theory; despite the wealth and might of the British empire; despite all the odds favoring a quick triumph, the problems facing the King and his ministers and the armed forces were formidable ones indeed. Surpassing all others in sheer magnitude was the immense distance between the mother country and the rebellious colonies. As Edmund Burke described the situation in his last, most eloquent appeal for conciliation, "Three thousand miles of ocean lie between you and them. No contrivance can prevent the effect of this distance in weakening government. Seas roll, and months pass, between the order and the execution; and the want of a speedy explanation of a single point is enough to defeat a whole system.'' Often the westerly passage took three months, and every soldier, every weapon, every button and gaiter and musket ball, every article of clothing and great quantities of food and even fuel, had to be shipped across those three thousand miles of the Atlantic. It was not only immensely costly and time consuming, but there was a terrifying wastefulness to it. Ships sank or were blown hundreds of miles off course, supplies spoiled, animals died en route. Worse yet, men died, and in substantial numbers: returns from regiments sent from the British Isles to the West Indies between 1776 and 1780 reveal that an average of 11 per cent of the troops was lost on these crossings.

Beyond the water lay the North American land mass, and it was an article of faith on the part of many a British military man that certain ruin lay in fighting an enemy on any large scale in that savage wilderness. In the House of Lords in November, 1775, the Duke of Richmond warned the peers to consult their geographies before turning their backs on a peaceful settlement. There was, he said, ''one insuperable difficulty with which an army would have to struggle'' — America abounded in vast rivers that provided natural barriers to the progress of troops; it was a country in which every bush might conceal an enemy, a land whose cultivated parts would be laid waste, so that ''the army (if any army could march or subsist) would be obliged to draw all its provisions from Europe, and all its fresh meat from Smithfield market.'' The French, the mortal enemies of Great Britain, who had seen a good deal more of the North American wilds than the English had, were already laying plans to capitalize on the situation when the British army was bogged down there. In Paris, watchfully eyeing his adversary's every move, France's foreign minister, the Comte de Vergennes, predicted in July, 1775, that ''it will be vain for the English to multiply their forces'' in the colonies; ''no longer can they bring that vast

continent back to dependence by force of arms.'' Seven years later, as the war drew to a close, one of Rochambeau's aides told a friend of Charles James Fox: ''No opinion was clearer than that though the people of America might be conquered by well disciplined European troops, the country of America was unconquerable.''

Yet even in 1775 some thoughtful Englishmen doubted if the American people or their army could be defeated. Before the news of Bunker Hill arrived in London, the adjutant general declared that a plan to defeat the colonials militarily was ''as wild an idea as ever controverted common sense,'' and the secretary-of-war, Lord Barrington, had similar reservations. As early as 1774 Barrington ventured the opinion that a war in the wilderness of North America would cost Britain far more than she could ever gain from it; that the size of the country and the colonials' familiarity with firearms would make victory questionable — or at best achievable only at the cost of enormous suffering; and finally, even if Britain should win such a contest, Barrington believed that the cost of maintaining the colonies in any state of subjection would be staggering. John Wilkes, taunting Lord North on this matter of military conquest, suggested that North — even if he rode out at the head of the entire English cavalry — would not venture ten miles into the countryside for fear of guerrilla fighters. ''The Americans,'' Wilkes promised, ''will dispute every inch of territory with you, every narrow pass, every strong defile, every Thermopylae, every Bunker's Hill.''

It was left to the great William Pitt to provide the most stirring warning against fighting the Americans. Now Earl of Chatham, he was so crippled in mind and body that he rarely appeared in the House of Lords, but in May, 1777, he made the supreme effort, determined to raise his voice once again in behalf of conciliation. Supported on canes, his eyes flashing with the old fire and his beak-like face thrust forward belligerently, he warned the peers: "You cannot conquer the Americans. You talk of your numerous friends to annihilate the Congress, and of your powerful forces to disperse their army, but I might as well talk of driving them before me with this crutch. . . . You have been three years teaching them the art of war, and they are apt scholars. I will venture to tell your lordships that the American gentry will make officers enough fit to command the troops of all the European powers. What you have sent there are too many to make peace, too few to make war. You cannot make them respect you. You cannot make them wear your cloth. You will plant an invincible hatred in their breast against you. . . ."

"My lords," he went on, "you have been the aggressors from the beginning. I say again, this country has been the aggressor. You have made descents upon their coasts. You have burnt their towns, plundered their country, made war upon the inhabitants, confiscated their property, proscribed and imprisoned their persons. . . . The people of America look upon Parliament as the authors of their miseries. Their affections are estranged from their sovereign. Let, then, reparation come from the hands that inflicted the injuries. Let conciliation succeed chastisement. . . ." But there was no persuading the majority; Chatham's appeal was rejected and the war went on unabated.

It began to appear, however, that destruction of the Continental Army — even if that goal could be achieved — might not be conclusive. After the disastrous campaign around Manhattan in 1776, George Washington had determined not to risk his army in a major engagement, and he began moving away from the European battle style in which two armies confronted each other head to head. His tactical method became that of the small, outweighed prizefighter who depends on his legs to keep him out of range of his opponent and who, when the bigger man begins to tire, darts in quickly to throw a quick punch, then retreats again. It was an approach to fighting described by Nathanael Greene, writing of the cam-

paign in the South in 1780: "We fight, get beat, rise, and fight again." In fact, between January and September of the following year, Greene, short of money, troops, and supplies, won a major campaign without ever really winning a battle. The battle at Guilford Courthouse, which was won by the British, was typical of the results. As Horace Walpole observed, "Lord Cornwallis has conquered his troops out of shoes and provisions and himself out of troops."

There was, in the colonies, no great political center like Paris or London, whose loss might have been demoralizing to the Americans; indeed, Boston, New York, and Philadelphia, the seat of government, were all held at one time or another by the British without irreparable damage to the rebel cause. The fragmented political and military structure of the colonies was often a help to the rebels, rather than a hindrance, for it meant that there was almost no chance of the enemy striking a single crushing blow. The difficulty, as General Frederick Haldimand, who succeeded Carleton in Canada, saw it, was the seemingly unending availability of colonial militiamen who rose up out of nowhere to fight in support of the nucleus of regular troops called the Continental Army. "It is not the number of troops Mr. Washington can spare from his army that is to be apprehended," Haldimand wrote, "it is the multitude of militia and men in arms ready to turn out at an hour's notice at the shew of a single regiment of Continental Troops. . . ." So long as the British were able to split up their forces and fan out over the countryside in relatively small units, they were fairly successful in putting down the irregulars' activities and cutting off their supplies; but the moment they had to concentrate again to fight the Continentals, guerrilla warfare burst out like so many small brush fires on their flank and rear. No British regular could tell if an American was friend or foe, for loyalty to King George was easy to attest; and the man who was a farmer or merchant when a British battalion marched by his home was a militiaman as soon as it had passed by, ready to shoulder his musket when an emergency or an opportunity to confound the enemy arose.

Against an unnumberable supply of irregular forces the British could bring to bear only a fixed quantity of troops — however many, that is, they happened to have on the western side of the Atlantic Ocean at any given moment. Early in the war General James Murray had foreseen the difficulties that would undoubtedly arise. Writing to Lord Barrington, he warned that military conquest was no real answer. If the war proved to be a long one, their advantage in numbers would heavily favor the rebels, who could replace their losses while the British could not. Not only did every musket and grain of powder have to be shipped across the ocean; but if a man was killed or wounded, the only way to replace him was to send another man in full kit across the Atlantic. And troop transports were slow and small: three or four were required to move a single battalion.

During the summer of 1775 recruiting went badly in England and Ireland, for the war was not popular with a lot of the people who would have to fight it, and there were jobs to be had. It was evident that the only means of assembling a force large enough to suppress the rebellion in the one massive stroke that had been determined upon was to hire foreign troops. And immediately this word was out, the rapacious petty princes of Brunswick, Hesse-Cassel, and Waldeck, and the Margrave of Anspach-Bayreuth, generously offered up a number of their subjects — at a price — fully equipped and ready for duty, to serve His Majesty George III. Frederick the Great of Prussia, seeing the plan for what it was, announced that he would "make all the Hessian troops, marching through his dominions to America, pay the usual cattle tax, because, although human beings, they had been sold as beasts." But George III and the princes regarded it as a business deal, in the manner of such dubious alliances ever since: each foot soldier and trooper supplied by the Duke of Brunswick,

for instance, was to be worth seven pounds, four shillings, fourpence halfpenny in levy money to his Most Serene Highness. Three wounded men were to count as one killed in action, and it was stipulated that a soldier killed in combat would be paid for at the same rate as levy money. In other words the life of a subject was worth precisely seven pounds, four shillings, fourpence halfpenny to the Duke.

As it turned out, the large army that was assembled in 1776 to strike a quick, overpowering blow that would put a sudden end to the rebellion proved — when that decisive victory never came to pass — to be a distinct liability, a hideously expensive and at times vulnerable weapon. In the indecisive hands of men like William Howe and Henry Clinton, who never seemed absolutely certain about what they should do or how they should do it, the great army rarely had an opportunity to realize its potential; yet, it remained a ponderous and insatiable consumer of supplies, food, and money.

The loyalists, on whom many Englishmen had placed such high hopes, proved a will-o'the-wisp. Largely ignored by the policy makers early in the war despite their pleas for assistance, the loyalists were numerous enough but were neither well organized nor evenly distributed throughout the colonies. Where the optimists in Britain went wrong in thinking that loyalist strength would be an important factor was to imagine that anything like a majority of Americans *could* remain loyal to the Crown if they were not continuously supported and sustained by the mother country. Especially as the war went on, as opinions hardened, and as the possibility increased that the new government in America might actually survive, it was a very difficult matter to retain one's loyalty to the King unless friends and neighbors were of like mind and unless there was British force nearby to safeguard such a belief. Furthermore, it proved almost impossible for the British command to satisfy the loyalists, who were bitterly angry over the persecution and physical violence and robbery they had to endure and who charged constantly that the British generals were too lax in their treatment of rebels.

While the problems of fighting the war in distant America mounted, Britain found herself unhappily confronted with the combination of circumstances the Foreign Office dreaded most: with her armies tied down, the great European maritime powers — France and Spain — vengeful and adventurous and undistracted by war in the Old World, formed a coalition against her. When the American war began, the risk of foreign intervention was regarded as minimal, and the decision to fight was made on the premise that victory would be early and complete and that the armed forces would be released before any threatening European power could take advantage of the situation. But as the war continued without any definite signs of American collapse, France and Spain seized the chance to embarrass and perhaps humiliate their old antagonist. At first they supported the rebels surreptitiously with shipments of weapons and other supplies; then, when the situation appeared more auspicious, France in particular furnished active support in the form of an army and a navy, with catastrophic results for Great Britain.

One fascinating might-have-been is what would have happened had the Opposition in Parliament been more powerful politically. It consisted, after all, of some of the most forceful and eloquent orators imaginable, men whose words still have the power to send shivers up the spine. Not simply vocal, they were highly intelligent men whose concern went beyond the injustice and inhumanity of war. They were quick to see that the personal liberty of the King's subjects was as much an issue in London as it was in the colonies, and they foresaw irreparable damage to the empire if the government followed its unthinking policy of coercion. Given a stronger power base, they might have headed off war or the ultimate disaster; had the government been in the hands of men like Chatham or Burke or their followers, some accommodation with America might conceivably have evolved from the various proposals for reconciliation. But the King and

North had the votes in their pockets, and the antiwar Opposition failed because a majority that was largely indifferent to reason supported the North ministry until the bitter end came with Cornwallis' surrender. Time and again a member of the Opposition would rise to speak out against the war for one reason or another: "This country," the Earl of Shelburne protested, "already burdened much beyond its abilities, is now on the eve of groaning under new taxes, for the purpose of carrying on this cruel and destructive war." Or, from Dr. Franklin's friend David Hartley: "Every proposition for reconciliation has so constantly and uniformly been crushed by Administration, that I think they seem not even to wish for the appearance of justice. The law of force is that which they appeal to. . . ." Or, from Sir James Lowther, when he learned that the King had rejected an "Olive Branch Petition" from the provincials: "Why have we not peace with a people who, it is evident, desire peace with us?" Or this, from General Henry Seymour Conway, inviting Lord North to inform members of the House of Commons about his overall program: "I do not desire the detail; let us have general outline, to be able to judge of the probability of its success. It is indecent not to lay before the House some plan, or the outlines of a plan. . . . If [the] plan is conciliation, let us see it, that we may form some opinion of it; if it be hostility and coercion, I do repeat, that we have no cause for a minute's consideration; for I can with confidence pronounce, that the present military armament will never succeed." But all unavailing, year after year, as each appeal to reason and humanity fell on ears deafened by self-righteousness and minds hardened against change.

Although it might be said that the arguments raised by the Opposition did not change the course of the war, they nevertheless affected the manner in which it was conducted, which in turn led to the ultimate British defeat. Whether Lord North was uncertain of that silent majority's loyalty is difficult to determine, but it seems clear that he was sufficiently nervous about public support to decide that a bold policy which risked defeats was not for him. As a result the war of the American Revolution was a limited war — limited from the standpoint of its objectives and the force with which Britain waged it.

In some respects the aspect of the struggle that may have had the greatest influence on the outcome was an intangible one. Until the outbreak of hostilities in 1775 no more than a small minority of the colonials had seriously contemplated independence, but after a year of war the situation was radically different. Now the mood was reflected in words such as these — instructions prepared by the county of Buckingham, in Virginia, for its delegates to a General Convention in Williamsburg: ". . . as far as your voices are admitted, you [will] cause a free and happy Constitution to be established, with a renunciation of the old, and so much thereof as has been found inconvenient and oppressive." That simple and powerful idea — renunciation of the old and its replacement with something new, independently conceived — was destined to sweep all obstacles before it. In Boston, James Warren was writing the news of home to John Adams in Philadelphia and told him: "Your Declaration of Independence came on Saturday and diffused a general joy. Every one of us feels more important than ever; we now congratulate each other as Freemen." Such winds of change were strong, and by contrast all Britain had to offer was a return to the status quo. Indeed, it was difficult for the average Englishman to comprehend the appeal that personal freedom and independence held for a growing number of Americans. As William Innes put it in a debate in Commons, all the government had to do to put an end to the nonsense in the colonies was to "convince the lower class of those infatuated people that the imaginary liberty they are so eagerly pursuing is not by any means to be compared to that which the Constitution of this happy country already permits them to enjoy."

With everything to gain from victory and everything to lose by defeat, the Americans could follow Livy's advice, that "in desperate matters the boldest counsels are the safest." Frequently beaten and disheartened, inadequately trained and fed and clothed, they fought on against unreasonably long odds because of that slim hope of attaining a distant goal. And as they fought on, increasing with each passing year the possibility that independence might be achieved, the people of Britain finally lost the will to keep going.

In England the goal had not been high enough while the cost was too high. There was nothing compelling about the limited objective of bringing the colonies back into the empire, nothing inspiring about punishing the rebels, nothing noble in proving that retribution awaited those who would change the nature of things.

After the war had been lost and the treaty of peace signed [in 1783], Lord North looked back on the whole affair and sadly informed the members of the House of Commons where, in his opinion, the fault lay. . . . "The American war," he said, "has been suggested to have been the war of the Crown, contrary to the wishes of the people. I deny it. It was the war of Parliament. There was not a step taken in it that had not the sanction of Parliament. It was the war of the people, for it was undertaken for the express purpose of maintaining the just rights of Parliament, or, in other words, of the people of Great Britain, over the dependencies of the empire. For this reason, it was popular at its commencement, and eagerly embraced by the people and Parliament. . . . Nor did it ever cease to be popular until a series of unparalleled disasters and calamities caused the people, wearied out with almost uninterrupted ill-success and misfortune, to call out as loudly for peace as they had formerly done for war."

QUESTIONS TO CONSIDER

1 Examine the role of King George III in the British decision to use military force to put down the rebellion in the American colonies. What are the

implications of basing foreign policy on the question of personal loyalty?

2   What was the importance of American loyalists in British military plans? Was it realistic for the British to hope to use them as they did?

3   What did Charles James Fox mean when he said, "Though the people of America might be conquered . . . the country of America was unconquerable"?

4   Analyze the role played by England's antiwar protesters in Parliament. What arguments did men like Edmund Burke and William Pitt offer in opposition to England's military policy, and what effect did they have on the conduct of the war?

5   How were George Washington's military tactics perfectly designed to win the Revolutionary War without necessarily winning a single battle?

V

BIRTH
OF THE
REPUBLIC

9

Sunrise at Philadelphia

Brian McGinty

Once the Revolution began, Americans set about creating the political machinery necessary to sustain an independent nation. The Second Continental Congress, called in 1775, continued as an emergency, all-purpose central government until 1781, when the Articles of Confederation were finally ratified and a new one-house Congress was elected to function as the national government. Wary of central authority because of the British experience, Americans now had precisely the kind of government most of them wanted: an impotent Congress that lacked the authority to tax, regulate commerce, or enforce its own ordinances and resolutions. Subordinate to the states, which supplied it with funds as they chose, Congress was little more than "a stately debating society," whose delegates wandered about the country from Princeton to Annapolis to Trenton to New York, endlessly discussing where they should settle. A beggar at home and abroad, Congress was powerless to run the country.

Patriots like Madison, Hamilton, and the venerable Washington fretted in their correspondence about the near paralysis of the central government and the unstable conditions that plagued the land. "An opinion begins to prevail, that a General Convention for revising the Articles of Confederation would be expedient," John Jay wrote Washington in March 1787. Washington agreed that the "fabrick" was "tottering." When Massachusetts farmers rose in rebellion under Daniel Shays, Washington was horror-stricken. "Are your people getting mad? . . . What is the cause of all this? When and how is it to end? . . . What, gracious God, is man! that there should be such inconsistency and perfidiousness in his conduct? . . . We are fast verging to anarchy and confusion!"

Many of his colleagues agreed. There followed a series of maneuvers and meetings that culminated in the great convention of 1787, a gathering of fifty-five notables sent to Philadelphia to overhaul the feeble Articles of Confederation. Without authority, they proceeded to draft an entirely new Constitution that scrapped the Articles, created a new government, and undoubtedly saved the country and America's experiment in popular government. As James MacGregor Burns has noted, it was a convention of "the well-bred, the well-fed, the well-read, and the well-wed." Most of the delegates were wealthy, formally educated, and youngish (their average age was the early forties), and more than a third of them were slaveowners. The poor, the uneducated, the backcountry farmers, and women, blacks, and Indians were not represented. Throughout their deliberations, moreover, they compromised on the volatile slavery issue. "For these white men," wrote one scholar, "the black man was always a brooding and unsettling presence (the black woman, even more than the white woman, was beyond the pale, beyond calculation)." For most of the framers of the Constitution, order and national strength were more important than the inalienable rights of blacks or women. Like their countrymen, most of them could simultaneously love liberty, recognize the injustice of slavery, and yet tolerate bondage as a necessary evil.

As we enter our third century under the Constitution, we need more than ever to remember that the framers were not saints but human beings — paradoxical, complex, unpredictable, and motivated by selfishness as well as high idealism. Yet, as Brian McGinty shows in his account of "the miracle of Philadelphia," the founders were able to rise above petty self-interest to fashion what remains the oldest written national constitution, which in turn created one of the oldest and most successful federal systems in history. McGinty tells the full story of the great convention; he describes the remarkable personalities gathered there, the debates and the compromises that shaped the new Constitution, the battle for ratification, and the forging of a Bill of Rights in the form of the first ten amendments.

AS BENJAMIN FRANKLIN looked over the roster of delegates at the start of the Constitutional Convention, he confessed that he was well pleased. "We

From "Sunrise at Philadelphia" by Brian McGinty, *American History Illustrated* (Summer 1987), excerpted from pp. 22–47. Reprinted through the courtesy of Cowles Magazines, Inc. publisher of *American History Illustrated*.

have here at present," Franklin wrote a friend, "what the French call *une assemblée des notables,* a convention composed of some of the principal people from the several states of our Confederation." [Thomas] Jefferson, examining the same roster in Paris, proclaimed the convention "an assembly of demi-gods."

Most prominent among the "demigods" was

George Washington. Early on the morning of May 9, 1787, he had left Mount Vernon in his carriage. Washington was no stranger to the road from the Potomac to Philadelphia, for he had traveled it often during the days of the First and Second Continental Congresses, oftener still while he was leading the military struggle for independence. He would have liked to travel with Martha this time, but the mistress of the plantation on the Potomac had "become too domestic and too attentive to her two little grandchildren to leave home." The retired general's progress was impeded more than a little by the joyful greetings he received at every town and stage stop along the way. When he arrived in Philadelphia on May 13, the biggest celebration of all began. Senior officers of the Continental Army greeted him on the outskirts of the city, and citizens on horseback formed an escort. Guns fired a salute and the bells of Christ Church pealed as the great man rode into the city.

Washington had reflected carefully before deciding to attend the Philadelphia convention. He was fifty-five years old now, and his once-powerful physique was wracked with rheumatism. He was far from certain that the Philadelphia convention would find a solution to the nation's political problems and had little wish to risk his reputation in an effort that might be doomed to failure. More important, when he had resigned his military commission in December 1783 he had clearly stated his intention of spending the rest of his days in private life. But his friends had urged him to reconsider his decision and lend his commanding influence and prestige to the Philadelphia assembly.

Despite his lingering doubts about the convention's ultimate outcome, Washington had no reservations about its purpose. "The discerning part of the community," he wrote a friend, "have long since seen the necessity of giving adequate powers to Congress for national purposes; and the ignorant and designing must yield to it ere long." What most troubled the Virginian was the realization that his failure to go to Philadelphia might be interpreted as a rejection of the convention. And so he decided, more out of a sense of duty than with any enthusiasm, to make the long trip to Philadelphia. Although Washington arrived there the day before the assembly was set to convene, he found that some delegates were already in the city. The Pennsylvania delegates, who all lived in Philadelphia, were there, of course, headed by the venerable Dr. Benjamin Franklin. Franklin received Washington in the courtyard of his home just off Market Street above Third, after which the general repaired to the luxurious home of Robert Morris on Market just east of Sixth, where he was to be a guest during the convention.

Franklin was eighty-one years old and beset by infirmities (gout and gall stones) that made it all but impossible for him to walk. But his mind was bright and alert, and he continued to play an active role in the affairs of his city and state. He had returned in 1785 from Paris, where he had been American minister to France, to enjoy comforts of a well-earned retirement, but relented when members of the Supreme Executive Council of Pennsylvania asked him to accept the post of president, an office that corresponded to the position of governor in other states. By late March, on the motion of Robert Morris, Franklin had accepted a commission to attend the upcoming convention as a Pennsylvania delegate. . . .

Although Washington was the most celebrated of the Virginia delegates, he was not the first to arrive in Philadelphia. Thirty-six-year-old James Madison of Montpelier in the Old Dominion's Orange County arrived in Philadelphia on May 3, 1787, from New York, where he had been serving in Congress. A slight man, barely five feet, six

A view of the Philadelphia State House (Independence Hall), where the delegates to the Constitutional Convention assembled in May 1787. During these meetings, the United States government, as we know it, took shape. In the tower of the State House hung the Liberty Bell, which tolled the news of the signing of the Declaration of Independence and of American victories in the Revolution. An impassioned motto girdled the bell: "Proclaim Liberty throughout the land, and to all the inhabitants thereof." But given all the inhabitants excluded from the blessings of liberty, the motto seems more than a little ironic today. (By permission of the Houghton Library, Harvard University)

inches tall, Madison was shy and bookish. What he lacked in force and dynamism, the little Virginian more than made up in thought and scholarship. After graduating from the College of New Jersey (later Princeton), he had returned to his home state to take an active interest in public affairs. He served in the Virginia House of Delegates and Council of State before accepting election to Congress, where he served twice (in 1780–83 and again in 1786–88). A close friend of Thomas Jefferson, Madison came to the convention with well-developed ideas about democratic processes and republican institutions. . . .

In all, seventy-four delegates were selected to attend the convention, and fifty-five actually appeared in Philadelphia. Although not all of the fifty-five would attend all of the sessions, it was a sizable group — large enough to give the spacious, paneled assembly room on the east side of the ground floor of the Pennsylvania State House (the same room in which the Declaration of Independence had been signed in 1776) an air of excitement when the convention was in session.

In some ways the convention was as notable for the men who were not there as for those who were. The absence of John Adams and Thomas Jefferson was sharply felt, for both of these veterans of 1776 were widely regarded as American giants. Important diplomatic assignments kept them away from Philadelphia: Jefferson was American minister in Paris, while Adams filled the same post in London. Both were apprised of developments in the Pennsylvania city by faithful correspondents on the scene. Adams's intellectual presence was strongly felt at the convention, for he had recently published *A Defence of the Constitutions of Government of the United States of America,* a treatise that explained and analyzed the constitutional structures of a half-dozen American states. Jefferson exchanged letters with James Madison and, at the younger man's request, sent him books on constitutional theory and history, for Madison was particularly interested in the histories of ancient confederacies. . . .

George Washington's presence in Philadelphia was enough to reassure all those who worried about the absence of Adams, Jefferson, [Richard Henry], Lee, [Patrick] Henry, and [John] Jay. When the hero of the Revolution entered Philadelphia at the head of a parade of cheering well-wishers, nearly everyone in the city was able to breathe more easily. If anyone could guarantee the results of the Philadelphia assembly, surely the Squire of Mount Vernon could. New York's Henry Knox wrote the Marquis de Lafayette: "General Washington's attendance at the convention adds, in my opinion, new lustre to his character. Secure as he was in his fame, he has again committed it to the mercy of events." "This great patriot," said the *Pennsylvania Herald,* "will never think his duty performed, while anything remains to be done."

It is not surprising that so many of the delegates (more than half) were lawyers, for members of the legal profession had long led the struggle for independence. Nor was it remarkable that many were present or former public officials. Fully four-fifths of the delegates were serving in or had been members of Congress, while even more had been involved, at one time or another, in colonial, state, and local governments. Many had helped draft their states' constitutions, and about half were veterans of military service. There were merchants, farmers, and one or two men who described themselves as "bankers" in the group. Three of the delegates were physicians, and one, Franklin, was a printer.

On the whole, the delegates were remarkably young: The average age was forty-three. Jonathan Dayton of New Jersey, at twenty-six, was the youngest; Franklin, at eighty-one, the oldest. Many had humble origins. Franklin had once been an indentured servant, and [Roger] Sherman of Connecticut had begun his working life as a cobbler's apprentice. But most delegates had acquired comfortable positions in life. A few ranked among the richest men in the country.

In a letter to Jefferson, Franklin expressed cautious optimism about the convention. The delegates were men of character and ability, Franklin said, "so that I hope Good from their meeting. Indeed," he added, "if it does not do good it must do Harm, as it will show that we have not Wisdom enough among us to govern ourselves; and will strengthen the opinion of some Political writers, that popular Governments cannot long support themselves." . . .

George Washington appeared regularly in the State House (the historic building would not be known as Independence Hall until the nineteenth century) at the appointed time each day, waiting patiently for the stragglers to appear and be recorded as present. When on May 25, the delegates of seven states were at last in their chairs, the convention was ready to begin.

First, a presiding officer has to be selected. Nobody in attendance had any doubt that the honor would be conferred on Washington; the only uncertainty was who would nominate him. Benjamin Franklin had planned to do so, but it was raining on May 25 and he was not well enough to make the trip from his home to the State House in poor weather. The motion was made in his stead by Robert Morris (Pennsylvania) and seconded by John Rutledge (South Carolina). Without discussion, the question was put to a vote, and Washington was unanimously elected president of the convention. Morris and Rutledge escorted the Virginian to the President's Chair. The chair belonged to the Pennsylvania Assembly and had been used by all the presidents of the Continental Congress when it had met in Philadelphia. Surmounting its back was the carved and gilded image of a sun that, before the assembly was concluded, would become a symbol for the convention and its work.

Second, rules for the convention's proceedings had to be adopted. One rule . . . was readily approved. It provided that "no copy be taken of any entry on the journal during the sitting of the House without the leave of the House. That members only be permitted to inspect the journal. That nothing spoken in the House be printed, or otherwise published, or communicated without leave." . . .

To impress on the delegates the seriousness with which the rule of secrecy was to be enforced, armed sentries were posted in the hall beyond the assembly chamber and on the street outside the State House. . . .

The delegates, on the whole, were scrupulous in their observance of the "rule of secrecy"; so scrupulous, in fact, that for nearly a generation after the convention the positions taken during the debates were still largely unknown to the public. Washington even refused to write about the debates in his diary. A few delegates kept private records that found their way into print long after the events at Philadelphia had become history. The best record was kept by James Madison. "I chose a seat," the Virginian later explained, "in front of the presiding member, with the other members on my right hand and left hand. In this favorable position for hearing all that passed I noted in terms legible and abbreviations and marks intelligible to [no one but] myself what was read from the Chair or spoken by the members; and losing not a moment unnecessarily between the adjournment and reassembling of the Convention I was enabled to write out my daily notes during the session or within a few finishing days after its close. . . . I was not absent a single day, nor more than a casual fraction of any hour in any day, so that I could not have lost a single speech, unless a very short one." Published in 1840, Madison's notes form the single best record of the convention's proceedings.

The Virginia delegates came to the convention's first deliberative session on May 29 equipped with a comprehensive plan for a new charter of government. Although the "Virginia Plan" had been discussed at length by members of that state's delegation, it bore the mark of Madison's careful thought and planning on every page. Edmund Randolph, who, as governor of the state, was titular leader of the Virginia delegation, presented the plan to the convention. The Virginia Plan proclaimed that it was designed to "correct and enlarge" the Articles of Confederation, but it was actually a blueprint for a whole new structure of government. Under it, the "national legislature" would consist of not one, but two houses, with the lower elected by the people and the upper chosen by the lower. There would be a "national executive," with veto power over legislative acts, and a "national judiciary," with authority to decide cases involving "national peace or harmony."

The Virginia plan was a tempting subject for debate, but the convention's leaders believed more fundamental questions had to be decided first — questions upon which all other as yet undecided questions depended.

First among these threshold questions was whether the convention ought to content itself with revising the Articles of Confederation or propose an entirely new government with truly national purposes and powers. Delegates from at least four of the states had been sent to Philadelphia with strict instructions to consider revisions of the Articles and nothing else; and Congress, in its resolution approving the convention, had purported to limit the convention to revising the old charter.

Next the delegates resolved to organize into a Committee of the Whole. The purpose of this parliamentary maneuver was to keep discussions informal and to allow the representatives to change their votes until near the end of the convention. The device promoted open minds and frank speech.

As discussion began, South Carolina's Charles Pinckney expressed concern that, if the convention proposed a national government, the states might cease to exist. But Edmund Randolph (Virginia) assured him that a national government would not prevent the states from continuing to exercise authority in their proper spheres. John Dickinson (Delaware) and Elbridge Gerry (Massachusetts) admitted that the Articles of Confederation were defective, but they thought that the convention should correct their defects, not toss them aside.

Gouverneur Morris (Pennsylvania) expressed his belief that a national government was essential to the future of the country. "We had better take a supreme government now," Morris warned his fellow-delegates, "than a despot twenty years hence — for come he must." Agreeing with Morris, George Mason (Virginia) argued that the country needed a government that could govern directly, without the intervention of the states.

On May 30, on the motion of Gouverneur Morris, the convention decided, by a vote of six states to one, that "a *national* government ought to be established consisting of a *supreme* Legislative, Executive and Judiciary." Almost before they knew it, the delegates had decided what was to be the single most important issue of the convention. From that day forward, the convention would be irrevocably dedicated to the construction of a national government for the United States.

On May 31 the Committee of the Whole (the convention delegates) proceeded to consider other potentially explosive questions: whether the "national legislature" should have two houses or one; whether either or both houses should be elected by the people; and how the national government should function in terms of the citizens and the states. . . . Surprisingly, the delegates quickly agreed that there should be two houses in the legislature, that the lower house should be popularly elected, and that the legislature should have broad powers "to legislate in all cases to which the separate States are incompetent."

After deliberating for two weeks, the Committee of the Whole presented its recommendations to the convention. The proposed form of government followed the terms of the "Virginia Plan" closely — too closely, some delegates thought. Elbridge Gerry (Massachusetts) protested that some decisions might have been made too hastily, "that it was necessary to consider what the people would approve." Taking his cue from Gerry, William Paterson (New Jersey) proposed an alternative to the "Virginia Plan." Introduced on June 15, Paterson's "New Jersey Plan" suggested an entirely different frame of government: a unicameral legislature with members chosen by the state legislatures but with powers to "pass Acts for the regulation of trade and commerce." . . .

The delegates now decided to refer both the New Jersey Plan and the Virginia Plan to the Committee of the Whole for discussion.

The debates were now becoming contentious. The large states, led in size by Virginia, believed it was essential to do away with the old principle embodied in the Articles of Confederation of "one state, one vote." Under this rule, voters in the large states were effectively disfranchised by those in the small states. For their part, the small states insisted they could never consent to any rule that would deprive them of an equal voice in the federal government. If such a resolution were passed, Delaware's George Read announced, he would have no choice but to leave the convention, for his credentials forbade him to consent to such a measure.

Washington had been pleased when, in the early days of the convention, the delegates quickly and readily reached agreement on difficult questions. Now, it seemed, they were arguing about every issue that came before them. Discouraged, he wrote home for additional clothing, explaining that he saw "no end to my staying here." The sweltering heat (some Philadelphians thought the summer of 1787 was the worst since 1750) added to the bad humor of the delegates. Franklin, noting the rancor of the debates, suggested the representatives invite clergymen to attend their sessions and offer daily prayers. Roger Sherman (Connecticut) seconded the motion, but Alexander Hamilton (New York) doubted the wisdom of calling for "foreign aid." Many different faiths were represented among the delegates, and it would have been difficult to meet the demands of them all. Besides, a call for prayer might signal to the public outside the hall that all was not well inside. After some discussion, Franklin's proposal was dropped.

Sensing that the convention was approaching an impasse, Roger Sherman (Connecticut) rose to propose the convention's first important compromise.

Representation in the lower house, Sherman suggested, should be based on population, while representation in the upper house should be equal. Sherman's proposal was ingenious. Its chief virtue was that it satisfied neither the large states nor the small states. Hamilton called it a "motley measure," and Madison said it was a "novelty & a compound." Because it met the demands of neither interest, however, it was acceptable to both. On July 16, by a vote of five states in favor, four states against, and one (Massachusetts) evenly divided, the "Connecticut Compromise" was passed. Another major hurdle to agreement had been overcome.

But many difficult questions still remained to be resolved. After spirited debate, the convention decided that each state would be allotted two representatives (senators) in the upper house of the national legislature and that the senators would vote "per capita," that is, individually. Additional debate prompted the delegates to decide that the "national executive" (the president) would be chosen neither by the national legislature nor by the people directly, but by a body of men (the electoral college) specially chosen for the purpose. George Mason (Virginia) proposed that membership in the national legislature be limited to "citizens of the United States," and no one objected.

By July 26, the convention felt it had made enough progress on the broad questions that faced it to safely proceed to more particular issues. To this end, it referred the proposed Constitution to a Committee of Detail with instructions to report back on August 6 with specific proposals to implement the convention's broad intentions. Its five members, John Rutledge (South Carolina), Edmund Randolph (Virginia), James Wilson (Pennsylvania), Oliver Ellsworth (Connecticut), and Nathaniel Gorham (Massachusetts) represented all sections of the country; the committee constituted a kind of "miniature convention."

From July 26 to August 6, the committee proposed, debated, revised, and, finally, resolved a host of important questions. It spelled out the powers of the national legislature, including a power that the Articles of Confederation had never given the old Congress: "to lay and collect taxes, duties, imposts and excises." The committee proposed to grant the national legislature the power to make all laws that should be "necessary and proper" for carrying out its specific powers. The "necessary and proper" clause would later become one of the chief building blocks of a strong central government. The committee decided the Supreme Court should have jurisdiction to decide all "Cases arising under the Laws passed by the general Legislature." And, significantly, the Committee of Detail provided that acts of the national legislature, treaties, and "this Constitution" should all be the "supreme Law of the Land."

With the basic structure of the proposed government now agreed upon, the convention appointed a Committee of Style and Arrangement to draft the Constitution. Some of the best penmen of the convention were appointed to the committee — James Madison (Virginia), Alexander Hamilton (New York), William Samuel Johnson (Connecticut), and Rufus King (Massachusetts). But the chief responsibility for drafting the document fell to the talented Gouverneur Morris (Pennsylvania). Years later, Morris would write that the Constitution "was written by the fingers, which write this letter." Madison, who was responsible for much of the substance of the document, admitted "the finish given to the style and arrangement of the Constitution fairly belongs to the pen of Mr. Morris."

Morris worked quickly and apparently with inspiration. One of the last sections he composed was the Preamble. As originally drafted by the Committee of Detail, the Preamble had stated:

"We the People of the States of New-Hampshire, Massachusetts, Rhode-Island and Providence Plantations, Connecticut, New-York, New-Jersey, Pennsylvania, Delaware, Maryland, Virginia, North Carolina, South-Carolina, and Georgia, do ordain,

declare, and establish the following Constitution for the Government of Ourselves and our Posterity."

The Committee of Style and Arrangement rewrote the same passage to read:

"We the People of the United States, in Order to form a more perfect Union, to establish Justice, insure domestic Tranquility, provide for the common defence, promote the general Welfare, and secure the Blessings of Liberty to ourselves and our Posterity, do ordain and establish this Constitution for the United States of America."

The change from "We the People" of named states to "We the People of the United States" did not seem particularly significant to the delegates when they read and considered Morris's draft. To history, however, it became one of the single most important acts of the Constitutional Convention. It would signify that the Union was the product, not of thirteen states, but of more than three million citizens. It was not a compact between sovereign governments, but a contract to which the citizens were parties.

When the Committee of Style presented its draft to the convention, there was a flurry of last-minute objections. Some delegates thought that Congress's right to overrule presidential vetoes should be by a vote of two-thirds rather than three-fourths of both houses. Others thought the document ought to guarantee the right of trial by jury in all civil cases. George Mason (Virginia) demanded that a bill of rights (similar to the precedent-setting Bill of Rights he drafted for the Virginia Constitution in 1776) be appended to the Constitution. But the hour was late, and the delegates were opposed to making major revisions. All states on the convention floor (including Mason's own Virginia) voted "no" to adopting a bill of rights.

Some delegates left the convention before the final copy of the Constitution was prepared. Others remained in Philadelphia, but only to express their opposition to the final version of the charter. George Mason, obstinate on the point of a bill of rights, announced that he "would sooner chop off his right hand than put it to the Constitution." Another Virginian, Edmund Randolph, who had first proposed the "Virginia Plan" that had formed the basis for many of the Constitution's major provisions, now doubted whether the people of his state would approve the document, and announced that he could not sign it. Elbridge Gerry (Massachusetts) thought that members of the Senate would hold their offices too long, that Massachusetts would not be fairly represented in the House of Representatives, and that a Supreme Court without juries would be a "Star-Chamber as to civil cases." He announced that he would not sign.

Word was circulating in Philadelphia that Pennsylvania's Benjamin Franklin also objected to the Constitution, but the philosopher-statesman soon put an end to such speculation. On Monday morning, September 17, after the secretary of the convention read a newly engrossed copy of the document, Franklin asked for permission to present a speech he had written. Because it was painful for him to stand, he asked James Wilson to read it for him:

"I confess that there are several parts of this constitution which I do not at present approve, but I am not sure I shall never approve them: For having lived long, I have experienced many instances of being obliged by better information or fuller consideration, to change opinions even on important subjects, which I once thought right, but found to be otherwise. . . . Thus I consent, Sir, to this Constitution because I expect no better, and because I am not sure, that it is not the best."

Before the Constitution could be signed, Nathaniel Gorham (Massachusetts) proposed that one final change be made in the document. Where the charter provided that each member of the House of Representatives would represent 40,000 citizens, Gorham suggested that the number be changed to 30,000. Several of the delegates felt that 40,000 was too large a constituency to be represented by one man. Rufus King (Massachusetts), Daniel Carroll (Maryland), and, finally, George Washington announced their agreement with Gorham. Although Washington had previously maintained a rigorous silence on disputed questions, he felt that he should express his opinion on this matter. He hoped that grounds for objection to the Constitution would, wherever possible, be eliminated. He believed that 40,000 was too large a constituency, and, although the hour was late, he still favored the change. Without objection, the word "forty" was erased and the word "thirty" written in its place on the engrossed copy.

The question now arose as to the manner in which the Constitution should be signed. Quorums in all of the represented states (although not all of the delegates in those states) were in favor of submitting the document to ratification. Most delegates wished to present the document to the public in the most favorable light possible and, to that end, hoped to give the impression of unanimity. Accordingly, Franklin moved that the signature clause be made to read: "Done in Convention by the Unanimous Consent of the States present." The motion was passed by a vote of eleven states to one. (South Carolina was divided on the issue. Charles Pinckney and Pierce Butler thought the clause too ambiguous.)

That same day, September 17, nearly four months after the convention began, the engrossed copy of the Constitution was signed. Proceeding in the traditional order of states from north to south, the delegates walked to the front of the room, bent over the table in front of the President's Chair and, with quill pen dipped in iron gall ink, signed their names on the last of the four pages of parchment. There were thirty-eight delegates and thirty-nine signatures (George Read of Delaware, who had overcome his earlier opposition to the document, signed both for himself and for John Dickinson, who was feeling ill and had gone home to Wilmington). Only three members present — Edmund Randolph (Virginia), George Mason (Virginia), and Elbridge

Gerry (Massachusetts) — abstained. Thirteen members had left the convention before the final day.

Appropriately, Benjamin Franklin had a few last words. While the other delegates signed their names, the old patriot looked thoughtfully toward the President's Chair. He told a few delegates near him that painters had found it difficult "to distinguish in their art a rising from a setting sun. I have," said he, "often and often in the course of the Session, and the vicissitudes of my hopes and fears as to its issue, looked at that behind the President without being able to tell whether it was rising or setting: But now at length I have the happiness to know that it is a rising and not a setting Sun."

After the Constitution was signed and the last gavel fell, the delegates filed out of the State House, then proceeded to the City Tavern on Second Street near Walnut. The City Tavern was one of old Philadelphia's most enjoyable gathering places and had been a favorite haunt of the delegates during the convention. The members shared a last dinner together, complete with toasts and speeches, then bade each other a fond farewell. George Washington's mind was still excited when he returned to his room at Robert Morris's house. Washington tended to some business matters and then, in the words of his diary, "retired to meditate on the momentous work which had been executed."

The newspapers were full of news from the convention. The delegates' self-imposed "rule of secrecy" had heightened the air of mystery surrounding the meeting, and now it seemed as if the public could not hear enough about what had happened during the convention. In Philadelphia on September 19, the *Pennsylvania Packet and Daily Advertiser* published the full text of the Constitution. Just under the newspaper's masthead, in boldface type, were the words of the Preamble, beginning with the soon-to-be memorable phrase: "We, the People of the United States." Within weeks, the Constitution was reprinted in newspapers, pamphlets, and booklets all over the country. . . .

Article VII of the Constitution prescribed the process by which the charter was to be ratified. When conventions in at least nine states had approved the document, the Constitution would be "established" between the ratifying states. Until ratifying conventions had assembled, deliberated, and expressed their approval, however, the document would be nothing more than a hope for a better future. . . .

When Congress received the document, some of its members were baffled. The Articles of Confederation, from which Congress derived its authority, did not authorize it to do away with the Confederation and replace it with a *national government*. Those members of Congress who had also attended the Philadelphia assembly argued strongly that Congress should follow the wishes of the convention and submit the Constitution to state ratifying conventions. Richard Henry Lee, a Congressman from Virginia, objected. Lee thought the "Federalists" (as proponents of the Constitution were now being called) were trying "to push the business on with dispatch . . . that it might be adopted before it had stood the test of reflection and due examination." But a majority of Congress favored the document, paving the way for passage of a resolution referring the Constitution to the legislatures, by them to be "submitted to a convention of Delegates chosen in each state by the people thereof in conformity to the resolves of the Convention. . . ."

[Meanwhile], proponents and opponents of the Constitution began to argue their cases. James Madison [noted:] "The advocates for it come forward more promptly than the adversaries. . . . The sea coast seems everywhere fond of it."

Indeed, many were "fond" of the Constitution — but hardly anyone entertained the notion that it was "perfect." The charter was the work of different men with various ideas, the product of a long string of concessions and compromises. To be sure, it called for the establishment of some notable features: three autonomous branches of government, each invested with power and authority to check the excesses of the others; a Congress consisting of two houses with specifically enumerated powers; a national judiciary; and a strong executive. And it provided the framework for a federal government that combined national supremacy with state autonomy and made both subservient to the popular will.

But the document was not free of anomalies. For instance, members of the House of Representatives were to be apportioned among the states "according to their respective numbers," but the "numbers" were to be calculated in a curious way: all "free persons" were to be counted, as were persons "bound to service for a term of years," but "Indians not taxed" were to be excluded, and only three-fifths of "all other persons" were to be counted. The delegates knew, of course, that the words "all other persons" referred to slaves and that, by allowing the southern states to count three-fifths of their slaves, the document gave tacit recognition to slavery. But the Constitution by no means *approved* slavery; indeed, many delegates believed the institution should be abolished throughout the country. The document did require enforcement of fugitive slave laws, but it also empowered Congress to forbid the importation of new slaves into the country after the year 1808. In its curious and conflicting references to slavery, the Constitution was reflecting the concessions and compromises by which it was produced.

In many ways, the charter was a hodgepodge. And yet it was bound together by common values: dedication to the ideals of American independence and liberty, and a conviction that a strong federal government was the best way to safeguard those ideals. . . .

By the end of October, however, Madison could see that the tide of opinion in the country was beginning to turn away from the Constitution. In Virginia, Richard Henry Lee and Patrick Henry announced their intention to work against ratification. In Massachusetts, James Winthrop (writing under the pseudonym of "Agrippa") published letters that charged that the Constitution gave too much power to the central government and not enough to the states. In New York, Melancton Smith published an *Address to the People of the State of New York* in which he warned that the Constitution would create an "aristocratic tyranny." Meanwhile, in Pennsylvania, Samuel Bryan published a broadside predicting that, under the Constitution, the United States would be "melted down into one empire" with a government "devoid of all responsibility or accountability to the great body of the people."

Richard Henry Lee's views were recorded in his *Letters from the Federal Farmer.* Forgetting for the moment his own privileged background, Lee said that the Constitution was the work of "the artful and ever active aristocracy." He agreed with George Mason that the Constitution should include a bill of rights. He also thought that it should provide for a council to assist and advise the president and guarantee the right of jury trial. "If our countrymen are so soon changed," Lee charged, "and the language of 1774 is become odious to them, it will be in vain to use the language of freedom, or attempt to rouse them to free inquiries."

Patrick Henry warned Virginians who lived in the region called Kentucky (it would not become a state until 1792) that the Constitution favored the eastern part of the country at the expense of the west and that it would inevitably lead to loss of navigation rights on the Mississippi. Henry was angered by the Preamble's reference to "We the People" and challenged the right of the Philadelphia delegates to use such an all-encompassing term. "[W]ho authorized them to speak the language of *We the people,*" Henry demanded, "instead of, *We the states*? States are the characteristics and the soul of a confederation. If the states be not the agents of this compact, it must be one great consolidated national government, of the people of all the states."

In New York on September 27 the newspapers began to publish a series of articles attacking the Constitution and the Philadelphia convention. Signed with the pseudonym "Cato," the letters were widely supposed to have been written by New York's staunchly antifederalist governor, George Clinton. Other letters, similar in tone and content, appeared under the names of "Sydney" and "Brutus" and were widely recognized as pseudonyms for Clinton's supporters. Alarmed by the vigor of the "anti-Federalist" letters, Alexander Hamilton decided to mount a reply.

Hamilton had been the only New Yorker to sign the Constitution. He now tried to use the influence he had with other New York politicians. Hamilton was one of the state's most brilliant lawyers and effective writers. His home and law office on Wall Street were not far from the residences of John Jay and James Madison. The three soon joined forces to answer the attacks of "Cato," "Sydney," and "Brutus" with a series of letters [to various newspapers] signed with the name of "Publius." . . .

There were eighty-five letters from "Publius" — fifty-five written by Hamilton, twenty-nine by Madison, and five by Jay. Never one to lose the opportunity to publicize his views, Hamilton arranged with a printing firm to publish the letters in book form, and on May 28, 1788, a two-volume edition bearing the title of *The Federalist* was issued by J. and A. McLean in New York. . . . The book was both a reasoned defense of the Constitution and a ringing call for its ratification. "The establishment of a Constitution," Hamilton wrote in his last *Federalist* paper, "in time of profound peace, by the voluntary consent of a whole people, is a prodigy, to the completion of which I look forward with trembling anxiety." . . .

The demand for a bill of rights had become a clarion call of the antifederalists. In his speeches and

letters, George Mason, who had written the Virginia Bill of Rights, argued that the people needed protection against a strong and powerful central government and that they could secure that protection only by specifically limiting the government's powers. Supporting Mason, Richard Henry Lee complained of the Constitution's lack of provisions to protect "those essential rights of mankind without which liberty cannot exist."

Prominent supporters of the Constitution generally opposed a bill of rights. Hamilton thought such a declaration not only unnecessary, but "dangerous." Under the Constitution, the federal government would have only the powers that the people granted it. Therefore, Hamilton argued, the government could have no power to abridge the people's rights unless they *gave it* that power. He pointed out that the Constitution already contained many provisions guaranteeing basic civil rights: protection of the writ of *habeas corpus,* a prohibition against bills of attainder and *ex post facto* laws, strict proof requirements in all prosecutions for treason, and a guarantee of the right of trial by jury in all criminal cases except impeachments. A bill of rights, Hamilton said, would inevitably "contain various exceptions to powers which are not granted; and on this very account would afford a colourable pretext to claim more than were granted. For why declare that things shall not be done which there is no power to do?"

South Carolina's Charles Cotesworth Pinckney pointed out that bills of rights "generally begin with declaring that all men are by nature born free." "Now, we should make that declaration with a very bad grace," Pinckney said, "when a large part of our property consists in men who are actually born slaves." Connecticut's Roger Sherman said, "No bill of rights ever yet bound the supreme power longer than the honeymoon of a new married couple, unless the rulers were interested in preserving the rights." And Pennsylvania's James Wilson sneered: "Enumerate all the rights of men? I am sure that no gentlemen in the late Convention would have attempted such a thing."

James Madison at first agreed with Hamilton that a bill of rights was unnecessary and potentially dangerous. But, by the fall of 1788, he had become convinced that such a declaration was not only desirable but essential to ratification of the Constitution. On October 17, 1788, Madison expressed his belief that an enumeration of the "fundamental maxims of free Government" would be "a good ground for an appeal to the sense of community" and "counteract the impulses of interest and passion." Madison pledged that, if the new Constitution went into effect, he would do everything in his power to see that it was amended in such a way as to protect basic human rights from federal infringement. . . .

[The ratification process began in Delaware, whose convention voted unanimously to endorse the new Constitution. The conventions of several other states did likewise. New Hampshire was the ninth and deciding state to ratify. The federalists found themselves hard-pressed in Virginia, where Patrick Henry and other antifederalists resisted tenaciously. "Whither is the spirit of America gone?" Patrick Henry cried. "Sir, the American spirit, assisted by the ropes and chains of consolidation, is about to convert this country into a powerful and mighty empire." Virginia narrowly approved the Constitution, as did New York. North Carolina was the twelfth state to ratify, but tiny Rhode Island, the only state that had refused to send a delegation to Philadelphia, held out until May, 1790, when it finally approved the Constitution and joined the new Union. Meanwhile, Congress had adopted] an "ordinance" setting March 4, 1789, as the date and New York City as the place for the first meeting of the first Congress under the Constitution. Members of the electoral college were chosen, and on February 4 they cast their ballots. To nobody's surprise, their unanimous choice as the

first president under the Constitution was George Washington.

James Madison attended the new Congress as a member of the House of Representatives from Orange County, Virginia. He was denied a Senate seat by a vindictive Patrick Henry, who declared him "unworthy of the confidence of the people." In the House, Madison took responsibility for introducing the Bill of Rights that Henry, George Mason, and other antifederalists had demanded. . . . [This took the form of seventeen amendments to the new Constitution; Congress approved most of them and sent them to the states for ratification. By the end of 1791, the requisite three-fourths of the states had approved ten of the amendments, which afterward became known as the American "Bill of Rights."] Now United States citizens everywhere could be sure that their most valued civic rights — freedom of speech and of the press, freedom of assembly and of religion, freedom from unreasonable searches and seizures, the right to bear arms, the privilege against self-incrimination, the right to due process of law, the right to trial by jury, and the right to representation by counsel — would be protected from federal abridgment.

The process was complete. . . . The United States had become a nation.

QUESTIONS TO CONSIDER

1 James Madison was not destined to be a happy president (1809–1817), but he was a brilliant statesman and the true father of the Constitution. In what ways did he shape the drafting and passage of the Constitution? How did he overcome his own prejudices and the pressures exerted on him by his fellow Virginians in order to ensure the final success of the document?

2 In selection 7 Carl Degler concluded that Americans fought a conservative revolution to preserve the status quo. Discuss the possible revolutionary or

counterrevolutionary nature of the Constitutional Convention, whose delegates, instead of revising the Articles of Confederation as they were charged to do, scrapped that document and came up with an entirely new plan of government.

3   The framers of the Constitution were all well-to-do, socially prominent Americans. Did they produce a document that was fundamentally democratic or undemocratic? How did they feel about the will of the majority? What steps did they take to control that majority?

4   In many ways, as author McGinty says, the charter was a "hodgepodge," a collection of ideas based on northern or southern biases, agricultural or commercial interests, federalist or antifederalist sentiments. What kinds of compromises did the representatives of these divergent interests finally accept?

5   How did the framers deal with the issue of slavery? Where, in particular, did they find it an embarrassment? Wherein did they sow the seeds of future discord?

6   The Constitution nearly failed the battle for ratification. What was the largest area of dissension? What forms of suasion and compromise did both federalists and antifederalists employ?

10

George Washington and the
Use of Power

EDMUND S. MORGAN

In polls taken in 1948, 1962, and 1982, American historians and presidential scholars ranked George Washington as the second-best president in American history (the first in all three surveys was Abraham Lincoln). More than any other statesman, specialists contend, Washington defined the presidency and set the standard for executive leadership. "It is no exaggeration to say that but for George Washington, the office of president might not exist," one historian maintains. Washington was so respected in his day, so much above factional bickering and regional jealousies, that he was probably the only leader behind whom the country could unite. "One of the problems with Washington," says writer Garry Wills, "is that we think of him in the wrong company as a peer of Franklin and Jefferson, when he belongs in the select company of Caesar, Napoleon and Cromwell as a charismatic nation-builder who personified an epoch."

Not that Washington was the cherry-tree saint of mythology. As historian Edmund S. Morgan makes clear, the first president had human flaws — among them, an aloofness that made and makes him a hard man to know. Washington was also a slaveowner who shared the antiblack prejudice of most whites of his time. But in spite of Washington's shortcomings, Morgan believes him unsurpassed among his contemporaries in understanding the use of power.

WHEN A CROWD OF AMERICAN FARMERS opened fire on the regular troops of the British army some 200 years ago, the action must have seemed foolhardy to any impartial observer. Such an observer might have been a little surprised at the events that immediately followed, when the farmers put the regulars to rout, chased them from Concord to Boston, and laid siege to that town. But however impressive this performance, it did not alter the fact that the British army was probably the most powerful in the world, having succeeded scarcely a dozen years before in defeating the armies of France, England's only serious rival. For a handful of colonists, unorganized, without any regular source of arms or ammunition, with no army and no navy, to take on the world's greatest power in open war must still have looked like a foolhardy enterprise.

Somehow or other it proved not to be. Yet it remains something of a puzzle that the farmers were able to bring it off. With the benefit of hindsight we can offer a number of explanations. For one thing, the generals whom the British sent to put down the rebels proved to be somewhat less than brilliant in using the immense force at their disposal. For another thing, the colonists got a great deal of assistance from England's old enemy, France. But perhaps most important, the American Revolution seems to have elicited from those who participated in it a response that no other event or situation in American history has been able to do.

It was not that extraordinarily large numbers of people were ready to sacrifice their lives or their fortunes for the common good. That has often happened in times of crisis. And the revolution did not in fact induce this kind of sacrifice very widely. It was always difficult to fill up enlistments in the

Continental Army. What was extraordinary about the revolution was the talent it generated, the number of men of genius who stepped out of farmyards and plantations, out of countinghouses and courtrooms, to play a leading role in winning the war and then in building a national government. Prominent among them was George Washington, who more than any other single man was responsible for bringing success to this seemingly foolhardy enterprise. Since there was nothing in his previous career to suggest that he could play so large a role, it may be worth asking what there was in him that enabled him to do what he did.

This is not an easy task, for George Washington is and was a hard man to know. Part of the difficulty in approaching him comes from the heroic image in which we have cast him and which already enveloped him in his own lifetime. But it is not simply the plaster image that stands between him and us. We have other national heroes who also became legendary figures in their own lifetimes, a Benjamin Franklin, an Andrew Jackson, an Abraham Lincoln; and yet with them we find no great difficulty in pushing past the image to find the man. In their letters and other writings, in the countless anecdotes they inspired, we can meet them on familiar terms and feel comfortable in their company.

But not George Washington. The familiar anecdotes about Washington tell us to keep our distance. The most arresting one is told about a gathering at the time of the Constitutional Convention in 1787. One evening during the sessions of the convention a group of Washington's old friends from wartime days were remarking on the extraordinarily reserved and remote manner he maintained, even among his most intimate acquaintances. One of them, Gouverneur Morris, who was always full of boldness and wit, had the nerve to disagree with the rest about Washington's aloofness. He could be as familiar with Washington, he said, as with any of his other friends. Alexander Hamilton called his bluff by offering to provide a dinner with the best of wine for a dozen of them if Morris would, at the next reception Washington gave, simply walk up to him, gently slap him on the shoulder, and say, "My dear general, how happy I am to see you look so well." On the appointed evening a substantial number were already present when Morris arrived, walked up to Washington, bowed, shook hands, and then placed his left hand on Washington's shoulder and said, "My dear General, I am very happy to see you look so well." The response was immediate and icy. Washington reached up and removed the hand, stepped back, and fixed his eyes in silence on Morris, until Morris retreated abashed

"Washington's genius," says Edmund S. Morgan, "lay in his understanding of power, both military and political. . . . But he accepted the premises of a Republican government as an Oliver Cromwell never did . . . [and] he never sought power on any other terms than those on which he had initially accepted it, as a servant of the people." (The Metropolitan Museum of Art, Bequest of Charles Allen Munn, 1924)

into the crowd. The company looked on in dismay, and no one ever tried it again.

It seems today a rather extravagant reaction on the part of our national hero, a bit of overkill. It makes us almost as embarrassed for Washington as for poor Morris. Yet it may serve as an appropriate starting place for our inquiry, because Washington's dignity and reserve, the aloofness that separated him from his contemporaries and still separates him from us, were, I believe, an integral part of the genius that enabled him to defeat the armies of Great Britain and to establish the United States as an independent world power.

Washington's genius lay in his understanding of power, both military power and political power, an understanding unmatched by that of any of his contemporaries. At a time when the United States needed nothing quite so much as military power but had very little, this hitherto obscure Virginia planter knew how to make the best possible use of what there was. And after securing independence, when the United States was trying to establish itself in a war-torn world, he knew how to deal with foreign countries to the maximum advantage of his own. He was not a bookish man. He contributed nothing to the formal political thought of the American Revolution, nor did he produce any treatises on military strategy or tactics. But he did understand power in every form.

At the simplest level Washington's understanding of power showed itself in the ability to take command. Some men have the quality; others do not. Washington had it, and in exercising it he nourished the aloofness that became his most conspicuous trait. That aloofness was deliberate, as it may be in many men who have the gift of command. In Washington it may have grown around a nucleus of inborn native reserve, but Washington purposely cultivated it. We should not mistake it for arrogance. Washington did crave honor and pursued it relentlessly, but he did not deceive himself with that spurious substitute for honor which is arrogance. His aloofness had nothing to do with arrogance. It had to do with command.

He explained the matter in a letter to a fledgling colonel in the Continental Army in 1775: "Be easy and condescending in your deportment to your officers," he wrote, "but not too familiar, lest you subject yourself to a want of that respect, which is necessary to support a proper command."

Washington practiced what he preached, and as his talents for command developed there were fewer and fewer persons with whom he could allow himself to be familiar. As commander in chief and later as president, he could scarcely afford it with anyone. The remoteness that still surrounds him was a necessary adjunct of the power he was called upon to exercise.

But Washington's understanding of power went far beyond mere posture. Although he had not had a great deal of military experience before he took charge of the Continental Army in 1775, his participation in the French and Indian War from 1754 to 1758 had exposed him to the geographical conditions of warfare on the American continent and the way in which they must affect the exercise of military power. As commander of the revolutionary army he was quick to perceive the significance of geographical factors that his opponents seem never to have grasped. At the outset of the war, when the British almost caught him in the Battle of Long Island, he learned the danger of allowing his forces to be bottled up in any location where their retreat might be cut off. Having learned that lesson, he did not make the same mistake again. Though he was not always able to prevent his subordinates from making it, his constant alertness to it enabled him to keep his precarious army in existence. In September 1777, for example, he sent a letter on the subject to Brigadier General Thomas Nelson in Virginia. In the light of future events it was a remarkable letter. Nelson had proposed to station his forces at Hampton and Yorktown, which lay at the end of the peninsula between the James and the York rivers. Here,

of course, they would be in a position to observe the movement of any British troops into the area by sea. But the location, Washington perceived at once, was one where they could be trapped, and he quickly warned Nelson against it. The troops, he said,

by being upon a [narrow] neck of land would be in danger of being cut off. The Enemy might very easily throw up a few Ships into York and James's river, as far as Queens Creek; and land a body of men there, who by throwing up a few Redoubts, would intercept their retreat and oblige them to surrender at discretion.

Four years later Lord Cornwallis made the mistake that Washington warned Nelson against, and Washington pounced. It was almost like taking candy from a child. For Cornwallis it was the world turned upside down, but for Washington it was a lesson learned long before in the geography of power.

Of course, if the British navy had been on hand in sufficient strength Cornwallis might have escaped by sea. But Washington did not move until he had the French navy to dominate the seas nearby. He had realized early in the war that without local naval superiority to stand off the British warships, he could not capture a British army at any point on the coast. Washington understood this better than his more experienced French helpers. The Comte de Grasse, in command of the French navy, seems to have missed the whole point of the Yorktown strategy, complaining to Washington that he would prefer to cruise off New York where he might encounter the main British fleet, rather than be an idle spectator in the Cheasapeake. Washington knew, however, that even with de Grasse on hand, he was not strong enough to attack the main British force in New York. But by picking off Cornwallis at Yorktown he could deal the British a crippling blow.

Washington's appreciation of geographical factors made him not only wary of being trapped like Cornwallis but also averse to defending any particular point, including cities. The British armies were much more powerful than his and capable of taking any place they wanted. It was therefore not worthwhile to erect elaborate stationary defenses. When General Howe was approaching Philadelphia and Congress wanted Washington to divert troops to the preparation of fortifications for the city's defense, he refused. If he could defeat Howe in the field, he said, the defenses would be unnecessary. If he could not, then the time and labor spent on them would be lost, for the fortifications would sooner or later fall to Howe's superior forces and could then be used against the Americans. It was imperative, he believed, to keep his small force concentrated and mobile, so that he could strike effectively when opportunity presented. "It would give me infinite pleasure," he assured the Congress, "to afford protection to every individual and to every Spot of Ground on the whole of the United States." But that was not the way wars were won. Wars were won by destroying or disarming the enemy, not by trying to spare civilians from occupation. And Washington was bent on winning.

Washington, in other words, was or became a good field general. But his understanding of military power did not stop at the ability to command troops and deploy them effectively. He also understood that the power he could wield in battle depended on the willingness of the civil government to supply him with men and money. He understood the political basis of military power, and he also understood that in the new United States this was a very precarious basis. His army was the creature of a Congress that never quite dared to act like a government. Congress declared independence. It authorized the creation of the army. It even authorized the creation of a navy. But it did not attempt to levy taxes to pay for these things. Instead, it recommended to the states that they make contributions, specifying the amount for each state. Whether a state followed

the recommendation depended on public opinion. And public opinion was as fickle then as now. Rumors of peace and of British surrender came with every skirmish, and each one produced a debilitating effect on the willingness of taxpayers in the different states to advance money for a war that might soon be over.

Men were almost as hard to get as the money to pay and clothe and feed them. As a result Washington was never able to build an army strong enough to face the British on even terms. At the outset of the war he had hoped to enlist soldiers for the duration. Instead, Congress provided for enlistments of a year only. It took almost that long to collect and build a disciplined fighting force, even from men who already knew how to fire a gun. By the time he had them trained, their terms would be up, and off they would go, frequently taking with them the guns he had issued them. In their place would often come raw militia on even shorter terms, men who were not used to obeying commands and who did not take kindly to them, men who were ready to head for home and tend the crops the moment they were offended by some officer's efforts to bring them in line. In 1780, after the war had dragged on for five years, Washington was still trying to get Congress to place the army on a more lasting basis. If they had done so at the beginning, he reminded them, his forces would

not have been the greatest part of the War inferior to the enemy, indebted for our safety to their inactivity, enduring frequently the mortification of seeing inviting opportunities to ruin them, pass unimproved for want of a force which the Country was completely able to afford.

Although Washington's complaints to Congress were fruitless, he never appealed over the heads of Congress to their constituents. He refrained from doing so in part because the very effort to explain the situation to the public would also have explained it to the enemy. He did not dare to advertise the weakness of his force, when the only thing between him and defeat was the fact that the enemy did not realize how weak he was. But his restraint was also based on principle. In spite of the imperious manner with which he bolstered his ability to command, Washington was a republican. He had been fully persuaded that the king of England and the minions surrounding him were conspiring to destroy the liberties of Americans. More than that, he was persuaded that kings in general were a bad lot. He welcomed Thomas Paine's devastating attack not only on George III but on monarchy itself. He never doubted that the United States must be a republic. And the principles of republican liberty as he saw them dictated that the military must be forever subordinate to the civil power. Although he could lament the short-sightedness exhibited by Congress and the state legislatures, he never even suggested that he and his army should be anything but their servants.

Washington realized that he could have commanded an immense popular following in defiance of the do-nothing Congress and that he could have counted on the backing of his officers and troops in such an adventure. But he accepted the premises of republican government as an Oliver Cromwell never did. Although it meant submitting to a body that became increasingly incompetent, irresponsible, and corrupt, he never sought power on any other terms than those on which he had initially accepted it, as servant of the people. And when his men grew exasperated with the failure of the government to feed, arm, or pay them, he stood between them and Congress and thwarted every threat against the civil power. Enlisted men mounted mutinies, and he faced them down with his steely authority. Some of his officers conspired to seize power, and he nipped the movement in the bud.

Washington was fighting not simply for independence but for an independent republic. He was fighting a people's war, and he knew that he would lose what he was fighting for if he tried to take more power than the people would freely give. One of the difficulties of republican government, as he explained later to uncomprehending foreigners, was that the people must always feel an evil before they can see it. "This," he admitted, "is productive of errors and temporary evils, but generally these evils are of a nature to work their own cure." In the end, he believed the people would do the right thing.

Washington's patience in waiting for the people to do the right thing is the more remarkable because he knew that the ineffectiveness of Congress not only prolonged the war needlessly but also exposed the country to needless perils. Because Congress lacked the nerve to vote him the needed men and money, he had to rely on assistance from the French in order to bring the war to a successful conclusion. And reliance on the French could have meant the loss of the very independence Americans were fighting for. Once French forces were engaged on the American continent, Washington feared that they would wish to invade and occupy Canada. Ostensibly the United States would be the sole beneficiary of such a move, for the French agreed to forgo any territorial claims on the continent in their treaty of alliance with the United States. But Washington had no illusions about the binding power of treaties.

Unfortunately Congress did have illusions. At the beginning of the war Americans had hoped that Canada would join them in rebellion against England, and Washington himself thought it highly desirable to eliminate this bastion of British power. He had sent an expedition to effect the liberation of the province, but the inhabitants had not responded in the manner hoped for, and the expedition was a disaster. With the arrival of French troops, congressmen developed an enthusiasm for trying again with French forces. The population of Canada was mainly French, and it was plausible to suppose that they would welcome their countrymen more warmly than they had the Americans. But Washington was alarmed. He would not have been in a position to refuse if the French had decided to employ their troops in this way, but he did not want Congress encouraging them to do so. He wrote out all the tactical reasons he could think of against the expedition and sent them in an official communication to Congress. Then he wrote out a private, confidential letter to Henry Laurens, the president of Congress, explaining his real objection. The letter remains one of the more striking examples of the quick perception of political realities that lay behind Washington's understanding of power.

The expedition, he explained to Laurens, would mean

the introduction of a large body of French troops into Canada, and putting them in possession of the capital of that Province, attached to them by all the ties of blood, habits, manners, religion and former connexions of government. I fear this would be too great a temptation to be resisted by any power actuated by the common maxims of national policy.

He went on to outline all the economic and political benefits that France would gain by holding on to the province in violation of the treaty. It would not be difficult to find a plausible pretext. The United States had borrowed funds from France on a large scale; and the United States government, if one could dignify Congress by that name, had no power to tax its citizens in order to repay the debt. The United States could scarcely object if France retained Canada as security for the payment. "Resentment, reproaches, and submission" would be the only recourse left to the United States. And Washington went on to read a gentle lecture to the gullible members of Congress: "Men are very apt," he said,

to run into extremes; hatred to England may carry some into an excess of Confidence in France; especially when motives of gratitude are thrown into the scale. Men of this description would be unwilling to suppose France capable of acting so ungenerous a part. I am heartily disposed to entertain the most favourable sentiments of our

new ally and to cherish them in others to a reasonable degree; but it is a maxim founded on the universal experience of mankind, that no nation is to be trusted farther than it is bound by its interest; and no prudent statesman or politician will venture to depart from it.

☆ 2 ☆

With the victory at Yorktown and the peace that followed, the United States had no further need of the military wisdom of which it had made such poor use. But Washington as a civilian was no less cogent in his understanding of power than he had been as commander in chief. His response to the postwar vicissitudes of the nation matched that of the most constructive political thinkers on the scene, and his influence may have been greater than theirs because of the enormous prestige he now carried.

The ineffectiveness of Congress that had hampered Washington's prosecution of the war continued to threaten the viability of the new republic in peacetime. Having submitted to the military loss of her mainland colonies, England set about to regain them by economic warfare, or so it seemed. In the early years of peace English merchants, offering liberal credits, sent shiploads of goods to their old customers in America, and Americans rang up a huge debt. But when Americans tried to ship their own goods to their old prewar markets in the British West Indies and elsewhere, England closed the ports to them. Before the Americans could gain new outlets for their produce many found themselves bankrupt. Washington's reaction was that power should be met with power. If England barred American ships, Americans should bar English ships until England relented. But for some states to do so and others not would defeat the strategy, and Congress had no authority to regulate trade for the whole nation. Washington supported every move to give it such authority, but at the same time he despaired of putting power in the hands of men who had demonstrated again and again their timidity in using it. What was the use of giving them more powers, he asked, when "the members seem to be so much afraid of exerting those which they already have, that no opportunity is slipped of surrending them, or referring the exercise of them, to the States individually?"

Washington had been convinced, long before the war ended, that the national government as it operated under the Articles of Confederation was not adequate to carry out its functions; and he feared it had in effect written its own death warrant by failing to exercise what powers it had. "Extensive powers not exercised," he once observed, ". . . have I believe scarcely ever failed to ruin the possessor." But he hoped against hope that this would not be the case with the United States. When the inhabitants of western Massachusetts rose in arms against their own elected government in Shays' Rebellion, and neither the state nor the national government seemed ready to do anything about it, it looked as though the case was hopeless. Henry Lee urged Washington to use his influence to quiet the troubles, but Washington snapped back, "Influence is no Government. . . . If they have *real* grievances, redress them. . . . If they have not, employ the force of government against them at once." It was mortifying to see the new American republic exhibiting the weakness that doctrinaire European political philosophers had always attributed to republics. "How melancholy is the reflection," Washington wrote to James Madison,

that in so short a space, we should have made such large strides towards fulfilling the predictions of our transatlantic foe! 'Leave them to themselves, and their government will soon dissolve.' . . . What stronger evidence can be given of the want of energy in our governments than these disorders? If there exists not a power to check them, what security has a man for life, liberty, or property?

But the weakness of the American republic did not diminish Washington's republican ardor. He was outraged by the very idea of rebellion against a republican government, but he was also outraged by the reaction of Americans who talked without horror of substituting a monarch for the ineffective Congress. And after the Massachusetts government finally succeeded in putting down the rebels, he objected to the fact that they had been disfranchised. To deprive them of political rights was as much an abuse of power as the failure to use power effectively against them in the first place.

When Washington became the first president of the United States, he brought to the office a determination to establish what he called "a national character," by which he meant something like national reputation. It was essential, in his view, that the country gain a reputation that would oblige other countries to respect it. "We are a young Nation," he had written in 1783, "and have a character to establish. It behooves us therefore to set out right for first impressions will be lasting, indeed are all in all." And in the years that followed the winning of independence, as the power of Congress continued to wane, his great worry had been that the failure of the states to support the union would "destroy our National character, and render us as contemptible in the eyes of Europe as we have it in our power to be respectable." With an effective national government in operation at last, it became possible to establish a proper national character, a reputation that would command respect both at home and abroad. And in his conduct of the presidency Washington bent his every effort toward that end.

He recognized that he was on trial, that the character of the government and the respect accorded it would be measured by the respect that he himself demanded and commanded. As president of a republic he aimed at an elegant simplicity in his style of living, sumptuous enough to escape any imputation of ostentatious poverty, but restrained enough to avoid outright splendor. At the same time he cultivated his characteristic aloofness, even to the point where his critics charged that his condescension smacked of monarchy.

Washington identified the national interest so closely and so personally with the new national government that he could scarcely recognize the validity of any kind of dissent. It is all too easy at the present day to see his impatience with public criticism as intolerance bordering on paranoia. But Washington had borne the brunt of a war that was needlessly prolonged because of the supineness of the central government. He had watched the nation approach the point of dissolution in the 1780s, a development that threatened everything he had fought for. And in the 1790s it was by no means clear that the new government was there to stay. If he greeted criticism with distrust, it was because domestic dissent might belie the character he was seeking to establish for his government, might return the nation to the impotence of the 1780s, might signal to the watching world the predicted collapse of the republic.

In spite of his determination to establish a strong character for the nation, Washington had no yearning for personal power, nor did he want any military adventures of the kind that so often infatuate men who are obsessed with power for its own sake. He did want the United States to grow in strength, for strength must be the ultimate basis of respect. And strength, he was sure, would not come to the United States by going to war. He had had ample experience that war was the way to poverty, and poverty meant impotence. The way for the country to grow strong, he believed, was to eschew internal dissension and steer clear of the quarrels which he saw were about to envelop the nations of Europe. The United States was encumbered with a French alliance, but as Washington read the terms of it, it did not require the United States to become involved in any quarrel that France might have with other countries, including England. And although he was grateful for the assistance received from France in the winning of American independence,

he did not think that gratitude had a place in the determination of national policy. As he had pointed out some years earlier to Henry Laurens, the nation, like other nations, should not be counted on to act beyond its own interest. France in helping Americans during the Revolution had acted out of self-interest — her interest to have England weakened by loss of the colonies. Now, as Washington saw it, the main interest of the United States was to recover from the economic exhaustion incurred, however needlessly, in the Revolutionary War. The means of recovery, he thought, lay in exploiting the American land to produce as much as possible for sale to nations less fruitfully engaged in quarreling with one another.

Washington had no difficulty in persuading the new Congress or the advisers whom he appointed to his cabinet that a policy of neutrality was the way to let the United States develop its powers. But his advisers never understood the operation of the policy as well as Washington did. Jefferson was bent on making a weapon of neutrality, on wringing concessions, especially from England, in return for American neutrality. Hamilton, on the other hand, was highly conciliatory in trying to restore commercial relations with England, and went almost past the limits of neutrality in his obsession with the ideological dangers presented by the French Revolution. Although Washington was closer to Hamilton than to Jefferson, neither of the two men fully grasped the sophistication of their chief's policy for the nation.

Washington realized that the people of the United States would benefit from high prices for their agricultural exports while European farmers were distracted by war. But other than this benefit, he did not propose to take advantage of the distress of any country in order to wring concessions from it, because he was convinced that benefits thus obtained would not last. In 1791, when he was about to appoint Gouverneur Morris (he of the slap on the back) as minister to France, he warned him against seeking to obtain favorable treaties from countries in distress, "for unless," he said, "treaties are mutually beneficial to the Parties, it is in vain to hope for a continuance of them beyond the moment when the one which conceives itself to be over-reached is in a situation to break off the connexion." A treaty had to match the powers and interests of the parties making it. Otherwise it would be indeed a scrap of paper. Washington signed two treaties as president of the United States. The first one, Jay's Treaty with England, was extremely unpopular; and Washington himself did not think well of it. But he signed it because he thought that commercial relations with England would be worse with no treaty than with this one. The popular outcry against it did not move him and indeed struck him as senseless, because he believed that the United States in 1795 was not sufficiently powerful and England was not sufficiently weak to have negotiated a better treaty. And even if Jay had been able to get a better treaty, Washington thought there was no reason to suppose that it would have been better kept than the peace treaty, in which England had agreed to give up her posts in the Northwest Territory. The fact that England had not yet given up the posts and the fact that Jay had not secured any further agreement for her to give them up was no surprise to Washington. The American negotiators at the peace conference had got more from England than America's bargaining powers really entitled her to. England's retention of the northwest posts was therefore to be expected and was no reason for rejecting Jay's treaty if it might improve the commercial situation of the United States in any way.

Washington could afford to be equally calm about Pinckney's Treaty with Spain. That treaty was almost as popular with the American people as Jay's had been unpopular, and it had generally been hailed as a triumph because it secured the American right to navigate the Mississippi. Yet it merely obtained what Washington was certain the United States would get anyhow. After the Revolutionary War settlers had poured into the western country in such numbers that by 1795 Spain could not safely have denied them the right to export their produce down the Mississippi. What prompted the concession was not Pinckney's negotiating skill but the expanding American strength in the west and the strong character that Washington had conferred on the national government. Treaties, in Washington's view, were not important. What was important was power.

Washington was not a man of many talents. He had none of the range of the brilliant men around him, the intellectual curiosity of a Jefferson, the fiscal genius of a Hamilton. But in his understanding of power he left them all behind, as he did the British generals who opposed him and the French who assisted him. When he retired from the presidency after eight years, he had placed the United States on the way to achieving the power that he had aspired to for it. In the years that have followed, that power has grown until there are those who wonder whether it has been a good thing for the world. But at the time it looked like a very good thing indeed. And for better or for worse, it was the work of George Washington, the man who still keeps us all at a distance.

QUESTIONS TO CONSIDER

1   Contrast the image of George Washington with the reality of the man. In what ways does Morgan's biographical portrait demythologize Washington and restore his humanity?

2   How much credit should we give to individuals, particularly to one man — George Washington — for achieving what at first must have seemed impossible: the defeat of the most powerful army in the world, winning independence from England, and establishing a viable national government in the former colonies?

3   Do you agree with Morgan that Washington was a genius in his understanding of the use of power? On that score, how does he compare to such modern presidents as Ronald Reagan and George Bush?

4   In what ways did Washington, as president, help to establish the national reputation of the new Republic? What were his greatest fears for the new nation?

5   Washington's goal as president was to make the new Republic strong. Today the United States may be the most powerful country in the world. If Washington could speak to us now, what advice do you think he might offer?

VI

TO HAVE AND
HAVE NOT

II

Benjamin Banneker:
He Overcame

LERONE BENNETT, JR.

The United States was conceived in idealism and in paradox. America joined the family of nations dedicated to the proposition that all men are "created equal" and that all are endowed with the inalienable rights of life, liberty, and the pursuit of happiness. These were truths Americans had learned in the Age of Enlightenment, when men and women had searched for more rational, humane ways to order their universe. Yet in 1789, the year the Constitution was ratified and George Washington was chosen president, this same enlightened America held some 800,000 blacks in chains, most of them in the South. The first president himself embodied the paradox, for he was a wealthy planter who owned some 250 human beings; he even brought slave servants to the president's house in Philadelphia. He said he "regretted" that slavery existed and wished it could be abolished, but he shrank from doing anything about it.

Back in 1776, when the Revolution began, slavery existed in all thirteen states and was an indispensable labor force for the patriot cause. Hoping to disrupt the American war effort, the British invited the slaves to desert their American masters and join the British side, ultimately promising freedom if they did so. This promise horrified the American patriots. "Hell itself," one cried, "could not have vomited anything more black than this design of emanicpating our slaves."

The Americans had reason to be worried, for their slaves went over to the British in ever increasing numbers. That American blacks fought against the Revolution turns received notions of freedom and oppression on their heads. From the view of fleeing slaves, the redcoats *were the liberators, the American patriots the oppressors. To forestall mass slave defections, the Americans started recruiting black soldiers too; some states even offered freedom in exchange for military service (South Carolina, however, offered white volunteers a bounty in slaves, in the form of one grown black to each private, three grown blacks and a child to each colonel). Altogether some 5,000 blacks served the American cause. But approximately 100,000 blacks, a fifth of the slave population in revolutionary America, were "loyalists," who sided with the British. When the war ended, General Washington, angry because some of his own slaves had fled, demanded that the defeated British return the black loyalists to their American masters. The British, however, asserted that the blacks had been emancipated in accordance with royal policy. In the end, the British did give up blacks who had been seized by royal forces and refugees who had come to British lines after the war had ended. Other black loyalists wound up in slavery in the British West Indies; 3,000 more were colonized in Nova Scotia, where they braved discrimination and established a black community that still exists.*

The black patriots, by contrast, gained a measure of freedom during the Revolutionary era. The northern states either liberated their slaves outright or started gradual emancipation programs. New Jersey even allowed blacks to vote — for a while.

But the story was dramatically different for blacks in the South. Because the northern states had so few slaves in relation to their white population, as southern whites liked to say, what did the Yankees have to lose in adopting emancipation? Southern whites were not about to abolish slavery, not with their heavy concentration of blacks (in some places they outnumbered whites) and their correspondingly large investments. What was more, most northerners were content to leave slavery alone in the South, even if they did believe in liberty and the equality of men. For whites in North and South alike, slavery was always more than a labor system; it was also a crucial means of race control, keeping blacks and whites apart. Moreover, some of America's most prominent leaders were southerners who owned other human beings. Like Washington, Thomas Jefferson, James Madison, and James Monroe all dedicated themselves to the triumph of republican government and human liberty — and all supported their careers through slave labor. By the end of the eighteenth century, slavery was institutionalized in the southern states, safeguarded by the property clause in the Fifth Amendment of the federal Constitution and by a web of national and state laws. The central paradox in American history — the existence of slavery in a nation based on the ideals of liberty in Jefferson's Declaration — remained for later generations to resolve.

Yet not all blacks in America languished in chains or in the twilight zone between bondage and full liberty that was the lot of free blacks on these shores. Some overcame the obstacles against them and managed to lead prominent and influential lives. Phillis Wheatley, a free black in Boston, was an internationally known poet, whose Poems on Various Subjects, Religious and Moral, *was the first book published by a black woman in America and only the second by an American woman. Prince Hall, one of several thousand blacks who fought for America in the Revolution, formed the first black Masonic lodge. And Benjamin Banneker, born a free black in slaveholding Maryland, became a celebrated astronomer and the most famous black in the young republic. Lerone Bennett, Jr., the author of many books of African-American history and biography, restores this remarkable man to his proper place in the annals of the American past.*

EVERY NIGHT, as soon as the moon appeared over the hills on the Patapsco River, the black farmer stole from his cabin with a cloak and pencil and paper. Spreading the cloak on the ground, oblivious of the startled gaze of prying neighbors, the man took up his favorite position: flat on his back, hands under his head, eyes fixed on the fireflies of stars and suns hundreds of light-years away. Until dawn, until the stars melted away in light, the stargazer maintained his vigil. Then, brushing himself off, he retreated, absentmindedly, into the cabin where neighbors, in search of salt or information, found him asleep at midday.

The good dull farmers of Ellicott's Lower Mills (now Ellicott City), near Baltimore, were shocked. Good farmers didn't act that way. A farmer, it was said, should be up and doing in the morning and early to bed at night.

What kind of behavior was this?

What kind of house was the man operating?

People who understood such things tried to explain. They said the man was studying the motions of the heavenly bodies or something of the kind —

an explanation, under the circumstances, that did more harm than good. The stolid, unimaginative farmers listened to the explanations with the mounting anger the normal mind throws up to fend off the unusual. In an age when few white men read books, and even fewer considered scientific careers, it was worse than useless to tell people that a black man was studying the stars. One can almost hear the peals of laughter as the stories made the rounds. A black man studying the motions of the heavenly bodies! Who ever heard of such goings-on?

Before too many years had passed, the whole world had heard of Benjamin Banneker, the first American black scholar and the first black man of national stature to give vent to the Negro protest. As an advocate, and as an example, Banneker made a fundamental contribution during the formative years of the American people. In the years of the Revolution, and after, when Thomas Jefferson and others expressed doubts about the mental endowment of black people, Banneker stood out, like a rock in a raging stream, as a center of safety and truth for blacks and whites who lost their footing and surrendered to the deception of appearances. He preached eloquently in letters and in private conversation against "the long-established illiberal prejudice against the blacks." Of even more importance

From *Pioneers in Protest* by Lerone Bennett, Jr. Reprinted by permission of Johnson Publishing Company, Inc., © 1969.

SELECTION 11 BENJAMIN BANNEKER: HE OVERCAME

Benjamin Banneker, a self-educated scientific genius, was the first American black scholar and the first black man of national stature to give vent to the Negro protest. As Lerone Bennett comments, "Wherever the doctrine [of black phylogenetic inferiority] was preached, men had to overcome the hurdle of Banneker, who not only beat white men at their own games, but also devised new games for white men to play." Banneker is shown here on the cover of a 1795 edition of his Almanac. *(Maryland Historical Society)*

was the propaganda of his deeds. As a mathematician, as an astronomer, surveyor, poet, mechanic, philosopher, clock-maker, and zoologist, Banneker startled men and made them question their assumptions.

All over the world, at this juncture, reason followed profit; and men, as usual, found it easy to believe what served their pocketbooks. They believed, in other words, that black men were phylogenetically incapable of absorbing "the wonders and mysteries" of Western civilization. Whenever this doctrine was preached, men had to overcome the hurdle of Banneker, who not only beat white men at their own games but also devised new games for white men to play. In Paris, the founders of the *Société des Amis des Noirs* discussed the phenomenon of "America's African Astronomer." So did Pitt and Wilberforce and Buxton in the House of Commons in London. After 1791, when Banneker participated in the survey of Washington, D.C., Americans admitted his weight, though some, characteristically, looked upon him as a biological sport who proved only that it was dangerous to mix black people and alphabets.

The Banneker years and the Banneker protests were one with the founding of America. Banneker's grandfather came to America on a slave ship. But so, in a manner of speaking, did his white grandmother.

The grandmother, an extraordinary personage named Molly Welsh, was a poor English worker who ran afoul of the harsh laws regulating employers and employees. For a minor offense, she was shipped to America and sold to a planter for seven years to pay the cost of her passage. Molly Welsh, in short, was an indentured servant — as were many, perhaps most, of the first settlers.

Most white indentured servants were singularly free of racial prejudice. They worked in the fields with black slaves and black indentured servants; they shared huts and tankards of rum with blacks — and they married them, even in the South. The relationship between black and white indentured servants was close in Maryland, where Molly Welsh worked out her term of servitude and acquired, by stringent economies, a small nest egg. After completing her term of service, she bought a small farm and acquired, as another token of upward mobility, two slaves from a ship in Chesapeake Bay. One of the slaves was an African of some importance who continued to worship African gods. According to tradition, he was the son of an African king. However that may be, the African in question, one Bannaky, certainly had airs of a royal person. Or so it seemed to Molly Welsh, who worked the two slaves for a spell and then freed them. Immediately thereafter she married Bannaky and took his name, which was subsequently Anglicized to Bannaker or Banneker.

To Banneker and his English wife were born four children, only one of whom concerns us here. Mary, the oldest, followed her mother's example and married a native African, Robert, who took her name. Among their children was Benjamin Banneker, who was born on November 9, 1731. Six years later, Robert Banneker bought 102 acres in a thinly populated region near Baltimore and built a family home on the brow of a hill overlooking the Patapsco Valley.

Young Benjamin Banneker grew up in a world of ambiguity and change. The status of free Afro-Americans at that time was relatively high. They could vote, marry anyone who wanted to marry them, hold property and dispose of it. Although free Afro-Americans had a place, the place was not well-defined; it depended on a multiplicity of variables and an ingenious black man could rise by exploiting fissures in the wall.

Banneker, like his famous contemporary Phillis Wheatley, exploited and eventually transcended the wall that hemmed black people in. Like Wheatley, he was a bookworm. His grandmother taught him letters and he was soon reading the Bible. The family arranged for the precocious youngster to attend an integrated neighborhood school. With his black and white schoolmates, Banneker learned the rudiments of arithmetic, writing, and reading. Then he dropped out of school to help his father with the farm. But he was no longer the same boy. Farm work irked him now, for he had caught a vision of

a larger world. He wanted books, pencil, and paper. But the little farming community near Baltimore provided few opportunities for scholars — black or white. Most of Banneker's white neighbors were illiterate, books were hard to come by, and learning was considered a luxury. Here and there, provisions were made for bright and well-to-do white boys. But a black scholar and scientist! Everyone — or almost everyone — knew that blacks could not learn — a "fact" that was related in some way to the color of their skin.

Perceiving the drift of the age, probing into the web of relationships that bound and separated black and white folk, Banneker retreated within himself and made his own world. While tending cows or tilling the ground, he chewed over the basic problems he had learned in school. Within a few years, he had thoroughly digested the basic principles of mathematics. Retreating further inward, the farm boy concentrated on his senses and sensations. The whole world — the sky, the ground, the rain, the seasons — became a school to him. By the time he reached twenty, Banneker had a photographic memory and the eye and instincts of a man of science. Although he had never seen a clock, he made one, using as a model a borrowed watch. All parts of the clock, which was probably the first homemade clock in America, were chipped laboriously out of wood. Banneker's clock, which was completed about 1761, worked perfectly for more than twenty years and people came from miles around to hear it sound the hours.

By 1770, Banneker was a community celebrity. It was the fashion in this age for men of leisure to exchange difficult mathematical problems. In this game, Banneker had few peers. He often returned the answers in rhyme. His fame, as a result, leaped the bounds of Maryland. From all over Colonial America came problems and questions for the African mathematician.

But Banneker's primary problem — a vocation — remained unsolved. On the death of his father and mother, he became the sole proprietor of the farm. There are indications that the idealistic young man considered this windfall a calamity. He was appalled by the time he would have to spend away from his musings and meditations.

A stroke of fate saved the scholar from the pig pen. On the eve of the Revolutionary War, the Ellicotts, a talented and humane Quaker family, settled in the community and erected a flour mill. Three sons of this distinguished family were mathematicians and astronomers of note. They immediately perceived what their duller peers missed: that Banneker was a man of unusual talents. George Ellicott gave Banneker three books, Mayer's *Tables,* Ferguson's *Astronomy,* Leadbetter's *Lunar Tables,* and some astronomical instruments. The Ellicotts also solved Banneker's domestic problems. In return for an annuity of twelve pounds, and a life interest in the farm, Banneker conveyed his property to his white friends.

Freed now from cows and corn, with leisure for contemplation and books for study, Banneker gave himself up to scholarly pursuits. Astronomy became the burning passion of his life. Within a few years, he could predict eclipses. In 1791, he completed calculations for his first almanac, which was published in 1792.

James McHenry, a prominent Baltimore politician who later served as secretary of war, helped Banneker find a publisher for the almanac. In a letter to Goddard & Angel, the Baltimore publishers, he underlined Banneker's importance as an advocate in the flesh. "I consider this Negro as fresh proof that the powers of the mind are disconnected with the color of the skin, or, in other words, a striking contrast to Mr. Hume's doctrine, that 'the Negroes are naturally inferior to the whites, and unsusceptible of attainments in arts and sciences.' In every civilized country, we shall find thousands of whites liberally educated and who have enjoyed greater opportunities for instruction than this Negro, his inferiors in those intellectual acquirements and capacities that

form the most characteristic features in the human race."

McHenry was one of several powerful whites who came within the orbit of Banneker's influence. In his dealings with men of substance, Banneker was artful in his advocacy of the Afro-American's cause. He always urged upon his friends the emancipation of slaves and the elevation of free Negroes. To deprive Afro-Americans of ambition and hope, he said, was to rob them of the credentials of manhood.

Another influential friend, Major Andrew Ellicott, succeeded in getting Banneker appointed to the commission that laid out the city of Washington, D.C. With the approval of George Washington, Banneker and Ellicott were named to assist Pierre Charles L'Enfant, the brilliant and temperamental French engineer who conceived and drew up the original plan for the ten-mile-square area set aside for the nation's Capital. The naming of Banneker to the Capital commission marked the first presidential appointment received by a Negro.

The African astronomer accompanied Ellicott and L'Enfant to Washington and shared in the deliberations and computations of the commission. The *Georgetown Weekly Ledger* of March 12, 1791, noted the arrival of L'Enfant and Ellicott, who were "attended by Benjamin Banneker, an Ethiopian, whose abilities as surveyor and astronomer already prove that Mr. Jefferson's concluding that that race of men were void of mental endowment was without foundation."

L'Enfant was the moving spirit behind the Washington plan. With Ellicott and Banneker assisting, he laid out a show city with great avenues and vistas and open spaces. When a major property owner and political power erected a mansion that obstructed one of his vistas, L'Enfant, the temperamental artist, immediately tore it down. Washington reluctantly dismissed him, and L'Enfant departed in a huff, leaving the calculations to Ellicott and Banneker.

In the middle of 1791, Banneker returned to his home near Baltimore. He was now fifty-five, and he was the best known black man in America. Invitations were pressed upon him from all quarters and strangers beat a path to his farm. On a favorite horse, Banneker made the rounds and related his experiences in Washington. People who had ridiculed him for wasting his time now gathered close to hear words from his lips. Sitting in the middle of a group in the combination post office and store, leaning on his staff, Banneker told his neighbors of the currents at work in the outside world. Of medium stature, running to fat around the middle, white-haired, pleasant-miened, with dreamy, otherwordly eyes, the country celebrity made a noble appearance. He dressed in "superfine broadcloth" cut in the current mode: a plain coat with straight collar and long waistcoat topped by a broad-brimmed hat.

By all standards, Banneker should have been the happiest of men. His work was going well. Scholars had acclaimed his dissertation on bees and a study which proved that the locust plague recurred in seventeen-year cycles. Now, in the middle of 1791, publishers were bringing out his first almanac. It is true that he had no family. But he seemed to prefer it that way. With no wife, with no responsibilities, he was free to study stars at night and sleep during the day. In his spare time, he washed his own clothes, cooked his own food and corresponded with scholars. For relaxation, he sat under a huge chestnut tree in his orchard and played the flute or the violin. He was famous, free, and comparatively well-to-do. What else could he want?

There was something. Banneker had returned from Washington with a sense of impending doom. The winds of change were blowing in the new nation called America, and they were blowing the Afro-American no good. Banneker concluded that the wave of revolutionary idealism in America had reached its peak. The great tide of interracial amity that followed the Revolutionary War was receding, leaving in its wake fear and hate and anxiety. All about him were signs. Free black men were being hemmed in by restrictions and oppressive rules: they were insulted on the streets, barred from employment, and proscribed in the church. Laws were being devised that stripped slaves of every vestige of human personality. Walls — walls of hate and fear and guilt — were closing off every avenue of black advancement. In Banneker's youth, it had been possible for blacks and whites to marry. He himself had attended an integrated school. Now, a scant fifty years later, these things were no longer possible. There were 757,000 black people in America, two out of every ten persons. Of this number, 59,000 were free. But the differences between slaves and free Afro-Americans were being flattened out and obscured. It seemed almost that men feared free Afro-Americans more than they feared slaves. Something, Banneker told himself — something must be done. Why, he wondered, didn't the Afro-American's friends speak out? A word at this critical juncture, when the moulds of a nation and a people were being poured — a word now could make a great deal of difference.

Banneker's mind turned to Thomas Jefferson, who was the great and brooding symbol of the age. Jefferson had, when his blood was hot, championed emancipation and manumission of slaves. In a burst of revolutionary idealism, he had written: "All men are created equal." But Jefferson was not the first, nor the last, to set down words that frightened him. As the years wore on, as the black population increased, Jefferson hedged his bet with polysyllabic rationalizations. He had not disowned the Declaration of Independence. But he seemed to be saying now that white men were created more equal than black people. And worse: he had not manumitted the hundred or more slaves he held at Monticello. Thinking about these things, following the eddies and currents of the age, Banneker decided that the time was ripe for an act. There had been individual acts of protest in Boston and Philadelphia, but these protests were muted. Free Afro-Americans claimed, with good cause, that their lifelines were too exposed to make an open protest. Banneker proposed to abandon caution and speak openly — as a man. To whom? To Thomas Jefferson, of course. Banneker gathered the manuscript pages of his first almanac and sat down at the oval table in his living room. Dipping pen in ink, he put down these words:

Maryland, Baltimore Country,
August 19, 1791

Sir: I am fully sensible of the greatness of the freedom I take with you on the present occasion; a liberty which seemed to me scarcely allowable, when I reflected on that distinguished and dignified station in which you stand, and the almost general prejudice and prepossession, which is so prevalent in the world against those of my complexion.

I suppose it is a truth too well attested to you, to need a proof here, that we are a race of beings, who have long laboured under the abuse and censure of the world; that we have long been looked upon with an eye of contempt; and that we have long been considered rather as brutish than human, and scarcely capable of mental endowments.

Sir, I hope I may safely admit, in consequence of the report which has reached me, that you are a man less inflexible in sentiments of this nature, than many others; that you are measurably friendly, and well disposed towards us; and that you are willing and ready to lend your aid and assistance to our relief, from those many distresses, and numerous calamities, to which we are reduced.

Now Sir, if this is founded in truth, I apprehend you will embrace every opportunity, to eradicate that train of absurd and false ideas and opinions, which so generally prevail with respect to us; and that your sentiments are concurrent with mine, which are, that one universal Father hath given being to us all; and that He hath not only made us all of one flesh, but that He hath also, without partiality, afforded us all the same sensations, and endowed us all with the same faculties; and that however variable we may be in society or religion, however diversified in situation or colour, we are all of the same family, and stand in the same relation to Him.

Sir, if these are sentiments of which you are fully persuaded, I hope you cannot but acknowledge, that it is the indispensable duty of those, who maintain for themselves the rights of human nature, and who profess the obligations of Christianity, to extend their power and influence to the relief of every part of the human race, from whatever burden of oppression they may unjustly labour under. . . .

Sir, I freely and cheerfully acknowledge, that I am of the African race, and in that colour which is natural to them, of the deepest dye; and it is under a sense of the most profound gratitude to the Supreme Ruler of the Universe, that I now confess to you, that I am not under that state of tyrannical thralldom, and inhuman captivity, to which too many of my brethren are doomed, but that I have abundantly tasted of the fruition of those blessings, which proceeded from that free and unequalled liberty with which you are favoured; and which, I hope, you will willingly allow you have mercifully received, from the immediate hand of that Being from whom proceedeth every good and perfect gift.

Sir, suffer me to recall to your mind that time, in which the arms and tyranny of the British crown were exerted, with every powerful effort, in order to reduce you to a state of servitude; look back, I entreat you, on the variety of dangers to which you were exposed; reflect on that time, in which every human aid appeared unavailable . . . and you cannot but be led to a serious and grateful sense of your miraculous and providential preservation. . . .

This, Sir, was a time when you clearly saw into the injustice of a state of slavery, and in which you had just apprehensions of the horrors of its condition. It was then that your abhorrence thereof was so excited that you publicly held forth this true and invaluable doctrine, which is worthy to be recorded and remembered in all succeeding ages: "We hold these truths to be self-evident, that all men are created equal; that they are endowed by their Creator with certain inalienable rights, and that among these are life, liberty, and the pursuit of happiness."

Here was a time, in which your tender feelings for yourselves had engaged you thus to declare; you were then impressed with proper ideas of the great violation of liberty, and the free possession of those blessings, to which you were entitled by nature; but, sir, how pitiable it is to reflect, that although you were so fully convinced of the benevolence of the Father of Mankind, and of His equal and impartial distribution of these rights and privileges, which He hath conferred upon them, that you should at the same time counteract His mercies, in detaining by fraud and violence, so numerous a part of my brethren under groaning captivity, and cruel oppression, that you should at the same time be found guilty of that most criminal act, which you professedly detested in others, with respect to yourselves.

I suppose that your knowledge of the situation of my brethren is too extensive to need a recital here; neither shall I presume to prescribe methods by which they may be relieved, otherwise than by recommending to you and all others, to wean yourself from those narrow prejudices which you have imbibed with respect to them, and as Job proposed to his friends, "put your soul in their soul's stead"; thus shall your hearts be enlarged with kindness and benevolence towards them; and thus shall you need neither the direction of myself or others, in what manners to proceed herein.

Banneker stopped and reread his lines. Perhaps he had been too bold. After all, it was not the custom for black people to speak thus to white people. It was certainly not customary for black people to speak frankly to a man of Jefferson's stature. Banneker thought for a moment and then added a modest and clever disclaimer.

And now, Sir, although my sympathy and affection for my brethren has caused my enlargement thus far, I ardently hope that your candour and generosity will plead with you in my behalf, when I make known to you that it was not originally my design; but having taken up my pen in order to direct to you, as a present, a copy of an Almanac which I have calculated for the succeeding year, I was unexpectedly and unavoidably led thereto.

This calculation is the product of my arduous study, in this my advanced stage of life. . . . I have taken the liberty to direct a copy to you which I humbly request you will favourably receive and although you may have the opportunity of persuing it after its publication, yet I desire to send it to you in manuscript previous thereto, thereby you might not only have an earlier inspection, but that you might also view it in my own handwriting.

And now, Sir, I shall conclude, and subscribe myself, with the most profound respect.

Your most obedient humble servant,
Benjamin Banneker

The letter reached Jefferson, who was then secretary of state in George Washington's cabinet, at Philadelphia. Jefferson's immediate impressions are not a matter of record. Over the next decade, he said various things about Benjamin Banneker, some of them quite harsh. But to Banneker himself he presented his best face in reply.

Philadelphia, Aug. 30, 1791

Sir: I thank you most sincerely, for your letter of the 19th instant, and for the Almanac it contained. Nobody wishes more than I do, to see such proofs as you exhibit, that nature has given to our black brethren talents equal to those of the other color of men; and that the appearance of the want of them is owing merely to the degraded condition of their existence, both in Africa and America. I can add with truth, that nobody wishes more ardently to see a good system commenced, for raising the condition, both of their body and mind, to what it ought to be, as far as the imbecility of their present existence, and other circumstances, which cannot be neglected, will admit.

I have taken the liberty of sending your Almanac to Monsieur de Condorcet, Secretary of the Academy of Sciences, at Paris, and Member of the Philanthropic Society, because I considered it as a document to which your whole coulour have a right for their justification against the doubts which have been entertained of them.

I am, with great esteem, Sir,
Your most obedient humble servant,
Tho. Jefferson

Mr. Benjamin Banneker, near
Ellicot's Lower Mills, Baltimore County.

Banneker's letter and Jefferson's answer made a big ripple in the events of the day. The correspondence was discussed in France, England, and the South. But nothing happened. Slavery continued its ominous march across the soul of America. Frightened by the successful Haitian Revolution and abortive slave revolts in Virginia and other states, masters elaborated increasingly severe rules for the control of slaves and free Afro-Americans.

In dwindling hope, then, and with foreboding for the country he loved, Banneker lived out his measured days. A gentle, Christian man who never joined a church, he turned in his winter days to the advocacy of peace. His plan for *A Lasting Peace* anticipated many of the principles of the League of Nations and the United Nations. But neither in peace nor in tolerance did he overcome. The whole drift of the age was against him. Wars and rumors of wars and the clanking of slave chains: these things were in the wind of October, 1806. Banneker was resting in his home one day in that month when he seemed to hear voices beckoning him to another world. On an impulse, he rose and started down the path leading from his house. He had not gone far when his strength gave out and he sank helplessly to the ground. He died later that day and was buried in an unmarked grave. But the idea the gentle scholar and advocate symbolized could not be disposed of so easily. Within twenty years, Banneker was disturbing the peace of racists from the grave. His name and his letter ("Look back, I entreat you") were cited repeatedly by abolitionists in their successful assault on the intellectual props of the slave South. Banneker has been no less persuasive in our own times. For men who dare and dream, for men who appeal from the gutters to the stars, for men who stand up and protest, no matter what the odds, the stargazer remains a persuasive and articulate example.

QUESTIONS TO CONSIDER

1 How did Benjamin Banneker's life contradict prevalent white myths about blacks? In what ways did his example make whites question their own assumptions of racial superiority?

2 Benjamin Banneker was an educated man. What effect did education have on Banneker's life? Can you hypothesize why white Americans, particularly southerners, would come to regard black education fearfully as a potential threat to their society?

3 When Banneker returned from Washington, D.C., to Baltimore in 1791, the best-known black man in America, he felt uneasy. What signs did Banneker see that the status of blacks was changing for the worse in postrevolutionary America? How can we explain this waning of idealism after the winning of a war fought on behalf of human liberty?

4 Compare Banneker with Benjamin Franklin in selection 6. In what ways did Banneker embody the American ideal Franklin described in his own autobiography? Was Banneker also a "representative man" of the eighteenth century?

12

Abigail Adams:
"Remember the Ladies"

NORMAN K. RISJORD

In this selection Norman K. Risjord views the birth of the Republic from the perspective of another class of Americans excluded from the Revolutionary promise of freedom and equality. Although men like Alexander Hamilton, Benjamin Franklin, and John Jay worried about the discrepancy between the idealism of the Declaration of Independence and the reality of slavery, no statesmen of note thought to extend the equality doctrine to white women, who, though not slaves in a legal sense, were not free either. Women in the young Republic could not vote or hold political office. Unmarried women and widows could own landed property, but few occupations were open to them. Indeed, custom held that the only proper sphere for women was in the home. Once a woman married, the law treated her like a child. A married woman could not own property or sue in court without her husband. If a married woman did work outside the home, her husband legally commanded her wages. He was also the sole guardian of their children. If he died without a will and there were children, the woman was entitled to only one-third of her husband's estate. In certain cases, she could keep only her dowry — the property she had brought to the marriage. If she wedded again (and widows usually did remarry in order to survive), she had to surrender her property to her new husband. If the woman was black, she faced a double wall of discrimination — one because she was a woman, the other because she was black.

Educational restrictions hampered women further. Northern elementary schools did admit females, and southern planters hired tutors for their daughters as they did for their sons. But before 1820, that was about all the education a woman could expect. "As a result," as Norman Risjold says, "adult women received politeness from men-folk, but rarely intellectual companionship or conversation." Only a rare woman could overcome such formidable barriers and make a mark on history. One who did was Abigail Adams, the subject of Risjord's striking portrait.

Abigail not only gave invaluable moral support to her husband and the second president, John Adams, but also spoke out against slavery and became an advocate of woman's rights. In addition to her significant moral concerns, her life affords delightful glimpses into the home front during the Revolution and into the workings of government and society from the view of a perceptive First Lady. She was one of the most remarkable figures of her time — a woman who, in striving to liberate the human spirit, lived by the dictum that "life stagnates without action. I could never bear merely to vegetate."

☆

ABIGAIL SMITH

ABIGAIL SMITH was more advantaged than the average woman. Her father, Reverend William Smith, was a Congregational minister whose forebears had amassed a considerable fortune in trade. Her mother was a Quincy, a family that was interlocked by blood and marriage with the elite of the Massachusetts Bay Colony. She grew up in the pristine atmosphere of a parsonage in rural Weymouth. Her religious training was liberal Congregationalist, and she adhered to that faith all her life (except for her sojourn in New York, while her husband served as vice president, when she found the sermons of the Episcopalian minister more congenial).

She was a sickly child; recurrent illness kept her from attending school. Her father gave her some personal instruction, and she had access to his well-stocked library. Her letters and those of her two sisters indicate an early acquaintance with the English greats — Shakespeare, Milton, Dryden, and Pope — and she knew well the histories, travel diaries, and church literature of her own time. She taught herself French, and her later success with her husband's accounts indicates that she was well versed in arithmetic.

In 1759, at the age of fourteen, she met John Adams, a struggling young lawyer from nearby Braintree. Adams was more interested in her older sister at first, but by 1762 they were in ardent courtship. They married two years later, on the eve of her twentieth birthday. Although both came from pious, rural backgrounds, there was nothing puritanical about either. Their love letters were amazingly open and uninhibited. And their marriage, though broken by long separations while Adams pursued revolutionary politics and diplomacy, was one of the happiest ever recorded.

From *Representative Americans* by Normand Risjord. Copyright 1980 by D. C. Heath and Company. Reprinted by permission of the publisher.

Abigail Smith was a striking nineteen-year-old when Benjamin Blyth painted this portrait of her in 1763. She married John Adams the next year, on the eve of her twentieth birthday. "Their love letters," writes Norman K. Risjord, "were amazingly open and uninhibited." (Massachusetts Historical Society)

Seldom has a love been more deeply felt or more exquisitely expressed. But their marriage was more than that: it was a partnership to which each contributed in equal measure. John Adams was a man of extraordinary gifts. His many essays on government were without equal even in that age of spangled brilliance. He was a shrewd and realistic diplomat, an honest and sensible politician. Yet he needed a counterweight. He was a man full of anxieties and hostilities. He wavered continually between a suspicion that others were plotting against him and a fear that he was undoing himself. Though glorying in

his reputation as philosopher-statesman, he hungered for the contentment of a rural law practice. John Adams's best biographer states flatly: "Abigail insured his sanity." With her devotion, her intellectual companionship, and her competent management of his affairs, she was "a gyroscope that brought him safely through the stormiest seas."

☆

"REMEMBER THE LADIES"

Elizabeth Quincy Smith, Abigail's mother, considered John Adams a small-town attorney of second-rate family and uncertain future. Yet he prospered quickly enough. Before long his casework forced him to divide his time between Braintree and the superior court in Boston. In 1767 Adams moved his family, which by then included daughter Abigail and son John Quincy Adams, to Boston. The prospects there were better, cousin Samuel had pointed out, for a career in the law or in politics. He was soon deeply involved in Samuel Adams's revolutionary machine, attending sessions of the Caucus and serving in the colonial assembly. In 1774 the assembly, barring the doors against General Gage's orders to dissolve, sent him to the First Continental Congress. Abigail returned to Braintree, and, except for brief intervals, the two were apart for the next ten years while Adams served as delegate to Congress and minister in Europe.

They remained in close contact by letter, however. His notes were hastily written, yet intimately descriptive. Hers were splendidly crafted, graced with lines of poetry, and full of suggestion and insight. It was, says the editor of the Adams family papers, "one of the greatest epistolary dialogues between husband and wife in all history."

Abigail Adams shared all her husband's political trials. She favored full independence for the United States at least as early as he did, and she was more open in advocating it. Adams considered it "the choice blessing" of his life that she had "the capacity to comprehend" the great issues of the day. So well formed were her political opinions that Adams raided her letters for apt quotations to use in his own writings. He sent her a copy of Tom Paine's *Common Sense* as soon as it came off the press in early 1776. Abigail was "charmed" with its arguments in favor of independence and wondered how anyone could "hestiate one moment at adopting them." She was, of course, delighted when Congress finally approved the Declaration. "May the foundation of our new constitution be Justice, Truth, Righteousness!" she exclaimed.

That she picked those virtues for the new nation is itself revealing. She was not content simply with self-rule. The creation of new governments, she felt, presented a unique opportunity to repair some of the injustices in American society. The disparities in the educational system particularly bothered her, possibly because of her own lack of formal schooling. In a republic, where the citizenry had an important voice in government, it was essential that education be available to all. The discrimination against women, she suspected, was due to men's "ungenerous jealousy of rivals near the Throne." Equal educational opportunities would ensure future greatness, for women, as mothers, had the greatest effect on the young. "If we mean to have heroes, statesmen and philosophers," she told her husband, "we should have learned women."

He doubtless realized that education would also expand the horizons of women, perhaps even foster a desire for political power; but in the male-dominated world of the eighteenth century such arguments would have been self-defeating. It was first necessary to remove some of the legal chains that fettered women, and that she did try to do. Independence, she reminded her husband, meant the drafting of state constitutions and the revision of legal codes. When Adams and his colleagues set about this task, she begged, "Remember the Ladies, and be more generous and favourable to them

than your ancestors. Do not put such unlimited power into the hands of husbands. Remember all Men would be tyrants if they could. If particular care and attention is not paid to the Ladies we are determined to foment a Rebellion, and will not hold ourselves bound by any Laws in which we have no voice, or Representation." The popular slogan "No taxation without representation" had all sorts of revolutionary implications.

Realizing, perhaps, the futility of her crusade, husband John chose to treat her plea as a joke. "I cannot but laugh," he replied. "We have been told that our struggle has loosened the bonds of government everywhere: that children and apprentices were disobedient; that schools and colleges were grown turbulent; that Indians slighted their guardians, and Negroes grew insolent to their masters. But your letter was the first intimation that another tribe, more numerous and powerful than all the rest, were grown discontented." Perhaps, he concluded still with tongue in cheek, the British ministry was responsible. Having without success appealed to "Tories, land jobbers, bigots, Canadians, Indians, Negroes, Hessians, Russians, Irish Roman Catholics, and Scotch renegades, at last they have stimulated the most dangerous group of all to demand new privileges and threaten to rebel."

Abigail's tone had been jocular, but she was deadly serious. Not satisfied with John's reply, she wrote her friend Mercy Warren to ask her "to join me in a petition to Congress." She wanted to rid the country of the ancient "laws of England, which give unlimited power to the husband to use his wife ill," and to institute a new legal code "in our favor upon just and liberal principles." Mercy Warren disappointingly failed to respond. Abigail, not yet through, wrote to John:

I cannot say that I think you are very generous to the ladies, for whilst you are proclaiming peace and good will to men, emancipating all nations, you insist upon retaining an absolute power over wives. But you must remember that arbitrary power is, like most other things which are very hard, very liable to be broken; and, notwithstanding all your wise laws and maxims, we have it in our power, not only to free ourselves, but to subdue our masters, and without violence, throw both your natural and legal authority at our feet —

"Charm by accepting, by submitting sway,
Yet have our humor most when we obey."

At least she had the last word. What could John reply to that?

Women's rights were not her only concern. She abhorred slavery and thought that it, too, ought to be abolished in the new order of things. How, she wondered openly, could the Virginians be considered leaders in the cause of liberty when they "have been accustomed to deprive their fellow creatures of theirs"? Some years later — indeed, after her husband had been elected president — she sent a young black servant of hers to night school at the lad's request. When a father of two of the white pupils appeared at her door to protest, she gave him a lecture on "equality of rights. The Boy is a Freeman as much as any of the young Men," she told him, "and merely because his Face is Black, is he to be denied instruction? How is he to be qualified to procure a livelihood? . . . I have not thought it any disgrace to myself to take him into my parlour and teach him both to read and write." For a president's wife it was a becoming posture. And she won. Nothing further was said.

☆

LIFE ON THE HOME FRONT

Not least among the treasures in the correspondence of Abigail Adams is the picture it gives of civilian life during the Revolution. Even though Massachusetts saw little fighting after the British evacuated Boston, it suffered the usual wartime poblems.

Goods were short, labor scarce, and disease rampant.

When John Adams departed for the Continental Congress in 1774, Abigail was left with the care of their Braintree farm. Although she knew little of farming, she proved a capable superintendent of the hired help. When John returned late in the autumn, he found the fields plowed and manured for the spring planting, and the pasture was fertilized with seaweed brought up from the beach. With the outbreak of fighting his absences became more prolonged, her work ever more professional. In the spring of 1776 she wrote to him that "the barley looks charmingly" after good spring rains and that they were about to plant the summer crops. She had let one incompetent hand go and had hired two others at a shilling a day. With the money he had sent her, she had paid yearly taxes, wages to the hired men, and rent on the loan of her father's horse. Impressed, her husband replied playfully that he was beginning "to be jealous that our Neighbors will think Affairs more discreetly conducted in my Absence than at any other Time."

Toward the end of the war she purchased out of her own savings a tract of land that she knew her husband had long wanted. It had once belonged to John's uncle, and he had tromped its woods as a youth. For seven acres she paid two hundred dollars. John doubtless would have bought it anyway for sentimental reasons, but she prudently analyzed the value of the investment. The parcel held, she estimated, forty-five cords of firewood (John had earlier complained that firewood sold for twenty dollars a cord in Philadelphia). He was, of course, delighted with the purchase.

Life in Braintree was exciting while Washington besieged the British in Boston. In February 1776 Mrs. Adams was at her writing table when Washington's newly acquired artillery began booming on Dorchester Heights. The cannon roared all night long, and the next day the town militia marched off to Boston to join the fight. Abigail climbed a nearby hill to watch the artillery duel. The sound, she wrote, "is one of the grandest in nature, and is of the true species of the sublime! 'Tis now an incessant roar; but oh! the fatal ideas which are connected with the sound! How many of our dear countrymen must fall!"

When the militia returned with news that Washington had occupied Dorchester Heights, she was disappointed. "I would not have suffered all I have for two such hills," she wrote with a true appreciation of the ratio between human life and bits of land. Nor was she much comforted when she discovered that the victory enabled Washington to menace the city and harbor. She feared that the cannonade would leave the city a flattened wreckage. From her hilltop perch she watched the British evacuate Boston. Their fleet of 170 ships, the largest ever assembled in America, filled the bay as far as she could see. Afterwards she hastened into Boston to inspect the damage. Their own house had been occupied by a British army physician, and, though it was stripped and dirty, it was intact. The rest of the city was likewise in fair shape. With relief she bade farewell to the war, though she would continue to suffer its privations.

As the fighting shifted to the South, the revolutionary fervor that had gripped Massachusetts began to ebb. Patriotism gave way to profiteering and speculation. A *nouveau riche* of war profiteers came to dominate the social life of Braintree. Abigail ignored them, and they her. "I have not the *honor* to be known to many of them," she wrote with icy disapproval. Wartime disruption also brought a decline in moral standards. "Matrimony is not in vogue here," Abigail reported. "We have ladies but not a gentleman in the whole town. . . . Licentiousness and freedom of manners are predominant."

As the war dragged on, goods became scarce and prices rose. The assembly passed an act regulating prices, but it proved impossible to enforce. Merchants charged what the traffic would bear. Sugar, molasses, rum, and coffee could not be had at any price. Labor, too, was scarce after Braintree's Minutemen went off to war. Without teachers, the schools had ceased to function, and the town children were left to "range the streets." Farmhands were unavailable, and Abigail thought that the women of the town would have to bring in the crops. "I believe I could gather corn and husk it," she wrote John, "but I should make a poor figure at digging potatoes." She was even prepared to fight. If General Howe returned to Massachusetts, she predicted, "an army of women would oppose him." She assured her husband: "We possess a spirit that will not be conquered. If our men are drawn off and we should be attacked, you would find a race of Amazons in America."

In early 1778 John Adams departed for France to replace Silas Deane. Except for a brief reunion in 1780, he and Abigail would be separated for the next six years. In his absence the farm and the family accounts were left completely to her. Ministerial expenses easily ate up the meager pay allotted him by Congress. Abigail and the children had to subsist on the income from the Braintree farm. As prices rose, that became increasingly difficult. To make ends meet, she asked John to send her goods from Paris, which she could sell through friends. John obliged with a trunkful of French cloth and ribbons. Abigail turned the articles over to merchant friends, who sold them on a commission basis. The proceeds enabled her to survive the war in some comfort. Peace brought a collapse in prices and ruin to some of the war speculators. Abigail hastily wrapped up her own "mercantile affairs" and wrung new economies from her family.

☆

AMERICAN ABROAD

Peace did not bring John Adams home. At the request of Congress he and Franklin stayed on in Europe to negotiate commercial treaties for the new republic. Then in 1784 Congress appointed him minister to Great Britain, while simultaneously sending his friend Jefferson to replace Franklin in Paris. Adams was delighted with the honor, but the prospect of further separation was more than he or Abigail could bear. With his encouragement Abigail decided to join him in Europe.

The voyage required extensive preparations. Abigail left the town house in the care of Phoebe, the black maid she had inherited from her father (and her lifetime companion), and found tenants for the farm. She placed the younger boys with her sister and took her daughter, Nabby, with her. The voyage also disentangled Nabby from a suitor of whom Abigail disapproved. (Abigail's judgment of the young man, Royall Tyler, seemed correct at the time, but he later straightened himself out and became a respected chief justice of Vermont. Nabby ultimately married a feckless New Yorker, who was in constant financial difficulties.)

The day before her vessel was to sail, Thomas Jefferson appeared in Boston. Also bound for Europe, the Virginian had made a special trip to persuade her to accompany him on a vessel sailing from New York. Though flattered by his gracious gesture, she refused to change plans at the last minute. The act marked the beginning of a new friendship, however.

After a joyous reunion in London, the Adamses set out for Paris, where John was to join Jefferson in trade negotiations. Abigail's first impressions of France were unfavorable. Farms, she noted, were poorly cultivated, and the villages they passed through seemed "the most wretched habitations of man." Paris, she declared, was "the dirtiest place I ever saw," and, she might have added, the smelliest. Garbage littered the streets; raw sewage trickled down the gutters.

Setting up housekeeping in Paris was a chore. Each servant considered herself a specialist. The upstairs maid would only dust; making beds was the department of a *femme de chambre*. The coachman did nothing but attend to the horses; the cook would not think of washing a dish. With a staff of eight Abigail could find no one willing to do the family wash. Had she not persuaded the two American servants she had brought with her to do double duty, Abigail complained, she would have had to hire eight more "lazy wretches." Nor did she like the constant handouts. At New Year's every servant expected a special gift, as did the clerk of the parish and the newspaper boy. Foreign ministers were also expected to visit the royal court on that occasion with gifts for all the king's servants. "If we miss one of these harpies," Abigail observed caustically, "they will follow you from Versailles to Paris."

Nevertheless, Abigail soon learned to appreciate the French. The men she found charming and attentive, full of flirtatious compliments; and the women were graceful, easy in manner, and interesting conversationalists. Their superiority over American women she attributed to better education. The Adamses enjoyed French cooking and attended the theater regularly. Life in Paris was a world away from Braintree, or even Boston, yet the experience also reinforced their pride in home. When the Dutch minister arrived for dinner in a coach drawn by six horses and attended by five liveried servants, Abigail wished that she was back in America "where frugality and economy are considered as virtues."

England, where the Adamses removed at the end of 1784, charmed Abigail at once. The countryside was clean and tidy, she wrote Jefferson, and London was a magnificent city. She admitted, however, that the English could not compare with the French in cooking and in dress. After lecturing Jefferson on the superiority of English life, she commissioned the Virginian to purchase her four pairs of shoes in Paris.

The stay in England further reinforced her Americanism. Both the Adamses detested the caste system into which English society was divided and the snobbery that it produced. The treatment of women was especially appalling to Abigail, who resented being herded off to a special room after dinner while the men drew port and lit cigars. Cards, the only pastime in which women were included, she considered a waste of time. To improve their manners and widen their horizons, Abigail suggested, Englishmen ought to reside for a time in America. In England, she complained, she had heard "more narrow prejudice, more illiberality of sentiment . . . than I ever saw or heard in my whole life."

Still, she was not one to romanticize her homeland. She criticized Congress for its weakness and fretted over the seeming paralysis that had overtaken Americans since the end of the war. The Shaysites, debt-ridden farmers who interrupted court proceedings in Massachusetts during the fall of 1786, aroused her wrath. They were "ignorant, restless desperadoes, without conscience or principles," she exploded to Jefferson. Nor was she happy with the Virginian's mild reply: "I like a little rebellion now and then. It is like a storm in the atmosphere."

The Adamses greeted with joy the new American Constitution, drafted at Philadelphia in the summer of 1787. The expanded powers given to both Congress and the Executive gave promise of order and stability. The change in government also increased John Adams's desire to return home. A decade of service abroad was enough; besides, he had a good chance of winning a post in the new regime. Adams signified his wishes to Secretary of Foreign Affairs John Jay, and Congress duly recalled him. The Adamses landed in New York in July 1788, just as New York gave its approval to the Constitution (all but North Carolina and Rhode Island had earlier ratified).

☆

First Lady

After the stately mansions they occupied in Europe, Abigail worried that the Braintree farmhouse was too small for her family. When her business agent at home (who superintended the farm, purchased securities for her, and provided funds for John Quincy at Harvard) informed her that a particularly nice house in Quincy was for sale, she quickly instructed him to buy it. She got it for six hundred dollars. The purchase was just the beginning of her new responsibilities. After years of freedom from such mundane concerns, husband John took no interest in their income or expenses.

More than housewife, Abigail was quite literally a home economist. She managed the farm, put the boys through college, and invested their extra cash in securities for their old age. The instructions that she left when she journeyed to New York to attend the birth of Nabby's first baby reveal her many concerns. Briesler, the hired man, was to slaughter a steer and hang it in the cellar, guard the winter stores against rats and mice, bottle the apple cider before it turned to vinegar, and pick through the harvest of pears and apples to remove the rotten ones. If she failed to return in time for Christmas, she authorized John to slaughter a pig so that he could have roast pork for Christmas dinner. He was to save the legs, however, for smoked bacon.

When Adams was chosen vice president in the first federal elections, Abigail supervised the move to New York. She found tenants for the farm, paid their local debts, and saw to the crating of furniture. Richmond Hill, their residence in Manhattan, was a splendid house ("perfectly romantic," exclaimed Abigail), though it was some distance from the center of town.

Adams soon found that his principal job as vice president (a position that he eventually derided as the most insignificant office ever contrived by the mind of man) was to preside over the Senate. Unfamiliar with the role and unable to sit quietly for long periods of time, Adams took an active part in the debates. Enemies were shocked, and even friends were irritated at his lack of presidential impartiality. The early weeks of the first Congress were occupied with a discussion of titles — how to address the president, what to call fellow congressmen, whether to bow upon entering the Senate.

Feeling, as Washington did, that the first essential of the new government was to win the respect of the people, Adams held out for titles and ceremonies of all kinds. Every European government relied on pomp and ceremony, he informed the astonished Senate. Jefferson and other critics of the government began to suspect him of being a monarchist at heart. Abigail loyally echoed John's political views but with garnishment of her own. When a Federalist friend suggested titling her ''Autocratix of the United States,'' she responded with barbed wit. ''I do not know what he means by abusing me so,'' she wrote. ''I was always for equality as my husband can witness.''

Abigail did not enjoy the political limelight. Aside from the proximity of her daughter, who lived on Long Island, the only bright spot for her in New York was Martha Washington. The president, the Adamses found, was quiet and reserved, but Martha was a delight. The two ''first ladies'' quickly became friends. As Abigail had found with Jefferson, the difference between Yankee and Virginian was not a barrier but a source of fascination.

Toward the end of Washington's first term, Abigail's health worsened and she returned to Quincy. Like her husband, she was never robust, and advancing age brought diabetes and a susceptibility to ''fevers'' (influenza would probably be the modern diagnosis). She remained there until her husband was elected president in 1796. Her interest in politics never flagged, however. When John Jay's accommodation with Great Britain came before Congress for approval, she helped to circulate a pro-treaty petition. Canvassing the town, she encountered a company of militia drilling on the Quincy Common. The captain was reluctant to sign anything, but she brought him around by reading one of her husband's letters, which predicted that anarchy and war would result if the treaty were re-jected. To her delight the captain then prevailed upon his entire company to sign.

Washington's retirement she greeted with mixed emotions, for her husband was the logical choice among Federalists to succeed him. ''My ambition leads me not to be first in Rome,'' she wrote John. ''If personal considerations alone were to weigh, I should immediately say retire with [him].'' For her it meant leaving the peaceful intimacy of her native village for the boisterous pageantry of the capital. And it meant a new sort of confinement. ''I must impose a silence upon myself,'' she said, reflecting on her habit of speaking her mind. She was sure that the presidency would be ''a most unpleasant seat, full of thorns, briars, thistles, murmuring, faultfinding, calumny, obloquy.'' But, she added philosophically, ''the Hand of Providence ought to be attended to and what is designed, cheerfully submitted to.''

Of one thing she was certain — John must never accept second place should Thomas Jefferson win the presidency. The party battles of the 1790s had utterly destroyed her affection for the lanky Virginian. Jefferson, she now felt, was a cheap demagogue determined to destroy the government. Like Washington and her own husband, Abigail did not understand the function or the value of political parties.

Adams won the election, though by the slimmest of margins — three votes in the electoral college. Jefferson, who placed second in the balloting, became vice president. More flexible than the Adamses, he accepted the job. Tensions within the administration and troubles with France, which had reacted angrily to the Jay Treaty, meant a difficult four years for both president and vice president.

Abigail set out from Quincy at the end of April 1797, some six weeks after her husband was inaugurated. John met her just outside New York and drove her in the presidential carriage to the new seat of government, Philadelphia. The executive mansion had been stocked with their own furniture from Quincy after the Washingtons moved out, and the servants had put all in good order. Within a few days after her arrival Abigail held her first formal reception — "thirty-two ladies and near as many gentlemen."

She adapted swiftly to the role of First Lady. The president relied on her heavily for opinions and advice. He was not inclined to consult his cabinet, a contentious collection of second-rate politicians, who (he later discovered) owed their allegiance to party leader Alexander Hamilton. Abigail usually reflected the president's own views, but the discussion helped him reach decisions. She also kept up an extensive correspondence, mostly with old political allies, explaining and reinforcing the president's public statements. But most important was her function as family economist: she directed a corporate household in Philadelphia while overseeing the Quincy farms by mail.

On a typical day she rose at five and spent the early hours reading, at prayer, writing letters, or watching the sunrise. Family breakfast was at eight, and the remainder of the morning she spent supervising the household. Maids had to be checked, meals planned, and food ordered. Entertaining was part of the daily routine, for she often had thirty or forty guests to dinner. On one occasion she invited the entire Senate. From noon until three she received visitors. Dinner, served in the middle or late afternoon was an elaborate affair, usually lasting two hours. Afterward she "rode out," visiting friends in the city, shopping, or exploring the Pennsylvania countryside.

Philadelphia was a deadly place in the summer, swept annually by yellow fever, and the entire government fled for home. On the road to Quincy in the summer of 1798 Abigail herself was struck by fever, complicated by diarrhea. The common prescription for fever was bleeding, and that, of course, only made her weaker. She recovered slowly and did not accompany John when he returned to the capital city. Indeed, she remained in Quincy for the next two years.

The intervening years were trying ones for President Adams. The French crisis came to a head with the failure of a special commission sent to Paris, and fighting broke out on the high seas. Ultra-Federalists wished for a formal declaration of war against France and were enraged when Adams sent over a new peace mission in 1799. Adams upheld his stand by dismissing two members of his cabinet, but the action left his party bitterly divided. The division helped cost him the election of 1800.

The seat of government moved again in early 1800, this time to its permanent location on the banks of the Potomac, where a city had been carved out of the wooded flats of southern Maryland. No one liked the new capital, except the Virginians, who had contrived the removal. Buildings were unfinished; trees grew in the middle of streets because no one had taken time to remove them. Pennsylvania Avenue, the principal thoroughfare, bogged down in a swamp halfway between the Capitol and the President's house. The executive mansion was a damp and drafty place, barren of furnishings. Mindful of their health, the Adamses kept fires burning in every room.

Nor did Abigail like the South. She always abhorred slavery, but she had never realized the debilitating effect that the institution had on whites. It was impossible to get them to do anything, she complained, because any sort of manual labor was scorned as "nigger's work." The lower class in white society she considered a step below the slaves "in point of intelligence and ten below them in point of civility."

Abigail greeted Adams's loss to Jefferson in the election of 1800 with sympathy for her husband, but without regret. "Neither my habits, or my education or inclinations," she told a Quincy cousin, "have led me to an expensive style of living. . . . If I did not rise with dignity, I can at least fall with ease, which is the more difficult task." Shortly after his victory became known, Jefferson paid a call on her, offering to be of service in

Gilbert Stuart's painting, done in Boston in 1815, captures an aging but still striking Abigail, after she and her husband had retired from public life. She superintended their crowded "mansion" in Quincy and refused to slow down, saying, "Life stagnates without action." (National Gallery of Art, Washington, Gift of Mrs. Robert Homans, 1954)

any way that he could. Abigail was gratified at this gracious gesture, but it failed to still her partisan distaste. It would be a decade before the wounds of party strife were healed and the old friendship of Jefferson and the Adamses was restored.

Retirement was a tonic after thirty years of public service, and the health of both Adamses returned. Money was scarce, as ever, but with the cash from the securities that Abigail had secretly bought over the years they lived comfortably enough. The Quincy "mansion" was crowded with grandchildren, first the daughter of Charles, who died in

1800, and then Nabby's children after she died of breast cancer. In 1811 they also took the children of John Quincy Adams after their eldest son, having turned Republican, was rewarded with the post of minister to Russia. There was also a constant stream of visitors and overnight guests. Abigail superintended it all, and when friends suggested that she ought to slow down, she replied: "I had rather have too much than too little. Life stagnates without action. I could never bear merely to vegetate."

In 1818 she suffered a stroke and died swiftly. John survived her another eight years, living long enough to see their son elected president. But the beautiful partnership had ended.

QUESTIONS TO CONSIDER

1 Abigail Adams was her husband's intellectual companion; she was, as author Risjord says, "the gyroscope that brought him safely through the stormiest seas." Do you think, according to the evidence given in this selection, that she expanded her husband's awareness of the position of women — or that she ever got him to alter his ideas?

2 Although Abigail Adams was a Federalist like her husband, it could be argued that she was in many ways a representative American republican. In this light discuss her attitudes toward women, blacks, and Europeans and her own role as First Lady. In what ways was she elitist?

3 How were Abigail Adams's responsibilities similar to those of other women of her day and social class? Where did she differ from them and from women of other social classes? How much of what she did could be considered work usually performed by men?

4 Why do we seem to know so much about Abigail Adams and so little about almost every other woman of her era? What tools and techniques might historians employ to find out about the lives of women less prominent than presidents' wives?

VII

PATTERNS
OF SOCIETY

13

The Personal Side
of a Developing People

JACK LARKIN

The study of everyday life is one of the most fascinating new fields of American history. Like biography, it is firmly grounded in specific experience; it allows us to see the people of the past going about the daily business of living, and it invites us to compare their patterns of behavior with our own. The differences can be astounding, but so can the similarities. In the following selection, Jack Larkin, chief historian of Old Sturbridge Village in Massachusetts, relies on contemporary observers of the young Republic to answer some provocative questions: What were people then really like? What did they eat and drink? What did they wear? What did they do for amusement? How did they occupy their leisure time? How did they deal with tension and stress? How did they make love?

The picture that emerges is of a vibrant, busy, contentious people who drank too much liquor (one historian termed it the era of "the alcoholic Republic"), spat tobacco, wore dour expressions, slept in bug-ridden beds, dumped their sewage in the streets, and pursued the pleasures of the flesh more than we might have imagined. It would be well to contrast Larkin's portrait with John C. Miller's account of "courtship, marriage, and children" in the colonial era (selection 4). Note what happened to bundling in the nineteenth century. And note, too, how significant were patterns of regional, ethnic, and class distinctiveness in the early Republic. Larkin even goes into the plight of the slaves, virtually picking up that unhappy story where Carl Degler leaves off in selection 3.

☆

DOUR VISAGES

CONTEMPORARY OBSERVERS of early-nineteenth-century America left a fragmentary but nonetheless fascinating and revealing picture of the manner in which rich and poor, Southerner and Northerner, farmer and city dweller, freeman and slave presented themselves to the world. To begin with, a wide variety of characteristic facial expressions, gestures, and ways of carrying the body reflected the extraordinary regional and social diversity of the young republic.

When two farmers met in early-nineteenth-century New England, wrote Francis Underwood, of Enfield, Massachusetts, the author of a pioneering 1893 study of small-town life, "their greeting might seem to a stranger gruff or surly, since the facial muscles were so inexpressive, while, in fact, they were on excellent terms." In courtship and marriage, countrymen and women were equally constrained, with couples "wearing all unconsciously the masks which custom had prescribed; and the onlookers who did not know the secret would think them cold and indifferent."

Underwood noted a pervasive physical as well as emotional constraint among the people of Enfield; it was rooted, he thought, not only in the self-denying ethic of their Calvinist tradition but in the nature of their work. The great physical demands of unmechanized agriculture gave New England men, like other rural Americans, a distinctively ponderous gait and posture. Despite their strength and endurance, farmers were "heavy, awkward and slouching

Excerpt from *The Reshaping of Everyday Life in the United States 1790–1840* by Jack Larkin. Copyright © 1988 by Jack Larkin. Reprinted by permission of Harper & Row, Publishers, Inc., and American Heritage.

in movement" and walked with a "slow inclination from side to side."

Yankee visages were captured by itinerant New England portraitists during the early nineteenth century, as rural storekeepers, physicians, and master craftsmen became the first more or less ordinary Americans to have their portraits done. The portraits caught their caution and immobility of expression as well as recording their angular, long-jawed features, thus creating good collective likenesses of whole communities.

The Yankees, however, were not the stiffest Americans. Even by their own impassive standards, New Englanders found New York Dutchmen and Pennsylvania German farmers "clumsy and chill" or "dull and stolid." But the "wild Irish" stood out in America for precisely the opposite reason. They were not "chill" or "stolid" enough, but loud and expansive. Their expressiveness made Anglo-Americans uncomfortable.

The seemingly uncontrolled physical energy of American blacks left many whites ill at ease. Of the slaves celebrating at a plantation ball, it was "impossible to describe the things these people did with their bodies," Frances Kemble Butler, an English-born actress who married a Georgia slave owner, observed, "and above all with their faces. . . ." Blacks' expressions and gestures, their preference for rhythmic rather than rigid bodily motion, their alternations of energy and rest made no cultural sense to observers who saw only "antics and frolics," "laziness," or "savagery." Sometimes perceived as obsequious, childlike, and dependent, or sullen and inexpressive, slaves also wore masks — not "all unconsciously" as Northern farm folk did, but as part of their self-protective strategies for controlling what masters, mistresses, and other whites could know about their feelings and motivations.

American city dwellers, whose daily routines were driven by the quicker pace of commerce, were easy to distinguish from "heavy and slouching" farmers attuned to slow seasonal rhythms. New

Country revelers at a quilting "frolic" in the days of the Early Republic. This 1813 painting, by German-born John Lewis Krimmel, is conspicuous for its fine detail and racial contrasts. Notice how well dressed the newly arrived whites are in comparison to the black fiddler. Krimmel's comic portrayal marked the start of an almost constant popular association of blacks with music and music-making. It also contributed to the development of degrading racial stereotypes: note that both the fiddler and the black serving girl have toothy grins and oversized red lips, and both are presented in the darkest shade of color. (Courtesy The Henry Francis duPont Winterthur Museum)

Yorkers, in particular, had already acquired their own characteristic body language. The clerks and commercial men who crowded Broadway, intent on their business, had a universal "contraction of the brow, knitting of the eyebrows, and compression of the lips . . . and a hurried walk." It was a popular American saying in the 1830s, reported Frederick Marryat, an Englishman who traveled extensively in the period, that "a New York merchant always walks as if he had a good dinner before him, and a bailiff behind him."

Northern and Southern farmers and city merchants alike, to say nothing of Irishmen and blacks, fell well short of the standard of genteel "bodily carriage'' enshrined in both English and American etiquette books and the instructions of dancing masters: ''flexibility in the arms . . . erectness in the spinal column . . . easy carriage of the head.'' It was the ideal of the British aristocracy, and Southern planters came closest to it, expressing the power of their class in the way they stood and moved. Slave owners accustomed to command, imbued with an ethic of honor and pride, at ease in the saddle, carried themselves more gracefully than men hardened by toil or preoccupied with commerce. Visiting Washington in 1835, the Englishwoman Harriet Martineau contrasted not the politics but the postures of Northern and Southern congressmen. She marked the confident bearing, the ''ease and frank courtesy . . . with an occasional touch of arrogance'' of the slaveholders alongside the ''cautious . . . and too deferential air of the members of the North.'' She could recognize a New Englander ''in the open air,'' she claimed, ''by his deprecatory walk.''

Local inhabitants' faces became more open, travelers observed, as one went west. Nathaniel Hawthorne found a dramatic contrast in public appearances only a few days' travel west of Boston. ''The people out here,'' in New York State just west of the Berkshires, he confided to his notebook in 1839, ''show out their character much more strongly than they do with us,'' in his native eastern Massachusetts. He compared the ''quiet, silent, dull decency . . . in our public assemblages'' with Westerners' wider gamut of expressiveness, ''mirth, anger, eccentricity, all showing themselves freely.'' Westerners in general, the clergyman and publicist Henry Ward Beecher observed, had ''far more freedom of manners, and more frankness and spontaneous geniality'' than did the city or country people of the New England and Middle Atlantic states, as did the ''odd mortals that wander in from the western border,'' that Martineau observed in Washington's political population.

☆

A PUNGENT FOLK

Early-nineteenth-century Americans lived in a world of dirt, insects, and pungent smells. Farmyards were strewn with animal wastes, and farmers wore manure-spattered boots and trousers everywhere. Men's and women's working clothes alike were often stiff with dirt and dried sweat, and men's shirts were often stained with ''yellow rivulets'' of tobacco juice. The locations of privies were all too obvious on warm or windy days. Unemptied chamber pots advertised their presence. Wet baby ''napkins,'' today's diapers, were not immediately washed but simply put by the fire to dry. Vats of ''chamber lye'' — highly concentrated urine used for cleaning type or degreasing wool — perfumed all printing offices and many households. ''The breath of that fiery bar-room,'' as Underwood described a country tavern, ''was overpowering. The odors of the hostlers' boots, redolent of fish-oil and tallow, and of buffalo-robes and horse-blankets, the latter reminiscent of equine ammonia, almost got the better of the all-pervading fumes of spirits and tobacco.''

Densely populated, but poorly cleaned and drained, America's cities were often far more noisome than its farmyards. Horse manure thickly covered city streets, and few neighborhoods were free from the spreading stench of tanneries and slaughterhouses. New York City accumulated so much refuse that it was generally believed the actual surfaces of the streets had not been seen for decades. During her stay in Cincinnati, the English writer Frances Trollope followed the practice of the vast majority of American city housewives when she threw her household ''slops'' — refuse food and dirty dishwater — out into the street. An irate neighbor soon informed her that municipal ordinances forbade ''throwing such things at the sides of the streets'' as she had done; "they must just all be cast right into the middle and the pigs soon takes them off." In most cities hundreds, sometimes thousands, of free-roaming pigs scavenged the garbage; one exception was Charleston, South Carolina, where buzzards patrolled the streets. By converting garbage into pork, pigs kept city streets cleaner than they would otherwise have been, but the pigs themselves befouled the streets and those who ate their meat — primarily poor families — ran greater then usual risks of infection.

☆

PRIVY MATTERS

The most visible symbols of early American sanitation were privies or "necessary houses." But Americans did not always use them; many rural householders simply took to the closest available patch of woods or brush. However, in more densely settled communities and in regions with cold winters, privies were in widespread use. They were not usually put in out-of-the-way locations. The fashion of some Northern farm families, according to Robert B. Thomas's *Farmer's Almanack* in 1826, had long been to have their "necessary planted in a garden or other conspicuous place." Other countryfolk went even further in turning human wastes to agricultural account and built their outhouses "within the territory of a hog yard, that the swine may root and ruminate and devour the nastiness thereof." Thomas was a long-standing critic of primitive manners in the countryside and roundly condemned these traditional sanitary arrangements as demonstrating a "want of taste, decency, and propriety." The better arranged necessaries of the prosperous emptied into vaults that could be opened and cleaned out. The dripping horse-drawn carts of the "nocturnal goldfinders," who emptied the vaults and

took their loads out for burial or water disposal — "night soil" was almost never used as manure — were a familiar part of nighttime traffic on city streets.

The humblest pieces of American household furniture were the chamber pots that allowed people to avoid dark and often cold nighttime journeys outdoors. Kept under beds or in corners of rooms, "chambers" were used primarily upon retiring and arising. Collecting, emptying, and cleaning them remained an unspoken, daily part of every housewife's routine.

Nineteenth-century inventory takers became considerably more reticent about naming chamber pots than their predecessors, usually lumping them with miscellaneous "crockery," but most households probably had a couple of chamber pots; genteel families reached the optimum of one for each bedchamber. English-made ceramic pots had become cheap enough by 1820 that few American families within the reach of commerce needed to go without one. "Without a pot to piss in" was a vulgar tag of long standing for extreme poverty; those poorest households without one, perhaps more common in the warm South, used the outdoors at all times and seasons.

The most decorous way for householders to deal with chamber-pot wastes accumulated during the night was to throw them down the privy hole. But more casual and unsavory methods of disposal were still in wide use. Farm families often dumped their chamber pots out the most convenient door or window. In densely settled communities like York, Pennsylvania, the results could be more serious. In 1801, the York diarist Lewis Miller drew and then described an event in North George Street when "Mr. Day an English man [as the German-American Miller was quick to point out] had a bad practice by pouring out of the upper window his filthiness . . . one day came the discharge . . . on a man and wife going to a wedding, her silk dress was fouled."

☆

LETTING THE BEDBUGS BITE

Sleeping accommodations in American country taverns were often dirty and insect-ridden. The eighteenth-century observer of American life Isaac Weld saw "filthy beds swarming with bugs" in 1794; in 1840 Charles Dickens noted "a sort of game not on the bill of fare." Complaints increased in intensity as travelers went south or west. Tavern beds were uniquely vulnerable to infestation by whatever insect guests travelers brought with them. The bedding of most American households was surely less foul. Yet it was dirty enough. New England farmers were still too often "tormented all night by bed bugs," complained *The Farmer's Almanack* in 1837, and books of domestic advice contained extensive instructions on removing them from feather beds and straw ticks.

Journeying between Washington and New Orleans in 1828, Margaret Hall, a well-to-do and cultivated Scottish woman, became far more familiar with intimate insect life than she had ever been in the genteel houses of London or Edinburgh. Her letters home, never intended for publication, gave a graphic and unsparing account of American sanitary conditions. After sleeping in a succession of beds with the "usual complement of fleas and bugs," she and her party had themselves become infested: "We bring them along with us in our clothes and when I undress I find them crawling on my skin, nasty wretches." New and distasteful to her, such discoveries were commonplace among the ordinary folk with whom she lodged. The American children she saw on her Southern journey were "kept in such a state of filth," with clothes "dirty and slovenly to a degree," but this was "nothing in comparison with their heads . . . [which] are absolutely crawling!" In New Orleans she observed women picking through children's heads for lice, "catching them

according to the method depicted in an engraving of a similar proceeding in the streets of Naples."

☆

BIRTH OF THE BATH

Americans were not "clean and decent" by today's standards, and it was virtually impossible that they should be. The furnishings and use of rooms in most American houses made more than the most elementary washing difficult. In a New England farmer's household, wrote Underwood, each household member would "go down to the 'sink' in the lean-to, next to the kitchen, fortunate if he had not to break ice in order to wash his face and hands, or more fortunate if a little warm water was poured into his basin from the kettle swung over the kitchen fire." Even in the comfortable household of the prominent minister Lyman Beecher in Litchfield, Connecticut, around 1815, all family members washed in the kitchen, using a stone sink and "a couple of basins."

Southerners washing in their detached kitchens or, like Westerners in warm weather, washed outside, "at the doors . . . or at the wells" of their houses. Using basins and sinks outdoors or in full view of others, most Americans found anything more than "washing the face and hands once a-day," usually in cold water, difficult, even unthinkable. Most men and women also washed without soap, reserving it for laundering clothes; instead they used a brisk rubbing with a course towel to scrub the dirt off their skins.

Gradually the practice of complete bathing spread beyond the topmost levels of American society and into smaller towns and villages. This became possible as families moved washing equipment out of kitchens and into bedchambers, from shared space to space that could be made private. As more prosperous households furnished one or two of their chambers with washing equipment — a washstand, a basin, and a ewer, or large-mouthed pitcher — family members could shut the chamber door, undress, and wash themselves completely. The daughters of the Larcom family, living in Lowell, Massachusetts, in the late 1830s, began to bathe in a bedchamber in this way; Lucy Larcom described how her oldest sister started to take "a full cold bath every morning before she went to her work . . . in a room without a fire," and the other young Larcoms "did the same whenever we could be resolute enough." By the 1830s better city hotels and even some country taverns were providing individual basins and pitchers in their rooms.

At a far remove from "primitive manners" and "bad practices" was the genteel ideal of domestic sanitation embodied in the "chamber sets" — matching basin and ewer for private bathing, a cup for brushing the teeth, and a chamber pot with cover to minimize odor and spillage — that American stores were beginning to stock. By 1840 a significant minority of American households owned chamber sets and washstands to hold them in their bedchambers. For a handful there was the very faint dawning of an entirely new age of sanitary arrangements. In 1829 the new Tremont House hotel in Boston offered its patrons indoor plumbing: eight chambers with bathtubs and eight "water closets." In New York City and Philadelphia, which had developed rudimentary public water systems, a few wealthy households had water taps and, more rarely, water closets by the 1830s. For all others flush toilets and bathtubs remained far in the future.

The American people moved very slowly toward cleanliness. In "the backcountry at the present day," commented the fastidious author of the *Lady's Book* in 1836, custom still "requires that everyone should wash at the pump in the yard, or at the sink in the kitchen." Writing in 1846, the physician and health reformer William Alcott rejoiced that to "wash the surface of the whole body in water daily" had now been accepted as a genteel standard of personal cleanliness. But, he added, there were "multitudes who pass for models of neatness and cleanliness, who do not perform this work for themselves half a dozen times — nay once — a year." As the better-off became cleaner than ever before, the poor stayed dirty.

☆

Besotted Era

In the early part of the century America was a bawdy, hard-edged, and violent land. We drank more than we ever had before or ever would again. We smoked and chewed tobacco like addicts and fought and quarreled on the flimsiest pretexts. The tavern was the most important gateway to the primarily male world of drink and disorder: in sight of the village church in most American communities, observed Daniel Drake, a Cincinnati physician who wrote a reminiscence of his Kentucky boyhood, stood the village tavern, and the two structures "did in fact represent two great opposing principles."

The great majority of American men in every region were taverngoers. The printed street directories of American cities listed tavernkeepers in staggering numbers, and even the best-churched parts of New England could show more "licensed houses" than meetinghouses. In 1827 the fast-growing city of Rochester, New York, with a population of approximately eight thousand, had nearly one hundred establishments licensed to sell liquor, or one for every eighty inhabitants.

America's most important centers of male sociability, taverns were often the scene of excited gaming and vicious fights and always of hard drinking, heavy smoking, and an enormous amount of alcohol-stimulated talk. City men came to their neighborhood taverns daily, and "tavern haunting, tippling, and gaming," as Samuel Goodrich, a New

England historian and publisher, remembered, "were the chief resources of men in the dead and dreary winter months" in the countryside.

City taverns catered to clienteles of different classes: sordid sailors' grog-shops near the waterfront were rife with brawling and prostitution; neighborhood taverns and liquor-selling groceries were visited by craftsmen and clerks; well-appointed and relatively decorous places were favored by substantial merchants. Taverns on busy highways often specialized in teamsters or stage passengers, while country inns took their patrons as they came.

Taverns accommodated women as travelers, but their barroom clienteles were almost exclusively male. Apart from the dockside dives frequented by prostitutes, or the liquor-selling groceries of poor city neighborhoods, women rarely drank in public.

Gambling was a substantial preoccupation for many male citizens of the early republic. Men played billiards at tavern tables for money stakes. They threw dice in "hazard," slamming the dice boxes down so hard and so often that tavern tables wore the characteristic scars of their play. Even more often Americans sat down to cards, playing brag, similar to modern-day poker, or an elaborate table game called faro. Outdoors they wagered with each other on horse races or bet on cockfights and wrestling matches.

Drink permeated and propelled the social world of early-nineteenth-century America — first as an unquestioned presence and later as a serious and divisive problem. "Liquor at that time," recalled the builder and architect Elbridge Boyden, "was used as commonly as the food we ate." Before 1820 the vast majority of Americans considered alcohol an essential stimulant to exertion as well as a symbol of hospitality and fellowship. Like the Kentuckians with whom Daniel Drake grew up, they "regarded it as a duty to their families and visitors . . . to keep the bottle well replenished." Weddings, funerals, frolics, even a casual "gathering of two or three neighbors for an evening's social chat" required the obligatory "spirituous liquor" — rum, whiskey, or gin — "at all seasons and on all occasions."

Northern householders drank hard cider as their common table beverage, and all ages drank it freely. Dramming — taking a fortifying glass in the forenoon and again in the afternoon — was part of the daily regimen of many men. Clergymen took sustaining libations between services, lawyers before going to court, and physicians at their patients' bedsides. To raise a barn or get through a long day's haying without fortifying drink seemed a virtual impossibility. Slaves enjoyed hard drinking at festival times and at Saturday-night barbecues as much as any of their countrymen. But of all Americans they probably drank the least on a daily basis because their masters could usually control their access to liquor.

In Parma, Ohio, in the mid-1820s, Lyndon Freeman, a farmer, and his brothers were used to seeing men "in their cups" and passed them by without comment. But one dark and rainy night they discovered something far more shocking, "nothing less than a *woman beastly drunk* . . . with a flask of whiskey by her side." American women drank as well as men, but usually much less heavily. They were more likely to make themselves "tipsy" with hard cider and alcohol-containing patent medicines than to become inebriated with rum or whiskey. Temperance advocates in the late 1820s estimated that men consumed fifteen times the volume of distilled spirits that women did; this may have been a considerable exaggeration, but there was a great difference in drinking habits between the sexes. Americans traditionally found drunkenness tolerable and forgivable in men but deeply shameful in women.

By almost any standard, Americans drank not only nearly universally but in large quantities. Their yearly consumption at the time of the Revolution has been estimated at the equivalent of three and one-half gallons of pure two-hundred-proof alcohol for each person. After 1790 American men began to drink even more. By the late 1820s their imbibing

LIFE IN AN AMERICAN HOTEL?

This British cartoon suggests the American propensity to violence in a hard-edged, hard-drinking era, when people fought often and with relish. Perhaps the irritable fellow with the gun spent a sleepless night battling the hotel's bed bugs. (Punch, June 28, 1856)

had risen to an all-time high of almost four gallons per capita.

Along with drinking went fighting. Americans fought often and with great relish. York, Pennsylvania, for example, was a peaceable place as American communities went, but the Miller and Weaver families had a long-running quarrel. It had begun in 1800 when the Millers found young George Weaver stealing apples in their yard and punished him by "throwing him over the fence," injuring him painfully. Over the years hostilities broke out periodically. Lewis Miller remembered walking down the street as a teenaged boy and meeting Mrs. Weaver, who drenched him with the bucket of water she was carrying. He retaliated by "turning about and giving her a kick, laughing at her, this is for your politeness." Other York households had their quarrels too; in "a general fight on Beaver Street," Mistress Hess and Mistress Forsch tore each other's caps from their heads. Their husbands and then the

186

neighbors interfered, and "all of them had a knock down."

When Peter Lung's wife, Abigail, refused "to get up and dig some potatoes" for supper from the yard of their small house, the Hartford, Connecticut, laborer recalled in his confession, he "kicked her on the side . . . then gave her a violent push" and went out to dig the potatoes himself. He returned and "again kicked her against the shoulder and neck." Both had been drinking, and loud arguments and blows within the Lung household, as in many others, were routine. But this time the outcome was not. Abigail Lung was dead the next day, and Peter Lung was arrested, tried, and hanged for murder in 1815.

In the most isolated, least literate and commercialized parts of the United States, it was "by no means uncommon," wrote Isaac Weld, "to meet with those who have lost an eye in a combat, and there are men who pride themselves upon the dexterity with which they can scoop one out. This is called *gouging.*"

☆

THE SLAVE'S LOT

Slaves wrestled among themselves, sometimes fought one another bitterly over quarrels in the quarters, and even at times stood up to the vastly superior force of masters and overseers. They rarely, if ever, reduced themselves to the ferocity of eye gouging. White Southerners lived with a pervasive fear of the violent potential of their slaves, and the Nat Turner uprising in Virginia in 1831, when a party of slaves rebelled and killed whites before being overcome, gave rise to tighter and harsher controls. But in daily reality slaves had far more to fear from their masters.

Margaret Hall was no proponent of abolition and had little sympathy for black Americans. Yet in her travels south she confronted incidents of what she ironically called the "good treatment of slaves" that were impossible to ignore. At a country tavern in Georgia, she summoned the slave chambermaid, but "she could not come" because "the mistress had been whipping her and she was not fit to be seen. Next morning she made her appearance with her face marked in several places by the cuts of the cow-skin and her neck handkerchief covered with spots of blood."

Southern stores were very much like Northern ones, Francis Kemble Butler observed, except that they stocked "negro-whips" and "mantraps" on their shelves. A few slaves were never beaten at all, and for most, whippings were not a daily or weekly occurrence. But they were, of all Americans, by far the most vulnerable to violence. All slaves had, as William Wells Brown, an ex-slave himself, said, often "heard the crack of the whip, and the screams of the slave" and knew that they were never more than a white man's or women's whim away from a beating. With masters' unchecked power came worse than whipping: the mutilating punishments of the old penal law including branding, ear crop-ping, and even occasionally castration and burning alive as penalties for severe offenses. In public places or along the road blacks were also subject to casual kicks, shoves, and cuffs, for which they could retali-ate only at great peril. "Six or seven feet in length, made of cowhide, with a platted wire on the end of it," as Brown recalled it, the negro-whip, for sale in most stores and brandished by masters and over-seers in the fields, stood for a pervasive climate of force and intimidation.

☆

PUBLIC PUNISHMENT

The penal codes of the American states were far less bloodthirsty than those of England. Capital punish-ment was not often imposed on whites for crimes other than murder. Yet at the beginning of the nine-teenth century many criminal offenses were pun-ished by the public infliction of pain and suffering.

"The whipping post and stocks stood on the green near the meetinghouse" in most of the towns of New England and near courthouses everywhere. In Massachusetts before 1805 a counterfeiter was liable to have an ear cut off, and a forger to have one cropped or partially amputated, after spending an hour in the pillory. A criminal convicted of man-slaughter was set up on the gallows to have his fore-head branded with a letter M. In most jurisdictions town officials flogged petty thieves as punishment for their crime. In New Haven, Connecticut, around 1810, Charles Fowler, a local historian, re-called seeing the "admiring students of [Yale] col-lege" gathered around to watch petty criminals re-ceive "five or ten lashes . . . with a rawhide whip."

Throughout the United States public hangings brought enormous crowds to the seats of justice and sometimes seemed like brutal festivals. Thousands of spectators arrived to pack the streets of courthouse towns. On the day of a hanging near Mount Holly, New Jersey, in the 1820s, the scene was that of a holiday: "around the place in every direction were the assembled multitudes — some in tents, and by-wagons, engaged in gambling and other vices of the sort, in open day." In order to accommodate the throngs, hangings were usually held not in the pub-lic square but on the outskirts of town. The gallows erected on a hill or set up at the bottom of a natural amphitheater allowed onlookers an unobstructed view. A reprieve or stay of execution might disap-point a crowd intent on witnessing the deadly drama and provoke a riot, as it did in Pembroke, New Hampshire, in 1834.

☆

RISE OF
RESPECTABILITY

At a drunkard's funeral in Enfield, Massachusetts, in the 1830s — the man had strayed out of the road while walking home and fallen over a cliff, "his stiffened fingers still grasping the handle of the

187

jug'' — Rev. Sumner G. Clapp, the Congregation-alist minister of Enfield, mounted a log by the woodpile and preached the town's first temperance sermon before a crowd full of hardened drinkers. In this way Clapp began a campaign to ''civilize'' the manners of his parishioners, and ''before many years there was a great change in the town; the incorrigi-ble were removed by death, and others took warn-ing.'' Drinking declined sharply, and along with it went ''a general reform in conduct.''

Although it remained a powerful force in many parts of the United States, the American way of drunkenness began to lose ground as early as the mid–1820s. The powerful upsurge in liquor con-sumption had provoked a powerful reaction, an un-precedented attack on all forms of drink that gath-ered momentum in the Northeast. Some New England clergymen had been campaigning in their own communities as early as 1810, but their con-cerns took on organized impetus with the founding of the American Temperance Society in 1826. Ener-gized in part by a concern for social order, in part by evangelical piety, temperance reformers popular-ized a radically new way of looking at alcohol. The ''good creature'' became ''demon rum''; promi-nent physicians and writers on physiology, like Ben-jamin Rush, told Americans that alcohol, tradition-ally considered healthy and fortifying, was actually a physical and moral poison. National and state soci-eties distributed anti-liquor tracts, at first calling for moderation in drink but increasingly demanding to-tal abstinence from alcohol.

To a surprising degree these aggressive temper-ance campaigns worked. By 1840 the consumption of alcohol had declined by more than two-thirds, from close to four gallons per person each year to less than one and one-half. Country storekeepers gave up the sale of spirits, local authorities limited the number of tavern licenses, and farmers even abandoned hard cider and cut down their apple or-chards. The shift to temperance was a striking trans-formation in the everyday habits of an enormous number of Americans. ''A great, though silent change,'' in Horace Greeley's words, had been ''wrought in public sentiment.'' . . .

Closely linked as they were to drink, such diver-sions as gambling, racing, and blood sports also fell to the same forces of change. In the central Massa-chusetts region that George Davis, a lawyer in Stur-bridge, knew well, until 1820 or so gaming had ''continued to prevail, more and more extensively.'' After that ''a blessed change had succeeded,'' over-turning the scenes of high-stakes dice and card games that he knew in his young manhood. Im-pelled by a new perception of its ''pernicious ef-fects,'' local leaders gave it up and placed ''men of respectable standing'' firmly in opposition. Race-courses were abandoned and ''planted to corn.'' Likewise, ''bear-baiting, cock-fighting, and other cruel amusements'' began to dwindle in the North-ern countryside. Elsewhere the rude life of the tav-ern and ''cruel amusements'' remained widespread, but some of their excesses of ''sin and shame'' did diminish gradually.

Over the first four decades of the nineteenth cen-tury the American people increasingly made church-going an obligatory ritual. The proportion of fami-lies affiliated with a local church or Methodist circuit rose dramatically, particularly after 1820, and there were fewer stretches of the wholly pagan, un-churched territory that travelers had noted around 1800. ''Since 1830,'' maintained Emerson Davis in his retrospect of America, *The Half Century,* ''. . . the friends of the Sabbath have been gaining ground. . . . In 1800, good men slumbered over the desecra-tion of the Sabbath. They have since awoke. . . .'' The number of Sunday mails declined, and the cam-paign to eliminate the delivery of mail on the Sabbath entirely grew stronger. ''In the smaller cities and towns,'' wrote Mrs. Trollope in 1832, worship and ''prayer meetings'' had come to ''take the place of almost all other amusements.'' There were still com-munities near the edge of settlement where a traveler would ''rarely find either churches or chapels, prayer or preacher," but it was the working-class neighborhoods of America's larger cities that were increasingly the chief strongholds of "Sunday dissipation" and "Sabbath-breaking."

Whipping and the pillory, with their attentive audiences, began to disappear from the statute book, to be replaced by terms of imprisonment in another new American institution, the state penitentiary. Beginning with Pennsylvania's abolition of flogging in 1790 and Massachusetts's elimination of mutilating punishments in 1805, several American states gradually accepted John Hancock's view of 1796 that "mutilating or lacerating the body" was less an effective punishment than "an indignity to human nature." Connecticut's town constables whipped petty criminals for the last time in 1828.

Slaveholding states were far slower to change their provisions for public punishment. The whipping and mutilation of blacks may have become a little less ferocious over the decades, but the whip remained the essential instrument of punishment and discipline. "The secret of our success," thought a slave owner, looking back after emancipation, had been "the great motive power contained in that little instrument." Delaware achieved notoriety by keeping flogging on the books for whites and blacks alike through most of the twentieth century.

Although there were important stirrings of sentiment against capital punishment, all American states continued to execute convicted murders before the mid–1840s. Public hangings never lost their drawing power. But a number of American public officials began to abandon the long-standing view of executions as instructive communal rituals. They saw the crowd's holiday mood and eager participation as sharing too much in the condemned killer's own brutality. Starting with Pennsylvania, New York, and Massachusetts in the mid-1830s, several state legislatures voted to take executions away from the crowd, out of the public realm. Sheriffs began to carry out death sentences behind the walls of the jailyard, before a small assembly of representative onlookers. Other states clung much longer to tradition and continued public executions into the twentieth century.

☆

SEX LIFE
OF THE NATIVES

Early-nineteenth-century Americans were more licentious than we ordinarily imagine them to be.

"On the 20th day of July" in 1830, Harriet Winter, a young woman working as a domestic in Joseph Dunham's household in Brimfield, Massachusetts, "was gathering raspberries" in a field west of the house. "Near the close of day," Charles Phelps, a farm laborer then living in the town, "came to the field where she was," and in the gathering dusk they made love — and, Justice of the Peace Asa Lincoln added in his account, "it was the Sabbath." American communities did not usually document their inhabitants' amorous rendezvous, and Harriet's tryst with Charles was a commonplace event in early-nineteenth-century America. It escaped historical oblivion because she was unlucky, less in becoming pregnant than in Charles's refusal to marry her. Asa Lincoln did not approve of Sabbath evening indiscretions, but he was not pursuing Harriet for immorality. He was concerned instead with economic responsibility for the child. Thus he interrogated Harriet about the baby's father — while she was in labor, as was the long-customary practice — in order to force Charles to contribute to the maintenance of the child, who was going to be "born a bastard and chargeable to the town."

Some foreign travelers found that the Americans they met were reluctant to admit that such things happened in the United States. They were remarkably straitlaced about sexual matters in public and eager to insist upon the "purity" of their manners. But to take such protestations at face value, the unusually candid Englishman Frederick Marryat thought, would be "to suppose that human nature is not the same everywhere."

The well-organized birth and marriage records of a number of American communities reveal that in late-eighteenth-century America pregnancy was frequently the prelude to marriage. The proportion of brides who were pregnant at the time of their weddings had been rising since the late seventeenth century and peaked in the turbulent decades during and after the Revolution. In the 1780s and 1790s nearly one-third of rural New England's brides were already with child. The frequency of sexual intercourse before marriage was surely higher, since some couples would have escaped early pregnancy. For many couples sexual relations were part of serious courtship. Premarital pregnancies in late-eighteenth-century Dedham, Massachusetts, observed the local historian Erastus Worthington in 1828, were occasioned by "the custom then prevalent of females admitting young men to their beds, who sought their company in marriage."

Pregnancies usually simply accelerated a marriage that would have taken place in any case, but community and parental pressure worked strongly to assure it. Most rural communities simply accepted the "early" pregnancies that marked so many marriages, although in Hingham, Massachusetts, tax records suggest that the families of well-to-do brides were considerably less generous to couples who had had "early babies" than to those who had avoided pregnancy.

"Bundling very much abounds," wrote the anonymous author of "A New Bundling Song," still circulating in Boston in 1812, "in many parts in country towns." Noah Webster's first *Dictionary of the American Language* defined it as the custom that allowed couples "to sleep on the same bed without undressing" — with, a later commentator added, "the shared understanding that innocent endearments should not be exceeded." Folklore and local tradition, from Maine south to New York, had American mothers tucking bundling couples into bed with special chastity-protecting garments for the young woman or a "bundling board" to separate them.

In actuality, if bundling had been intended to allow courting couples privacy and emotional intimacy but not sexual contact, it clearly failed. Couples may have begun with bundling, but as courtship advanced, they clearly pushed beyond its restraints, like the "bundling maid" in "A New Bundling Song" who would "sometimes say when she lies down/She can't be cumbered with a gown."

Young black men and women shared American whites' freedom in courtship and sexuality and sometimes exceeded it. Echoing the cultural traditions of West Africa, and reflecting the fact that their marriages were not given legal status and security, slave communities were somewhat more tolerant and accepting of sex before marriage.

Gradations of color and facial features among the slaves were testimony that "thousands," as the abolitionist and former slave Frederick Douglass wrote, were "ushered into the world annually, who, like myself, owe the existence to white fathers, and those fathers most frequently their own masters." Sex crossed the boundaries of race and servitude more often than slavery's defenders wanted to admit, if less frequently than the most outspoken abolitionists claimed. Slave women had little protection from whatever sexual demands masters or overseers might make, so that rapes, short liaisons, and long-term "concubinage" all were part of plantation life.

As Nathaniel Hawthorne stood talking with a group of men on the porch of a tavern in Augusta, Maine, in 1836, a young man "in a laborer's dress" came up and asked if anyone knew the whereabouts of Mary Ann Russell. "Do you want to use her?" asked one of the bystanders. Mary Ann was, in fact, the young laborer's wife, but she had left him and their child in Portland to become "one of a knot of whores." A few years earlier the young men of

York, Pennsylvania, made up a party for "overturning and pulling to the ground" Eve Geese's "shameful house" of prostitution in Queen Street. The frightened women fled out the back door as the chimney collapsed around them; the apprentices and young journeymen — many of whom had surely been previous customers — were treated by local officials "to wine, for the good work."

From medium-sized towns like Augusta and York to great cities, poor American women were sometimes pulled into a darker, harsher sexual world, one of vulnerability, exploitation, and commerce. Many prostitutes took up their trade out of poverty and domestic disaster. A young widow or a country girl arrived in the city and, thrown on her own resources, often faced desperate economic choices because most women's work paid too poorly to provide decent food, clothing, and shelter, while other women sought excitement and independence from their families.

As cities grew, and changes in transportation involved more men in long-distance travel, prostitution became more visible. Men of all ages, married and unmarried, from city lawyers to visiting country storekeepers to sailors on the docks, turned to brothels for sexual release, but most of the customers were young men, living away from home and unlikely to marry until their late twenties. Sexual commerce in New York City was elaborately graded by price and the economic status of clients, from the "parlor houses" situated not far from the city's best hotels on Broadway to the more numerous and moderately priced houses that drew artisans and clerks, and finally to the broken and dissipated women who haunted dockside grogshops in the Five Points neighborhood.

From New Orleans to Boston, city theaters were important sexual marketplaces. Men often bought tickets less to see the performance than to make assignations with the prostitutes, who sat by custom in the topmost gallery of seats. The women usually received free admission from theater managers, who claimed that they could not stay in business without the male theatergoers drawn by the "guilty third tier."

Most Americans — and the American common law — still did not regard abortion as a crime until the fetus had "quickened" or began to move perceptibly in the womb. Books of medical advice actually contained prescriptions for bringing on delayed menstrual periods, which would also produce an abortion if the woman happened to be pregnant. They suggested heavy doses of purgatives that created violent cramps, powerful douches, or extreme kinds of physical activity, like the "violent exercise, raising great weights . . . strokes on the belly . . . [and] falls" noted in William Buchan's *Domestic Medicine,* a manual read widely through the 1820s. Women's folklore echoed most of these prescriptions and added others, particularly the use of two American herbal preparations — savin, or the extract of juniper berries, and Seneca snakeroot — as abortion-producing drugs. They were dangerous procedures but sometimes effective.

☆

REINING IN
THE PASSIONS

Starting at the turn of the nineteenth century, the sexual lives of many Americans began to change, shaped by a growing insistence on control: reining in the passions in courtship, limiting family size, and even redefining male and female sexual desire.

Bundling was already on the wane in rural America before 1800; by the 1820s it was written about as a rare and antique custom. It had ceased, thought an elderly man from East Haddam, Connecticut, "as a consequence of education and refinement." Decade by decade the proportion of young women who had conceived a child before marriage declined. In most of the towns of New England the rate had dropped from nearly one pregnant bride in three to one in five or six by 1840; in some places prenuptial pregnancy dropped to 5 percent. For many young Americans this marked the acceptance of new limits on sexual behavior, imposed not by their parents or other authorities in their communities but by themselves.

These young men and women were not more closely supervised by their parents than earlier generations had been; in fact, they had more mobility and greater freedom. The couples that courted in the new style put a far greater emphasis on control of the passions. For some of them — young Northern merchants and professional men and their intended brides — revealing love letters have survived for the years after 1820. Their intimate correspondence reveals that they did not give up sexual expression but gave it new boundaries, reserving sexual intercourse for marriage. Many of them were marrying later than their parents, often living through long engagements while the husband-to-be strove to establish his place in the world. They chose not to risk a pregnancy that would precipitate them into an early marriage.

Many American husbands and wives were also breaking with tradition as they began to limit the size of their families. Clearly, married couples were renegotiating the terms of their sexual lives together, but they remained resolutely silent about how they did it. In the first two decades of the nineteenth century, they almost certainly set about avoiding childbirth through abstinence, coitus interruptus, or male withdrawal, and perhaps sometimes abortion. These contraceptive techniques had long been traditional in preindustrial Europe, although previously little used in America.

As they entered the 1830s, Americans had their first opportunity to learn, at least in print, about more effective or less self-denying forms of birth control. They could read reasonably inexpensive editions of the first works on contraception published in the United States: Robert Dale Owen's *Moral Physiology* of 1831 and Dr. Charles Knowlton's *The Fruits of Philosophy* of 1832. Both authors frankly described the full range of contraceptive techniques, although they solemnly rejected physical intervention in the sexual act and recommended only douching after intercourse and coitus interruptus. Official opinion, legal and religious, was deeply hostile. Knowlton, who had trained as a physician in rural Massachusetts, was prosecuted in three different counties for obscenity, convicted once, and imprisoned for three months.

But both works found substantial numbers of Americans eager to read them. By 1839 each book had gone through nine editions, putting a combined total of twenty to thirty thousand copies in circulation. An American physician could write in 1850 that contraception had "been of late years so much talked of." Greater knowledge about contraception surely played a part in the continuing decline of the American birthrate after 1830.

New ways of thinking about sexuality emerged that stressed control and channeling of the passions. Into the 1820s almost all Americans would have subscribed to the commonplace notion that sex, within proper social confines, was enjoyable and healthy and that prolonged sexual abstinence could be injurious to health. They also would have assumed that women had powerful sexual drives.

Starting with his "Lecture to Young Men on Chastity" in 1832, Sylvester Graham articulated very different counsels about health and sex. Sexual indulgence, he argued, was not only morally suspect but psychologically and physiologically risky. The sexual overstimulation involved in young men's lives produced anxiety and nervous disorders, "a shocking state of debility and excessive irritability." The remedy was diet, exercise, and a regular routine that pulled the mind away from animal lusts. Medical writings that discussed the evils of masturbation, or "solitary vice," began to appear. Popular books of advice, like William Alcott's *Young Man's Guide,* gave similar warnings. They tried to persuade young men that their health could be ruined, and their prospects for success darkened, by consorting with prostitutes or becoming sexually entangled before marriage.

A new belief about women's sexual nature appeared, one that elevated them above "carnal passion." Many American men and women came to believe during the nineteenth century that in their true and proper nature as mothers and guardians of the home, women were far less interested in sex than men were. Women who defined themselves as passionless were in a strong position to control or deny men's sexual demands either during courtship or in limiting their childbearing within marriage.

Graham went considerably farther than this, advising restraint not only in early life and courtship but in marriage itself. It was far healthier, he maintained, for couples to have sexual relations "very seldom."

Neither contraception nor the new style of courtship had become anything like universal by 1840. Prenuptial pregnancy rates had fallen, but they remained high enough to indicate that many couples simply continued in familiar ways. American husbands and wives in the cities and the Northern countryside were limiting the number of their children, but it was clear that those living on the farms of the West or in the slave quarters had not yet begun to. There is strong evidence that many American women felt far from passionless, although others restrained or renounced their sexuality. For many people in the United States, there had been a profound change. Reining in the passions had become part of everyday life.

☆

SMOKING AND SPITTING

Everyone smokes and some chew in America," wrote Isaac Weld in 1795. Americans turned tobacco, a new and controversial stimulant at the time

of colonial settlement, into a crucially important staple crop and made its heavy use a commonplace — and a never-ending source of surprise and indignation to visitors. Tobacco use spread in the United States because it was comparatively cheap, a home-grown product free from the heavy import duties levied on it by European governments. A number of slave rations described in plantation documents included "one hand of tobacco per month." Through the eighteenth century most American smokers used clay pipes, which are abundant in colonial archeological sites, although some men and women dipped snuff or inhaled powdered tobacco.

Where the smokers of early colonial America "drank" or gulped smoke through the short, thick stems of their seventeenth-century pipes, those of 1800 inhaled it more slowly and gradually; from the early seventeenth to the late eighteenth century, pipe stems became steadily longer and narrower, increasingly distancing smokers from their burning tobacco.

In the 1790s cigars, or "segars," were introduced from the Caribbean. Prosperous men widely took them up; they were the most expensive way to consume tobacco, and it was a sign of financial security to puff away on "long-nines" or "principe cigars at three cents each" while the poor used clay pipes and much cheaper "cut plug" tobacco. After 1800 in American streets, barrooms, stores, public conveyances, and even private homes it became nearly impossible to avoid tobacco chewers. Chewing extended tobacco use, particularly into workplaces; men who smoked pipes at home or in the tavern barroom could chew while working in barns or workshops where smoking carried the danger of fire.

"In all the public places of America," wrote Charles Dickens, multitudes of men engaged in "the odious practice of chewing and expectorating," a recreation practiced by all ranks of American society. Chewing stimulated salivation and gave rise to a public environment of frequent and copious spitting, where men every few minutes were "squirting a mouthful of saliva through the room."

Spittoons were provided in the more meticulous establishments, but men often ignored them. The floors of American public buildings were not pleasant to contemplate. A courtroom in New York City in 1833 was decorated by a "mass of abomination" contributed to by "judges, counsel, jury, witnesses, officers, and audience." The floor of the Virginia House of Burgesses in 1827 was "actually flooded with their horrible spitting," and even the aisle of a Connecticut meetinghouse was black with the "ejection after ejection, incessant from twenty mouths," of the men singing in the choir. In order to drink, an American man might remove his quid, put it in a pocket or hold it in his hand, take his glassful, and then restore it to his mouth. Women's dresses might even be in danger at fashionable balls. "One night as I was walking upstairs to valse," reported Margaret Hall of a dance in Washington in 1828, "my partner began clearing his throat. This I thought ominous. However, I said to myself, 'surely he will turn his head to the other side.' The gentleman, however, had no such thought but deliberately shot across me. I had not courage enough to examine whether the result landed in the flounce of my dress."

The segar and the quid were almost entirely male appurtenances, but as the nineteenth century began, many rural and lower-class urban women were smoking pipes or dipping snuff. During his boyhood in New Hampshire, Horace Greeley remembered, "it was often my filial duty to fill and light my mother's pipe."

After 1820 or so tobacco use among women in the North began to decline. Northern women remembered or depicted with pipe or snuffbox were almost all elderly. More and more Americans adopted a genteel standard that saw tobacco use and womanliness — delicate and nurturing — as antithetical, and young women avoided it as a pollutant.

For them, tobacco use marked off male from female territory with increasing sharpness.

In the households of small Southern and Western farmers, however, smoking and snuff taking remained common. When women visited "among the country people" of North Carolina, Frances Kemble Butler reported in 1837, the "proffer of the snuffbox, and its passing from hand to hand, is the usual civility." By the late 1830s visiting New Englanders were profoundly shocked when they saw the women of Methodist congregations in Illinois, including nursing mothers, taking out their pipes for a smoke between worship services.

☆

FROM DEFERENCE TO EQUALITY

The Americans of 1820 would have been more recognizable to us in the informal and egalitarian way they treated one another. The traditional signs of deference before social superiors — the deep bow, the "courtesy," the doffed cap, lowered head, and averted eyes — had been a part of social relationships in colonial America. In the 1780s, wrote the American poetess Lydia Huntley Sigourney in 1824, there were still "individuals . . . in every grade of society" who had grown up "when a bow was not an offense to fashion nor . . . a relic of monarchy." But in the early nineteenth century such signals of subordination rapidly fell away. It was a natural consequence of the Revolution, she maintained, which, "in giving us liberty, obliterated almost every vestige of politeness of the 'old school.'" Shaking hands became the accustomed American greeting between men, a gesture whose symmetry and mutuality signified equality. Frederick Marryat found in 1835 that it was "invariably the custom to shake hands" when he was introduced to Americans and that he could not carefully grade the acknowledgment he would give to new acquaintances according to their signs of wealth and breeding. He found instead that he had to "go on shaking hands here, there and everywhere, and with everybody." Americans were not blind to inequalities of economic and social power, but they less and less gave them overt physical expression. Bred in a society where such distinctions were far more clearly spelled out, Marryat was somewhat disoriented in the United States; "it is impossible to know who is who," he claimed, "in this land of equality."

Well-born British travelers encountered not just confusion but conflict when they failed to receive the signs of respect they expected. Margaret Hall's letters home during her Southern travels outlined a true comedy of manners. At every stage stop in the Carolinas, Georgia, and Alabama, she demanded that country tavernkeepers and their households give her deferential service and well-prepared meals; she received instead rancid bacon and "such an absence of all kindness of feeling, such unbending frigid heartlessness." But she and her family had a far greater share than they realized in creating this chilly reception. Squeezed between the pride and poise of the great planters and the social debasement of the slaves, small Southern farmers often displayed a prickly insolence, a considered lack of response, to those who too obviously considered themselves their betters. Greatly to their discomfort and incomprehension, the Halls were experiencing what a British traveler more sympathetic to American ways, Patrick Shirreff, called "the democratic rudeness which assumed or presumptuous superiority seldom fails to experience."

☆

LAND OF ABUNDANCE

In the seventeenth century white American colonials were no taller than their European counterparts, but by the time of the Revolution they were close to their late-twentieth-century average height for men of slightly over five feet eight inches. The citizens of the early republic towered over most Europeans. Americans' early achievement of modern stature — by a full century and more — was a striking consequence of American abundance. Americans were taller because they were better nourished than the great majority of the world's peoples.

Yet not all Americans participated equally in the nation's abundance. Differences in stature between whites and blacks, and between city and country dwellers, echoed those between Europeans and Americans. Enslaved blacks were a full inch shorter than whites. But they remained a full inch taller than European peasants and laborers and were taller still than their fellow slaves eating the scanty diets afforded by the more savagely oppressive plantation system of the West Indies. And by 1820 those who lived in the expanding cities of the United States — even excluding immigrants, whose heights would have reflected European, not American, conditions — were noticeably shorter than the people of the countryside, suggesting an increasing concentration of poverty and poorer diets in urban places.

Across the United States almost all country households ate the two great American staples: corn and "the eternal pork," as one surfeited traveler called it, "which makes its appearance on every American table, high and low, rich and poor." Families in the cattle-raising, dairying country of New England, New York, and northern Ohio ate butter, cheese, and salted beef as well as pork and made their bread from wheat flour or rye and Indian corn. In Pennsylvania, as well as Maryland, Delaware, and Virginia, Americans ate the same breadstuffs as their Northern neighbors, but their consumption of cheese and beef declined every mile southward in favor of pork.

Farther to the south, and in the West, corn and corn-fed pork were truly "eternal"; where reliance on them reached its peak in the Southern uplands, they were still the only crops many small farmers raised. Most Southern and Western families built their diets around smoked and salted bacon, rather than the Northerners' salt pork, and, instead of wheat or rye bread, made cornpone or hoecake, a coarse, strong bread, and hominy, pounded Indian corn boiled together with milk.

Before 1800, a game — venison, possum, raccoon, and wild fowl — was for many American households "a substantial portion of the supply of food at certain seasons of the year," although only on the frontier was it a regular part of the diet. In the West and South this continued to be true, but in the Northeast game became increasingly rare as forests gave way to open farmland, where wild animals could not live.

Through the first half of the eighteenth century, Americans had been primarily concerned with obtaining a sufficiency of meat and bread for their families; they paid relatively little attention to foodstuffs other than these two "staffs of life," but since that time the daily fare of many households had grown substantially more diverse. . . .

Important patterns of regional, class, and ethnic distinctiveness remain in American everyday life. But they are far less powerful, and less central to understanding American experience, than they once were. Through the rest of the nineteenth century and into the twentieth, the United States became ever more diverse, with new waves of Eastern and Southern European immigrants joining the older Americans of Northern European stock. Yet the new arrivals — and even more, their descendants — have experienced the attractiveness and reshaping power of a national culture formed by department stores, newspapers, radios, movies, and universal public education. America, the developing nation,

developed into us. And perhaps our manners and morals, to some future observer, will seem as idiosyncratic and astonishing as this portrait of our earlier self.

QUESTIONS TO CONSIDER

1 Compare Larkin's description of American urban conditions, crime, disorder, and drunkenness with the conditions Page Smith found in seventeenth-century London (selection 2). Were these Americans worse or better off than their English forbears? How did the American legal response to crime and disorder compare to the earlier British model?

2 Bacterial pollution from animal and human wastes, offal, open drains, and contaminated water were major threats to American health in the early nineteenth century. Are we more fortunate nearly two centuries later, or have we found new ways to poison our environment? Which era do you think is the more deadly?

3 Larkin is a social and cultural historian. What sources has he used to compile his vivid account of everyday life among ordinary Americans in the early nineteenth century? What are the advantages of using these sources? Potential disadvantages?

4 Larkin points out that American women drank less than a third as much as American men at the turn of the nineteenth century and that alcohol consumption by slaves was also limited. A few decades later women spearheaded the temperance movement in communities all over the country. What issues of social control do you suppose were in operation throughout this period?

5 In what personal ways are these ordinary nineteenth-century Americans different from us today? How are they the same? What distinctively American traits does Larkin suggest were born in this era?

14

The Labor of Life:
Changing Customs of Childbirth

Catherine M. Scholten

Before the 1760s, as Catherine Scholten suggests, the midwife was one of the most important figures in American family and social life. Summoned to the bedside of a woman in labor, she took full charge, with the assistance of other women. The midwife comforted the expectant mother, gave her hard liquor or wine, and helped her as she gave birth, which she did by squatting on a midwife's stool, kneeling on a pallet, or sitting on another woman's lap. In addition to her work in childbirth, the midwife might serve as the mother's confidante and even attend her child's baptism. In those days, people regarded childbearing as something that women must suffer with the help and encouragement of other women while the men stayed away.

But after the 1760s, all this began to change in the urban areas of the Republic. With the growth of medical knowledge on both sides of the Atlantic, male physicians gradually assumed the practice of midwifery, and increasing numbers of well-to-do women turned to them for advice and attendance in childbearing. By 1825, the male doctor had largely supplanted the midwife in urban America, shutting her out of an area of medicine that had once been her particular domain. Scholten explains why this shift occurred and draws a vivid and often troubling comparison between the art of midwifery as practiced by women and the "science" of male-dominated obstetrics that eventually replaced it. Scholten's story illuminates significant changes in attitude toward women as patients and professionals, changes that foreshadowed the Victorian views of women that gained ascendancy in the mid-nineteenth century.

IN OCTOBER 1799, as Sally Downing of Philadelphia labored to give birth to her sixth child, her mother, Elizabeth Drinker, watched her suffer "in great distress." Finally, on the third day of fruitless labor, Sally's physician, William Shippen, Jr., announced that "the child must be brought forward." Elizabeth Drinker wrote in her diary that, happily, Sally delivered naturally, although Dr. Shippen had said that "he thought he should have had occasion for instruments" and clapped his hand on his side, so that the forceps rattled in his pocket.

Elizabeth Drinker's account of her daughter's delivery is one of the few descriptions by an eighteenth-century American woman of a commonplace aspect of women's lives — childbirth. It is of special interest to social historians because it records the participation of a man in the capacity of physician. Shippen was a prominent member of the first generation of American doctors trained in obstetrics and, commencing in 1763, the first to maintain a regular practice attending women in childbirth. Until that time midwives managed almost all deliveries, but with Shippen male physicians began to supplant the midwives.

The changing social customs and medical management of childbirth from 1760 to 1825 . . . show that, beginning among well-to-do women in Philadelphia, New York, and Boston, childbirth became less a communal experience and more a private event confined within the intimate family. In consequence of new perceptions of urban life and of women, as well as of the development of medical science, birth became increasingly regarded as a medical problem to be managed by physicians. For when Shippen, fresh from medical studies in London, announced his intention to practice midwifery in Philadelphia

in 1763, he was proposing to enter a field considered the legitimate province of women. Childbearing had been viewed as the inevitable, even the divinely ordained, occasion of suffering for women; childbirth was an event shared by the female community; and delivery was supervised by a midwife.

During the colonial period childbearing occupied a central portion of the lives of women between their twentieth and fortieth years. Six to eight pregnancies were typical, and pregnant women were commonly described as "breeding" and "teeming." Such was women's natural lot; though theologians attributed dignity to carrying the "living soul" of a child and saluted mothers in their congregations with "Blessed are you among women," they also depicted the pains of childbirth as the appropriate special curse of "the Travailing Daughters of Eve." Two American tracts written specifically for lying-in women dwelt on the divinely ordained hazards of childbirth and advised a hearty course of meditation on death, "such as their pregnant condition must reasonably awaken them to."

Cotton Mather's pamphlet, *Elizabeth in Her Holy Retirement,* which he distributed to midwives to give to the women they cared for, described pregnancy as a virtually lethal condition. "For ought you know," it warned, "your Death has entered into you, you may have conceived that which determines but about Nine Months more at the most, for you to live in the World." Pregnancy was thus intended to inspire piety. . . .

Surely women did not need to be reminded of the risks of childbirth. The fears of Mary Clap, wife of Thomas Clap, president of Yale College, surface even through the ritual phrases of the elegy written by her husband after her death in childbirth at the age of twenty-four. Thomas remembered that before each of her six lyings-in his wife had asked him to pray with her that God would continue their lives together. Elizabeth Drinker probably echoed

Excerpts from "'On the Importance of the Obstetrick Art': Changing Customs of Childbirth in America, 1760 to 1825" by Catherine M. Scholten, *William and Mary Quarterly,* vol. 34 (1977), pp. 426–445. Reprinted by permission.

the sentiments of most women when she reflected, "I have often thought that women who live to get over the time of Child-bareing, if other things are favourable to them, experience more comfort and satisfaction than at any other period of their lives."

Facing the hazards of childbirth, women depended on the community of their sex for companionship and medical assistance. Women who had moved away at marriage frequently returned to their parents' home for the delivery, either because they had no neighbors or because they preferred the care of their mothers to that of their in-laws. Other women summoned mothers, aunts, and sisters on both sides of the family, as well as female friends, when birth was imminent. Above all, they relied on the experience of midwives to guide them through labor.

Women monopolized the practice of midwifery in America, as in Europe, through the middle of the eighteenth century. As the recognized experts in the conduct of childbirth, they advised the mother-to-be if troubles arose during pregnancy, supervised the activities of lying-in, and used their skills to assure safe delivery. Until educated male physicians began to practice obstetrics, midwives enjoyed some status in the medical profession, enhanced by their legal responsibilities in the communities they served.

English civil authorities required midwives to take oaths in order to be licensed but imposed no official test of their skills. The oaths indicate that midwives had responsibilities which were serious enough to warrant supervision. They swore not to allow any infant to be baptized outside the Church of England, and promised to help both rich and poor, to report the true parentage of a child, and to abstain from performing abortions. Oath-breaking midwives could be excommunicated or fined.

Some American midwives learned their art in Europe, where midwifery was almost exclusively the professional province of women. Though barber surgeons and physicians increasingly asserted their interest in midwifery during the seventeenth cen-

tury, midwives and patients resisted the intruders. The midwives' levels of skill varied. Some acquired their medical education in the same way as many surgeons and physicians, by apprenticeship; some read manuals by more learned midwives and physicians; and after 1739, when the first British lying-in hospital was founded, a few were taught by the physicians who directed such hospitals. But more often than not, women undertook midwifery equipped only with folk knowledge and the experience of their own pregnancies.

Disparity of skills also existed among American midwives. Experienced midwives practiced alongside women who were, one physician observed, "as ignorant of their business as the women they deliver." By the end of the eighteenth century physicians thought that the "greater part" of the midwives in America took up the occupation by accident, "having first been *catched,* as they express it, with a woman in labour." The more diligent sought help from books, probably popular medical manuals such as *Aristotle's Master Piece.*

American midwives conducted their practice free, on the whole, from governmental supervision and control. Only two colonies appear to have enacted regulatory statutes, and it does not seem that these were rigorously enforced. In the seventeenth century Massachusetts and New York required midwives, together with surgeons and physicians, not to act contrary to the accepted rules of their art. More specifically, in 1716 the common council of New York City prescribed a licensing oath for midwives, which was similar to the oaths of England, though without the provision on baptism. The oath included an injunction — significant for the theme of this article — that midwives not "open any matter Appertaining to your Office in the presence of any Man unless Nessessity or Great Urgent Cause do Constrain you to do so." This oath, which was regularly re-enacted until 1763, suggests the common restriction of midwifery to women, excluding male physicians or barber surgeons, who, in any

This early engraving shows the crowded birthing room typical of American childbirth practices well into the nineteenth century, before the advent of the male obstetrician. "Facing the hazards of childbirth," says Catherine Scholten, "women depended on the community of their sex for companionship and medical assistance." Laboring women summoned mothers, sisters, aunts, friends, and neighbors to their bedsides. "Above all, they relied on the experience of midwives to guide them through labor." (The Bettmann Archive)

case, were few and usually ill trained. There are records of male midwives in New York, Philadelphia, Charleston, and Annapolis after 1740, but only one, a Dr. Spencer of Philadelphia, had London training in midwifery, and it was said of another that "he attended very few natural labors."

Though their duties were not as well defined by law, American midwives served the community in ways similar to those of their British counterparts. In addition to assisting at childbed, they testified in court in cases of bastardy, verified birthdates, and examined female prisoners who pleaded pregnancy to escape punishment. Some colonials also observed the English custom of having the midwife attend the baptism and burial of infants. Samuel Sewall reported that Elizabeth Weeden brought his son John to church for christening in 1677, and at the funeral of little Henry in 1685 "Midwife Weeden and Nurse Hill carried the Corps by turns."

The inclusion of the midwife in these ceremonies

of birth and death shows how women's relationships with their midwives went beyond mere respect for the latters' skill. Women with gynecologic problems would freely tell a midwife things "that they had rather die than discover to the Doctor." Grateful patients eulogized midwives. The acknowledgment of the services of one Boston midwife, recorded on her tombstone, has inspired comment since 1761. The stone informs the curious that Mrs. Phillips was "born in Westminster in Great Britain, and Commission'd by John Laud, Bishop of London in ye Year 1718 to ye Office of a Midwife," came to "this Country" in 1719, and "by ye Blessing of God has brought into this world above 3000 Children."

We may picture Mrs. Phillip's professional milieu as a small room, lit and warmed by a large fire, and crowded by a gathering of family and friends. In daytime, during the early stages of labor, children might be present, and while labor proceeded female friends dropped in to offer encouragement and help; securing refreshments for such visitors was a part of the preparation for childbirth, especially among the well-to-do families with which we are concerned. Men did not usually remain at the bedside. They might be summoned in to pray, but as delivery approached they waited elsewhere with the children and with women who were "not able to endure" the tension in the room.

During the final stages of labor the midwife took full charge, assisted by other women. As much as possible, midwives managed deliveries by letting nature do the work; they caught the child, tied the umbilical cord, and if necessary fetched the afterbirth. In complicated cases they might turn the child and deliver it feet first, but if this failed, the fetus had to be destroyed. In all circumstances the midwife's chief duty was to comfort the woman in labor while they both waited on nature, and this task she could, as a woman, fulfill with social ease. Under the midwife's direction the woman in labor was liberally fortified with hard liquor or mulled wine. From time to time the midwife examined her cervix to gauge the progress of labor and encouraged her to walk about until the pains became too strong. There was no standard posture for giving birth, but apparently few women lay flat in bed. Some squatted on a midwife's stool, a low chair with an open seat. Others knelt on a pallet, sat on another woman's lap, or stood supported by two friends.

Friends were "welcome companions," according to one manual for midwives, because they enabled the woman in labor "to bear her pains to more advantage," and "their cheerful conversation supports her spirits and inspires her with confidence." Elizabeth Drinker endeavored to talk her daughter into better spirits by telling her that as she was thirty-nine "this might possibly be the last trial of this sort." Some women attempted to cheer the mother-to-be by assuring her that her labor was easy compared to others they had seen, or provoked laughter by making bawdy jokes.

For some attendants, a delivery could be a wrenching experience. Elizabeth Drinker relived her own difficult deliveries when her daughters suffered their labors, and on one such occasion she noted with irony, "This day is 38 years since I was in agonies bringing her into this world of troubles; she told me with tears that this was her birthday." For others the experience of assisting the labors of friends was a reminder of their sex. Sarah Eve, an unmarried twenty-two-year-old, attended the labor of a friend in 1772 and carried the tidings of birth to the waiting father. "None but those that were like anxious could be sensible of a joy like theirs," she wrote in her journal that night, "Oh! Eve! Adam's wife I mean — who could forget her today?"

After delivery, the mother was covered up snugly and confined to her bed, ideally for three to four weeks. For fear of catching cold she was not allowed to put her feet on the floor and was constantly supplied with hot drinks. Family members relieved her of household duties. Restless women, and those who could not afford weeks of idleness, got up in a week or less, but not without occasioning censure.

The social and medical hold of midwives on childbirth loosened during the half century after 1770, as male physicians assumed the practice of midwifery among urban women of social rank. Initially, physicians entered the field as trained practitioners who could help women in difficult labors through the use of instruments, but ultimately they presided over normal deliveries as well. The presence of male physicians in the lying-in chamber signaled a general change in attitudes toward childbirth, including a modification of the dictum that women had to suffer. At the same time, because medical training was restricted to men, women lost their position as assistants at childbirth, and an event traditionally managed by a community of women became an experience shared primarily by a woman and her doctor.

William Shippen, the first American physician to establish a steady practice of midwifery, quietly overcame resistance to the presence of a man in the lying-in room. Casper Wistar's *Eulogies on Dr. Shippen,* published in 1809, states that when Shippen began in 1763, male practitioners were resorted to only in a crisis. "This was altogether the effect of prejudice," Wistar remarked, adding that "by Shippen this prejudice was so done away, that in the course of ten years he became very fully employed." A few figures testify to the trend. The Philadelphia city directory in 1815 listed twenty-one women as midwives, and twenty-three men as practitioners of midwifery. In 1819 it listed only thirteen female midwives, while the number of men had risen to forty-two; and by 1824 only six female midwives remained in the directory. "Prejudice" similarly dissolved in Boston, where in 1781 the physicians advertised that they expected immediate payment for

their services in midwifery; by 1820 midwifery in Boston was almost "entirely confined" to physicians. By 1826 Dr. William Dewees, professor of midwifery at the University of Pennsylvania and the outstanding American obstetrician of the early nineteenth century, could preface his textbook on midwifery with an injunction to every American medical student to study the subject because "everyone almost" must practice it. He wrote that "a change of manners within a few years" had "resulted in almost exclusive employment of the male practitioner." . . .

On one level the change was a direct consequence of the fact that after 1750 growing numbers of American men traveled to Europe for medical education. Young men with paternal means, like Shippen, spent three to four years studying medicine, including midwifery, with leading physicians in the hospitals of London and the classrooms of Edinburgh. When they returned to the colonies they brought back not only a superior set of skills but also British ideas about hospitals, medical schools, and professional standards.

In the latter part of the eighteenth century advanced medical training became available in North America. At the time of Shippen's return in 1762 there was only one hospital in the colonies, the Pennsylvania Hospital, built ten years earlier to care for the sick poor. Shippen and his London-educated colleagues saw that the hospital could be used for the clinical training of physicians, as in Europe. Within three years the Philadelphia doctors, led by John Morgan, established formal, systematic instruction at a school of medicine, supplemented by clinical work in the hospital. Morgan maintained that the growth of the colonies "called aloud" for a medical school "to increase the number of those who exercise the profession of medicine and surgery." Dr. Samuel Bard successfully addressed the same argument to the citizens of New York in 1768.

In addition to promoting medical schools, Morgan and Bard defined the proper practitioner of medicine as a man learned in a science. To languages and liberal arts their ideal physician added anatomy, material medicine, botany, chemistry, and clinical experience. He was highly conscious not only of his duty to preserve "the life and health of mankind," but also of his professional status, and this new emphasis on professionalism extended to midwifery.

The trustees of the first American medical schools recognized midwifery as a branch of medical science. From its founding in 1768, Kings College in New York devoted one professorship solely to midwifery, and the University of Pennsylvania elected Shippen professor of anatomy, surgery, and midwifery in 1791. By 1807 five reputable American medical schools provided courses in midwifery. In the early years of the nineteenth century some professors of midwifery began to call themselves obstetricians or professors of obstetrics, a scientific-sounding title free of the feminine connotations of the word midwife. Though not compulsory for all medical students, the new field was considered worthy of detailed study along the paths pioneered by English physicians.

Dr. William Smellie contributed more to the development of obstetrics than any other eighteenth-century physician. His influence was established by his teaching career in London from 1741 to 1758, and by his treatise on midwifery, first published in 1752. Through precise measurement and observation Smellie discovered the mechanics of parturition. He found that the child's head turned throughout delivery, adapting the widest part to the widest diameter of the pelvic canal. Accordingly, he defined maneuvers for manipulating an improperly presented child. He also recognized that obstetrical forceps, generally known for only twenty years when he wrote in 1754, should be used to rectify the position of an infant wedged in the mouth of the cervix, in preference to the "common method" of simply jerking the child out. He perfected the design of the forceps and taught its proper use, so that physicians could save both mother and child in difficult deliveries, instead of being forced to dismember the infant with hooks.

To Smellie and the men who learned from him, the time seemed ripe to apply science to a field hitherto built on ignorance and supported by prejudice. Smellie commented on the novelty of scientific interest in midwifery. "We ought to be ashamed of ourselves," he admonished the readers of his *Treatise*, "for the little improvement we have made in so many centuries." Only recently have "we established a better method of delivering in laborious and preternatural cases." Smellie's countryman Dr. Charles White reflected in his text on midwifery in 1793 that "the bringing of the art of midwifery to perfection upon scientific and medical principles seems to have been reserved for the present generation."

Some American physicians shared this sense of the new "Importance of the Obstetrick Art." Midwifery was not a "trifling" matter to be left to the uneducated, Thomas Jones of the College of Medicine of Maryland wrote in 1812. Broadly defined as the care of "all the indispositions incident to women from the commencement of pregnancy to the termination of lactation," it ranked among the most important branches of medicine. "With the cultivation of this branch of science," women could now "reasonably look to men for safety in the perilous conditions" of childbirth. . . .

Social as well as medical reasons account for the innovations in the practice of midwifery in such cities as Boston, Philadelphia, and New York. Physicians received their medical education in cities, and cities offered the best opportunities to acquire patients and live comfortably. Urban families of some means could afford the $12 to $15 minimum fee which Boston physicians demanded for midwife services in 1806. Obstetrics was found to be a good way to establish a successful general practice. The man who conducted himself well in the lying-in room won the gratitude and confidence of his patient and her family, and they naturally called him to serve in other medical emergencies. It was midwifery, concluded Dr. Walter Channing of Boston, that ensured doctors "the permanency and security of all their other business."

The possibility of summoning a physician, who could perhaps insure a safer and faster delivery, opened first to urban women. The dramatic rescue of one mother and child given up by a midwife could be enough to convince a neighborhood of women of a physician's value and secure him their practice. Doctors asserted that women increasingly hired physicians because they became convinced "that the well instructed physician is best calculated to avert danger and surmount difficulties." Certainly by 1795 the women of the Drinker family believed that none but a physician should order medicine for a woman in childbed, and had no doubts that Dr. Shippen or his colleague Dr. Nicholas Way was the best help that they could summon.

Although she accepted a male physician as midwife, Elizabeth Drinker still had reservations about the use of instruments to facilitate childbirth and was relieved when Shippen did not have to use forceps on her daughter. Other women feared to call a physician because they assumed that any instruments he used would destroy the child. However, once the capabilities of obstetrical forceps became known, some women may have turned to them by choice in hope of faster deliveries. Such hope stimulated a medical fashion. By about 1820 Dewees and Bard felt it necessary to condemn nervous young doctors for resorting unnecessarily to forceps.

The formal education of American physicians and the development of midwifery as a science, the desire of women for the best help in childbirth, the utility of midwifery as a means of building a physician's practice, and, ultimately, the gigantic social changes labeled urbanization explain why physicians assumed the ordinary practice of midwifery among well-to-do urban women in the late eighteenth and early nineteenth centuries. This development provides insight into the changing condition of women in American society.

The development of obstetrics signified a partial rejection of the assumption that women had to suffer in childbirth and implied a new social appreciation of women, as admonitions to women for forbearance under the pain of labor turned to the desire to relieve their pain. . . . In his doctoral dissertation in 1812 one American medical student drew a distinction between childbirth in primitive societies and his own. In the former, "women are generally looked on by their rugged lords as unworthy of any particular attention," and death or injury in childbirth is "not deemed a matter of any importance." Well-instructed assistants to women in childbirth were one sign of the value placed on women in civilized societies.

The desire to relieve women in childbirth also signified a more liberal interpretation of scripture. At the University of Pennsylvania in 1804, Peter Miller, a medical student, modified the theological dictum that women must bear in sorrow. The anxieties of pregnancy and the anguish caused by the death of so many infants constituted sorrow enough for women, argued Miller. They did not need to be subjected to bodily pain as well. Reiterating this argument, Dewees bluntly asked, "Why should the female alone incur the penalty of God?" To relieve the pain of labor Dewees and his fellows analyzed the anatomy and physiology of childbirth and defined techniques for the use of instruments.

If the development of obstetrics suggests the rise of a "special tenderness for women" on the part of men, it also meant that women's participation in medical practice was diminished and disparaged. A few American physicians instructed midwives or wrote manuals for them, but these efforts were private and sporadic, and had ceased by 1820. The increasing professionalization of medicine, in the minds of the physicians who formed medical associations that set the standards of the field, left little room for female midwives, who lacked the prescribed measure of scientific training and professional identity.

William Shippen initially invited midwives as well as medical students to attend his private courses in midwifery. His advertisement in the *Pennsylvania Gazette* in January 1765 related his experience assisting women in the country in difficult labors, "most of which was made so by the unskillful old women about them," and announced that he "thought it his duty to immediately begin" courses in midwifery "in order to instruct those women who have virtue enough to own their ignorance and apply for instructions, as well as those young gentlemen now engaged in the study of that useful and necessary branch of surgery." Shippen taught these private lessons until after the Revolution, when he lectured only to the students at the University of Pennsylvania, who, of course, were male.

At the turn of the century Dr. Valentine Seaman conducted the only other known formal instruction of midwives. He was distressed by the ignorance of many midwives, yet convinced that midwives ought to manage childbirth because, unlike physicians, they had time to wait out lingering labors, and, as women, they could deal easily with female patients. Seaman offered his private lectures and demonstrations at the New York Almshouse lying-in ward, and in 1800 published them as the *Midwives Monitor and Mothers Mirror*. A handful of other men wrote texts at least nominally directed to midwives between 1800 and 1810; some of these, like Seaman's, discussed the use of instruments. In 1817 Dr. Thomas Ewell proposed that midwives be trained at a national school of midwifery in Washington, D.C., to be supported by a collection taken up by ministers. There is no evidence that Ewell's scheme, presented in his medical manual, *Letters to Ladies,* ever gained a hearing.

Seaman and Ewell, and other authors of midwives' manuals, presumed that if women mastered some of the fundamentals of obstetrics they would be desirable assistants in ordinary midwifery cases. In 1820 Dr. Channing of Boston went further in his pamphlet, *Remarks on the Employment of Females as Practitioners of Midwifery,* in which he maintained that no one could thoroughly understand the management of labor who did not understand "thoroughly the profession of medicine as a whole." Channing's principle would have totally excluded women from midwifery, because no one favored professional medical education for women. It was generally assumed that they could not easily master the necessary languages, mathematics, and chemistry, or withstand the trials of dissecting room and hospital. Channing added that women's moral character disqualified them for medical practice: "Their feelings of sympathy are too powerful for the cool exercise of judgement" in medical emergencies, he wrote; "they do not have the power of action, nor the active power of mind which is essential to the practice of the surgeon."

Denied formal medical training, midwives of the early nineteenth century could not claim any other professional or legal status. Unlike Great Britain, the United States had no extensive record of licensing laws or oaths defining the practice of midwifery. Nor were there any vocal groups of midwives who, conscious of their tradition of practice or associated with lying-in hospitals, were able to defend themselves against competition from physicians. American midwives ceased practice among women of social rank with few words uttered in their defense.

The victory of the physicians produced its own problems. The doctor's sex affected the relationships between women and their attendants in childbirth, and transformed the atmosphere of the lying-in room. In his advice to his male students Dewees acknowledged that summoning a man to assist at childbed "cost females a severe struggle." Other doctors knew that even the ordinary gynecologic services of a physician occasioned embarrassment and violated woman's "natural delicacy of feeling," and that every sensitive woman felt "deeply humiliated" at the least bodily exposure. Doctors recognized an almost universal repugnance on the part of women to male assistance in time of labor. Because of "whim or false delicacy" women often refused to call a man until their condition had become critical. It is unlikely that physicians exaggerated these observations, although there is little testimony from women themselves about their childbed experience in the early nineteenth century.

The uneasiness of women who were treated by men was sometimes shared by their husbands. In 1772 the *Virginia Gazette* printed a denunciation of male midwifery as immoral. The author, probably an Englishman, attributed many cases of adultery in England to the custom of employing men at deliveries. Even in labor a woman had intervals of ease, and these, he thought, were the moments when the doctor infringed on the privileges of the husband. It would be a matter of utmost indifference to him "whether my wife had spent the night in a bagnio, or an hour of the forenoon locked up with a man midwife in her dressing room." Such arguments were frequently and seriously raised in England during the eighteenth century. They may seem ludicrous, but at least one American man of Dr. Ewell's acquaintance suffered emotional conflict over hiring a male midwife. He sent for a physician to help his wife in her labor, yet "very solemnly he declared to the doctor, he would demolish him if he touched or looked at his wife."

Physicians dealt with the embarrassment of patients and the suspicion of husbands by observing the drawing-room behavior of "well-bred gen-

tlemen." Dewees told his students to "endeavor, by well chosen conversation, to divert your patient's mind from the purpose of your visit." All questions of a delicate nature were to be communicated through a third party, perhaps the only other person in the room, either a nurse or an elderly friend or relative. The professional man was advised "never to seem to know anything about the parts of generation, further than that there is an orifice near the rectum leading to an os."

Physicians did not perform vaginal examinations unless it was absolutely important to do so, and they often had to cajole women into permitting an examination at all. Nothing could be more shocking to a woman, Shippen lectured his students, "than for a young man the moment he enters the Chamber to ask for Pomatum and proceed to examine the uterus." Doctors waited until a labor pain clutched their patients and then suggested an examination by calling it "taking a pain." During examination and delivery the patient lay completely covered in her bed, a posture more modest, if less comfortable, than squatting on a pallet or a birth stool. The light in the room was dimmed by closing the shutters during the day and covering the lamps at night. If a physician used forceps, he had to manipulate them under the covers, using his free hand as a guide. On this point doctors who read Thomas Denman's *Obstetrical Remembrancer* were reminded that "Degorges, one of the best obstetricians of his time, was blind."

The crowd of supportive friends and family disappeared with the arrival of the doctor. The physician guarded against "too many attendants; where there are women, they must talk." The presence of other women might increase the doctor's nervousness, and they certainly did not help the woman in labor. Medical men interpreted women's talk of other experiences with childbirth as mere gossip "of all the dangerous and difficult labours they ever heard any story about in their lives," which ought to be stopped lest it disturb the patient. Especially distracting were the bawdy stories visitors told, expecting the physician to laugh, too. Medical professors recommended "grave deportment," warning that levity would "hurt your patient or yourself in her esteem." Far from providing the consolation of a friend, the physician was often a stranger who needed to "get a little acquainted" with his patient. One medical text went so far as to coach him in a series of conversational ice breakers about children and the weather.

Etiquette and prudery in the lying-in chamber affected medical care. Physicians were frustrated by their inability to examine their patients thoroughly, for they knew full well that learning midwifery from a book was "like learning shipbuilding without touching timber." Examinations were inadequate, and the dangers of manipulating instruments without benefit of sight were tremendous. Dewees cautioned his students to take great care before pulling the forceps that "no part of the mother is included in the locking of the blades. This accident is frequent." Accidental mutilation of infants was also reported, as the navel string had to be cut under the covers. Lecturers passed on the story of the incautious doctor who included the penis of an infant within the blades of his scissors.

In view of such dangers, the conflict between social values and medical practice is striking. The expansion of medical knowledge brought men and women face to face with social taboos in family life. They had to ask themselves the question, Who should watch a woman give birth? For centuries the answer had unhesitatingly been female relatives and friends, and the midwife. The science of obstetrics, developing in the eighteenth century, changed the answer. Though women might socially be the most acceptable assistants at a delivery, men were potentially more useful.

In consequence of the attendance of male physicians, by 1825, for some American women, childbirth was ceasing to be an open ceremony. Though birth still took place at home, and though friends and relatives still lent a helping hand, visiting women no longer dominated the activities in the lying-in room. Birth became increasingly a private affair conducted in a quiet, darkened room. The physician limited visitors because they hindered proper medical care, but the process of birth was also concealed because it embarrassed both patient and physician.

Between 1760 and 1825 childbirth was thus transformed from an open affair to a restricted one. As one consequence of the development of obstetrics as a legitimate branch of medicine, male physicians began replacing midwives. They began to reduce childbirth to a scientifically managed event and deprived it of its folk aspects. Strengthened by the professionalization of their fields, these physicians also responded to the hopes of women in Philadelphia, New York, and Boston for safe delivery. Although they helped some pregnant women, they hurt midwives, who were shut out of an era of medicine that had been traditionally their domain. All these innovations took place in the large urban centers in response to distinctly urban phenomena. They reflected the increasing privatization of family life, and they foreshadowed mid-nineteenth-century attitudes toward childbirth, mother, and woman.

QUESTIONS TO CONSIDER

1   What role did the female community, and not just the midwife, play in the childbirth experience before male physicians began practicing obstetric medicine?

2   How do the changes in eighteenth- and nineteenth-century childbirth practices reveal an important shift in American attitudes toward women as patients and as professionals?

3   Discuss the ways in which the experience of childbirth changed when male physicians replaced

midwives in the birthing room. What gains and losses resulted from this change?

4 What were the motives of male physicians for professionalizing obstetric medicine, taking over the birthing procedure, and pushing midwives out of the field?

5 What were the benefits and drawbacks of medical technological improvements, like the invention and use of forceps? Comment on the fact that the scientific developments making childbirth less risky and less painful also increased female dependence on male physicians.

VIII

FIGURES
IN THE
LANDSCAPE

15

"We Are All Federalists, All Republicans"

MAX LERNER

Students of the past have long debated what determines the course of history. There are those who maintain that great "forces" shape the direction and composition of human societies; some even argue that people, individuals, are not important. There are others, however, who focus on the human side of the past, examining how the interaction of people and events dictates the course of subsequent events. From this view, human beings are not mere cogs in the engines of history; they can and do make a difference. Portrait of America, *of course, stresses the latter view of history. The authors of the next three selections attempt to show the political course of the young Republic, from the dawn of the nineteenth century to the Age of Jackson, through the lives of some of the leading participants — Thomas Jefferson, John Marshall, and John Quincy Adams, son of Abigail and John Adams.*

Let us pick up political events where Edmund S. Morgan leaves off in his assessment of George Washington in selection 10. When John Adams replaced Washington as president in 1796, Federalist leaders were extremely apprehensive about the French Revolution and the anarchy and violence that seemed to characterize it. Might the French virus not spread to America as it appeared to be spreading across Europe? Might not a conspiracy already be under way in the United States to fan the flames of revolution, to unleash the American mob on Federalist leaders, to destroy the order and stability they had worked so hard to establish? Since 1793, when Citizen Genêt had tried to enlist American men and privateers for the French cause, the Federalists had feared revolution in their midst. Champions of a strong government to maintain order, apostles of elitist rule and the sanctity of private property, the Federalists soon equated the Republicans under Madison and Jefferson with revolution, chaos, and destruction. After all, did the Republicans not support the French? Did they not defend the mob here at home? Did they not call for more democracy in government (although many of their leaders paradoxically were southern slave owners)?

The harried Federalists barely fought off a Republican attempt to seize the government in 1796, when Adams defeated Jefferson by only three votes in the electoral college. Then, as though the Republican threat were not bad enough, trouble broke out with revolutionary France. In the notorious XYZ affair, French agents tried to extract a bribe from American representatives sent to negotiate about deteriorating Franco-American relations. Many Americans thought the nation's honor had been besmirched and demanded a war of revenge. In response, the Federalists undertook an undeclared sea war against France that lasted from 1798 to 1800. Using the war as a pretext to consolidate their power, bridle the Republicans, and prevent revolution in the United States, the Federalists passed the Alien and Sedition Acts. These, they declared, were necessary for the nation's security in the war with France.

The Alien Acts severely restricted the rights and political influence of immigrants, who usually joined the Republicans after they were naturalized and who might be carrying the French virus. The Sedition Act made hostile criticism of Federalist policies punishable by fine and imprisonment. The Republicans, decrying such government censorship, launched a counterattack against Federalist "despotism." The Federalists were so discredited by the alien and sedition laws, and so divided by an irreconcilable feud between Adams and Hamilton, that the Republicans were able to win the government in 1801. Their victory marked the decline and eventually the end of the Federalist party as a national political organization.

Jefferson liked to describe his rise to power as "the revolution of 1800." But was it really a revolution? True, the Republicans allowed the hated Alien and Sedition Acts to expire in 1801, reduced the residence requirement for naturalized citizenship from fourteen years to five so that America could again function as an "asylum" for "oppressed humanity," inaugurated a new fiscal policy of government frugality and efficiency, and strove to retire the national debt of $83 million in sixteen years. Jefferson also repudiated the idea of government by and for a political elite. Yet he and his top administrators were as educated, talented, and upper-class as their Federalist predecessors. Moreover, while Jefferson embraced the laissez-faire principle that that government is best which governs least, he found that reversing all Federalist commitments could cause confusion and consternation across the land. Therefore he and his followers permitted the United States Bank to continue operating (it closed in 1811 when its charter ran out), and they maintained Federalist measures for refunding the national debt, stimulating American shipping, and assuming the states' Revolutionary War debts. Nor did Jefferson's "revolution of 1800" change the condition of Ameri-

ca's enslaved blacks. As president, the author of the Declaration of Independence, himself a slaveholder, carefully avoided the subject of bondage.

"What is practicable," Jefferson said, "must often control what is pure theory." For Max Lerner, a distinguished student of American civilization, this statement is the key to the essential Jefferson. Lerner's sprightly profile reveals a many-sided man who had follies as well as triumphs, who by turns was philosophical, practical, passionate, and contradictory, and who still has meaning for our time.

ON MARCH 4, 1801, THOMAS JEFFERSON, attended by some friends, walked from Conrad and Mc-Munn's boardinghouse, in the raw village called Washington, to the new Capitol. In a crowded Senate chamber, Chief Justice John Marshall, his old political enemy, swore him in as President. He was a tall, freckled, redheaded planter-scholar-aristocrat, with a loose-jointed figure, casually worn clothes, strong but kindly features, and an air of gentleness that belied the sharpness of purpose and will behind it. His inauguration marked the first peaceful succession of power from one party to another in a modern republic. But the power base itself was being shifted. What had started as an armed revolution against the British monarchy and had then become a constitutional government of the owning groups was now being completed by the peaceful revolution of 1800 against privilege and the dead hand of the past.

No wonder he had worked hard on his inaugural address, putting it through three drafts, polishing every sentence and phrase. His words were conciliatory in tone: "We are all republicans; we are all federalists." In his manuscript he put it in lower case, meaning the principles of republicanism and federalism, not the parties. Yet the real theme of the address was Jefferson's vision of where the strength (or "energy") of the new American experiment lay — not in the idea of power but in the power of the idea of a self-governing republic, continually remaking itself by the will of the people.

He knew there were fears about him because he wanted to turn power back to the states, cut both government costs and taxes, reduce the army and navy, and retire the public debt. He had repeatedly said "Peace is my passion," which caused many to wonder whether he would expose the new nation naked to its enemies.

His answer was a ringing affirmation of the democratic potential. "I believe this . . . the strongest government on earth. I believe it to be the only one where every man, at the call of the laws, would fly to the standard of the law. . . . Sometimes it is said that man cannot be trusted with the government of himself. Can he, then, be trusted with the government of others? Or have we found angels in the form of kings to govern him? Let history answer the question."

Every new President starts, in his campaign, as a suppliant at the door of power and ends as a suppliant at the door of history, to learn how it will judge him. And history puts the old and ever-new questions about him: how much power he wielded, and

From "The Real Mr. America: Thomas Jefferson" by Max Lerner in *Quest/77*, March–April 1977. Reprinted by permission of the author.

how; what he was like in mind, character, appetites, neuroses, psyche, vision; how many lives he blasted in war, how securely he built the peace. They are the old questions Freud took from the Greeks — of Eros and Thanatos.

There is a streak of Golden Age thinking in Americans, a cult of primitivism which makes them dream of the early days as always the good ones. If anyone should have made a good President, it is the writer, thinker, and statesman who has come down through history as a demigod. Jefferson is the only philosopher-king America has had, unless we include the unschooled Lincoln as a philosopher. He hated kings, yet for a time reigned as an uncrowned one. As revolutionary spokesman and as draftsman of the Declaration of Independence, as Ambassador to France, as Secretary of State under Washington, as party leader and polemicist, he was brilliantly effective. But put to the test of sustained power at the summit, he proved a great man but an indifferent President, a better philosopher than he was a king.

By his nature and conviction he was — in James Barber's classification — a passive President rather than an active one, and an inward-looking one rather than an extrovert. His conception of the presidency was not the dynamic one that Roosevelt, Kennedy, and Johnson made familiar to our own time. It reached back — in his theory at least — to his basic philosophy.

His view of government and society was part of his view of the cosmos — that it had been formed all of a piece by a divine Intelligence and operated by the laws of Nature, that in the moral universe as well as the physical there were laws and principles that men must discover and live by. He had few illusions about man's essential goodness: "The lions and tigers are mere lambs compared with man as a destroyer." He saw man as a predator and prey alike, but he saw governments — unless their tyranny was checked — as the embodiment of the predator. His remedy was a double one: to set limits on the powers and actions of the government, and to educate the people to resist the predators and escape being prey. This meant direct intervention by the people to narrow the powers of government and set up checks and balances on power.

Although he was a revolutionary, he didn't believe that revolutions changed institutions. He thought they were not utopian but purgative: they couldn't create an ideal society, but they could get rid of obstructions from the past, and prevent old forms from hardening into tyrannical ones. Unlike Burke, he had little feel for tradition and the continuities of the social organism over time. This man, himself so deeply rooted in soil, family, party, state, nation, time, kept rootedness out of his political philosophy except in his aversion to cities. He felt, unlike the French *philosophes,* that the present owed no debts to the past and could make no claims on the future. Rarely has America had a thinker for whom the generational struggle was so crucial. He calculated a generational span as 18 years and eight months, and felt that every generation had a right to pry away the dead hand of the past, start with a clean slate, and work out its own lines of development.

This left Jefferson open to a pragmatism which has marked liberalism in America ever since. It gave flexibility to one whose firm sense of principle might otherwise have turned him into a rigid doctrinaire.

In doctrine he did not believe in a strong executive power nor an activist presidency; in practice he tried to hold sway over his administration — effectively in his first term, disastrously in his second. In doctrine he believed in constructing the Constitution strictly; in practice, as the Louisiana Purchase showed, he used the Constitution flexibly enough to accommodate an "empire for freedom." In doctrine he was a champion of legislative supremacy; in practice he kept a tight rein on Congress through his party lieutenants in both houses, with whom he was in constant touch. In doctrine he saw a "happy variety of minds" as part of the scheme of creation;

in practice, when the going got hard, he engineered the impeachment of judges in his first term and tried to harass and jail hostile editors in his second.

He played host to all the 138 congressmen at dinner, inviting them in groups of eight or ten from the same party every other day, so that usually (counting the diplomats and others) he had a dozen to eighteen guests. In the village of 3,000 that called itself the nation's capital, where the social life was sparse and bleak, an invitation to dine with the President was unlikely to be refused. The guests arrived around 3:30, when Congress was through for the day, chatted for a half hour, found places at the round table (there was no protocol: everything was done by "the principle of equality, or pele-mele"), and enjoyed a hearty dinner, with good and plentiful wine, and with conversation as the main course throughout.

There were no blessings at the start, no toasts were drunk, and talk of politics was discouraged at any time. The conversation ranged widely because the host, who led it, knew something about everything and everything about some things. The talk was of travel, crops, farming techniques, animals, music, cities, wines, literature, building, medicine, science, history, fossils, wars, revolutions. "You never can be an hour in this man's company," wrote John Quincy Adams in his diary, "without something of the marvelous. . . ."

His dinners were a costly burden to him, but they were also an intellectual delight, an arena for the quiet and effortless display of everything he knew and had done, everyone he had met. Although they were nonpolitical in tone, they were in the deepest sense political — a way of holding his party in Congress together, while undercutting some of the attacks on him that were mounting in the federalist press.

Although a deeply convinced pacifist, Jefferson came to believe in extending America's "empire for liberty" on its own continent. Dreaming of an American empire of his own, Napoleon had forced a declining Spanish monarchy to cede to him the

immense, vaguely outlined Mississippi Valley. This set in motion strong pressures on Jefferson from the frontier settlers, who needed New Orleans as a transshipping port for their products. Jefferson sent James Monroe to Paris to talk about buying New Orleans and west Florida, but before he arrived, Napoleon — his forces decimated in Santo Domingo — had decided to move his imperial ambitions toward the East rather than America, and Talleyrand offered to sell the whole of the Louisiana Territory.

Jefferson was staggered by the new nation's chance, sudden and immense, to extend its domain beyond any dream of the most fervent nationalists. The price — $15 million — seems tiny to us, but it was four or five times the annual cost of running the government, and added to the debt [Secretary of Treasury Albert] Gallatin had whittled down. But the real problem was constitutional, since the President had no explicit power under the Constitution to buy land. At first Jefferson thought of asking for a constitutional amendment, but speed was essential. So he did what history has admired him for: he closed the deal, and rationalized it by saying the people would have wanted him to decide as he did.

When the treaty of purchase came before the Senate, a number of Federalists denounced it as "Jefferson's Folly." Yet later generations of Americans have preferred to see it as Jefferson's glory — the greatest single geopolitical event of American history since the discovery by Columbus.

The new land doubled America's expanse, gave it a structure of agricultural and manufacturing power, and propelled it decisively into becoming in time a world power. It also upset the balance of power between the two major parties, broadening the base of the Republicans and making them a national party with an impulsion westward. While it did not make Jefferson an "imperialist" in today's sense, it made him part of what was to be called the "manifest destiny" of America. Himself a naturalist and ethnographer, and the son of a surveyor, Jefferson sent out

214

Thomas Jefferson, an oil painting done in 1805 by Charles Willson Peale. Jefferson was tall and slender, with a freckled face, gray eyes, and short, powdered, red hair. The color of his hair inspired one correspondent to salute him as "you redheaded son of a bitch." Despite his aristocratic upbringing, he was largely indifferent about his clothes, which rarely fit him. A Federalist senator once mistook Jefferson for a servant, observing with a sniff that his shirt was dirty. (Independence National Historical Park Collection)

the Lewis and Clark expedition to map the new domain, report on its resources and people, and dramatize its meaning for the rising American national consciousness. He had not abandoned his dream of an agrarian society: he had only found a larger sitting in which the dream could be renewed and pursued.

By a stroke of fortune history had offered Jefferson, at an unsuspected moment, a great navigable stream and a vast land empire almost for the asking. Had he been merely doctrinaire, he would have turned a stony face to Napoleon and Talleyrand and rejected the great historic chance because it ran counter to what he had argued and written about the Constitution. But he didn't, and thereby he laid the basis for the place of his first term in history.

In 1804 Jefferson was overwhelmingly reelected, despite a bitter campaign in the Federalist press against his personal life and morals. He took his success as fresh evidence of the people's mandate. But in 1805 his troubles began. In his first term, very little seemed to go wrong for him. In his second, nothing seemed to go right — not the [Aaron] Burr conspiracy and trial, nor the embargo, nor the impeachment of Supreme Court Justice Samuel Chase, nor his vendetta with the anti-Republican press.

Burr was brilliant, cynical, persuasive, unscrupulous, with a flaring imagination — in short, a fascinating rascal. After being dropped as vice-presidential candidate in 1804, he cooked up a grandiose scheme for carving out of the Louisiana Territory an independent republic over which he could rule. Jefferson could have played it cool, and let the legal authorities deal with his actual conspiracy. Instead he overreacted, made a treason trial out of it, and Chief Justice Marshall — who had outmaneuvered Jefferson in the case of the "midnight judges" in *Marbury* v. *Madison* — was now able, in presiding over the trial, to apply a strict definition of treason as overt acts of war or betrayal against the United States. The crucial evidence for treason in this sense was lacking; Burr was acquitted, and Jefferson was left looking both foolish and vindictive.

He had an even more hapless time with the French and British depredations on American commerce. It was Jefferson's fate to act out his entire presidential career against the background of swirling struggle between the great European powers — a struggle that locked him into dilemmas not of his own making, presented him with options not of his choosing, and finally proved the undoing of much he had hoped to accomplish.

When the British and French both seized American vessels if they touched at the ports of the other, Jefferson decided to test one of his favorite doctrines — that war was both intolerable and unnecessary, and that the best weapon against both powers lay in economic sanctions. He got Congress to pass a series of five Embargo Acts, stringently forbidding U.S. trade with Britain and France not only overseas but even along the Canadian border.

Not surprisingly, the tactic failed. The British and French were unmoved by a measure that didn't hurt them decisively. That Jefferson had stripped the armed forces, out of pacifist principle and for economy, made them contemptuous. Within the U.S. there was sporadic resistance, which infuriated Jefferson. It made him turn each new Embargo Act into a Force Act, with searches and seizures by the army and navy. These in turn embittered the resistance, which Jefferson saw as "insurrection."

When an embargo case involving the port of Charleston came before the Supreme Court, and Justice Johnson held that presidential acts were subject to due process of law, Jefferson insisted on his "coequal" power to interpret the Constitution and therefore to defy the Supreme Court view. When a lumber-laden raft in Vermont was snatched away from an army guard and hauled to Canada, the culprits were arrested and — on Jefferson's insistence — tried for treason, to set an example to others. Justice Livingston, himself a Republican, was shocked by the treason charge, and lashed out at Jefferson for seeking to use the doctrine of constructive treason in a domestic legislative case.

One must judge Jefferson's embargo strategy a dismal failure as an instrument of foreign policy, and a dangerous adventure as domestic policy. Jefferson's idea of passive resistance to the European blockades might have worked if he had used intermediate means. He could have armed American merchant ships and equipped them with convoys, or used a policy of nonintercourse with Britain and France, or both measures together. The embargo was too broad and ineffectual, and did more harm to the U.S. by paralyzing commerce and manufactures than it did to the offending European powers.

Jefferson made the embargo his personal project, watching over its day-to-day operation but doing little to educate Congress and the people on why extreme measures were necessary. Like some later American Presidents, he made the mistake of attributing his failure not to his policy but to the opposition to it. He isolated himself from the people, calling the congressional vote to remove the embargo (just as he left office) a "sudden unaccountable revolution of opinion." The pathos of it was that in 1787 he had mocked the fears about Shays' Rebellion, and had written that "the tree of liberty must be refreshed from time to time by the blood of patriots and tyrants. It is its natural manure." When people resist and take up arms, he had said, "the remedy is to set them right as to facts, pardon and pacify them." As President he did none of these.

One must remember about Jefferson that he had a strong will, not easily diverted from its purpose, nor softened by adversity. While out of power, resisting attacks on freedom of criticism, he had achieved some abiding victories. When he was in power, he still had his old sense of being surrounded by enemies, and his strength of will became an instrument of repression. Jefferson in opposition met constantly with his fellow party leaders, exchanged letters with countless colleagues, and was deflected by them from potential blunders. Jefferson in power lost the habit of subjecting his policies to prior criticism and — especially after his reelection victory in 1804 — he was confident that the people were with him, and came to equate his own thinking and intuitions with the will of the people.

Leonard Levy, a Pulitzer Prize–winning constitutional historian at Claremont Graduate School, courageously took Jefferson as libertarian apart in his *Jefferson and Civil Liberties: The Darker Side,* to the dismay of the established Jefferson scholars who are protective of him. Quite apart from the Jefferson image, the facts are troubling. A number of Republican theorists of press freedom emerged at the turn of the 19th century, broke with the English common law of seditious libel, and spoke up for a wholly unfettered press, much as Justice Hugo Black was to do in our own time. This new libertarianism was bold and radical, condemning not only prior restraints against publication but also prosecution after it, and condemning state as well as national trials.

Jefferson was wary of it. He condemned national but not state antisedition action. When, as President, he felt that the Federalist press had reached "licentiousness" and "a degree of prostitution as to deprive it of all credit," he suggested to a Pennsylvania governor "a few prosecutions of the most prominent offenders. . . . Not a general prosecution, for that would look like persecution, but a selected one." There followed the trial of an editor in Philadelphia, one in New York, several in New England. They all failed, and Jefferson looked foolish.

He could veer wildly on the theme of press freedom. He said at one point, "Were it left to me to decide whether we should have a government without newspapers, or newspapers without a government, I should not hesitate a moment to prefer the latter." Yet this didn't keep him from harassing editors by prosecution. A few years before his death he found a middle ground in seeing press freedom as "a formidable censor of the public functionaries," and noting that "it produces reform peaceably, which must otherwise be done by revolution."

As President, he was as foolish about politically overzealous judges as about vituperative journalists. The bone that struck in his throat was the Federalist judges whom the Adams administration had appointed to lifetime jobs in federal courts just as it left office. Many of them were crassly unjudicial. They galled Jefferson because, massively and symbolically, they stood in the way of his transfer of power. He tried to wait them out, or make life diffi-

cult for them, but complained that "few die and none resign." His effort at a purge came to a crisis in 1804 with the House of Representatives' impeachment of Justice Chase of the Supreme Court, who had said intemperate things about Jefferson from the bench. The House presented the charge of malfeasance in office, the Senate sat as a court in 1805, but fortunately — both for Jefferson and for judicial independence — Chase was acquitted. No member of the Supreme Court has been impeached since, although there were rumblings of thunder around the heads of Chief Justice Warren and Justice Douglas.

One may guess that part of Jefferson's thin-skinned sensitivity to his critics derived from their attacks on his private life and morals. At one point a gutter journalist, James Callendar — who had been part of the Republican press stable — failed in his effort to blackmail Jefferson, and then published the story of Jefferson's supposed seduction of a close friend and neighbor, Mrs. Betsy Walker. Jefferson later wrote a friend about the episode: "When young and single I offered love to a handsome lady. I acknowledge its incorrectness." But there is no way of telling whether the husband's charge that Jefferson had made repeated efforts to seduce his wife, or the lady's own charge of a 10-year siege by Jefferson, amounted to more than the fantasies of a wife and the wounded vanity of a husband.

Jefferson's relationships with women have become the thorniest problem for his biographers. He had a strong commitment to his wife, Martha, who died when he was still a young man of 39, and whose death shook him. But the assumption of most who have written about him, that this great and good man must have forsworn sexuality of the rest of his life, doesn't necessarily follow. The efforts to sanctify him, as if he were a spinsterish clergyman figure, do justice neither to his intense, passionate nature nor to his basic character as a complex, many-sided, total person.

The storm has raged around the question of Jefferson's relationship to two women — Maria Cosway, American wife of a dandified British miniature painter, who lived in London and visited Paris while Jefferson was Minister; and Sally Hemings, a slave girl at Jefferson's Monticello home, who was also an illegitimate half sister to Jefferson's wife. Jefferson and Maria Cosway unquestionably had a romantic love affair, as evidenced by Jefferson's famous long letter, "Dialogue between My Head and My Heart," which he wrote out of his heartbreak when Maria had to leave Paris for London. They exchanged 25 more letters, described by Fawn Brodie as "the most remarkable collection of love letters in the history of the American presidency." Mrs. Brodie's detailed and scholarly psychohistory, *Thomas Jefferson: An Intimate History,* argues persuasively that their relationship was sexual as well as romantic, but that neither of the lovers dared make the break into a marriage which both must have thought of.

The scholarly controversy over Sally Hemings has been even stormier, with Jefferson's traditional biographers dismissing as libel the contention that she was Jefferson's mistress from the days of his Paris household and bore him four children, and with Fawn Brodie marshaling her artillery of evidence to assert it was true. The reader who wants to decide for himself must go to Dumas Malone's masterly five volumes on Jefferson's life and to Mrs. Brodie's massive and lively 800-page book. It is interesting that recent black writers, who uniformly attack Jefferson for having continued to own slaves despite his passionate defense of human freedom, are inclined to accept the Sally Hemings story as part of the facts of life about Virginia plantation morals.

My own guess is that they and Fawn Brodie have the better of the controversy. In his relationships with women, Jefferson seems to have been attracted to the difficult and the forbidden. He was trapped in an age, a class, and a society where miscegenation was practiced but severely punished when made public. He couldn't have escaped a feeling of guilt

about this relationship, as suggested by his long history of migraine headaches. This doesn't negate my view of him as a whole man, although a complex and guilt-ridden one. Yeats put it well: "Nothing can be sole or whole/ That has not been rent."

A week after he left the presidency, Jefferson (at 66) set out for Monticello, riding for days on horseback and for eight hours through a snowstorm. "I have more confidence in my *vis vitae* than I had before entertained," he wrote Madison. For 17 years he was to live out his life at Monticello, in the groves he loved, on his farms, busy with letters and books and guests, and with a brick factory and mill. He was a world-famous figure. Streams of visitors came to Monticello, some only to see him walk across the lawn. He restored his friendship with John Adams, breaking their long feud, and the two former Presidents — lonely, solitary on the American landscape stripped of most of its Revolutionary leaders — exchanged some 160 letters whose learning, high spirits, and versatility of theme are unmatched in the history of American letter writing. "You and I," Adams wrote, "ought not to die before We have explained ourselves to each other."

Of the two men's letters, Jefferson's are more urbane and mellow, expressing an unshattered belief in man's power by reason and education to make his society work. Adams was more convinced of the force of the irrational in human events. When Jefferson wrote him about his plans for his beloved new University of Virginia, which occupied the last decade of his life, Adams answered with the hope that the twin elements of superstition and force "may never blow up all your benevolent and phylanthropic lucubrations. But the History of all Ages is against you."

Jefferson was undaunted. Even the fact that his last years were shallowed by sickness and debts (he was a poor plantation manager and had to sell his library to meet his obligations) didn't shake his basic optimism. The end came, symbolically, exactly 50 years after the Declaration of Independence he had written. He survived the night of July 3rd, and toward midnight — after a fitful sleep — asked, "Is it the Fourth?" He was told, stretching it a little, that it was, and he fell into a coma which passed into death around noon on July 4, 1826.

In Quincy, Massachusetts, John Adams was also dying, equally intent on lasting until Independence Day. Since he didn't know that Jefferson had died five hours earlier, his last words were reported as being "Thomas Jefferson still . . ." The legend was that he murmured either "lives" or "survives" to end the sentence and his life. There is something eerie about the fact that both men died on exactly the day when the nation was celebrating the 50th anniversary of the independence they had both helped to win. (It was more than coincidence: it was a linked act of will on the part of both.)

Even in his last years Jefferson lost little of his political shrewdness. "Take care of me when I am dead," he wrote Madison, his old comrade in the political wars. Surely few political figures could have needed less caretaking for the judgement of posterity. The legend that crystallized after his death made him out to have been bigger than life, so complex that his name and writings were invoked for every cause — conservative, liberal, and radical angles of vision, weak and strong presidencies. Everyone saw him through the prism of his own political coloration. But of one fact there could be no doubt — the many-sidedness of his devouring mind. As one reads his letters to Adams the breathtaking web of his interests is revealed: in the sciences, linguistics, anthropology, archaeology and fossil remains, the humanities and classics, music, architecture, farming, in the earth and the skies and the meaning of the cosmos, in the dispersion and variety of the races and their inherent equality as well as differences, in religion, government, aristocracies, morals, education.

As he looked back at his long life, what swam through his crowded memories? He was of the little band of young Virginians who, in their hedonic but intellectually tempestuous life, had shaped themselves into a great governing generation. He had become the spokesman of the American Revolution to the world, drawing on the basic ideas of the European Enlightenment whose child he was, but giving them an analytic sweep and verbal elegance all his own. He had celebrated his state in his *Notes on Virginia,* and his nation in his great public papers. His European education, during his days as American Minister, was an intellectual overlay on his essential Americanism, yet without those European years he could not have become the assured man of the world and statesman he became.

He misread much about the French Revolution (he was no disciplined social thinker), but his French experience stood him in good stead as he carried through his own "Revolution of 1800." In his struggles with Hamilton, both were romantics; Hamilton romanticized the nation, Jefferson the people. Yet it was Jefferson's hard organizing capacity that made him the victor. I count Jefferson, for all his intellectualizing and his lofty revolutionary sentiments, the most brilliant party leader in American political history — at least until Franklin Roosevelt. The miracle was that he managed to project a public image of himself as at once a militant popular leader and a serene philosopher.

In an age like our own, of expanding problems, wary specialization, shrinking perspectives, Jefferson remains witness to the truth that to be a generalist need not keep a man from action, and to be a philosopher need not keep him from power and passion.

QUESTIONS TO CONSIDER

1   What evidence does Lerner provide to support his conclusion that Thomas Jefferson "proved a great man but an indifferent President, a better philosopher than he was a king"? Do you agree?

2 Jefferson did not believe that revolution could create an ideal society. Why, then, did he become a revolutionary during the American colonists' fight for independence? How were his ideas on revolution linked to liberal pragmatism?

3 Contrast Jefferson's principles with his practices as president. Was Jefferson simply a hypocrite who talked out of both sides of his mouth? What lessons does Jefferson's example teach us about the words and behavior of an individual out of office and an individual in office?

4 In 1787, Jefferson had mocked the fears of men like Washington about Shays's Rebellion. When people take up arms to resist some unpopular government action, Jefferson advised, "the remedy is to set them right as to facts, pardon and pacify them." How well did Jefferson follow his own advice once in office?

5 Jefferson was a complex person, and like Columbus, Benjamin Franklin, and George Washington, the myths that surround him have obscured the real man. Discuss how effectively Lerner has stripped away the legends around Jefferson the demigod to reveal Jefferson the many-sided human being.

16

The Great Chief Justice

BRIAN McGINTY

As the court of last appeal in all matters involving the Constitution, the United States Supreme Court may be the most powerful branch of the federal government. It has the authority to uphold or strike down federal and state legislation, overturn decisions by lower courts, and determine the rights of individuals. Consequently, as in the modern struggle over abortion, the Court often stands at the center of national controversy.

You may be surprised to read in this selection that the Court was not always supreme, that in the first decade of its existence it was a maligned junior branch of the federal government, ignored by lawyers and scorned by politicians. How did it change into the powerful national tribunal we know today? As Brian McGinty points out, Chief Justice John Marshall made the nation's high tribunal a court that is supreme in fact as well as in name. During his thirty-four years on the bench (from 1801 to 1835), Marshall, a dedicated Federalist, also read the basic tenets of federalism into American constitutional law: the supremacy of the nation over the states, the sanctity of contracts, the protection of property rights, and the superiority of business over agriculture.

If you fear you are about to read a dull and dreary essay on constitutional law, don't despair. McGinty's warm portrait of the chief justice personalizes the major currents of the period and captures Marshall the human being in vivid scenes. We see him doing his own shopping for groceries, frequenting taverns and grog shops (he loves wine so much that a colleague quips, "the Chief was brought up on Federalism and Madeira"), and carrying a turkey for a young jurist who is too embarrassed to do so in public. Marshall clashes repeatedly with Jefferson over fundamental political and constitutional issues; here we see Jefferson from a somewhat different perspective than we did in selection 15. Later Marshall tangles with Andrew Jackson in defending the treaty rights of the Cherokee Indians, a subject to be treated in more detail in selection 22.

It was Marshall's court decisions, however, that had the largest impact on his country. As McGinty says, Marshall's ruling in Marbury v. Madison, which established the principle of judicial review, was perhaps the most important decision ever to come from the United States Supreme Court. Judicial review empowered the Supreme Court to interpret the meaning of the Constitution and so to define the authority of the national government and the states. The system of judicial review helped ensure the flexibility of the Constitution — so much so that a document originally designed for a small, scattered, largely agrarian population on the East Coast could endure for two centuries, during which the United States became a transcontinental, then a transpacific urban and industrial nation. That the Constitution has been able to grow and change with the country owes much to John Marshall.

HE WAS a tall man with long legs, gangling arms, and a round, friendly face. He had a thick head of dark hair and strong, black eyes — "penetrating eyes," a friend called them, "beaming with intelligence and good nature." He was born in a log cabin in western Virginia and never wholly lost his rough frontier manners. Yet John Marshall became a lawyer, a member of Congress, a diplomat, an advisor to presidents, and the most influential and respected judge in the history of the United States. "If American law were to be represented by a single figure," Supreme Court Justice Oliver Wendell Holmes, Jr., once said, "sceptic and worshipper alike would agree without dispute that the figure could be but one alone, and that one John Marshall."

From "The Great Chief Justice" by Brian McGinty, *American History Illustrated* (September 1988), pp. 8–14, 46–47. Reprinted by permission from American History Illustrated Magazine.

To understand Marshall's preeminence in American legal history it is necessary to understand the marvelous rebirth the United States Supreme Court experienced after he became its chief justice in 1801. During all of the previous eleven years of its existence, the highest judicial court in the federal system had been weak and ineffectual — ignored by most of the nation's lawyers and judges and scorned by its principal politicians. Under Marshall's leadership, the court became a strong and vital participant in national affairs. During his more than thirty-four years as chief justice of the United States, Marshall welded the Supreme Court into an effective and cohesive whole. With the support of his colleagues on the high bench, he declared acts of Congress and of the president unconstitutional, struck down laws that infringed on federal prerogatives, and gave force and dignity to basic guarantees of life and liberty and property. Without John Marshall, the Supreme Court might never have been anything but an inconsequential junior partner of the executive and legislative branches of the national government. Under his guidance and inspiration, it became what the Constitution intended it to be — a court system in fact as well as in name.

Born on September 4, 1755, in Fauquier County, Virginia, John Marshall was the oldest of fifteen children born to Thomas Marshall and Mary Randolph Keith. On his mother's side, the young Virginian was distantly related to Thomas Jefferson, the gentlemanly squire of Monticello and author of the Declaration of Independence. Aside from this kinship, there was little similarity between Marshall and Jefferson. A son of the frontier, Marshall was a backwoodsman at heart, more comfortable in the company of farmers than intellectuals or scholars. Jefferson was a polished aristocrat who liked to relax in the library of his mansion near Charlottesville and meditate on the subtleties of philosophy and political theory.

The contrast between the two men was most clearly drawn in their opposing political beliefs. An advocate of limiting the powers of central government, Thomas Jefferson thought of himself first and foremost as a Virginian (his epitaph did not even mention the fact that he had once been president of the United States). Marshall, in contrast, had, even as a young man, come to transcend his state roots, to look to Congress rather than the Virginia legislature as his government, to think of himself first, last, and always as an American. Throughout their careers, their contrasting philosophies would place the two men at odds.

Marshall's national outlook was furthered by his father's close association with George Washington and his own unflinching admiration for the nation's first president. Thomas Marshall had been a schoolmate of Washington and, as a young man, helped him survey the Fairfax estates in northern Virginia. John Marshall served under Washington during the bitter winter at Valley Forge and later became one of the planter-turned-statesman's most loyal supporters.

Years after the Revolution was over, Marshall attributed his political views to his experiences as a foot soldier in the great conflict, recalling that he grew up "at a time when a love of union and resistance to the claims of Great Britain were the inseparable inmates of the same bosom — when patriotism and a strong fellow feeling with our suffering fellow citizens of Boston were identical; — when the maxim 'united we stand, divided we fall' was the maxim of every orthodox American . . ." "I had imbibed these sentiments so thoughroughly (sic) that they constituted a part of my being," wrote Marshall. "I carried them with me into the army where I found myself associated with brave men from different states who were risking life and everything valuable in a common cause believed by all to be most precious; and where I was confirmed in the habit of considering America as my country, and Congress as my government."

After Washington's death, Marshall became the great man's biographer, penning a long and admiring account of Washington's life as a farmer, soldier, and statesman, expounding the Federalist philosophy represented by Washington and attacking those who stood in opposition to it. Jefferson, who detested Federalism as much as he disliked Marshall, was incensed by the biography, which he branded a "five-volume libel."

Frontiersman though he was, Marshall was no bumpkin. His father had personally attended to his earliest schooling, teaching him to read and write and giving him a taste for history and poetry (by the age of twelve he had already transcribed the whole of Alexander Pope's *Essay on Man*). When he was fourteen, Marshall was sent to a school a hundred miles from home, where future president James Monroe was one of his classmates. After a year, he returned home to be tutored by a Scottish pastor who had come to live in the Marshall house. The future lawyer read Horace and Livy, pored

Chester Harding's 1829 portrait of John Marshall. The Chief Justice, writes Brian McGinty, "was a tall man with long legs, gangling arms, and a round, friendly face. He had a thick head of dark hair and strong, black eyes — 'penetrating eyes,' a friend called them, 'beaming with intelligence and good nature.'" (Washington and Lee University, Virginia)

through the English dictionary, and scraped at least a passing acquaintance with the "Bible of the Common Law," William Blackstone's celebrated *Commentaries on the Laws of England.*

In 1779, during a lull in the Revolution, young Marshall attended lectures at the College of William and Mary in Williamsburg. He remained at the college only a few weeks, but the impression made on him by his professor there, George Wythe, was lasting. A lawyer, judge, and signer of the Declaration of Independence, Wythe is best remembered today as the first professor of law at any institution of higher learning in the United States. As a teacher, he was a seminal influence in the development of American law, counting among his many distinguished students Thomas Jefferson, John Breckinridge, and Henry Clay.

Marshall did not remain long at William and Mary. It was the nearly universal custom then for budding lawyers to "read law" in the office of an older lawyer or judge or, failing that, to appeal to the greatest teacher of all — experience — for instruction. In August 1780, a few weeks before his twenty-fifth birthday, Marshall appeared at the Fauquier County Courthouse where, armed with a license signed by Governor Thomas Jefferson of Virginia, he was promptly admitted to the bar.

His first cases were not important, but he handled them well and made a favorable impression on his neighbors; so favorable that they sent him to Richmond in 1782 as a member of the Virginia House of Delegates. Though he retained a farm in Fauquier County all his life, Richmond became Marshall's home after his election to the legislature. The general courts of Virginia held their sessions in the new capital, and the commonwealth's most distinguished lawyers crowded its bar. When Marshall's fortunes improved, he built a comfortable brick house on the outskirts of the city, in which he and his beloved wife Polly raised five sons and one daughter (four other offspring died during childhood).

Marshall's skill as a lawyer earned him an enthusiastic coterie of admirers and his honest country manners an even warmer circle of friends. He liked to frequent the city's taverns and grog shops, more for conviviality than for refreshment, and he was an enthusiastic member of the Barbecue Club, which met each Saturday to eat, drink, "josh," and play quoits.

Marshall liked to do his own shopping for groceries. Each morning he marched through the streets with a basket under his arm, collecting fresh fruits, vegetables, and poultry for the Marshall family larder. Years after his death, Richmonders were fond of recalling the day when a stranger came into the city in search of a lawyer and found Marshall in front of the Eagle Hotel, holding a hat filled with cherries and speaking casually with the hotel proprietor. After Marshall went on his way, the stranger approached the proprietor and asked if he could direct him to the best lawyer in Richmond. The proprietor replied quite readily that the best lawyer was John Marshall, the tall man with the hat full of cherries who had just walked down the street.

But the stranger could not believe that a man who walked through town so casually could be a really "proper barrister" and chose instead to hire a lawyer who wore a black suit and powdered wig. On the day set for the stranger's trial, several cases were scheduled to be argued. In the first that was called, the visitor was surprised to see that John Marshall and his own lawyer were to speak on opposite sides. As he listened to the arguments, he quickly realized that he had made a serious mistake. At the first recess, he approached Marshall and confessed that he had come to Richmond with a hundred dollars to hire the best lawyer in the city, but he had chosen the wrong one and now had only five dollars left. Would Marshall agree to represent him for such a small fee? Smiling good-naturedly, Marshall accepted the five dollars, then proceeded to make a brilliant legal argument that quickly won the stranger's case.

Marshall was not an eloquent man; not eloquent, that is, in the sense that his great contemporary, Patrick Henry, a spellbinding courtroom orator, was eloquent. Marshall was an effective enough speaker; but, more importantly, he was a rigorously logical thinker. He had the ability to reduce complex issues to bare essentials and easily and effortlessly apply abstract principles to resolve them.

Thomas Jefferson (himself a brilliant lawyer) was awed, even intimidated, by Marshall's powers of persuasion. "When conversing with Marshall," Jefferson once said, "I never admit anything. So sure as you admit any position to be good, no matter how remote from the conclusion he seeks to establish, you are gone. . . . Why, if he were to ask me if it were daylight or not, I'd reply, 'Sir, I don't know, I can't tell.'"

Though Marshall's legal prowess and genial manner won him many friends in Richmond, his political views did little to endear him to the Old Dominion's political establishment. While Jefferson and his followers preached the virtues of agrarian democracy, viewing with alarm every step by which the fledgling national government extended its powers through the young nation, Marshall clearly allied himself with Washington, Alexander Hamilton, and John Adams and the Federalist policies they espoused.

Marshall was not a delegate to the convention that met in Philadelphia in 1787 to draft a constitution for the United States, but he took a prominent part in efforts to secure ratification of the Constitution, thereby winning the special admiration of George Washington. After taking office as president, Washington offered Marshall the post of attorney general. Marshall declined the appointment, as he did a later offer of the prestigious post of American minister to France, explaining that he preferred to stay in Richmond with his family and law practice.

He did agree, however, to go to Paris in 1798 as one of three envoys from President John Adams to the government of revolutionary France. He did this, in part, because he was assured that his duties in Paris would be temporary only, in part because he believed he could perform a real service for his country, helping to preserve peaceful relations between it and France during a time of unusual diplomatic tension.

After Marshall joined his colleagues Elbridge Gerry and Charles Pinckney in Paris, he was outraged to learn that the French government expected to be paid before it would receive the American emissaries. Marshall recognized the French request as a solicitation for a bribe (the recipients of the payments were mysteriously identified as "X," "Y," and "Z"), and he refused to consider it.

Thomas Jefferson, who was smitten with the ardor and ideals of the French Revolution, suspected that Marshall and his Federalist "cronies" were planning war with France to promote the interests of their friends in England. But the American people believed otherwise. When they received news of the "XYZ Affair," they were outraged. "Millions for defense," the newspapers thundered, "but not one cent for tribute!" When Marshall returned home in the summer of 1798, he was welcomed as a hero. In the elections of the following fall, he was sent to Congress as a Federalist representative from Richmond.

Jefferson was not pleased. He declined to attend a dinner honoring Marshall in Philadelphia and wrote worried letters to his friends. Though he deprecated his fellow Virginian's popularity, alternatively attributing it to his "lax, lounging manners" and his "profound hypocrisy," Jefferson knew that Marshall was a potentially dangerous adversary. A half-dozen years before the Richmonder's triumphal return from Paris, Jefferson had written James Madison a cutting letter about Marshall that included words he would one day rue: "I think nothing better could be done than to make him a judge."

In Congress, Marshall vigorously supported the Federalist policies of President John Adams. Adams took note of the Virginian's ability in 1800 when he appointed him to the important post of secretary of state, a position that not only charged him with conduct of the country's foreign affairs but also left him in effective charge of the government during Adam's frequent absences in Massachusetts.

John Marshall's future in government seemed rosy and secure in 1800. But the elections in November of that year changed all that, sweeping Adams and the Federalists from power and replacing them with Jefferson and the Democratic Republicans.

After the election, but before Adam's term as president expired, ailing Supreme Court Chief Justice Oliver Ellsworth submitted his resignation. Casting about for a successor to Ellsworth, Adams sent John Jay's name to the Senate, only to have Jay demand that it be withdrawn. The thought of leaving the appointment of a new chief justice to Jefferson was abhorrent to Adams, and the president was growing anxious. He summoned Marshall to his office to confer about the problem.

"Who shall I nominate now?" Adams asked dejectedly. Marshall answered that he did not know. He had previously suggested that Associate Justice William Paterson be elevated to the chief justiceship, but Adams had opposed Paterson then and Marshall supposed that he still did. The president pondered for a moment, then turned to Marshall and announced: "I believe I shall nominate you!"

Adams's statement astounded Marshall. Only two years before, Marshall had declined the president's offer of an associate justiceship, explaining that he still hoped to return to his law practice in Richmond. "I had never before heard myself named for the office," Marshall recalled later, "and had not even thought of it. I was pleased as well as surprized (sic), and bowed my head in silence."

Marshall's nomination was sent to the Senate and promptly confirmed, and on February 4, 1801, he took his seat as the nation's fourth Chief Justice. As subsequent events would prove, it was one of the most important dates in American history.

With Thomas Jefferson in the Executive Mansion and John Marshall in the Chief Justice's chair, it was inevitable that the Supreme Court and the executive branch of the government should come into conflict. Marshall believed firmly in a strong national government and was willing to do all he could to strengthen federal institutions. Jefferson believed as firmly in state sovereignty and the necessity for maintaining constant vigilance against federal "usurpations." In legal matters, Jefferson believed that the Constitution should be interpreted strictly, so as to reduce rather than expand federal power.

Marshall, in contrast, believed that the Constitution should be construed fairly so as to carry out the intentions of its framers. Any law or executive act that violated the terms of the Constitution was, in Marshall's view, a nullity, of no force or effect; and it was the peculiar prerogative of the courts, as custodians of the laws of the land, to strike down any law that offended the Supreme Law of the Land.

Jefferson did not question the authority of the courts to decide whether a law or executive act violated the Constitution, but he believed that the other branches of the government also had a duty and a right to decide constitutional questions. In a controversy between the Supreme Court and the president, for example, the Supreme Court could order the president to do whatever the Court thought the Constitution required him to do; but the president could decide for himself whether the Supreme Court's order was proper and whether or not it should be obeyed.

As he took up the duties of the chief justiceship, Marshall contemplated his role with uncertainty. The Supreme Court in 1801 was certainly not the kind of strong, vital institution that might have been expected to provide direction in national affairs. There were six justices when Marshall joined the Court, but none (save the Chief Justice himself) was particularly distinguished. One or two men of national prominence had accepted appointment to the Court in the first eleven years of its existence, but none had remained there long. John Jay, the first Chief Justice, had resigned his seat in 1795 to become governor of New York. During the two years that John Rutledge was an associate justice, he had regarded the Court's business as so trifling that he did not bother to attend a single session, and he finally resigned to become chief justice of South

Carolina. The Court itself had counted for so little when the new capitol at Washington was being planned that the architects had made no provision for either a courtroom or judges' chambers, and the justices (to everyone's embarrassment) found that they had to meet in a dingy basement room originally designed for the clerk of the Senate.

How could Chief Justice Marshall use his new office to further the legal principles in which he believed so strongly? How could he strengthen the weak and undeveloped federal judiciary when most of the nation's lawyers and judges regarded that judiciary as superfluous and unnecessary? How could he implement his view of the Supreme Court as the final arbiter of constitutional questions when the President of the United States — his old nemesis, Thomas Jefferson — disagreed with that view so sharply? It was not an easy task, but John Marshall was a resourceful man, and he found a way to accomplish it.

His opportunity came in 1803 in the case of *Marbury* v. *Madison*. William Marbury was one of several minor federal judges who had been appointed during the closing days of John Adams's administration. When Jefferson's secretary of state, James Madison, refused to deliver the commissions of their offices, the judges sued Madison to compel delivery. In 1789, Congress had passed a law granting the Supreme Court authority to issue writs of mandamus, that is, legally enforceable orders compelling public officials to do their legal duties. Following the mandate of Congress, Marbury and the other appointees filed a petition for writ of mandamus in the Supreme Court.

Marshall pondered the possibilities of the case. He was sure that Marbury and his colleagues were entitled to their commissions, and he was just as sure that Jefferson and Madison had no intention of letting them have them. He could order Madison to deliver the commissions, but the secretary of state would certainly defy the order; and, as a practical matter, the Court could not compel obedience to any order that the president refused to acknowledge. Such an impasse would weaken, not strengthen, the federal union, and it would engender unprecedented controversy. No, there must be a better way. . . .

All eyes and ears in the capitol were trained on the lanky Chief Justice as he took his seat at the head of the high bench on February 24, 1803, and began to read the Supreme Court's opinion in *Marbury* v. *Madison.*

The evidence, Marshall said, clearly showed that Marbury and the other judges were entitled to their commissions. The commissions had been signed and sealed before John Adams left office and were, for all legal purposes, complete and effective. To withhold them, as Jefferson and Madison insisted on doing, was an illegal act. But the Supreme Court would not order the secretary of state to deliver the commissions because the law authorizing it to issue writs of mandamus was unconstitutional: the Constitution does not authorize the Supreme Court to issue writs of mandamus; in fact, it prohibits it from doing so. And any law that violates the Constitution is void. Since the law purporting to authorize the Supreme Court to act was unconstitutional, the Court would not — indeed, it could not — order Madison to do his legal duty.

If historians and constitutional lawyers were asked to name the single most important case ever decided in the United States Supreme Court, there is little doubt that the case would be *Marbury* v. *Madison.* Though the dispute that gave rise to the decision was in itself insignificant, John Marshall used it as a springboard to a great constitutional pronouncement. The rule of the case — that the courts of the United States have the right to declare laws unconstitutional — was immediately recognized as the cornerstone of American constitutional law, and it has remained so ever since.

More than a half-century would pass before the Supreme Court would again declare an act of Con-

gress unconstitutional, but its authority to do so would never again be seriously doubted. Marshall had made a bold stroke, and he had done so in such a way that neither Congress, nor the president, nor any other public official had any power to resist it. By denying relief to Marbury, he had made the Supreme Court's order marvelously self-enforcing!

Predictably, Thomas Jefferson was angry. If the Supreme Court could not issue writs of mandamus, Jefferson asked, why did Marshall spend so much time discussing Marbury's entitlement to a commission? And why did the Chief Justice lecture Madison that withholding the commission was an illegal act?

The president thought for a time that he might have the Chief Justice and his allies on the bench impeached. After a mentally unstable federal judge in New Hampshire was removed from office, Jefferson's supporters in the House of Representatives brought a bill of impeachment against Marshall's colleague on the Supreme Court, Associate Justice Samuel Chase. Chase was a Federalist who had occasionally badgered witnesses and made intemperate speeches, but no one seriously contended that he had committed an impeachable offense (which the Constitution defines as "treason, bribery, or other high crimes and misdemeanors"). So the Senate, three-quarters of whose members were Jeffersonians, refused to remove Chase from office. Marshall breathed a deep sigh of relief. Had the associate justice been impeached, the chief had no doubt that he himself would have been Jefferson's next target.

Though he never again had occasion to strike down an act of Congress, Marshall delivered opinions in many cases of national significance; and, in his capacity as circuit judge (all Supreme Court justices "rode circuit" in the early years of the nineteenth century), he presided over important, sometimes controversial, trials. He was the presiding judge when Jefferson's political arch rival, Aaron Burr, was charged with treason in 1807. Interpreting the constitutional provision defining treason against the United States, Marshall helped to acquit Burr, though he did so with obvious distaste. The

Burr prosecution, Marshall said, was "the most unpleasant case which has been brought before a judge in this or perhaps any other country which affected to be governed by law."

On the high bench, Marshall presided over scores of precedent-setting cases. In *Fletcher* v. *Peck* (1810) and *Dartmouth College* v. *Woodward* (1819), he construed the contracts clause of the Constitution so as to afford important protection for the country's growing business community. In *McCulloch* v. *Maryland* (1819), he upheld the constitutionality of the first Bank of the United States and struck down the Maryland law that purported to tax it. In *Gibbons* v. *Ogden* (1824), he upheld federal jurisdiction over interstate commerce and lectured those (mainly Jeffersonians) who persistently sought to enlarge state powers at the expense of legitimate federal authority.

Though Marshall's opinions always commanded respect, they were frequently unpopular. When, in *Worcester* v. *Georgia* (1832), he upheld the treaty rights of the Cherokee Indians against encroachments by the State of Georgia, he incurred the wrath of President Andrew Jackson. "John Marshall has made his decision," "Old Hickory" snapped contemptuously. "Now let him enforce it!" Marshall knew, of course, that he could not enforce the decision; that he could not enforce any decision that did not have the moral respect and acquiescence of the public and the officials they elected. And so he bowed his head in sadness and hoped that officials other than Andrew Jackson would one day show greater respect for the nation's legal principles and institutions.

Despite the controversy that some of his decisions inspired, the Chief Justice remained personally popular; and, during the whole of his more than thirty-four years as head of the federal judiciary, the Court grew steadily in authority and respect.

Well into his seventies, Marshall continued to ride circuit in Virginia and North Carolina, to travel each year to his farm in Fauquier County, to attend to his shopping duties in Richmond, and to preside over the high court each winter and spring in Washington. On one of his visits to a neighborhood market in Richmond, the Chief Justice happened on a young man who had been sent to fetch a turkey for his mother. The youth wanted to comply with his mother's request, but thought it was undignified to carry a turkey in the streets "like a servant." Marshall offered to carry it for him. When the jurist got as far as his own home, he turned to the young man and said, "This is where I live. Your house is not far off; can't you carry the turkey the balance of the way?" The young man's face turned crimson as he suddenly realized that his benefactor was none other than the Chief Justice of the United States.

Joseph Story, who served as an associate justice of the Supreme Court for more than twenty years of Marshall's term as chief justice, spent many hours with the Virginian in and out of Washington. Wherever Story observed Marshall, he was impressed by his modesty and geniality. "Meet him in a stagecoach, as a stranger, and travel with him a whole day," Story said, "and you would only be struck with his readiness to administer to the accommodations of others, and his anxiety to appropriate the least to himself. Be with him, the unknown guest at an inn, and he seemed adjusted to the very scene, partaking of the warm welcome of its comforts, wherever found; and if not found, resigning himself without complaint to its meanest arrangements. You would never suspect, in either case, that he was a great man; far less that he was the Chief Justice of the United States."

In his youth, Marshall had been fond of corn whiskey. As he grew older, he lost his appetite for spirits but not for wine. He formulated a "rule" under which the Supreme Court judges abstained from wine except in wet weather, but Story said he was liberal in allowing "exceptions." "It does sometimes happen," Story once said, "the Chief Justice will say to me, when the cloth is removed, 'Brother Story, step to the window and see if it does not look like rain.' And if I tell him that the sun is shining brightly, Judge Marshall will sometimes reply, 'All the better; for our jurisdiction extends over so large a territory that it must be raining somewhere.'" "You know," Story added, "that the Chief was brought up upon Federalism and Madeira, and he is not the man to outgrow his early prejudices."

In Richmond, Marshall held regular dinners for local lawyers, swapped stories with old friends, and tossed quoits with his neighbors in the Barbecue Club. An artist named Chester Harding remembered seeing the chief justice at a session of the Barbecue Club in 1829. Harding said Marshall was "the best pitcher of the party, and could throw heavier quoits than any other member of the club." "There were several ties," he added, "and, before long, I saw the great Chief Justice of the United States, down on his knees, measuring the contested distance with a straw, with as much earnestness as if it had been a point of law; and if he proved to be in the right, the woods would ring with his triumphant shout."

In 1830, a young Pennsylvania congressman and future president of the United States commented on Marshall's enduring popularity among his neighbors. "His decisions upon constitutional questions have ever been hostile to the opinions of a vast majority of the people in his own State," James Buchanan said, "and yet with what respect and veneration has he been viewed by Virginia? Is there a Virginian whose heart does not beat with honest pride when the just fame of the Chief Justice is the subject of conversation? They consider him, as he truly is, one of the great and best men which this country has ever produced."

Marshall was nearly eighty years old when he died in Philadelphia on July 6, 1835. His body was brought back to Virginia for burial, where it was met by the longest procession the city of Richmond had ever seen.

In the contrast between proponents of strong and weak national government, Marshall had been one of the foremost and clearest advocates of strength. The struggle — between union and disunion, between federation and confederation, between the belief that the Constitution created a nation and the theory that it aligned the states in a loose league — was not finally resolved until 1865. But the struggle *was* resolved. "Time has been on Marshall's side," Oliver Wendell Holmes, Jr., said in 1901. "The theory for which Hamilton argued, and he decided, and Webster spoke, and Grant fought, is now our cornerstone."

Justice Story thought that Marshall's appointment to the Supreme Court contributed more "to the preservation of the true principles of the Constitution than any other circumstances in our domestic history." "He was a great man," Story said. "I go farther; and insist, that he would have been deemed a great man in any age, and of all ages. He was one of those, to whom centuries alone give birth."

John Adams and Thomas Jefferson both lived long and distinguished lives, but neither ever gave an inch in their differences of opinion over Marshall. Jefferson went to his grave bemoaning the "cunning and sophistry" of his fellow Virginian. Adams died secure in the belief that his decision to make Marshall chief justice had been both wise and provident. Years later, Adams called Marshall's appointment "the pride of my life." Time has accorded Thomas Jefferson a great place in the affections of the American people, but, in the controversy over John Marshall, the judgment of history has come down with quiet strength on the side of John Adams.

QUESTIONS TO CONSIDER

1   John Marshall and Thomas Jefferson were both Virginians; they were also distant relatives. How did they turn out to be so different from each other?

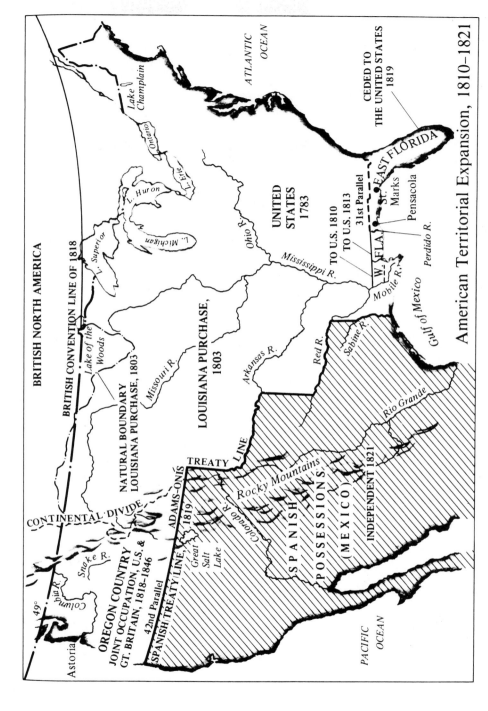

American Territorial Expansion, 1810–1821

BRITISH NORTH AMERICA

BRITISH CONVENTION LINE OF 1818

Lake Champlain

L. Ontario

L. Erie

L. Huron

L. Michigan

L. Superior

Lake of the Woods

NATURAL BOUNDARY
LOUISIANA PURCHASE, 1803

CONTINENTAL DIVIDE

49°

Astoria

Columbia R.

Snake R.

OREGON COUNTRY
JOINT OCCUPATION, U.S. &
GT. BRITAIN, 1818–1846

42nd Parallel
SPANISH TREATY LINE

ADAMS-ONÍS
1819

TREATY LINE

Great Salt Lake

Colorado R.

Rocky Mountains

SPANISH POSSESSIONS
(MEXICO)

INDEPENDENT 1821

Rio Grande

Sabine R.

Red R.

Arkansas R.

LOUISIANA PURCHASE, 1803

Missouri R.

Ohio R.

Mississippi R.

UNITED STATES 1783

TO U.S. 1810
TO U.S. 1813
31st Parallel

W. FLA.

Mobile R.

Perdido R.

Pensacola

St. Marks

EAST FLORIDA

CEDED TO
THE UNITED STATES
1819

ATLANTIC OCEAN

Gulf of Mexico

PACIFIC OCEAN

Transcontinental map of the United States (From The Course of American Diplomacy: From the Revolution to the Present by Howard Jones. © 1985 by Howard Jones. Reprinted by permission of Wadsworth.

235

did most of his life, Benton felt that the United States could probably not extend its sovereignty to Oregon — indeed he pictured the "fabled god Terminus" astride the Rocky Mountains preventing future mass migrations in that direction — but he saw Oregon and the Columbia as a strategic trading outpost on the road to India: hence of supreme importance to American interests. A settlement of republican-minded emigrants from the United States at the mouth of the Columbia would give the new nation a window on the Pacific, keep the British out, and make the Columbia, and what came to be the Oregon Trail (discovered by Robert Stuart in 1813) a vital path of inland commerce between the Mississippi Valley and the Pacific with its sea otter and China trade. Benton's grandiose rhetoric in defense of this aggressive plan more than matched the audacity of the plan itself, which had once been the dream of John Jacob Astor and of Thomas Jefferson.

Given these pressures, the results of the negotiations of 1818 were at least satisfactory. No boundary west of the Rocky Mountains was agreed upon. In August, 1818, Astoria was returned to American sovereignty and an official American claim was established north of the Columbia River, although it took a warship, the U.S.S. *Ontario,* to do it. And finally the negotiators agreed to a joint occupation treaty to extend for ten years which left both the British and Americans free to trade in the Oregon country, but which did not prejudice the claims of either nation to political sovereignty over the region. Spanish interests in the Northwest were for the time being ignored.

Adams was not, however, unmindful of Spain. The object of his immediate attention was Florida, both East Florida, "the pistol pointed at the heart of the United States," and West Florida, the region extending from the Mississippi to the present-day Florida line. The latter, Spain claimed, was not properly part of the Louisiana Purchase, and the former, though she held it loosely under tolerance from the Indians, she regarded as having great strategic

if not sentimental value. Both of these areas were troublesome to the United States: from them, spurred on by British and Spanish soldiers of fortune and agents of the Panton-Leslie Company, bands of brigands, red men and white, terrorized settlements on the American southwestern frontier. It fell to Adams to extinguish these conflagrations by acquiring the Floridas by any peaceful means possible. In performing this task he had powerful aid from his future lifelong political antagonist, General Andrew Jackson.

Under Monroe's orders Jackson employed the doctrine of "hot pursuit" and invaded Florida, capturing Pensacola and St. Mark's. There, with 3,000 men, he chastised the Indians, humiliated the Spanish officials, and precipitated a serious international crisis by executing two British filibusters. . . . Weak-minded, vindictive or politically opportunistic members of Monroe's cabinet wished to disavow or publicly condemn Jackson's actions. But Adams persuaded Monroe against this action, despite the possibility of war with England and Spain. This course proved to be an expedient one. Lord Castlereagh and the British negotiators in London acknowledged the justice of Jackson's actions and proceeded in good spirits to negotiate the other issues of the treaty of 1818. Spain, on the other hand, although she protested vehemently, saw clearly that the Floridas were beyond her practical control. This increased her willingness to trade them for some more secure piece of property, in point of fact Texas, and if possible the entire Trans-Mississippi West, as far north as the upper Missouri.

Adams' negotiation of the transcontinental boundary treaty of 1819 thus began as a swap: Texas (whatever that was) for the Floridas. As a student of history, Adams could not help being aware of Spain's insecurity over Texas and New Mexico. In 1806, Zebulon Pike was captured on the upper Rio Grande and held prisoner, his papers and maps were confiscated, and he was summarily sent back to the United States by the quickest possible route. Shortly afterward, in 1807, Captains Freeman and Sparks were turned back on the Red River. That same year the fur trader Anthony Glass was repeatedly threatened by Spanish authorities as he intruded on what they regarded as their territory. An 1812 trading expedition by Robert McKnight to Santa Fe landed him in a Chihuahua prison for nine years. The Gutierrez-Magee filibustering expedition into Texas in 1813 was put down and its leaders executed. In 1818 the fur trader Auguste Chouteau and his partner Jules DeMun were captured on the upper Arkansas. Their furs were confiscated; they were forced to kneel and kiss the document sentencing them; and then they were sent home with a bare minimum of equipment. These were convincing demonstrations of Spanish insecurities regarding Texas, but what made them seem outrageous to the United States was the fact that, if the limits of the Louisiana Purchase included the watershed of the Mississippi, then the territory to the headwaters of the Arkansas and Red Rivers belonged to the United States. Indeed, certain enthusiasts with a poor knowledge of geography claimed even the Rio Grande on this basis.

Needless to say, faced by a threatened American penetration of its territories, Spain, by 1819, was ready to negotiate a boundary that would give her a buffer against American invasion. Though Adams never knew it, she was willing to retreat all the way to the Rio Grande.

The negotiations with the Spanish minister Onís . . . began with Adams offering a Texas boundary and indemnity for the Floridas. The Spanish sought a larger buffer to the West, however, and attempted to extend the Texas border from the high point of land between two creeks near Natchitoches, Louisiana, north to the Missouri River. In this way they could acquire most of Louisiana in exchange for the Floridas, which they could not hold in any case. This strategy, however, caused Adams to revise his own thinking. Previously he had been concerned with southern and southwestern problems; now the vision of a continental empire arose, and he shifted

ground. If in exchange for Texas he could acquire the Floridas and also an extension of Louisiana in a wide swath to the Pacific, he would have opened the way to an American empire on the Pacific and gained the key to the continent.

Thus began a series of new negotiations, with the implied threat of an American invasion of the Floridas and Texas hanging in the background. On July 16 Adams, using [John] Melish's inaccurate map of 1818 [which accompanied his book *A Geographical Description of the World*], offered a line up the Colorado River of Texas to the Red River, and then across from the Red River to the crest of the Rocky Mountains, thence along the 41st parallel to the Pacific. Onís countered with a line northward from Natchitoches to the Missouri, then along the Missouri to its headwaters at the Three Forks, the line west from there not specified. And so the negotiations went throughout the fall and winter of 1818–1819, with Onís trying ultimately to get a Missouri-Columbia line to the Pacific with rights of trade on these rivers, and Adams stumping for the Colorado River of Texas or the Sabine River and the 41st parallel. Even an ultimatum offer of October 31, 1818, made at the behest of President Monroe, who had grown impatient, failed to impress Onís. Then Monroe began to give ground and seemed almost inclined to accept Onís' proposal of February 1, 1819, which was a line up the Arkansas River to the mythical San Clemente River, to the 43rd parallel and along it to the sea. But Adams held firm, and eventually on February 22, 1819, he had his transcontinental boundary treaty. The major provisions of the treaty included the Spanish cession of the Floridas, East and West, to the United States, the assumption by the United States of American claims against Spain up to $5 million, and a western boundary line which began at the mouth of the Sabine River, continued north along the western bank of that river to the 32nd parallel of latitude, thence by a line due north to the Red River, thence westward up the south bank of the Red River to the

100th meridian of longitude, thence across the Red River due north on the 100th meridian to the south bank of the Arkansas River, thence up that river to its source in latitude 42° north, and westward from that point along the 42nd parallel to the Pacific, as laid down in Melish's map of 1818.

Adams had thus bartered away Texas, but he had gained the Floridas and, equally important, he had gained his coveted transcontinental corridor to the Pacific. In accomplishing this he had served the New England sea traders well. But, in addition, despite much western opposition, he had served the West equally well since the acquisition of the Spanish claims to the Northwest opened the way for the development of the Rocky Mountain fur trade. However, Westerners fretted that he had given up Texas and the potential riches of the Southwest. Present-day knowledge of Spanish documents indicates that he had indeed done so. But Adams could not have known this at the time, and thus he did the best he could. As his biographer remarks,

Even without Texas the Transcontinental Treaty with Spain was the greatest diplomatic victory won by any single individual in the history of the United States.

One further course of diplomatic events that took place while Adams was Secretary of State continued — indeed exaggerated — the emergence of America on the horizon of world diplomacy. This involved the development or formulation of an American policy for the entire western hemisphere that culminated in the Monroe Doctrine.

During the time Adams was negotiating with Spain, the countries of Latin America, encouraged by tradesmen from England and the United States, revolted against Spain, and in a long series of civil wars succeeded in establishing a de facto independence. Since the delicate negotiations with Spain were in progress, Adams was reluctant to recognize the new revolutionary nations although, like Jefferson, he sympathized with their desire for indepen-

Austere, cold, determined, and tenacious, John Quincy Adams was nevertheless a visionary, and one of the most brilliant secretaries of state in United States history. The Monroe Doctrine, for which he was primarily responsible, was a cornerstone of American foreign policy from its inception. (The Metropolitan Museum of Art, Gift of I. N. Phelps Stokes, Edward S. Hawes, Alice Mary Hawes, Marion Augusta Hawes, 1937)

dence. As a New Englander, however, Adams also deplored the outfitting by the new countries of privateers which preyed on world shipping, including that of neutrals. He stood for the principle of freedom of the seas, and the violation of that principle by any power, however just its cause, threatened the principle itself. At least during the Spanish treaty negotiations the canny Braintree moralist used this as an argument to counter the enthusiastic trumpetings of Henry Clay, who was demanding immediate recognition of the new republics, partly out of sincerity and partly because of a desire to embarrass the Monroe administration.

Eventually the new Latin republics ceased their privateering. American business representatives were established in the major ports. And, in 1821, Spain ratified the transcontinental treaty. Between 1822 and 1826 the United States recognized the independence of the seven new Latin American countries, although not all of them were republics patterned after the Jeffersonian democratic model. The United States was the first major nation to recognize formally the independence of the Latin states, and she did so at the risk of offending the major powers of Europe.

After the defeat of Napoleon [1815], the chief continental powers led by the Czar of Russia formed the Holy Alliance with the avowed purpose of keeping peace in Europe through pacts of mutual assistance. Although we now know that there was little chance of a continental nation coming to the aid of Spain in her attempt to regain her lost New World colonies, this did not necessarily appear to be the case when the United States extended its recognition. Rather than a feat of diplomatic daring, however, the recognition of the Latin states appears to have been a response to demands by American trading and maritime interests for official government support in their competition with Britain for the trade of South and Central America.

[Meanwhile], Adams faced still another challenge to his dream of a continental empire. In 1816 the Russians had landed at Bodega Bay north of San Francisco and established a colony, Fort Ross. Subsequently Russia claimed all of the Pacific coast from Alaska to the latitude of Fort Ross, which of course encompassed the newly won Spanish claims above the 42nd parallel. Adams sternly rebuked the Russian expansionists in a note which was later to become the model for the Monroe Doctrine. He wrote to the Russian minister in Washington that the United States contested the right of Russia to her coastal claims, and furthermore he declared, ''We

should assume distinctly the principle that the American continents are no longer subjects for any new European colonial establishments.'' Russia retreated from her untenable and unprofitable position in the face of opposition not only from the United States but also from Britain, and in 1824 concluded a treaty with the United States limiting her territorial aspirations to 54°40', the present Alaskan boundary. In 1825 a similar treaty with Britain was consummated. Adams had forestalled still another threat by a major power, although the United States had no way of defending her position by anything like the force of arms.

The Monroe Doctrine grew out of this anti-European position. Interested in maintaining good relations with South America, the British Minister, George Canning, proposed in 1823 that the United States join with England in making a declaration against any further attempts by the continental powers to colonize the New World. At Adams' insistence Monroe refused to join the British plan. Instead he issued an independent American statement, since known as the Monroe Doctrine, although Adams claimed to be its primary author. The Monroe Doctrine declared:

1   That the United States did not wish to take part in the politics or wars of Europe.

2   That the United States would regard as manifestations of an unfriendly disposition to itself the effort of any European power to interfere with the political system of the American continents, or to acquire any new territory on these continents.

The Monroe Doctrine . . . was something more and something less than tradition has made it seem. Enforcement of the doctrine depended . . . on the British fleet, and in this sense many have considered it a hollow gesture although it was a true commitment. Later generations have seen it as a weapon or facade behind which the United States was able to interfere unduly in the internal affairs of its neighbors, and it has also on occasion served this purpose. Still others regard it as one more inflexible American principle that by its unyielding quality has limited American maneuverability in Latin American affairs, and this is certainly correct. But understood in the context of its own day, the Monroe Doctrine would appear to have several other legitimate purposes. First, it was a refusal to allow Latin America to become exclusively a British protectorate. Second, it reinforced American trading interests in the hemisphere. Third, it announced America's emergence as a power among nations that had to be reckoned with. Fourth, it was a gesture of genuine goodwill and concern for the new Latin republics. Fifth, it was a continual renunciation of European political alliances and a strategic refusal to play the balance-of-power game on Britain's terms. And finally, it was a rallying cry, a nationalistic symbol for Americans at home, that drew the nation together in terms of its ultimate ideals of republican democracy for all. Only the fact of slavery beclouded the lofty pretensions of such a democratic mission.

By the time Adams became president, the United States had acquired a continental empire of its own that looked both inward and outward, south toward the Caribbean, and west toward China and the Pacific. It had, moreover, taken an important place in the world family of nations and, following Jefferson's prophecy, it had spawned sister republics based on the American model as far as Cape Horn. The French had been ousted from North America, and the British, Spanish, and Russians severely circumscribed. This was not the work of a nation that sought or needed a comfortable security. It was the missionary impulse of individuals who had fought their way to freedom and independence, and therefore appreciated their virtues, an impulse making itself felt for the first time around the world.

QUESTIONS TO CONSIDER

1 How was John Quincy Adams, in Goetzmann's words, both the incarnation of "the staunch, introspective New England puritan" and also "a man of the world"?

2 In what ways were John Quincy Adams and Thomas Jefferson both "architects of American westward expansion"? Compare the two men's motives for acquiring new lands. How did Adams's motives reflect local as well as national interests?

3 Adams's biographer calls the Adams-Onís Treaty "the greatest diplomatic victory won by any single individual in the history of the United States." Does the available evidence support or contradict this judgment?

4 Examine American motives in extending formal recognition to seven newly independent Latin American countries between 1822 and 1826. Weigh the idealistic and materialistic reasons. What significance do these deliberations have for present United States relations with Latin America?

5 The Monroe Doctrine, as Goetzmann points out, has come under much-warranted criticism since President Monroe issued the declaration in 1824. But Goetzmann also says that, judged in the context of its own times, the Monroe Doctrine had several legitimate purposes. What were these purposes? Do you think earlier presidents like Washington and Jefferson would have approved of the Monroe Doctrine?

IX

THE
AGE OF
JACKSON

18

"I Will Die with the Union": Andrew Jackson and the Nullification Crisis

ROBERT V. REMINI

The Age of Jackson was a turbulent era — a period of boom and bust, of great population shifts into the cities and out to the frontier, of institutionalized violence and racial antagonisms, of utopian communities, reform movements, the abolitionist crusade, and the "great Southern reaction" in defense of slavery. It was also a time of graft and corruption, of machine politics and ruthless political bosses. But above all it was an age of the self-made man, a time when privilege and elitist rule gave way to the vestiges of popular democracy — at least for white males. Between the 1820s and the 1840s, America witnessed the rise of universal manhood suffrage for whites, long ballots, national nominating conventions, and grassroots political parties.

The man who gave the age its name was a self-made planter and slaveholder of considerable wealth. Like most aristocrats from the Tennessee country of his day, Andrew Jackson could not spell, he lacked education and culture, but he did aspire to wealth and military glory, both of which he won. Despite his harsh, gaunt features, he looked like a gentleman and a soldier, and in calm moods he could be gentle, even grave. Though anything but "a common man," he was a symbol for the typical American of that day — an "expectant capitalist," as historian Richard Hofstadter has described him, who also wanted to become a self-made success. Ambitious and hardworking, the expectant capitalist looked to the Jacksonian government to remove monopolies and other special interests that prevented him from entering American *enterprise and making his fortune as well. This entrepreneurial impulse was the driving spirit of the Jacksonian movement, which by 1845 had expanded economic as well as political opportunity for America's lower- and middle-class white males and contributed considerably to the notion that America was a country of self-made men.*

But Jackson was more than a symbol for an age. In office, he asserted his executive powers more aggressively than any president before him. Nowhere was this more in evidence than in his handling of the nullification crisis of 1832, which threatened the survival of the United States as a nation. Robert V. Remini, today's foremost Jackson scholar and author of many books about Jackson, including a prize-winning three-volume biography, guides us confidently through Jackson's role in the nullification crisis, describing how Jackson drew on all his political skills to preserve the Union and uphold the supremacy of national law. In this and other ways, says Remini, Jackson inaugurated the history of powerful executive leadership in this country.

DURING THE FIRST YEARS OF HIS PRESIDENCY Jackson's own thinking about issues and policies tended to be neo-Jeffersonian and conservative, leaning toward States' rights and the economics of laissez faire, but fundamentally pragmatic in concept, and suffused with a strong sense of popular need. Later in his administration he edged closer to the notion of a strong central government, but as he moved he was invariably motivated by sheer political necessity. Consequently whenever there was disagreement between sections on practically any political issue, Jackson tended to equivocate and, where possible, to seek a compromise. For example, the question of federally-sponsored internal improvements provoked sharp differences of opinion. The National Republican party of Clay, Webster, and Adams supported the principle in general. Since westerners also favored public works, the Hero deliberately fuzzed his position on the issue, rather than risk western hostility. Yet he was not equivocal when it came to the Maysville Road, a stretch of proposed highway from Maysville to Lexington within the state of Kentucky, the home of Henry Clay. Friends of the projected road argued that it would be an extension of the National Road and therefore not something local in character; but [Martin] Van Buren, when still Secretary of State, denied this and characterized the bill as purely intrastate and therefore unconstitutional. It is not surprising that the Magician argued this way, since his own state had constructed the Erie Canal at its own expense and did not relish the idea of the federal government aiding other states to build similar improvements.

Despite such objections, and the inflexible opposition of States' righters, the Maysville Road bill passed Congress in May, 1830. Jackson vetoed it. In his message, he not only negated the Maysville Road, but he challenged the principle that internal improvements were a federal responsibility. "If it be the wish of the people that the construction of roads and canals should be conducted by the Federal

Government," he wrote, "it is not only highly expedient, but indispensably necessary, that a previous amendment to the Constitution, delegating the necessary power and defining and restricting its exercise with reference to the sovereignty of the States, should be made." What gave the veto special significance was the apparent hostility of the administration to the concept of an energetic central government in Washington — that it was reacting from a basic commitment to States' rights. But this was false. Jackson was not as much opposed to public works as his message implied, and he later approved several bills authorizing federal assistance for internal improvements. Fundamentally, the purpose of the veto was twofold: kill this particular bill because of its connection with Clay; and slap down what Van Buren called the "Internal Improvements party" (otherwise known as the National Republican party), which opposed his administration.

There was a tremendous uproar in the country over the veto, much of it organized by Clay and much of it ridiculous wailings about the dismal failure of public works. But the message, recorded Van Buren, was "the entering wedge" by which "the Internal Improvement party was broken asunder and finally annihilated." It was the first significant lunge against "a triumvirate of active and young statesmen" who were seeking "power . . . to achieve for themselves the glittering prize of the Presidency, operating in conjunction with minor classes of politicians . . . and backed by a little army of cunning contractors. . . ." The veto, in other words, was another of Jackson's carefully calculated political moves — not an expression of administration philosophy to be taken as immutable party doctrine. Although he continued throughout his administration to fret over the constitutional difficulties involved in public works, Jackson never regarded the Maysville veto as an absolute canon against improvements — at least not when they were sponsored by loyal Democrats. Said he to Congress, the first time both houses were won by his

party, "I am not hostile to internal improvements and wish to see them extended to every part of the country." . . .

But if there was misunderstanding about the President's intention [regarding internal improvements], there was no possible confusion over his intentions with respect to South Carolina and the problem of the tariff.

Trouble had been brewing for a long time. Southerners resented the tariff protection accorded northern industries because, among other things, it meant they had to buy their manufactured goods on a closed market, while they sold their cotton abroad on an open one. They were caught in a squeeze that drained them at both ends. Northerners, on the other hand, argued that they had to have government protection if they were to sustain themselves against competition from Europe, particularly Great Britain. Unfortunately the 1828 tariff, which jacked up the rates as high as their manipulators could get them, was conceived solely as a vehicle for Jackson's election, but now that he was safely ensconced in the White House, Southerners expected him to haul the rates down again. Indeed, if he did not, some of them were ready to do it for him, using the nullification device suggested by John C. Calhoun, South Carolina planter and Jackson's vice-president. Acting on the request of James Hamilton, Jr., Calhoun further explained his doctrine of nullification in a statement dated July 26, 1831, which became known as the "Fort Hill Address." According to his view, the Union was a compact of states, in which each state retained the right to examine the acts of Congress, and when necessary nullify within its borders any it felt was a violation of its sovereignty and rights. Thus, Calhoun would assign judicial review to each state, thereby destroying the fundamental concept of the tripartite national government constructed under the Constitution. To his credit, he did not favor secession. Nothing so blunt and sudden. What he proposed was the slow but inevitable dissolution of the Union through long legal and constitutional procedures. However, Southerners never really cared for the slow process. They preferred the quick bang. They never lost their affection for secession even when they trifled with nullification.

The testing of these various attitudes and doctrines came with the introduction of a new tariff in Congress by Henry Clay on January 9, 1832. . . .

The President promptly snatched leadership of the tariff question away from Clay — whose bill he mistrusted — by substituting another more to his liking. The southern "nullies" naturally prepared to resist any tariff, unless it completely capitulated to their terms, and just as naturally the President rejected their excessive terms. Instead, he tried to shape a bill which was satisfactory to the North and West without inflicting severe penalties on the South. What resulted was the Tariff of 1832. . . . Generally, the rates of the bill hovered near those imposed by the Tariff of 1824; and although it was not a low tariff, it did include several new items on the free list. Even so, high duties were again imposed on such political essentials as wool, woolens, iron, and hemp. Jackson signed the tariff on July 14, 1832, under the genuine conviction that it represented a compromise, one that would win approval in the North and quell the discontent in the South. Indeed, many Democrats and National Republicans applauded it as a reasonable and judicious "middle course," perhaps not wholly satisfactory to all, but one with which all sections and classes of the country could live.

This tariff reform, approaching sectional balance and accommodation, was totally unacceptable to the South Carolina Nullifiers. Representing none but a small radical fringe, they planned to subvert protection by threatening disunion. Their objective clearly in mind, they organized themselves in South Carolina during the presidential election of 1832 to strengthen their position before applying Calhoun's doctrine of nullification. So effective was their organization that they won a thumping victory at the polls, whereupon the governor of the state, James Hamilton, Jr., summoned a special session of the South Carolina legislature, which in turn called for the election of a convention to meet at Columbia on November 19, 1832, to take appropriate action.

As South Carolina sped toward nullification, possible disunion and civil war, the President countered with several effective actions. First he examined and prepared his military strength. He alerted naval authorities at Norfolk, Virginia, to stand ready to dispatch a squadron to South Carolina if trouble should arise. He ordered the Secretary of the Navy to take appropriate action to check any attempt by the "nullies" to undermine the loyalty of naval officers and men at Charleston Harbor; then he warned the commanders of the forts in that harbor to stand by for a possible emergency; and finally, he hurried Major-General Winfield Scott southward to take command of the Charleston garrison that had recently been changed. Yet none of these measures seemed sufficient to cool the hotheads gathered at Columbia, and on November 24, 1832 the convention, by a vote of 136 to 26, adopted an Ordinance of Nullification declaring the tariffs of 1828 and 1832 null and void and forbidding the collection of duties required by these laws within the state of South Carolina. Also it warned the federal government that if force were used to coerce the state, South Carolina would secede from the Union.

Jackson's reaction to this threat was masterful. He did not, as many contend, respond in a wild outburst of promises to scourge the state with violence unless it immediately capitulated and obeyed the tariff laws. He proceeded cautiously, trying to be conciliatory. Nevertheless, he would not be bullied, nor would he tolerate the humiliation of the country. What he did was alternate between the gesture of conciliation and the menace of retaliation. At one moment, he professed his willingness to forgive and grant concessions; at the next, he let it be known that he was preparing an army to put down treason. And it was this change of pace that threw the "nullies" completely off balance, weakening their resolve to experiment with the most extreme form of protest.

In implementing his approach, Jackson did several things at once. He encouraged Unionists within South Carolina, such as Joel Poinsett, the former minister to Mexico, assuring them that munitions would be available to them if it came to a question of saving the Union. "I repeat to the union men again," he wrote Poinsett, "fear not, *the union will be preserved* and treason and rebellion promptly put down, when and where it may shew its monster head." And, good to his word, he transported arms and ammunition a short distance away in North Carolina. Also, he sent George Breathitt, the brother of the governor of Kentucky, to South Carolina, ostensibly as a postal inspector but actually to serve as a liaison with the Unionists and to keep the President informed of developments lest they suddenly deteriorate to the point of secession and require vigorous action. Then, shifting his approach, Jackson delivered to Congress his annual message in which he urged a policy of conciliation. ". . . In justice," he wrote, ". . . the protection afforded by existing laws to any branches of the national industry should not exceed what may be necessary to counteract the regulations of foreign nations and to secure a supply of those articles of manufacture essential to the national independence and safety in time of war. If upon investigation it shall be found, as it is believed it will be, that the legislative protection granted to any particular interest is greater than is indispensably requisite for these objects, I recommend that it be gradually diminished, and that . . . the whole scheme of duties be reduced. . . ." Jackson ended by noticing the danger in South Carolina but ventured that the laws were sufficient to handle any eventuality. Privately, he admitted something more was necessary. "The union . . . will now be tested by the support I get by the people," he wisely said. "I will die with the union."

Then, in a Proclamation dated December 10,

President Jackson spoke directly to the people of South Carolina. In his message, he blended words of warning with entreaty, demand with understanding, threat with conciliation. He appealed to their fears, their pride, their interests; at the same time he categorically rejected nullification and secession. The nation was supreme, he said; not the states. "The laws of the United States must be executed. I have no discretionary power on the subject; my duty· is emphatically pronounced in the Constitution. Those who told you that you might peaceably prevent their execution deceived you. . . . Their object is disunion. But be not deceived by names. Disunion by armed force is *treason*. Are you really ready to incur its guilt?"

Much of the message was the work of the Secretary of State, Edward Livingston, particularly in its strong constitutional arguments about the nature of the Union, arguments very similar to those advanced by John Marshall and Daniel Webster. But the fire in it was pure Jackson; and that fire was what gave the Proclamation its special strength and power.

The publication of the Proclamation produced a chorus of patriotic shouts around the country. Meetings were organized to express support of the President; parades and bonfires demonstrated the ardor of Americans to stand behind Jackson. Thus, the Proclamation not only rallied the people to the President's side, prompting state legislatures (including those in the South) to denounce nullification and assure the General of their loyalty, but it also warned the nullifiers that if they rejected a peaceful settlement he was quite prepared to summon an armed force to execute the laws. In this respect, Jackson quietly let it be known that he could have fifty thousand men inside South Carolina within forty days and another fifty thousand forty days after that. Then, in a public display of his intention, he asked Congress for the necessary legislation to permit him to insure obedience of the tariff laws in South Carolina and the collection of the custom duties. When introduced into Congress the Force Bill (or Bloody Bill as it was called by some) received widespread support on a nonpartisan and intersectional basis.

Precisely within a week after Jackson's annual message, South Carolina indicated a willingness to respond to reason. Indeed, even when the Ordinance of Nullification was first adopted, it was apparent that a negotiated settlement was possible by the very fact that the date for the Ordinance to go into effect was advanced to February 1, 1833, giving the national government enough time to suggest an agreeable compromise. On December 10, the South Carolina legislature went further and elected as governor, Robert Y. Hayne, who was much more moderate on the nullification issue than his predecessor. Two days later, it elected John C. Calhoun U.S. Senator, thereby stationing the state's strongest bargainer inside the Congress to work out a settlement. Calhoun resigned the vice-presidency on December 28, 1832, to take his new office and begin the task of finding a consensus that would spare his state the humiliation of military defeat. As he was sworn in, one observer said, "I could not help thinking when he took the oath to support the Constitution of the United States that he made a mental reservation that it would be as 'he understood it.' "

Gratified by South Carolina's seeming efforts at moderation, Jackson quickly responded to show the state that any favorable move to avoid violence would be met with similar forbearance. For example, although General Scott had been sent to take command of the South Carolina troops, he was repeatedly warned to avoid trouble and any unnecessary display of force. Meanwhile, the administration threw its full weight behind a new tariff bill, introduced by Gulian C. Verplanck of New York and written with the assistance of the Secretary of the Treasury, which would lower protection by 50 per cent within two years. The bill elicited strong support from many northerners worried about the possibility of secession and civil war. Unfortunately,

protectionists howled their fears over such a sharp reduction of duties proposed by the Verplanck Bill. To make matters worse, Henry Clay tried to steer a land bill through Congress that would distribute revenue from the sale of land to the states, thus reducing the government's revenue and forcing it to raise the tariff. It was "mischievous" business, to use Silas Wright's apt description of it, completely unworthy of its author, but Clay had just been dealt a decisive defeat by Jackson in the presidential election of 1832, and he was bitter, angry, and resentful over his loss of prestige. Despite his nationalistic sentiments, he refused to assist the President in his efforts at compromise. Instead, he plotted to scuttle any legitimate accommodation of the tariff question. He seemed more worried by Jackson's triumphs and popularity than South Carolina's defiance of law. To strengthen his tactical position in Congress, therefore, he concluded an alliance with Senator Calhoun on the assumption that such a coalition would operate to their mutual benefit and the President's discomfort. Working together, Clay and Calhoun would kill the Verplanck Bill and emasculate the Force Bill.

On February 12, 1833 Clay introduced into the Senate what was euphemistically called a "compromise" tariff. The bill provided for the reduction of rates over a ten-year period, at the end of which time, no duty would be higher than 20 per cent. But there was a joker buried in it: only the tiniest reductions would occur during the first years of the bill's operation, the major changes coming nine years later at the tail end of the period. And, as it turned out, they would prove so sharp a drop as to threaten the economy of the country. It was a bad law, written without regard to compromise, and done for political advantage and the caressing of Clay's *amour propre*. However, if it could extinguish the fires of nullification and disunion the administration would go along with it, however apparent the bill's defects. The measure passed the Senate on March 1 by a vote of 29 to 16, and the House on

February 26 by a vote of 119 to 85. Almost all the South voted to accept it — the Congressmen literally falling over themselves to agree to any solution that would end the dispute and the possibility of civil war. New England and some of the Middle Atlantic states tended to vote against the bill, while the Northwest was split. That the passage of the Compromise Tariff of 1833 should be due almost entirely to the massive support it received from the South proved to some men how ridiculous politics could be.

While the tariff hared its way through Congress, the Force Bill was brought up for debate. Calhoun denounced the measure, finding it a suitable occasion to reargue his interpretation of the nature of the Union. He made a final effort to kill the bill by forcing an adjournment, but the Congress, conscious of the meaning of compromise, vetoed this maneuver. When the vote on the Force Bill was taken in the Senate, Calhoun and his followers strode out of the chamber. Only John Tyler of Virginia remained in his seat to cast the single vote against the bill. Reluctantly, Clay voiced approval of the measure during the debate, but on the day of the final vote he failed to appear, claiming poor health and the need to stay home and rest. The bill passed the House on March 1 by a vote of 149 to 48.

With great pride, Jackson signed both the Compromise Tariff and the Force Bill on March 2, 1833 just as his first term in office ended. South Carolina reassembled its convention on March 11 and repealed its nullification of the tariff laws but then proceeded to nullify the Force Bill. It was a pathetic gesture to save face, and the President chose not to quarrel with that.

Jackson's victory was an extraordinary display of tact and rare wisdom. He did not gain a total victory over South Carolina, nor did he want one. In politics total victory usually means eventual defeat. What he did was spare the Union the agony of civil conflict. He accomplished it not by waging war but by initiating compromise. That he did everything in his power to oblige South Carolina can be seen in the remark of John Quincy Adams, who thought the controversy was won by the Nullifiers, not Jackson. Of course, Calhoun and his henchmen claimed victory, and some even thought the real victor was Henry Clay, who, through it all, had managed to preserve his precious tariff. But Jackson's accomplishment can not be dismissed so lightly. Through the careful use of presidential powers, rallying the people to his side, alerting the military, offering compromise while preparing for treason, he preserved the Union and upheld the supremacy of federal law.

Because he had grown tremendously in political sagacity during the past few years Jackson took off on a long tour of the country just as soon as he could escape Washington. His purpose was to encourage demonstrations of popular approval for his recent conduct in handling South Carolina. The trip enabled the public to see their President close up as well as express their "detestation of nullification." Leaving the capital in late spring, 1833, and accompanied by Van Buren, Levi Woodbury, Lewis Cass, Major Donelson and others, Jackson journeyed to Baltimore, Philadelphia, Trenton, New York, Boston, Newport, Salem and many other cities. Those who witnessed any part of the grand tour never forgot "the long processions; the crowded roofs and windows; the thundering salutes of artillery; steamboats gay with a thousand flags and streamers; the erect, gray-headed old man, sitting his horse like a centaur, and bowing to the wild hurrahs of the Unterrified with matchless grace; the rushing forward of interminable crowds to shake the President's hand; the banquets, public and private; the toasts, addresses, responses; and all the other items of the price which a popular hero has to pay for his popularity."

In New York City, Jackson took a steamboat to Staten Island and while staring at the city's magnificent harbor he suddenly turned to a companion and

Ralph Earl's 1833 portrait of President Andrew Jackson shows him with anxious eyes and furrowed brow as he faced the greatest challenge of his presidency, the Nullification Crisis. "Jackson's victory," says Robert Remini, "was an extraordinary display of tact and rare wisdom. He did not gain a total victory over South Carolina, nor did he want one. In politics, total victory usually means eventual defeat. What he did was spare the Union the agony of civil conflict. He accomplished it not by waging war but by initiating compromise." (Brooks Memorial Art Gallery, Memphis, Tennessee)

blurted out, "What a country God has given us! . . . We have the best country and the best institutions in the world. No people have so much to be grateful for as we."

Further along in his tour, at Cambridge, Massachusetts, the President received an honorary degree of Doctor of Laws from Harvard — much to John Quincy Adams' intense disgust. Later, when Jackson addressed a small audience in another town someone called out from the crowd, "You must

give them a little Latin, *Doctor.*" Whereupon the President, his eyes twinkling, responded: "*E pluribus unum,* my friends, *sine qua non!*"

Jackson was forced to cut short the tour at Concord because of extreme fatigue and "bleeding at the lungs," but by that time he had succeeded in his primary mission of summoning popular support for a strong federal government in its quarrel with a rebellious state. Here was Jackson at his political best, using his office and popularity to unite the American people.

Indeed, it was Jackson's profound understanding of his presidential powers and the extent to which he used them that reveals his greatness as a President. For it was Jackson who first explored the full dynamic potential of the American government. That potential largely depends on the initiative and aggressiveness of the chief executive, and none of the previous presidents had sought this kind of leadership while in office. Jackson was different. . . .

More than any other president before him, Jackson used his office to reach the people, employing messages, Proclamations, Protests, and any number of party devices, such as newspapers, to close the distance between the chief executive and the American electorate. He also used his office to reach into Congress and control legislation. Not only did his advisers work closely with Democratic leaders in both houses, but he himself repeatedly sought to control the membership of Congressional committees. . . .

Thus, with Jackson begins the history of dynamic and aggressive executive leadership in the United States. Those in his own generation and later who, for one reason or another, insisted on characterizing him as an arrogant, militaristic hothead, slamming around the White House and shooting from the hip and lip at the slightest provocation, will never admit to his statesmanship or understand his contribution to the presidency. But those who will gage his skills and insights into the political process, and measure the distance he stretched the executive powers, will

249

discover some of the factors that constitute his greatness as an American President.

QUESTIONS TO CONSIDER

1 How did President Jackson and President Jefferson adjust their principles to meet practical needs while they were in office?

2 Remini describes President Jackson's handling of the South Carolina nullification crisis as "masterful." Would you agree? How did Jackson use both "carrot" and "stick" to overcome this potential threat to the stability and future of the Union?

3 Henry Clay is often called the Great Compromiser. Examine Clay's behavior during the nullification crisis. Is it Clay — or Jackson — who deserves credit for being willing to compromise?

4 Comment on the argument that Andrew Jackson — in his use of presidential powers, his public relations efforts, his ability to handle Congress, the states, and individual rivals — was our first modern president.

19

"Woe If It Comes with Storm and Blood and Fire"

RALPH KORNGOLD

In the Jacksonian era, slavery remained the central paradox of American society. While white men enjoyed greater opportunity and more political rights, while the nation attempted to mold itself into a popular democracy, two-and-a-half million southern blacks remained in chains. Moreover, most northern states either retained or now enacted black codes that discriminated against free blacks, denying them the right to vote, hold political office, work at skilled jobs, live in white neighborhoods, or attend public schools (even though they had to pay school taxes). Only in Massachusetts and a few other New England states did African-American citizens enjoy more or less the same rights as white people. But white racial hostility often flared up in New England, too. In fact, hundreds of race riots broke out all over the North during the Age of Jackson; in many of the riots, angry whites — including leaders of the community — burned black ghettos and beat up and killed black people.

It was inevitable that some whites would become upset about such injustice, would become distressed and then angered about the contradiction of slavery and racial discrimination in a self-proclaimed free and just society. Some Americans — southern and northern Quakers particularly — had, in fact, opposed slavery since the colonial period. But in the 1820s — a decade of religious and political ferment, a decade when the struggle began for universal manhood suffrage — the antislavery movement truly took shape. The American Colonization Society, founded in 1816, distributed pamphlets and gathered petitions that called for the voluntary colonization of blacks in Africa. Quakers and free blacks also collected antislavery petitions and sent them to Congress (where intimidated southerners had them tabled); and Benjamin Lundy, a Baltimore Quaker, not only started publishing The Genius of Universal Emancipation, but organized antislavery societies in the South itself. At this time, most antislavery whites (a distinct minority of the population) were both gradualists and colonizationists. But by the 1830s some would emphatically change their minds, would champion immediate emancipation, organize a national antislavery society, and start an abolitionist crusade that would haunt the American conscience and arouse latent racism everywhere in the land.

The best-known leader of the crusade was William Lloyd Garrison. An intense, bespectacled young man who came from a broken home (his father had run away), he was raised by his mother as an ardent Baptist; later he became a radical Christian perfectionist. Initially, Garrison too was a gradualist and a colonizer. But in 1829, after he went to work for Lundy's paper, Garrison renounced colonization and came out for immediate emancipation. Ralph Korngold speculates that Garrison was influenced by the abolitionist writings of James Duncan and the Reverend George Bourne, who denounced slavery as a sin and demanded that blacks be freed at once.

At any rate, in the columns of Lundy's paper, Garrison conducted a stunning moral attack against slavery and anybody who condoned or perpetuated it. For example, when he learned that a ship belonging to a man from Newburyport, Massachusetts (Garrison's hometown), was taking a cargo of slaves from Baltimore to New Orleans, Garrison castigated him as a highway robber and a murderer. The man, a highly respected citizen and a church deacon, slapped Garrison with a $5,000 libel suit. The court decided against Garrison and fined him $50, but he couldn't pay and had to go to jail. Korngold's narrative opens with Garrison in prison. It follows his career as he founded the Liberator and not only crusaded against slavery but championed the rights of free blacks.

☆ 1 ☆

WHILE IN PRISON Garrison had prepared three lectures. The first contrasted the program of the Colonization Society with his own; the second gave a vivid description of the slavery system; the third showed the extent to which the North shared responsibility for the "peculiar institution." After his release he left Baltimore for the North, intending to make a lecture tour of several months' duration and then launch an antislavery weekly in Washington. If he later chose Boston, it was because Lundy moved the *Genius* to the National Capital. Garrison had become convinced the North needed enlightenment even more than the South. In the first issue of his new paper he was to write:

"During my recent tour for the purpose of exciting the minds of the people by a series of discourses on the subject of slavery, every place that I visited gave fresh evidence of the fact, that a greater revolution in public sentiment was to be effected in the free States — *and particularly in New England* — than at the South. I found contempt more bitter, opposition more active, detraction more relentless, prejudice more stubborn, and apathy more frozen, than among slaveowners themselves."

He delivered his lectures in Philadelphia, where he was the guest of James and Lucretia Mott, whose influence was to be largely responsible for his abandonment of religious orthodoxy. "If my mind has since become liberalized in any degree (and I think it has burst every sectarian trammel)," he wrote, "if theological dogmas which I once regarded as essential to Christianity, I now repudiate as absurd and pernicious, — I am largely indebted to them for the changes." When he reached Massachusetts he

From pages 42–64 in *Two Friends of Man* by Ralph Korngold, published by Little, Brown & Co., 1950. Reprinted by special permission of Mrs. Ralph Korngold.

decided that his native Newburyport should be the first to hear his message. But he had reckoned without Mr. [Frances] Todd, whose influence was sufficiently great to have the trustees of the Presbyterian Church intervene when the minister offered Garrison the use of the church auditorium. The pastor of the Second Congregational Church came to the rescue and he was able to deliver his first lecture. Then again Todd intervened. Garrison made no further attempt to enlighten his native town, and left for Boston.

☆ 2 ☆

In Boston Garrison took lodgings as usual at Parson Collier's, and then called on the Reverend Lyman Beecher, hoping to enlist his moral support. Dr. Beecher, however, was not the man to identify himself with an unpopular cause. ("True wisdom," he said in one of his Seminary lectures, "consists in advocating a cause only so far as the community will sustain the reformer.") He now excused himself, saying: "I have too many irons in the fire already."

"Then," replied the young zealot, "you had better let them all burn than to neglect your duty to the slave."

Dr. Beecher did not think so. "Your zeal," he said, "is commendable, but you are misguided. If you will give up your fanatical notions and be guided by us [the clergy] we will make you the Wilberforce of America."

When not looking for a hall in which to deliver his message Garrison wrote letters to public men imploring them to declare themselves for immediate emancipation. He wrote to [William Ellery] Channing, to [Daniel] Webster and to several others, but received no reply. His search for a meeting place likewise remained unrewarded. Finally he inserted the following advertisement in the Boston *Courier:*

WANTED — For three evenings, a Hall or meeting-house (the latter would be preferred), in which to vindicate the rights of TWO MILLIONS of American citizens who are now groaning in servile chains in this boasted land of liberty; and also to propose just, benevolent, and constitutional measures for their relief. As the addresses will be gratuitous, and as the cause is of public benefit, I cannot consent to remunerate any society for the use of its building. If this application fails, I propose to address the citizens of Boston in the open air, on the Common.

Wm. Lloyd Garrison
No. 30, Federal Street, Oct. 11, 1830

The advertisement attracted the attention of sexagenarian Abner Kneeland, founder of the First Society of Free Enquirers. Kneeland was an atheist, and his society made war on religion. A few years later he was to be indicted for having published in his paper, the Boston *Enquirer,* a "scandalous, injurious, obscene, blasphemous and profane libel of and concerning God." His society was the lessee of Julian Hall, on the northwest corner of Milk and Congress Streets. He had no sooner read Garrison's advertisement than he offered him the use of the hall.

It was only a couple of years since Garrison had written about "the depravity and wickedness of those . . . who reject the gospel of Jesus Christ," but he now saw no reason why he should "reject the co-operation of those who . . . make no pretense to evangelical piety" when "the religious portion of the community are indifferent to the cries of suffering humanity."

☆ 3 ☆

The hall was filled. Dr. Beecher and other notables were present. Three men were there who were destined to become Garrison's staunch friends and supporters. They had come together and were seated side by side. The eldest was Samuel J. May, a Unitarian minister from Brooklyn, Connecticut, who was visiting his father, Colonel Joseph May, a prosperous Boston merchant. His friends called him "God's chore boy," for while far less combative than Garrison, he was just as ready to rush to the succor of anyone in need of assistance. Sitting beside him was his brother-in-law, Bronson Alcott, whose daughter Louisa May Alcott was to become a popular novelist. He was a philosopher and a mystic who combined great profundity with great extravagance of thought. The Sage of Concord has called him "the most refined and the most advanced soul we have ever had in New England," and "the most remarkable and the highest genius of his time." Along with gems of thought worthy of Aristotle, Alcott propounded such absurdities as that the atmosphere surrounding the earth was the accumulated exhalation of mankind, and that the weather was fair or foul depending on whether good or evil thought predominated! He would say in all seriousness to a friend: "Men must have behaved well today to have such fine sunshine." The third man was May's cousin, Samuel E. Sewall, a Boston attorney and a direct descendant of the judge of that name who a hundred and thirty years before had written the first antislavery pamphlet in America.

When the speaker had finished, May turned to his two companions and said: "That is a providential man; he is a prophet; he will shake our nation to its center, but he will shake slavery out of it. We ought to know him, we ought to help him. Come, let us go and give him our hands." When they had done so, May said to the young lecturer: "Mr. Garrison, I am not sure that I can endorse all you have said this evening. Much of it requires careful consideration. But I am prepared to embrace you. I am sure you are called to a great work, and I mean to help you."

Alcott suggested that all come home with him. They accepted and remained in animated conversation until after midnight. Garrison told his new friends of his plan to launch an antislavery paper in Boston, which he intended to call the *Liberator.* Sewall thought the name too provoking and suggested the *Safety Lamp.* Garrison would not hear of it. "Provoking!" That was exactly what he meant it to be. Slavery in the United States had now lasted over two hundred years. During nearly three quarters of that time the Quakers had agitated against it in their inoffensive, conciliatory fashion. What had been accomplished? There were now more than four times as many slaves as when they began their propaganda. New Slave States had been added to the Union. The slave laws were more oppressive than ever. He meant to agitate. He meant to call hard names. He meant to make it impossible for any man to confess without shame that he was the owner of slaves. He was prepared for any sacrifice: "A few white victims must be sacrificed to open the eyes of this nation and show the tyranny of our laws. I expect and am willing to be persecuted, imprisoned and bound for advocating African rights; and I should deserve to be a slave myself if I shrunk from that duty or danger."

May was so fascinated by the young man's enthusiasm that the following morning, immediately after breakfast, he called on him at his boardinghouse and remained until two in the afternoon. Before the week was over he and Sewall had made arrangements for Garrison to repeat his lectures at Athenaeum Hall.

The Sunday following, May occupied the pulpit at "Church Green," in Summer Street. So filled was he with Garrison's message that he interpolated his sermon with frequent references to slavery and finished with an appeal to the congregation to help abolish the institution before it destroyed the Republic. He was aware of the mounting uneasiness among his listeners, and having pronounced the benediction, said: "Every one present must be conscious that the closing remarks of my sermon have caused an unusual emotion throughout the church. I am glad. . . . I have been prompted to speak thus

by the words I have heard during the past week from a young man hitherto unknown, but who is, I believe, called of God to do a greater work for the good of our country than has been done by any one since the Revolution. I mean William Lloyd Garrison. He is going to repeat his lectures the coming week. I advise, I exhort, I entreat — would that I could compel! — you to go and hear him."

The following day May's father, Colonel Joseph

William Lloyd Garrison, celebrated abolitionist and editor of the controversial Liberator. *"I will be as harsh as truth, and as uncompromising as justice," wrote Garrison in his manifesto in the first issue of the* Liberator. *On the subject of slavery, "I do not wish to think, or speak, or write, with moderation. . . . I am in earnest — I will not equivocate — I will not excuse — I will not retreat a single inch — AND I WILL BE HEARD." (Department of Special Collections, Wichita State University Library)*

May, was walking down State Street when a friend rushed up to him and impuslively grasped his hand.

"Colonel," he said, "you have my sympathy. I cannot tell you how much I pity you."

The old man looked at him astounded. "Sympathy? Pity? For what?"

The other appeared embarrassed. "Well," he said, "I hear your son went mad at 'Church Green' yesterday."

☆   4   ☆

> In a small chamber, friendless and unseen,
>   Toiled o'er his types one poor, unlearned
>   young man;
> The place was dark, unfurnitured and mean,
>   Yet there the freedom of a race began.
>
> Help came but slowly; surely, no man yet
>   Put lever to the heavy world with less;
> What need of help? He knew how types were
>   set,
>   He had a dauntless spirit and a press.

James Russell Lowell, the author of these lines, has availed himself of the usual poetic license. The room on the third floor of Merchants' Hall, in Boston, where on January 1, 1831, Garrison launched the *Liberator,* was not particularly small, being eighteen feet square, and not one, but two unlearned young men "toiled over the types," for he and Isaac Knapp of Newburyport had joined forces. Later they were aided by a Negro apprentice. The windows were grimy and spattered with printer's ink, as were the dingy walls. There was a press, picked up at a bargain, a couple of composing stands with worn secondhand type, a few chairs and a long table covered with exchanges, at which the editor attended to his correspondence. In a corner of the room was a mattress on which the two friends slept,

for they could not afford the luxury of a boardinghouse. They lived on bread, milk and a little fruit, sharing the first two with a cat who, when Garrison sat down to write, would jump on the table and rub her fur caressingly against his bald forehead. Although the paper advocated temperance as well as abolition, Knapp found it impossible to wean himself from his craving for strong drink, a weakness which eventually led to his undoing.

In the literature of social protest few lines are more stirring than the following paragraph from Garrison's salutatory to the public in the first number of the *Liberator:*

"I am aware that many object to the severity of my language; but is there not cause for severity? I *will* be as harsh as truth, and as uncompromising as justice. On this subject, I do not wish to think, or speak, or write, with moderation. No! No! Tell a man whose house is on fire to give a moderate alarm; tell him to moderately rescue his wife from the hands of the ravisher; tell the mother to gradually extricate her babe from the fire into which it has fallen — but urge me not to use moderation in a cause like the present. I am in earnest — I will not equivocate — I will not excuse — I will not retreat a single inch — AND I WILL BE HEARD."

The last statement proved prophetic. The *Liberator* never paid expenses, never had over three thousand subscribers, but its message became known from coast to coast and across the Atlantic. The paper had a fertilizing influence that caused the sprouting of various forms of opposition to slavery, of most of which Garrison disapproved, but for all of which he was directly or indirectly responsible. There were to be Abolitionists who formed political parties and others who abstained from voting; those who were orthodox churchmen and those who set out to destroy organized religion; those who believed in nonresistance and those who advocated armed intervention; those who wished to arouse the slaves to revolt and those who opposed this; those determined to remain within constitutional limits and those who scoffed at the Constitution. The Liberty Party, the Free-Soil Movement, the Republican Party — all, to a greater extent than their leaders cared to acknowledge, owed their existence to Garrison. He was the sower who went forth to sow and whose seed fell onto fertile ground, blossoming forth in a variety of shapes. He was the spiritual father of innumerable children, most of whom disowned him. He shamed a reluctant nation into doing what it did not wish to do, and the nation has never forgiven him. In 1853, Wendell Phillips said:

"The community has come to hate its reproving Nathan so bitterly, that even those whom the relenting part of it is beginning to regard as standard-bearers of the antislavery host think it unwise to avow any connection or sympathy with him. I refer to some of the leaders of the political movement against slavery. . . . They are willing to confess privately, that our movement produced theirs, and that its continued existence is the very breath of their life. But, at the same time, they would fain walk on the road without being soiled by too close contact with the rough pioneers who threw it up. . . . If you tell me that they cherished all these principles in their own breasts before Mr. Garrison appeared, I can only say, if the antislavery movement did not give them their ideas, it surely gave them the courage to utter them."

☆ 5 ☆

"Why so hot my little man?" wrote Ralph Waldo Emerson; and at another time: "There is a sublime prudence which, believing in a vast future, sure of more to come than is yet seen, postpones always the present hour to the whole life." But now see Emerson, returning from Boston in 1850, a copy of the Fugitive Slave Law in his pocket, writing in his Journal: "This filthy enactment was made in the nineteenth century — I will not obey it — by

God!" What has become of the "sublime prudence"? To refuse to obey the Fugitive Slave Law meant to incur a thousand dollar fine and be liable to pay another thousand to the claimant of the fugitive, not to speak of a possible six months in jail. Was it that Emerson had come to agree with Whittier that a civilized man could no more obey the Fugitive Slave Law, even when a Lincoln set out to enforce it, than he could become a cannibal?

Garrison never worried about keeping cool. He agreed with Burke that "To speak of atrocious crimes in mild language is treason to virtue," with Luther that "Those things that are softly dealt with, in a corrupt age, give people but little concern, and are presently forgotten." Samuel J. May once said to him: "O, my friend, do try to moderate your indignation, and keep more cool; why, you are all on fire." His friend replied: "Brother May, I have need to be *all on fire,* for I have mountains of ice about me to melt."

Was the method effective? That it made well-nigh impossible to spread the gospel of emancipation in the South admits of no doubt. But except among Southern Quakers such propaganda had borne no fruit. Indeed, while at one time the slaveholders had been willing to concede that slavery was an evil and a curse, foisted upon the South by the mother country, after years of propaganda by Quakers and others they had arrived at the conclusion that it was the best of all possible labor systems, far superior to that prevailing in the North. This change of outlook was clearly perceptible at the time of the Missouri Compromise, long before the appearance of the *Liberator.* It was due to the fact that the invention of the cotton gin had made slavery far more profitable.

When Garrison began publication of his paper nearly all opposition to slavery had disappeared, North as well as South. Albert Bushnell Hart, in a profound study of the subject, wrote: "When Jackson became President in 1829, anti-slavery seemed, after fifty years of effort, to have spent its force. The voice of the churches was no longer heard in protest; the abolitionist societies were dying out; there was hardly an abolitionist militant in the field. . . . In Congress there was only one anti-slavery man and his efforts were without avail.'' But in 1839 the managers of the Massachusetts Anti-Slavery Society were able to declare: ''Ten years ago a solitary individual stood up as the advocate of immediate and unconditional emancipation. Now, that individual sees about him hundreds of thousands of persons, of both sexes, members of every sect and party, from the most elevated to the humblest rank of life. In 1829 not an Anti-Slavery Society of a genuine stamp was in existence. In 1839 there are nearly two thousand such societies swarming and multiplying in all parts of the free States. In 1829 there was but one Anti-Slavery periodical in the land. In 1839 there are fourteen. In 1829 there was scarcely a newspaper of any religious or political party which was willing to disturb the 'delicate' question of slavery. In 1839 there are multitudes of journals that either openly advocate the doctrine of immediate and unconditional emancipation, or permit its free discussion in their columns. Then scarcely a church made slaveholding a bar to communion. Now, multitudes refuse to hear a slaveholder preach, or to recognize one as a brother. Then, no one petitioned Congress to abolish slavery in the District of Columbia. Now, in one day, a single member of the House of Representatives (John Quincy Adams) has presented one hundred and seventy-six such petitions in detail; while no less than seven hundred thousand persons have memorialized Congress on that and kindred subjects.''

Garrison was to say: ''In seizing the trump of God, I had indeed to blow a 'jarring blast' — but it was necessary to wake up a nation then slumbering in the lap of moral death. . . . What else but the *Liberator* primarily, (and of course instrumentally,) has effected this change? Greater success than I have had, no man could reasonably desire, or humbly expect.''

When in 1837 Dr. William Ellery Channing complimented James G. Birney on the reasonableness and moderation of his antislavery paper, in contrast with the *Liberator,* which he accused of being ''blemished by a spirit of intolerance, sweeping censure and rash, injurious judgment,'' the former Kentucky slaveholder and Solicitor General of Alabama replied: ''Our country was asleep, whilst slavery was preparing to pour its 'leprous distilment' into her ears. So deep was becoming her sleep that nothing but a rude and almost ruffian-like shake could rouse her to a contemplation of her danger. If she is saved, it is because she has been thus treated.'' He left no doubt about whom he had in mind when he said on another occasion: ''My anti-slavery trumpet would never have roused the country — Garrison alone could do it.''

Another former Kentucky slaveholder, the famous Cassius Marcellus Clay, who while a student at Yale heard Garrison speak and became a convert, wrote: ''There is one saying of his [Garrison's] traducers, and the traducers of those who act with him, . . . that 'they have set back the cause of emancipation by agitation'! Nothing is more false. The cause of emancipation advances only with agitation: let that cease and despotism is complete.''

☆ 6 ☆

Garrison did not expect to convert the slaveholders. He considered such an attempt a waste of time. In 1837 he wrote to Elizabeth Pease: ''I have relinquished the expectation that they [the slaveholders] will ever, by mere moral suasion, consent to emancipate their victims.'' In 1840 he wrote to Elizabeth's brother Joseph: ''There is not any instance recorded either in sacred or profane history, in which the oppressors and enslavers of mankind, except in individual cases, have been induced, by mere moral suasion, to surrender their despotic power, and let the oppressed go free; but in nearly every instance, from the time that Pharaoh and his hosts were drowned in the Red Sea, down to the present day, they have persisted in their evil course until sudden destruction came upon them, or they were compelled to surrender their ill-gotten power in some other manner."

Others were of the same opinion. Cassius M. Clay wrote: "The slaveholders have just as much intention of yielding up their slaves as the sum of the kings of the earth have of laying down, for the benefit of the people, their sceptres." In August, 1855, Abraham Lincoln was to write to George Robertson of Kentucky that the Tsar of Russia would abdicate and free his serfs sooner than American slaveholders would voluntarily give up their slaves. "Experience has demonstrated, I think, that there is no peaceful extinction of slavery in prospect for us."

Garrison feared, like Lincoln, that slavery would never be abolished except by force of arms, but he believed there was one other method worth trying. When Jesus of Nazareth called the Pharisees "fools," "hypocrites," "devourers of widows' houses," "serpents," "generation of vipers" — and asked, "How can ye escape the damnation of hell?" — he was obviously not using moral *suasion,* but moral *pressure.* This was the method Garrison had decided to adopt. Shortly after he founded the *Liberator,* he told Samuel J. May: "Until the term 'slaveholder' sends as deep a feeling of horror to the hearts of those who hear it applied to any one as the term, 'robber,' 'pirate,' 'murderer' do, we must use and multiply epithets when condemning the sins of him who is guilty of 'the sum of all villainies.'" He hoped to arouse such a feeling of abhorrence and storm of disapproval in the North (and in fact throughout the civilized world) that the South would be forced to yield. That the method offered some hope of success was acknowledged by General Duff Green, who wrote: "We believe that we have

most to fear from the organized action upon the conscience and fears of the slaveholders themselves. . . . It is only by alarming the consciences of the weak and feeble, and diffusing among our own people a morbid sensibility on the question of slavery, that the abolitionists can accomplish their object."

The method did not succeed any more than it had succeeded in Christ's time; but who will say that it was not worth trying? Nor can it be said that it produced no results. If Garrison failed to shame and intimidate the South, he yet succeeded in arousing such an aversion to, and fear of, slavery in the North that war seemed preferable to allowing it to spread. Archibald H. Grimké has well said: "The public sentiment which Lincoln obeyed, [Garrison and] Phillips created."

☆ 7 ☆

About a year before the appearance of the *Liberator,* David Walker, a Boston Negro who made a living as an old-clothes man, published a pamphlet entitled *Walker's Appeal.* He boldly called upon the slaves to revolt. "If you commence," he wrote, "make sure work — do not trifle, for they will not trifle with you — they want us for their slaves, and think nothing of murdering us in order to subject us to that wretched condition — therefore, if there is an attempt made by us, kill or be killed." There were three editions of the pamphlet, copies of which found their way into the Slave States. The consternation these produced in the South bordered on the ridiculous and was eloquent testimony of the fear that lurked under the South's brave exterior. Governors sent special messages to Legislatures. Repressive laws were hastily passed. Incoming ships and trains were searched. Colored seamen were taken from Northern ships entering Southern ports and imprisoned. "How much is it to be regretted," declared *Niles' Weekly Register,* "that a negro dealer in old clothes, should thus excite two states to legislative action." Walker, however, died in June, 1830, and the South breathed a sigh of relief.

Then, in January, 1831, again in the city of Boston, appeared the *Liberator,* and in an early issue of the paper a poem from the editor's pen warning of the danger of a slave uprising if emancipation were delayed. One stanza read:

> Woe if it come with storm, and blood, and
> fire,
> When midnight darkness veils the earth and
> sky!
> Woe to the innocent babe — the guilty
> sire —
> Mother and daughter — friends of kindred tie!
> *Stranger and citizen alike shall die!*
> Red-handed slaughter his revenge shall feed,
> And Havoc yell his ominous death-cry;
> And wild Despair in vain for mercy plead —
> While Hell itself shall shrink, and sicken at
> the deed!

The slave uprising in the French colony of San Domingo towards the close of the eighteenth century proved there were reasons for the warning. Garrison, however, did not advise the slaves to revolt. He had condemned *Walker's Appeal* in the *Genius,* and the last stanza of his poem read:

> Not by the sword shall your deliverance be;
> Not by the shedding of your masters' blood,
> Not by rebellion — or foul treachery,
> Upspringing suddenly, like swelling flood:
> Revenge and rapine ne'er did bring forth good.
> God's *time is best!* — nor will it long delay:
> Even now your barren cause begins to bud,
> And glorious shall the fruit be! — Watch and
> pray,

> For, lo! the kindling dawn, that ushers in the
> day!

Shortly after the appearance of this poem, on August 22, 1831, there took place in Southampton County, Virginia, the most sanguinary slave uprising in the annals of American slavery. A Negro mystic named Nat Turner, a slave belonging to a small planter, gathered a band of followers variously estimated at from forty to two hundred, and after killing his master and the latter's family, moved from plantation to plantation, slaughtering between fifty and sixty persons, men, women and children. Bands of white men and the state militia finally subdued the rebels, but not without committing outrages upon innocent Negroes surpassing in cruelty anything of which Turner had been guilty. Finally, the Negro leader and nineteen of his followers were hanged. The uprising was responsible for a sensational debate in the Virginia Legislature during which slavery was condemned in language as violent as any Garrison had ever used. For a while indeed it seemed that what years of propaganda by the Quakers had failed to accomplish would come as a result of Turner's bloodletting. Governor John Floyd of Virginia noted in his diary: "Before I leave this Government I will have contrived to have a law passed gradually abolishing slavery in this state." But the people and the authorities eventually got over their fright and began looking about for a scapegoat. Walker was read, but there was Garrison and his paper. Turner and his confederates had denied that they had read either *Walker's Appeal* or the *Liberator,* and no evidence to the contrary was introduced; but Governor Floyd wrote to Governor James Hamilton of South Carolina that black preachers had read from the pulpit the inflammatory writings of Walker and Garrison, which may or may not have been true. Anyway, Harrison Gray Otis, Mayor of Boston, received letters from the Governors of Virginia and Georgia "severally remonstrating against an incendiary newspaper published in Boston, and, as they alleged, thrown broadcast among their plantations, inciting to insurrection and its horrid results.''

Mayor Otis was puzzled. Although the *Liberator* had now been published in Boston for nearly a year, he had never seen a copy or even heard of the paper's existence. "It appeared on enquiry," he wrote, "that no member of the city government, nor any person of my acquaintance, had ever heard of the publication. Some time afterward, it was reported to me by the city officers that they had ferreted out the paper and its editor; that his office was an obscure hole, his only visible auxiliary a negro boy, and his supporters a very few insignificant persons of all colors. This information, with the consent of the aldermen, I communicated to the above-named governors, with an assurance of my belief that the new fanaticism had not made, nor was likely to make, proselytes among the respectable classes of our people. In this, however, I was mistaken.''

Neither the Mayor of Boston nor the Governor of Massachusetts felt he possessed the power to stop publication of the *Liberator,* though both regretted that shortcoming in the law. The South was indignant. The Columbia (South Carolina) *Telescope* believed the matter called for armed intervention. "They [the people of Massachusetts] permit a battery to be erected upon their territory, which fires upon us, and we should be justified in invading that territory to silence their guns," the editor declared. A Vigilance Committee in Columbia offered a reward of fifteen hundred dollars for the arrest and conviction of any person "distributing or circulating the *Liberator* or any other publication of a seditious nature." Georgetown, District of Columbia, passed a law forbidding any colored person to take the *Liberator* from the post-office on pain of twenty dollars' fine and thirty days' imprisonment. In Raleigh, North Carolina, the grand jury found a true bill against Garrison and Knapp in the hope of ex-

trading them. A correspondent in the *Washington National Intelligence* proposed that the President of the United States or the Governor of Virginia demand Garrison's extradition, and in case of refusal by the Governor of Massachusetts "the people of the South offer an adequate reward to any person who will deliver him dead or alive, into the hands of the authorities of any State South of the Potomac." He did not have long to wait. On November 30, 1831, the Senate and the House of Representa-

Helen Eliza Benson Garrison not only shared her husband's commitment to reform but provided him with the refuge of a stable personal life. "By her unwearied attentions to my want, her sympathetic regards, her perfect equanimity of mind," Garrison said, "she is no trifling support to abolitionism, inasmuch as she lightens my labors, and enables me to find exquisite delight in the family circle, as an off-set to public adversity." (The Bettmann Archive)

tives of Georgia appropriated five thousand dollars to be paid by the Governor "to any person or persons who shall arrest, bring to trial and prosecute to conviction, under the laws of the State, the editor or publisher of a certain paper called the *Liberator,* published in the town of Boston and State of Massachusetts."

Garrison was not in the least intimidated and wrote defiantly: "A price upon the head of a citizen of Massachusetts — for what? For daring to give his opinion of the moral aspect of slavery! . . . Know this, ye Senatorial Patrons of kidnappers! that we despise your threats as much as we deplore your infatuation; nay, more — know that a hundred men stand ready to fill our place as soon as it is made vacant by violence."

☆ 8 ☆

On his last visit to the United States, General Lafayette expressed his astonishment at the increase in racial prejudice. He recalled that in Washington's army, white and black had fought side by side and had messed together in harmony. Now, however, in the Free as well as in the Slave States, free Negroes were despised, persecuted, deprived of most of the prerogatives of the free man, permitted to earn a living only at the most menial and ill-paid employments.

A glance at some of the laws governing the free people of color leaves no doubt concerning the tenuous nature of the freedom they enjoyed. In Maryland a Justice of the Peace could order a free Negro's ears cropped for striking a white man even in self-defense. A free Negro entering that State incurred a penalty of fifty dollars for every week spent within its borders, and if unable to pay was sold into slavery. In Georgia the penalty for teaching a free Ne-

gro to read or write was five hundred dollars if the offender was white, if colored he was fined and flogged at the discretion of the court. In Virginia and South Carolina any Justice of the Peace could disband a school where free Negroes or their offspring were taught to read or write, fine the teacher five hundred dollars and have twenty lashes administered to each pupil. In Louisiana a fine of like amount awaited the zealous Christian who taught a free Negro in Sunday School. In Mississippi and the District of Columbia a Negro unable to prove his legal right to freedom could be sold into slavery. In South Carolina a Negro who "entertained" a runaway slave by giving him as much as a crust of bread was fined fifty dollars, and if unable to pay was sold. In several Slave States free Negroes were not permitted to assemble for religious purposes unless white people were present, and they were forbidden to preach. In Ohio a white man who hired a Negro or mulatto even for a day made himself liable for his future support. In the Free States, Negro children could not attend public school and little or no provision was made for their instruction. In several Free and of course in all the Slave States, free people of color were denied the right of suffrage.

Custom solidified this edifice of injustice. It made it well-nigh impossible for an artisan, mechanic or shopkeeper to employ a colored apprentice. In the North as well as in the South, Negroes were required to travel in the steerage of a boat or on the outside of a stagecoach, when they were not barred altogether. When a convention of colored people in Philadelphia made a brave attempt to establish a manual labor school for Negroes in New Haven, Connecticut, the Mayor called a mass meeting of the citizens, and such a hue and cry arose that the plan had to be abandoned. When Noyes Academy, in Canaan, New Hampshire, admitted a few colored students, three hundred citizens with a hundred yoke of oxen dragged the building from its foundation and deposited it outside the town. In church,

Negroes had to sit in separate pews — which in the Baptist Church at Hartford, Connecticut, were boarded up and provided with peepholes. When in Houghton, Massachusetts, a colored man acquired a white man's pew, the church authorities had the floor removed in that part of the edifice. . . .

☆ 9 ☆

Garrison championed the free people of color as fervently as the slaves. "This then is my consolation," he wrote on one occasion: "if I cannot do much in this quarter towards abolishing slavery, I may be able to elevate our free colored population in the scale of society." Speaking before a colored convention in Philadelphia he said with feeling: "I never rise to address a colored audience without feeling ashamed of my color; ashamed of being identified with a race of men who have done you so much injustice and yet retain so large a portion of your brethren in servitude."

No matter how pressing his work, he would lay it aside when invited to address a colored audience. He did not flatter his listeners, but urged them to be worthy of liberty, to be temperate, industrious and to surpass the white man in virtue, which, he assured them, was no difficult task. They must not resort to violence, but should incessantly petition to be permitted to vote, to send their children to public school and to exercise every other right of the freeman. "If your petition is denied seven times, send it seven times seven."

His influence was great among them. Once in Boston, when he had addressed them on temperance, they immediately formed a temperance society, which within a few days counted one hundred and fifty members. "Such acts as these, brethren, give me strength and boldness in your cause," he assured

them. Henry E. Benson, in a letter to Isaac Knapp, described a scene that took place in Providence, Rhode Island, after Garrison had addressed a colored audience. "After the meeting," he wrote, "the poor creatures wept and sobbed like children — they gathered round him anxious to express their gratitude for what he had done for them, and tell him how well they loved him."

So persistent was he in their defense that some believed him to be colored, and when he advocated the repeal of the Massachusetts law against intermarriage, the rumor spread that he meant to marry a Negress. No resentment at the rumor is noticeable in this mild denial he published in the *Liberator*: "We declare that our heart is neither affected *by,* nor pledged *to,* any lady, black or white, bond or free."

☆ 10 ☆

If "the style is the man," then one might have expected Garrison in his maturity to have been a scowling, brusque, bitter, opinionated individual. Such in fact was the mental image formed by many. The reality confounded Buffon's maxim. Josiah Copley, editor of a religious paper in Pittsburgh, Pennsylvania, happening to be in Boston in 1832, called on Garrison after some hesitation. "I never was more astonished," he wrote. "All my preconceptions were at fault. My ideal of the man was that of a stout, rugged, dark-visaged desperado — something like we picture a pirate. He was a quiet, gentle and I might say handsome man — a gentleman indeed, in every sense of the word."

William H. Herndon, Lincoln's law partner, who visited Garrison in the latter's old age, wrote: "I had imagined him a shriveled, cold, selfish, haughty man, one who was weak and fanatically blind to the charities and equities of life, at once whining and insulting, mean and miserable, but I was pleasantly disappointed. I found him warm, generous, approachable, communicative; he has some mirth, some wit, and a deep abiding faith in coming universal charity. I was better and more warmly received by him than by any man in Boston.''

Harriet Martineau, famous British authoress, who met Garrison in 1835, declared: ''His aspect put to flight in an instant what prejudices his slanderers had raised in me. I was wholly taken by surprise. It was a countenance glowing with health and wholly expressive of purity, animation and gentleness. I did not now wonder at the citizen who, seeing a print of Garrison at a shop window without a name to it, went in and bought it and framed it as the most saintlike of countenances. The end of the story is, that when the citizen found whose portrait he had been hanging in his parlor, he took the print out of the frame and huddled it away.''

The preponderance of opinion is that his conversation was the very opposite of his writing — mild, tolerant, disarming. Miss Martineau wrote: ''Garrison had a good deal of a Quaker air; and his speech is deliberate like a Quaker's but gentle as a woman's. . . . Every conversation I had with him confirmed my opinion that sagacity is the most striking attribute of his conversation. It has none of the severity, the harshness, the bad taste of his writing; it is as gladsome as his countenance, and as gentle as his voice.''

Harriet Beecher Stowe, who had confided to one of Garrison's sons that she was ''dreadfully afraid'' of his father, having made the editor's acquaintance, wrote to him: ''You have a remarkable tact at conversation.''

Ralph Waldo Emerson, who for a long time had been prejudiced against him, in 1844 wrote in his Journal: ''The haters of Garrison have lived to rejoice in that grand world movement which, every

age or two, casts out so masterly an agent for good. I cannot speak of the gentleman without respect.''

☆ **11** ☆

In the first number of the *Liberator*, where appeared Garrison's immortal challenge to the slaveholders, one may read these lines from the editor's pen:

''An attempt has been made — it is still making — we regret to say, with considerable success — to inflame the minds of our working classes against the more opulent, and to persuade them that they are contemned and oppressed by a wealthy aristocracy. That public grievances exist, is unquestionably true; but they are not confined to any one class of society. Every profession is interested in their removal — the rich as well as the poor. It is in the highest degree criminal, therefore, to exasperate our mechanics to deeds of violence, or to array them under a party banner; for it is not true, that, at any time, they have been the objects of reproach. . . . We are the friends of reform; but that is not reform, which, in curing one evil, threatens to inflict a thousand others.''

The reason for this outburst was an attempt by Seth Luther and others to organize a Working Men's Party and to form labor unions.

In the fifth number of the paper a correspondent pointed out to Garrison that he was wrong in trying to discourage labor's attempts to organize:

''Although you do not appear to have perceived it, I think there is a very intimate connexion between the interests of the working men's party and your own. . . . In the history of the origin of slavery is to be found the explanation of the evils we deplore and seek to remove, as well as those you have attacked. . . . We seek to enlighten our brethren in the knowledge of their rights and duties. . . . It is a duty owed by working men to themselves and the world to exert their power through the ballot-box."

Garrison replied: "There is a prevalent opinion that . . . the poor and vulgar are taught to consider the opulent as their natural enemies. Where is the evidence that our wealthy citizens, as a body, are hostile to the interests of the laboring classes? It is not in their commercial enterprises, which whiten the ocean with canvas and give employment to a useful and numerous class of men. It is not found in the manufacturing establishments, which multiply labor and cheapen the necessities of the poor. It is not found in the luxuries of their tables, or the adornments of their dwellings, for which they must pay in proportion to their extravagance. . . . Perhaps it would be the truth to affirm, that mechanics are more inimical to the success of each other, more unjust toward each other, than the rich are toward them."

Yet in 1831, and for a long time thereafter, the hours of labor in New England factories were from five in the morning until seven-thirty in the evening — the working day being thirteen and one half hours. The two half hours allowed for breakfast and midday dinner were as tiring as any, since the workers had to hurry home, bolt their food and hasten back to the factory to escape a fine. In 1849 a report submitted to the American Medical Association by one of its members contained the statement that "there is not a State's prison, or house of correction in New England, where the hours of labor are so long, the hours for meals so short, or the ventilation so much neglected, as in all the cotton mills with which I am acquainted." In Boston Irish workmen were forced to labor fifteen hours a day, including Sunday. The death rate among them was so appalling that it was claimed the Irish lived on an average only fourteen years after reaching Boston. The Cochee Manufacturing Company required its workers to sign an agreement to "conform in all respects to the regulations which are now, or may be here-

after adopted . . . and to work for such wages as the company may see fit to pay." Workers were commonly required to buy at the company store and were usually in debt to their employers. If they attempted to leave their employment without paying what they owed they were imprisoned. In 1831 there were over fifteen hundred people imprisoned for debt in Boston alone, more than half of whom owed less than twenty dollars. It may therefore be said that a system of veritable peonage prevailed.

Strikes were frequent, but prior to 1860 not a single strike was won in Massachusetts, and not until 1874 did that State have any legal restriction on the number of hours adult wageworkers could be required to work. Employers in other parts of the country often gave working conditions in New England as an excuse for not improving labor's lot.

In view of all this, how could a man ready for almost any sacrifice for the sake of the Negro have remained indifferent to the lot of white wageworkers?

Garrison was an individualist. In his opinion, if a man was not a chattel, he was master of his own fate. If he was poor the fault was his. In the days of handicraft, poverty had indeed usually been the result of shiftlessness; but the poverty of the factory worker was more often due to the greed of the employer. The handicraftsman, having finished his apprenticeship, looked forward to being his own master. If he worked long hours he was buoyed up by the hope of getting ahead in the world. But later, only the exceptional man could hope to become a factory owner or even a foreman. Garrison, grown to maturity in a transition period, failed to grasp that the average wageworker's only hope of improving his lot was to unite with his fellows.

When Garrison wrote "Mechanics are more inimical to the success of each other, more unjust toward each other than the rich are towards them," he failed to comprehend that fear was at the bottom of this. Yankee workmen feared the competition of

Irish immigrants and sometimes rioted against them. White workmen were hostile to Negroes for the same reason and opposed emancipation fearing it would result in hordes of Negroes from the South invading the North and lowering their standard of living, already sufficiently low. Southern leaders shrewdly exploited this fear. In 1843, Henry Clay wrote to the Reverend Calvin Colton, urging him to prepare a popular tract whose "great aim and object . . . should be to arouse the laboring classes of the free States against abolition. The slaves, being free, would be dispersed throughout the Union; they would enter into competition with the free laborer; with the American, the Irish, the German; reduce his wages; be confounded with him, and affect his moral and social standing. And as the ultras go for both abolition and amalgamation, show that their object is to unite in marriage the laboring white man and the laboring black man, and to reduce the white laboring man to the despised and degraded condition of the black man."

The situation required shrewd and careful handling. Most of all it required a thorough understanding of the problem. Garrison lacked that understanding, and antagonized his natural allies. As a result American wageworkers remained indifferent, if not hostile, to Abolition. Some regarded it as a plot of the employers to lower wages. Others saw it as a scheme of professional philanthropists. The editor of the *Chronicle,* a Massachusetts weekly devoted to the interests of labor, wrote: "Philanthropists may speak of negro slavery, but it would be well first to emancipate the slaves at home. Let us not stretch our ears to catch the sound of the lash on the flesh of our oppressed black, while the oppressed in our midst are crying in thunder tones, and calling upon us for assistance."

QUESTIONS TO CONSIDER

1 Garrison always insisted that he was a Christian pacifist who expected to abolish slavery through nonviolent methods. How, then, can you explain his words in 1850 that in order to achieve black emancipation "a few white victims must be sacrificed to open the eyes of this nation and show the tyranny of our laws"?

2 When Samuel May spoke from the pulpit at "Church Green" in Boston in 1830, condemning slavery and exhorting the congregation to help destroy the institution before the institution destroyed the nation, his amazed audience thought he had lost his mind. What conclusions can you draw from this incident about the attitudes of northern whites toward blacks, slavery, and abolitionists?

3 Analyze the effectiveness of Garrison's method of achieving the abolition of slavery. Would a cooler, more moderate approach than his have made more headway, especially in the South? In what national context did Garrison propose his radical objective of immediate emancipation? How did that context affect his choice of tactics?

4 Compare the treatment of free blacks in the North and in the South. Was racial prejudice, like the institution of slavery, confined below the Mason-Dixon Line?

5 Southern proslavery apologists frequently pointed to the evils of what they called "wage slavery" among the northern working classes. They accused abolitionists of hypocrisy in ignoring the harsh "slavery" in their own backyards while condemning the South's more "benevolent" institution of black slavery. How valid were these accusations when leveled at Garrison?

X

THE GROWTH OF TECHNOLOGY

20

The Lords and the
Mill Girls

MAURY KLEIN

One group of Massachusetts businessmen tried to avoid the ugly factory towns and horrible working conditions that Korngold describes in his profile of Garrison (selection 19). They formed the Boston Associates, an organization of financiers who built a model mill town in Massachusetts called Lowell. The story of Lowell — America's first planned industrial community — tells us a great deal about the dreams and realities of a nation already undergoing considerable industrial and urban growth. Maury Klein relates that story with a vivid pen — the landscaped town on the banks of the Concord and Merrimack rivers that commanded worldwide attention, the healthy farm girls who worked its looms. In 1833, President Andrew Jackson and Vice President Martin Van Buren visited Lowell and watched transfixed as 2,500 mill girls, clad in blue sashes and white dresses, with parasols above their heads, marched by two abreast. "Very pretty women, by the Eternal!" exclaimed the president. Though they loathed Jackson, the members of the Boston Associates were pleased with his observation, for they were proud of their working girls — the show-pieces for what they believed was an industrial utopia. But it was not to last. By 1860 Lowell had become another grim and crowded mill town, and its once-prized girls had been replaced by Irish immigrants who were desperate for employment and would work for lower wages. What happened to Lowell, Klein writes, revealed some harsh truths about the incompatibility of democratic ideals and the profit motive.

☆

THE ASSOCIATES

THEY FLOCKED TO THE VILLAGE OF LOWELL, these visitors from abroad, as if it were a compulsory stop on the grand tour, eager to verify rumors of a utopian system of manufacturers. Their skepticism was natural, based as it was on the European experience where industry had degraded workers and blighted the landscape. In English manufacturing centers such as Manchester, observers had stared into the pits of hell and shrank in horror from the sight. Charles Dickens used this gloomy, putrid cesspool of misery as a model in *Hard Times,* while Alexis de Tocqueville wrinkled his nose at the "heaps of dung, rubble from buildings, putrid, stagnant pools" amid the "huge palaces of industry" that kept "air and light out of the human habitations which they dominate. . . . A sort of black smoke covers the city. . . . Under this half daylight 300,000 human beings are ceaselessly at work. A thousand noises disturb this damp, dark labyrinth, but they are not at all the ordinary sounds one hears in great cities."

Was it possible that America could produce an alternative to this hideous scene? It seemed so to the visitors who gaped in wonderment at the village above the confluence of the Concord and Merrimack rivers. What they saw a planned community with mills five to seven stories high flanked by dormitories for the workers, not jammed together but surrounded by open space filled with trees and flower gardens set against a backdrop of the river and hills beyond. Dwelling houses, shops, hotels, churches, banks, even a library lined the streets in orderly, uncrowded rows. Taken whole, the scene bore a

flavor of meticulous composition, as if a painting had sprung to life.

The contrast between so pristine a vision and the nightmare of Manchester startled the most jaded of foreigners. "It was new and fresh, like a setting at the opera," proclaimed Michel Chevalier, a Frenchman who visited Lowell in 1834. The Reverend William Scoresby, an Englishman, marveled at how the buildings seemed "as fresh-looking as if built within a year." The indefatigable Harriet Martineau agreed, as did J. S. Buckingham, who pronounced Lowell to be "one of the most remarkable places under the sun." Even Dickens, whose tour of America rendered him immune to most of its charms, was moved to lavish praise on the town. "One would swear," he added "that every 'Bakery,' 'Grocery' and 'Bookbindery' and every other kind of store, took its shutters down for the first time, and started in business yesterday."

If Lowell and its social engineering impressed visitors, the mill workers dazzled them. Here was nothing resembling Europe's *Untermenschen,* that doomed proletariat whose brief, wretched lives were squeezed between child labor and a pauper's grave. These were not men or children or even families as found in the Rhode Island mills. Instead Lowell employed young women, most of them fresh off New England farms, paid them higher wages than females earned anywhere else (but still only half of what men earned), and installed them in dormitories under strict supervision. They were young and industrious, intelligent, and entirely respectable. Like model citizens of a burgeoning republic they saved their money, went to church, and spent their leisure hours in self-improvement.

More than one visitor hurried home to announce the arrival of a new industrial order, one capable of producing goods in abundance without breaking its working class on the rack of poverty. Time proved them wrong, or at best premature. The Lowell ex-

From "From Utopia to Mill Town" by Maury Klein in *American History Illustrated,* October and November 1981. Reprinted by permission of *American History Illustrated.*

Lowell, Massachusetts, was a model mill town located on the banks of the Concord and Merrimack rivers. The community attracted worldwide attention because it presented a sharp contrast to the squalor of manufacturing centers in England and Europe. The buildings stood in groups separated by trees, shrubs, and strips of lawn that were attractively landscaped and reminiscent of a college campus. (Worcester Art Museum, Worcester, Massachusetts)

periment lasted barely a generation before sliding back into the grinding bleakness of a conventional mill town. It had survived long enough to tantalize admirers with its unfulfilled promise and to reveal some harsh truths about the incompatibility of certain democratic ideals and the profit motive.

The founding fathers of Lowell were a group known as the Boston Associates, all of whom belonged to that tight knit elite whose dominance of Boston society was exceeded only by their strangehold on its financial institutions. The seed had been planted by Francis Cabot Lowell, a shrewd, far-sighted merchant who took up the manufacture of cotton cloth late in life. A trip abroad in 1810 introduced him to the cottom mills of Lancashire and to a fellow Boston merchant named Nathan Appleton.

Blessed with a superb memory and trained in mathematics, Lowell packed his mind with details about the machinery shown him by unsuspecting mill owners. The Manchester owners jealously hoarded their secrets and patents, but none regarded the wealthy American living abroad for his health as a rival.

Once back in America, Lowell recruited a mechanical genius named Paul Moody to help replicate the machines he had seen in Manchester. After much tinkering they designed a power loom, cottonspinning frame, and some other machines that in fact improved upon the English versions. As a hedge against inexperience Lowell decided to produce only cheap, unbleached cotton sheeting. The choice also enabled him to use unskilled labor, but where was he to find even that? Manchester drew its workers from the poorhouses, a source lacking in America. Both the family system and use of apprentices had been tried in Rhode Island with little success. Most men preferred farming their own land to working in a factory for someone else.

But what about women? They were familiar with spinning and weaving, and would make obedient workers. Rural New England had a surplus of daughters who were considered little more than drains on the family larder. To obtain their services Lowell need only pay decent wages and overcome parental reservations about permitting girls to live away from home. This could be done by providing boarding houses where the girls would be subject to the strict supervision of older women acting as chaperones. There would be religious and moral instruction enough to satisfy the most scrupulous of parents. It was an ingenious concept, one that cloaked economic necessity in the appealing garb of republican ideals.

Lowell added yet another wrinkle. Instead of forming a partnership like most larger businesses, he obtained a charter for a corporation named the Boston Manufacturing Company. Capitalized at $300,000 the firm started with $100,000 subscribed by Lowell and a circle of his caste and kin: Patrick Tracy Jackson and his two brothers, Nathan Appleton, Israel Thorndike and his son, two brothers-in-law, and two other merchants. Jackson agreed to manage the new company, which chose a site at the falls on the Charles River at Waltham. By late 1814 the first large integrated cotton factory in America stood complete, along with its machine shop where Lowell and Moody reinvented the power loom and spinner.

Production began in 1815, just as the war with England drew to a close. The mill not only survived the return of British competition but prospered in spectacular fashion: during the years 1817–1824 dividends averaged more than nineteen percent. Moody's fertile mind devised one new invention

after another, including a warp-yarn dresser and double speeder. His innovations made the firm's production methods so unique that they soon became known as the "Waltham system." As Gilman Ostrander observed, "The Waltham method was characterized by an overriding emphasis upon standardization, integration, and mechanization." The shop began to build machinery for sale to other mills. Even more, the company's management techniques became the prototype on which virtually the entire textile industry of New England would later model itself.

Lowell did not live to witness this triumph. He died in 1817 at the age of forty-two, having provided his associates with the ingredients of success. During the next three years they showed their gratitude by constructing two more mills and a bleachery, which exhausted the available water power at Waltham. Eager to expand, the Associates scoured the rivers of New England for new sites. In 1821 Moody found a spot on the Merrimack River at East Chelmsford that seemed ideal. The river fell thirty-two feet in a series of rapids and there were two canals, one belonging to the Pawtucket Canal Company and another connecting to Boston. For about $70,000 the Associates purchased control of the Canal Company and much of the farmland along the banks.

From that transaction arose the largest and most unique mill town in the nation. In this novel enterprise the Associates seemed to depart from all precedent, but in reality they borrowed much from Waltham. A new corporation, the Merrimack Manufacturing Company, was formed with Nathan Appleton and Jackson as its largest stockholders. The circle of inventors was widened to include other members of the Boston elite such as Daniel Webster and the Boott brothers, Kirk and John. Moody took some shares but his ambitions went no further; he was content to remain a mechanic for the rest of his life. The memory of Francis Cabot Lowell was honored by giving the new village his name.

The task of planning and overseeing construction was entrusted to Kirk Boott. The son of a wealthy Boston Anglophile, Boott's disposition and education straddled the Atlantic. He obtained a commission in the British army and fought under Wellington until the War of 1812 forced his resignation. For several years he studied engineering before returning home in 1817 to take up his father's business. A brilliant, energetic, imperious martinet, Boott leaped at the opportunity to take charge of the new enterprise. As Hannah Josephson observed, he became "its town planner, its architect, its engineer, its agent in charge of production, and the leading citizen of the new community."

The immensity of the challenge appealed to Boott's ordered mind. He recruited an army of 500 Irish laborers, installed them in a tent city, and began transforming a pastoral landscape into a mill town. A dam was put across the river, the old canal was widened, new locks were added, and two more canals were started. The mills bordered the river but not with the monotony of a wall. Three buildings stood parallel to the water and three at right angles in a grouping that reminded some of Harvard College. Trees and shrubs filled the space between them. The boarding houses, semi-detached dwellings two-and-a-half stories high separated by strips of lawn, were set on nearby streets along with the superintendents' houses and long brick tenements for male mechanics and their families. It was a standard of housing unknown to working people anywhere in the country or in Europe. For himself Boott designed a Georgian mansion ornamented with a formidable Ionic portico.

Lowell emerged as the nation's first planned industrial community largely because of Boott's care in realizing the overall concept. At Waltham the boarding houses had evolved piecemeal rather than as an integral part of the design. The Associates took care to avoid competition between the sites by confining Lowell's production to printed calicoes for the higher priced market. While Waltham remained profitable, it quickly took a back seat to the new works. The machine shop provided a true barometer of change. It not only produced machinery and water wheels for Lowell but also oversaw the construction of mills and housing. Shortly before Lowell began production in 1823, the Associates, in Nathan Appleton's words, "arranged to equalize the interest of all the stockholders in both companies" by formally purchasing Waltham's patterns and patent rights and securing Moody's transfer to Lowell. A year later the entire machine shop was moved to Lowell, leaving Waltham with only a maintenance facility.

The success of the Lowell plant prompted the Associates to unfold ambitious new plans. East Chelmsford offered abundant water power for an expanding industry; the sites were themselves a priceless asset. To use them profitably the Associates revived the old Canal Company under a new name, the Locks and Canals Company, and transferred to it all the land and water rights owned by the Merrimack Company. The latter then bought back its own mill sites and leased the water power it required. Thereafter the Locks and Canals Company sold land to other mill companies, leased water power to them at fixed rates per spindle, and built machinery, mills, and housing for them.

This organizational arrangement was as far advanced for the times as the rest of the Lowell concept. It brought the Associates handsome returns from the mills and enormous profits from the Locks and Canals Company, which averaged twenty-four percent in dividends between 1825 and 1845. As new companies like the Hamilton, Appleton, and Lowell corporations were formed, the Associates dispersed part of their stock among a widening network of fellow Brahmins. New partners entered their exclusive circle, including the Lawrence brothers, Abbott and Amos. Directories of the companies were so interlocked as to avoid any competition between them. In effect the Associates had created industrial harmony of the sort J. P. Morgan would later promote under the rubric "community of interest."

By 1836 the Associates had invested $6.2 million in eight major firms controlling twenty five-story mills with more than 6,000 employees. Lowell had grown into a town of 18,000 and acquired a city charter. It boasted ten churches, several banks to accommodate the virtue of thrift on the part of the workers, long rows of shops, a brewery, taverns, schools, and other appurtenances of progress. Worldwide attention had transformed it into a showcase. Apart from the influx of foreigners and other dignitaries, it had already been visited by a president the Associates despised (Andrew Jackson), and by a man who would try three times to become president (Henry Clay).

The Associates basked in his attention because they viewed themselves as benevolent, far-seeing men whose sense of duty extended far beyond wealth. To be sure the life blood of the New England economy flowed through their counting houses from their domination of banks, insurance companies, railroads, shipping, and mills elsewhere in New England. Yet such were the rigors of their stern Puritan consciences that for them acquisition was all consuming without being all fulfilling. Duty taught that no fortune was so ample that more was not required. Economist Thorstein Veblen later marveled at the "steadfast cupidity" that drove these men "under pain of moral turpitude, to acquire a 'competence,' and then unremittingly to augment any competence acquired."

Not content with being an economic and social aristocracy, the Associates extended their influence to politics, religion, education, and morality. Lowell fit their *raison d'être* so ideally because it filled their coffers while at the same time reflecting their notion of an orderly, paternal community imbued with the proper values. The operatives knew their place, deferred to the leadership of the Associates, shared their values. . . .

☆

THE MILL GIRLS

In promoting their mills as an industrial utopia [the Associates] were quick to realize that the girls were the prime attraction, the trump card in their game of benevolent paternalism. As early as 1827 Captain Basil Hall, an Englishman, marveled at the girls on their way to work at six in the morning, "nicely dressed, and glittering with bright shawls and showy-colored gowns and gay bonnets . . . with an air of lightness, and an elasticity of step, implying an obvious desire to get to their work."

Observers who went home to rhapsodize about Lowell and its operatives as a model for what the factory system should become trapped themselves in an unwitting irony. While there was much about the Lowell corporations that served later firms as model, the same did not hold true for their labor force. The young women who filled the mills, regarded by many as the heart of the Lowell system, were in fact its most unique element and ultimately its most transient feature. They were of the same stock and shared much the same culture as the men who employed them. This relative homogeneity gave them a kinship of values absent in later generations of workers. Benita Eisler has called them "the last WASP labor force in America."

The women who flocked to Lowell's mills came mostly from New England farms. Some came to augment the incomes of poor families, others to earn money for gowns and finery, to escape the bleak monotony of rural life, or sample the adventure of a fresh start in a new village. Although their motives were mixed, they chose the mills over such alternatives as teaching or domestic service because the pay was better and the work gave them a sense of independence. Lucy Larcom, one of the most talented and articulate of the mill girls, observed that:

Country girls were naturally independent, and the feeling that at this new work for the few hours they had of everyday leisure were entirely their own was a satisfaction to them. They preferred it to going out as "hired help." It was like a young man's pleasure in entering upon business for himself.

Leisure hours were a scarce commodity. The mill tower bells tolled the girls to work before the light of day and released them at dusk six days a week, with the Sabbath reserved for solemn observance. The work day averaged twelve-and-a-half hours, depending on the season, and there were only three holidays a year, all unpaid: Fast Day, the Fourth of July, and Thanksgiving. Wages ranged between $2 and $4 a week, about half what men earned. Of this amount $1.25 was deducted for board, to which the company contributed another twenty-five cents. Meager as these sums appear, they exceeded the pay offered by most other mills.

The work rooms were clean and bright for a factory, the walls whitewashed and windows often garnished with potted flowers. But the air was clogged with lint and fumes from the whale-oil lamps hung above every loom. Since threads would snap unless the humidity was kept high, windows were nailed shut even in the summer's heat, and the air was sprayed with water. Delicate lungs were vulnerable to the ravages of tuberculosis and other respiratory ailments. More than one critic attributed the high turnover rate to the number of girls "going home to die."

The machines terrified newcomers with their thunderous clatter that shook the floor. Belts and wheels, pulleys and rollers, spindles and flyers, twisted and whirled, hissing and buzzing, always in motion, a cacophonous jungle alien to rural ears. At first the machines looked too formidable to master.

One girl, in the story recalling her first days at Lowell, noted that:

she felt afraid to touch the loom, and she was almost sure she could never learn to weave; the harness puzzled and the reed perplexed her; the shuttle flew out and made a new bump on her head; and the first time she tried to spring the lathe she broke a quarter of the threads. It seemed as if the girls all stared at her, and the overseers watched every motion, and the day appeared as long as a month had at home. . . . At last it was night. . . . There was a dull pain in her head, and a sharp pain in her ankles; every bone was aching, and there was in her ears a strange noise, as of crickets, frogs and jews-harps, all mingling together.

Once the novelty wore off, the strangeness of it all gave way to a more serious menace: monotony.

The boarding houses provided welcome havens from such trials. These were dwellings of different sizes, leased to respectable high-toned widows who served as housemothers for fifteen to thirty girls. They kept the place clean and enforced the company rules, which were as strict as any parent might want. Among other things they regulated conduct, imposed a ten o'clock curfew, and required church attendance. The girls were packed six to a bedroom, with three beds. One visitor described the small rooms as "absolutely choked with beds, trunks, band-boxes, clothes, umbrellas and people," with little space for other furniture. The dining room doubled as sitting room, but in early evening it was often besieged by peddlers of all sorts.

This cramped arrangement suited the Associates nicely because it was economical and reinforced a sense of group standards and conformity. Lack of privacy was old hat to most rural girls, though a few complained. Most housemothers set a good table and did not cater to dainty appetites. One girl reported dinner as consisting of "meat and potatoes, with vegetables, tomatoes and pickles, pudding or pie, with bread, butter, coffee or tea." English novelist Anthony Trollope was both impressed and repulsed by the discovery that meat was served twice a day, declaring that for Americans "to live a day without meat would be as great a privation as to pass a night without a bed."

The corporations usually painted each house once a year, an act attributed by some to benevolence and others to a shrewd eye for public relations and property values. Their zeal for cleanliness did not extend to bathing facilities, which were minimal at best. More than one visitor spread tales of dirt and vermin in the boarding houses, but these too were no strangers to rural homes. Like the mills, later boarding houses were built as long dormitory rows unleavened by strips of lawn or shrubbery, but the earlier versions retained a quaint charm for visitors and inhabitants.

Above all the boarding houses were, as Hannah Josephson stressed, "a woman's world." In these cluttered cloisters the operatives chatted, read, sewed, wrote letters, or dreamed about the day when marriage or some better opportunity would take them from the mills. They stayed in Lowell about four years on the average, and most married after leaving. The mill experience was, in Thomas Dublin's phrase, simply "a stage in a woman's life cycle before marriage." For many girls the strangeness of it all was mitigated by the presence of sisters, cousins, or friends who had undertaken the same adventure.

Outside the boarding house the girls strolled and picnicked in the nearby countryside, attended church socials, paid calls, and shopped for the things they had never had. Dozens of shops vied with the savings banks for their hard-earned dollars and won more than their share of them. Those eager to improve their minds, and there were many, patronized the library and the Lyceum, which for fifty cents offered a season ticket for twenty-five lectures by such luminaries as Ralph Waldo Emerson, Horace

Mann, John Quincy Adams, Horace Greeley, Robert Owen, and Edward Everett. Some were ambitious enough to attend evening classes or form study groups of their own in everything from art to German.

Above all the girls read. Their appetite for literature was voracious and often indiscriminate. So strong was this ardor that many slipped their books into the mills, where such distractions were strictly forbidden. It must have pained overseers to confiscate even Bibles from transgressors, but the large number that filled their drawers revealed clearly the Associates' determination to preserve the sharp distinction between the Lord's business and their own.

No one knows how many of the girls were avid readers, but the number probably exceeded the norm for any comparable group. Where so many read, it was inevitable that some would try their hand at writing. By the early 1840s Lowell boasted seven Mutual Self-Improvement Clubs. These were the first women's literary clubs in America, and the members consisted entirely of operatives. From two of these groups emerged a monthly magazine known as the *Lowell Offering* which in its brief life span (1841–1845) achieved a notoriety and reputation far in excess of its literary merits. The banner on its cover described the contents as *A Repository of Original Articles, Written Exclusively by Females Actively Employed in the Mills.*

No other aspect of Lowell rivaled the *Offering* as a symbol for the heights to which an industrial utopia might aspire. Observers at home and abroad were astounded at the spectacle of factory workers — women no less — capable of producing a literary magazine. Even Charles Dickens, that harsh critic of both English industrialism and American foibles, hurried this revelation to his readers:

I am now going to state three facts, which will startle a large class of readers on this side of the Atlantic very

Women factory workers at the Lowell mills were avid readers. They also formed self-improvement clubs and published their own monthly magazine, the Lowell Offering. *The* Offering *became a symbol for the heights to which an industrial utopia might aspire. As Maury Klein comments, "Observers at home and abroad were astounded at the spectacle of factory workers — women no less — capable of producing a literary magazine." (University of Lowell, Lowell, Massachusetts)*

much. First, there is a joint-stock piano in a great many of the boarding-houses. Secondly, nearly all these young ladies subscribe to circulating libraries. Thirdly, they have got up among themselves a periodical . . . which is duly printed, published, and sold; and whereof I brought away from Lowell four hundred good solid pages, which I have read from beginning to end.

As the *Offering's* fame grew, the Associates were not slow to appreciate its value. Nothing did more to elevate their esteem on both sides of the Atlantic. Contrary to the belief of some, the magazine never became a house organ. Both editors, Harriet Farley and Harriott Curtis, were veterans of the mills who opened their columns to critics and reformers while keeping their own editorial views within more discreet and refined bounds. For their part the Associates were too shrewd not to recognize that the *Offering's* appeal, its effectiveness as a symbol of republican virtues, lay in its independence. To serve them best it must not smack of self-serving, and it did not.

Although the magazine's prose and poetry seldom rose above mediocre, the material offered revealing insights into every aspect of factory life. Inevitably it attracted authors eager to voice grievances or promote remedies. The editors trod a difficult path between the genteel pretensions of a literary organ and a growing militancy among operatives concerned with gut issues. Few of the girls subscribed to the *Offering* anyway; most of the copies went to patrons in other states or overseas. Small wonder that critics charged the magazine had lost touch with actual conditions in the mills or the real concerns of their operatives.

The *Offering* folded in part because it reflected a system hurrying toward extinction. By the 1840s, when Lowell's reputation as an industrial utopia was still at its peak, significant changes had already taken place. Hard times and swollen ranks of stockholders clamoring for dividends had dulled the Associates' interest in benevolent paternalism. It had always been less a goal than a by-product and not likely to survive a direct conflict with the profit motive. The result was a period of several years during which Lowell coasted on its earlier image while the Associates dismantled utopia in favor of a more cost-efficent system.

The self-esteem of the Associates did not permit them to view their actions in this light, but the operatives felt the change in obvious ways. Their work week increased to seventy-five hours with four annual holidays compared to sixty-nine hours and six holidays for the much maligned British textile workers. To reduce unit costs, girls tended faster machines and were paid lower wages for piecework. That was called speedup; in another practice known as stretch-out, girls were given three or four looms where earlier they had tended one or two. Overseers and second hands were offered bonuses for wringing more productivity out of the workers.

At heart the utopian image of Lowell, indeed the system itself, rested on the assumption that grateful, obedient workers would not bite the hand of their masters. When operatives declined to accept this role, factory agents countered with dismissals and blacklists. The result was a growing sense of militancy among the girls and the first stirrings of a labor movement. In 1834 and 1836 there occurred spontaneous "turnouts" or strikes in Lowell, the first protesting wage cuts and the second an increase in the board charge. Neither achieved much, although a large number of girls (800 and 2,500) took part. The Associates showed their mettle in one instance by turning a widow with four children out of her boarding house because her eleven-year-old daughter, a bobbin girl, had followed the others out. "Mrs. Hanson, you could not prevent the older girls from turning out," the corporate agent explained sternly, "but your daughter is a child, and *her* you could control."

Between 1837 and 1842 a national depression drove wages down and quieted labor unrest at Lowell. When conditions improved and wages still fell, the disturbances began anew. In December 1844 five mill girls met to form the Lowell Female Labor Reform Association; within a year the organization had grown to 600 members in Lowell and had branches elsewhere in New England. Since unions had no legal status or power to bargain directly, LFLRA could only appeal to public opinion and petition the General Court (state legislature) for redress.

For three years the organization dispatched petitions and testified before legislative commissions on behalf of one issue in particular; the ten hour workday. Led by Sarah Bagley and other women of remarkable energy and intelligence, LFLRA joined hands with workingmen's groups in the push for shorter hours. Their efforts were dogged, impressive, and ultimately futile. As their ranks swelled, they suffered the usual problems of divided aims and disagreement over tactics. More than that, the LFLRA failed in the end simply because it had determination but no leverage. Legislators and other officials did not take them seriously because they were women who had no business being involved in such matters and could not vote anyway. By 1847 LFLRA was little more than a memory. The ten-hour movement lived on, but did not succeed until 1874.

During its brief life LFLRA did much to shatter the image of Lowell as an industrial utopia. The Associates held aloof from controversy and allowed editors, ministers, and distinguished visitors to make their case. There were those who preserved Lowell as a symbol because they wanted to believe, needed to believe in what it represented. After several years of constant labor strife, however, few could overlook the problems pointed up by LFLRA: more work for less pay, deteriorating conditions in the mills and boarding houses, blacklists, and more repressive regulations. Lowell had lost much of what had made it special and was on the verge of becoming another bleak and stifling mill town.

Gradually the river and countryside disappeared behind unbroken walls of factory or dormitory. Nature approached extinction in Lowell, and so did the girls who had always been the core of its system. In 1845 about ninety percent of the operatives were native Americans, mostly farm girls; by 1850 half the mill workers were Irish, part of the flood that migrated after the famine years of 1845–46. The Irish girls were illiterate, docile, and desperate enough to work for low wages. They preferred tenements with their friends and family to boarding houses, which relieved the Associates of that burden. It did not take the Associates long to appreciate the virtues of so helpless and undemanding a work force. In these immigrants they saw great promise for cheap labor comparable to that found in English mill towns like Manchester.

The Associates had lost their bloom as models of propriety and benevolence. Some called them "lords of the loom" and consigned them to the same terrace of Inferno as the South's "lords of the lash." How ironic it was for Nathan Appleton, the most beloved of souls with an unmatched reputation for philanthropy and civic virtue, that his mills were the first to be called "soulless corporations."

So it was that Lowell's utopian vision ended where industrialism began. In time the Irish would rise up in protest as their predecessors had done, but behind them came waves of Dutch, Greek, and French Canadian immigrants to take their places in the mills. The native New England girls continued to flee the mills or shy away from them in droves, until by 1860 they were but a small minority. Their departure marked the emergence of Lowell as a mill town no different than any other mill town. One of the girls, peering from her boarding house window, watched the growing stories of a new mill snuff out her view of the scenery beyond and caught the significance of her loss. In her lament could be found an epitaph for Lowell itself:

Then I began to measure . . . and to calculate how long I would retain this or that beauty. I hoped that the brow of the hill would remain when the structure was complete. But no! I had not calculated wisely. It began to recede from me . . . for the building rose still higher and higher. One hope after another is gone . . . one image after another, that has been beautiful to our eye, and dear to our heart has forever disappeared. How has the scene changed! How is our window darkened!

QUESTIONS TO CONSIDER

1 Thomas Jefferson, an agrarian idealist, hated the idea of America's becoming an industrial nation, basing his feelings on the evils of European cities. How did the city of Lowell, at least in its early years, escape the evils Jefferson believed inherent in urban industrial life?

2 Klein says that what happened at Lowell reveals that the profit motive and certain democratic ideals are incompatible. Do you agree? Was the Lowell experiment doomed from its inception because of conflicting goals?

3 Why did the Boston Associates choose young females from rural parts of New England to be operatives in their Lowell textile mills? What were the advantages of a female labor force?

4 Examine boarding-house life at Lowell from the perspective of the female mill workers. What were the advantages and drawbacks to living in the boarding houses? In what way, if any, was boarding-house life conducive to the development of a positive female subculture?

5 By the 1840s, changes taking place in the Lowell boarding houses and in the factories indicated the breakdown of that model factory town. Describe these changes and the reasons for growing labor militancy among the once "docile" female work force.

21

"Hell in Harness": The Iron Horse and the Go-Ahead Age

PAGE SMITH

The development of steam power was one of the great technological accomplishments of the late eighteenth and nineteenth centuries. In an age of giant rockets, space shuttles, and satellite probes of other planets, we tend to forget that the "advanced" steam engine, patented by England's James Watts in 1769, fostered myriad technological innovations that came to characterize industrial society.

A significant improvement over an earlier "atmospheric" engine, Watts's machine transformed the textile industry in Europe as well as in America. The steam engine had an equally profound effect on the history of transportation. As train historian David Plowden said in a recent issue of Timeline *magazine, "the railroad builder and the locomotive shattered a fixed distance-time equation for overland travel" that had existed for centuries. Until the advent of the steam engine, people had relied on nature for locomotion — on wind, water, and animals. In the "turnpike and canal eras," which lasted from around 1790 to the 1830s, Americans tried to alter nature by creating roads and waterways, but nature still furnished the power for the boats and barges, wagons and stages. The emergence of the steam-powered locomotive in the 1820s and 1830s was a quantum leap forward. In Plowden's words, "it was a symbol of man's will to rise above nature." Soon a locomotive driven by the steam engine could pull a train of cars at 30 miles per hour, doing so with a chugging roar and puffs of black smoke that would thrill generations of Americans.*

The early railroad promoters, however, found themselves in a bitter struggle with canal and steamboat interests for transportation supremacy. But with the advantages of speed, year-round operation, and location almost anywhere, the railroads were the way of the future. By the 1850s, the Age of the Iron Horse had arrived: thousands of miles of railroad track, shining beneath iron wheels that transported the cargo of a nation, lay across a bustling land. The railroads tied the East to the Middle West; they caused astonishing growth in existing cities like Chicago that lay along their routes; they spawned foundries, machine shops, new tools, and "a dizzying proliferation of inventions and improvements," as Page Smith says in this selection. Railroads also inspired the American imagination, as poets and storytellers heard America singing in the music of the trains, in the clang of their bells, in the hum of their wheels, and in the throb of their engines. The train even attracted a new breed of artist — the photographer. Railroads were to become America's principal form of transportation, remaining so until the interstate highway system replaced them in the middle of the next century.

Yet, as Smith notes, there was a down side to the railroad boom: along with it came an insatiable American need to "go ahead," to travel faster and make more money regardless of the consequences to human life. In truth, the locomotives smoking up the sky presaged an industrial society whose pollutants and destructive forces would eventually imperil humankind itself. But all that lay in the future. For Americans of the mid-nineteenth century, the train was the supreme example of the illimitable aspiration and resourcefulness of the human spirit.

TRACKS PRECEDED TRAINS. Enterprising entrepreneurs began laying crude tracks in the 1820s to carry horse-drawn carriages. The advantages were that a horse could pull a much heavier load faster and passengers much more comfortably on tracks than on the commonly rutted and unpaved roads of the time. Rails were usually made of wood with bands of iron on top. In Maryland experiments were conducted with stone ''rails'' covered with iron. The iron-covered wooden rails proved unsatisfactory as soon as the first steam engines were introduced; they had a tendency to tear loose and curl up, especially at the high rates of speed that the steam engines were soon capable of attaining — as much as fifteen miles an hour.

In England, steam engines at first seemed most promising in carrying passengers over ordinary roads and turnpikes. The Duke of Wellington's barouche was drawn by a steam engine and attained a speed of more than twenty-five miles an hour. English experiments in the use of rails were confined primarily to the hauling of heavy loads by horse or mule and, more and more frequently, by the use of some kind of steam engine.

In America, Peter Cooper, a successful business-

Extracts from *A People's History of the American Revolution,* Vol IV, *The Nation Comes of Age,* pages 262–282, copyright McGraw-Hill Publishing Company. Used by permission of the publisher.

man, saw the possibilities of combining rails and steam engines. While Cooper was neither an engineer nor an artisan, he did not hesitate to involve himself in the design of a locomotive, buying up unmounted gun barrels to use as tubes in the engine's boiler. When the locomotive failed to perform satisfactorily, Cooper turned the job of making a better one over to George Johnson, the owner of a machine shop and a skilled mechanic, who set to work with his young apprentice, James Milholland. While Johnson and Milholland were working on an improved version of Cooper's train, the *Stourbridge Lion,* imported from England, arrived in New York, followed by several other engines which were eagerly studied; the best features were quickly incorporated into the American machine.

Fourteen miles of railroad had meanwhile been laid between Baltimore and Ellicott's Mills, allowing horse-drawn carriages to make the trip in record time. The run to Ellicott's Mills was made by the horse carriage three times a day at a charge of twenty-five cents.

By May 30, 1830, Cooper's steam engine was ready to be tested. Cooper himself took the throttle of the *Tom Thumb,* with the president and the treasurer of the Baltimore & Ohio Company beside him. The *Tom Thumb* had a fourteen-inch piston stroke, weighed barely a ton, and developed slightly more than one horsepower, but it drew a weight of more than four tons at the rate of fifteen miles an hour. To draw attention to this new machine, Cooper advertised "a race between a Gray Horse and *Tom Thumb.*" The race took place on August 28, 1830, and a passenger on the coach drawn by the locomotive wrote: "The trip was most interesting. The curves were passed without difficulty, at a speed of fifteen miles an hour. . . . The day was fine, the company in the highest spirits, and some excited gentlemen of the party pulled out memorandum books, and when at the highest speed, which was eighteen miles an hour, wrote their names and some connected sentences, to prove that even at that great velocity it was possible to do so." It was on the way back to Baltimore that the famous race occurred. At first the horse, with quicker acceleration, raced out ahead but as the engine got up steam it overtook and passed the gray. Just at that moment the safety valve on the engine blew open and the train lost pressure and fell behind, despite Peter Cooper's frantic efforts to repair the damage.

George Stephenson, the great British engineer, had been working for almost a decade to perfect a practical engine. He had, in the process, built a dozen locomotives of various types in the well-equipped workshops of the Liverpool and Manchester Railroad and he had the stimulus of half a dozen active competitors. The United States had entered the field late and with far more modest resources, but within two years Cooper had produced the first practical passenger railroad locomotive. Engines designed by Stephenson soon outstripped the *Tom Thumb,* but American railroad building was on its way. When the Baltimore and Ohio offered a four-thousand-dollar reward for the most improved engine, Johnson and Milholland had one waiting. Its most serious rival was one designed and built by Phineas Davis, a watchmaker. Three other engines were also entered, each with important original features and all differing greatly in design. The *York,* built by Davis, won the first prize and Davis became an employee of the Baltimore and Ohio Railroad. It soon seemed as though every ambitious young engineer in the United States who could round up a few financial backers was making a locomotive. A year after the *Tom Thumb* made its historic run, the Mohawk and Hudson Railroad was completed and an engine named the *DeWitt Clinton* drew three cars at speeds that at times reached thirty miles an hour.

The Baltimore and Ohio Railroad Company had been formed on July 4, 1828, and the cornerstone laid by ninety-year-old Charles Carroll of Carrollton. But the course of the railroads, as they were soon called, proved far from smooth. They were opposed by the farmers, through whose lands their right-of-ways must run, in an alliance with the officers and stockholders of canal and highway companies (who rightly saw the railroads as dangerous competition), and by the teamsters (whose jobs were threatened). The engines themselves were so unpredictable that teams of horses had to be kept at way stations to pull broken-down trains to their destination. . . .

By 1832 — two years after *Tom Thumb's* famous trip — Pennsylvania alone had sixty-seven railroad tracks from a few hundred yards to twenty-two miles in length, many of them constructed of wood. When the Baltimore and Ohio built a passenger carriage with seats on either side of a center aisle, there were strong objections that such an aisle would simply become an extended spittoon, but this seating arrangement soon became standard on most lines. (Davy Crockett was widely reported to have exclaimed at his first sight of a train: "Hell in harness, by the 'tarnal!'")

Locomotives proved easier to build and to improve in efficiency than rails. Many rails were imported from England at an exorbitant cost. The six miles of railroad between Philadelphia and Germantown, for example, cost some thirty thousand dollars per mile and the rails, weighing thirty-nine pounds to the yard, were English-made.

On his way from Quincy to Washington in the fall of 1833 to take his seat in Congress, John Quincy Adams rode on the Amboy railroad from Amboy to Philadelphia. The train consisted of two locomotives, "each drawing an accommodation car, a sort of moving stage, in a square, with open railing, a platform and a row of benches holding forty or fifty persons; then four or five cars in the form of large stage coaches, each in three compartments, with doors of entrance on both sides." Each train ended with a high-piled baggage car, in which the passengers' luggage was covered with an oilcloth. The train sped along at almost thirty miles an hour, but after ten miles it had to stop to allow the wheels to be oiled. Despite this precaution, in another five

miles a wheel on one of the cars caught fire and slipped off, killing one passenger and badly maiming another. Of the sixteen passengers in the coach only one escaped injury.

Boilers on the early trains were wood-fired and, like steamboats, trains had to stop frequently to take on fresh supplies of wood. The remarkable thing is that in spite of all these difficulties — the constraints imposed by state legislatures under the control of the canal and highway interests, the scarcity of money, the inadequacy of the rails themselves, the constant litigation, the restrictive municipal ordinances that for a time forbade the building of railroad stations in cities, the disastrous accidents that plagued every line, the barns and fields set afire by sparks that showered from primitive smokestacks — the building of engines and railway tracks went inexorably on.

Boston, which had seen the greater part of the vast commerce with the Mississippi Valley West go to New York with the construction of the Erie Canal, took the lead in developing railroad links with the West, thereby regaining much of its lost financial eminence. New York, anxious to protect the investment of the state and its citizens in the canal, did all it could to impede the development of competing railroads.

Bu 1850 there were some three thousand miles of track running from Boston to the principal cities of New England and westward to Ohio, representing an investment of seventy million dollars. Of even greater significance was the fact that most of the lines made money. . . .

The railroad mania exceeded, if possible, the earlier canal mania. Canals still continued to be built, of course, and fierce competition developed between canals and railroads, but an extraordinary amount of technical skill and ingenuity was channeled into the development of railroads and the locomotives and the cars that passed over them. Hardly a month passed without some important innovation which, as soon as it had proved itself (and often before),

Hell in Harness: The Iron Horse and the Go-Ahead Age *is an oil painting of the first railway on the Mohawk and Hudson Road, completed in 1831. Because boilers on the early trains were wood-fired, they had to stop frequently for fresh* supplies of wood. *(Painting by Edward Lamson Henry, Collection of Albany Institute of History and Art, Albany, New York. Gift of Catherine Gansevoort Lansing)*

was adopted by other designers and builders. It was as though a particular quality in the American character, until now more or less dormant, had been activated. For forty years — from 1789 to 1830 — the canal, the steamboat, and the bridge had been the primary fields of engineering development. Now, with the "discovery" of the railroad, the machine shop claimed equal importance with the farm or factory and Americans revealed more dramatically than ever before their astonishing facility for marshaling human energies and material resources to meet a particular challenge. Barns became foundries, warehouses were converted into machine shops. New tools were built and old tools improved. Moreover, the primary activity of building locomotives spawned a host of subsidiary and only indirectly related undertakings. Farmers with a bent for mechanics began working on an improved plow. Longer and stronger bridges had to be built to carry

heavier and heavier trains, and there were tunnels to be built through mountains that blocked the way. It was clear that principles developed in making locomotives — such elements as pistons and valves — were adaptable to other processes. So there was a dizzying proliferation of inventions and improvements. Dedicated from the first moment to finding labor-saving methods and building labor-saving tools, thereby improving the ratio between work and its monetary return, a new breed of Americans — men like Peter Cooper and Mathias Baldwin and thousands of their less well-known compatriots — ushered in the "go-ahead age," the age of technology wherein any ambitious and dexterous farm boy might dream of becoming as rich as John Jacob Astor or Peter Cooper. A disposition to see the world in terms of practical problems to be solved was both the condition and the consequence of such a habit of mind, and it certainly contributed directly to the optimistic strain in American character. Wherever one looked he or she could see signs of "progress" and improvement in man's long war against nature. Everywhere "nature" was in retreat and civilization in advance. The Indian was nature, the natural man, and he was giving way to the determination of the American to cultivate the land and obey the biblical injunction to make it fruitful and to be fruitful himself, the determination to organize space and apply ideas to landscape with such single-minded zeal and unwearying industry that the landscape must succumb. Philip Hone noted proudly in his diary: "There was never a nation on the face of the earth which equalled this in rapid locomotion." A message had been carried from President Tyler in Washington to New York, a distance of some 225 miles, in twenty-four hours.

In the face of every obstacle the promoters of the railroads pushed ahead, raising their capital primarily by public subscription. A train of seventeen cars ran from Baltimore to Washington in 1835 in two hours and fifteen minutes, carrying relatives of Washington, Adams, Jefferson, and Madison. But antirailroad teamsters still waylaid trains and shot at crews from ambush, and two years later the Depression of 1837 brought railroad building to a virtual halt. It was eleven years before stockholders in the Baltimore and Ohio got any return on their investment and then it was a mere 2 percent. Construction had gone on during that period to connect Baltimore with the Ohio River commerce at the cost of $7,500,000, and only the intervention of the famous British banking house of Alexander Baring made it possible to avoid bankruptcy.

The biggest impediments to the railroads were laws designed to protect the investors in canals. The Chesapeake and Ohio canal, for example, cost $60,000 a mile to build and took twenty-two years to complete, by which time many of the original investors had died. The most notable feature of the canal was a tunnel 3,118 feet long which required the use of headlamps on barges through it, and de-

spite the fact that the Baltimore and Ohio Railroad ran its tracks parallel to the river, the transportation of Cumberland coal down the canal brought in substantial revenues for years, although not enough to pay its enormous costs. Protracted and expensive as its construction was, the canal was by any standard one of the great engineering feats of the century, second only to the Erie Canal. Legislators were under enormous pressure to protect such a huge investment.

A number of states passed laws requiring the railroads, after they had recouped the cost of their construction, to pay all profits above 10 percent to rival canal companies. Other laws prohibited trains from entering into or passing through the incorporated areas of cities and towns. Some states included in railroad franchises the requirement that railroads sell their tracks and stock to the state after twenty years — at the state's evaluation. Other provisions limited the carrying of freight by train to those times of the year when the canals were frozen. Freight and passenger rates of trains were frequently tied to those of canal transportation to keep the trains from drawing off business. A more practical obstacle was the fact that virtually every railroad company, many of which ran no more then fifty to a hundred miles, had a different gauge, so that freight and passengers had to be unloaded and loaded again at the boundary of every company. Everything in America was bound to have a moral dimension; the railroads must be seen as not merely having a remarkable effect on commerce but as improving morals. In this spirit the Western Railroad Company of Massachusetts sent a circular to all the clergy of the state pointing out "the moral effects of rail-roads" and urging them "to take an early opportunity to deliver a discourse before your congregation, on the moral effect of rail-roads on our wide extended country" — thereby, presumably, encouraging investment.

Since nature and morality (and, indeed, religion) were intertwined, the railroad train must be somehow reconciled with nature. [Ralph Waldo] Emerson, who believed that everything worked for the best, had no trouble in effecting the reconciliation. He was entranced by the technological revolution ushered in by the train. In 1834 he wrote in his journal: "One has dim foresight of the hitherto uncomputed mechanical advantages who rides on the rail-road and moreover a practical confirmation of the ideal philosophy that Matter is phenomenal whilst men & trees & barns whiz by you as fast as the leaves of a dictionary. As our teakettle hissed along through a field of mayflowers, we could judge of the sensations of a swallow who skims by trees & bushes with about the same speed. The very permanence of matter seems compromised & oaks, fields, hills, hitherto esteemed symbols of stability do absolutely dance by you." The railroads had introduced a "multitude of picturesque traits into our pastoral scenery," Emerson wrote, "the tunneling of the mountains, the bridging of streams . . . the encounter at short distances along the track of gangs of laborers . . . the character of the work itself which so violates and revolutionizes the primal and immemorial forms of nature; the villages of shanties at the edge of the beautiful lakes . . . the blowing of rocks, explosions all day, with the occasional alarm of a frightful accident." These all served to "keep the senses and the imagination active."

The train, Emerson believed, would complete the conquest of the continent, carrying Americans to every corner and making the United States "Nature's nation." The ambivalence of Emerson's own view of nature is suggested by his remark that "Nature is the noblest engineer, yet uses a grinding economy, working up all that is wasted to-day into to-morrow's creation. . . ." Thus nature was a good Puritan after all, a hard worker who wasted nothing.

In fairness to Emerson it must be said that, visiting the industrial midlands of England, he had second thoughts about the happy union of nature and technology. "A terrible machine has possessed itself of the ground, the air, the men and women, and hardly even thought is free," he wrote. Everything was centered in and conditioned by the omnipresent factory. In 1853, no longer rhapsodic about railroads, he wrote: "The Railroad has proved too strong for all our farmers & has corrupted them like a war, or the incursion of another race — has made them all amateurs, given the young men an air their fathers never had; they look as if they might be railroad agents any day."

By the early 1840s the railroads had an irresistible momentum. Small lines constantly consolidated in an effort to increase their access to capital and improve their service. New lines were established and as soon as they proved themselves (or went bankrupt) they were taken up by larger lines and incorporated into a "system." This process of consolidation was noted by Sidney George Fisher in 1839. "The whole route from Washington to N. York," he wrote, "is now owned by gigantic corporations, who of course manage the lines solely with a view to profit, without reference to the convenience or accommodation of passengers. Heretofore the line on the Chesapeake has been unrivalled for speed, cleanliness, civility of officers & servants, and admirable accommodations of every kind. Secure now from any competition, & sure that all persons must travel by their conveyance, they charge what they please, and the fare & accommodations will I doubt not be as wretched as that of the line to N. York." British capital and the labor of Irish immigrants were two essential ingredients in the extraordinary expansion of the railroads in the decade of the 1840s. The prize was the produce of the Mississippi Valley, the great bulk of which had to be carried down the Mississippi and its tributaries to New Orleans. To carry it by rail to New York and the large East Coast cities and ports would generate enormous profits. The Pennsylvania Railroad took the lead in building a "through line" of uniform gauge (this meant a shift from primarily passenger service to freight and passenger) and in dressing its train "captain'' or conductor in a uniform with blue coat and brass buttons. Coal was the principal freight on short hauls within states. Wheat and lumber were common loads on long hauls. Perhaps most important were the changes in the patterns of urban and rural life that the building of innumerable feeder lines brought about. Farmers within a radius of a hundred miles or more of a city could now ship fresh produce — milk, eggs, fruit and vegetables — to city markets. The farmer was thus disposed to specialize, to raise cash crops in sufficient quantity to make it practical to ship them to city markets. Dairy farms and one-crop farms thus began to replace general farming. As the farmer came to depend on distant city markets, he also became vulnerable to the operations of middlemen or wholesalers, who offered the lowest possible price for his produce, and from fluctuations in demand resulting from economic cycles. The farmer thus lost a measure of his cherished independence in return for more hard money. In turn the city, guaranteed a supply of essential foods, was able to grow at an unprecedented rate.

Much of the capital required to build railroads and develop coal mines as ancillary to them came from England. An English family named Morrison started the Hazelton Coal Company at Hazelton, Pennsylvania. Sidney George Fisher's brother Henry was the American representative for the coal company and for the Reading Railroad, which the Morrison family also owned. "The railroad," Sidney wrote, "is excellent, you roll along with great speed and great smoothness, and there is very little jar or noise, the cars are very comfortable, and there is but one source of annoyance, the cinders & smoke from the engine." The mining town of Tamaqua, not far from the Hazelton mine, was "a miserable village, wretched houses & population, produced by and dependent on the Little Schuylkill mines which are all around the town & make the whole place black with coal dust." Hazelton was a pleasant "new town" located in a pine forest under which lay "im-

mense and rich veins of coal." The ground was undermined for miles around with diggings and the Morrisons, Fisher reported, owned "1800 acres of the finest coal land in the state, the buildings, mines, railroad & machinery."

In the time the legal impediments to railroad building were struck down by courts or repealed by state legislatures. The emphasis now shifted to providing incentives for building railroads, especially in the Mississippi Valley region, where vast expanses of lands were unsold and unsettled because of their distance from markets. Most settlement took place along rivers and waterways that provided access to markets. Illinois set aside eleven million dollars in 1837, the year of the depression, to build a railroad that would run through the center of the state down to the Ohio River, but the state was in such desperate financial circumstances that it was fourteen years before any substantial progress was made in building the Central Illinois Railroad to link the Great Lakes with the Ohio and the Mississippi, making Chicago the terminus for the proposed route. Irishmen again provided the workers, and the death toll from disease was a heavy one. Cholera was especially deadly in the crowded and unsanitary work camps. "Our laborers," an engineer wrote, "numbered from 5,000 to 8,000 men. We had to recruit in New York and New Orleans paying transportation to Illinois . . . but the men would desert when the cholera epidemics broke out and scatter like frightened sheep. Men at work one day, were in their graves the next. . . . It was dangerous during the summer months to eat beef, butter, or drink milk. Our difficulties were increased by the groggeries and whisky that got in our camps. Drunken frolics ended in riots, when a contractor was murdered and state troops called out. One hundred and fifty laborers left in a body after the riot." . . .

The Central Illinois cost ten million dollars more to build than its projectors had estimated. The state gave the company 2,595,000 acres of land along its right-of-way. Abraham Lincoln was an attorney for the railroad; when he submitted a bill for $2,000 for his services and the railroad protested that that was more than Daniel Webster would have charged, Lincoln raised his fee to $5,000, took the railroad to court, and won his claim. Land through which the railroad passed rose in value from sixteen cents an acre to ten dollars an acre in a five-year period and a decade later to thirty dollars an acre.

The South now lagged behind the North and West in railroad building. All told, the feverish decade of building in the forties resulted in quadrupling the number of miles of railroad. This was all accomplished at enormous cost (the better part of it never recovered) and great loss of life (primarily Irish). When Alexander Mackay visited the United States in 1846 he found "an unbroken line of railway communication extending from Boston . . . to beyond Macon in Georgia, a distance of upwards of 1,200 miles." Lines reached out from Philadelphia to Pittsburgh, and the Baltimore and Ohio was pushing through the Cumberland Gap into the Mississippi Valley. Over 5,700 miles of railway had been completed, 2,000 of it within New England and New York state, and more than 4,000 miles of additional railway were under construction. In the 1850s the railroad mileage of the nation quadrupled once more.

Of all those who profited from the incredible expansion of the railroads none rose as dizzily as the city of Chicago. As Gustaf Unonius wrote in 1860, "The web of railroads which Chicago has spun around itself during the last ten years is the thing that more than anything else haas contributed to its wealth and progress." The first locomotive reached the city in 1851. Seven years later it was the terminus of more than a dozen trunk lines. Three lines ran from Chicago to New York in less than thirty-six hours (it once had taken ten days to make the trip). Daily 120 trains, some of them hauling as many as forty freight cars, arrived and departed from the stations in various parts of the city. "It should be mentioned," Unonius wrote, "that all

these railroads, altogether measuring five thousand miles in length, which radiate from Chicago as a central point in that immense iron web, the threads of which cross each other everywhere in the extensive Mississippi valley, are private undertakings." Private undertakings, as we have noted, with considerable public encouragement.

The passion to "go ahead," the endless emphasis on speed, exacted a heavy price in lives and serious injuries. In 1838 alone 496 persons died and many more were seriously injured in boiler explosions, not to mention those killed or injured in wrecks. Sidney George Fisher noted in his diary that there had been an accident on the North Pennsylvania Railroad in which thirty-nine persons had been killed and seventy-two wounded. One of the cars had caught fire and seventeen people had been burned to death. "These horrible scenes," he added, "are constantly recurring, and there seems no remedy." And Philip Hone wrote: "I never open a newspaper that does not contain some account of disasters and loss of life on railroads. They do a retail business in human slaughter, whilst the wholesale trade is carried on (especially on Western waters) by the steamboats. This world is going on too fast. Improvements, Politics, Reform, Religion — all fly. Railroads, steamers, packets, race against time and beat it hollow. Flying is dangerous. By and by we shall have balloons and pass over to Europe between sun and sun. Oh, for the good old days of heavy postcoaches and speed at the rate of six miles an hour!"

Captain Marryat ascribed such American "recklessness" to "the insatiate pursuit of gain among a people who consider that time is money, and who are blinded by their eagerness in the race for it. . . . At present, it certainly is more dangerous to travel one week in America than to cross the Atlantic a dozen times. The number of lives lost in one year by accidents in steamboats, railroads, and coaches was estimated . . . at *one thousand seven hundred and fifty!*" To Hone such disasters were "a stigma on our country; for these accidents (as they are called) seldom occur in Europe. . . . But we have become the most careless, reckless, headlong people on the face of the earth. 'Go ahead' is our maxim and password; and we do go ahead with a vengeance, regardless of the consequences and indifferent about the value of human life.'' His reflections were prompted by a report of the burning of the *Ben Sherrod.* The boat's crew, according to newspaper reports, was drunk and the wood took fire. ''Out of 235 persons, 175 were drowned or burned to death.'' By the end of the year fifty-five steamboats had blown up, burned, or run aground and sunk on the Mississippi River alone; thirteen sunk on the Ohio and two on the Missouri.

When Marryat ventured by rail around the United States in the 1830s he wrote: ''At every fifteen miles of the railroads there are refreshment rooms; the cars stop, all the doors are thrown open, and out rush the passengers, like boys out of school, and crowd around the tables to solace themselves with pies, patties, cakes, hard-boiled eggs, ham, custards, and a variety of railroad luxuries, too numerous to mention. The bell rings for departure, in they all hurry with their hands and mouths full, and off they go again, until the next stopping place induces them to relieve the monotony of the journey by masticating without being hungry.'' By the time Isabella Bird traveled west twenty years later there were numerous conveniences not available to Marryat. Bird reported that ''water-carriers, book, bonbon, and peach vendors'' were ''forever passing backwards and forewards.'' Baggage could be checked with metal checks, which was a novelty and a great convenience. Bird also discovered ''through tickets,'' a single long ticket bought at the station of origin, for an entire trip of fifteen hundred miles on a dozen different lines.

Since Americans traveled so perpetually, travelers' accommodations were generally excellent, clean, and comfortably and virtually interchangeable. Marryat observed that ''the wayside inns are remarkable for their uniformity; the furniture of the bar-room is invariably the same: a wooden clock, map of the United States, a map of the state, the Declaration of Independence, a looking-glass, with a hair-brush and comb hanging on it, *pro bono publico;* sometimes with the extra embellishment of one or two miserable pictures, such as General Jackson scrambling upon a horse, with fire and steam coming out of his nostrils, going to the battle of New Orleans, etc. etc.'' . . .

The feverish railroad building of the 1840s and 1850s opened up a large part of the still undeveloped land of the Mississippi Valley and provided a tremendous stimulus to business activity, although it did not prevent the devastating Depression of 1857. Perhaps most important of all, it had tied the Old West or the Near West to the Northeast and thereby laid the foundation for preserving the Union.

One can only attempt to convey the nature of the railroad boom by such phrases as ''reckless enthusiasm'' and ''extravagant passion.'' The American public, which had so recently fallen in love with canals, now made trains the objects of its collective affection. Canals suddenly seemed hopelessly pokey and out of date although they continued to be an important part of the transportation network. The loss of money and loss of life attendant upon the marvelous new invention seemed to most people an in-no-way unacceptable price to pay for the intoxicating sense of *speed,* of being drawn along as fast as the wind. So began a hundred-year-long love affair between Americans and railroads. If any one invention or device can be said to have had a determining effect on the history of a people, it was certainly the railroad train on the history of the people of the United States. In the beginning everything was [by water]. Water was the element on which Americans moved — lakes, rivers, and canals provided the initial circulatory system of American travel and American commerce. Now it was iron and soon it would be steel. The canal was an adaption of nature to human needs. The train, with its relentless disposition to go straight and level to its destination, was the subjugation of nature, man's greatest triumph over a world of curves and declivities.

QUESTIONS TO CONSIDER

1 Even more than the factory, the railroad is a symbol of mid-nineteenth-century America, for it was the railroad that linked the agricultural heartland to the industrial cities. How did the growth of the railroad change the way farmers farmed? How did it influence changes in industry?

2 What effect do you think fast travel to practically everywhere may have had on family life? What effect would increased mobility via railroad have had on westward expansion? On immigration?

3 Where does the railroad fit into nineteenth-century America's long philosophic love affair with nature? What did people dislike about the railroad?

4 Which technologies in our own day do you think have expanded with the rapidity of railroads in the mid-nineteenth century and with similar impact?

5 It seems ironic that in present-day America trains evoke nostalgia for a way of life that was slower, safer, and more gracious than our own, for safety and graciousness were the very qualities that nineteenth-century people thought the railroads had destroyed. What do you see as the future of railroads in the United States? What advantages do trains have over airplanes and automobiles? What disadvantages? In a world clouded by pollution and threatened with a scarcity of fossil fuels, what role might the railroads play?

XI

BEYOND THE MISSISSIPPI

22

The Trail of Tears

DEE BROWN

One of the most unhappy chapters in American history is the way whites treated Indians. American Indian policy, though, must be seen in the context of the entire European conquest of the New World. That conquest began with Columbus, who gave the people the name Indios *and kidnapped ten San Salvador Indians, taking them back to Spain to learn the white man's ways. In the ensuing four centuries, as Dee Brown writes in* Bury My Heart at Wounded Knee, *"several million Europeans and their descendants undertook to enforce their ways upon the people of the New World," and when these people would not accept European ways, they were fought, enslaved, or exterminated.*

Whites in North America joined the conquest in the colonial period, when they drove the eastern tribes into the interior. This pattern of "Indian removal" continued through the eighteenth and nineteenth centuries. When Jefferson came to power, his administration began an official United States policy of Indian removal either by treaty or by outright warfare. But the most impassioned champion of removal was Andrew Jackson, whom the Indians called Sharp Knife. Jackson was an incorrigible Indian hater. In his frontier years he had waged war against the Cherokees, Choctaws, Chicasaws, Creeks, and Seminoles, but they were still clinging to their tribal lands in the South when Jackson took office. At once he announced that these tribes must be sent away to "an ample district west of the Mississippi," and Congress responded with a law that embodied his recommendations. In a subsequent act, passed in 1830, Congress guaranteed that all of the United States west of the Mississippi "and not within the states of Missouri and Louisiana or the Territory of Arkansas" would constitute a permanent Indian frontier.

But settlers moved into Indian country before Washington could put the law into effect. So United States policy makers were obliged to shift the "permanent Indian frontier" from the Mississippi to the ninety-fifth meridian, again promising that everything west of this imaginary line would belong to the Indians "for as long as trees grow and water flows." In the late 1830s, United States soldiers rounded up the Cherokees and herded them west into Indian country in what ranks among the saddest episodes in the sordid story of white-Indian relations in the United States. That episode is related with grace and sensitivity by Dee Brown, a prolific historian of the West and the American Indians.

IN THE SPRING OF 1838, Brigadier General Winfield Scott with a regiment of artillery, a regiment of infantry, and six companies of dragoons marched unopposed into the Cherokee country of northern Georgia. On May 10 at New Echota, the capital of what had been one of the greatest Indian nations in eastern America, Scott issued a proclamation:

The President of the United States sent me with a powerful army to cause you, in obedience to the treaty of 1835, to join that part of your people who are already established in prosperity on the other side of the Mississippi. . . . The emigration must be commenced in haste. . . . The full moon of May is already on the wane, and before another shall have passed away every Cherokee man, woman and child . . . must be in motion to join their brethren in the west. . . . My troops already occupy many positions . . . and thousands and thousands are approaching from every quarter to render resistance and escape alike hopeless. . . . Will you then by resistance compel us to resort to arms? Or will you by flight seek to hide yourselves in mountains and forests and thus oblige us to hunt you down? Remember that in pursuit it may

be impossible to avoid conflicts. The blood of the white man or the blood of the red man may be spilt, and if spilt, however accidentally, it may be impossible for the discreet and humane among you, or among us, to prevent a general war and carnage.

For more than a century the Cherokees had been ceding their land, thousands of acres by thousands of acres. They had lost all of Kentucky and much of Tennessee, but after the last treaty of 1819 they still had remaining about 35,000 square miles of forested mountains, clean, swift-running rivers, and fine meadows. In this country which lay across parts of Georgia, North Carolina, and Tennessee they cultivated fields, planted orchards, fenced pastures, and built roads, houses, and towns. Sequoya had invented a syllabary for the Cherokee language so that thousands of his tribesmen quickly learned to read and write. The Cherokees had adopted the white man's way — his clothing, his constitutional form of government, even his religion. But it had all been for nothing. Now these men who had come across the great ocean many years ago wanted all of the Cherokees' land. In exchange for their 35,000 square miles the tribe was to receive five million dollars and another tract of land somewhere in the wilderness beyond the Mississippi River.

From "The Trail of Tears" by Dee Brown in *American History Illustrated,* June 1972. Reprinted by permission of *American History Illustrated.*

This was a crushing blow to a proud people. "They are extremely proud, despising the lower class of Europeans," said Henry Timberlake, who visited them before the Revolutionary War. William Bartram, the botanist, said the Cherokees were not only a handsome people, tall, graceful, and olive-skinned, but "their countenance and actions exhibit an air of magnanimity, superiority and independence."

Ever since the signing of the treaties of 1819, Major General Andrew Jackson, a man they once believed to be their friend, had been urging Cherokees to move beyond the Mississippi. Indians and white settlers, Jackson told them, could never get along together. Even if the government wanted to protect the Cherokees from harassment, he added, it would be unable to do so. "If you cannot protect us in Georgia," a chief retorted, "how can you protect us from similar evils in the West?"

During the period of polite urging, a few hundred Cherokee families did move west, but the tribe remained united and refused to give up any more territory. In fact, the council leaders passed a law forbidding any chief to sell or trade a single acre of Cherokee land on penalty of death.

In 1828, when Andrew Jackson was running for President, he knew that in order to win he must sweep the frontier states. Free land for the land-hungry settlers became Jackson's major policy. He hammered away at this theme especially hard in Georgia, where waves of settlers from the coastal low-lands were pushing into the highly desirable Cherokee country. He promised the Georgians that if they would help elect him President, he would lend his support to opening up the Cherokee lands for settlement. The Cherokees, of course, were not citizens and could not vote in opposition. To the Cherokees and their friends who protested this promise, Jackson justified his position by saying that the Cherokees had fought on the side of the British during the Revolutionary War. He conveniently forgot that the Cherokees had been his allies during the desperate War of 1812, and had saved the day for him in his decisive victory over the British-backed Creeks at Horseshoe Bend. (One of the Cherokee chiefs who aided Jackson was Junaluska. Said he afterward: "If I had known that Jackson would drive us from our homes I would have killed him that day at the Horseshoe.")

Three weeks after Jackson was elected President, the Georgia legislature passed a law annexing all the Cherokee country within that state's borders. As most of the Cherokee land was in Georgia and three-fourths of the tribe lived there, this meant an end to their independence as a nation. The Georgia legislature also abolished all Cherokee laws and customs and sent surveyors to map out land lots of 160 acres each. The 160-acre lots were to be distributed to white citizens of Georgia through public lotteries.

To add to the pressures on the Cherokees, gold was discovered near Dahlonega in the heart of their country. For many years the Cherokees had concealed the gold deposits, but now the secret was out and a rabble of gold-hungry prospectors descended upon them.

John Ross, the Cherokees' leader, hurried to Washington to protest the Georgia legislature's actions and to plead for justice. In that year Ross was 38 years old; he was well-educated and had been active in Cherokee government matters since he was 19. He was adjutant of the Cherokee regiment that served with Jackson at Horseshoe Bend. His father had been one of a group of Scottish emigrants who settled near the Cherokees and married into the tribe.

In Washington, Ross found sympathizers in Congress, but most of them were anti-Jackson men and the Cherokee case was thus drawn into the whirlpool of politics. When Ross called upon Andrew Jackson to request his aid, the President bluntly told him that "no protection could be afforded the Cherokees" unless they were willing to move west of the Mississippi.

While Ross was vainly seeking help in Washington, alarming messages reached him from Georgia. White citizens of that state were claiming the homes of Cherokees through the land lottery, seizing some of them by force. Joseph Vann, a hardworking half-breed, had carved out an 800-acre plantation at Spring Place and built a fine brick house for his residence. Two men arrived to claim it, dueled for it, and the winner drove Vann and his family into the hills. When John Ross rushed home he found that the same thing had happened to his family. A lottery claimant was living in his beautiful home on the Coosa River, and Ross had to turn north toward Tennessee to find his fleeing wife and children.

During all this turmoil, President Jackson and the governor of Georgia pressed the Cherokee leaders hard in attempts to persuade them to cede all their territory and move to the West. But the chiefs stood firm. Somehow they managed to hold the tribe together, and helped dispossessed families find new homes back in the wilderness areas. John Ross and his family lived in a one-room log cabin across the Tennessee line.

In 1834, the chiefs appealed to Congress with a memorial in which they stated that they would never voluntarily abandon their homeland, but proposed a compromise in which they agreed to cede the state of Georgia a part of their territory provided that they would be protected from invasion in the remainder. Furthermore, at the end of a definite period of years to be fixed by the United States they would be willing to become citizens of the various states in which they resided.

"Cupidity has fastened its eye upon our lands and our homes," they said, "and is seeking by force and by every variety of oppression and wrong to expel us from our lands and our homes and to tear from us all that has become endeared to us. In our distress we have appealed to the judiciary of the United States, where our rights have been solemnly established. We have appealed to the Executive of the United States to protect those rights according to the obligation of treaties and the injunctions of the laws. But this appeal to the Executive has been made in vain."

This new petition to Congress was no more effectual than their appeals to President Jackson. Again they were told that their difficulties could be remedied only by their removal to the west of the Mississippi.

For the first time now, a serious split occurred among the Cherokees. A small group of subchiefs decided that further resistance to the demands of the Georgia and United States governments was futile. It would be better, they believed, to exchange their land and go west rather than risk bloodshed and the possible loss of everything. Leaders of this group were Major Ridge and Elias Boudinot. Ridge had adopted his first name after Andrew Jackson gave him that rank during the War of 1812. Boudinot was Ridge's nephew. Originally known as Buck Watie, he had taken the name of a New England philanthropist who sent him through a mission school in Connecticut. Stand Watie, who later became a Confederate general, was his brother. Upon Boudinot's return from school to Georgia he founded the first tribal newspaper, the *Cherokee Phoenix,* in 1827, but during the turbulence following the Georgia land lotteries he was forced to suspend publication.

And so in February 1835 when John Ross journeyed to Washington to resume his campaign to save the Cherokee nation, a rival delegation headed by Ridge and Boudinot arrived there to seek terms for removal to the West. The pro-removal forces in the government leaped at this opportunity to bypass Ross's authority, and within a few days drafted a preliminary treaty for the Ridge delegation. It was then announced that a council would be held later in the year at New Echota, Georgia, for the purpose of negotiating and agreeing upon final terms.

During the months that followed, bitterness increased between the two Cherokee factions. Ridge's group was a very small minority, but they had the full weight of the United States government behind them, and threats and inducements were used to force a full attendance at the council which was set for December 22, 1835. Handbills were printed in Cherokee and distributed throughout the nation, informing the Indians that those who did not attend would be counted as assenting to any treaty that might be made.

During the seven days which followed the opening of the treaty council, fewer than five hundred Cherokees, or about 2 percent of the tribe, came to New Echota to participate in the discussions. Most of the other Cherokees were busy endorsing a petition to be sent to Congress stating their opposition to the treaty. But on December 29, Ridge, Boudinot and their followers signed away all the lands of the great Cherokee nation. Ironically, thirty years earlier Major Ridge had personally executed a Cherokee chief named Doublehead for committing one of the few capital crimes of the tribe. That crime was the signing of a treaty which gave away Cherokee lands.

Charges of bribery by the Ross forces were denied by government officials, but some years afterward it was discovered that the Secretary of War had sent secret agents into the Cherokee country with authority to expend money to bribe chiefs to support the treaty of cession and removal. And certainly the treaty signers were handsomely rewarded. In an era when a dollar would buy many times its worth today, Major Ridge was paid $30,000 and

his followers received several thousand dollars each. Ostensibly they were being paid for their improved farmlands, but the amounts were far in excess of contemporary land values.

John Ross meanwhile completed gathering signatures of Cherokees who were opposed to the treaty. Early in the following spring, 1836, he took the petition to Washington. More than three-fourths of the tribe, 15,964, had signed in protest against the treaty.

When the governor of Georgia was informed of the overwhelming vote against the treaty, he replied: "Nineteen-twentieths of the Cherokees are too ignorant and depraved to entitle their opinions to any weight or consideration in such matters."

The Cherokees, however, did have friends in Congress. Representative Davy Crockett of Tennessee denounced the treatment of the Cherokees as unjust, dishonest, and cruel. He admitted that he represented a body of frontier constituents who would like to have the Cherokee lands opened for settlement, and he doubted if a single one of them would second what he was saying. Even though his support of the Cherokees might remove him from public life, he added, he could not do otherwise except at the expense of his honor and conscience. Daniel Webster, Henry Clay, Edward Everett, and other great orators of the Congress also spoke for the Cherokees.

When the treaty came to a final decision in the Senate, it passed by only one vote. On May 23, 1836, President Jackson signed the document. According to its terms, the Cherokees were allowed two years from that day in which to leave their homeland forever.

The few Cherokees who had favored the treaty now began making their final preparations for departure. About three hundred left during that year and then early in 1837 Major Ridge and 465 followers departed by boats for the new land in the West. About 17,000 others, ignoring the treaty, remained steadfast in their homeland with John Ross.

For a while it seemed that Ross might win his long fight, that perhaps the treaty might be declared void. After the Secretary of War, acting under instructions from President Jackson, sent Major William M. Davis to the Cherokee country to expedite removal to the West, Davis submitted a frank report: "That paper called a treaty is no treaty at all," he wrote, "because it is not sanctioned by the great body of the Cherokees and was made without their participation or assent. . . . The Cherokees are a peaceable, harmless people, but you may drive them to desperation, and this treaty cannot be carried into effect except by the strong arm of force."

In September 1836, Brigadier General Dunlap, who had been sent with a brigade of Tennessee volunteers to force the removal, indignantly disbanded his troops after making a strong speech in favor of the Indians: "I would never dishonor the Tennessee arms in a servile service by aiding to carry into execution at the point of the bayonet a treaty made by a lean minority against the will and authority of the Cherokee people."

Even Inspector General John E. Wool, commanding United States troops in the area, was impressed by the united Cherokee resistance, and warned the Secretary of War not to send any civilians who had any part in the making of the treaty back into the Cherokee country. During the summer of 1837, the Secretary of War sent a confidential agent, John Mason, Jr., to observe and report. "Opposition to the treaty is unanimous and irreconcilable," Mason wrote. "They say it cannot bind them because they did not make it; that it was made by a few unauthorized individuals; that the nation is not party to it."

The inexorable machinery of government was already in motion, however, and when the expiration date of the waiting period, May 23, 1838, came near, Winfield Scott was ordered in with his army to force compliance. As already stated, Scott issued his proclamation on May 10. His soldiers were already building thirteen stockaded forts — six in North Carolina, five in Georgia, one in Tennessee, and one in Alabama. At these points the Cherokees would be concentrated to await transportation to the West. Scott then ordered the roundup started, instructing his officers not to fire on the Cherokees except in case of resistance. "If we get possession of the women and children first," he said, "or first capture the men, the other members of the same family will readily come in."

James Mooney, an ethnologist who afterwards talked with Cherokees who endured this ordeal, said that squads of troops moved into the forested mountains to search out every small cabin and make prisoners of all the occupants however or wherever they might be found. "Families at dinner were startled by the sudden gleam of bayonets in the doorway and rose up to be driven with blows and oaths along the weary miles of trail that led to the stockades. Men were seized in their fields or going along the road, women were taken from their spinning wheels and children from their play. In many cases, on turning for one last look as they crossed a ridge, they saw their homes in flames, fired by the lawless rabble that followed on the heels of the soldiers to loot and pillage. So keen were these outlaws on the scent that in some instances they were driving off the cattle and other stock of the Indians almost before the soldiers had fairly started their owners in the other direction."

Long afterward one of the Georgia militiamen who participated in the roundup said: "I fought through the Civil War and have seen men shot to pieces and slaughtered by thousands, but the Cherokee removal was the cruelest work I ever knew."

Knowing that resistance was futile, most of the Cherokees surrendered quietly. Within a month, thousands were enclosed in the stockades. On June 6 at Ross's Landing near the site of present-day Chattanooga, the first of many departures began. Eight hundred Cherokees were forcibly crowded onto a flotilla of six flatboats lashed to the side of a steamboat. After surviving a passage over rough rapids which smashed the sides of the flatboats, they landed at Decatur, Alabama, boarded a railroad train (which was a new and terrifying experience for most of them), and after reaching Tuscumbia were crowded upon a Tennessee River steamboat again.

Throughout June and July similar shipments of several hundred Cherokees were transported by this long water route — north on the Tennessee River to the Ohio and then down the Mississippi and up the Arkansas to their new homeland. A few managed to escape and make their way back to the Cherokee country, but most of them were eventually recaptured. Along the route of travel of this forced migration, the summer was hot and dry. Drinking water and food were often contaminated. First the young children would die, then the older people, and sometimes as many as half the adults were stricken with dysentery and other ailments. On each boat deaths ran as high as five per day. On one of the first boats to reach Little Rock, Arkansas, at least a hundred had died. A compassionate lieutenant who was with the military escort recorded in his diary for August 1: "My blood chills as I write at the remembrance of the scenes I have gone through."

When John Ross and other Cherokee leaders back in the concentration camps learned of the high mortality among those who had gone ahead, they petitioned General Scott to postpone further departures until autumn. Although only three thousand Cherokees had been removed, Scott agreed to wait until the summer drought was broken, or no later than October. The Cherokees in turn agreed to organize and manage the migration themselves. After a lengthy council, they asked and received permission to travel overland in wagons, hoping that by camping along the way they would not suffer as many deaths as occurred among those who had gone on the river boats.

During this waiting period, Scott's soldiers continued their searches for more than a thousand Cherokees known to be still hiding out in the deep wilderness of the Great Smoky Mountains. These Cherokees had organized themselves under the leadership of a chief named Utsala, and had developed warning systems to prevent captures by the bands of soldiers. Occasionally, however, some of the fugitives were caught and herded back to the nearest stockade.

One of the fugitive families was that of Tsali, an aging Cherokee. With his wife, his brother, three sons and their families, Tsali had built a hideout somewhere on the border between North Carolina and Tennessee. Soldiers surrounded their shelters one day, and the Cherokees surrendered without resistance. As they were being taken back toward Fort Cass (Calhoun, Tennessee) a soldier prodded Tsali's wife sharply with a bayonet, ordering her to walk faster. Angered by the brutality, Tsali grappled with the soldier, tore away his rifle, and bayoneted him to the ground. At the same time, Tsali's brother leaped upon another soldier and bayoneted him. Before the remainder of the military detachment could act, the Cherokees fled, vanishing back into the Smokies where they sought refuge with Chief Utsala. Both bayoneted soldiers died.

Upon learning of the incident, Scott immediately ordered that Tsali must be brought in and punished. Because some of his regiments were being transferred elsewhere for other duties, however, the general realized that his reduced force might be occupied for months in hunting down and capturing the escaped Cherokee. He would have to use guile to accomplish the capture of Tsali.

Scott therefore dispatched a messenger — a white man who had been adopted as a child by the Cherokees — to find Chief Utsala. The messenger was instructed to inform Utsala that if he would surrender Tsali to General Scott, the Army would withdraw from the Smokies and leave the remaining fugitives alone.

When Chief Utsala received the message, he was suspicious of Scott's sincerity, but he considered the general's offer as an opportunity to gain time. Perhaps with the passage of time, the few Cherokees remaining in the Smokies might be forgotten and left alone forever. Utsala put the proposition to Tsali: If he went in and surrendered, he would probably be put to death, but his death might insure the freedom of a thousand fugitive Cherokees.

Tsali did not hesitate. He announced that he would go and surrender to General Scott. To make certain that he was treated well, several members of Tsali's band went with him.

When the Cherokees reached Scott's headquarters, the general ordered Tsali, his brother, and three sons arrested, and then condemned them all to be shot to death. To impress upon the tribe their utter helplessness before the might of the government, Scott selected the firing squad from Cherokee prisoners in one of the stockades. At the last moment, the general spared Tsali's youngest son because he was only a child.

(By this sacrifice, however, Tsali and his family gave the Smoky Mountain Cherokees a chance at survival in their homeland. Time was on their side, as Chief Utsala had hoped, and that is why today there is a small Cherokee reservation on the North Carolina slope of the Great Smoky Mountains.)

With the ending of the drought of 1838, John Ross and the 13,000 stockaded Cherokees began preparing for their long overland journey to the West. They assembled several hundred wagons, filled them with blankets, cooking pots, their old people and small children, and moved out in separate contingents along a trail that followed the Hiwassee River. The first party of 1,103 started on October 1.

"At noon all was in readiness for moving," said an observer of the departure. "The teams were stretched out in a line along the road through a heavy forest, groups of persons formed about each wagon. The day was bright and beautiful, but a gloomy thoughtfulness was depicted in the lineaments of every face. In all the bustle of preparation there was a silence and stillness of the voice that betrayed the sadness of the heart. At length the word was given to move on. Going Snake, an aged and respected chief whose head eighty summers had whitened, mounted on his favorite pony and led the way in silence, followed by a number of younger men on horseback. At this very moment a low sound of distant thunder fell upon my ear . . . a voice of divine indignation for the wrong of my poor and unhappy countrymen, driven by brutal power from all they loved and cherished in the land of their fathers to gratify the cravings of avarice. The sun was unclouded — no rain fell — the thunder rolled away and seemed hushed in the distance."

Throughout October, eleven wagon trains departed and then on November 4, the last Cherokee exiles moved out for the West. The overland route for these endless lines of wagons, horsemen, and people on foot ran from the mouth of the Hiwassee in Tennessee across the Cumberland plateau to McMinnville and then north to Nashville where they crossed the Cumberland River. From there they followed an old trail to Hopkinsville, Kentucky, and continued northwestward to the Ohio River, crossing into southern Illinois near the mouth of the Cumberland. Moving straight westward they passed through Jonesboro and crossed the Mississippi at Cape Girardeau, Missouri. Some of the first parties turned southward through Arkansas; the

Trail of Tears, *an oil painting by Robert Lindneux. The first group of Cherokees started on their journey west on October 1, 1838. When all the groups had reached the new Indian Territory, as Dee Brown indicates, "the Cherokees had lost about four thousand by deaths — or one out of every four members of the tribe — most of the deaths brought about as the direct result of the enforced removal." (Woolaroc Museum, Bartlesville, Oklahoma)*

later ones continued westward through Springfield, Missouri, and on to Indian Territory.

A New Englander traveling eastward across Kentucky in November and December met several contingents, each a day apart from the others. "Many of the aged Indians were suffering extremely from the fatigue of the journey," he said, "and several were quite ill. Even aged females, apparently nearly ready to drop into the grave, were traveling with heavy burdens attached to their backs — on the sometimes frozen ground and sometimes muddy streets, with no covering for the feet except what nature had given them. . . . We learned from the inhabitants on the road where the Indians passed, that they buried fourteen or fifteen at every stopping place, and they make a journey of ten miles per day only on an average. They will not travel on the Sabbath . . . they must stop, and not merely stop — they must worship the Great Spirit, too; for they had divine service on the Sabbath — a camp meeting in truth."

Autumn rains softened the roads, and the hundreds of wagons and horsed cut them into molasses, slowing movement to a crawl. To add to their difficulties, tollgate operators overcharged them for passage. Their horses were stolen or seized on pretext of unpaid debts, and they had no recourse to the law. With the coming of cold damp weather, measles and whooping cough became epidemic. Supplies had to be dumped to make room for the sick in the jolting wagons.

By the time the last detachments reached the Mississippi at Cape Girardeau it was January, with the river running full of ice so that several thousand had to wait on the east bank almost a month before the channel cleared. James Mooney, who later heard the story from survivors, said that "the lapse of over half a century had not sufficed to wipe out the memory of the miseries of that halt beside the frozen river, with hundreds of sick and dying penned up in wagons or stretched upon the ground, with only a blanket overhead to keep out the January blast."

Meanwhile the parties that left early in October were beginning to reach Indian Territory. (The first arrived on January 4, 1839.) Each group had lost from thirty to forty members by death. The later detachments suffered much heavier losses, especially toward the end of their journey. Among the victims was the wife of John Ross.

Not until March 1839 did the last of the Cherokees reach their new home in the West. Counts were made of the survivors and balanced against the counts made at the beginning of the removal. As well as could be estimated, the Cherokees had lost about four thousand by deaths — or one out of every four members of the tribe — most of the deaths brought about as the direct result of the enforced removal. From that day to this the Cherokees

remember it as "the trail where they cried," or the Trail of Tears.

QUESTIONS TO CONSIDER

1 Columbus and the European adventurers who first came to the New World brought with them assumptions of their own cultural superiority and the inferiority of all non-Europeans, as we saw in selections 1 and 2. Compare these early Europeans' attitudes and treatment of the *Indios* they met with Americans' attitudes toward and treatment of the Cherokees.

2 How did factionalism within the Cherokee nation help the state of Georgia and the federal government to carry out their policy of Indian removal?

3 On December 29, 1835, a Cherokee treaty council signed away the Cherokees' tribal lands and agreed to the tribe's being moved west of the Mississippi. What methods did the United States government use to obtain this treaty? Discuss the paradox of how a nation like the United States, founded on democratic principles of government, could justify signing such a fraudulent treaty.

4 The framers of the Constitution were men of property who also held republican ideals (see selection 9). The Boston Associates, who founded Lowell, Massachusetts, were also wealthy men who tried and ultimately failed to combine benevolent and material ideas, (see selection 20). How does the experience of Indian removal also illustrate America's conflict between benevolence and greed, idealism and pragmatism?

23

Women and Their Families
on the
Overland Trails

JOHNNY FARAGHER
AND CHRISTINE STANSELL

After the War of 1812, America turned away from Old World entanglements and sought to extend her "natural sphere of influence" westward. Pioneers moved in sporadic waves out to the Mississippi River and beyond. Jefferson had made this westward movement possible by purchasing the vast Louisiana Territory from France in 1803. He had also begun American dreams of a transcontinental empire when he sent Lewis and Clark out to the Pacific and back. In the next two decades, Americans occupied the fertile Mississippi Valley, creating the new states of Louisiana, Indiana, Mississippi, Illinois, Alabama, and Missouri. At the same time, army explorers and scientists undertook expeditions up the Arkansas and Missouri rivers, finding that the complex river systems offered tremendous possibilities for commerce and trade. In the Adams-Onís Treaty of 1819, Spain gave the United States her claims to the Oregon country, an expansive region lying north of the Red and Arkansas rivers and the forty-second parallel. After Mexico revolted from Spain in 1822, the Mexican Republic also ratified the Adams-Onís Treaty, thus clearing the way for an American march to the Pacific.

American fur companies, operating out of St. Louis and Independence, Missouri, had already sent trappers and traders out into the awesome Rocky Mountains. These fabled mountain men blazed trails and explored rich mountain valleys across the

Oregon country, reporting back that the region was excellent for settlement. In the 1830s and 1840s, Americans from the fringes of the South and the old northwestern states headed across the trails the mountain men had blazed, establishing American outposts in Oregon and California. Meanwhile, other settlers — most of them from the Border South — migrated into Mexican-held Texas, where they eventually revolted and set up an independent republic.

In the 1840s — an era of unprecedented westward expansion — the United States virtually doubled her territory. She annexed the Republic of Texas, drove the British out of Oregon with threats of violence, and acquired California and the rest of the Southwest in a highly controversial war with Mexico.

The "glacial inexorability" of this westward sweep, as historian T. H. Watkins phrased it, gave birth to a faith called Manifest Destiny, a belief that Americans had a natural, God-given right to expand their superior institutions and way of life across the continent. And woe indeed to anybody — British, Mexican, or Indian — who stood in the way. To clear the way for Anglo-American settlement, the government rescinded the "permanent" frontier it had granted the Indians west of the ninety-fifth meridian and in the 1850s adopted a policy of concentration, which forced them into specified areas in various parts of the West. To justify their broken promises and treaties, white Americans contended that they were the dominant race and so were responsible for the Indians — "along with their lands, their forest, and their mineral wealth." God wished the white men to have all the lands of the West, because they knew how to use the soil and the pagan Indians did not.

Still, as historian Bernard De Voto has reminded us, other energies besides Manifest Destiny thrust America westward. Some southerners, for example, desired the empty lands for southern expansion, in order to maintain an equilibrium of power in Washington between slave and free states. Both southern and northern interests sought to control the Middle West for political and economic gain; and American industrial interests exhibited a "blind drive" to establish ports on the West Coast, thereby opening the Pacific Ocean and distant Asia to United States commercial expansion. There was another story in America's inexorable westward march — the story of the people who made the grueling trek across the overland trails to start new lives. The pioneers — men and women alike — are stock figures in frontier mythology. What were they really like? In their discussion of the conditions of life for women and their families on the Oregon and California trails, Johnny Faragher and Christine Stansell draw on contemporary diaries and letters to take us beyond the stereotypes. In the process, they raise some provocative questions. Did members of a westering family share the same attitudes? Was the women's experience different from the men's? Did the overland emigration alter eastern conventions about family structure and "proper" *women's roles? In answering such questions, the authors paint a vivid and realistic portrait of daily life, family roles, work tasks, cultural expectations, and women's ties with one another, as the wagons headed toward the Pacific.*

FROM 1841 UNTIL 1867, the year in which the transcontinental railroad was completed, nearly 350,000 North Americans emigrated to the Pacific coast along the western wagon road known variously as the Oregon, the California, or simply the Overland Trail. This migration was essentially a family phenomenon. Although single men constituted the majority of the party which pioneered large-scale emigration on the Overland Trail in 1841, significant numbers of women and children were already present in the wagon trains of the next season. Families made up the preponderant proportion of the migrations throughout the 1840s. In 1849, during the overwhelmingly male Gold Rush, the number dropped precipitously, but after 1851 families once again assumed dominance in the overland migration. The contention that "the family was the one substantial social institution" on the frontier is too sweeping, yet it is undeniable that the white family largely mediated the incorporation of the western territories into the American nation.

The emigrating families were a heterogeneous lot. Some came from farms in the midwest and upper South, many from small midwestern towns, and others from northeastern and midwestern cities. Clerks and shopkeepers as well as farmers outfitted their wagons in Independence, St. Louis, or Westport Landing on the Missouri. Since costs for supplies, travel, and settlement were not negligible, few

of the very poor were present, nor were the exceptionally prosperous. The dreams of fortune which lured the wagon trains into new lands were those of modest men whose hopes were pinned to small farms or larger dry-goods stores, more fertile soil or more customers, better market prospects and a steadily expanding economy.

For every member of the family, the trip West was exhausting, toilsome, and often grueling. Each year in late spring, westbound emigrants gathered for the journey at spots along the Missouri River and moved out in parties of ten to several hundred wagons. Aggregates of nuclear families, loosely attached by kinship or friendship, traveled together or joined an even larger caravan. Coast-bound families traveled by ox-drawn wagons at the frustratingly slow pace of fifteen to twenty miles per day. They worked their way up the Platte River valley through what is now Kansas and Nebraska, crossing the Rockies at South Pass in southwestern Wyoming by mid-summer. The Platte route was relatively easy going, but from present-day Idaho, where the roads to California and Oregon diverged, to their final destinations, the pioneers faced disastrous conditions: scorching deserts, boggy salt flats, and rugged mountains. By this time, families had been on the road some three months and were only at the midpoint of the journey; the environment, along with the wear of the road, made the last months difficult almost beyond endurance. Finally, in late fall or early winter the pioneers straggled into their promised lands, after six months and over two thousand miles of hardship.

As this journey progressed, bare necessity became the determinant of most of each day's activities. The

This article is reprinted from *Feminist Studies,* Volume 2, Number 2/3 (1975): 150–166, by permission of the publisher, Feminist Studies, Inc., c/o Women's Studies Program, University of Maryland, College Park, MD 20742.

primary task of surviving and getting to the coast gradually suspended accustomed patterns of dividing work between women and men. All able-bodied adults worked all day in one way or another to keep the family moving. Women's work was no less indispensable than men's; indeed, as the summer wore on, the boundaries dividing the work of the sexes were threatened, blurred, and transgressed.

The vicissitudes of the trail opened new possibilities for expanded work roles for women, and in the cooperative work of the family there existed a basis for a vigorous struggle for female-male equality. But most women did not see the experience in this way. They viewed it as a male enterprise from its very inception. Women experienced the breakdown of the sexual division of labor as a dissolution of their own autonomous "sphere." Bereft of the footing which this independent base gave them, they lacked a cultural rationale for the work they did, and remained estranged from the possibilities of the enlarged scope and power of family life on the trail. Instead, women fought *against* the forces of necessity to hold together the few fragments of female subculture left to them. We have been bequeathed a remarkable record of this struggle in the diaries, journals, and memoirs of emigrating women. In this study, we will examine a particular habit of living, or culture, in conflict with the new material circumstances of the Trail, and the efforts of women to maintain a place, a sphere of their own.

The overland family was not a homogeneous unit, its members imbued with identical aspirations and desires. On the contrary, the period of westward movement was also one of multiplying schisms within those families whose location and social status placed them in the mainstream of national culture. Child-rearing tracts, housekeeping manuals, and etiquette books by the hundreds prescribed and rationalized to these Americans a radical separation of the work responsibilities and social duties of

mothers and fathers; popular thought assigned unique personality traits, spiritual capacities, and forms of experience to the respective categories of man, woman, and child. In many families, the tensions inherent in this separatist ideology, often repressed in the everyday routines of the East, erupted under the strain of the overland crossing. The difficulties of the emigrants, while inextricably linked to the duress of the journey itself, also revealed family dynamics which had been submerged in the less eventful life "back home."

A full-blown ideology of "woman's place" was absent in preindustrial America. On farms, in artisan shops, and in town market-places, women and children made essential contributions to family income and subsistence; it was the family which functioned as the basic unit of production in the colony and the young nation. As commercial exchanges displaced the local markets where women had sold surplus dairy products and textiles, and the workplace drifted away from the household, women and children lost their bread-winning prerogatives.

In Jacksonian America, a doctrine of "sexual spheres" arose to facilitate and justify the segregation of women into the home and men into productive work. While the latter attended to politics, economics, and wage-earning, popular thought assigned women the refurbished and newly professionalized tasks of child-rearing and housekeeping. A host of corollaries followed on the heels of these shifts. Men were physically strong, women naturally delicate; men were skilled in practical matters, women in moral and emotional concerns; men were prone to corruption, women to virtue; men belonged in the world, women in the home. For women, the system of sexual spheres represented a decline in social status and isolation from political and economic power. Yet it also provided them with a psychological power base of undeniable importance. The "cult of true womanhood" was more than simply a retreat. Catharine Beecher, one of the chief theorists of "woman's influence," proudly quoted Tocqueville's observation that "in no country has such constant care been taken, as in America, to trace two clearly distinct lines of action for the two sexes, and to make them keep pace with the other, but in two pathways which are always different." Neither Beecher nor her sisters were simply dupes of a masculine imperialism. The supervision of child-rearing, household economy, and the moral and religious life of the family granted women a certain degree of real autonomy and control over their lives as well as those of their husbands and children. . . .

At its very inception, the western emigration sent tremors through the foundations of this carefully compartmentalized family structure. The rationale behind pulling up stakes was nearly always economic advancement; since breadwinning was a masculine concern, the husband and father introduced the idea of going West and made the final decision. Family participation in the intervening time ran the gamut from enthusiastic support to stolid resistance. Many women cooperated with their ambitious spouses: "The motive that induced us to part with pleasant associations and the dear friends of our childhood days, was to obtain from the government of the United States a grant of land that 'Uncle Sam' had promised to give to the head of each family who settled in this new country." Others, however, only acquiesced. "Poor Ma said only this morning, 'Oh, I wish we never had started,'" Lucy Cooke wrote her first day on the trail, "and she looks so sorrowful and dejected. I think if Pa had not passengers to take through she would urge him to return; not that he should be so inclined." Huddled with her children in a cold, damp wagon, trying to calm them despite the ominous chanting of visiting Indians, another woman wondered "what had possessed my husband, anyway, that he should have thought of bringing us away out through this God forsaken country." Similar alienation from the "pioneer spirit" haunted Lavinia Porter's leave-taking:

I never recall that sad parting from my dear sister on the plains of Kansas without the tears flowing fast and free. . . . We were the eldest of a large family, and the bond of affection and love that existed between us was strong indeed . . . as she with the other friends turned to leave me for the ferry which was to take them back to home and civilization, I stood alone on that wild prairie. Looking westward I saw my husband driving slowly over the plain; turning my face once more to the east, my dear sister's footsteps were fast widening the distance between us. For the time I knew not which way to go, nor whom to follow. But in a few moments I rallied my forces . . . and soon overtook the slowly moving oxen who were bearing my husband and child over the green prairie . . . the unbidden tears would flow in spite of my brave resolve to be the courageous and valiant frontierswoman.

Her dazed vacillation soon gave way to a private conviction that the family had made a dire mistake: "I would make a brave effort to be cheerful and patient until the camp work was done. Then starting out ahead of the team and my men folks, when I thought I had gone beyond hearing distance, I would throw myself down on the unfriendly desert and give way like a child to sobs and tears, wishing myself back home with my friends and chiding myself for consenting to take this wild goose chase." Men viewed drudgery, calamity, and privation as trials along the road to prosperity, unfortunate but inevitable corollaries of the rational decision they had made. But to those women who were unable to appropriate the vision of the upwardly mobile pilgrimage, hardship and the loss only testified to the inherent folly of the emigration, "this wild goose chase."

If women were reluctant to accompany their men, however, they were often equally unwilling to let them go alone. In the late 1840s, the conflict between wives and their gold-crazed husbands reveals the determination with which women enforced the cohesion of the nuclear family. In the name of family unity, some obdurate wives simply chose to blockbust the sexually segregated Gold Rush: "My husband grew enthusiastic and wanted to start immediately," one woman recalled, "but I would not be left behind. I thought where he could go I could and where I went I could take my two little toddling babies." Her family departed intact. Other women used their moral authority to smash the enterprise in its planning stages. "We were married to live together," a wife acidly reminded her spouse when he informed her of his intention to join the Rush: "I am willing to go with you to any part of *God's Foot Stool* where you think you can do best, and under these circumstances you have no right to go where I cannot, and if you do you need never return for I shall look upon you as dead." Roundly chastised, the man postponed his journey until the next season, when his family could leave with him. When included in the plans, women seldom wrote of their husbands' decisions to emigrate in their diaries or memoirs. A breadwinner who tried to leave alone, however, threatened the family unity upon which his authority was based; only then did a wife challenge his dominance in worldly affairs.

There was an economic reason for the preponderance of families on the Trail. Women and children, but especially women, formed an essential supplementary work force in the settlements. The ideal wife in the West resembled a hired hand more than a nurturant Christian housekeeper. Narcissa Whitman wrote frankly to aspiring settlers of the functional necessity of women on the new farms: "Let every young man bring a wife, for he will want one after he gets here, if he never did before." In a letter from California, another seasoned woman warned a friend in Missouri that in the West women became "hewers of wood and drawers of water everywhere." Mrs. Whitman's fellow missionary Elkanah Walker was unabashedly practical in beseeching his wife to join him: "I am tired of keeping an old bachelor's hall. I want someone to get me a good supper and let me take my ease and when I am very tired in the morning I want someone to get up and get breakfast and let me lay in bed and take my rest." It would be both simplistic and harsh to argue that men brought their families West or married because of the labor power of women and children; there is no doubt, however, that the new Westerners appreciated the advantages of familial labor. Women were not superfluous; they were workers. The migration of women helped to solve the problem of labor scarcity, not only in the early years of the American settlement on the coast, but throughout the history of the continental frontier.

In the first days of the overland trip, new work requirements were not yet pressing and the division of labor among family members still replicated familiar patterns. Esther Hanna reported in one of her first diary entries that "our men have gone to build a bridge across the stream, which is impassable," while she baked her first bread on the prairie. Elizabeth Smith similarly described her party's day: "rainy . . . Men making rafts. Women cooking and washing. Children crying." When travel was suspended, "the men were generally busy mending wagons, harnesses, yokes, shoeing the animals etc., and the women washed clothes, boiled a big mess of beans, to warm over for several meals, or perhaps mended clothes." At first, even in emergencies, women and men hardly considered integrating their work. "None but those who have cooked for a family of eight, crossing the plains, have any idea of what it takes," a disgruntled woman recalled: "My sister-in-law was sick, my niece was much younger than I, and consequently I had the management of all the cooking and planning on my young shoulders." To ask a man to help was a possibility she was unable even to consider.

The relegation of women to purely domestic duties, however, soon broke down under the vicissitudes of the Trail. Within the first few weeks, the unladylike task of gathering buffalo dung for fuel (little firewood was available *en route*) became women's work. As one traveler astutely noted, "force of surroundings was a great leveler"; miles of grass, dust, glare, and mud erased some of the most rudimentary distinctions between female and male responsibilities. By summer, women often helped drive the wagons and the livestock. At one Platte crossing, "the men drawed the wagons over by hand and the women all crossed in safety"; but at the next, calamity struck when the bridge collapsed, "and then commenced the hurry and bustle of repairing; all were at work, even the women and children." Such crises, which compounded daily as the wagons moved past the Platte up the long stretches of desert and coastal mountains, generated equity in work; at times of Indian threats, for example, both women and men made bullets and stood guard. When mountain fever struck the Pengra family as they crossed the Rockies, Charlotte relieved her incapacitated husband of the driving while he took care of the youngest child. Only such severe afflictions forced men to take on traditionally female chores. While women did men's work, there is little evidence that men reciprocated.

Following a few days in the life of an overland woman discloses the magnitude of her work. During the hours her party traveled, Charlotte Pengra walked beside the wagons, driving the cattle and gathering buffalo chips. At night she cooked, baked bread for the next noon meal, and washed clothes. Three successive summer days illustrate how trying these small chores could be. Her train pulled out early on a Monday morning, only to be halted by rain and a flash flood; Mrs. Pengra washed and dried her family's wet clothes in the afternoon while doing her daily baking. On Tuesday the wagons pushed hard to make up for lost time, forcing her to trot all day to keep up. In camp that night there was no time to rest. Before going to bed, she wrote, "Kept busy in preparing tea and doing other things preparatory for the morrow. I baked a cracker pudding, warm biscuits and made tea, and after supper stewed two pans of dried apples, and made two

loaves of bread, got my work done up, beds made, and child asleep, and have written in my journal. Pretty tired of course." The same routine devoured the next day and evening: "I have done a washing. Stewed apples, made pies and baked a rice pudding, and mended our wagon cover. Rather tired." And the next: "baked biscuits, stewed berries, fried meat, boiled and mashed potatoes, and made tea for supper, afterward baked bread. Thus you see I have not much rest." Children also burdened women's work and leisure. During one quiet time, Helen Stewart retreated in mild defiance from her small charges to a tent in order to salvage some private time: "It exceeding hot . . . some of the men is out hunting and some of them sleeping. The children is grumbling and crying and laughing and howling and playing all around." Although children are notably absent in women's journals, they do appear, frightened and imploring, during an Indian scare or a storm, or intrude into a rare and precious moment of relaxation, "grumbling and crying."

Because the rhythm of their chores was out of phase with that of the men, the division of labor could be especially taxing to women. Men's days were toilsome but broken up at regular intervals with periods of rest. Men hitched the teams, drove or walked until noon, relaxed at dinner, traveled until the evening camp, unhitched the oxen, ate supper, and in the evening sat at the campfire, mended equipment, or stood guard. They also provided most of the labor in emergencies, pulling the wagons through mires, across treacherous river crossings, up long grades, and down precipitous slopes. In the pandemonium of a steep descent,

you would see the women and children in advance seeking the best way, some of them slipping down, or holding on to the rocks, now taking an "otter slide," and then a run til some natural obstacle presented itself to stop their accelerated progress and those who get down safely without a hurt or a bruise, are fortunate indeed. Looking back to the train, you would see some of the men holding on to the wagons, others slipping under the oxen's feet, some throwing articles out of the way that had fallen out, and all have enough to do to keep them busily occupied.

Women were responsible for staying out of the way and getting themselves and the children to safety, men for getting the wagons down. Women's work, far less demanding of brute strength and endurance, was nevertheless distributed without significant respite over all waking hours: mealtimes offered no leisure to the cooks. "The plain fact of the matter is," a young woman complained,

we *have no time for sociability.* From the time we get up in the morning, until we are on the road, it is hurry scurry to get breakfast and put away the things that necessarily had to be pulled out last night — while under way there is no room in the wagon for a visitor, nooning is barely long enough to eat a cold bite — and at night all the cooking utensils and provisions are to be gotten about the camp fire, and cooking enough to last until the next night.

After supper, the men gathered together, "lolling and smoking their pipes and guessing, or maybe betting, how many miles we had covered during the day," while the women baked, washed, and put the children to bed before they finally sat down. Charlotte Pengra found "as I was told before I started that there is no rest in such a journey."

Unaccustomed tasks beset the travelers, who were equipped with only the familiar expectation that work was divided along gender lines. The solutions which sexual "spheres" offered were usually irrelevant to the new problems facing families. Women, for example, could not afford to be delicate: their new duties demanded far greater stamina and hardiness than their traditional domestic tasks. With no tradition to deal with the new exigencies of fuel-gathering, cattle-driving, and cooking, families found that "the division of labor in a party . . .

was a prolific cause of quarrel." Within the Vincent party, "assignments to duty were not accomplished without grumbling and objection . . . there were occasional angry debates while the various burdens were being adjusted," while in "the camps of others who sometimes jogged along the trail in our

A frontier woman and her children stand at the Grand Canyon in Arizona. Drudgery and deprivation, the fragility of children, and the hostile environment were not the only problems facing women on the westward journey. Many bitterly regretted the loss of the homes, companionship, and responsibilities that had been theirs in the East. Surely, as Stansell and Faragher tell us, "Harriet Ward's cry — 'Oh, shall we ever live like civilized beings again?' — reverberated through the thoughts of many of her sisters." (Keystone-Mast Collection, California Museum of Photography, University of California, Riverside)

company . . . we saw not a little fighting . . . and these bloody fisticuffs were invariably the outcome of disputes over division of labor." At home, these assignments were familiar and accepted, not subject to questioning. New work opened the division of labor to debate and conflict.

By midjourney, most women worked at male tasks. The men still retained dominance within their "sphere," despite the fact that it was no longer exclusively masculine. Like most women, Lavinia Porter was responsible for gathering buffalo chips for fuel. One afternoon, spying a grove of cottonwoods half a mile away, she asked her husband to branch off the trail so that the party could fell trees for firewood, thus easing her work. "But men on the plains I had found were not so accommodating, nor so ready to wait upon women as they were in more civilized communities." Her husband refused and Porter fought back: "I was feeling somewhat under the weather and unusually tired, and crawling into the wagon told them if they wanted fuel for the evening meal they could get it themselves and cook the meal also, and laying my head down on a pillow, I cried myself to sleep." Later that evening her husband awakened her with a belated dinner he had prepared himself, but despite his conciliatory spirit their relations were strained for weeks: "James and I had gradually grown silent and taciturn and had unwittingly partaken of the gloom and somberness of the dreary landscape." No longer a housewife or a domestic ornament, but a laborer in a male arena, Porter was still subordinate to her husband in practical matters.

Lydia Waters recorded another clash between new work and old consciousness: "I had learned to drive an ox team on the Platte and my driving was admired by an officer and his wife who were going with the mail to Salt Lake City." Pleased with the compliment, she later overheard them "laughing at the thought of a woman driving oxen." By no means did censure come only from men. The officer's wife as well as the officer derided Lydia Wa-

ters, while her own mother indirectly reprimanded teenaged Mary Ellen Todd. "All along our journey, I had tried to crack that big whip," Mary Ellen remembered years later:

Now while out at the wagon we kept trying until I was fairly successful. How my heart bounded a few days later when I chanced to hear father say to mother, "Do you know that Mary Ellen is beginning to crack the whip." Then how it fell again when mother replied, "I am afraid it isn't a very lady-like thing for a girl to do." After this, while I felt a secret joy in being able to have a power that set things going, there was also a sense of shame over this new accomplishment.

To understand Mrs. Todd's primness, so incongruous in the rugged setting of the Trail, we must see it in the context of a broader struggle on the part of women to preserve the home in transit. Against the leveling forces of the Plains, women tried to maintain the standards of cleanliness and order that had prevailed in their homes back East.

Our caravan had a good many women and children and although we were probably longer on the journey owing to their presence — they exerted a good influence, as the men did not take such risks with Indians . . . were more alert about the care of teams and seldom had accidents; more attention was paid to cleanliness and sanitation and, lastly, but not of less importance, meals were more regular and better cooked thus preventing much sickness and there was less waste of food.

Sarah Royce remembered that family wagons "were easily distinguished by the greater number of conveniences, and household articles they carried." In the evenings, or when the trains stopped for a day, women had a chance to create with few props a flimsy facsimile of the home.

Even in camp women had little leisure time, but within the "hurry scurry" of work they managed to re-create the routine of the home. Indeed, a female subculture, central to the communities women had left behind, reemerged in these settings. At night, women often clustered together, chatting, working, or commiserating, instead of joining the men: "High teas were not popular, but tatting, knitting, crochetting, exchanging recipes for cooking beans or dried apples or swopping food for the sake of variety kept us in practice of feminine occupations and diversions." Besides using the domestic concerns of the Trail to reconstruct a female sphere, women also consciously invoked fantasy: "Mrs. Fox and her daughter are with us and everything is so still and quiet we can almost imagine ourselves at home again. We took out our Daguerreotypes and tried to live over again some of the happy days of 'Auld Lang Syne.'" Sisterly contact kept "feminine occupations" from withering away from disuse: "In the evening the young ladies came over to our house and we had a concert with both guitars. Indeed it seemed almost like a pleasant evening at home. We could none of us realize that we were almost at the summit of the Rocky Mountains." The hostess added with somewhat strained sanguinity that her young daughter seemed "just as happy sitting on the ground playing her guitar as she was at home, although she does not love it as much as her piano." Although a guitar was no substitute for the more refined instrument, it at least kept the girl "in practice with feminine occupations and diversions": unlike Mary Ellen Todd, no big whip would tempt her to unwomanly pleasure in the power to "set things going."

But books, furniture, knick-knacks, china, the daguerreotypes that Mrs. Fox shared, or the guitars of young musicians — the "various articles of ornament and convenience" — were among the first things discarded on the epic trash heap which trailed over the mountains. On long uphill grades and over sandy deserts, the wagons had to be lightened; any materials not essential to survival were fair game for disposal. Such commodities of woman's sphere, although functionally useless, provided women with

a psychological lifeline to their abandoned homes and communities, as well as to elements of their identities which the westward journey threatened to mutilate or entirely extinguish. Losing homely treasures and memorabilia was yet another defeat within an accelerating process of dispossession.

The male-directed venture likewise encroached upon the Sabbath, another female preserve. Through the influence of women's magazines, by mid-century Sunday had become a veritable ladies' day; women zealously exercised their religious influence and moral skill on the day of their families' retirement from the world. Although parties on the Trail often suspended travel on Sundays, the time only provided the opportunity to unload and dry the precious cargo of the wagons — seeds, food, and clothing — which otherwise would rot from dampness. For women whose creed forbade any worldly activity on the Sabbath, the work was not only irksome and tedious but profane.

This is Sabath it is a beautiful day indeed we do not use it as such for we have not traveled far when we stop in a most lovely place oh it is such a beautiful spot and take everything out of our wagon to air them and it is well we done it as the flower was damp and there was some of the other ones flower was rotten . . . and we baked and boiled and washed oh dear me I did not think we would have abused the sabeth in such a manner. I do not see how we can expect to get along but we did not intend to do so before we started.

Denied a voice in the male sphere that surrounded them, women were also unable to partake of the limited yet meaningful power of women with homes. On almost every Sunday, Helen Stewart lamented the disruption of a familiar and sustaining order of life, symbolized by the household goods strewn about the ground to dry: "We took everything out the wagons and the side of the hill is covered with flower biscut meat rice oat meal clothes and such a quantity of articles of all discertions to many to mention and childre[n] included in the number. And hobos that is neather men nor yet boys being in and out hang about.''

The disintegration of the physical base of domesticity was symptomatic of an even more serious disruption in the female subculture. Because the wagon trains so often broke into smaller units, many women were stranded in parties without other women. Since there were usually two or more men in the same family party, some male friendships and bonds remained intact for the duration of the journey. But by midway in the trip, female companionship, so valued by nineteenth-century women, was unavailable to the solitary wife in a party of hired men, husband, and children that had broken away from a larger train. Emergencies and quarrels, usually between men, broke up the parties. Dr. Powers, a particularly ill-tempered man, decided after many disagreements with others in his train to make the crossing alone with his family. His wife shared neither his misanthropy nor his grim independence. On the day they separated from the others, she wrote in her journal: ''The women came over to bid me goodbye, for we were to go alone, all alone. They said there was no color in my face. I felt as if there was none.'' She perceived the separation as a banishment, almost a death sentence: ''There is something peculiar in such a parting on the Plains, one there realizes what a goodbye is. Miss Turner and Mrs. Hendricks were the last to leave, and they bade me adieu the tears running down their sunburnt cheeks. I felt as though my last friends were leaving me, for what — as I thought then — was a Maniac.'' Charlotte Pengra likewise left Missouri with her family in a large train. Several weeks out, mechanical problems detained some of the wagons, including those of the other three women. During the month they were separated, Pengra became increasingly dispirited and anxious: ''The roads have been good today — I feel lonely and almost disheartened. . . . Can hear the wolves howl very distinctly. Rather ominis, perhaps you think . . .

Feel very tired and lonely — our folks not having come — I fear some of them ar sick.'' Having waited as long as possible for the others, the advance group made a major river crossing. ''Then I felt that indeed I had left all my friends,'' Pengra wrote, ''save my husband and his brother, to journey over the dreaded Plains, without one female acquaintance even for a companion — of course I wept and grieved about it but to no purpose.''

Other echoed her mourning. ''The whipporwills are chirping,'' Helen Stewart wrote, ''they bring me in mind of our old farm in pensillvania the home of my childhood where I have spent the happiest days I will ever see again. . . . I feel rather lonesome today oh solitude solitude how I love it if I had about a dozen of my companions to enjoy it with me.'' Uprootedness took its toll in debilitation and numbness. After a hard week, men ''lolled around in the tents and on their blankets seeming to realize that the 'Sabbath was made for man,''' resting on the palpable achievements of miles covered and rivers crossed. In contrast, the women ''could not fully appreciate physical rest, and were rendered more uneasy by the continual passing of emigrant trains all day long. . . . To me, much of the day was spent in meditating over the past and in forebodings for the future.''

The ultimate expression of this alienation was the pressure to turn back, to retrace steps to the old life. Occasionally anxiety or bewilderment erupted into open revolt against going on.

This morning our company moved on, except one family. The woman got mad and wouldn't budge or let the children go. He had the cattle hitched on for three hours and coaxed her to go, but she wouldn't stir. I told my husband the circumstances and he and Adam Polk and Mr. Kimball went and each one took a young one and crammed them in the wagon, and the husband drove off and left her sitting. . . . She cut across and overtook her husband. Meantime he sent his boy back to camp after a horse he had left, and when she came up her husband said, "Did you meet John?" "Yes," was the reply, "and I picked up a stone and knocked out his brains." Her husband went back to ascertain the truth and while he was gone she set fire to one of the wagons. . . . He saw the flames and came running and put it out, and then mustered spunk enough to give her a good flogging.

Short of violent resistance, it was always possible that circumstances would force a family to reconsider and turn back. During a cholera scare in 1852, "women cried, begging their men to take them back." When the men reluctantly relented, the writer observed that "they did the hooking up of their oxen in a spiritless sort of way," while "some of the girls and women were laughing." There was little lost and much regained for women in a decision to abandon the migration.

Both sexes worked, and both sexes suffered. Yet women lacked a sense of inclusion and a cultural rationale to give meaning to the suffering and the work; no augmented sense of self or role emerged from augmented privation. Both women and men also complained, but women expanded their caviling to a generalized critique of the whole enterprise. Margaret Chambers felt "as if we had left all civilization behind us" after crossing the Missouri, and Harriet Ward's cry from South Pass — "Oh, shall we ever live like civilized beings again?" — reverberated through the thoughts of many of her sisters. Civilization was far more to these women than law, books, and municipal government; it was pianos, church societies, daguerreotypes, mirrors — in short, their homes. At their most hopeful, the exiles perceived the Trail as a hellish but necessary transition to a land where they could renew their domestic mission: "Each advanced step of the slow, plodding cattle carried us farther and farther from civilization into a desolate, barbarous country. . . . But our new home lay beyond all this and was a shining beacon that beckoned us on, inspiring our hearts with hope and courage." At worst, temporary exigencies became in the minds of the dispossessed the omens of an irrevocable exile: "We have been travelling with 25–18–14–129–64–3 wagons — now all alone — how dreary it seems. Can it be that I have left my quiet little home and taken this dreary land of solitude in exchange?"

Only a minority of the women who emigrated over the Overland Trail were from the northeastern middle classes where the cult of true womanhood reached its fullest bloom. Yet their responses to the labor demands of the Trail indicate that "womanliness" had penetrated the values, expectations, and personalities of midwestern farm women as well as New England "ladies." "Women's sphere" provided them with companionship, a sense of self-worth, and most important, independence from men in a patriarchal world. The Trail, in breaking down sexual segregation, offered women the opportunities of socially essential work. Yet this work was performed in a male arena, and many women saw themselves as draftees rather than partners. . . .

Nonetheless, the journals of overland women are irrefutable testimony to the importance of a separate female province. Such theorists as Catharine Beecher were acutely aware of the advantages in keeping life divvied up, in maintaining "two pathways which are always different" for women and men. The women who traveled on the Overland Trail experienced firsthand the tribulations of integration which Beecher and her colleagues could predict in theory.

QUESTIONS TO CONSIDER

1   How did necessity on the Overland Trail open up new work roles for women? Did women tend to regard these new "opportunities" to share in men's work as a gain or as a loss in status?

2   How does the "sphere theory," which emerges in Jacksonian America, lead to a decline in woman's social, political, and economic status but a gain in

her psychological and emotional status? Was the so-called cult of true womanhood simply a sexist ideology forced on oppressed American females?

3 Contrast the goals of men and women on the trail. Why did women feel particularly alienated by the migration experience?

4 How were women on the trail able to create a positive female subculture? What difficulties did they encounter?

5 Faragher and Stansell remind us that historians have often associated positive work roles for women with the absence of narrow definitions of woman's place. Why is this association inaccurate in describing women's experiences on the Overland Trail?

XII

LIFE
IN THE
MILITANT SOUTH

24

This Cargo of
Human Flesh

WILLIAM WELLS BROWN

Thanks to the influence of the motion picture Gone with the Wind, *many white Americans still think of the Old South as a romantic land of magnolias and landscaped manors, of cavalier gentlemen and happy darkies, of elegant ladies and breathless belles in crinoline — an ordered, leisurely world in which men and women, blacks and whites, all had their destined place. This view of Dixie is one of America's most enduring myths (*Gone with the Wind *still commands huge audiences when it runs on televison). The real world of the Old South was far more complex and cruel.*

Modern historical studies have demonstrated that antebellum Dixie was a rigidly patriarchal, slave-based social order that might have lasted indefinitely had not the Civil War broken out. At no time was slavery on the verge of dying out naturally. Tobacco cultivation may have become unprofitable by the Revolutionary period, but the invention of the cotton gin in 1793 stimulated cotton production immeasurably and created a tremendous demand for slave labor. Thanks to the cotton gin, slavery spread beyond the fertile black belt of Alabama and Mississippi, out to the Kansas-Missouri border, to the fringes of western Arkansas, and to south and east Texas. Although Congress outlawed the foreign slave trade in 1808 (it simply continued as illicit traffic), the number of slaves rose dramatically so that by 1860 there were nearly 4 million in fifteen slave states, including Delaware and Maryland. Slavery remained profitable, too, as evidenced by the fact that in 1860 a prime field hand sold for $1,250 in Virginia and $1,800 on the auction blocks in New Orleans. A "fancy girl" went for as high as $2,500. Still, from the southern white's viewpoint, *the profitability of slavery was not the crucial issue. Had slavery proved too costly in its plantation setting, southerners would have found other ways to utilize slave labor and keep blacks in chains, to maintain white male supremacy in the region.*

The following two selections portray life in the Old South from the point of view of two if its most significant figures: the slave and the planter's wife. The patriarchal South depended for its very existence on black slaves and white women, both of whom had strictly defined roles. We begin with a contemporary account of slavery written by William Wells Brown. The son of a white slaveholder and a black mother, Brown ran away from his master and escaped to the North, where he befriended William Lloyd Garrison and lectured widely on slavery for the Western New York Anti-Slavery Society and the Massachusetts Anti-Slavery Society. Brown became a successful author, writing the first novel, the first play, and the first black history by an African-American, in addition to his autobiography. In his account of life under the lash, excerpted here, we gain melancholy insight into what it was like to be a slave in antebellum Dixie.

☆ 1 ☆

MY MASTER OWNED ABOUT FORTY SLAVES, twenty-five of whom were field hands. He removed from Kentucky to Missouri, when I was quite young, and settled thirty or forty miles above St. Charles, on the Missouri, where, in addition to his practice as a physician, he carried on milling, merchandizing and farming. He had a large farm, the principal productions of which were tobacco and hemp. The slave cabins were situated on the back part of the farm, with the house of the overseer, whose name was Grove Cook, in their midst. He had the entire charge of the farm, and having no family, was allowed a woman to keep house for

From *Narrative of William W. Brown, A Fugitive Slave,* second edition, enlarged, by William Wells Brown. Boston: Published at the Anti-Slavery Office, 1848.

him, whose business it was to deal out the provisions for the hands.

A woman also kept at the quarters to do the cooking for the field hands, who were summoned to their unrequited toil every morning at four o'clock, by the ringing of a bell, hung on a post near the house of the overseer. They were allowed half an hour to eat their breakfast, and get to the field. At half past four, a horn was blown by the overseer, which was the signal to commence work; and every one that was not on the spot at the time, had to receive ten lashes from the negro-whip, with which the overseer always went armed. The handle was about three feet long, with the butt-end filled with lead, and the lash six or seven feet in length, made of cowhide, with platted wire on the end of it. This whip was put in requisition very frequently and freely, an a small offence on the part of a slave furnished an occasion for its use. During the time that Mr. Cook was overseer, I was a house servant — a situation preferable to that of a field hand, as I was better fed, better clothed, and not obliged to rise at the ringing of the bell, but about half an hour after. I have often laid and heard the crack of the whip, and the screams of the slave. My mother was a field hand, and one morning was ten or fifteen minutes behind the others in getting into the field. As soon as she reached the spot where they were at work, the overseer commenced whipping her. She cried, ''Oh! pray — Oh! pray — Oh! pray'' — these are generally the words of slaves when imploring mercy at the hands of their oppressors. I heard her voice, and knew it, and jumped out of my bunk, and went to the door. Though the field was some distance from the house, I could hear every crack of the whip, and every groan and cry of my poor mother. I remained at the door, not daring to venture any farther. The cold chills ran over me, and I wept aloud. After giving her ten lashes, the sound of the whip ceased, and I returned to my bed, and found no consolation but in my tears. It was not yet daylight.

☆ 2 ☆

My master being a political demagogue, soon found those who were ready to put him into office, for the favors he could render them; and a few years after his arrival in Missouri, he was elected to a seat in the Legislature. In his absence from home, everything was left in charge of Mr. Cook, the overseer, and he soon became more tyrannical and cruel. Among the slaves on the plantation, was one by the name of Randall. He was a man about six feet high, and well-proportioned, and known as a man of great strength and power. He was considered the most valuable and able-bodied slave on the plantation; but no matter how good or useful a slave may be, he seldom escapes the lash. But it was not so with Randall. He had been on the plantation since my earliest

recollection, and I had never known of his being flogged. No thanks were due to the master or overseer for this. I have often heard him declare, that no white man should ever whip him — that he would die first.

Cook, from the time that he came upon the plantation, had frequently declared, that he could and would flog any nigger that was put into the field to work under him. My master had repeatedly told him not to attempt to whip Randall, but he was determined to try it. As soon as he was left sole dictator, he thought the time had come to put his threats into execution. He soon began to find fault with Randall, and theatened to whip him, if he did not do better. One day he gave him a very hard task, — more than he could possibly do; and at night, the task not being performed, he told Randall that he should remember him the next morning. On the following morning, after the hands had taken breakfast, Cook called out to Randall, and told him that he intended to whip him, and ordered him to cross his hands and be tied. Randall asked why he wished to whip him. He answered, because he had not finished his task the day before. Randall said that the task was too great, or he should have done it. Cook said it made no difference, — he should whip him. Randall stood silent for a moment, and then said, ''Mr. Cook, I have always tried to please you since you have been on the plantation, and I find you are determined not to be satisfied with my work, let me do as well as I may. No man has laid hands on me, to whip me, for the last ten years, and I have long since come to the conclusion not to be whipped by any man living.'' Cook, finding by Randall's determined look and gestures, that he would resist, called three of the hands from their work, and commanded them to seize Randall, and tie him. The hands stood still — they knew Randall — and they also knew him to be a powerful man, and were afraid to grapple with him. As soon as Cook had ordered the men to seize him, Randall turned to them, and said — ''Boys, you all know me; you know that I can handle any three of you, and the man that lays hands on me shall die. This white man can't whip me himself, and therefore he has called you to help him.'' The overseer was unable to prevail upon them to seize and secure Randall, and finally ordered them all to go to their work together.

Nothing was said to Randall by the overseer, for more than a week. One morning, however, while the hands were at work in the field, he came into it, accompanied by three friends of his, Thompson, Woodbridge and Jones. They came up to where Randall was at work, and Cook ordered him to leave his work, and go with them to the barn. He refused to go; whereupon he was attacked by the overseer and his companions, when he turned upon them, and laid them, one after another, prostrate on the ground. Woodbridge drew out his pistol, and fired at him, and brought him to the ground by a pistol ball. The others rushed upon him with their clubs, and beat him over the head and face, until they succeeded in tying him. He was then taken to the barn, and tied to a beam. Cook gave him over one hundred lashes with a heavy cowhide, had him washed with salt and water, and left him tied during the day. The next day he was untied, and taken to a blacksmith's shop, and had a ball and chain attached to his leg. He was compelled to labor in the field, and perform the same amount of work that the other hands did. When his master returned home, he was much pleased to find that Randall has been subdued in his absence.

☆ 3 ☆

Soon afterwards, my master removed to the city of St. Louis, and purchased a farm four miles from there, which he placed under the charge of an overseer by the name of Friend Haskell. He was a regular Yankee from New England. The Yankees are noted for making the most cruel overseers.

My mother was hired out in the city, and I was also hired out there to Major Freeland, who kept a public house. He was formerly from Virginia, and was a horse-racer, cock-fighter, gambler, and withal an inveterate drunkard. There were ten or twelve servants in the house, and when he was present, it was cut and slash — knock down and drag out. In his fits of anger, he would take up a chair, and throw it at a servant; and in his more rational moments, when he wished to chastise one, he would tie them up in the smokehouse, and whip them; after which, he would cause a fire to be made of tobacco stems, and smoke them. This he called ''*Virginia play.*''

I complained to my master of the treatment which I received from Major Freeland; but it made no difference. He cared nothing about it, so long as he received the money for my labor. After living with Major Freeland five or six months, I ran away, and went into the woods back of the city; and when night came on, I made my way to my master's farm, but was afraid to be seen, knowing that if Mr. Haskell, the overseer, should discover me, I should be again carried back to Major Freeland; so I kept in the woods. One day, while in the woods, I heard the barking and howling of dogs, and in a short time they came so near, that I knew them to be the bloodhounds of Major Benjamin O'Fallon. He kept five or six, to hunt runaway slaves with.

As soon as I was convinced that it was them, I knew there was no chance of escape. I took refuge in the top of a tree, and the hounds were soon at its base, and there remained until the hunters came up in a half or three quarters of an hour afterwards. There were two men with the dogs, who, as soon as they came up, ordered me to descend. I came down, was tied, and taken to St. Louis jail. Major Freeland soon made his appearance, and took me out, and ordered me to follow him, which I did. After we returned home, I was tied up in the

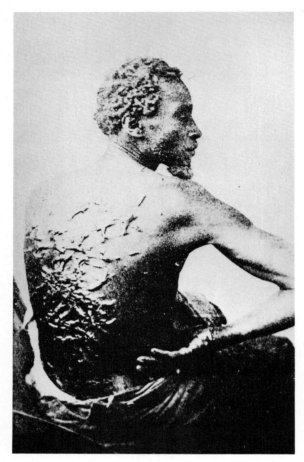

The scars on the back of this Louisiana bondsman testify to the violence inherent in the slave system. Overseers and slave traders meted out punishment with a sinister weapon called the "negro whip." The handle was some three feet long, with the butt-end filled with lead; the lash was six or seven feet long and made of cowhide, with platted wire on the end of it. According to William Wells Brown, "this whip was put in requisition very frequently and freely, and a small offence on the part of a slave furnished an occasion for its use." (Photograph by Chandler Seever, circa 1860, Massachusetts Historical Society)

smokehouse, and was very severely whipped. After the Major had flogged me to his satisfaction, he sent out his son Robert, a young man eighteen or twenty years of age, to see that I was well smoked. He made a fire of tobacco stems, which soon set me to coughing and sneezing. This, Robert told me, was the way his father used to do to his slaves in Virginia. After giving me what they conceived to be a decent smoking, I was untied and again set to work.

Robert Freeland was a "chip off the old block." Though quite young, it was not unfrequently that he came home in a state of intoxication. He is now, I believe, a popular commander of a steamboat on the Mississippi River. Major Freeland soon after failed in business, and I was put on board the steamboat Missouri, which plied between St. Louis and Galena. The commander of the boat was William B. Culver. I remained on her during the sailing season, which was the most pleasant time for me that I had ever experienced. At the close of navigation, I was hired to Mr. John Colburn, keeper of the Missouri Hotel. He was from one of the Free States; but a more inveterate hater of the negro, I do not believe ever walked on God's green earth. This hotel was at that time one of the largest in the city, and there were employed in it twenty or thirty servants, mostly slaves.

Mr. Colburn was very abusive, not only to the servants, but to his wife also, who was an excellent woman, and one from whom I never knew a servant to receive a harsh word; but never did I know a kind one to a servant from her husband. Among the slaves employed in the hotel, was one by the name of Aaron, who belonged to Mr. John F. Darby, a lawyer. Aaron was the knife-cleaner. One day, one of the knives was put on the table, not as clean as it might have been. Mr. Colburn, for this offence, tied Aaron up in the woodhouse, and gave him over fifty lashes on the bare back with a cowhide, after which, he made me wash him down with rum. This seemed to put him into more agony than the whipping. After being untied, he went home to his master, and complained of the treatment which he had received. Mr. Darby would give no heed to anything he had to say, but sent him directly back. Colburn, learning that he had been to his master with complaints, tied him up again, and gave him a more severe whipping than before. The poor fellow's back was literally cut to pieces; so much so, that he was not able to work for ten or twelve days.

There was also, among the servants, a girl whose master resided in the country. Her name was Patsey. Mr. Colburn tied her up one evening, and whipped her until several of the boarders came out and begged him to desist. The reason for whipping her was this. She was engaged to be married to a man belonging to Major William Christy, who resided four or five miles north of the city. Mr. Colburn had forbid her to see John Christy. The reason of this was said to be the regard which he himself had for Patsey. She went to meeting that evening, and John returned home with her. Mr. Colburn had intended to flog John, if he came within the inclosure; but John knew too well the temper of his rival, and kept at a safe distance — so he took vengeance on the poor girl. If all the slave-drivers had been called together, I do not think a more cruel man than John Colburn, — and he too a northern man, — could have been found among them.

While living at the Missouri Hotel, a circumstance occurred which caused me great unhappiness. My master sold my mother, and all her children, except myself. They were sold to different persons in the city of St. Louis.

☆   4   ☆

I was soon after taken from Mr. Colburn's, and hired to Elijah P. Lovejoy, who was at that time publisher and editor of the "St. Louis Times." My work, while with him, was mainly in the printing office, waiting on the hands, working the press, &c. Mr. Lovejoy was a very good man, and decidedly the best master that I had ever had. I am chiefly indebted to him, and to my employment in the printing office, for what little learning I obtained while in slavery.

Though slavery is thought, by some, to be mild in Missouri, when compared with the cotton, sugar and rice growing States, yet no part of our slave-holding country, is more noted for the barbarity of its inhabitants, than St. Louis. It was here that Col. Harney, a United States officer, whipped a slave woman to death. It was here that Francis McIntosh, a free colored man from Pittsburgh, was taken from the steamboat Flora, and burned at the stake. During a residence of eight years in this city, numerous cases of extreme cruelty came under my own observation — to record them all, would occupy more space than could possibly be allowed in this little volume. I shall, therefore, give but a few more, in addition to what I have already related.

Capt. J. B. Brunt, who resided near my master, had a slave named John. He was his body servant, carriage driver, &c. On one occasion, while driving his master through the city, — the streets being very muddy, and the horses going at a rapid rate, — some mud splattered upon a gentleman by the name of Robert More. More was determined to be revenged. Some three or four months after this occurrence, he purchased John, for the express purpose, as he said, "to take the d——d nigger." After the purchase, he took him to a blacksmith's shop, and had a ball and chain fastened to his leg, and then put him to driving a yoke of oxen, and kept him at hard labor, until the iron around his leg was so worn into the flesh, that it was thought mortification would ensue. In addition to this, John told me that his master whipped him regularly three times a week for the first two months: — and all this to "*tame him.*" A more noble looking man than he, was not to be found in all St. Louis, before he fell into the hands of More; and a more degraded and spirit-crushed looking being was never seen on a southern plantation, after he had been subjected to this "*taming*" process for three months. The last time that I saw him, he had nearly lost the entire use of his limbs.

While living with Mr. Lovejoy, I was often sent on errands to the office of the "Missouri Republican," published by Mr. Edward Charles. Once, while returning to the office with type, I was attacked by several large boys, sons of slaveholders, who pelted me with snow-balls. Having the heavy form of type in my hands, I could not make my escape by running; so I laid down the type and gave them a battle. They gathered around me, pelting me with stones and sticks, until they overpowered me, and would have captured me, if I had not resorted to my heels. Upon my retreat, they took possession of the type; and what to do to regain it I could not devise. Knowing Mr. Lovejoy to be a very humane man, I went to the office, and laid the case before him. He told me to remain in the office. He took one of the apprentices with him, and went after the type, and soon returned with it; but on his return informed me that Samuel McKinney had told him that he would whip me, because I had hurt his boy. Soon after, McKinney was seen making his way to the office by one of the printers, who informed me to the fact, and I made my escape through the back door.

McKinney not being able to find me on his arrival, left the office in a great rage, swearing that he would whip me to death. A few days after, as I was walking along Main Street, he seized me by the collar, and struck me over the head five or six times with a large cane, which caused the blood to gush from my nose and ears in such a manner that my clothes were completely saturated with blood. After beating me to his satisfaction, he let me go, and I returned to the office so weak from the loss of blood, that Mr. Lovejoy sent me home to my master. It was five weeks before I was able to walk again. During this time, it was necessary to have some one to supply my place at the office, and I lost the situation.

After my recovery, I was hired to Capt. Otis Reynolds, as a waiter on board the steamboat Enterprize, owned by Messrs. John and Edward Walsh, commission merchants at St. Louis. This boat was then running on the upper Mississippi. My employment on board was to wait on gentlemen, and the captain being a good man, the situation was a pleasant one to me — but in passing from place to place, and seeing new faces every day, and knowing that they could go where they pleased, I soon became unhappy, and several times thought of leaving the boat at some landing place, and trying to make my escape to Canada, which I had heard much about as a place where the slave might live, be free, and be protected.

But whenever such thoughts would come into my mind, my resolution would soon be shaken by the remembrance that my dear mother was a slave in St. Louis, and I could not bear the idea of leaving her in that condition. She had often taken me upon her knee, and told me how she had carried me upon her back to the field when I was an infant — how often she had been whipped for leaving her work to nurse me — and how happy I would appear when she would take me into her arms. When these thoughts came over me, I would resolve never to leave the land of slavery without my mother. I thought that to leave her in slavery, after she had undergone and suffered so much for me, would be proving recreant to the duty which I owed to her. Besides this, I had three brothers and a sister there, — two of my brothers having died. . . .

A few weeks after, on our downward passage, the boat took on board, at Hannibal, a drove of slaves, bound for the New Orleans market. They numbered from fifty to sixty, consisting of men and women from eighteen to forty years of age. A drove of slaves on a southern steamboat, bound for the cotton or sugar regions, is an occurrence so common, that no one, not even the passengers, appear to notice it, though they clank their chains at every step. There was, however, one in this gang that attracted the attention of the passengers and crew. It was a beautiful girl, apparently about twenty years of age, perfectly white, with straight light hair and blue eyes. But it was not the whiteness of her skin that created such a sensation among those who gazed upon her — it was her almost unparalleled beauty. She had been on the boat but a short time, before the attention of all the passengers, including the ladies, had been called to her, and the common topic of conversation was about the beautiful slave-girl. She was not in chains. The man who claimed this article of human merchandise was a Mr. Walker, — a well known slave-trader, residing in St. Louis. There was a general anxiety among the passengers and crew to learn the history of the girl. Her master kept close by her side, and it would have been considered impudent for any of the passengers to have spoken to her, and the crew were not allowed to have any conversation with them. When we reached St. Louis, the slaves were removed to a boat bound for New Orleans, and the history of the beautiful slave-girl remained a mystery.

I remained on the boat during the season, and it was not an unfrequent occurrence to have on board gangs of slaves on their way to the cotton, sugar and rice plantations of the South.

Toward the latter part of the summer, Captain Reynolds left the boat, and I was sent home. I was then placed on the farm under Mr. Haskell, the overseer. As I had been some time out of the field, and not accustomed to work in the burning sun, it was very hard; but I was compelled to keep up with the best of the hands.

I found a great difference between the work in a steamboat cabin and that in a corn-field.

My master, who was then living in the city, soon after removed to the farm, when I was taken out of the field to work in the house as a waiter. Though his wife was very peevish, and hard to please, I much preferred to be under her control than the overseer's. They brought with them Mr. Sloane, a Presbyterian minister; Miss Martha Tulley, a niece of theirs from Kentucky; and their nephew William. The latter had been in the family a number of years, but the others were all newcomers.

Mr. Sloane was a young minister, who had been [in] the South but a short time, and it seemed as if his whole aim was to please the slaveholders, especially my master and mistress. He was intending to make a visit during the winter, and he not only tried to please them, but I think he succeeded admirably. When they wanted singing, he sung; when they wanted praying, he prayed; when they wanted a story told, he told a story. Instead of his teaching my master theology, my master taught theology to him. While I was with captain Reynolds, my master "got religion," and new laws were made on the plantation. Formerly, we had the privilege of hunting, fishing, making splint brooms, baskets, &c. on Sunday; but this was all stopped. Every Sunday, we were all compelled to attend meeting. Master was so religious, that he induced some others to join him in hiring a preacher to preach to the slaves.

☆ 5 ☆

My master had family worship, night and morning. At night, the slaves were called in to attend; but in the mornings, they had to be at their work, and master did all the praying. My master and mistress were great lovers of mint julep, and every morning, a pitcher-full was made, of which they all partook freely, not excepting little master William. After drinking freely all around, they would have family worship, and then breakfast. I cannot say but I loved the julep as well as any of them, and during prayer was always careful to seat myself close to the table where it stood, so as to help myself when they were all busily engaged in their devotions. By the time prayer was over, I was about as happy as any of them. A sad accident happened one morning. In helping myself, and at the same time keeping an eye on my old mistress, I accidentally let the pitcher fall upon the floor, breaking it in pieces, and spilling the contents. This was a bad affair for me; for as soon as prayer was over, I was taken and severely chastised.

My master's family consisted of himself, his wife, and their nephew, William Moore. He was taken into the family, when only a few weeks of age. His name being that of my own, mine was changed, for the purpose of giving precedence to his, though I was his senior by ten or twelve years. The plantation being four miles from the city, I had to drive the family to church. I always dreaded the approach of the Sabbath; for, during service, I was obliged to stand by the horses in the hot broiling sun, or in the rain, just as it happened.

One Sabbath, as we were driving past the house of D. D. Page, a gentleman who owned a large baking establishment, as I was sitting upon the box of the carriage, which was very much elevated, I saw Mr. Page pursuing a slave around the yard, with a long whip, cutting him at every jump. The man soon escaped from the yard, and was followed by Mr. Page. They came running past us, and the slave perceiving that he would be overtaken, stopped suddenly, and Page stumbled over him, and falling on the stone pavement, fractured one of his legs, which crippled him for life. The same gentlemen, but a short time previous, tied up a woman of his, by the name of Delphia, and whipped her nearly to death; yet he was a deacon in the Baptist church, in good and regular standing. Poor Delphia! I was well acquainted with her, and called to see her while upon her sick bed; and I shall never forget her appearance. She was a member of the same church with her master.

Soon after this, I was hired out to Mr. Walker; the same man whom I have mentioned as having carried a gang of slaves down the river, on the steamboat Enterprize. Seeing me in the capacity of steward on the boat, and thinking that I would make a good hand to take care of slaves, he determined to have me for that purpose; and finding that my master would not sell me, he hired me for the term of one year.

When I learned the fact of my having been hired to a negro speculator, or a "soul-driver" as they are generally called among slaves, no one can tell my emotions. Mr. Walker had offered a high price for me, as I afterwards learned, but I suppose my master was restrained from selling me by the fact that I was a near relative of his. On entering the service of Mr. Walker, I found that my opportunity of getting to a land of liberty was gone, at least for the time being. He had a gang of slaves in readiness to start for New Orleans, and in a few days we were on our journey. I am at a loss of language to express my feelings on that occasion. Although my master had told me that he had not sold me, and Mr. Walker had told me that he had not purchased me, I did not believe them; and not until I had been to New Orleans, and was on my return, did I believe that I was not sold.

There was on the boat a large room on the lower deck, in which the slaves were kept, men and women, promiscuously — all chained two and two, and a strict watch kept that they did not get loose; for cases have occurred in which slaves have got off their chains, and made their escape at landing-places, while the boats were taking in wood — and with all our care, we lost one woman who had been taken from her husband and children, and having no desire to live without them, in the agony of her soul jumped overboard, and drowned herself. She was not chained.

It was almost impossible to keep that part of the boat clean.

On landing at Natchez, the slaves were all carried to the slave-pen, and there kept one week, during which time, several of them were sold. Mr. Walker fed his slaves well. We took on board, at St. Louis, several hundred pounds of bacon (smoked meat) and cornmeal, and his slaves were better fed than slaves generally were in Natchez, so far as my observation extended.

At the end of a week, we left for New Orleans, the place of our final destination, which we reached in two days. Here the slaves were placed in a negro-pen, where those who wished to purchase could call and examine them. The negro-pen is a small yard, surrounded by buildings, from fifteen to twenty feet wide, with the exception of a large gate with iron bars. The slaves are kept in the buildings during the night, and turned out into the yard during the day. After the best of the stock was sold at private sale at the pen, the balance were taken to the Exchange Coffee House Auctions Rooms, kept by Isaac L. McCoy, and sold at public auctions. After the sale of this lot of slaves, we left New Orleans for St. Louis.

☆ 6 ☆

On our arrival at St. Louis, I went to Dr. Young, and told him that I did not wish to live with Mr. Walker any longer. I was heart-sick at seeing my fellow-creatures bought and sold. But the Dr. had hired me for the year, and stay I must. Mr. Walker again commenced purchasing another gang of slaves. He bought a man of Colonel John O'Fallon, who resided in the suburbs of the city. This man had a wife and three children. As soon as the purchase was made, he was put in jail for safe keeping, until we should be ready to start for New Orleans. His wife visited him while there, several times, and several times when she went for that purpose was refused admittance.

In the course of eight or nine weeks Mr. Walker had his cargo of human flesh made up. There was in this lot a number of old men and women, some of them with gray locks. We left St. Louis in the steamboat Carlton, Captain Swan, bound for New Orleans. On our way down, and before we reached

Rodney,[1] the place where we made our first stop, I had to prepare the old slaves for market. I was ordered to have the old men's whiskers shaved off, and the gray hairs plucked out where they were not too numerous, in which case he had a preparation of blacking to color it, and with a blacking-brush we would put it on. This was new business to me, and was performed in a room where the passengers could not see us. These slaves were also taught how old they were by Mr. Walker, and after going through the blacking process, they looked ten or fifteen years younger; and I am sure that some of those who purchased slaves of Mr. Walker, were dreadfully cheated, especially in the ages of the slaves which they bought.

We landed at Rodney, and the slaves were driven to the pen in the back part of the village. Several were sold at this place, during our stay of four or five days, when we proceeded to Natchez. There we landed at night, and the gang were put in the warehouse until morning, when they were driven to the pen. As soon as the slaves are put in these pens, swarms of planters may be seen in and about them. They knew when Walker was expected, as he always had the time advertised beforehand when he would be in Rodney, Natchez, and New Orleans. These were the principal places where he offered his slaves for sale. . . .

The next day we proceeded to New Orleans, and put the gang in the same negro-pen which we occupied before. In a short time, the planters came flocking to the pen to purchase slaves. Before the slaves were exhibited for sale, they were dressed and driven out into the yard. Some were set to dancing, some to jumping, some to singing, and some to playing cards. This was done to make them appear cheerful and happy. My business was to see that they were placed in those situations before the arrival of the purchasers, and I have often set them to

[1]Mississippi.

dancing when their cheeks were wet with tears. As slaves were in good demand at that time, they were all soon disposed of, and we again set out for St. Louis.

On our arrival, Mr. Walker purchased a farm five or six miles from the city. He had no family, but made a housekeeper of one of his female slaves. Poor Cynthia! I knew her well. She was a quadroon, and one of the most beautiful women I ever saw. She was a native of St. Louis, and bore an irreproachable character for virtue and propriety of conduct. Mr. Walker bought her for the New Orleans market, and took her down with him on one of the trips that I made with him. Never shall I forget the circumstances of that voyage! On the first night that we were on board the steamboat, he directed me to put her into a stateroom he had provided for her, apart from the other slaves. I had seen too much of the workings of slavery, not to know what this meant. I accordingly watched him into the stateroom, and listened to hear what passed between them. I heard him make his base offers, and her reject them. He told her that if she would accept his vile proposals, he would take her back with him to St. Louis, and establish her as his housekeeper at his farm. But if she persisted in rejecting them, he would sell her as a field hand on the worst plantation on the river. Neither threats nor bribes prevailed, however, and he retired, disappointed of his prey.

The next morning, poor Cynthia told me what had past, and bewailed her sad fate with floods of tears. I comforted and encouraged her all I could; but I foresaw but too well what the result must be. Without entering into any farther particulars, suffice it to say that Walker performed his part of the contract, at that time. He took her back to St. Louis, established her as his mistress and housekeeper at his farm, and before I left, he had two children by her. But, mark the end! Since I have been at the North, I have been credibly informed that Walker has been married, and, as a previous

measure, sold poor Cynthia and her four children (she having had two more since I came away) into hopeless bondage!

He soon commenced purchasing to take up the third gang. We took steamboat, and went to Jefferson City, a town on the Missouri river. Here we landed, and took stage for the interior of the State. He bought a number of slaves as he passed the different farms and villages. After getting twenty-two or twenty-three men and women, we arrived at St. Charles, a village on the banks of the Missouri. Here he purchased a woman who had a child in her arms, appearing to be four or five weeks old.

We had been travelling by land for some days, and were in hopes to have found a boat at this place for St. Louis, but were disappointed. As no boat was expected for some days, we started for St. Louis by land. Mr. Walker had purchased two horses. He rode one, and I the other. The slaves were chained together, and we took up our line of march, Mr. Walker taking the lead, and I bringing up the rear. Though the distance was not more than twenty miles, we did not reach it the first day. The road was worse than any that I have ever travelled.

Soon after we left St. Charles, the young child grew very cross, and kept up a noise during the greater part of the day. Mr. Walker complained of its crying several times, and told the mother to stop the child's d——d noise, or he would. The woman tried to keep the child from crying, but could not. We put up at night with an acquaintance of Mr. Walker, and in the morning, just as we were about to start, the child again commenced crying. Walked stepped up to her, and told her to give the child to him. The mother tremblingly obeyed. He took the child by one arm, as you would a cat by the leg, walked into the house, and said to the lady,

"Madam, I will make you a present of this little nigger; it keeps such a noise that I can't bear it."

"Thank you, sir," said the lady.

The mother, as soon as she saw that her child was to be left, ran up to Mr. Walker, and falling upon her knees begged him to let her have her child; she clung around his legs, and cried, "Oh, my child! my child! master, do let me have my child! oh, do, do, do. I will stop its crying, if you will only let me have it again." . . .

Mr. Walker commanded her to return into the ranks with the other slaves. Women who had children were not chained, but those that had none were. As soon as her child was disposed of, she was chained in the gang. . . .

We finally arrived at Mr. Walker's farm. He had a house built during out absence to put slaves in. It was a kind of domestic jail. The slaves were put in the jail at night, and worked on the farm during the day. They were kept here until the gang was completed, when we again started for New Orleans, on board the steamboat North America, Capt. Alexander Scott. We had a large number of slaves in this gang. One, by the name of Joe, Mr. Walker was training up to take my place, as my time was nearly out, and glad was I. We made our first stop at Vicksburg, where we remained one week and sold several slaves.

Mr. Walker, though not a good master, had not flogged a slave since I had been with him, though he had threatened me. The slaves were kept in the pen, and he always put up at the best hotel, and kept his wines in his room, for the accommodation of those who called to negotiate with him for the purhase of slaves. One day while we were at Vicksburg, several gentlemen came to see him for this purpose, and as usual the wine was called for. I took the tray and started around with it, and having accidentally filled some of the glasses too full, the gentlemen spilled the wine on their clothes as they went to drink. Mr. Walker apologized to them for my carelessness, but looked at me as though he would see me again on this subject.

After the gentlemen had left the room, he asked me what I meant by my carelessness, and said that

he would attend to me. The next morning, he gave me a note to carry to the jailer, and a dollar in money to give to him. I suspected that all was not right, so I went down near the landing where I met with a sailor, and walking up to him, asked him if he would be so kind as to read the note for me. He read it over, and then looked at me. I asked him to tell me what was in it. Said he,

"They are going to give you hell."

"Why?" said I.

He said, "This is a note to have you whipped, and says that you have a dollar to pay for it."

He handed me back the note, and off I started. I knew not what to do, but was determined not to be whipped. I went up to the jail — took a look at it, and walked off again. As Mr. Walker was acquainted with the jailer, I feared that I should be found out if I did not go, and be treated in consequence of it still worse.

While I was meditating on the subject, I saw a colored man about my size walk up, and the thought struck me in a moment to send him with my note. I walked up to him, and asked him who he belonged to. He said he was a free man, and had been in the city but a short time. I told him I had a note to go into the jail, and get a trunk to carry to one of the steamboats; but was so busily engaged that I could not do it, although I had a dollar to pay for it. He asked me if I would not give him the job. I handed him the note and the dollar, and off he started for the jail.

I watched to see that he went in, and as soon as I saw the door close behind him, I walked around the corner, and took my station, intending to see how my friend looked when he came out. I had been there but a short time, when a colored man came around the corner, and said to another colored man with whom he was acquainted —

"They are giving a nigger scissors in the jail."

"What for?" said the other. The man continued,

"A nigger came into the jail, and asked for the jailer. The jailer came out, and he handed him a note, and said he wanted to get a trunk. The jailer told him to go with him, and he would give him the trunk. So he took him into the room, and told the nigger to give up the dollar. He said a man had given him the dollar to pay for getting the trunk. But that lie would not answer. So they made him strip himself, and then they tied him down, and are now whipping him.''

I stood by all the while listening to their talk, and soon found out that the person alluded to was my customer. I went into the street opposite the jail, and concealed myself in such a manner that I could not be seen by any one coming out. I had been there but a short time, when the young man made his appearance, and looked around for me. I, unobserved, came forth from my hiding-place, behind a pile of brick, and he pretty soon saw me and came up to me complaining bitterly, saying that I had played a trick upon him. I denied any knowledge of what the note contained and asked him what they had done to him. He told me in substance what I heard the man tell who had come out of the jail.

"Yes," said he, "they whipped me and took my dollar, and gave me this note."

He showed me the note which the jailer had given him, telling him to give it to his master. I told him I would give him fifty cents for it, — that being all the money I had. He gave it to me, and took his money. He had received twenty lashes on his bare back, with the negro-whip.

I took the note and started for the hotel where I had left Mr. Walker. Upon reaching the hotel, I handed it to a stranger whom I had not seen before, and requested him to read it to me. As near as I can recollect, it was as follows: —

Dear Sir: — By your direction, I have given your boy twenty lashes. He is a very saucy boy, and tried to make me believe that he did not belong to you, and I put it on to him well for lying to me. I remain,

Your obedient servant.

It is true that in most of the slave-holding cities, when a gentleman wishes his servants whipped, he can send him to the jail and have it done. Before I went in where Mr. Walker was, I wet my cheeks a little, as though I had been crying. He looked at me, and inquired what was the matter. I told him that I have never had such a whipping in my life, and handed him the note. He looked at it and laughed — "and so you told him that you did not belong to me." "Yes, sir," said I. "I did not know that there was any harm in that." He told me I must behave myself, if I did not want to be whipped again.

This incident shows how it is that slavery makes its victims lying and mean; for which vices it afterwards reproaches them, and uses them as arguments to prove that they deserve no better fate. I have often, since my escape, deeply regretted the deception I practised upon this poor fellow; and I heartily desire that it may be, at some time or other, in my power to make him amends for his vicarious sufferings in my behalf.

☆ 7 ☆

In a few days we reached New Orleans, and arriving there in the night, remained on board until morning. While at New Orleans this time, I saw a slave killed; an account of which had been published by Theodore D. Weld, in his book entitled, "Slavery as it is." The circumstances were as follows. In the evening, between seven and eight o'clock, a slave came running down the levee, followed by several men and boys. The whites were crying out, "Stop that nigger, stop that nigger"; while the poor panting slave, in almost breathless accents, was repeating, "I did not steal the meat — I did not steal the meat." The poor man at last took refuge in the river. The whites who were in pursuit of him, ran on board of one of the boats to see if they could discover him. They finally espied him under the bow of the steamboat Trenton. They got a pike-pole, and tried to drive him from his hiding place. When they would strike at him, he would dive under the water. The water was so cold, that it soon became evident that he must come out or be drowned.

While they were trying to drive him from under the bow of the boat or drown him, he would in broken and imploring accents say, "I did not steal the meat; I did not steal the meat. My master lives up the river. I want to see my master. I did not steal the meat. Do let me go home to master." After punching him, and striking him over the head for some time, he at last sunk in the water, to rise no more alive.

On the end of the pike-pole with which they were striking him was a hook which caught in his clothing, and they hauled him on the bow of the boat. Some said he was dead, others said he was "*playing possum*," while others kicked him to make him get up, but it was no use — he was dead.

As soon as they became satisfied of this, they commenced leaving, one after another. One of the hands on the boat informed the captain that they had killed the man, and that the dead body was lying on the deck. The captain came on deck, and said to those who were remaining, "You have killed this nigger; now take him off my boat." The captain's name was Hart. The dead body was dragged on shore and left there. I went on board of the boat where our gang of slaves were, and during the whole night my mind was occupied with what I had seen. Early in the morning, I went on shore to see if the dead body remained there. I found it in the same position that it was left the night before. I watched to see what they would do with it. It was left there until between eight and nine o'clock, when a cart, which takes up the trash out of the streets, came along, and the body was thrown in,

and in a few minutes more was covered over with dirt which they were removing from the streets. During the whole time, I did not see more than six or seven persons around it, who, from their manner, evidently regarded it as no uncommon occurrence.

During our stay in the city, I met with a young white man with whom I was well acquainted in St. Louis. He had been sold into slavery, under the following circumstances. His father was a drunkard, and very poor, with a family of five or six children. The father died, and left the mother to take care of and provide for the children as best she might. The eldest was a boy, named Burrill, about thirteen years of age, who did chores in a store kept by Mr. Riley, to assist his mother in procuring a living for the family. After working with him two years, Mr. Riley took him to New Orleans to wait on him while in that city on a visit, and when he returned to St. Louis, he told the mother of the boy that he had died with the yellow fever. Nothing more was heard from him, no one supposing him to be alive. I was much astonished when Burrill told me his story. Though I sympathized with him, I could not assist him. We were both slaves. He was poor, uneducated, and without friends; and if living, is, I presume, still held as a slave.

After selling out this cargo of human flesh, we returned to St. Louis, and my time was up with Mr. Walker. I had served him one year, and it was the longest year I ever lived.

QUESTIONS TO CONSIDER

1   When abolitionists like William Lloyd Garrison charged that slavery was a brutal institution, southern whites responded that slaves represented too large a financial investment for their owners to treat them cruelly (see selection 19). How would William Wells Brown had responded to this argument?

2   Southern whites insisted that under the benevo-

lent institution of slavery, blacks were contented Sambos who were too loyal and too cowardly to resist their bondage. How did the actual slave behavior that Wells witnessed compare with this image? Why do you think southern whites insisted on this picture of the slave's personality?

3 Contrast the image slaveholders projected about themselves — refined, cultured gentlemen and their ladies — with the reality that Wells encountered in his own life under the lash.

4 Wells's master was a religious man who considered himself a good Christian. What role did religion play in supporting slavery? How were ministers and slaveholders able to reconcile their Christianity with the owning of human beings?

5 Abolitionists accused slaveholders of licentious behavior and called the South "a giant brothel." Southern whites denied these accusations and defended the "purity" of southern civilization. How would Wells have responded?

25

The Myth of the
Southern Lady

ANNE FIROR SCOTT

The man of antebellum America was an enterprising builder of farms and plantations, factories and railroads, hard at work making his fortune in a bustling, materialistic society. For most white men of the period, the opportunities for individual advancement and self-fulfillment became increasingly plentiful. But it was not so for women. They were barred from polls and politics, most professions and occupations; if they were married, their earnings legally belonged to their husbands. As we have seen in "The Lords and the Mill Girls" (selection 20), farm and immigrant women might secure low-paying, low-skill jobs in mills and factories, but the only place for the "true woman" was the home — or at least so said the nineteenth-century women's magazines and religious journals, which reflected the pervasive attitudes of a male-dominated world. Most men — and a great many women — firmly held that the ideal woman was pious, pure, submissive, and domesticated, caring for her husband and rearing her children with a fragile, unquestioning sweetness. As historian Barbara Welter has wryly observed, "It was a fearful obligation, a solemn responsibility, which the nineteenth-century American woman had — to uphold the pillars of the temple with her frail white hand." Those who nurtured the cult of true womanhood thundered at those who questioned the old virtues, branding them all as enemies of God, of the Republic, of civilization itself.

This viewpoint especially prevailed in antebellum Dixie, where preachers, planters, novelists, and other molders of opinion were fanatical in idealizing and idolizing southern women. The southern belle, in fact, became an exaggerated image of the ideal woman so cherished in antebellum America. In the spirited essay that follows, historian Anne Firor Scott examines the myth of the southern lady as it flourished in the patriarchal South and explains that the need to preserve the slave system contributed in large part to the insistence on perfect, yet submissive, women. Readers may want to compare the role of the southern lady with that of the pioneer women discussed in selection 23.

IF TALKING COULD MAKE IT SO antebellum southern women of the upper class would have been the most perfect examples of womankind yet seen on earth. If praise could satisfy all of woman's needs, they would also have been the happiest. Literary journals, sermons, novels, commencement addresses — wherever men spoke there was praise of Woman, and exhortation to further perfection.

This marvelous creation was described as a submissive wife whose reason for being was to love, honor, obey, and occasionally amuse her husband, to bring up his children and manage his household. Physically weak, and "formed for the less laborious occupations," she depended upon male protection. To secure this protection she was endowed with the capacity to "create a magic spell" over any man in her vicinity. She was timid and modest, beautiful and graceful, "the most fascinating being in creation . . . the delight and charm of every circle she moves in."

Part of her charm lay in her innocence. The less a woman knew of life, Ellen Glasgow once remarked bitterly, the better she was supposed to be able to deal with it. Her mind was not logical, but in the absence of reasoning capacity her sensibility and intuition were highly developed. It was, indeed, to

her advantage that "the play of instincts and of the feelings is not cramped by the controlling influence of logic and reason." She was capable of acute perceptions about human relationships, and was a creature of tact, discernment, sympathy, and compassion. It was her nature to be self-denying, and she was given to suffering in silence, a charateristic said to endear her to men. Less endearing, perhaps, but no less natural, was her piety and her tendency to "restrain man's natural vice and immorality." She was thought to be "most deeply interested in the success of every scheme which curbs the passions and enforces a true morality." She was a natural teacher, and a wise counselor to her husband and children.

Thomas Nelson Page, writing many years after the Civil War, summed up the image:

Her life was one long act of devotion, — devotion to God, devotion to her husband, devotion to her children, devotion to her servants, to the poor, to humanity. Nothing happened within the range of her knowledge that her sympathy did not reach and her charity and wisdom did not ameliorate. She was the head and font of the church. . . . The training of her children was her work. She watched over them, inspired them, led them, governed them; her will impelled them; her word to them, as to her servants, was law. She reaped the reward . . . their sympathy and tenderness were hers always, and they worshipped her.

Selection from Anne Firor Scott, *The Southern Lady, from Pedestal to Politics,* pages 4–21, copyright © 1970 by The University of Chicago. Reprinted by permission of the publisher.

Even a realist like Augustus Baldwin Longstreet was obviously influenced by the image when he came to describe a southern matron in one of his stories:

. . . pious but not austere, cheerful, but not light; generous but not prodigal; economical, but not close; hospitable but not extravagant. . . . To have heard her converse you would have supposed she did nothing but read, to have looked through the departments of her household you would have supposed she never read. . . . Everything under her care went on with perfect system.

Oddly enough this paragon of virtue was thought to need the direction and control of some man. A person identified only as "president of the oldest college in Virginia" published a letter to his newly married daughter in an early issue of the *Southern Literary Messenger*. The wife's conduct alone, he asserted, determined the happiness or misery of a marriage. She must resolve at the outset never to oppose her husband, never to show displeasure, no matter what he might do. A man had a right to expect his wife to place perfect confidence in his judgment and to believe that he always knew best. "A difference with your husband ought to be considered the greatest calamity," wrote the father, adding that a woman who permitted differences to occur could expect to lose her husband's love and all hope of happiness. He concluded with the usual injunctions that she should be amiable, sweet, prudent, and devoted, that she should regulate her servants with a kind but firm hand, cultivate her mind by reading history and not currupt it with novels, and manage her domestic concerns with neatness, order, economy, and judgment.

A novelist echoed the opinions of the college president. "In the heart of woman, uncorrupted by a false philosophy which would unfit her for her proper sphere, the proudest feeling is that of admiration for her husband. . . . this is as God meant it should be. To this state the natural feelings of a woman's heart will tend, let quacks in education do what they will."

From earliest childhood girls were trained to the ideals of perfection and submission. A magazine for children published in Charleston, recording the death of a seven-year-old, spoke of her as "peculiarly amiable and engaging; her behaviour marked with a delicate sense of propriety, happily mingled with an artless innocence." She was praised for being kind and considerate to her servants. The fiction in the same magazine was filled with pious, obedient little girls. Boarding schools for young ladies, to which more and more girls were sent as the century wore on, emphasized correct female behavior more than intellectual development. In at least one school the girls wrote their English compositions on such subjects as modesty, benevolence, and the evils of reading novels.

By the time they arrived at their teens most girls had absorbed the injunctions of the myth. One young woman wrote in her diary that she longed to die because she had not found a husband, adding, "I know I would make a faithful, obedient wife, loving with all my heart, yielding entire trust in my husband."

The image of the submissive woman was reinforced by evangelical theology. Daniel R. Hundley, a young Alabama lawyer who wrote a sociological analysis of the antebelum South, relied on Saint Paul's authority for asserting that women should "content themselves with their humble household duties." Southern pulpits repeated the apostle's injunction that women should keep silent in the churches. One minister argued that women needed "the hope and prospects of religion more . . . than the other sex" to soften the pains of living and help women bear with patience and submission the inevitable trials of life, among which he suggested might be "a husband of acid temper." A North Carolina doctor wrote that "God in his inscrutable wisdom has appointed a place and duty for females *out of which* they can neither accomplish their destiny nor secure their happiness!!''

Southern women sought diligently to live up to the prescriptions, to attain the perfection and the submissiveness demanded of them by God and man. John Donald Wade, whose researches into the life of Augustus Baldwin Longstreet reinforced his understanding of the social history of middle Georgia, concluded that ''men found intelligence in woman a quality that in general distressed more than it pleased. When they did not openly condemn they treated it with insulting condescension. *The women*

Painting by Alice Ravenal Huger Smith, of a southern lady and her daughter in the "stack-yard" of the plantation. In patriarchal Dixie, the perfect lady was regal in bearing, but submissive in all things to her husband; she was the mistress of her household, her slaves, and her children, but not of herself. Living up to the idealized image of southern womanhood required intense inner struggle and self-repression; yet few women questioned the reality of the image or the need to maintain it. (Gibbes Museum of Art)

proved themselves marvelously adaptable.'' A woman novelist suggested something about the ongoing struggle to live up to the expectations of men:

To repress a harsh answer, to confess a fault, and to stop (right or wrong) in the midst of self-defence, in gentle submission, sometimes requires a struggle like life and death; but these *three* efforts are the golden threads with which domestic happiness is woven; once begin the fabric with this woof, and trials shall not break or sorrow tarnish it.

Men are not often unreasonable; their difficulties lie in not understanding the moral and physical structure of our sex. . . . How clear it is, then, that woman loses by petulance and recrimination! Her first study must be self-control, almost to hypocrisy. A good wife must smile amid a thousand perplexities, and clear her voice to tones of cheerfulness when her frame is drooping with disease or else languish alone.

Women made heroic efforts to live up to what was expected of them. One, who could hardly bear the sound of her husband tuning his violin, bit her lip and said nothing, murmuring about self-abnegation. There was no rest for the conscience. ''We owe it to our husbands, children and friends,'' wrote a Louisiana housewife, ''to represent as nearly as possible the ideal which they hold so dear.'' '''Tis man's to act, 'tis woman's to edure,'' reflected an Alabama novelist in the midst of trials with a husband she did not much respect, and financial problems beyond her power to solve. Women were made, indeed, the long-suffering wife of the violinist concluded, ''to suffer and be strong.'' ''Give me a double portion of the grace of thy Spirit that I may learn meekness,'' wrote the self-flagellating wife of a minister.

Even more effort, if possible, went into the struggle to live up to what God was presumed to expect of women. A young bride laid down a program for herself:

1   To read the Bible and pray after rising in the morning and sometime after breakfast.

2   To pray again before dinner and read the Bible in the evening and pray before bed.

3   To obey my husband in all things reasonable.

4   "I will endeavor to use patience and forebearance towards my son [her husband's son by an earlier marriage] and correct him in a spirit of mildness for every offense of which he may be guilty.

5   "I will endeavor to offend not with the tongue, but hold it in with bit and bridle and speak charitably of all persons."

6   "I will endeavor to do good unto all as far as it is in my power, especially unto the household of faith."

7   "I will endeavor to subdue every evil propensity by the assistance of Divine Grace, and by practicing that degree of fasting and abstinence which my health will admit of."

This same woman kept a religious diary devoted entirely to daily meditations and painful examination of her progress in the endless struggle for religious perfection. Shortly after her marriage she begged God to cleanse her of secret faults, to save her from impatience and hastiness of temper, and to give her "perfect resignation to Thy Holy Will concerning me." In succeeding entries she deplored her own hardness of heart and expressed guilt when she did not bear severe pain with Christian fortitude.

This was not just one aberrant perfectionist. There are numerous similar letters and diaries. "I feel this day heavy and sad and I would ask myself why and the answer is I feel cold in religious matters oh why am I thus?" "I feel that I am worthless and through the merits of Christ's all-atoning blood alone can I be saved." "Mr. B. [her husband] says we must try to live holier. Oh that I could. Spent some time today reading, weeping and praying." "Help me O Lord for I am poor and weak, help me for I am desolate, in Thee alone have I hope." As for myself I find my heart so full of sinful feelings that I am ready to say 'I am chief of sinners.'" "Lord I feel that my heart is a cage of unclean beasts." "I see so much of sin, so many things to correct, that I almost despair of being a perfect christian." "Oh! for an increased degree of peace to know and do my redeemers will, to live more as I should."

The biblical verse most frequently quoted in southern women's diaries was from Jeremiah: "The heart is deceitful above all things and desperately wicked: who can know it?" There are references to sins too awful even to be recorded in a private journal, accompanied by allusions to cold hearts.

Many women assumed that if they were unhappy or discontented in the "sphere to which God had appointed them" it must be their own fault and that by renewed effort they could do better. "My besetting sins are a roving mind and an impetuous spirit," wrote one woman whose diary is filled with admonitions to herself to be systematic, diligent, prudent, economical, and patient with her servants. Josephine Clay Habersham was a gentle and gifted woman who presided with skill and dignity over a large plantation in eastern Georgia. A devoted mother who could write, "I wish always to have a sweet babe to mind, care for and love," she still felt it necessary to make a constant effort to cultivate a cheerful spirit, to ask God for help with her "dull and wayward heart," and to ask forgiveness for not being a more faithful servant. A girl of eighteen prayed to be useful and bemoaned the "vain desires that every now and then trouble this prevailing one [to love God] and my flesh is so weak, I am always failing."

Women whose families and friends thought them "spotless" were themselves convinced that their souls were in danger. One prayed to God to be delivered from the "serpent whose folds are around my limbs; his sting in my heart." A Mississippi woman found her mind "sunk in a state of apathy from which I can with difficulty arouse myself'' and was sure that this was because she had neglected her duty and transgressed God's holy laws. She was constantly concerned lest "the world and its cares have too large a share of my time and affections.''

For many of these women the brief span of earthly life was chiefly important as preparation for eternity, and much of their self-exhortation centered on being ready to die. They prayed for the will to "overcome every evil propensity . . . to be calm and collected at all times," so as to be ready to depart from the world at a moment's notice in a state of grace, or for the power to bring other sinners to the "throne of peace.'' Such women were cast into deep depression when they gave way to temper, slapped a child, or admonished a slave. One woman scolded herself, "I am not as much engaged in religion as I should be . . . too worldly.'' An unattainable perfection was the only standard.

There is little doubt that religious faith served an important function at a time when many children and adults died for no apparent reason. A firm belief that death was a manifestation of God's will made it easier to bear what otherwise would have been an intolerable burden. It is also clear that the requirements for salvation dovetailed neatly with the secular image of women. Religious women were persuaded that the very qualities which made any human being a rich, interesting, assertive personality — a roving mind, spirit, ambition — were propensities to be curbed. No matter what secret thoughts a woman might have about her own abilities, religion confirmed what society told her — namely, that she was inferior to men.

The language of piety and the desire for salvation, the belief in an eternal life, were not, of course, confined to women. The same phrases abound in the letters, diaries, and sermons of many men. The significant difference was that for men submission to God's will in spiritual matters was considered to be perfectly compatible with aggressive behavior and a commanding position in life. Men expected to

be obeyed by women, children, and slaves, to be the decision makers and the ultimate source of secular authority.

Daniel Hundley's myth of the southern gentleman complements the image of the southern lady. The gentleman, Hundley insisted, in addition to being finely formed and highly educated, was firm, commanding, and a perfect patriarch. "The natural dignity of manner peculiar to the southern gentleman is doubtless owing to his habitual use of authority from his earliest years.'' The weakness and dependence of women was thrown into bold relief by his virility and mastery of his environment. Husbands were frequently referred to in the words used for God: Lord and Master.

The rigid definition of the proper role and behavior of southern women requires explanation. It is not that the constellation of ideas which constituted the image of the southern lady was peculiar to the American South; men in Victorian England conjured up a similar myth in poems like Coventry Patmore's "The Angel in the House." Harriet Martineau was speaking of all American women, not just those of the South, when she described them as lying down at night "full of self-reproach for the want of piety which they do not know how to attain." But, as Wiliam R. Taylor has noted, southern plantation novelists were "fanatical" in idolizing and idealizing southern women. The evidence adduced in this chapter bears out his observation with respect to southern men in general.

Such men continued an old tradition in Western history. The myth of the lady was associated with medieval chivalry. Books of advice on proper behavior for both men and women dated back to the invention of printing. Castiglione's *The Courtier,* a sixteenth-century book of etiquette, set the style for such books, and by the eighteenth century books specifically directed to women were widely read in England and in America. Usually written by men, they emphasized the softness, purity, and spirituality of women while denying them intellectual capacity. Women were instructed to please their husbands, attend to their physical needs, cover up their indiscretions, and give them no cause for worry. All such descriptions and injunctions were included in the southern creed.

But the fact that such ideas had been around for a long time does not explain why they were so enthusiastically embraced by antebellum southerners. Other models were available for a sparsely settled rural society. The good woman of Proverbs, for example, who worked willingly with her hands, got up early and set all in her household to work, bought and sold land, and didn't worry about her appearance might have been an excellent ideal. Why was she not chosen?

We know very little about the relationship of ideology to social structures and understand very little about the social consequences of unconscious needs. Even so, it is possible to speculate that, as with so much else in the antebellum South, slavery had a good deal to do with the ideal of the southern lady. Because they owned slaves and thus maintained a traditional landowning aristocracy, southerners tenaciously held on to the patriarchal family structure. The patriarchy had been the norm in seventeenth-century England. Transported to Virignia and adopted as a social pattern by the planters there, it lived on into the nineteenth century in the whole South. A future officer of the Confederacy explained the theory of the family common among his contemporaries, and related it directly to the institution of slavery:

The Slave Institution of the South increases the tendency to dignify the family. Each planter is in fact a Patriarch — his position compels him to be a ruler in his household. From early youth, his children and servants look up to him as the head, and obedience and subordination become important elements of education. . . . Domestic relations become those which are most prized.

Women, along with children and slaves, were expected to recognize their proper and subordinate place and to be obedient to the head of the family. Any tendency on the part of any of the members of the system to assert themselves against the master threatened the whole, and therefore slavery itself. It was no accident that the most articulate spokesmen for slavery were also eloquent exponents of the subordinate role of women. George Fitzhugh, perhaps the most noted and certainly among the most able of these spokesmen, wrote, for example:

So long as she is nervous, fickle, capricious, delicate, diffident and dependent, man will worship and adore her. Her weakness is her strength, and her true art is to cultivate and improve that weakness. Woman naturally shrinks from public gaze, and from the struggle and competition of life . . . in truth, woman, like children, has but one right and that is the right to protection. The right to protection involves the obligation to obey. A husband, a lord and master, whom she should love, honor and obey, nature designed for every woman. . . . If she be obedient she stands little danger of maltreatment.

If the need to maintain the slave system contributed to the insistence upon perfect, though submissive, women, so did the simple fact that a male-dominated society was good for men. Some of the characteristics demanded of the southern lady were also expected of women in other parts of the United States and require no more complex explanation than that any ruling group can find a theory to justify its position. Like aristocrats, Communists, and bourgeois businessmen, southern men had no trouble finding theoretical support for a way of life that was decidedly to their advantage. Obedient, faithful, submissive women strengthened the image of men who thought themselves vigorous, intelligent, commanding leaders.

Such women also contributed considerably to manly creature comforts. Ellen Glasgow put it this way in one of her novels:

The cares she met with such serenity had been too heavy for her strength; they had driven the bloom from her cheeks and the lustre from her eyes; and, though she had not faltered at her task, she had drooped daily and grown older than her years. The master might live with lavish disregard of the morrow, not the master's wife. For him were the open house, the shining table, the well-stocked wine cellar and the morning rides over the dewey fields; for her the care of her home and children, and of the souls and bodies of the black people that had been given into her hands.

Despite the vigor of their statements, there is some evidence that southern men did not feel altogether secure in their self-proclaimed position of lord and master of the whole patriarchy. Fear lay beneath the surface of the flowery praise of woman and the insistence that God had made her the way men wanted her to be. Otherwise it is hard to see why men spent so much time and energy stating their position. One of Beverly Tucker's leading characters discussed the way he proposed to educate his daughter. She must be raised, he said, to take for granted her husband's superiority, to rely on his wisdom, to take pride in his distinction. "Even should her faculties be superior to his, he cannot raise her so high but that she will still feel herself a creature of his hands."

What were they afraid of, these would-be patriarchs who threatened to withdraw their love from women who disagreed with them or aspired to any forbidden activity? Partly, perhaps, that the women to whom they had granted the custody of conscience and morality might apply that conscience to male behavior — to sharp trading in the market place, to inordinate addiction to alcohol, to nocturnal visits to the slave quarters. Men were aware, too, that the woman who had been so firmly put in her place, the home, often showed unusual power within that restricted domain. She raised the children; she set the standards for behavior. In 1802 a visiting Englishman commented that in North Carolina "the

legislative and executive powers of the house belong to the mistress, the master has nothing to do with administration; he is monument of uxoriousness and passive endurance." Two decades later a North Carolinian wrote to a friend contemplating matrimony that he must be "prepared to have his nose occasionally ground . . . and that he must not drink or play cards." If women could exert so much power even in their restricted position who could tell what they might do with more freedom?

The omens were there to see. Southern men often identified the work of the hated abolitionists with the work of "strong-minded" northern women. A Virginian wrote to a friend in 1853:

You have doubtless seen in the newspapers the struggle we had with the strong-minded women as they call themselves in the World Temperance Convention. If you have seen a true account of the matter you will see that we gained a perfect triumph, and I believe have given a rebuke to this most impudent clique of unsexed females and rampant abolitionists which must put down the petticoats — at least as far as their claim to take the platforms of public debate and enter into all the rough and tumble of the war of words.

His college professor correspondent replied: "I most heartily rejoice with you in the defeat of those shameless amazons." It was a paradox that men who asserted that God made woman as they wished her to be, or that the feminine qualities they admired were given by nature, were afraid that women would break out of the God-given and natural mode of behavior.

If these speculations ring true, one pressing question still remains. Since the ideal of perfection placed a great strain upon women, why did they tolerate their role? One reason is suggested by the early indoctrination already mentioned: the institutions and mores of the society all pointed in the same direction. Churches, schools, parents, books, magazines, all promulgated the same message: be a lady and you will be loved and respected and supported. If you defy the pattern and behave in ways considered unladylike you will be unsexed, rejected, unloved, and you will probably starve.

The presistence of the complementary images of the soft, submissive, perfect woman and of the strong, commanding, intelligent, and dominant man in the face of an exigent reality that often called for quite different qualities suggests that these images had deep significance for the men and women who believed in them. A society increasingly threatened from the outside had every reason to try to diminish internal threats to its stability. George Fitzhugh made this quite explicit when he equated any change in the role of women *or* in the institution of slavery with the downfall of the family and the consequent demise of society. If the distance between the myth and reality became so great that it could not be overlooked, then the situation might be threatening indeed.

Though many southern women were worried about slavery, few had any vision of a society different from the one they knew. Perhaps they, too, sensed a threat of social disorganization inherent in any challenge to male dominance. For whatever reasons, most of them tried to live up to the Sisyphean task expected of them.

QUESTIONS TO CONSIDER

1 Compare the role of the southern lady with that of the mill girl (selection 20) and the pioneer woman (selection 23). How does the reality of each female's life square with the image of the "true woman"?

2 Examine the role of evangelical Protestantism in reinforcing the passive image of women. What similarities do you see with Christianity's role in supporting black slavery?

3 The cult of true womanhood was an ideal of female behavior. What evidence does Scott present that real southern women took this ideal seriously and attempted to live up to its exacting standards? What were the costs and gains of these attempts?

4 Examine the words of southern writers like George Fitzhugh and Beverly Tucker on the subject of women. What fears and threats lurk behind their glorified praise of southern womanhood?

5 Why did southern whites, male and female, regard the maintenance of the feminine domestic ideal as crucial for the present and future stability of their slave-based society?

XIII

THE
DEATH OF
SLAVERY

26

God's Stone in the Pool of Slavery

STEPHEN B. OATES

Sectional conflict over slavery existed from the beginning of the Republic. It continued through the Federalist, Jeffersonian, and Jacksonian eras, becoming especially acute with the rise of the abolitionist crusade in the 1830s. Then, during the era of expansion and the Mexican War, the debate over slavery shifted to the western territories, which slave and free-soil elements alike sought to control for their own political interests. The decade of the 1850s was a time of spiraling violence over the slavery issue. It reached a shattering climax in John Brown's raid at Harpers Ferry in 1859, an event that traumatized the South and spun the nation irreversibly toward the Civil War.

The following essay discusses Brown's raid in the context of southern anxieties and apprehensions over slavery that had been growing for more than half a century. The essay demonstrates that on one score Brown himself was an extremely insightful man, for he correctly predicted the explosive impact that his raid would have on southern whites. For them, Harpers Ferry was no isolated outbreak of little historical import. It was an apocalyptic outgrowth of northern antislavery agitation, an act of "outside provocation" that caused white southerners to equate Brown's style of revolutionary violence with Abraham Lincoln and the Republican party and that escalated sectional tensions over slavery to the breaking point. In relating this, the essay stresses the fact that people respond to events according to their perception of reality. Therefore, what people think is true is quite as important as what is true when it comes to reconstructing the past or understanding the present.

☆ **1** ☆

ON A RAINSWEPT OCTOBER NIGHT IN 1859, grizzled old John Brown led a handful of revolutionaries — most of them young, five of them black — in a surprise attack against Harpers Ferry in northern Virginia, in what Brown envisioned as the first blow in an all-out war for slave liberation. With his twenty-one followers, he intended to incite a Southern-wide slave revolt and to establish a black state in the Southern mountains. Or, failing that, he hoped to ignite a sectional holocaust between North and South in which slavery would be destroyed.

For fifty-nine-year-old John Brown, a white man who had failed in virtually everything he had ever tried, this was the supreme moment of his life, the moment he had been working for since he had committed himself to violence in the Kansas civil war of 1856. All the years of trial, of affliction and sorrow, were behind him now. He and his men were going to liberate some four million human beings from bondage, thereby removing a monstrous wrong from American society. For Brown, slavery was an egregious "sin against God," a sin that violated the commandments of an all-wise, all-powerful Providence, and that contradicted the Declaration of Independence, too, which guaranteed all men the right to life, liberty, and the pursuit of happiness. Yes, slavery was "*foul and loathsome,*" Brown believed, a "*rotten whore*" of an institution which was not only criminally unjust to Negroes, but which offended him personally. When he was twelve years old, he had watched with growing rage — a rage he could not then articulate — as a Michigan innkeeper beat a slave boy with an iron fire shovel. In addition to his intense religious convictions, slavery violated Brown's secular views as well: his passionate commitment to the nuclear family (he had read about the inhuman breakup of slave families), his belief in the right of all men to enjoy the fruits of their labor and to raise themselves above the condition of their birth. Yet, instead of eradicating slavery, the United States had institutionalized that cruel institution, surrounding it with a network of legal and political safeguards quite as though the Declaration of Independence did not exist. Such hypocrisy enraged Brown. How could Americans sanction slavery and yet proclaim theirs the freest and most enlightened nation in the world? By 1859 he thought it impossible to remove slavery through regular political channels. For Southerners and their Northern allies dominated the crucial branches of the federal government and were using these agencies not only to preserve and perpetuate slavery, but also to extend it into the Western territories as well. Moreover, the United States Supreme Court, controlled by Southern Democrats, had denied Negroes the right of United States citizenship and had forbidden Congress to exclude slavery from the public lands. And in Brown's opinion few Northerners seemed to care. Northern Democrats, he declared, were all "doughfaces" who enjoyed licking up "Southern spittle." Republicans were too "wishy-washy" about slavery to do anything about that institution.

John Brown around 1857. By that time Brown had left Bleeding Kansas and gone east to solicit guns and money for a secret "military" operation he had conceived against the South. (Kansas State Historical Society, Topeka)

And the bona fide abolitionists were "milk-and-water" pacifists who preferred talk to action. By the late 1850s, Brown asserted, slavery had become too entrenched in American life ever to be expunged except by revolutionary violence — and by the extermination of this entire generation of men, women, and children, if that were the will of Almighty God. Such statements had electrified New England humanitarians like Ralph Waldo Emerson — who thought Brown was speaking symbolically — and had won him the outright support of six influential Northern reformers, who organized a secret committee to raise guns and money for his projected Virginia invasion.

On the eve of the attack, one or two of Brown's backers began to doubt the wisdom of the operation, but the old man was undaunted. He was convinced that Northern free blacks and Southern slaves would rally to his standard. He was equally certain that he was an instrument in the hands of God, a special angel of death called to remove slavery with the sword. So deeply did Brown — a devout Calvinist all his life — believe that God was directing the Harpers Ferry enterprise, that he thought it unnecessary to make battle plans, to examine the mountainous terrain about Harpers Ferry, to send out agents to contact slaves in the neighorhood, to work out escape plans in case militia or federal troops should mobilize. God would hurl Brown like a stone "into the black pool of slavery" and God alone would determine the outcome.

The outcome was never much in doubt. Brown and his little army seized the federal arsenal at Harpers Ferry and threw the town into bedlam. But militiamen soon surrounded the arsenal, and federal troops under Robert E. Lee, moving up from Washington at a killing pace, stormed the fire-engine house and captured the gnarled old captain and his surviving raiders. Virginia authorities brought Brown to a speedy trial and sentenced him to hang for murder, for inciting slaves to insurrection, and for treason against Virginia (although he was not a citizen of that state). But before he went to the gallows, Brown uttered some of the most eloquent words ever to come from a condemned man. What he said was not always the truth — he denied, for example, that he had ever intended to provoke a slave rebellion — but he did not care about that now. What he cared about was enlisting widespread Northern support for Negro freedom by playing on his own courage and self-sacrifice — and by playing on white guilts. "If it is deemed necessary," he told the Virginia court (and a divided nation beyond), "that I should forfeit my life for the furtherance of the ends of justice and mingle my blood with the blood of millions in this slave country whose rights are disregarded by wicked, cruel, and unjust enactments, I say let it be done.''

Brown's majestic statements, and the moral complexities surrounding the Harpers Ferry attack, plunged the North into what seemed a confusion of voices. The abolitionists, constituting a small minority there, heralded Brown as a saint who made the gallows — as Emerson phrased it — as glorious as the cross. This did not mean that the abolitionists now embraced revolutionary violence to rid the country of slavery. On the contrary, most of them remained committed to nonviolent protest. But in Brown they had an engaging symbol — of noble idealism and Christian sacrifice — and they used that symbol in a renewed effort to make Americans face the slavery curse forthrightly. Other Northerners agreed that Harpers Ferry involved extenuating circumstances — Brown's opposition to slavery was admirable — but thought the raid itself a criminal act which should not go unpunished. On the other hand, most members of the Republican party, with an eye on forthcoming state elections, disparaged Brown as a solitary fanatic who deserved to be hanged. And what they said reflected the opinions of a majority of Northern whites, who not only condemned Brown for taking the law into his own hands, but asserted the right of Southerners to own Negro slaves.

Southerners, though, were fatefully unable to believe that the mass of conservative Northern opinion was typical of the region. So Southern Democrats and their Northern colleagues branded the raid as a Republican party conspiracy, a wild and vicious scheme to destroy the whole Southern ''way of life.'' While the Republicans emphatically denied the charge, few in the South listened. The Virignia General Assembly, in an outburst of fear and defiance, declared that not just the ''Black'' Republicans, but the entire North was behind Harpers Ferry: the work of ''fanatics'' — all Northerners were fanatics — who wanted to incite the slaves to rape and murder. Even though no slaves had risen

to join Brown, rumors of slave ''stampedes'' and abolitionist invasions swept across the South, plunging the region into convulsions of hysteria. In a miasma of imagined revolts and attacks, Southerners mobilized their militia and slave patrols, imprisoned unattended slaves and suspicious-looking strangers, and imposed severe discipline in the slave compounds. As one historian phrased it, ''The raid of twenty-two men on one Virignia town had sent a spasm of uneasiness, resentment, and precautionary zeal from the Potomac to the Gulf.''

In truth, the raid had done a good deal more than that: it had so alarmed Southern whites that henceforth any compromise between them and Northern Republicans was impossible. And nobody was more exultant about the effects of Harpers Ferry than Southern secessionists, who used Brown's name to whip Southern crowds into a frenzy of anti-Republican, anti-Northern hatred. Harpers Ferry, raged one secessionist, ''is the first act in the grand tragedy of emanication, and the subjugation of the South in bloody treason. . . . The vanguard of the great army intended for our subjugation has crossed our borders on Southern soil and shed Southern blood.'' The only solution for the South, the only way to save ''our wives and daughters,'' was secession and an independent, slaveholding confederacy.

☆   2   ☆

Such massive overreaction to Brown's abortive venture may seem difficult to comprehend. After all, nothing really had happened. No slave rebellion had occurred, Brown had been summarily hanged, most Northerners thought he deserved it. But Southerners of that time were in no mood to treat Harpers Ferry as an isolated incident. For them, Brown's attack carried sinister implications about the entire past and future of the American Union; and it played on deep-seated anxieties about slavery — and about the safety of the South in the Union — that had been growing for decades.

In fact, from the very beginning of the nation, the planters — the South's master class — had felt uneasy about their slave regime. At the federal convention of 1787, Southern slaveowners refused to discuss the slavery issue, compelling the other delegates to avoid it or to forget about creating a stronger Union. So, apart from allowing the federal Congress to abolish the foreign slave trade (which it subsequently did), the Constitution maintained "a conspiracy of silence" about the slavery problem. In the 1790s, Southern congressmen demanded that all antislavery petitions be tabled, insisting that such documents were "an entering wedge for total emancipation." Although Thomas Jefferson and other enlightened Southerners talked about abolishing slavery in the South, few of them put their words into action. Their racist constituents would never have accepted emancipation anyway, even if it were gradual and even if slaveowners were compensated for their loss.

Why was this so? Because slavery in the South was always more than a labor device; it was also a rigid system of racial control to maintain white supremacy in a region brimming with Negroes. In this respect, slavery was quite as important to the mass of nonslaveholding whites — always a majority in the Old South — as to the small planter elite that controlled the region. For no matter how low the poor whites sank, no matter how miserable their lives, they were still better than the "nigger" in the levees and cotton fields. They were still white men. Moreover, yeomen and poor whites alike aspired to own Negroes, because slave ownership in the Old South was a tremendous status symbol. Many of these whites were also "expectant" planters who hoped some day to make a lot of money and live in a big white house like the gentry they admired and envied. Such aspirations and feelings melted away whatever class antagonism might have existed in the Old South and united nearly all

whites against the Negro himself — "our internal foe," Virginians called him, a common enemy in their midst, a sinister being of an alien and "inferior" race who if liberated would bring about social chaos and racial catastrophe.[1]

By the 1820s, the Old South seemed on the verge of another kind of catastrophe. A series of insurrection panics rocked the Deep South, especially the South Carolina tidewater where blacks heavily outnumbered whites. In 1822, authorities in Charleston uncovered a shocking slave plot — that of Denmark Vesey — which called for an all-out race war against the whites. Next there occurred the Charleston fire scare and the Georgetown conspiracy. While neither of these ranked as a rebellion, South Carolinians were terror-stricken. Then came 1831 and the bloody Nat Turner revolt in southeastern Virginia. A slave preacher who believed himself an instrument of God, Turner led sixty or seventy slave insurgents on a gruesome rampage: they hacked some sixty whites to death, including women and children. At last the militia crushed the rebellion and executed Turner and twenty other blacks, but not before vengeful whites had slaughtered more than 120 innocent Negroes.

The Turner uprising shook the Old South to its foundations. For who could be safe now in so grim and treacherous a time? How many more revolts would follow? Who among one's own slaves could be trusted? Virginians were so alarmed that they considered liberating all their slaves and then colonizing them at state expense. But in a dramatic debate over the feasibility of manumission, the Virginia legislature concluded that colonization was too

---

[1]Paradoxically, of course, Southern slaveowners often felt genuine affection for their Negroes (as long as they kept in their places), taught them Christianity, and pampered their house servants until some felt superior to "po white trash." And all the while Southerners trumpeted the glories of racial purity, many white slaveowners copulated clandestinely with black women.

costly and too complicated to implement. And since they were not about to emancipate the blacks and leave them as free people in their state, Virginians rejected abolition outright. Then they set about revising their slave codes and restricting their blacks so severely that they could never again mount an insurrection. Even so, whites in Virginia and everywhere else in the South could never escape the fear that somewhere, maybe in their own slave quarters, another Nat Turner was plotting to rise up and slit their throats.

For intimidated Southerners, it was no mere coincidence that the Turner rebellion came at a time of rising abolitionst militancy in the North. In fact, just six months before the Turner uprising, William Lloyd Garrison began publishing the *Liberator* in Boston, demanding in bold, strident editorials that the slaves be immediately and unconditionally emancipated. Desperately needing somebody to blame for Turner besides themselves, Southerners insisted that Garrison's rhetoric had incited the Turner outbreak, insisted that all abolitionists were bloodthirsty fanatics who wanted to obliterate the South in a carnage of racial violence. While this was hardly true (Garrison and his followers were Christian pacifists), Southerners believed what they wanted to believe. From 1831 on, slave rebellion and Yankee abolitionism were synonymous in the Southern mind.

Nor were threats to the South confined to the United States. A powerful antislavery movement seemed to be sweeping the entire Western world. In the 1830s, Great Britain abolished slavery in the Empire, and impassioned English emanicipators came to crusade in America as well. Inevitably, Southerners came to view their region as a lonely slave outpost in a hostile, changing world. Unable to change themselves, unable to free their blacks and surrender their cherished way of life, Southerners embarked on the Great Southern Reaction of the 1830s and 1840s, during which the Old South, threatened it seemed by internal and external enemies, became a closed, martial society determined to defend its slave-based civilization at all costs. Southern postmasters set about confiscating all abolitionist literature, lest these "incendiary" tracts invite the slaves to violence. Southerners also tightened up slave discipline, refusing to let blacks visit other plantations and vowing to hang any Negro who even looked rebellious. At the same time, Southerners eliminated slave schools and churches, revived their old slave patrols, and strengthened their militia forces. By the 1840s the Old South had devised such an oppressive slave system that organized insurrection was next to impossible.

Freedom of thought in the South was also difficult, as Southern zealots stamped out dissent at home and demanded total conformity to the Southern way. They seized "anti-Southern" books and burned them, expelled from classrooms any teacher suspected of abolitionist tendencies, and branded as a traitor anybody who questioned the right of slavery. Some states actually passed sedition laws and other restrictive measures which prohibited Negroes and whites alike from criticizing the peculiar institution.

In reaction to the abolitionists, Southern spokesmen began proclaiming the institution a positive good, asserting that it was justified by history, condoned by the Bible, and ordained by God from the beginning of time. They argued that "niggers" were subhuman anyway and belonged in chains as naturally as cattle in pens. Such inferior brutes were not fit for liberty and equality; these were rights reserved only for white men (for Anglo-Saxon white men). In fact, Southerners were doing "niggers" a huge Christian favor by enslaving them. On the floor of the United States Senate, John C. Calhoun declared slavery "a good — a positive good" and warned that it was indispensable for race control and could not be abolished "without drenching the country in blood." And cranky George Fitzhugh, writing pro-Southern tracts in a ramshackle, bat-ridden Virginia plantation, extolled Southern planters as enlightened reactionaries who ruled an insulated slave community, family based and proudly provincial. But to attain complete security, Fitzhugh contended, Southerners must free themselves from the competitive, market economy which governed the modern world; they must destroy capitalism — or "free society" — and revive the halcyon days of precapitalist Europe. Then the master class should enslave all workers, white as well as black, and the world would enjoy supreme order and stability. While few planters embraced Fitzhugh's economic views, they emphatically shared his assessment of the abolitionists. "For thirty years," Fitzhugh growled, "the South has been a field on which abolitionists, foreign and domestic, have carried on offensive warfare. Let us now, in turn, act on the offensive, transfer the seat of war, and invade the enemy's territory."

☆ 3 ☆

Southern leaders were anxious indeed to take the offensive, because only by doing so, they believed, could the South survive in a hostile world. They strove harder than ever to control the federal government, in order to prevent Northerners from enacting an abolition law or adopting any other measure that might harm the South. Because Southerners dominated the Democrats, the nation's majority party, they generally controlled the presidency, the Cabinet, the Senate, and the Supreme Court from the 1840s to 1860. They became consummate obstructionists, demolishing any bill that might facilitate the growth of the free states or the Yankee business community. In their zeal, Southerners seemed oblivious to the fact that Northern big businessmen were not their enemies but their friends; most of these businessmen despised the abolitionists and went out of their way to appease the South, because Southerners bought their manufac-

tured goods and sold them cotton. Northern capitalists would go to almost any length to hold the Union together with slavery, because they believed disunion would be economically devastating.

Until 1859, most Southerners wanted to remain in the Union, but at a high price. In additon to manipulating the federal government, they sought to open the Western territories to unrestrained slavery expansion. In fact, proslavery Missourians and other Southerners vowed to seize the new territory of Kansas and make it a gateway for slave expansion to the Pacific, thus creating a greater South with a world outlet on two oceans. In the late 1850s, Southern leaders in Washington clamored for a federal law guaranteeing what they regarded as their constitutional right to take slaves into the territories. In part, this was to prevent the free states from invading the West and ringing the South with hostile satellite territories. It would also set a precedent so that slavery could expand into Cuba and Central America, should the United States acquire those lands as Southern expansionists advocated.

In their efforts to extend slavery, Southern Democrats collided dramatically with the newly formed Republican party, a coalition of Northern free-soil elements out to contain slavery and dismantle Southern power in Washington. From 1856 on, Southern politicians engaged in a life-or-death struggle with the Republican party, regarding it as a demonic threat to slavery and the whole Southern way of life based on that institution.

The Republicans, for their part, denied any intention of menacing the South. While they were determined to exclude slavery from the territories, they vowed to leave it alone in the Southern states where it already existed. But the Southern people — who for twenty years had lived in a closed and suspicious society, dedicated to suppressing dissent and defending slavery — refused to believe anything the Republicans said. Were they not opposed to slavery in the territories? Then they must be against it in the

South as well. Did Republicans not denounce slavery as an evil which must perish some day? Then all Republicans must be abolitionists, radicals, and fanatics. Never mind their disavowals. Never mind their talk about "ultimate" extinction. Extinction was extinction. Once the Republicans attained power, pledges to leave slavery alone in the South would disappear like any other campaign promise, and the next thing Southerners would know, Republican troops would be invading their farms and plantations and liberating the slaves at gun point. "I shudder to contemplate it!" cried an Alabama white man. "What social monstrosities, what desolated fields, what civil broils, what robberies, rapes, and murders of the poorer whites by the emancipated blacks would then disfigure the whole fair face of this prosperous, smiling, and happy Southern land."

Anti-Republican feelings pervaded all classes in the Old South, and the fire-eaters — those already agitating for Southern independence — rushed to capitalize on those sentiments. On the stump and in the press, these spirited demagogues distorted Republican speeches and wrenched remarks out of context, molding these into inflammatory slogans to demonstrate that Republicans were warmongering abolitionists and that Southerners, for their own safety, had to get out of the Union. This is not to say that Southern discontent was a "manufactured crisis," created by a small bunch of rabble-rousers. On the contrary, the fire-eaters were telling Southern crowds precisely what they wanted to hear. Had Abraham Lincoln not proclaimed that a house divided against itself could not stand, that this nation could not endure half slave and half free? Had William H. Seward of New York not declared that North and South were locked in an irrepressible conflict? Were such statements not proof that Republicans desired a sectional war? Although both Seward and Lincoln hotly denied that they desired any such thing, their disclaimers fell on deaf ears.

☆ 4 ☆

By 1859, tensions between Republicans and Southern whites were at a combustible state. All that was needed was an overt act against the South — a spark to set a conflagration roaring. And that spark came in the form of John Brown, who for two years had been secretly plotting his bold and audacious attack against slavery in Virginia. That attack, one must remember, had alternative objectives: should it fail, Brown had repeatedly argued, it would nevertheless ignite a sectional powder keg that might explode into civil war. Though often maligned as a demented dreamer, Brown in one respect was an extremely perceptive man: he understood the depth of Southern anxieties about slavery, understood that all he had to do — being a Northerner and an abolitionist — was to set foot in the South with a gun, announce that he was here to free the slaves, and the effect on the South would be cataclysmic.

And so the Harpers Ferry raid took place. And so the South reacted with even greater hysteria than had followed Nat Turner's uprising. For thousands of Southerners, from poor whites in South Carolina to rich cotton planters in Mississippi, Harpers Ferry was the inevitable result of the "abolitionist" doctrines of the Republican party; the attack was dramatic, conclusive proof that slave insurrection was what the "Black" Republicans had wanted all along. From Harpers Ferry on, the Republican party and Brown-style revolutionary violence were forged like a ring of steel in the Southern mind.

Harpers Ferry, in sum, ensured that some kind of violent rupture would take place should the Republicans win the presidential election of 1860. There were, of course, a number of loyal Unionists in the South who pleaded for reason and restraint, who beseeched their fellow Southerners to wait for an overt Republican act against them before they did anything rash. For most, though, Brown's raid had been all the overt action they needed. "The Harper's Ferry invasion," exclaimed the Richmond *Enquirer,* "has advanced the cause of Disunion more than any other event that has happened since the formation of the Government." "I have said of Mr. Seward and his followers," cried a state senator of Mississippi, "that they are our enemies and we are theirs. He has declared that there is an 'irrepressible conflict' between us. So there is! He and his followers have declared war upon us, and I am fighting it out to the bitter end."

And to the bitter end, the Republicans kept trying to reach the South, kept denying any complicity in Brown's attack. "You charge that we stir up insurrections among your slaves," Lincoln told the South in his 1860 address at Cooper Union. "We deny it; and what is your proof? Harper's Ferry! John Brown!! John Brown was no Republican; and you have failed to implicate a single Republican in his Harper's Ferry enterprise." After he was nominated for the presidency and the Southern press viciously assailed him, Lincoln could not fathom why Southerners were so incensed. What had the Republicans done to them? What Southern rights had they violated? Did not Southerners still have the fugitive slave law? Did they not have the same Constitution they had lived under for seventy-odd years? "Why all this excitement" he asked a crowd at Cleveland, Ohio. "Why all these complaints?" He wrote Alexander H. Stephens of Georgia; "Do the people of the South really entertain fears that a Republican administration would, *directly,* or *indirectly,* interfere with their slaves . . . ? If they do, I wish to assure you, as once a friend, and still, I hope, not an enemy, that there is no cause for such fears." Lincoln added: "I suppose, however, this does not meet the case. You think slavery is *right* and ought to be extended; while we think it is *wrong* and ought to be restricted. That I suppose is the rub. It certainly is the only substantial difference between us."

CHARLESTON
MERCURY
EXTRA:

Passed unanimously at 1.15 o'clock, P. M., December 20th, 1860.

AN ORDINANCE

To dissolve the Union between the State of South Carolina and other States united with her under the compact entitled " The Constitution of the United States of America."

We, the People of the State of South Carolina, in Convention assembled, do declare and ordain, and it is hereby declared and ordained,

That the Ordinance adopted by us in Convention, on the twenty-third day of May, in the year of our Lord one thousand seven hundred and eighty-eight, whereby the Constitution of the United States of America was ratified, and also, all Acts and parts of Acts of the General Assembly of this State, ratifying amendments of the said Constitution, are hereby repealed; and that the union now subsisting between South Carolina and other States, under the name of " The United States of America," is hereby dissolved.

THE
UNION
IS
DISSOLVED!

Front-page headlines of the Charleston Mercury *announcing the secession of South Carolina, December 20, 1860. (Rare Books and Manuscript Division, The New York Public Library, Astor, Lenox and Tilden Foundations)*

Stephens and other Southern Unionists begged Lincoln to issue a public statement about his views. But he declined, remarking that he had made his opinions explicitly clear in previous speeches and that Southern militants would misconstrue anything he said. He was undoubtedly right. And anyway, Republicans and Southern whites were no longer speaking the same language. Words like *rights* and *constitution,* like *freedom* and *self-government,* meant one thing to the Republicans and quite another to distraught Southerners. For the latter, freedom meant escape from threats and invasions. And rights meant the right of white supremacy (Southern style), of self-determination and Southern independence. And Southerners were now ready for independence, if that was what it took to protect their slave-based social order from the "Black" Republican meance.

So when Lincoln was elected president, the seven states of the Deep South — with their heavy concentration of slaves — seceded from the Union. As the editor of the *Montgomery Mail* explained: "In the struggle for maintaining the ascendancy of our race in the South — our home — we see no chance for victory but in withdrawing from the Union. To remain in the Union is to lose all that white men hold dear in government. We vote to get out."

For the Republicans, all this was hard to comprehend. They had repeatedly asserted that they had no intention of freeing the slaves in the Southern states. And in any case, the Democrats, though divided themselves, had still won control of Congress and could demolish any abolition bill introduced there. But the Deep South was intractable all the same. And Lincoln himself decided to hold firm. He had won the presidency in a fair and legal contest. He would not compromise his election mandate. He would preserve the Union and the principle of self-government on which the Union was based: the right of a free people to choose their leaders and to expect the losers to acquiesce in that decision. And so the fateful events raced by in rapid-fire sequence: Fort Sumter, Lincoln's call for troops, the secession of the upper South, and the beginning of a civil war in which slavery itself would perish — the very thing old John Brown had hoped and prayed would be the ultimate consequences of the Harpers Ferry raid.

QUESTIONS TO CONSIDER

1   Given John Brown's deeply held abolitionist convictions, why do you think he did not join with moral suasionists like William Lloyd Garrison (selection 19) and instead embraced revolutionary violence as the best method to rid the country of slavery?

2   Compare the effects of John Brown's raid on northerners and southerners. Did the Harpers Ferry fiasco make civil war inevitable?

3   How did the instutition of slavery function in the South as a means of racial control, uniting slaveholders and nonslaveholders alike? Why did poor whites, in particular, support the slaveholders' regime?

4   Why, after the early 1830s, did the South become what one historian called the "Militant South" — suspicious, intolerant of dissent, ruthless in its attention to slave discipline?

5   Brown has been denounced by critics as a demented fanatic and praised by admirers as a clear-eyed visionary. Which, if either of these descriptions, do you feel is accurate?

27

Lincoln's Journey
to Emancipation

STEPHEN B. OATES

Throughout the first year and a half of the Civil War, Lincoln insisted that the North was fighting strictly to save the Union, not to free the slaves. But a combination of problems and pressures caused him to change his mind, and in September 1862 he issued the Preliminary Emancipation Proclamation, to take effect on January 1, 1863. The proclamation liberated the slaves in the rebellious states.

Ever since then, legends have flourished about Lincoln as the Great Emancipator — a man who dedicated his life to liberty and equality for all. On the other hand, counter-legends of Lincoln as a Great Racist eventually emerged in the South. Which view is the true one? Should Lincoln be applauded as a great humanitarian, or was he just another white bigot, as one writer recently contended? Or, as some of his contemporaries charged, was he an unscrupulous opportunist who eradicated slavery merely for political and military expediency? The following essay, drawing on modern scholarship about Lincoln's life and the times in which he lived, tries to answer the enduring questions about Lincoln as emancipator. It not only traces his changing views about slavery and race and discusses his evolving emancipation policy, but tries to present a realistic portrait of one of the most mythologized men in American history.

1

HE COMES TO US IN THE MISTS OF LEGEND as a kind of homespun Socrates, brimming with prairie wit and folk wisdom. He is as honest, upright, God-fearing, generous, and patriotic an American as the Almighty ever created. Impervious to material rewards and social station, the Lincoln of mythology is the Great Commoner, a saintly Rail Splitter who spoke in a deep, fatherly voice about the genius of the plain folk. He comes to us, too, as the Great Emancipator who led the North off to Civil War to free the slaves and afterward offered his fellow Southerners a tender and forgiving hand.

There is a counterlegend of Lincoln — one shared ironically enough by many white Southerners and certain black Americans of our time. This is the legend of Lincoln as bigot, as a white racist who championed segregation, opposed civil and political rights for black people, wanted them all thrown out of the country. This Lincoln is the great ancestor of racist James K. Vardaman of Mississippi, of ''Bull'' Connor of Birmingham, of the white citizens' councils, of the Knights of the Ku Klux Klan.

Neither of these views, of course, reveals much about the man who really lived — legends and politicized interpretations seldom do. The real Lincoln was not a saintly emancipator, and he was not an unswerving racist either. To understand him and the liberation of the slaves, one must eschew artificial, arbitary categories and focus on the man as he lived, on the flesh-and-blood Lincoln, on that flawed and fatalistic individual who struggled with himself and his countrymen over the profound moral paradox of slavery in a nation based on the Declaration of Independence. Only by viewing Lincoln scrupulously in the context of his own time can one under-

stand the painful, ironic, and troubled journey that led him to the Emancipation Proclamation and to the Thirteenth Amendment that made it permanent.

2

As a man, Lincoln was complex, many-sided, and richly human. He was almost entirely self-educated, with a talent for expression that in another time and place might have led him into a literary career. He wrote poetry himself and studied Shakespeare, Byron, and Oliver Wendell Holmes, attracted especially to writings with tragic and melancholy themes. He examined the way celebrated orators turned a phrase or employed a figure of speech, admiring great truths greatly told. Though never much at impromptu oratory, he could hold an audience of 15,000 spellbound when reading from a written speech, singing out in a shrill, high-pitched voice that became his trademark.

He was an intense, brooding person, plagued with chronic depression most of his life. ''I am now the most miserable man living,'' he said on one occasion in 1841. ''If what I feel were equally distributed to the whole human family, there would not be one cheerful face on the earth.'' He added, ''To remain as I am is impossible; I must die or be better.''

At the time he said this, Lincoln had fears of sexual inadequacy, doubting his ability to please or even care for a wife. In 1842 he confided in his closest friend, Joshua Speed, about his troubles, and both confessed that they had fears of ''nervous debility'' with women. Speed went ahead and married anyway and then wrote Lincoln that their anxieties were groundless. Lincoln rejoiced, ''I tell you, Speed, our forebodings, for which you and I are rather peculiar, are all the worst sort of nonsense.'' Encouraged by Speed's success, Lincoln finally wedded Mary Todd; and she obviously helped him over-

Reprinted from *Our Fiery Trial: Abraham Lincoln, John Brown, and the Civil War Era,* by Stephen B. Oates, copyright © 1978 by the University of Massachusetts press.

come his doubts, for they developed a strong and lasting physical love for one another.

Still, Lincoln remained a moody, melancholy man, given to long introspections about things like death and mortality. In truth, death was a lifelong obsession with him. His poetry, speeches, and letters are studded with allusions to it. He spoke of the transitory nature of human life, spoke of how all people in this world are fated to die in the end — all are fated to die. He saw himself as only a passing moment in a rushing river of time.

Preoccupied with death, he was also afraid of insanity, afraid (as he phrased it) of "the pangs that kill the mind." In his late thirties, he wrote and rewrote a poem about a boyhood friend, one Matthew Gentry, who became deranged and was locked "in mental night," condemned to a living death, spinning out of control in some inner void. Lincoln retained a morbid fascination with Gentry's condition, writing about how Gentry was more an object of dread than death itself: "A human form with reason fled, while wretched life remains." Yet, Lincoln was fascinated with madness, troubled by it, afraid that what had happened to Gentry could also happen to him — his own reason destroyed, Lincoln spinning in mindless night without the power to know.

Lincoln was a teetotaler because liquor left him "flabby and undone," blurring his mind and threatening his self-control. And he dreaded and avoided anything which threatened that. In one memorable speech, he heralded some great and distant day when all passions would be subdued, when reason would triumph and "*mind,* all conquering *mind,*" would rule the earth.

One side of Lincoln was always supremely logical and analytical. He was intrigued with the clarity of mathematics; and as an attorney he could command a mass of technical data. Yet he was also extremely superstitious, believed in signs and visions, contended that dreams were auguries of approaching triumph or calamity. He was skeptical of organized religion and never joined a church; yet he argued that all human destinies were controlled by an omnipotent God.

It is true that Lincoln told folksy anecdotes to illustrate a point. But humor was also tremendous therapy for his depressions — a device "to whistle down sadness," as a friend put it. Lincoln liked all kinds of jokes, from bawdy tales to pungent rib-ticklers like "Bass-Ackwards," a story he wrote down and handed a bailiff one day. Filled with hilarious spoonerisms, "Bass-Ackwards" is about a fellow who gets thrown from his horse and lands in "a great *tow-curd,*" which gives him a "*sick of fitness.*" About "*bray dake,*" he comes to and dashes home to find "the *door* sick abed, and his *wife* standing open. But thank goodness," the punch line goes, "she is getting right *hat* and *farty* again."

Contrary to legend, Lincoln was anything but a common man. In point of fact, he was one of the most ambitious human beings his friends had ever seen, with an aspiration for high station in life that burned in him like a furnace. Instead of reading with an accomplished attorney, as was customary in those days, he taught himself the law entirely on his own. He was literally a self-made lawyer. Moreover, he entered the Illinois legislature at the age of twenty-five and became a leader of the state Whig party, a tireless party campaigner, and a regular candidate for public office.

As a self-made man, Lincoln felt embarrassed about his log-cabin origins and never liked to talk about them. He seldom discussed his parents either and became permanently estranged from his father, who was all but illiterate. In truth, Lincoln had considerable hostility for his father's intellectual limitations, once remarking that Thomas "never did more in the way of writing than to bunglingly sign his own name." When his father died in a nearby Illinois county in 1851, Lincoln did not attend the funeral.

By the 1850s, Lincoln was one of the most sought-after attorneys in Illinois, with a reputation as a lawyer's lawyer — a knowledgeable jurist who argued appeal cases for other attorneys. He did his most influential legal work in the Supreme Court of Illinois, where he participated in 243 cases and won most of them. He commanded the respect of his colleagues, all of whom called him "Mr. Lincoln" or just "Lincoln." Nobody called him Abe — at least not to his face — because he loathed the nickname. It did not befit a respected professional who'd struggled hard to overcome the limitations of his frontier background. Frankly, Lincoln enjoyed his status as a lawyer and politician, and he liked money, too, and used it to measure his worth. By the mid–1850s, thanks to a combination of talent and sheer hard work, Lincoln was a man of substantial wealth. He had an annual income of around $5,000 — the equivalent of many times that today — and large financial and real-estate investments.

Though a man of status and influence, Lincoln was as honest in real life as in the legend. Even his enemies conceded that he was incorruptible. Moreover, he possessed broad humanitarian views, some of them in advance of his time. Even though he was a teetotaler, he was extremely tolerant of alcoholics, regarding them not as criminals — the way most temperance people did — but as unfortunates who deserved understanding, not vilification. He noted that some of the world's most gifted artists had succumbed to alcoholism, because they were too sensitive to cope with their insights into the human condition. He believed that women, like men, should vote so long as they all paid taxes. And he had no ethnic prejudices. His law partner William Herndon, who cursed the Irish with a flourish, reported that Lincoln was not at all prejudiced against "the foreign element, tolerating — as I never could — even the Irish."

Politically, Lincoln was always a nationalist in outlook, an outlook that began when he was an Indiana farm boy tilling hs father's mundane wheat field. While the plow horse was getting its breath at the end of a furrow, Lincoln would study Parson Weems's eulogistic biography of George Washington, and he would daydream about the Revolution and the origins of the Republic, daydream about Washington and Jefferson as great national statesmen who shaped the course of history. By the time he became a politician, Lincoln idolized the Founding Fathers as apostles of liberty (never mind for now that many of these apostles were also Southern slaveowners). Young Lincoln extolled the founders for beginning an experiment in popular government on this continent, to show a doubting Europe that people could govern themselves without hereditary monarchs an aristocracies. And the foundation of the American experiment was the Declaration of Independence, which in Lincoln's view contained the highest political truths in history: that all men are created equal and are entitled to freedom and the pursuit of happiness. Which for Lincoln meant that men like him were not chained to the condition of their births, that they could better their station in life and harvest the fruits of their own talents and industry. Thus he had a deep, personal reverence for the Declaration and insisted that all his political sentiment flowed from that document.

☆ **3** ☆

Which brings us to the problem and paradox of slavery in America. Lincoln maintained that he had always hated human bondage, as much as any abolitionist. His family had opposed the peculiar institution, and Lincoln had grown up and entered Illinois politics thinking it wrong. But before 1854 (and the significance of that date will become clear) Lincoln generally kept his own counsel about slavery and abolition. After all, slavery was the most inflammable issue of his generation, and Lincoln observed early on what violent passions Negro bondage — and the question of race that underlay it — could arouse in white Americans. In his day, as I have said, slavery was a tried and tested means of race control in a South absolutely dedicated to white supremacy. Moreover, the North was also a white supremacist region, where the vast majority of whites opposed emancipation lest it result in a flood of Southern blacks into the free states. And Illinois was no exception, as most whites there were against abolition and were anti-Negro to the core. Lincoln, who had elected to work within the system, was not going to ruin his career by espousing an extremely unpopular cause. To be branded as an abolitionist in central Illinois — his constituency as a legislator and a U.S. congressman — would have been certain political suicide. At the same time, attorney Lincoln conceded that Southern slavery had become a thoroughly entrenched institution, that bondage where it already existed was protected by the Constitution and could not be molested by the national government.

Still, slavery distressed him. He realized how wrong it was that slavery should exist at all in a self-proclaimed free and enlightened Republic. He who cherished the Declaration of Independence understood only too well how bondage mocked and contradicted that noble document. Too, he thought slavery a blight on the American experiment in popular government. It was, he believed, the one retrograde institution that robbed the Republic of its just example in the world, robbed the United States of the hope it should hold out to oppressed people everywhere.

He opposed slavery, too, because he had witnessed some of its evils firsthand. In 1841, on a steamboat journey down the Ohio River, he saw a group of manacled slaves on their way to the cruel cotton plantations of the Deep South. Lincoln was appalled at the sight of those chained Negroes. Fourteen years later he wrote that the spectacle "was a continual torment to me" and that he saw something like it every time he touched a slave border.

Slavery, he said, "had the power of making me miserable."

Again, while serving in Congress from 1847 to 1849, he passed slave auction blocks in Washington, D.C. In fact, from the windows of the Capitol, he could observe the infamous "Georgia pen" — "a sort of Negro livery stable," as he described it, "where droves of negroes were collected, temporarily kept, and finally taken to Southern markets, precisely like droves of horses." The spectacle offended him. He agreed with a Whig colleague that buying and selling of human beings in the United States capital was a national disgrace. Accordingly Lincoln drafted a gradual abolition bill for the District of Columbia. But powerful Southern politicians howled in protest, and his own Whig support fell away. At that, Lincoln dropped his bill and sat in glum silence as Congress rocked with debates — with drunken fights and rumbles of disunion — over the status of slavery out in the territories. Shocked at the behavior of his colleagues, Lincoln confessed that slavery was the one issue that threatened the stability of the Union.

What could be done? Slavery as an institution could not be removed, and yet it should not remain either. Trapped in what seemed an impossible dilemma, Lincoln persuaded himself that if slavery were confined to the South and left alone there, time would somehow solve the problem and slavery would ultimately die out. And he told himself that the Founding Fathers had felt the same way, that they too had expected slavery to perish some day. In Lincoln's interpretation, they had tolerated slavery as a necessary evil, agreeing that it could not be eradicated where it already flourished without causing wide-scale wreckage. But in his view they had taken steps to restrict its growth (had excluded slavery from the old Northwest territories, had outlawed the international slave trade) and so had placed the institution on the road to extinction.

So went Lincoln's argument before 1854. The solution was to bide one's time, trust the future to get rid of slavery and square America with her own ideals. And he convinced himself that when slavery was no longer workable, Southern whites would gradually liberate the blacks on their own. They would do so voluntarily.

To solve the ensuing problem of racial adjustment, Lincoln insisted that the federal government should colonize all blacks in Africa, an idea he got from his political idol, Whig national leader Henry Clay. Said Lincoln in 1852: if the Republic could remove the danger of slavery and restore "a captive people to their long-lost fatherland," and do both so gradually "that neither races nor individuals shall have suffered by the change," then "it will indeed be a glorious consummation."

☆ 4 ☆

Then came 1854 and the momentous Kansas-Nebraska Act, brainchild of Lincoln's archrival Stephen A. Douglas. The act overturned the old Missouri Compromise line, which excluded slavery from the vast northern area of the old Louisiana Purchase territory. The act then established a new formula for dealing with slavery in the national lands: now Congress would stay out of the matter, and the people of each territory would decide whether to retain or outlaw the institution. Until such time as the citizens of a territory voted on the issue, Southerners were free to take slavery into most western territories, including the new ones of Kansas and Nebraska. These were carved out of the northern section of the old Lousiana Purchase territory. Thanks to the Kansas-Nebraska Act, a northern domain once preserved for freedom now seemed open to proslavery invasion.

At once a storm of free-soil protest broke across the North, and scores of political leaders branded

the Kansas-Nebraska Act as part of a sinister Southern plot to extend slave territory and augment Southern political power in Washington. There followed a series of political upheavals. A civil war blazed up in Kansas, as proslavery and free-soil pioneers came into bloody collisions on the prairie there — proof that slavery was far too volatile ever to be solved as a purely local matter. At the same time, the old Whig party disintegrated. In its place emerged the all-Northern Republican party, dedicated to blocking slavery extension and to saving the cherished frontier for free white labor. Then in 1857 came the infamous Dred Scott decision, handed down by the pro-Southern Supreme Court, which ruled that neither Congress nor a territorial government could outlaw slavery, because that would violate Southern property rights. As Lincoln and many others observed, the net effect of the decision was to legalize slavery in all federal territories from Canada to Mexico.

The train of ominous events from Kansas-Nebraska to Dred Scott shook Lincoln to his foundations. In his view, the Southern-controlled Democratic party — the party that dominated the Senate, the Supreme Court, and the presidency — had instituted a revolt against the Founding Fathers and the entire course of the Republic so far as slavery was concerned. Now human bondage was not going to die out. Now it was going to expand and grow and continue indefinitely, as Southerners dragged manacled Negroes across the West, adapting slave labor to whatever conditions they found there, putting the blacks to work in mines and on farms. Now Southerners would create new slave states in the West and make slavery powerful and permanent in America. Now the Republic would never remove the cancer that infected its political system, would never remove the one institution that marred its global image, would never remove a "cruel wrong" that mocked the Declaration of Independence.

Lincoln waded into the middle of the antiextension fight. He campaigned for the national Senate. He joined the Republican party. He thundered against the evil designs of the "Slave Power." He spoke with an urgent sense of mission that gave his speeches a searching eloquence — a mission to save the Republic's noblest ideals, turn back the tide of slavery expansion, restrict the peculiar institution once again to the South, and place it back on the road to extinction, as Lincoln believed the Founding Fathers had so placed it.

By 1858, Lincoln, like a lot of other Republicans, began to see a grim proslavery conspiracy at work in the United States. The first stage was to betray the founders and send slavery flooding all over the West. At the same time, proslavery theorists were out to undermine the Declaration of Independence, to discredit its equality doctrine as "a self-evident lie" (as many Southern spokesmen were actually saying), and to replace the Declaration with the principles of inequality and human servitude.

The next step in the conspiracy would be to nationalize slavery: the Taney Court, Lincoln feared, would hand down another decision, one declaring that states could not prohibit slavery either. Then the institution would sweep into Illinois, sweep into Indiana and Ohio, sweep into Pennsylvania and New York, sweep into Massachusetts and New England, sweep all over the Northern states, until at last slavery would be nationalized and America would end up a slave house. At that, as George Fitzhugh advocated, the conspirators would enslave all American workers regardless of color. The Northern free-labor system would be expunged, the Declaration of Independence overthrown, self-government abolished, and the conspirators would restore despotism with class rule and an entrenched aristocracy. All the work since the Revolution of 1776 would be obliterated. The world's best hope — America's experiment in popular government — would be destroyed, and mankind would spin backward into feudalism.

For Lincoln and his Republican colleagues, it was imperative that the conspiracy be blocked in its ini-

tial stage — the expansion of slavery into the West. In 1858 Lincoln set out after Douglas's Senate seat, inveighing against the Little Giant for his part in the proslavery plot and warning Illinois — and Northerners beyond — that only the Republicans could save their free-labor system and their free government. Now Lincoln openly and fiercely declaimed his antislavery sentiments. He hated the institution. He hated slavery because it degraded blacks and whites alike. Because it prevented the Negro from "eating the bread which his own hand earns." Because it not only contradicted the Declaration, but violated the principles of free labor, self-help, social mobility, and economic independence, all of which lay at the center of Republican ideology, of Lincoln's ideology. Yet, while branding slavery as an evil and doing all they could to contain it in the South, Republicans would not, could not, molest the institution in those states where it already existed.

Douglas, fighting for his political life in freesoil Illinois, lashed back at Lincoln with unadulterated race-baiting. Throughout the Great Debates of 1858, Douglas smeared Lincoln and his party as Black Republicans, as a gang of radical abolitionists out to liberate all Southern slaves and bring them stampeding into Illinois and the rest of the North, where they would take away white jobs and copulate with white daughters. Again and again, Douglas accused Lincoln of desiring intermarriage and racial mongrelization.

Lincoln protested emphatically that race was not the issue between him and Douglas. The issue was whether slavery would ultimately triumph or ultimately perish in the United States. But Douglas understood the depth of anti-Negro feeling in Illinois, and he hoped to whip Lincoln by playing on white racial fears.

Forced to take a stand lest Douglas ruin him with his allegations, Lincoln conceded that he was not for Negro political or social equality. He was not for enfranchising Negroes, was not for intermarriage.

There was, he said, "a physical difference" between blacks and whites that would "probably" always prevent them from living together in perfect equality. Having confessed his racial views, Lincoln then qualified them: if Negroes were not the equal of Lincoln and Douglas in moral or intellectual endowment, they *were* equal to Lincoln, Douglas, and "every living man" in their right to liberty, equality of opportunity, and the fruits of their own labor. (Later he insisted that it was bondage that had "clouded" the slaves' intellects and that Negroes were capable of thinking like whites.) Moreover, Lincoln rejected "the counterfeit argument" that just because he did not want a black woman for a slave, he necessarily wanted her for a wife. He could just let her alone. He could let her alone so that she could also enjoy her freedom and "her natural right to eat the bread she earns with her own hands."

Exasperated with Douglas and white Negrophobia in general, Lincoln begged American whites "to discard all this quibbling about this man and the other man — this race and that race and the other race as being inferior," begged them to unite as one people and defend the ideals of the Declaration and its promise of liberty and opportunity for all.

Lincoln lost the 1858 Senate contest to Douglas. But in 1860 he won the Republican nomination for president and stood before the American electorate on the free-soil, free-labor principles of the Republican party. As the Republican standard bearer, Lincoln was uncompromising in his determination to prohibit slavery in the territories by national law and to save the Republic (as he put it) from returning to "class, caste, and despotism." He exhorted his fellow Republicans to stand firm in their duty: to brand slavery as an evil, contain it in the South, look to the future for slavery to die a gradual death, and promise colonization to solve the question of race. Some day, somehow, the American house must be free of slavery. That was the Republican vision, the distant horizon Lincoln saw.

Yet, for the benefit of Southerners, he repeated that he and his party would not harm slavery in the Southern states. The federal government had no constitutional authority in peace time to tamper with a state institution like slavery.

But Southerners refused to believe anything Lincoln said. In Dixie, orators and editors alike castigated him as a black-hearted radical, a "sooty and scoundrelly" abolitionist who wanted to free the slaves at once and mix the races. In Southern eyes, Lincoln was another John Brown, a mobocrat, a Southern hater, a chimpanzee, a lunatic, the "biggest ass in the United States," the evil chief of the North's "Black Republican, free love, free Nigger" party, whose victory would ring the bells of doom for the white man's South. Even if Southerners had to drench the Union in blood, cried an Atlanta man, "the South, the loyal South, the Constitution South, would never submit to such humiliation and degradation as the inauguration of Abraham Lincoln."

After Lincoln's victory and the secession of the Deep South, Lincoln beseeched Southerners to understand the Republican position on slavery. In his Inaugural Address of 1861, he assured them once again that the federal government would not free the slaves in the South, that it had no legal right to do so. He even gave his blessings to the original Thirteenth Amendment, just passed by Congress, that would have guaranteed slavery in the Southern states for as long as whites there wanted it. Lincoln endorsed the amendment because he thought it consistent with Republican ideology. Ironically, Southern secession and the outbreak of war prevented that amendment from ever being ratified.

When the rebels opened fire on Fort Sumter, the nation plunged into civil war, a conflict that began as a ninety-day skirmish for both sides, but that swelled instead into a vast and terrible carnage with consequences beyond calculation for those swept up in its flames. Lincoln, falling into a depression that would plague him through his embattled presidency, remarked that the war was the supreme irony of his life: that he who sickened at the sight of blood, who abhorred stridency and physical violence, was caught in a national holocaust, a tornado of blood and wreckage with Lincoln himself whirling in its center.

☆ 5 ☆

At the outset of the war, Lincoln strove to be consistent with all that he and his party had said about slavery: his purpose in the struggle was strictly to save the Union; it was not to free the slaves. He would crush the rebellion with his armies and restore the national authority in the South with slavery intact. Then Lincoln and his party would resume and implement their policy of slave containment.

There were other reasons for Lincoln's hands-off policy about slavery. Four slave states — Delaware, Maryland, Kentucky, and Missouri — remained in the Union. Should he try to free the slaves, Lincoln feared it would send the crucial border spiraling into the Confederacy, something that would be catastrophic for the Union. A Confederate Maryland would create an impossible situation for Washington, D.C. And a Confederate Missouri and Kentucky would give the rebels potential bases from which to invade Illinois, Indiana, and Ohio. So Lincoln rejected emancipation in part to appease the loyal border.

He was also waging a bipartisan war effort, with Northern Democrats and Republicans alike enlisting in his armies to save the Union. Lincoln encouraged this because he insisted that it would take a united North to win the war. An emancipation policy, he feared, would alienate Northern Democrats, ignite a racial powder keg in the Northern states, and possibly cause a civil war in the rear. Then the Union really would be lost.

But the pressures and problems of civil war caused Lincoln to change his mind, caused him to abandon his hands-off policy and hurl an executive fist at slavery in the rebel states, thus making emancipation a Union war objective. The pressures operating on Lincoln were complex and merit careful discussion.

First, from the summer of 1861 on, several Republican senators — chief among them, Charles Sumner of Massachusetts, Ben Wade of Ohio, and Zachariah Chandler of Michigan — sequestered themselves with Lincoln and implored and badgered him to free the slaves.[1] Sumner, as Lincoln's personal friend and one of his chief foreign policy advisers, was especially persistent. Before secession, of course, Sumner and his colleagues had all adhered to the Republican position on slavery in the South. But civil war had now removed their constitutional scruples about the peculiar institution. After all, they told Lincoln, the Southern people were in rebellion against the national government; they could not resist that government and yet enjoy the protection of its laws. Now the senators argued that the national government could eradicate slavery by the War Power, and they wanted Lincoln to do it in his capacity as commander-in-chief. If he emancipated the slaves, it would maim and cripple the Confedracy and hasten an end to the rebellion.

Second, they pointed out that slavery had caused the war, was the reason why the Southern states had seceded, and was now the cornerstone of the confederacy. It was absurd, the senators contended, to fight a war without removing the thing that had brought it about. Should the South return to the Union with slavery intact, as Lincoln desired, Southerners would just start another war over slav-

---

[1]These "more advanced Republicans," as the *Detroit Post and Tribune* referred to Sumner and his associates, belonged to a powerful minority faction of the party inaccurately categorized as "radicals," a misnomer that has persisted through the years. For a discussion of this point, see my article, "The Slaves Freed," *American Heritage* (December 1980), 74–83.

ery, whenever they thought it threatened again, so that the present struggle would have accomplished nothing, nothing at all. If Lincoln really wanted to save the Union, he must tear slavery out root and branch and smash the South's planter class — that mischievous class the senators thought had masterminded secession and fomented war.

Sumner, as a major Lincoln adviser on foreign affairs, also linked emancipation to foreign policy. On several occasions in 1861 and 1862, Britain seemed on the verge of recognizing the Confederacy as an independent nation — a move that would be calamitous for the Union. As a member of the family of nations, the Confederacy could form alliances and seek mediation and perhaps armed intervention in the American conflict. But, Sumner argued, if Lincoln made the obliteration of slavery a Union war aim, Britain would balk at recognition and intervention. Why so? Because she was proud of her antislavery tradition, Sumner contended, and would refrain from helping the South protect human bondage from Lincoln's armies. And whatever powerful Britain did, the rest of Europe was sure to follow.

Also, as Sumner kept reminding everyone, emancipation would break the chains of several million oppressed human beings and right America at last with her own ideals. Lincoln could no longer wait for the future to remove slavery. He must do it. The war, monstrous and terrible though it was, had given Lincoln the opportunity to do it.

There was still another argument for emancipation, an argument advanced not just by Sumner and his colleagues, but by members of Lincoln's cabinet as well. In 1862, his armies suffered from manpower shortages on every front. Thanks to repeated Union military failures and to a growing war weariness across the North, volunteering had fallen off sharply; and Union generals bombarded Washington with shrill complaints, insisting that they faced an overwhelming Southern foe and must have reinforcements before they could win battles or even fight. While Union commanders often exaggerated

rebel strength, Union forces *did* need reinforcements to carry out a successful offensive war. As Sumner reminded Lincoln, the slaves were an untapped reservoir of strength. "You need more men," Sumner said, "not only at the North, but at the South. You need the slaves." If Lincoln freed them, he could recruit black men into his armed forces, thus helping to solve his manpower woes.

Lincoln was sympathetic to the entire range of arguments Sumner and his associates rehearsed for him. Personally, Lincoln hated slavery as much as they did, and many of their points had already occurred to him. In fact, as early as November and December 1861, Lincoln began wavering in his hands-off policy about slavery, began searching about for some compromise — something short of a sweeping emancipation decree. Again he seemed caught in an impossible dilemma: how to remove the cause of the war, keep Britain out of the conflict, cripple the Confederacy and suppress the rebellion, and yet retain the allegiance of Northern Democrats and the critical border?

In March 1862, he proposed a plan to Congress he thought might work: a gradual, compensated emancipation program to commence in the loyal border states. According to Lincoln's plan, the border states would gradually abolish slavery themselves over the next thirty years, and the federal government would compensate slaveowners for their loss. The whole program was to be voluntary; the states would adopt their own emancipation laws without federal coercion.

At the same time, the federal government would sponsor a colonization program, which was also to be entirely voluntary. Without a promise of colonization, Lincoln understood only too well, most Northern whites would never accept emancipation, even if it were carried out by the states. From now on, every time he contemplated some new antislavery move, he made a great fuss about colonization: he embarked on a colonization project in central America and another in Haiti, and he held an interview about colonization with Washington's black leaders, an interview he published in the press. In part, the ritual of colonization was designed to calm white racial fears.

If his gradual, state-guided plan were adopted, Lincoln contended that a presidential decree — federally enforced emacipation — would never be necessary. Abolition would begin on the local level in the loyal border and then be extended into the rebel states as they were conquered. Thus by a slow and salubrious process would the cause of the rebellion be removed and the future of the Union guaranteed.

The plan failed. It failed because the border states refused to act. Lincoln couldn't even persuade Delaware, with its small and relatively harmless slave population, to adopt his program. In desperation, Lincoln on three different occasions — in the spring and summer of 1862 — pleaded with border-state congressmen to endorse his program. In their third meeting, held in the White House on July 12, Lincoln warned the border representatives that it was impossible now to restore the Union with slavery preserved. Slavery was doomed. They could not be blind to the signs, blind to the fact that his plan was the only aternative to a more drastic move against slavery, one that would cause tremendous destruction in the South. Please, he said, commend my gradual plan to your people.

But most of the border men turned him down. They thought his plan would cost too much, would only whip the flames of rebellion, would cause dangerous discontent in their own states. Their intransigence was a sober lesson to Lincoln. It was proof indeed that slaveowners — even loyal slaveowners — were too tied up in the slave system ever to free their own Negroes and voluntarily transform their way of life. If abolition must come, it must begin in the rebel South and then be extended into the loyal border later on. Which meant that the president must eradicate slavery himself. He could no longer avoid the responsibility. By mid-July 1862, the pressures of the war had forced him to abandon his hands-off policy and lay a "strong hand on the colored element."

On July 13, the day after his last talk with the border men, Lincoln took a carriage ride with a couple of his cabinet secretaries. His conversation, when recounted in full, reveals a tougher Lincoln than the lenient and compromising president of the legend-building biographies. Lincoln said he was convinced that the war could no longer be won through forbearance toward Southern rebels, that it was "a duty on our part to liberate the slaves." The time had come to take a bold new path and hurl Union armies at "the heart of the rebellion," using the military to destroy the very institution that caused and now sustained the insurrection. Southerners could not throw off the Constitution and at the same time invoke it to protect slavery. They had started the war and must now face its consequences.

He had given this a lot of grave and painful thought, he said, and had concluded that a presidential declaration of emancipation was the last alternative, that it was "a military necessity absolutely essential to the preservation of the Union." Because the slaves were a tremendous source of strength for the rebellion, Lincoln must invite them to desert and "come to us and uniting with us they must be made free from rebel authority and rebel masters." His interview with the border men yesterday, he said, "had forced him slowly but he believed correctly to this conclusion."

On July 22, 1862, Lincoln summoned his cabinet members and read them a draft of a preliminary Emancipation Proclamation. Come January 1, 1863, in his capacity as commander-in-chief of the armed forces in time of war, Lincoln would free all the slaves everywhere in the rebel states. He would thus make it a Union objective to annihilate slavery as an institution in the Confederate South.

Contrary to what many historians have said, Lincoln's projected Proclamation went further than anything Congress had done. True, Congress had just enacted (and Lincoln had just signed) the second confiscation act, which provided for the seizure and liberation of all slaves of people who supported or participated in the rebellion. Still, most slaves would be freed only after protracted case-by-case litigation in the federal courts. Another section of the act did liberate certain categories of slaves without court action, but the bill exempted loyal slaveowners in the rebel South, allowing them to keep their slaves and other property. Lincoln's Proclamation, on the other hand, was a sweeping blow against bondage as an institution in the rebel states, a blow that would free *all* the slaves there — those of secessionists and loyalists alike. Thus Lincoln would handle emancipation himself, avoid judicial red tape, and use the military to vanquish the cornerstone of the Confederacy. Again, he justified this as a military necessity to save the Union.

But Seward and other cabinet secretaries disuaded Lincoln from issuing his Proclamation in July. Seward argued that the Union had won no clear military victories, particulary in the showcase Eastern theater. As a consequence, Europe would misconstrue the Proclamation as "our last shriek on the retreat," as a wild and reckless attempt to compensate for Union military ineptitude by provoking a slave insurrection behind rebel lines. If Lincoln must give an emancipation order, Seward warned, he must wait until the Union won a military victory.

Lincoln finally agreed to wait, but he was not happy about it: the way George B. McClellan and his other generals had been fighting in the Eastern theater, Lincoln had no idea when he would ever have a victory.

One of the great ironies of the war was that McClellan presented Lincoln with the triumph he needed. A Democrat who sympathized with Southern slavery and opposed wartime emancipation with a passion, McClellan outfought Robert E. Lee at Antietam Creek in September 1862, and forced the rebel army to withdraw. Thereupon Lincoln issued his preliminary Proclamation, with its warning that if the rebellion did not cease by January 1, 1863, the executive branch, including the army and the navy, would destroy slavery in the rebel states.

As it turned out, the preliminary Proclamation ignited racial discontent in much of the lower North, especially the Midwest, and led to a Republican disaster in the fall by-elections of 1862. Already Northern Democrats were upset with Lincoln's harsh war measures, especially his use of martial law and military arrests. But Negro emancipation was more than they could stand, and they stumped the Northern states that fall, beating the drums of Negrophobia, warning of massive influxes of southern blacks into the North once emancipation came. Sullen, war weary, and racially aroused, Northern voters dealt the Republicans a smashing blow, as the North's five most populous states — all of which had gone for Lincoln in 1860 — now returned Democratic majorities to Congress. While the Republicans narrowly retained control of Congress, the future looked bleak indeed for 1864.

Republican analysts — and Lincoln himself — conceded that the preliminary Proclamation was a major factor in the Republican defeat. But Lincoln told a delegation from Kentucky that he would rather die than retract a single word in his Proclamation.

As the New Year approached, conservative Republicans begged Lincoln to abandon his "reckless" emancipation scheme lest he shatter their demoralized party and wreck what remained of their country. But Lincoln stood firm. On New Year's day, 1863, he officially signed the final Emancipation Proclamation in the White House. His hand trembled badly, not because he was nervous, but because he had shaken hands all morning in a White House reception. He assured everyone present that he was never more certain of what he was doing. "If my name ever goes into history," he said, "it will be for this act." Then slowly and deliberately he wrote out his full name.

In the final Proclamation, Lincoln temporarily exempted occupied Tennessee and certain occupied places in Louisiana and Virginia. (Later, in reconstructing those states, he withdrew the exemptions and made emancipation a mandatory part of his reconstruction program.) He also excluded the loyal slave states because they were not in rebellion and he lacked the legal authority to uproot slavery there. He would, however, keep goading them to obliterate slavery themselves — and would later push a constitutional amendment that liberated their slaves as well. With the exception of the loyal border and certain occupied areas, the final Proclamation declared that as of this day, all slaves in the rebellious states were *"forever free."* The document also asserted that black men — Southern and Northern alike — would now be enlisted in Union military forces.

Out the Proclamation went to an anxious and dissident nation. Later in the day an interracial crowd gathered on the White House lawn, and Lincoln greeted the people from an open window. The blacks cheered and sang, "Glory, Jubilee has come," and told Lincoln that if he would "come out of that palace, they would hug him to death." A black preacher named Henry M. Turner exclaimed that "it is indeed a time of times," that "nothing like it will ever be seen again in this life."

☆ 6 ☆

Lincoln's Proclamation was the most revolutionary measure ever to come from an American president up to that time. As Union armies punched into rebel territory, they would rip out slavery as an institution, automatically freeing all slaves in the areas and states they conquered. In this respect (as Lincoln said), the war brought on changes more vast, more fundamental and profound, than either side had expected when the struggle began. Now slavery would perish as the Confederacy perished, would die by degrees with every Union advance, every Union victory.

Moreover, word of the Proclamation hummed across the slave grapevine in the Confederacy; and as Union armies drew near, more slaves than ever abandoned rebel farms and plantations and (as one said) "demonstrated with their feet" their desire for freedom.

The Proclamation also opened the army to black volunteers, and Northern free Negroes and Southern ex-slaves now enlisted as Union soldiers. As Lincoln said, "the colored population is the great *available* and yet unavailed of, force for restoring the Union." And he now availed himself of that force. In all, some 180,000 Negro fighting men — most of them emancipated slaves — served in Union forces on every major battle front, helping to liberate their brothers and sisters in bondage and to save the Union. As Lincoln observed, the blacks added enormous and indispensable strength to the Union war machine.

Unhappily, the blacks fought in segregated units under white officers, and until late in the war received less pay than whites did. In 1864 Lincoln told Negro leader Frederick Douglass that he disliked the practice of unequal pay, but that the government had to make some concessions to white prejudices, noting that a great many Northern whites opposed the use of black soldiers altogether. But he promised that they would eventually get equal pay — and they did. Moreover, Lincoln was proud of the performance of his black soldiers: he publicly praised them for fighting "with clenched teeth, and steady eye, and well poised bayonet" to save the Union, while certain whites strove "with malignant heart" to hinder it.

After the Proclamation, Lincoln had to confront the problem of race adjustment, of what to do with all the blacks liberated in the South. By the spring of 1863, he had pretty well written off colonization as unworkable. His colonization schemes all floundered, in part because the white promoters were dis-

*Men of the 54th Massachusetts (Colored) Infantry Regiment.
Organized after the Emancipation Proclamation, the 54th became the most famous black fighting unit in the Union Army.
All the men in the regiment were volunteers, and nearly all of
them were free blacks from the North. They enlisted for various
reasons: to help free their brothers and sisters from bondage,
prove that black men were not inferior, and help save the
Union. The subject of the brilliant motion-picture* Glory, *the
54th led the Federal assault on Fort Wagner in Charleston
Harbor, losing its white officer and almost half its men. Although the attack was repulsed, the men of the 54th proved
that black soldiers could fight as well as white soldiers. All told,
some 186,000 blacks served in the Union army: they fought
in 450 engagements and won 21 Congressional Medals of
Honor. (Luis F. Emilio,* A Brave Black Regiment)

honest or incompetent. But the main reason colonization failed was because most blacks adamantly
refused to participate in Lincoln's voluntary program. Across the North, free Negroes denounced
Lincoln's colonization efforts — this was their country too! they cried — and they petitioned him to de-
port slaveholders instead.

As a consequence, Lincoln had just about concluded that whites and liberated blacks must somehow learn how to live together in this country.
Still, he needed some device for now, some program
that would pacify white Northerners and convince
them that Southern freedmen would not flock into
their communities, but would remain in the South
instead. What Lincoln worked out was a refugee
system, installed by his adjutant general in the occupied Mississippi Valley, which mobilized Southern
blacks in the South, utilizing them in military and
civilian pursuits there. According to the system, the
adjutant general enrolled all able-bodied freedmen in
the army, employed other ex-slaves as military laborers, and hired still others to work on farms and
plantations for wages set by the government. While
there were many faults with the system, it was
predicated on sound Republican dogma; it kept
Southern Negroes out of the North, and it got them
jobs as wage earners, thus helping them to help
themselves and preparing them for life in a free society.

Even so, emancipation remained the most explosive and unpopular act of Lincoln's presidency. By
mid–1863, thousands of Democrats were in open
revolt against his administration, denouncing Lincoln as an abolitionist dictator who had surrendered
to radicalism. In the Midwest, dissident Democrats
launched a peace movement to throw ''the shriek-
ing abolitionist faction'' out of office and negotiate
a peace with the Confederacy that would somehow
restore the Union with slavery unharmed. There
were large antiwar rallies against Lincoln's war for
slave liberation. Race and draft riots flared in several
Northern cities.

With all the public unrest behind the lines, conservative Republicans beseeched Lincoln to abandon emancipation and rescue his country "from the brink of ruin." But Lincoln seemed intractable. He had made up his mind to smash the slave society of the rebel South and eliminate "the cruel wrong" of Negro bondage, and no amount of public discontent, he indicated, was going to change his mind. "To use a coarse, but an expressive figure," he wrote one aggravated Democrat, "broken eggs cannot be mended. I have issued the Proclamation, and I cannot retract it." Congressman Owen Lovejoy applauded Lincoln's stand. "His mind acts slowly," Lovejoy said, "but when he moves, it is *forward*."

He wavered once — in August 1864, a time of unrelenting gloom for Lincoln when his popularity had sunk to an all-time low and it seemed he could not be reelected. He confessed that maybe the country would no longer sustain a war for slave emancipation, that maybe he shouldn't pull the nation down a road it did not want to travel. On August 24 he decided to offer Jefferson Davis peace terms that excluded emancipation as a condition, vaguely suggesting that slavery would be adjusted later "by peaceful means." But the next day Lincoln changed his mind. With awakened resolution, he vowed to fight the war through to unconditional surrender and to stick by emancipation come what may. He had made his promise of freedom to the slaves, and he meant to keep it so long as he was in office.

When he won the election of 1864, Lincoln interpreted it as a popular mandate for him and his emancipation policy. But in reality the election provided no clear referendum on slavery, since Republican campaigners had played down emancipation and concentrated on the peace plank in the Democratic platform. Nevertheless, Lincoln used his reelection to promote a constitutional amendment that would guarantee the freedom of all slaves, those in the loyal border as well as those in the rebel South. Since issuing his Proclamation, Lincoln had worried that it might be nullified in the courts or thrown out

by a later Congress or a subsequent administration. Consequently he wanted a constitutional amendment that would safeguard his Proclamation and prevent emancipation from ever being overturned.

As it happened, the Senate in May of 1864 had already passed an emancipation amendment — the present Thirteenth Amendment — but the House had failed to approve it. After that Lincoln had insisted that the Republican platform endorse the measure. And now, over the winter of 1864 and 1865, he put tremendous pressure on the House to endorse the amendment, using all his powers of persuasion and patronage to get it through. He buttonholed conservative Republicans and opposition Democrats and exhorted them to support the amendment. He singled out "sinners" among the Democrats who were "on praying ground," and informed them that they had a lot better chance for the federal jobs they desired if they voted for the measure. Soon two Democrats swung over in favor of it. With the outcome still in doubt, Lincoln participated in secret negotiations never made public — negotiations that allegedly involved the patronage, a New Jersey railroad monopoly, and the release of rebels related to Congressional Democrats — to bring wavering opponents into line. "The greatest measure of the nineteenth century," Thaddeus Stevens claimed, "was passed by corruption aided and abetted by the purest man in America." On January 31, 1865, the House adopted the present Thirteenth Amendment by just three votes more than the required two-thirds majority. At once a storm of cheers broke over House Republicans, who danced around, embraced one another, and waved their hats and canes overhead. "It seemed to me I had been born with a new life," one Republican recalled, "and that the world was overflowing with beauty and joy."

Lincoln, too, pronounced the amendment "a great moral victory" and "a King's cure" for the

The strain of war: at left, Abraham Lincoln in Springfield, Illinois, on June 3, 1860. At right, after four years of war, Lincoln posed for photographer Alexander Gardner in Wash- *ington, April 10, 1865. (Photo on left: Chicago Historical Society, photo on right: Brown University, McClennan Lincoln Collection)*

evils of slavery. When ratified by the states, the amendment would end human bondage everywhere in America. Lincoln pointed across the Potomac. "If the people over the river had behaved themselves, I could not have done what I have."

☆ 7 ☆

Lincoln conceded, though, that he had not controlled the events of the war, but that events had controlled him instead, that God had controlled him. He thought about this a great deal, especially at night when he couldn't sleep, trying to under-

stand the meaning of the war, to understand why it had begun and grown into such a massive revolutionary struggle, consuming hundreds of thousands of lives (the final casualties would come to 618,000 on both sides). By his second inaugural, he had reached an apocalyptic conclusion about the nature of the war — had come to see it as a divine punishment for the "great offense" of slavery, as a terrible retribution God had visited on a guilty people, in North as well as South. Lincoln's vision was close to that of old John Brown, who had prophesied on the day he was hanged, on that balmy December day back in 1859, that the crime of savery could not be purged away from this guilty land except by blood. Now, in his second Inaugural Address, Lin-

367

coln too contended that God perhaps had willed this "mighty scourge of War" on the United States, "until all the wealth piled by the bondman's two hundred and fifty years of unrequited toil shall be sunk, and until every drop of blood drawn with the lash, shall be paid by another drawn from the sword."

In the last paragraph of his address, Lincoln said he would bind the nation's wounds "with malice toward none" and "charity for all." Yet that did not mean he would be so gentle and forgiving in reconstruction as most biographers have contended. He would be magnanimous in the sense that he wouldn't resort to mass executions or even mass imprisonment of Southern "traitors," as he repeatedly called them. He would not even have the leaders tried and jailed, though he said he would like to "frighten them out of the country." Nevertheless, still preoccupied with the war as a grim purgation which would cleanse and regenerate his country, Lincoln endorsed a fairly tough policy toward the conquered South. After Lee surrendered in April 1865, Lincoln publicly endorsed limited suffrage for Southern blacks, announcing that the intelligent ex-slaves and especially those who had served in Union military forces should have the vote. This put him in advance of most Northern whites. And it put him ahead of most Republicans as well — including many of the so-called radicals — who in April 1865 shrank from Negro suffrage out of fear of their own white constituents. True, Sumner, Salmon Chase, and a few of their colleagues now demanded that all Southern black men be enfranchised in order to protect their freedom. But Lincoln was not far from their position. In a line in his last political speech, April 11, 1865, he granted that the Southern black man deserved the vote, though Lincoln was not quite ready to make that mandatory. But it seems clear in what direction he was heading.

Moreover, in a cabinet meeting on Good Friday, 1865, Lincoln and all his Secretaries endorsed the military approach to reconstruction and conceded that an army of occupation might be necessary to control the rebellious white majority in the conquered South. During the war, Lincoln had always thought the military indispensable in restoring civilian rule in the South. Without the army, he feared that the rebellious Southern majority would overwhelm the small Unionist minority there — and maybe even reenslave the blacks. And he was not about to let the latter happen. The army had liberated the blacks in the war, and the army might well have to safeguard their freedom in reconstruction.

☆ 8 ☆

He had come a long distance from the young Lincoln who entered politics, quiet on slavery lest he be branded an abolitionist, opposed to Negro political rights lest his political career be jeopardized, convinced that only the future could remove slavery in America. He had come a long way indeed. Frederick Douglass, who interviewed Lincoln in the White House in 1863, said he was "the first great man that I talked with in the United States freely who in no single instance reminded me of the difference between himself and myself, of the difference of color." Douglass, reflecting back on Lincoln's presidency, recalled how in the first year and a half of the war, Lincoln "was ready and willing" to sacrifice black people for the benefit and welfare of whites. But since the preliminary Emancipation Proclamation, Douglass said, American blacks had taken Lincoln's measure and had come to admire and some to love this enigmatic man. Though Lincoln had taxed Negroes to the limit, they had decided, in the roll and tumble of events, that "the how and the man of our redemption had somehow met in the person of Abraham Lincoln."

But perhaps it was Lincoln himself who best summed up his journey to emancipation — his own as well as that of the slaves. In December 1862, after the calamitous by-elections of that year, in the midst of rising racial protest against his emancipation policy, Lincoln asked Congress — and Northern whites beyond — for their support. "The dogmas of the quiet past," he reminded them, "are inadequate to the stormy present. The occasion is piled high with difficulty, and we must rise with the occasion. As our case is new, so we must think anew, and act anew. We must disenthrall our selves, and then we shall save our country.

"Fellow-citizens, *we* cannot escape history. . . . The fiery trial through which we pass, will light us down, in honor or dishonor, to the latest generation. . . . In *giving* freedom to the slave, we *assure* freedom to the *free* — honorable alike in what we give, and what we preserve. We shall nobly save, or meanly lose, the last best, hope of earth."

QUESTIONS TO CONSIDER

1   Most of us are familiar with the story of "Honest Abe" Lincoln, the unambitious rail-splitting man of the people. How does Oates's biographical portrait of Lincoln reveal the complex human being behind this mythical image?

2   How was Lincoln able to reconcile his reverence for the founders and the Constitution with the moral paradox of slavery in a free society? How did Lincoln hope to solve the problems of slavery and racial adjustment in America?

3   What was the so-called slave power conspiracy that Lincoln and many other Republicans feared by the late 1850s? How had the events of that crucial decade seemed to confirm their fears?

4   Oates says that the pressures and problems of fighting a civil war caused Lincoln to hurl an executive fist at slavery finally. What were the forces that led Lincoln to issue his Emancipation Proclamation?

5   Many of Lincoln's contemporaries as well as later scholars accused Lincoln of having made an empty gesture with the Emancipation Proclamation. How does Oates answer these accusations?

XIV

A Cruel War,
a Troubled Peace

28

How "the Lost Cause" Was Lost

HENRY STEELE COMMAGER

In early February 1861, delegates from six seceded states — South Carolina, Florida, Georgia, Alabama, Mississippi, and Louisiana (Texas delegates joined them later) — gathered in Montgomery, Alabama, and there established the southern Confederacy. The delegates not only wrote a constitution that guaranteed slavery and affirmed states' rights, but unanimously selected gaunt, aloof Jefferson Davis of Mississippi and Alexander H. Stephens of Georgia as the Confederate president and vice president respectively. Later, in a speech in Savannah, Stephens made it unmistakable clear what the Confederacy stood for; "Our new government is founded upon exactly the opposite idea [from that of equality in the Declaration of Independence]; its foundations are laid, its cornerstone rests, upon the great truth that the negro is not equal to the white man; that slavery — subordination to the superior race — is his natural and normal condition. This, our new government, is the first in the history of the world based upon this great physical, philosophical, and moral truth."

After the Confederates bombarded Fort Sumter and Lincoln called for 75,000 volunteers to suppress the rebellion, four border slave states — Virginia, North Carolina, Tennessee, and Arkansas — also seceded and joined the Confederacy. The Confederates transferred their capital to Richmond, which had better facilities for a national government than did Montgomery. Richmond was also the home of the Tredegar Iron Works, the only concern in the rebel South capable of producing heavy weapons.

From the outset, the Confederacy was beset with internal problems: she lacked sound money, guns, factories, food, railroads, and harmonious political leadership.

Still, with her excellent generals, the possibility of foreign intervention, and other advantages, the Confederacy faced better odds in her war for independence than had the American colonies. Why, then, did the Confederacy go down to defeat? Henry Steele Commager, one of America's greatest historians, contends that the rebel states never became a nation at all, that they were unable, with their inept political leadership and a Confederate constitution that guaranteed states' rights, to create truly viable national institutions. But more than anything else, Commager states, a failure of morality led to the Confederacy's ultimate defeat.

LOOKING BACK NOW THROUGH THE MISTS OF 100 years at the prodigious story of Gettysburg and Vicksburg, we are lost in admiration for the gallantry of those who led the ranks of gray in what we have come to call "the Lost Cause." And we know just when it was lost. It was lost in those fateful days of July, 1863, when Lee's bold thrust into Pennsylvania, which was to have threatened the capital and brought recognition of the Confederacy from Britain and France, was blunted and turned back, and when Vicksburg fell and the Father of Waters went again unvexed to the sea. It was high tide and ebb tide; it was the beginning of the end.

So, at least, most of us suppose. As we contemplate the fall of the Confederacy, we conclude that it was indeed inevitable and that the Confederacy was but a dream:

> Woe! woe! is us, how strange and sad,
> That all our glorious visions fled,
> Have left us nothing real but our dead,
> In the land where we were dreaming.

From "How 'the Lost Cause' Was Lost" by Henry Steele Commager, *New York Times,* August 4, 1963. © 1963 by The New York Times Company. Reprinted by permission.

To most of us it is inconceivable that the Civil War should have had any outcome but that registered at Appomattox. It is inconceivable that the territory which now constitutes the United States should have been fragmented — like that of Latin America — into 20 states. It is inconceivable that the Confederacy should have made good its bid for independent nationhood.

But the doctrine of inevitability confronts us with two insuperable difficulties. If it was clear from the beginning that the South must lose, how can we explain the fact that men like Jefferson Davis, Judah P. Benjamin, R. B. Rhett, Howell Cobb and scores of others, men who were upright, virtuous, intelligent and humane, were prepared to lead their people to certain destruction? If defeat was inevitable, they must have discerned this, too, and their conduct takes on the character of criminal imbecility. And second, how can we explain the widespread assumption in Europe — and even in parts of the North — that the South would make good her bid for independence? How does it happen that so many otherwise sensible and judicious men were misled?

It is not too much to say that the South held — or appeared to hold — at least two trump cards in 1861. The first was what we would now call grand strategy or ultimate war aims. For the fact is that the Confederacy did not need to win in order to

Unidentified Confederate and friends. When the Civil War began, young southern volunteers like this one rushed to enlist in the Confederate army. The war began as a ninety-day lark for both sides, only to swell into a holocaust of destruction that left few families in either section unscathed. (Collection of Larry Williford)

win; it was enough if she held the field long enough to weary the North with the war. But the North, in order to win, had to conquer the South, had to invade and hold an area as great as Western Europe minus Italy and Scandinavia — an achievement as yet without parallel in modern history. The Confederacy could afford to lose all the battles and all the campaigns if only she could persuade the North that the price of victory was too high. The South asked merely to be left alone, and she proposed to make the war so costly that the North would in the end prefer to leave her alone. After all, the American colonies, and the United Netherlands, had won their independence against even heavier odds than those which faced the Confederacy.

And this suggests the second trump card: foreign intervention. The leaders of the Confederacy had read well the history of the American Revolution, or had heard it from their fathers and their grandfathers — for the Virginians of 1860 were psychologically closer to the generation of Washington then were the Yankees of Massachusetts to the generation of Sam Adams. They knew that the intervention of France and then of other European nations had turned the tide in favor of the Americans, and they assumed that history would repeat itself. They counted with confidence on the intervention of Britain and France — intervention at a practical level on behalf of cotton, intervention at a higher level on behalf of freedom and self-determination.

Quite aside from these two major strategic considerations, the South held other advantages. She commanded interior lines and therefore the ability to shift her smaller forces rapidly from one front to another. She fought on the defensive, and that position (so it was thought) more than made up for her numerical inferiority, since offensive operations, with their implacable demands of transportation, supply and occupation, required a great superiority than she felt the Union forces could muster. She had a long and deeply indented coastline, one which presented almost insuperable obstacles to a successful blockade — and, after all, the Union Navy was not above contempt. She had, in her 3,000,000 Negro slaves, a large and, on the whole, loyal labor force which might relieve Southern whites of many civilian duties and permit them to fight in the ranks. She had, at the beginning, the best generals and a long military tradition. And she boasted — mistakenly as it proved — a broader and deeper unity than the heterogeneous North.

With all these advantages, why did the South lose? Since 1865, students and historians have speculated about this question but no one has answered it. Curiously enough, the leaders of the Lost Cause had little to say about the reasons for defeat. The greatest of them, R. E. Lee, preserved a dignified silence after Appomattox. President Davis wrote two ponderous volumes but they say nothing about the underlying causes of defeat except to blame his political enemies. Vice President Stephens also produced two unreadable volumes on the Confederacy and the war but failed conspicuously to speculate on the question (in his case, speculation might have proved too embarrassing). Judah P. Benjamin, the most philosophical mind in the Confederate Government, might have given us a really penetrating analysis of the problem, but he chose to forget his American past in a more glamorous English present.

Nor do the lesser figures help us much. The literature is voluminous but mostly elegiac and almost all of it is unreflective. Perhaps the Southerner of that generation was, as Henry Adams wrote of his classmate Rooney Lee, by nature unreflective: "Strictly," said Adams, "the Southerner had no mind; he had temperament. He was not a scholar, he had no intellectual training, he could not analyze an idea, and he could not even conceive of admitting two."

Or, more probably, reflection on the responsibility for so great a catastrophe was simply too uncomfortable. And as for the Northerners, by and large they were content with victory, or with easy assumptions about their superiority in arms and in men, or the righteousness of their cause, or the wickedness of the South, or the preference of Providence for the Union.

Why *did* the South lose? Was it because the Confederacy was hopelessly outnumbered? Until 1864, it was able to put almost as many soldiers into battle as the Union — in fact, the South had a numerical superiority at First Bull Run, Pea Ridge, Gaines's Mill, Seven Days, Corinth, Chickamauga, Peach Tree Creek and Atlanta. Was it for reasons of finance? Lack of money had not prevented the Americans from making good their bid for independence. (And besides, a financial explanation merely begs another question: *Why* did the Confederacy lack money?) Was it due to poor transportation? The South had a much smaller railroad mileage than the North, but she enjoyed interior lines and the advantage of a system of inland waterways. Southern transportation facilities were not, in fact, inadequate in themselves — or at least not irremediably inadequate. The real question is, why did the South fail to use what she had or to develop what she needed?

Was defeat atrributable to the failure of the Confederacy to win the border states — Maryland, Kentucky, Missouri? These were, after all, slave states and Southern in culture and social structure. There was every reason to suppose that they would throw in their lot with the South.

> Come! For thy shield is bright and strong,
> Come! for thy dalliance does these wrong,
> Maryland, my Maryland.

But she did not come, nor did the other border states — though Kentucky and Missouri were represented in the Confederate Congress! Why not? Was it lack of military skill or political prescience, or simply bad luck? Why did this calculation — like so many others — go wrong?

Or was the underlying fault, perhaps, in Jefferson Davis — so brittle, so temperamental, so arrogant? He took the conduct of the war into his own hands; he interfered with the military; he had favorites (like the wretched Braxton Bragg) and enemies (like the brilliant Joseph Johnston). He alienated state Governors and Congressmen and he never won the affections of the Southern people. Yet on balance Davis emerges as a reasonably good President — probably as good as any the Confederacy could have selected at that time. He was tireless, high-minded, courageous, intelligent, indomitable and more often right on major issues than his critics. The real question is why there were so few alternatives to Jefferson Davis.

Or was the South beaten by the blockade? This is perhaps the favorite of all explanations, for ever since Mahan, seapower has been the glamorous key to history. But at the beginning of the war, the North had only an excuse for a navy; not until 1863

was the blockade effective. Why did not the Confederacy bring in whatever she needed before that time? Why did she not utilize her swift privateers to the best advantage? And, why for that matter, were Britain and France willing to respect what was, for a long time, a mere paper blockade? If Cotton was King, why did Europeans refuse to recognize its sovereignty? If Cotton was *not* King, why did Southerners so delude themselves?

When we have considered, and dismissed, these surface reasons for the failure of the Confederacy, we come to more fundamental causes. Three of these, all interrelated, command our attention.

The first was the failure of Southern nationalism. Almost all the ingredients of nationalism were there — indeed, the Confederacy in 1860 had more of the ingredients of nationalism than the Colonies in 1775 — but somehow the Confederacy never really became a nation. For all its passionate devotion to Dixie Land, it seemed to lack a sense of nationalism and the will to nationalism. Given the circumstances of its birth, this is not surprising. The Southern states had broken away from the old Union beause the Federal Government — so they alleged — threatened their rights, and they defiantly founded their new nation on states' rights and state sovereignty. The new nation was therefore based on a repudiation of nationalism.

Even its political institutions reflected this, perhaps unconsciously. Military leadership in the South was splendid, but political leadership was weak and vacillating. The Confederacy had its Lee and its Jackson to match — perhaps to outmatch — Grant and Sherman, but where was its Lincoln? Where for that matter were its Seward, its Stanton, its Stevens, its Sumner, its Trumbull; its diplomats like Charles Francis Adams; its war Governors like Andrew of Massachusetts or Morton of Indiana? There were local factions but no political parties, and therefore no safety valve for political discontent. There were strong state supreme courts, but not-

Some 360,000 Northerners and 258,000 Southerners perished in the Civil War. Here is a photograph of a dead Confederate *soldier; he was killed in one of the last assaults against Petersburg in 1865. (Library of Congress)*

withstanding the provision of the Confederate constitution, Congress never created a Confederate Supreme Court.

State sovereignty is not necessarily fatal to nationalism or to union in time of peace and order, when no grave problems confront a government and no stern crises challenge the people. Had the North permitted the "wayward sisters to depart in peace," the Confederacy might have survived long enough to develop the essential institutions, political habits and administrative practices. But to build a nation on state sovereignty in time of war is to build upon a foundation of quicksand.

The second fundamental cause of failure was, in fact, this very issue of states' rights, which steadily eroded the strength of the Confederacy. State Representatives at Richmond devoted their energies to thwarting Jefferson Davis. Vice President Stephens retired to his Georgia home to wage relentless war on the President. State supreme courts nullified Confederate laws, and there was, as we have seen, no Confederate Supreme Court to which to appeal. States put their own interests ahead of the interests of the embryo nation. Even in the first year of the war, the states jealously held on to their arms and supplies. Had they surrendered them to the Confederacy at the begininng of the war, it could have put 600,000 men into the field instead of 400,000, and that might have made all the difference.

State Governors like Brown of Georgia and Vance of North Carolina exempted thousands of their citizens from conscription and their judges protected deserters and refugees from capture and restoration to the ranks of the Confederate armies. The Governor of Mississippi exempted over 4,500 militia officers and others in his state from the operation of the conscription laws, and the Governor of Alabama almost the same number.

All through the war, state Governors withheld desperately needed supplies. Thus Brown of Georgia not only kept his Georgia troops well supplied with uniforms and blankets but had a surplus in his warehouses — sufficient to have outfitted the whole of Lee's army — and kept it there! At a time when ''Lee's Miserables'' were going barefoot and freezing in the terrible trenches of Petersburg, Governor Vance of North Carolina had 5,000 complete uniforms and an equal quantity of shoes and blankets in his warehouses — and kept them there!

States' rights, instead of being the rock on which the nation was built, was the reef on which the nation foundered. There is a moral here, even for our own time.

The third fundamental cause of Southern defeat was slavery itself — that ''peculiar institution,'' as the South euphemistically called it. It was slavery that the war was ultimately about; it was slavery that ultimately doomed the South to defeat. For it was slavery that decisively prevented the one move which might have saved the South, even after Vicksburg and Gettysburg — European intervention. As late as 1863, British aristocrats — a Cecil, a Halifax, a Gregory, a Lindsay, a Vansittart — organized the Southern Independence Association which dedicated itself to intervention. It was in the summer of 1863 that the British navy yards were building the fa-

mous Laird rams that almost got away — almost, but not quite!

Had Britain intervened to break the blockade — and France would have followed her lead, and Mexico, of course — there is every likelihood that the Confederacy would have won her independence. With Britain ready to provide the Confederacy with money, arms, munitions, food and drugs, and ready to buy her cotton and other produce, the Confederacy could have fought on indefinitely, just as the Americans did once they had supplies and money from France after 1777. And had the Union Government responded to such intervention by a declaration of war — as it almost certainly would have done — it would probably have signed its own death warrant.

What prevented intervention from abroad? Not the failure of the South on the battlefield, for that failure was not decisive until after the midsummer of 1863. And it was not sympathy for the Government of the Union, for there was very little of that in the ruling circles of Britain or France. No, more than anything else, it was slavery. The upper classes might be sympathetic to the Confederacy, but the powerful middle and working classes were passionately on the side of the North. It was not merely that the North represented democracy — although that was a consideration; it was, far more, that the South represented slavery. Public opinion, that newly emerging and still amorphous thing, simply would not tolerate going in on the side of slavery.

But, it will be asked, why did not the South see what we now see? Why did not Southerners see the necessity of a strong national government in time of war and create one? Why did they not see the pernicious consequences of states' rights in time of crisis and restrict them? Why did they not see the blight of slavery and move against it, move to win public opinion abroad by some dramatic gesture of gradual emancipation?

Here we come to something very fundamental, indeed — to the psychology, the philosophy associated — perhaps inevitably associated — with slavery.

Slavery was the foundation of the South, and slavery carried with it the enslavement of the mind of a people. For 30 years the South had felt herself misunderstood, condemned and beleaguered. For 30 years she had rallied her resources to defend the "peculiar institution," and she had finally convinced herself that slavery was not a necessary evil but a positive good, not a curse but a blessing. She realized, however, that she was almost alone in this opinion and, feeling herself increasingly isolated, she withdrew into her own intellectual and moral fortress.

Whoever criticized slavery in the South was an enemy of society, a traitor to the Southern way of life. Preachers who questioned slavery from their pulpits were deprived of their churches; teachers who criticized slavery were driven out of the colleges and universities; editors who dared raise their voices against slavery saw their presses destroyed. If the United States mails carried abolition or anti-slavery literature, the mails were rifled, the pernicious literature burned. Libraries were purged of offensive books — even Hinton Helper's "The Impending Crisis of the South" was publicly burned. The whole South, in short, closed ranks to defend and exalt the "peculiar institution."

Now when you prevent the free discussion of the greatest of public issues, you prevent the discussion of almost all issues. When you drive out critics, you leave behind the noncritics. When you silence dissent, you assure only approval. When you intimidate criticism, you discourage the habit of critical inquiry. When you stop agitation, you guarantee complacency. We have learned in our own time the price that a society pays when it intimidates the liberal mind, when it silences criticism.

The habit of independent inquiry and criticism all but disappeared in the South of the eighteen-fifties and sixties. There was no real discussion of slavery, and because there was no discussion there was no probing of alternatives. There was no real debate over secession — at least, not on the principles at stake. As Southern political thought had gone slowly bankrupt after Calhoun, so Southern political discussion went bankrupt — in the Confederate Congress and in the newspapers of the Confederacy. There were a few bold spirits who questioned secession; there were some who doubted the ability of the South to win a war against the North; there were some who saw that slavery would become the Achilles' heel of the Confederacy. But there was no discussion of real issues, as in the North, and no statesman to lead the people out of the labyrinth in which they found themselves and on to a high plateau from which they could see their life and their society in perspective.

There is, perhaps, a certain poetic justice in all this. The Confederacy, which was founded on state sovereignty, was destroyed by state sovereignty. The Confederacy, which was founded on slavery, was destroyed by the state of mind which slavery imposed upon its other victims — the white people of the South. The failure of the Confederacy was ultimately a monument not to a failure of resolution or courage or will, but of intelligence and morality.

Questions to Consider

1   Many historians, weighing the material and numerical advantages of the North, have concluded that Confederate defeat was inevitable. According to Commager, what advantages did the Confederacy have at the start of the Civil War that could have offset northern economic might and superior numbers?

2   How much did poor political leadersip contribute to the defeat of the Confederacy?

3 How was it that the Confederacy was defeated, according to Commager, by the very causes for which it fought?

4 At the outset of the Civil War, Europeans generally believed that the Confederacy would win its independence. How, then, can you explain Europe's refusal to intervene militarily on the Confederate side?

5 What does Commager mean when he argues that the Confederacy was "destroyed by the state of mind which slavery imposed upon . . . the white people of the South"? Is Commager implying that the South lost the Civil War because it defended an immoral institution?

29

"Boys, War Is Hell"

STEPHEN E. AMBROSE

Thanks to conflicting political factions and pressure groups, it was extremely difficult for the Union to apply its enormous numerical and material superiority against Confederate armies. This, along with incompetent Union generalship and a deadlock on the battlefronts during the first two years, explains why the North took so long to defeat a divided and troubled South. Not until July 1863, with simultaneous Union victories at Gettysburg and Vicksburg, did the North at last seem able to utilize its superior strength. The Vicksburg campaign, moreover, made Union leaders aware of a new style of fighting that might break the military deadlock on the battlefields.

During the Vicksburg operations, General Ulysses S. Grant threw military theory to the winds, broke off from his supply base, and campaigned south of the rebel river garrison, subsisting etirely off the country and thus maximizing his freedom of movement. William Tecumseh Sherman, one of Grant's corps commanders, especially grasped the significance of Grant's style of fighting. But even more than Grant, Sherman realized that modern wars were won not simply by fighting enemy armies but by destroying the very ability of the enemy to wage war — that is, by wrecking railroads, burning fields, and destroying other economic resources. To southerners, he was a modern Attila the Hun; to many historians, a manic-depressive psychotic. In this reassessment of Sherman, Stephen E. Ambrose avoids emotion-charged labels and introduces us to a complex, brilliant, often erratic man who more than any other Civil War general understood the nature of modern warfare.

"GENERAL WILLIAM T. SHERMAN INSANE," the headline read. The *Cincinnati Commercial* of December 11, 1861, reported that the "late commander of the Department of the Cumberland is insane. It appears that he was at the time while commanding in Kentucky, stark mad." Details followed: Sherman overestimated the strength of the Rebels, underestimated his own, and gave preposterous orders. The Secretary of War had removed him from Kentucky and sent him to Missouri in a subordinate position in which he could presumably get a complete rest. While in Missouri he had once again panicked over supposed Confederate movements and ordered perfectly secure troops to fall back. His commander, Henry W. Halleck, at Mrs. Sherman's request, sent him home for a twenty-day leave.

In both Kentucky and Missouri Sherman had shown traits of extreme agitation and general nervousness highlighted by fits of depression and moments of exhilaration. When he returned home to Ohio he sat by the window and stared out into the street. He confessed to a neighbor who came to visit, "Sometimes I felt crazy in Kentucky: I couldn't get one word from Washington." He told his brother, U.S. Senator John Sherman, that he would have killed himself had it not been for his children.

Sherman's wife Ellen wrote John, "If there were no kind of insanity in your family and if his feelings were not already in a marked state, I would feel less concern about him . . ." but she was worried because of "that melancholy insanity to which your family is subject." Halleck, who was an old Army friend of Sherman's, did his best to reassure the family, but even Halleck thought Sherman "acted crazy." Still, when the twenty days ended, Halleck brought Sherman back. By giving him gradually increasing responsibilities (beginning with drilling recruits) Halleck nursed him back to health.

Through the remainder of his life Sherman exhibited the same tendency of high and low emotional levels, but never again did he have anything like a breakdown serious enough to lead to public charges of insanity. Once was enough, however, and historians borrowing from clinical concepts have diagnosed Sherman as a manic-depressive psychotic. This is an illness marked, in the manic phase, by rapid movement, little or no sleep, extreme self-confidence, an outburst of talk which often jumps from one subject to another without any real transition, and the making of grandiose schemes that are abandoned before they are finished. In the depressive stage the patient blames himself for all the ills around him, feels hopeless, is slow of movement and speech, and is suicidal. The two stages alternate, with one sometimes immediately following the other; each stage can last from a few days to many months.

Descriptions of Sherman by his contemporaries reinforce the manic-depressive diagnosis. While in Kentucky he would work until 3 A.M., then go to his hotel. He never seemed to sleep. "He lived at the Galt House on the ground floor," a reporter noted, "and he paced the corridor outside his rooms for hours, absorbed. The guests whispered about him and the gossip was that he was insane." A war correspondent in Missouri said "his eye had a half-wild expression. . . . He looks rather like an anxious man of business than an ideal soldier, suggesting the exchange and not the camp. Sometimes he works for twenty consecutive hours. He sleeps little; . . . indifferent to dress and to fare, he can live on hard bread and water and fancies any one else can do so." Another reporter said he "walked, talked or laughed all over. He perspired thought at every pore."

From "William T. Sherman" by Stephen E. Ambrose in *American History Illustrated,* January 1967. Reprinted by permission of *American History Illustrated.*

An officer who called on Sherman later in the war was fascinated. "If I were to write a dozen pages I could not tell you a tenth part of what he said, for he talked incessantly and more rapidly than any man I ever saw. General Sherman is the most American man I ever saw, tall and lank, with hair like thatch, which he rubs up with his hands. . . . It would be easier to say what he did not talk about than what he did. . . . At his departure I felt it a relief and experienced almost an exhaustion after the excitement of his vigorous presence."

The evidence, while impressive, is misleading. Sherman was all the things observers said he was. He was given to moods, and extreme ones at that. He did at one time contemplate suicide. His actions in late 1861 had little relation to reality. But the key to Sherman's character, and to his successes, cannot be found in clinical jargon. Those historians who try to apply psychiatric findings to this great general do not help us in our understanding of him or his contribution. He was not manic-depressive. He was Sherman, unique unto himself.

Sherman was the sixth child and third son of Charles Robert Sherman, a judge on the Ohio State Supreme Court. He had a happy childhood, with many playmates — he had ten brothers and sisters. His nickname, "Cump," stuck with him his entire life. He had red hair, a source of embarrassment, which he once dyed. It came out green and he left it alone thereafter.

When Cump was 9 his father died. A friend and neighbor, U.S. Senator Thomas Ewing, brought Cump into his home and he grew up there. In 1836 Ewing secured an appointment to West Point for the boy. Sherman, who had a sound education, did well at the Academy, graduating sixth in his class. His subsequent Army career was dull and routine. In 1850, after a seven-year engagement, he married Senator Ewing's daughter, Ellen. Three years later he resigned from the Army to become a partner in a branch bank in San Francisco.

In 1854, although banks all over the country were failing, Sherman's shrewd foresight and good management kept a run on his bank from occurring, and it weathered the storm. Sherman had, however, accepted $130,000 from old Army friends to invest for them; because of the depression he lost some $13,000. Although not obligated to do so, he personally repaid the money, considering it a debt of honor. This wiped out his savings.

Sherman unsuccessfully tried to get back into the Army. Then, having read law on his own, he formed a law partnership in Leavenworth, Kansas, with two of the Ewing boys. He lost his only case, again tried to get back into the Army, again failed, and finally applied for the superintendency of a new military college in Alexandria, Louisiana (now Louisiana State University). He got the post, and from October 1859 until January 1861, he was both happy and conspicuously successful.

Then Louisiana left the Union and Sherman, after resigning and refusing an offer of a commission in the [Confederate Army], went to St. Louis to work for a streetcar line.

This was a bitter and trying time for Sherman. At each of the positions he had held he had shown qualities of honesty, hard work, and ability, but at each one either he or the enterprise had failed. Time and again he had been forced to accept the hospitality of the Ewings; time and again he had had to tell his brother-in-law politely but firmly that he would not accept the sinecure of the management of the Ewing salt-works in Ohio.

Still, he was at the height of his powers. Forty-one years old, he was in excellent physical condition. He was indifferent to his dress, but he stood straight, was lean in features and build, and had the quick and sure movements that denoted good muscle tone. He smoked cigars incessantly, talked rapidly, and thought constantly. His mind was alive with plans, ideas, hopes. He had a military education and some experience; perhaps the war would give him his opportunity.

Sherman stayed only a short time in St. Louis. He had never had any doubts about fighting for the Union cause. He was pro-slavery, would always be something of a Negrophobe, and he had learned in Louisiana to love the South. But he loved the Union more. From Senator Ewing he had learned of its glories, and he followed the Senator into the Webster branch of the Federalist-Whig camp. Sherman was mystical about the flag and he valued order above all else. He was furious with the South for breaking up the nation. He thought the Confederacy ought to be punished severely for opening the way to chaos.

Sherman, like so many other West Pointers who had been out of the Army, went to Washington to offer his services. At this time most of his colleagues were joining the Volunteers. McClellan, Grant, Halleck, and the others who did so were not making the offer because of any high admiration for state-controlled volunteers — nearly all Academy men were contemptuous of these untrained troops — but because with the Volunteer Corps they could receive high rank immediately. The Federal Government was making only a slight increase in the Regular Army, and most of the positions in that Army were already filled. In any case the Regular Army was still so small that it needed only a few officers of general rank. Sherman, however, could not so easily overcome his aversion to Volunteers, and he decided to try for a Regular commission. It would be at a lower rank, but he would command better troops. Some historians have seen in this decision a neurotic tendency to avoid responsibility, or have claimed that Sherman had serious doubts about his own ability. Events showed, however, that Sher-

man's decision, and later ones like it, was — whatever the motive — a wise one.

In May 1861, Sherman arrived in Washington, where along with other former West Pointers he reported to Lincoln in person. The President told the men to ask for whatever positions they wanted. Sherman requested and received a colonelcy in one of the ten new regiments of Regulars that Congress had formed.

Leaving the White House, Sherman ran into an old West Point friend, Irvin McDowell, who was wearing the uniform of a brigadier general.

"Hello, Sherman," said McDowell, "What did you ask for?"

"A colonelcy."

"What?" exclaimed McDowell. "You should have asked for a brigadier general's rank. You're just as fit for it as I am."

"I know it," snapped Sherman. Then he went off to meet and train his Regulars.

In the first big battle, Bull Run, Sherman and his men were the only Union forces who acquitted themselves well. When the general retreat began he formed his regiment into a hollow square and covered the fleeing troops.

Later, feeling that every officer connected with the battle ought to be discharged — himself included — Sherman grew bitter and wild. "Nobody, no man can save the country," he told his wife. His agitation showed in other ways. One morning while he was riding by a camp site an officer called out to him. "Colonel, I'm going to New York today; what can I do for you?" Sherman said he did not remember signing a pass. The officer answered, "I need no leave. My time is up and I'm going."

Sherman looked at the man for a full minute, then quietly declared, "I will shoot you like a dog."

That afternoon Lincoln came to inspect the regiment. He gave a short speech; when he finished the officer stood up and declared, "Mr. President, I have a cause for grievance. This morning I went to speak to Colonel Sherman and he threatened to shoot me." Lincoln looked down, rubbed his chin, and repeated gravely, "Threatened to shoot you?" Then the President glanced at Sherman, who sat quietly on the front seat of a carriage and stared straight ahead. Bending over, Lincoln looked directly at the officer and loudly whispered, "Well, if I were you and he threatened to shoot, I wouldn't trust him, for I believe he would do it."

A month after Bull Run the President promoted Sherman to brigadier general and told him to go to Kentucky as second in command to General Robert Anderson. Sherman extracted a promise from Lincoln that under no circumstances would he be asked to replace Anderson, explaining that he was not ready for such an important post. He was right; the point he missed was that no other Union officer was ready either. But those who escaped high command in the first two years of the war, when the Northern public clamored for action before the troops were trained, were the lucky ones. Not a single Union officer who held an important post during the first half of the war held a significant position at the end.

Shortly after Sherman arrived in Kentucky, however, Anderson resigned. Over his violent protests Sherman took command of the Department of the Cumberland. He was plagued by problems common to commanders on both sides at this stage of the war. His troops were untrained, and he had no officers capable of giving them proper training. The men were poorly clad and armed, but his supply service was unable to meet their needs. He had no intelligence service, and he consistently exaggerated the enemy's force. The War Department, the President, and the public wanted a grand advance southward, but his troops were simply not prepared to fight. Even though his brother John had just begun his distinguished career as senator, Sherman abhorred politicians — the corollary to which was that

he had no political sense. The political situation was cloudy — even a master politician like Lincoln could not be sure which way Kentucky was headed. Sherman's estimate, however — that Kentucky was overwhelmingly secessionist — was far off the mark.

Sherman, refusing to launch an offensive in response to the clamor of the press and public, pulled back his troops. He was, in a way, like McClellan — he refused to sacrifice the men he was training. Sherman was a sensitive man (a secret ambition was to be a painter) who shrank from the thought of bloodshed. Neither in Kentucky, nor at any time later (except, possibly, at Kenesaw Mountain), did he fight a bloody battle. Sherman was the only important commander on either side in the Civil War who never subjected his men to a blood-bath.

The reporters were displeased. Their mood changed to one of anger when Sherman imposed censorship upon them. The General argued that their reports conveyed valuable information to the Confederates (they did); the reporters contended that the sacred principle of freedom of the press was in jeopardy. The press struck back with its strongest weapon — ridicule. Newspaper columns ignored his very real problems and concentrated on his more erratic behavior and statements.

In October, Secretary of War Simon Cameron came to visit Sherman. The general was delighted. He had been sending daily telegrams to Washington pleading for more of everything and not even receiving an answer. Now he could state his case to the head of the War Department, actually show him what the problems were, and thus get results.

Cameron arrived, accompanied by some reporters. He retired to his hotel room, ordered food and liquor, and then called Sherman in. The general found the secretary stretched full length on his bed. Cameron glanced up and declared, "Now, General Sherman, tell us your troubles." Sherman objected to talking in front of strangers; Cameron said they were all friends. The general locked the door and, in great excitement, recited his woes. He could not get any reinforcements; the Confederates could take Louisville in a day's time if they chose; Kentucky was going to join the South.

"You astonish me!" Cameron exclaimed. Sherman pressed his point. To defend Kentucky he needed 60,000 men, and "for offense, before we are done, 200,000."

"Great God!" Cameron declared. "Where are they to come from?" (There would later be dispute about this conversation. If Sherman meant he needed 200,000 men to clear Kentucky, he was indeed insane. If he meant it would take 200,000 men to clear the Mississippi Valley, he had made one of the shrewdest predictions of the war. Sherman always contended he meant the latter. Major General Thomas J. Wood, who was present at the time, later agreed that Sherman had specified that 200,000 men would be needed to clear the Mississippi Valley.)

The two men talked a little longer. Cameron sent a telegram to Washington ordering 10,000 reinforcements to Kentucky, and Sherman left in an elated mood. He thought he had won the Secretary over to his side. In fact he had been betrayed to the newspaper reporters.

In the next few days the columns carried rumors about Sherman's insanity. Cameron meanwhile relieved him, sending Don Carlos Buell as his replacement. The *Cincinnati Commercial* congratulated Kentucky on escaping from "the peevishness, prejudice and persecution" of a man who "is a perfect monomaniac. . . ." Sherman's "favorite often proclaimed plan for the successful management of the war," the story continued, "is the suppression of every newspaper in the country — a theory which he advocates the more strongly since the comments of the press on his requisition of only 200,000 men."

Sherman went to Missouri to work for Henry Halleck. Halleck sent him on an inspection trip; Sherman misjudged Confederate strength and ordered the troops to fall back. Halleck countermanded the order and gave Sherman a furlough. The newspapers only proclaimed that he was insane.

But Sherman was no psychotic. He was an intensely emotional man who had a highly developed imagination. His quickness of mind, his ability to see in a flash all the possibilities, eventually led him to greatness — in 1861 it led him into serious errors of judgment. Perhaps the reason was that he loved his men so much. In 1861 he could not bear to sacrifice them; in 1864, in Georgia, he knew that they were ready and could do anything. His general mood in 1861 was one of depression and fear; given the way the North was conducting the war, these were appropriate feelings. In 1864 he was elated, for equally good reason.

Whatever the cause of his difficulties, Halleck's therapy worked, and Sherman was soon back in the field. He was, as commander at Cairo, Illinois, Grant's staunchest supporter during the Donelson campaign. Afterwards he took command of a corps in Grant's army and acquitted himself well at Shiloh. When Halleck assumed personal command of the army for the march to Corinth and Grant, disgruntled, muttered that he was going to resign, Sherman talked him out of it. Years later, half jokingly, Sherman remarked, "General Grant is a great general. I know him well. He stood by me when I was crazy and I stood by him when he was drunk; and now, sir, we stand by each other always."

With Grant, Sherman had found the rock upon which he could stand. For the next two years they operated together in perfect harmony. . . . Grant's qualities of determination, calm stability, and steadfastness complemented Sherman's more excitable and, let it be said, more intelligent nature. Sherman was well aware of Grant's effect on him; he analyzed it well in a letter to Grant. Sherman thought Grant's strongest feature was a "simple faith in success. . . . Also, when you have completed your best preparations you go into battle without hesitation . . . no doubts, no reserve; and I tell you that it was this that made me act with confidence."

General James Harrison Wilson served under both Grant and Sherman; to a friend Wilson once declared that "to say the least Sherman is *very erratic.* I don't believe him guilty of *vaulting ambition,* but I have never been entirely willing to trust his mental processes and special idiosyncrasies. Grant has a great moral breadth and stability, a reliable honesty, and certainty of character which make him the superior of all such men as Sherman however brilliant." What Wilson did not see was that men like Sherman, although usually dependent upon men like Grant and unable to operate effectively without them, are the men who take society forward. Brilliance is often erratic; it is also necessary to progress. Grant's great contribution to America was his dogged determination to see the war through, to preserve the Union. Sherman's contribution was to give the world a new way of looking at things, in his case military matters. Each man helped the other.

Together Grant and Sherman at Vicksburg returned the Mississippi River to the Union; at Chattanooga they opened the gateway to the heart of what remained of the Confederacy. Following these victories Grant in 1864 went east to assume the post of General in Chief while Sherman stayed in Chattanooga to direct the advance on Atlanta. For the first time since 1861, when he was in Kentucky, Sherman would operate alone in the field as senior commander.

This time there was no exaggeration, no doubts, no lack of grip on the situation. Sherman conducted a masterful campaign, maneuvering the enemy from position after position without sacrificing his men in bloody but fruitless frontal attacks. Confederate President Jefferson Davis, growing desperate, removed Joseph Johnston in favor of John Bell Hood. The new Rebel leader tried to defeat Sherman in a series of engagements around Atlanta, failed, and withdrew from Atlanta. Sherman followed Hood's army for a short time, then returned to Atlanta.

For a month and a half Sherman brooded over his next move. The obvious one was to follow Hood and destroy his army, but Sherman was not sure he could catch the Confederates. Beyond that, he was not sure he wanted to. Hood's force was no longer a major threat to anything; Sherman felt he could use his magnificent troops to a better purpose. He could, in short, burn Atlanta, then detach one corps back to Nashville to keep Hood out of Tennessee, and thus free the bulk of his army to make a new kind of war.

For three years Sherman had been thinking about the nature of war; now, in a blinding insight, his genius had come to grips with both the nature of modern warfare and the solution to its unique problem. "This war," he told Halleck, "differs from European wars in this particular; we are not only fighting hostile armies, but a hostile people, and must make old and young, rich and poor, feel the hard hand of war." What would in the next century be called the home front, Sherman saw, was at least as important as the fighing front.

Sherman realized, before anyone else, that the modern nation-state has tremendous staying power. Any nation that has the will to continue the battle can carry on. Only total war can break this will.

The real problem in modern war is not how to win battles, but how to destroy the enemy's will. One way to do this is to destroy his armies, but this is the most expensive possible approach. Advocates of air power since Billy Mitchell's day, and modern atomic strategists, have found a quicker way, but it works only at a fearful cost.

Sherman's solution was something approaching total war. He said he would make Georgia howl and he did. He decided to wage war on property — not, it must be said, on women and children (an advantage his method had over modern air doctrines). The women of Georgia, however, would help him, through their letters to soldiers in Lee's army in Virginia describing the destruction and chaos Sherman brought. A soldier in Sherman's army marching through Georgia expressed Sherman's intentions best when he lectured an indignant housewife from whom he had liberated some chickens. "You, in wild enthusiasm, urge young men to the battlefield where men are being killed by the thousand, while you stay at home and sing 'The Bonnie Blue Flag'; but you set up a howl when you see the Yankees down here getting your chickens. Many of your young men have told us that they are tired of war and would quit, but you women would shame them and drive them back."

William Tecumseh Sherman, apostle of total war. "We are not only fighting hostile armies, but a hostile people," Sherman argued in 1864, "and must make old and young, rich and poor, feel the hard hand of war." (Library of Congress)

Beyond the personal application of Northern power, Sherman wanted to show the entire South and the world that the Confederacy was a hollow shell. The result of seeing Union troops marching unimpeded through Georgia, he knew, would be a sense of helplessness; soldiers in Lee's army, planters in Mississippi, the ladies of Charleston would know that there was no hope for a nation that could not even resist, much less repel, a march through one of its most important states. Southerners could make excuses for and recover from the shock of the destruction of Hood's army — they could read news of such an event and keep their will to fight. For a march through Georgia there could be no excuse, and no recovery of spirits.

Sherman proposed to make war, not on the South's armies, but on its will to resist.

He broached the idea to Grant, who did not like it. Grant questioned the idea of ignoring Hood and at first did not see the potential in Sherman's plan. Still, Cump won his friend over, and made his preparations.

On November 15, 1864, Sherman and 62,000 men marched out of Atlanta, destination unknown. Sherman kept his plans so secret that Chief of Staff Halleck had to create two supply depots for him when he reached the sea, one on the Gulf of Mexico and the other on the Atlantic coast. Even Lincoln did not know where Sherman was going. John Sherman asked the President one evening if it were true that no one knew where Cump was headed. "Oh, no," answered Lincoln. "I know the hole he went in at, but I can't tell you what hole he will come out of.''

The British *Army and Navy Gazette,* more perceptive than most professional journals, stated, "If Sherman has really left his army in the air and started off without a base to march from Georgia to South Carolina, he had done either one of the most brilliant or one of the most foolish things ever performed by a military leader. . . . The date on which he goes and the plan on which he acts must really place him among the great generals or the very little ones.''

The march itself has often been described; it is now part of America's folklore. After it was over Sherman summarized for Lincoln the damage he had done. "I estimate one hundred million dollars, at least twenty millions of which has inured to our advantage, and the remainder is simple waste and destruction.'' He then justified himself. "This may seem a hard species of warfare, but it brings the sad realities of war home to those who have been directly or indirectly instrumental in involving us in its attendant calamities.'' All later Southern charges to the contrary, Sherman was no war criminal. What he was doing was new, to be sure, but it was designed to end the war in the quickest and least bloody manner possible. Years later Sherman put the whole matter in proper perspective. "The South should not complain,'' he declared, "because they deliberetely put their slaves in the balance and lost them. They bet on the wrong card and lost.''

After reaching the Atlantic coast at Savannah, Sherman rested his army — weary from marching, not fighting — and then set out for the Carolinas. The men burned and looted. The Confederates mounted feeble efforts at resistance, but the Confederacy was doomed. Sherman was destroying its will to resist. Nothing illustrates this better, or describes the effect of Sherman's army on the South more succinctly, than a letter one of Sherman's soldiers picked up from a dead Confederate in North Carolina. "deer sister Lizy: i hev conkludid that the dam fulishness uv trying to lick shurmin had better be stoped. we have ben gettin nuthin, but hell & lots uv it ever sinse we saw the dam yanks & i am tirde uv it. shurmin has a lots of pimps that dont car a dam what they doo. and its no use trying to whip em. . . . if i cood git home ide tri dam hard to git thare. my old horse is plaid out or ide trie to go now. maibee ile start to nite fur ime dam tired uv this war fur nothing. if the dam yankees Havent got thair yit its a dam wunder. Thair thicker an lise on a hen and a dam site ornraier. your brother jim.''

When the Confederate forces facing him surrendered in North Carolina, Sherman demonstrated that he had neither lost his love for the South nor become a victim of war psychosis. On the assumption that Southerners were ready to resume their place in the Union, Sherman gave very generous peace terms, allowing the South to resume self-government under its old leaders although he had no such authority.

It has been said that if Lincoln had not been assassinated and Sherman's terms allowed to go into effect, there would have been no Reconstruction. This is nonsense. Sherman's terms were not farseeing; in giving them he was making a serious political error, one equal in magnitude to his 1861 judgment of Kentucky's intentions. Sherman was trying, in his own way, to deny any meaning, beyond the preservation of the Union, to the war. In 1863 that may have been possible; in 1865 the North demanded, almost unanimously, that the South be punished. Further, a significant proportion of the population — perhaps even a majority — wanted some safeguards for the Negro. There was never any possibility, even had Lincoln lived, that Sherman's terms would have gone into effect.

The "hard hand of war" left Columbia, South Carolina, in ruins. After cutting a swath of destruction through Georgia, Sherman's army stormed into South Carolina with a vengeance, for South Carolina had been the first state to secede, and the war had begun there with the firing on Fort Sumter in Charleston harbor. Sherman's relentless columns wrecked the state, tearing up railroads, destroying cotton gins, burning fields and barns, killing livestock, wiping out everything that might sustain dwindling Confederate forces. Columbia, the state capital, went up in an inferno of smoke, the conflagration started either by Confederates or by Union troops. "South Carolina may have been the cause of the whole thing," said a Union officer, "but she has had an awful punishment." (National Archives)

After this venture into politics Sherman avoided that field. During Reconstruction he concentrated on the Army (he became General in Chief in 1868), trying to protect it from Congress, prepare it for Indian wars, and keep it out of Reconstruction politics. Occasionally he commented, privately, on the course of Reconstruction. When he did he displayed his usual lack of political sense, his penchant for trying to solve political problems by ignoring them. "If all hands would stop talking and writing," he declared, "and let the sun shine and the rains fall for two or three years, we would be nearer reconstruction than we are likely to be with the three and four hundred statesmen trying to legislate amid the prejudices begotten for four centuries." Sherman became so disgusted with politicians that he moved his headquarters out of Washington to St. Louis.

He was often spoken of for the Presidency, at first by Democrats who wanted to run him against Grant, later by Republicans who wanted to cash in on his popularity as they had on Grant's. Unable to believe Sherman meant his constant denials of desire for the office, politicians again and again spoke of drafting him. Sherman's reply was always the same: "If nominated I will not run, if elected I will not serve."

As the years went by, Sherman became more and more a testy old general, beloved for his pungent statements to the press on politicians, always looking for opportunities to defend the Army's honor and virtue, the man who more than any other American recalled to millions the glorious days of 1861–1865. He himself loved best to get together with his boys, to hear them shout for "Uncle Billy." The boys were all old men now, but when the Grand Army of the Republic held its encampments they showed up ready to follow Uncle Billy once again through Georgia or anywhere else he might choose to lead them.

Sherman must have spoken to at least a thousand veterans' reunions. He always talked directly to the men, knowing that they would understand him even if the world did not. "Now my friends," he told the members of the Society of the Army of the Tennessee, "there is nothing in life more beautiful than the soldier. A knight errant with steel casque, lance in hand, has always commanded the admiration of men and women. The modern soldier is his legitimate successor and you, my comrades, were not hirelings; you never were, but knight errants transformed into modern soldiers, as good as they were and better." Sherman thought for a moment about the causes knight errants fought for, looked out at his boys, then slowly declared, "Now the truth is we fought the holiest fight ever fought on God's earth."

On August 11, 1880, Sherman made his most famous speech. Five thousand G.A.R. veterans had gathered at Columbus, Ohio, along with unnumbered masses of civilians, for the state fair. It was raining. Sherman escorted President Hayes to the stand. Hayes was the last scheduled speaker; when he finished the program was over and the dignitaries began to move off the stand. The old soldiers in the crowd began shouting, "Sherman! Speech! Uncle Billy!"

This had happened countless times before and Sherman, not surprised, stepped forward. The crowd grew quiet. Rain pattered on the assembly.

"Fellow soldiers," Sherman began, deliberately ignoring the civilians before him and the statesmen behind him, "my speech is not written, nor has been even thought of by me. It delights my soul to look on you and see so many of the good old boys left yet. They are not afraid of rain; we have stood it many a time.

"I came as part of the escort to the President, and not for the purpose of speaking to you, but simply to look on and let the boys look at Old Billy again. We are to each other all in all as man and wife, and every soldier here today knows that Uncle Billy loves him as his own flesh and blood. . . .

"The war is now away back in the past and you can tell what books cannot. When you talk you come down to the practical realities just as they happened. You all know that this is not soldiering here.

"There is many a boy here today who looks on war as all glory, but, boys, it is all hell. You can bear this warning voice to generations yet to come. I look upon war with horror," — and then he grinned — "but if it has to come I am here."

Sherman died on February 14, 1891. At his funeral the band played, in dirge tempo, "Marching Through Georgia."

QUESTIONS TO CONSIDER

1 Sherman was proslavery, Negrophobic, and living in the South at the time of secession. Why, then, did he fight for the Union?

2 Sherman's reputation, particulary among south-

ern whites, is like that of Attila the Hun, a warmonger who thirsted for blood. But Ambrose insists that Sherman was a sensitive man who hated bloodshed. How does the evidence sustain or refute either portrait of Sherman?

3 Ambrose notes that Sherman felt depressed in 1861 and elated in 1864, but he disagrees with those who label Sherman a manic-depressive psychotic. Analyze the pros and cons of Ambrose's argument. Can human emotions be removed from the context of time and place, be put on a psychiatrist's couch, and be diagnosed as sane or insane?

4 Compare Sherman with Ulysses S. Grant. What qualities did each man bring to the Union military cause? In what ways did each man complement the other?

5 Analyze the complicated web of Sherman's motives for "marching through Georgia." How did his reasoning reflect a sophisticated understanding of the nature of modern war?

30

Reconstruction:
The Revolution That Failed

JAMES MACGREGOR BURNS

In the closing days of the Civil War, the pace of momentous events was almost too much to comprehend. On April 2, 1865, Confederate President Jefferson Davis fled a blazing Richmond with his family and Cabinet members; the next day Union troops occupied the rebel capital. On April 9, Robert E. Lee surrendered the Army of Northern Virginia; five days later, on Good Friday, John Wilkes Booth shot Lincoln at Ford's Theater, and Lincoln joined the 360,000 Union dead he himself had immortalized. By then, the dream of an independent slaveowning South was dead as well.

In the mansion of a Virginia plantation, a young black woman found whites crying over a report that Yankee troops had captured Jefferson Davis. The young woman went down to a spring, alone, and there cried out, "Glory, glory, halleleujah to Jesus! I's free! I's free!" Suddenly afraid, she looked about, then fell to the ground and kissed it, thanking "Master Jesus" over and over. For her, freedom meant hope — hope that she could find her husband and four children who had been sold to a slave trader.

Other blacks celebrated their liberation in public. In Athens, Georgia, they danced around a liberty pole; in Charleston, they paraded through the streets. Many blacks, however, were wary and uncertain. "You're joking me," a black man said when his master told him he was free. He asked some neighbors if they were free also. "I couldn't believe we was all free alike," he said. Some blacks, out of feelings of obligation or compassion, remained on the home place to help their former masters.

But others were hostile. Through generations of one black family comes the story of Caddy, who had been badly treated as a slave. When she heard that the war was over, she threw her hoe down, marched up to the big house, found the mistress, and flipped her dress up. She told the white woman, "kiss my ass!"

Southern whites, by turns, were angry, helpless, vindictive, resigned, and heartsick. Their cherished South was not just defeated; it was annihilated. Some 260,000 rebel soldiers, the flower of southern manhood, were dead, and thousands more were maimed and crippled for life. The South's major cities were in ruins, her railroads and industry desolated, her commerce paralyzed, and two-thirds of her assessed wealth, including billions of dollars in slaves, destroyed. As James MacGregor Burns says in The Workshop of Democracy (1985), from which this selection is excerpted, "Many [white Southerners] were already grieving over sons, plantations, and fortunes taken by war; losing their blacks was the final blow." Some masters shot or hanged blacks who proclaimed their freedom. That was a harbinger of what was to follow in the years of Reconstruction, for most white southerners were certain that their cause had been just and were entirely unrepentant about fighting against the Union. A popular ballad captured the current mood in conquered Dixie:

> Oh, I'm a good ole Rebel, now that's just what I am
> For this fair land of freedom I do not care a damn,
> I'm glad I fit against it, I only wish't we'd won
> And I don't want no pardon for nothin' what I done. . . .
>
> I hates the Yankee nation and everything they do
> I hates the Declaration of Independence too
> I hates the glorious Union, 'tis dripping with our blood
> And I hate the striped banner, I fit it all I could. . . .
>
> I can't take up my musket and fight 'em now no mo'
> But I ain't gonna love 'em and that is certain sho'
> And I don't want no pardon for what I was and am
> And I won't be reconstructed and I don't care a damn.

In Washington, Republican leaders were jubilant in victory and determined to deal firmly with southern whites in order to preserve the fruits of the war. But what about the new president, Andrew Johnson? A profane, hard-drinking Tennessee Democrat who bragged about his plebeian origins, Johnson had been the only southern senator to oppose secession openly. He had sided with the Union, had served as war governor of Tennessee, and had become Lincoln's running mate in 1864, on a Union ticket comprising both Republicans and War Democrats. Thanks to Booth's pistol shot,

Johnson was now president, and he faced one of the most difficult tasks ever to confront an American chief executive: how to bind the nation's wounds, preserve black freedom, and restore the southern states to their proper places in the Union.

As we saw in "Lincoln's Journey to Emancipation" (selection 27), Lincoln had contemplated an army of occupation for the South, thinking that military force might be necessary to protect the former slaves and prevent the old southern leadership from returning to power. Now there was such an army in the South: some 200,000 Union troops had moved in to restore order there and to perform whatever reconstruction duties Johnson might ask of them.

Initially, Republican leaders were hopeful about Johnson, for in talking about his native region he seemed tough, even uncompromising. But as he set about restoring defeated Dixie, Johnson alarmed and then enraged congressional Republicans by adopting a soft, conciliatory reconstruction policy. The president not only opposed granting blacks the right to vote, but allowed former Confederates to return to power in the southern states. He stood by as they adopted black codes that reduced blacks to a virtual condition of peonage, and he hotly opposed congressional interference in the reconstruction process. He even urged southern states to reject the Fourteenth Amendment, pushed through Congress by the Republicans, which would protect southern blacks. The projected amendment would prevent the states from enacting laws that abridged "the privileges or immunities of citizens of the United States." It would also bar the states from depriving "any person of life, liberty, or property, without due process of law," or from denying any person the "equal protection of the law." Johnson did more than just oppose the amendment; he damned Republican leaders like Charles Sumner of Massachusetts and Thaddeus Stevens of Pennsylvania, calling them tyrants and traitors. He even campaigned against the Republican party in the 1866 off-year elections. As a consequence, he alienated moderate as well as radical Republicans, who soon united against him. When the 1866 elections gave the Republicans huge majorities in both houses of Congress, they set out to take control of Reconstruction and to reform the South themselves.

This sets the scene for Burns's account of Republican Reconstruction. Burns believes that it was a revolutionary experiment that failed. He does not, of course, subscribe to the outmoded interpretation of Reconstruction as a misguided attempt to "put the colored people on top" in the South and turn the region over to hordes of beady-eyed carpetbaggers and roguish scalawags intent on "stealing the South blind." In the old view, Reconstruction was "a blackout of honest government," a time when the "Southern people were put to the torch," a period so rife with "political rancor, and social violence and disorder," that nothing good came out of it. Since the 1930s, modern scholarship has systematically rejected this interpretation and the antiblack prejudice that underlay it. Drawing on modern studies of the period, Burns argues that the

Republican Congress did go too far in trying to centralize power in the legislative branch. But he is sympathetic to Republican efforts to bring southern blacks into the American mainstream, to grant them political, social, and educational opportunities for self-advancement. On this score, however, the Republicans did not go far enough, for they failed to provide blacks with the economic security they needed to be truly free in America. Alas, that failure was to plague black Americans for generations to come.

FOR A BRIEF FLEETING MOMENT in history — from late 1866 to almost the end of the decade — radical senators and congressmen led the Republican party in an audacious venture in both the organization and the goals of political power. To a degree that would have astonished the constitution-makers of earlier years, they converted the eighty-year-old system of checks and balances into a highly centralized, majoritarian system that elevated the legislative branch, subordinated the executive and judicial branches, and suspended federalism and "states' rights" in the South. They turned the Constitution on its head. The aims of these leaders were indeed revolutionary — to reverse age-old human and class relationships in the South and to raise millions of people to a much higher level of economic, political, social, and educational self-fulfillment. That such potent means could not in the end produce such humane and democratic ends was the ultimate tragedy of this revolutionary experiment.

This heroic effort was not conducted by men on white horses, but rather by quarrelsome parliamentarians — by a Congress that seemed to one of its members as never "more querulous, distracted, in-

coherent and ignoble." In the Senate, [Charles] Sumner had good reason to be distracted, for he had married a woman half his age shortly before the [1866] election and was preoccupied first by marital bliss and very soon by marital distress as he and his wife found themselves hopelessly incompatible. His colleagues found him more remote and unpredictable than ever. In the House, [Thaddeus] Stevens worked closely with his Radical allies, but he was now desperately anxious to move swiftly ahead, for he knew that time was running out for him and perhaps for his cause. Rising on the House floor, he now presented the countenance of death, with his dourly twisted mouth, deeply sunken eyes, parchment skin, and a body so wasted that he often conducted business from a couch just outside the chamber. But the old man never lost his ferocious drive to dominate; as he spoke, his eyes lighted up in a fierce gleam and his croaking voice turned thunderous, while he stretched his bony arm out in a wide sweep and punctuated his arguments with sudden thrusts of his long yellow forefinger.

The strength of the Republican party lay in the advanced positions of these two men but even more in the quality and commitment of other party leaders in both houses. Some of these men — John Sherman, James A. Garfield, James G. Blaine — would gain fame in the decades ahead. Others . . . would fade into the mists of history. Occupying almost every hue on the party rainbow, these men differed sharply and disputed mightily, but they felt they had a clear election mandate to establish civil and other rights in the South; they had a strong sense of party solidarity; and they had the backing of rank-and-file senators and representatives and of party organizations throughout the North.

They also had a common adversary in Andrew Johnson. The President stewed over his election defeat, but he would make no fundamental change in his political and legislative strategy. Setbacks seemed only to mire him more deeply in his own resentments. . . . He received little independent advice from his Cabinet, which appeared to believe that the beleaguered President needed above all their loyalty. [Secretary of War Edwin] Stanton dissented on occasion but, characteristically, Johnson did not wholly trust him. As the President stuck to the disintegrating political center and the Republicans moved toward a radical posture, the legislative stage was set for drama and conflict.

The upshot was a burst of legislative creativity in the "hundred days" of winter 1866–67:

December 14, 1866: Congress enacts black suffrage for the District of Columbia, later reenacts it over Johnson's veto. *January 7, 1867:* the House adopts [James M.] Ashley's resolution instructing the Judiciary Committee to "inquire into the conduct of Andrew Johnson." *January 22:* Congress grants itself authority to call itself into special session, a right recognized until now as belonging only to the President. *March 2:* all on the same day, Congress passes a basic act laying out its general plan of political reconstruction; in effect deprives the President of command of the army; and enacts the Tenure of Office Act barring the Chief Executive from removing officials appointed by and with the advice of the Senate, without Senate approval. *March 23:* Congress passes a supplementary Reconstruction Act requiring military commanders to start registering "loyal" voters.

The heart of congressional strategy to democra-

tize the South lay in the first Reconstruction Act of March 2, 1867, as clarified, strengthened, and implemented in later acts. With the ostensible purpose of restoring social order and republican government in the South, and on the premise that the existing "Johnson" state regimes there could not realize these ends or even protect life or property, the South was divided into five military districts subject to martial law. The commanders were empowered not only to govern — to suppress disorder, protect life and property, remove civil officeholders — but to initiate political reconstruction by enrolling qualified voters including blacks, and excluding the disloyal. To be restored to the Union, the Southern states must call new constitutional conventions that, elected under universal manhood suffrage, in turn must establish new state governments that would guarantee black suffrage and ratify the Fourteenth Amendment. These states would be eligible for representation in the national legislature only after Congress had approved their state constitutions and after the Fourteenth Amendment had become part of the Constitution.

It was a radical's dream, a centralist's heaven — and a states'-righter's nightmare. Congress held all the governmental strings in its hands. No more exquisite punishment could have been devised for secessionists than to make them conform to national standards in reconstructing their own state governments and gaining restoration to the Union. Congress did not stop with upsetting the division of powers between nation and states; it overturned the separation of powers [between the executive and legislative branches of the national government. In 1868, congressional Republicans sought to remove Johnson by a method never before used against an American president. The Republican-controlled House impeached Johnson on various partisan charges, including his defiance of the Tenure of Office Act and his efforts to undermine the Reconstruction Act, but the Senate failed to convict him by just one vote short of the two-thirds required for removal. Thus ended the first and last attempt to impeach an American president for political reasons. Even so, Johnson's presidency was irreparably damaged; he served out his last year in office, as truculent as ever. The Republicans, meanwhile, nominated war hero Ulysses S. Grant as their candidate in the 1868 presidential elections. Since Grant had maintained ties with congressional Republicans and seemed genuinely militant in his stance on reconstruction, congressional Republicans were certain that he would cooperate with them. That November, Grant defeated Democratic candidate Horatio Seymour by winning all but three northern states and polling 52.7 percent of the popular vote.]

Some Radical Republicans now were more optimistic than ever. Grant's election, they felt, provided a supreme and perhaps final opportunity to reconstruct the South. Now the Republicans had their own men in the White House; they still controlled both houses of Congress; they had established their supremacy over the Supreme Court; they had considerable influence over the federal military and civilian bureaucracy in the South. They still had the power to discipline the Southern states, by admitting them to the Union or expelling them. The Republicans had pushed through the Thirteenth and Fourteenth Amendments. They still possessed the ablest, most experienced political leadership in the nation. Stevens had died during the campaign, but Sumner had been handsomely reelected in Massachusetts. "So at last I have conquered; after a life of struggle," the senator said.

Other Radicals were less sanguine. They knew that far more than Andrew Johnson had thwarted Reconstruction. The national commitment to black equality was weak, the mechanisms of government faulty, and even with the best of intentions and machinery, the connecting line between a decision in Washington and an actual outcome affecting a black family in Virginia or Mississippi was long and fragile. Time and again, voters had opposed black wrongs without favoring black rights. Before the

war, they had fought the extension of slavery but not slavery where it existed. During the war, they had come to approve emancipation only after Lincoln issued his proclamation. After the war, in a number of state elections — especially those of 1867 — Northerners had shown that they favored black suffrage in the South but not at home.

Spurred by effective leaders, Americans were moving toward racial justice, but the journey was agonizingly slow and meandering. "It took America three-quarters of a century of agitation and four years of war to learn the meaning of the word 'Liberty,'" the *American Freedman* editorialized. "God grant to teach us by easier lessons the meaning of the words 'equal rights.'" How quickly and firmly Americans moved ahead on black rights could turn significantly on continuing moral and political leadership.

The crucial issue after Grant's election was the right of blacks to vote. Republican leaders in Congress quickly pushed ahead with the Fifteenth Amendment, which declared in its final form that the "right of the citizens of the United States to vote shall not be denied or abridged by the United States or by any State on account of race, color, or previous condition of servitude." It was a noble sentiment that had emerged out of a set of highly mixed motives. Democrats charged, with some reason, that the majority party was far less interested in legalizing the freedman's vote in the South than in winning the black vote in the North. But the Republican leadership, knowing that countless whites in the North opposed black voting there, were responding to the demands of morality as well as practicality. Senator Henry Wilson reminded his colleagues that the "whole struggle in this country to give equal rights and equal privileges to all citizens of the United States has been an unpopular one; that we have been forced to struggle against passions and prejudices engendered by generations of wrong and oppression." He estimated that that struggle had cost his party a quarter of a million votes. Another Republican senator, however, contended that in the long run adherence to "equality of rights among men" had been not a source of party weakness but of its strength and power. . . .

If political morality in the long run meant political practicality, the Fifteenth Amendment nevertheless bore all the markings of compromise. To gain the two-thirds support constitutionally required in each chamber, the sponsors were compelled to jettison clauses that would have outlawed property qualifications and literacy tests. The amendment provided only that Congress and the states could not deny the vote, rather than requiring them to take positive action to secure black suffrage; nor was there any provision against denial of vote by mobs or other private groups. And of course the amendment did not provide for female voting — and so the National Woman Suffrage Association opposed it.

Still, radicals in and out of Congress were elated when the Fifteenth cleared Congress, elated even more when the measure became part of the Constitution in March 1870, after Republican state parties helped drive it through the required number of legislatures. . . .

The legal right of blacks to vote soon produced a phenomenon in Southern politics — black legislators, judges, superintendents of education, lieutenant governors and other state officials, members of Congress, and even two United States senators. These, however, made up only a fraction of Southern officeholders: in none of the legislatures did blacks hold a majority, except briefly in South Carolina's lower house. Usually black leaders shared power with "carpetbaggers" — white Northerners who came south and became active in politics as Republicans — and "scalawags" — white Southerners who cooperated with Republicans and blacks. While many black leaders were men of "ability and integrity," in [historian] Kenneth Stampp's view, the whites and blacks together comprised a mixed lot of the corrupt and the incorruptible, moderate

and extreme, opportunistic and principled, competent and ignorant. The quality of state government under such leadership also was mixed, but on the whole probably no worse than that of many state and local governments of the time. The state governments in the South bore unusually heavy burdens, moreover — demoralization and poverty in the wake of a devastating war, the need to build or rebuild public services throughout the region, the corrupting influence of contractors, speculators, and promoters seeking subsidies, grants, contracts, franchises, and land.

Far more important than the reality of black-and-white rule in the South was the perverted image of it refracted through the distorted lenses of Southern eyes. It was not easy for the white leadership to see newly freed men . . . occupy positions of prestige and power; and it was perhaps inevitable that they would caricature the new rulers to the world. A picture emerged of insolent boors indulging in legislative license, lording it over downtrodden whites, looting the public treasury, bankrupting the state, threatening white traditions, womanhood, and purity. . . .

The worst fear of the old white leadership — that black-and-white rule would produce a social revolution — turned out to be the least warranted of all. The mixed rule of blacks, scalawags, and carpetbaggers produced a few symbolic and actual changes: rhetoric drawn directly from the Declaration of Independence proclaiming liberty, "equality of all persons before the law," various civil and political rights; a mild effort in two or three states to integrate certain educational institutions; a feeble effort at land reform. [Southern state] constitutions were made somewhat more democratic, legislative apportionment less discriminatory, more offices elective; "rights of women were enlarged, tax systems were made more equitable, penal codes were reformed, and the number of crimes punishable by death was reduced," in Stampp's summation. The constitution of South Carolina — the state that had served as the South's political and ideological heartland, and the state that now paradoxically had elevated the most blacks to leadership positions — was converted almost into a model state charter, with provisions for manhood suffrage, public education, extension of women's rights, and even the state's first divorce law. . . .

But what the black-and-white leadership failed to do was of far more profound consequence than what it did. Both radicals and moderates understood that education was a fundamental need for Southern blacks, but the obstacles were formidable and progress slow. Even the best educational system could hardly have compensated for decades of illiteracy and ignorance. "The children," James McPherson noted, "came from a cultural environment almost entirely devoid of intellectual stimulus. Many of them had never heard of the alphabet, geography, or arithmetic when they first came to school. Few of them knew their right hand from their left, or could tell the date of their birth. Most of them realized only vaguely that there was a world outside their own plantation or town." In the early years, teachers sponsored by "Freedmen's Aid" and missionary groups met the challenge, often finding to their surprise that black children had a passion to learn, could be taught to read as quickly as white children, and might be found laboriously teaching their own parents the alphabet and the multiplication table.

These private educational efforts were never adequate, however, to teach more than a fraction of the South's black children. The question was whether the reconstructed black-and-white state governments would take over the task in a comprehensive way, and here they failed. The difficulties were at least as great as ever: inadequate facilities, insufficient money, lack of teachers, inadequate student motivation, discipline problems (black teachers tended to be the harsher disciplinarians). But the biggest hurdle was the constant, pervasive, and continuing hostility of many Southern whites to schooling for blacks. "I have seen many an absurdity in my lifetime," said a Louisiana legislator on observing black pupils for the first time, "but this is the climax of absurdities." A Southern white woman warned a teacher that "you might as well try to teach your horse or mule to read, as to teach these niggers. They *can't* learn."

Behind these white Southern attitudes toward schooling for black children lay a host of fears. One was their old worry that blacks would be educated above their station and out of the labor supply. "To talk about educating this drudge," opined the Paducah (Kentucky) *Herald,* "is to talk without thinking. Either to 'educate,' or to teach him merely to read and write, is to ruin him as a laborer. Thousands of them have already been ruined by it." Even more pervasive was the white fear of integration, although most black leaders made it clear that their main interest was education, whether segregated or not. Southern fears often took the form of harassing and humiliating teachers or, more ingeniously, depriving them of white housing so that some teachers lived with blacks — and hence could be arrested as vagrants. Defending the arrest of a freedmen's teacher, the mayor of Enterprise, Mississippi, said that the teacher had been "living on terms of equality with negroes, living in their houses, boarding with them, and at one time gave a party at which there were no persons present (except himself) but negroes, all of which are offenses against the laws of the state and declared acts of vagrancy." Black-and-white governments could not overcome such deep-seated attitudes.

To many blacks, even more important than education was land — "forty acres and a mule." During the war, when workers on a South Carolina plantation had rejected a wage offer from their master, one of them had said, "I mean to own my own manhood, and I'm goin' on to my own land, just as soon as when I git dis crop in. . . ." Declared a black preacher in Florida to a group of field hands: "It's de white man's turn ter labor now. He ain't got nothin' lef' but his lan', an' de lan' won't be his'n long, fur de Guverment is gwine ter gie ter ev'ry Nigger forty acres of lan' an' a mule.'' Black hopes for their own plots had dwindled sharply after the war, when Johnson's amnesty proclamation restored property as well as civil rights to most former rebels who would take an oath of allegiance. His expectations dashed, a Virginia black said now that he would ask for only a single acre of land — ''ef you make it de acre dat Marsa's house sets on.''

Black hopes for land soared again after the congressional Republicans took control of Reconstruction in the late 1860s, only to collapse when Republican moderates — and even some radicals — refused to support a program of land confiscation. Black hopes rose still again when black-and-white regimes took over state governments; some freedmen heard rumors that they need only go to the polls and vote and they would return home with a mule and a deed to a forty-acre lot. But, curiously, ''radical'' rule in no state produced systematic effort at land redistribution. Some delegates to the Louisiana constitutional convention proposed that purchases of more than 150 acres be prohibited when planters sold their estates, and the South Carolina convention authorized the creation of a commission to buy land for sale to blacks, but little came of these efforts. One reason was clear: Southern whites who had resisted black voting and black education would have reacted with even greater fury to as radical a program as land redistribution, with all its implications for white pride, white property — and the white labor supply.

Black leaders themselves were wary of the freedmen's lust for ''forty acres and a mule.'' In part, this caution may have been due to the class divisions between the black Southern masses and their leaders, many of whom had been artisans or ministers, had been free before the war, and had never experienced plantation life and closeness to the soil. Some of these leaders were, indeed, virtually middle-class in their attitudes toward property, frugality, ''nega-

tive'' liberty, and hard work, and in their fear that radical blacks might infuriate white power elites by talking ''confiscation.'' Such leaders preferred to bargain with the white power structure rather than threaten its control over land and other property. Prizing liberal values of individual liberty, the need for schooling, and above all the right to vote, they played down the economic and social needs of the blacks. And they based their whole strategy on the suffrage, arguing that all the other rights that blacks claimed — land, education, homes — were dependent on their using the potential power inherent in their right to vote.

Would black voting make the crucial difference? Of the three prongs of black advance in the South — schools, land, and the vote — the limited success of the first and the essential failure of the second left black suffrage as the great battlefield of Southern reform. Certainly Southern whites realized this and, as the Republican commitment faltered during the Grant Administration, they stepped up their efforts to thwart black voting. They used a battery of stratagems: opening polling places late or closing them early or changing their location; gerrymandering districts in order to neutralize the black vote; requiring the payment of a poll tax to vote; ''losing'' or disregarding black ballots; counting Democratic ballots more than once; making local offices appointive rather than elective; plying blacks with liquor. These devices had long been used against white Americans, and by no means did all Southern whites use them now, but fraud and trickery were especially effective against inexperienced and unlettered blacks.

When nonviolent methods failed, many Southern whites turned to other weapons against voting: intimidation, harassment, and terror. Mobs drove blacks away from the polls. Whites blocked polling entrances or crowded around ballot boxes so blacks could not vote. Rowdies with guns or whips followed black voters away from the polling place. When a group of black voters in Gibson County,

Tennessee, returned the fire of a band of masked men, the authorities put the blacks in jail, from which an armed mob took them by force to a nearby riverbank and shot them down. Fifty-three defendants were arrested by federal authorities and tried, none convicted.

Some of this violence erupted spontaneously as young firebrands, emboldened by liquor, rode into polling areas with their guns blazing. But as the stakes of voting rose, terrorists organized themselves. Most notable was the Ku Klux Klan, with its white robes and hoods, sheeted horses, and its weird hierarchies of wizards, genii, dragons, hydras, ghouls, and cyclopes. Proclaiming its devotion to "Chivalry, Humanity, Mercy, and Patriotism," the Klan proposed to protect the "weak, the innocent, and the defenseless" — and the "Constitution of the United States." The Klan had allies in the Knights of the White Camelia, the White Brotherhood, and other secret societies.

Incensed by mob violence, the Republicans in Washington tried to counter it with legislation. The Enforcement Act of May 1870 outlawed the use of force, bribery, or intimidation that hindered the right to vote because of race in state and local eletions. Two more enforcement acts during the next twelve months extended and tightened enforcement machinery, and in April 1871 Congress in effect outlawed the Klan and similar groups. But actual enforcement in the thousands of far-flung polling places required an enormous number of marshals and soldiers. As army garrisons in the South thinned out, enforcement appropriations dwindled, and the number of both prosecutions by white prosecutors and convictions by white juries dropped, black voting was more and more choked off.

After his election to a second term Grant tried vigorously though spasmodically to support black rights for the sake of both Republican principle and Republican victories. In a final effort, the Republicans were able to push through the Civil Rights Act of 1875, designed to guarantee equal rights for blacks in public places, but the act was weak in coverage and enforcement, and later would be struck down by the Supreme Court.

By the mid-seventies Republicanism, Reconstruction, and reform were all running out of steam. Southern Democrats were extending their grip over political machinery; the Republican leadership was shaken by an economic panic in 1873, and the party lost badly in the 1874 midterm elections. The *coup de grâce* for Reconstruction came after Rutherford Hayes's razor-thin electoral-college victory in 1876 over [Democrat] Samuel J. Tilden. Awarded the office as a result of Republican control over three Southern states where voting returns were in doubt, and as a result too of a Republican majority on the Electoral Commission, Hayes bolstered his position by offering assurances about future treatment of the South. While these were in the soft political currency of veiled promises and delphic utterances, the currency was hard enough for the Democrats — and for Hayes as well. Within two months of his inauguration, he ordered the last federal troops out of the South and turned over political control of Louisiana, South Carolina, and Florida to the Southern [Democrats].

*   *   *

And what of the objects of this long political struggle — the black people of the South? The vast majority were in the same socioeconomic situation as ten years before, at the end of the war. They had gained certain personal liberties, such as the right to marry, and a modicum of legal and civil and political rights, including the right to vote in certain areas; but their everyday lot was much the same as before. Most still lacked land, property, money, capital; they were still dependent on the planters, sometimes the same old "massa." It was not a black man but a prominent white Georgian who said of the freedman late in 1865: "The negro's first want is, not

When the war ended, most of the former slaves owned little more than the skin on their backs. To secure their liberty, they needed their own land, schools, and the right to vote. During Reconstruction, they did gain personal liberties like the right to marry and a modicum of political, civil, and legal rights. But their every-day lot improved little. When Reconstruction ended, as James MacGregor Burns says, most southern blacks "still lacked land, property, money, capital; they were still dependent on the planters, sometimes the same old 'massa.'" (Collection of William Gladstone)

the ballot, but a chance to live, — yes, sir, *a chance to live.* Why, he can't even live without the consent of the white man! He has no land; he can make no crops except the white man gives him a chance. He hasn't any timber; he can't get a stick of wood without leave from a white man. We crowd him into the fewest possible employments, and then he can scarcely get work anywhere but in the rice-fields and cotton plantations of a white man who has owned him and given up slavery only at the point of the bayonet. . . . What sort of freedom is that?''

Many a freedman had exchanged bondage for a kind of bargaining relationship with employers, but his bargaining position was woefully weak. If he held out for better terms, he could be evicted; if he left, he might be denied work elsewhere and arrested for vagrancy; if he struck, he had no unions or money to sustain him. So the "bargains" were usually one-sided; contracts sometimes literally required "perfect obedience" from employees. Some blacks had had the worst of both worlds — they had left the security of old age and sickness in bondage, under masters who cared for them because they were valuable property, for a strange "free-market" world in which they developed new dependencies on old masters.

Could Reconstruction have turned out differently? Many have concluded that the impotence of the blacks was too deeply rooted, the white intransigence too powerful, the institutions of change too faulty, and the human mind too limited to begin to meet the requirements of a genuine Reconstruction. Yet the human mind had already conducted a stupendous social revolution with the blacks. For a hundred years and more, Southern planters, assisted by slave recruiters in Africa, masters of slaving ships, various middlemen, auctioneers, and drivers, had been uprooting blacks by the hundreds of thousands out of far-off tribal civilizations, bringing most of them safely across broad expanses of water, establishing them in a new and very different culture, and converting them into productive an profit-creating slaves. Somehow the human mind seemed wholly capable of malign ''social engineering,'' incapable of benign.

Yet there were some Americans who did understand the kind of broad social planning and governmental action that was needed to reconstruct genuine democracy in the South and truly to liberate the freed people. [Abolitionist] Wendell Phillips understood the depth of the problem, the need for a ''social revolution.'' He said: '' You must plant at the South the elements which make a different society. You cannot enact four millions of slaves, ignorant, down-trodden, and despised, into personal equals of the old leaders of the South.'' He wanted to ''give the negroes land, ballot and education and to hold the arm of the Federal government over the whole Southern Territory until these seeds have begun to bear fruit beyond any possibility of blighting.'' We must see to it, said Senator Henry Wilson, that ''the man made free by the Constitution is a freeman indeed; that he can go where he pleases, work when and for whom he pleases; that he can sue and be sued; that he can lease and buy and sell and own property, real and personal; that he can go into the schools and educate himself and his children. . . .'' [Black leader Frederick] Douglass and Stevens and Sumner took similar positions.

These men were not typical of Republicans or even of Radical Republicans, but many other radicals and moderates recognized that the freed people needed an array of economic, political, social, and legal supports, and that these were interrelated. Congressman George Hoar lamented that blacks had been given universal suffrage without universal education. Some radicals believed that voting was the black's first need and others that land or sustenance came first, but most recognized that no single ''solution'' was adequate. Antislavery men, said Phillips, ''will believe the negro safe when we see him with 40 acres under his feet, a schoolhouse behind him, a ballot in his right hand, the sceptre of the Federal Government over his head, and no State Government to interfere with him, until more than one-half of the white men of the Southern States are in their graves.'' . . .

The critical failure of Reconstruction probably lay . . . in the realm of leadership — especially that of opinion-makers. Editors, ministers, and others preached liberty and equality without always comprehending the full dimensions of these values and the means necessary — in the South of the 1870s — to accomplish such ends. The radicals ''seemed to have little conception,'' according to Stampp, ''of what might be called the sociology of freedom, the ease with which mere laws can be flouted when they alone support an economically dependent class, especially a minority group against whom is directed an intense racial prejudice.'' Reconstruction could have succeeded only through use of a strategy employed in a number of successful postwar reconstructions of a comprehensive nature — a strategy of combining ideological, economic, political, educational, and institutional forces in such a firm and coordinated way as truly to transform the social environment in which Southerners, both black and white, were trying to remake their lives after the Civil War. And such a strategy, it should be noted, would have imposed heavy intellectual, economic, and psychological burdens on the North as well.

Not only would such a strategy have called for

rare political leadership — especially for a leader, in William Gillette's words, able to "fashion a means and then persevere in it, bending men to his purpose by vigorous initiative, skillful influence, and masterful policy." Even more it called for a rare kind of *intellectual* leadership — political thinkers who could translate the component elements of values such as liberty and equality into policy priorities and operational guidelines. But aside from a few radicals such as Phillips, most of the liberals and many of the radicals had a stunted view of the necessary role of public authority in achieving libertarian and egalitarian purposes. *The Nation,* the most influential liberal weekly in the postwar period, under Edwin L. Godkin shrank from using the only means — government — that could have marshaled the resources necessary for genuine reconstruction. "To Govern Well," *The Nation* proclaimed, "Govern Little." A decisive number of otherwise liberal-minded and generously inclined intellectual leaders held similar views. . . . There were many reasons for the failure of Reconstruction, but the decisive one — because it occurred in people's conceptualizing and analyzing processes and not merely in ineluctable social and economic circumstances — took place in the liberal mind. Most of the liberals were effective transactional leaders, or brokers; few displayed transforming leadership.

That liberal mind seemed to have closed itself off even to the results of practical experimentation. During the war, General Sherman had set aside for freedmen several hundred thousand acres on the Sea Islands south of Charleston and on the abandoned rice lands inland for thirty miles along the coast. Each black family was to receive its forty acres until Congress should rule on their final disposition. Federal officials helped settle 40,000 blacks on these lands. When the whole enterprise was terminated by Johnson's pardon and amnesty program, and land turned back to former onwers, the black farmers were incredulous. Some had to be driven off their land by force. The program had lasted long

enough, however, to demonstrate that freed people could make a success of independent farming, and that "forty acres and a mule" could serve as the foundation of Reconstruction. But the lesson seemed lost on Northerners who shuddered at the thought of "land confiscation."

Thus the great majority of black people were left in a condition of dependency, a decade after war's end, that was not decisively different, in terms of everyday existence, from their prewar status. They were still landless farm laborers, lacking schooling, the suffrage, and self-respect. They achieved certain civil and legal rights, but their expectations had been greatly raised too, so the Golden Shore for many seemed more distant than ever. Said a black woman: "De slaves, where I lived, knowed after de war dat they had abundance of dat somethin' called freedom, what they could not eat, wear, and sleep in. Yes, sir, they soon found out dat freedom ain't nothin', 'less you is got somethin' to live on and a place to call home. Dis livin' on liberty is lak young folks livin' on love after they gits married. It just don't work."

Or as an Alabama freedman said more tersely when asked what price tag he bore — and perhaps with two meanings of the word in mind:

"I'se free. Ain't wuf nuffin."

QUESTIONS TO CONSIDER

1   Why does Burns call Reconstruction a revolution? Why does he consider the actions of federal officials, especially congressmen, to be revolutionary? What happened to the Constitution during Reconstruction? Why was Reconstruction "a radicalist's dream, a centralist's heaven, and a states'-righter's nightmare"?

2   What compromises and weaknesses vitiated the strength of the Fifteenth (voting rights) Amendment?

3   Reconstructionists realized that blacks needed education, land, and the vote if equality was to be-

come a reality in the South. What fundamental fears and racist attitudes in both the South and the North kept these goals from being realized? What practical steps does Burns feel ought to have been taken to ensure the success of Reconstruction policies? Do you see any potential problems in aggressive governmental policies temporarily adopted to make Reconstruction work? Or do you think the Constitution is strong enough to protect us from government excesses?

4 Discuss Burns's contention that the failure of liberal intellectual leaders to shape public opinion was responsible for the failure of Reconstruction.

Were the leaders more to blame than the weak enforcement policies of the federal government or the repressive, sometimes violent reactions of white southerners?

5 Imagine for a moment that Reconstruction was a success, that American blacks in the late nineteenth century achieved lives founded on a sound economic and legal base, with equal access to land, education, and the franchise. How would the United States be different today? Would Americans have elected a black president by now? How might other issues of social justice, such as women's rights, have been affected?